T0381350

# Communications
# in Computer and Information Science     2374

Series Editors

Gang Li⊙, *School of Information Technology, Deakin University, Burwood, VIC,*
*Australia*
Joaquim Filipe⊙, *Polytechnic Institute of Setúbal, Setúbal, Portugal*
Zhiwei Xu, *Chinese Academy of Sciences, Beijing, China*

**Rationale**

The CCIS series is devoted to the publication of proceedings of computer science conferences. Its aim is to efficiently disseminate original research results in informatics in printed and electronic form. While the focus is on publication of peer-reviewed full papers presenting mature work, inclusion of reviewed short papers reporting on work in progress is welcome, too. Besides globally relevant meetings with internationally representative program committees guaranteeing a strict peer-reviewing and paper selection process, conferences run by societies or of high regional or national relevance are also considered for publication.

**Topics**

The topical scope of CCIS spans the entire spectrum of informatics ranging from foundational topics in the theory of computing to information and communications science and technology and a broad variety of interdisciplinary application fields.

**Information for Volume Editors and Authors**

Publication in CCIS is free of charge. No royalties are paid, however, we offer registered conference participants temporary free access to the online version of the conference proceedings on SpringerLink (http://link.springer.com) by means of an http referrer from the conference website and/or a number of complimentary printed copies, as specified in the official acceptance email of the event.

CCIS proceedings can be published in time for distribution at conferences or as post-proceedings, and delivered in the form of printed books and/or electronically as USBs and/or e-content licenses for accessing proceedings at SpringerLink. Furthermore, CCIS proceedings are included in the CCIS electronic book series hosted in the SpringerLink digital library at http://link.springer.com/bookseries/7899. Conferences publishing in CCIS are allowed to use Online Conference Service (OCS) for managing the whole proceedings lifecycle (from submission and reviewing to preparing for publication) free of charge.

**Publication process**

The language of publication is exclusively English. Authors publishing in CCIS have to sign the Springer CCIS copyright transfer form, however, they are free to use their material published in CCIS for substantially changed, more elaborate subsequent publications elsewhere. For the preparation of the camera-ready papers/files, authors have to strictly adhere to the Springer CCIS Authors' Instructions and are strongly encouraged to use the CCIS LaTeX style files or templates.

**Abstracting/Indexing**

CCIS is abstracted/indexed in DBLP, Google Scholar, EI-Compendex, Mathematical Reviews, SCImago, Scopus. CCIS volumes are also submitted for the inclusion in ISI Proceedings.

**How to start**

To start the evaluation of your proposal for inclusion in the CCIS series, please send an e-mail to ccis@springer.com.

Nadia Magnenat Thalmann · Xinrong Hu ·
Bin Sheng · Daniel Thalmann · Tao Peng ·
Weiliang Meng · Jin Huang · Lei Zhu · Xiong Wei
Editors

# Computer Animation and Social Agents

37th International Conference, CASA 2024
Wuhan, China, June 5–7, 2024
Revised Selected Papers, Part I

Springer

*Editors*

Nadia Magnenat Thalmann
MIRALab-University of Geneva
Geneva, Switzerland

Bin Sheng
Shanghai Jiao Tong University
Shanghai, China

Tao Peng
Wuhan Textile University
Wuhan, China

Jin Huang
Wuhan Textile University
Wuhan, China

Xiong Wei
Wuhan Textile University
Wuhan, China

Xinrong Hu
Wuhan Textile University
Wuhan, China

Daniel Thalmann
Swiss Federal Institute of Technology
Lausanne, Switzerland

Weiliang Meng
University of Chinese Academy of Sciences
Beijing, China

Lei Zhu
The Hong Kong University of Science
and Technology
Guangzhou, China

ISSN 1865-0929    ISSN 1865-0937 (electronic)
Communications in Computer and Information Science
ISBN 978-981-96-2680-9    ISBN 978-981-96-2681-6 (eBook)
https://doi.org/10.1007/978-981-96-2681-6

# Preface

CASA is the oldest international conference on computer animation and social agents in the world. It was founded in Geneva in 1988 under the name of Computer Animation (CA) by the Computer Graphics Society (CGS). In the past few years, CASA was held in Europe (Belgium, Netherlands, France, Switzerland, UK, etc.), Asia (South Korea, China, Singapore) and the USA. CASA 2024 provided a great opportunity to interact with leading experts, share your own work, and educate yourself through exposure to the research of your peers from around the world.

The 37th International Conference on Computer Animation and Social Agents (CASA 2024) was held on June 5–7, 2024, in Wuhan, China. The conference was organized by the Wuhan Textile University (WTU), Shanghai Jiao Tong University (SJTU), State Key Laboratory of Computer Science, Institute of Software, Chinese Academy of Sciences and State Key Laboratory of Multimodal Artificial Intelligence Systems/National Laboratory of Pattern Recognition, Institute of Automation, Chinese Academy of Sciences.

These CASA 2024 CCIS proceedings are composed of 60 papers from a total of 208 submissions. To ensure the high quality of the publications, each paper was reviewed by at least two experts in the field and authors of accepted papers were asked to revise their paper according to the review comments prior to publication.

We would like to express our deepest gratitude to all the PC members and external reviewers who provided timely high-quality reviews. We would also like to thank all the authors for contributing to the conference by submitting their work.

November 2024

Nadia Magnenat Thalmann
Xinrong Hu
Bin Sheng
Daniel Thalmann
Tao Peng
Weiliang Meng
Jin Huang
Lei Zhu
Xiong Wei

# Organization

## Honorary Conference Co-chairs

| | |
|---|---|
| Weilin Xu | Wuhan Textile University, China |
| Enhua Wu | Chinese Academy of Sciences and University of Macao, China |
| Dagan Feng | University of Sydney, Australia |

## Conference Co-chairs

| | |
|---|---|
| Minghua Jiang | Wuhan Textile University, China |
| Nadia Magnenat Thalmann | Nanyang Technological University, Singapore |
| Bin Sheng | Shanghai Jiao Tong University, China |

## Program Co-chairs

| | |
|---|---|
| Jun Feng | Wuhan Textile University, China |
| Daniel Thalmann | École Polytechnique Fédérale de Lausanne, Switzerland |
| Weiliang Meng | Inst. of Automation, Chinese Academy of Sciences, China |
| Xuequan Lu | La Trobe University, Australia |

## Organization Co-chairs

| | |
|---|---|
| Xinrong Hu | Wuhan Textile University, China |
| Ping Li | Hong Kong Polytechnic University, China |
| Sheng Li | Peking University, China |
| Jin Huang | Wuhan Textile University, China |
| Lei Zhu | Hong Kong University of Science and Technology, China |

## Publication Co-chairs

| | |
|---|---|
| Yongtian Wang | Beijing Institute of Technology, China |
| Jian Zhu | Guangdong University of Technology, China |
| Xiao Lin | Shanghai Normal University, China |
| Chunwei Tian | Northwestern Polytechnical University, China |

## Publicity Co-chairs

| | |
|---|---|
| Tao Peng | Wuhan Textile University, China |
| Xiong Wei | Wuhan Textile University, China |
| Anton Bardera | University of Girona, Spain |
| Jun Tie | South-Central Minzu University, China |
| Kai Zhang | Wuhan University of Science and Technology, China |
| Zhiwei Ye | Hubei University of Technology, China |
| Tao Lu | Wuhan Institute of Technology, China |
| Jinxing Liang | Wuhan Textile University, China |
| Feng Yu | Wuhan Textile University, China |
| Bangchao Wang | Wuhan Textile University, China |

## Technical Chair

| | |
|---|---|
| Kunfang Song | Wuhan Textile University, China |

## Workshop Co-chairs

| | |
|---|---|
| Guangzheng Fei | Communication University of China, China |
| Ye Pan | Shanghai Jiao Tong University, China |
| Zixin Huang | Wuhan Institute of Technology, China |
| Ruhan He | Wuhan Textile University, China |

## Poster Co-chairs

| | |
|---|---|
| Jia Chen | Wuhan Textile University, China |
| Li Li | Wuhan Textile University, China |

Zixin Huang                     Wuhan Institute of Technology, China
Peng Ye                         Wuhan Textile University, China

## Program Committee

Weilin Xu                       Wuhan Textile University; Chinese Academy of
                                    Engineering, China
Nadia Magnenat Thalmann         University of Geneva, Switzerland
Enhua Wu                        Chinese Academy of Sciences and University of
                                    Macau, China
Daniel Thalmann                 École Polytechnique Fédérale de Lausanne,
                                    Switzerland
Xinrong Hu                      Wuhan Textile University, China
Sheng Li                        Peking University, China
Bin Sheng                       Shanghai Jiao Tong University, China
Weiliang Meng                   Chinese Academy of Sciences, China
Ping Li                         Hong Kong Polytechnic University, China
Ruhan He                        Wuhan Textile University, China
Jian Zhu                        Guangdong University of Technology, China
Tao Peng                        Wuhan Textile University, China
Xiao Lin                        Shanghai Normal University, China
Feng Yu                         Wuhan Textile University, China
Guangzheng Fei                  Communication University of China, China
Min Li                          Wuhan Textile University, China
Ye Pan                          Shanghai Jiao Tong University, China
Jinxing Liang                   Wuhan Textile University, China
Ran Yi                          Shanghai Jiao Tong University, China
Junping Liu                     Wuhan Textile University, China
Youquan Liu                     Chang 'an University, China
Jia Chen                        Wuhan Textile University, China
Andrea Bönsch                   RWTH Aachen University, Germany
Carlo Harvey                    Birmingham City University, UK
Changhe Tu                      Shandong University, China
Jin Huang                       Wuhan Textile University, China
Dominik Michels                 KAUST, Saudi Arabia
Edmond S. L. Ho                 University of Glasgow, UK
Etienne Vouga                   University of Texas at Austin, USA
Hui Chen                        Institute of Software, Chinese Academy of
                                    Sciences, China
James Hahn                      George Washington University, USA
Jason Peng                      Simon Fraser University, Canada

| | |
|---|---|
| Li Li | Wuhan Textile University, China |
| Jian Chang | Bournemouth University, UK |
| Jianmin Zheng | Nanyang Technological University, Singapore |
| Libin Liu | Peking University, China |
| Marcelo Kallmann | University of California Merced, USA |
| Nadine Aburumman | Brunel University London, UK |
| Qiong Zeng | Shandong University, China |
| Sehoon Ha | Georgia Institute of Technology, USA |
| Shihui Guo | Xiamen University, China |
| Xiong Pan | Wuhan Textile University, China |
| Shinjiro Sueda | Texas A&M University, USA |
| Taesoo Kwon | Hanyang University, South Korea |
| Taku Komura | Hong Kong University, China |
| Xiaokun Wang | University of Science and Technology Beijing, China |
| Yi Zhang | Sichuan University, China |
| Yoonsang Lee | Hanyang University, South Korea |
| Xiao Zhang | South-Central Minzu University, China |
| Ximing Yang | South-Central Minzu University, China |
| Bo Meng | South-Central Minzu University, China |
| Shihua Zhang | South-Central Minzu University, China |
| Wan Tang | South-Central Minzu University, China |
| Zheng Ye | South-Central Minzu University, China |
| Shengzhou Xu | South-Central Minzu University, China |
| Pan Lai | South-Central Minzu University, China |
| Dejun Wang | South-Central Minzu University, China |
| Jun Wang | South-Central Minzu University, China |
| Lingyun Zhou | South-Central Minzu University, China |
| Yuanai Xie | South-Central Minzu University, China |
| Ke Xu | South-Central Minzu University, China |
| Tongzhou Zhao | Wuhan Institute of Technology, China |
| Tongwei Lu | Wuhan Institute of Technology, China |
| Hui Li | Wuhan Institute of Technology, China |
| Bin Zhang | Wuhan Institute of Technology, China |
| Juan Li | Wuhan Institute of Technology, China |
| Xin Nie | Wuhan Institute of Technology, China |
| Tao Lu | Wuhan Institute of Technology, China |
| Wei Liu | Wuhan Institute of Technology, China |
| Yanan Li | Wuhan Institute of Technology, China |
| Jun Liu | Wuhan Institute of Technology, China |
| Xin Xu | Wuhan University of Science and Technology, China |

| | |
|---|---|
| Bo Li | Wuhan University of Science and Technology, China |
| He Deng | Wuhan University of Science and Technology, China |
| Peng Li | Wuhan University of Science and Technology, China |
| Jianfeng Lu | Wuhan University of Science and Technology, China |
| Ling Zhang | Wuhan University of Science and Technology, China |
| Jun Pang | Wuhan University of Science and Technology, China |
| Jianfeng Lu | Wuhan University of Science and Technology, China |
| Xiaoming Liu | Wuhan University of Science and Technology, China |
| Jinguang Gu | Wuhan University of Science and Technology, China |
| Maofu Liu | Wuhan University of Science and Technology, China |
| Feng Gao | Wuhan University of Science and Technology, China |
| Mingwei Wang | Hubei University of Technology, China |
| Jinshan Cao | Hubei University of Technology, China |
| Ran Zhou | Hubei University of Technology, China |
| Guangqi Xie | Hubei University of Technology, China |
| Yepei Chen | Hubei University of Technology, China |
| Zhina Song | Hubei University of Technology, China |
| Teng Xiao | Hubei University of Technology, China |

# Contents – Part I

# Contents – Part II

# YOLOv8_ODY: An Object Detection Model for Traffic Signs

JiaHui Lv[✉] and Xiang Li

China University of Geosciences (Wuhan), Wuhan, China
1016886595@qq.com

**Abstract.** Autonomous driving, as part of the intelligent transportation system, is increasingly becoming prevalent in people's daily lives, and the ability to correctly recognize traffic signs is a crucial step in autonomous driving technology. Traditional traffic sign detection techniques primarily rely on color and shape-based methods. However, due to the influence of complex real-world factors such as weather and visibility, the detection performance often falls short of expectations. This paper introduces a new detection model called YOLOv8_ODY, built upon YOLOv8. To address the challenge of detecting small-sized traffic signs, YOLOv8_ODY incorporates a novel approach in its model backbone by introducing the full-dimensional dynamic convolution, referred to as ODConv. ODConv learns complementary attention from four dimensions of the convolutional kernel space, significantly enhancing the model's ability to capture traffic sign objects. Furthermore, to improve the detection performance of the model's head, a dynamic detection framework called DyHead is introduced, enhancing the perception of spatial position, spatial size, and task regions within the head. Experimental results demonstrate that, without altering the model's depth, YOLOv8_ODY achieves a 2.6% improvement in mAP@0.5 compared to the original model. On the TT100k dataset, YOLOv8_ODY achieves an mAP@0.5 of 87.7%.

**Keywords:** Traffic Sign Detection · Deep Learning · Object Detection · ODConv · DyHead

## 1 Introduction

With the rapid advancement of technology, driver assistance systems and autonomous driving technologies are gradually emerging. In this context, the traffic sign detection system, as an essential component of intelligent transportation systems, plays a crucial role in providing current traffic information to drivers and enhancing driving safety. Therefore, the accurate recognition of traffic signs has become a focal point of research. Many methods have already yielded satisfactory results on some publicly available traffic sign detection datasets. Current traffic sign detection technologies exhibit several shortcomings: Firstly, traffic signs typically occupy a small proportion of real-world road scenes, making it challenging for traffic sign detection systems to capture accurate information. Secondly, within the same image, there can be both large and small-scale traffic signs, and the scale differences can lead to false positives or misses by the detector, significantly impacting detection accuracy. Lastly, the deployment of traffic sign detection technology not only demands high accuracy but also requires high inference speed to meet real-time detection requirements in complex traffic environments. To address these issues, this paper proposes a traffic sign detection model called YOLOv8_ODY based on YOLOv8. Experimental results demonstrate that the model introduced in this paper achieves desirable detection and classification accuracy. The primary contributions of this paper are as follows:

1. To tackle the challenge of small-sized traffic sign detection in real-world road scenes, this paper introduces Omni-dimensional dynamic convolution (ODConv) into the Backbone of YOLOv8. ODConv adapts the weight of each convolutional kernel based on the input image, overcoming the limitations of static convolution. Furthermore, learning complementary attention from four dimensions significantly enhances the capture of traffic signs.
2. To improve the detection performance of the original model's head, a dynamic detection framework called DyHead is introduced to enhance spatial position, spatial scale, and task region perception.
3. The paper achieves improved detection performance without altering the depth of the model network.

## 2   Related Work

### 2.1   Object Detection

Object detection is a technology that locates objects within input images and assigns them respective categories. Currently, popular object detection algorithms can be categorized into two main types: One-stage detection algorithms (One-Stage [1]) and Two-stage detection algorithms (Two-Stage [2]). The earlier Two-Stage algorithms gained widespread attention due to their high precision in localization and recognition. Two-Stage object detection algorithms consist of two stages: first, they employ a region proposal network to generate candidate object bounding boxes, and then they utilize classification and regression networks to further classify the generated candidates and refine the bounding boxes, ultimately providing the final object detection results. Classic Two-Stage object detection algorithms include R-CNN [3], Fast R-CNN [4], Faster R-CNN [5], and SPP-Net [6]. In contrast to traditional Two-Stage methods, One-Stage object detection algorithms directly complete the object detection task within a single stage. They predict object bounding boxes and category confidences directly through regression networks, transforming the object detection problem into an end-to-end regression problem. By eliminating the need for candidate box generation, One-Stage algorithms typically offer higher detection speed. Typical One-Stage algorithms include the SSD [7] and YOLO [8] series. In 2016, Redmon and others introduced the YOLO algorithm, which revolutionized object detection by converting it into a regression problem. It used convolutional neural networks to directly predict object boundaries and determine object categories, achieving real-time object detection and heralding a new era of One-Stage object detection algorithms. With ongoing optimizations and improvements, the YOLO series has evolved to YOLOv8.However, it's worth noting that YOLO series algorithms are primarily designed for detecting common objects, and their performance in detecting small objects like traffic signs still requires further improvement.

## 2.2 Small Object Detection

Small object detection is typically defined in two ways: relative size definition, where the object size is less than 10% of the original image size, and absolute size definition, where the object size is smaller than 32 × 32 pixels. Therefore, in object detection tasks, detecting small objects is often more challenging. On one hand, this is because small objects have low resolution, limited visual information, and are highly susceptible to environmental interference. On the other hand, small objects occupy a small area in the image, and even a slight offset in the predicted bounding box can result in significant errors during the prediction process. Currently, improvements in small object detection primarily fall into the following categories: multi-scale detection, high resolution, and context awareness. For multi-scale detection, in 2018, the Cui [9] team used shallow feature maps to detect smaller objects and deep feature maps to detect larger objects. Regarding context awareness, there are several methods such as FPN [10] and PAN [11], which use top-down and bottom-up pathways to fuse features from different layers. Additionally, more powerful prediction heads also have an impact on the detection results of small objects.

## 2.3 Traffic Sign Detection

Traffic Sign Detection (TSD) is a branch of object detection that has gained prominence in recent years with the rise of technologies such as driver assistance systems and autonomous driving. Traditional methods for traffic sign recognition primarily rely on color and shape-based approaches, involving the manual extraction of specific image features. For example, in 2009, the Belaroussi [12] team used corner vertices and corner unions to detect triangular traffic signs. In 2013, the Fleyeh [13] team employed color segmentation based on AdaBoost binary classifiers and cyclic Hough transform for traffic sign detection. In 2014, the Yang [14] team introduced the Ohta color probability model for traffic sign detection by creating color probability maps. However, traditional detection methods often suffer from limited generalization, leading to a sharp decline in detection performance when colors fade or shapes change. With the development of convolutional neural networks (CNNs), deep learning-based approaches have been widely adopted in traffic sign detection. In 2020, the Zhang [15] team proposed the Cascade R-CNN, building upon the Two-Stage detection algorithm. Cascade R-CNN obtains multi-scale features of a pyramid, refines features by dot products and softmax-weighted multi-scale features, and utilizes their phases to highlight traffic sign features, thereby improving the accuracy of traffic sign detection. However, it's worth noting that Two-Stage models tend to have complex structures and require more computational resources.

## 3   Improvements Based on YOLOv8

This paper introduces an effective traffic sign detection algorithm called YOLOv8_ODY. In this model, two modules are incorporated into the Backbone and Head of YOLOv8, respectively. The following sections will provide a detailed overview of the overall structure of the improved model and the two modules introduced, along with their advantages.

### 3.1   The Architecture of YOLOv8_ODY

This section will provide a detailed introduction to the network architecture of YOLOv8_ODY. Similar to YOLOv8, the new model is still composed of three parts: Backbone, Neck, and Head, as shown in Fig. 1 of the network structure. In comparison to the YOLOv8 model, to enhance the model's feature capturing and extraction capabilities, we introduce ODConv [16] to replace the C2f structure in the Backbone. This convolution learns complementary attention in four dimensions: spatial, input channels, output channels, and the number of convolutional kernels. It then adaptively determines the weight of each kernel based on the input, overcoming the limitations of static convolution. Furthermore, by introducing DyHead [17] in the Head, we enhance the model's feature perception from three aspects: spatial position, spatial scale, and task region, adding self-attention mechanisms.

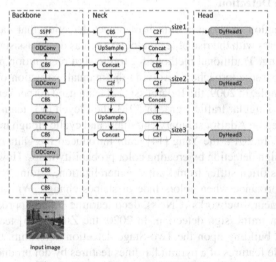

**Fig. 1.**  The architecture of YOLOv8_ODY

### 3.2   ODConv

YOLOv8 uses traditional static convolution to generate features. In traditional static convolution, convolution kernel parameters are determined through training, and the same convolution kernel is used to perform the same operation on all input images. In other words, static convolution applies the same network structure and parameters to all input data. The number of output channels in the convolution layer is equal to the number of filters, and the dimension of each filter depends on the dimension of the input features. Its calculation can be described using Eq. 3.1:

$$y = W * x \tag{3.1}$$

Here, 'x' represents the input features, and 'W' represents the convolution layer. It's evident that the convolution kernels for each filter do not change under different inputs. To address this issue, this paper introduces Dynamic Convolution (ODConv) into the YOLOv8 network structure.

Unlike traditional static convolution kernels, dynamic convolution kernels can adaptively adjust their shape and weight based on the input data's features, thereby obtaining better representation capability in different scenarios. Dynamic convolution employs 'n' convolution kernels combined linearly through attention mechanisms, making the convolution operation input-dependent. The computation of dynamic convolution is described by Eq. 3.2:

$$y = (\alpha_{w1} W_1 + \alpha_{w2} W_2 + \cdots \alpha_{wn} W_n) * x \tag{3.2}$$

Here, $W\_i$ represents a given convolution kernel. Existing dynamic convolutions like CondConv [18] and DyConv [19] compute a single attention scalar $\alpha_{wi}$ for each convolution kernel. However, for the given 'n' convolution kernels, corresponding to four-dimensional kernel space dimensions including kernel size $k * k$, input channels $C_{in}$, output channels $C_{out}$, and the number of convolution kernels 'n', adopting a single attention scalar for each convolution kernel as in CondConv or DyConv implies that the output filters have the same attention values for the input. This results in a coarse utilization of kernel space when designing attention mechanisms to provide dynamic features for 'n' convolution kernels. In contrast, ODConv employs a multi-dimensional attention mechanism through a parallel strategy. It learns complementary attention scalars along the four dimensions of kernel space, providing better performance to capture rich contextual information and significantly enhancing the feature extraction capabilities of the fundamental CNN convolution operation. The computation of ODConv can be represented by Eq. 3.3:

$$y = \begin{pmatrix} \alpha_{s1} \odot \alpha_{c1} \odot \alpha_{f1} \odot \alpha_{w1} \odot W_1 + \\ \cdots \\ +\alpha_{sn} \odot \alpha_{cn} \odot \alpha_{fn} \odot \alpha_{wn} \odot W_n \end{pmatrix} * x \tag{3.3}$$

Here, $\alpha_{si}$, $\alpha_{ci}$, $\alpha_{fi}$, $\alpha_{wi}$ represent attention scalars along the four dimensions of the convolution kernel $W_i$: spatial, input channels, output channels, and the number of convolution kernels, respectively. These scalars are computed through the attention function $\pi_{wi}(x)$. The process of generating attention scalars by the attention function is illustrated in Fig. 2. First, the input values 'x' are compressed into a feature vector of length '$C_{in}$' through channel-wise Global Average Pooling (GAP) operations. Subsequently, this feature vector passes through a fully connected layer (FC) and a Rectified Linear Unit

(ReLU). For each of the four branches, there is an FC layer with output sizes of '$k * k$', '$C_{in1}$', '$C_{out1}$', and 'n1', respectively, followed by a Softmax or Sigmoid function, which generates normalized attention scalars $\alpha_{si}$, $\alpha_{ci}$, $\alpha_{fi}$, $\alpha_{wi}$.

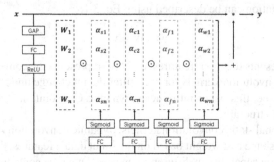

**Fig. 2.** The process of generating attention scalars by ODConv

The proposed YOLOv8_ODY utilizes ODConv, replacing the original C2f structure in the Backbone in a plug-and-play manner. It adaptively adjusts convolution kernels based on different input traffic sign images, significantly enhancing the model's feature extraction capabilities without increasing network width and depth. This strengthens the network's learning ability and greatly improves the model's accuracy in recognizing traffic sign targets.

### 3.3  DyHead

In YOLOv8_ODY, to enhance the perception capability of the Head, we introduce the Dynamic Detection Framework (DyHead) as a detector. This framework combines spatial scale, spatial position, and task perception with a multi-head self-attention mechanism. Compared to the original Head, both expressive power and detection accuracy are significantly improved. In order to achieve scale awareness, spatial awareness, and task awareness simultaneously in a unified object detection head, DyHead designs attention mechanisms in three parts:

1. Spatial Awareness Attention: Relies on deformable convolution to extract the target positions from feature maps.
2. Scale Awareness Attention: Utilizes a $1 \times 1$ convolution structure, sequentially applying Rectified Linear Units (RELU) and hard sigmoid activation functions. By fusing feature maps of different scales, it obtains spatial scale information.
3. Task Awareness Attention: Employs a fully connected network as a classifier, expanding input information for classification.

As shown in Fig. 3, DyHead first uses spatial awareness attention to obtain three feature maps at different scales, namely temp3, temp4, and temp5. These maps are then upsampled or downsampled to a uniform scale and fused with each other to form new three-dimensional tensors $F_1$, $F_2$, $F_3$ ($F_i \in R^{L \times S \times C}$), where L represents the number of feature levels, S represents feature map size, and C represents the number of channels.

Subsequently, through scale awareness and task awareness attention mechanisms, feature tensors $F_1$, $F_2$ and $F_3$ are processed to generate anchor box information.

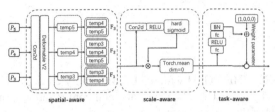

**Fig. 3.** The implementation mechanism of DyHead

## 4  Experimental Results and Analysis

This chapter will introduce the dataset used, experimental configurations and evaluation metrics, ablation and comparative experimental results, and analysis.

### 4.1  TT100K Dataset

This paper utilizes the Tsinghua-Tencent 100K dataset to validate the proposed YOLOv8_ODY model. This dataset was jointly developed by Tsinghua University and Tencent, encompassing various instances of traffic signs under complex weather and environmental conditions. It aims to provide a more challenging training and test set for traffic sign detection and recognition tasks, further advancing research and applications in fields like autonomous driving and intelligent transportation systems.

The complete dataset comprises 221 types of traffic signs, with each data sample having a resolution of $2048 \times 2048$ pixels. In total, there are approximately 100,000 images containing 230,000 traffic signs. However, during experimental analysis, it was discovered that the original dataset contained a large number of traffic signs with extremely low proportions, leading to data imbalance and making effective learning difficult. To address this issue, the dataset underwent further analysis and processing before experiments were conducted. Ultimately, 45 types of traffic signs with more than 100 samples each were selected. Signs starting with 'w' indicate warning signs, those starting with 'p' represent prohibition signs, and those starting with 'i' denote regulatory signs, as detailed in Table 1. The processed dataset was designed to improve data balance and effectiveness, consisting of a total of 8,764 images. The training set contains 7,011 images, while the test set contains 1,653 images.

### 4.2  Experimental Configuration and Evaluation Criteria

#### 4.2.1  Experimental Configuration

The experimental environment for this study includes the Ubuntu 18.06 operating system and hardware consisting of a dual-core CPU with 32 GB of memory. Additionally, it is

**Table 1.** Specific categories of the dataset

| Category | Sign Name |
|---|---|
| Warning signs | w13,w55,w32,w57,w59 |
| Forbidden signs | pl80,p6,p5,pm55,pl60,p11,p23,pg,ph4,pl70,pne,ph4.5,p12,p3,pl5,pl30,p10, pn,p26,p13,pr40,pl20,pm30,pl40,pl120,ph5,pl100,p19,pm20,p27,pl50 |
| Indicating signs | ip,i2r,il80,i4,i41,i2,il60,il100,i5 |

equipped with an RTX 3090 GPU with a 24 GB memory capacity. The deep learning framework used is PyTorch 1.7. The environmental configuration remains unchanged for the experiments in the following sections.

### 4.2.2 Evaluation Criteria

In object detection tasks, precision (P) represents the proportion of correctly detected objects to the total predicted objects, while recall (R) represents the proportion of correctly detected objects to the total number of objects. Their calculation formulas are shown in Eqs. 4.1 and 4.2, respectively:

$$P = \frac{TP}{TP+FP} \times 100\% \tag{4.1}$$

$$R = \frac{TP}{TP+FN} \times 100\% \tag{4.2}$$

Here, TP represents the count of accurately recognized objects, FP represents the count of incorrectly detected objects, and FN represents the count of undetected objects. Average Precision (AP) represents the precision values at different recall points for a single category. It is computed by calculating the area enclosed by the P-R curve, as defined in Eq. 4.3. mAP is the average of AP values across all categories, calculated using the formula in Eq. 4.4. A higher mAP value indicates a higher accuracy of the algorithm. In the experiments of this paper, mAP@0.5 is the average precision for traffic sign categories with an IOU threshold set to 0.5 and serves as the primary evaluation metric.

$$AP = \int_0^1 P_i(R_i)dR_i \tag{4.3}$$

$$mAP = \frac{\sum_{i=1}^{C} AP_i}{C} \times 100\% \tag{4.4}$$

### 4.3 Experimental Results and Analysis

### 4.3.1 Ablation Experiments

This paper evaluates the effectiveness of the ODConv and DyHead modules on the public TT100k dataset, and the experimental results are shown in Table 2. The results indicate that both introduced modules contribute to the improvement of the model's performance.

A total of four sets of experiments were conducted, and from the table, it can be observed that the ODConv module had a relatively significant improvement in the

**Table 2.** Ablation Experiments Results

|            | ODConv | DyHead | mAP@0.5 (%) |
|------------|--------|--------|-------------|
| YOLOv8_ODY |        |        | 85.1        |
| YOLOv8_ODY | √      |        | 86.5        |
| YOLOv8_ODY |        | √      | 86.0        |
| YOLOv8_ODY | √      | √      | 87.7        |

algorithm's detection performance, increasing mAP@0.5 by 1.1%. While the addition of DyHead was not as effective as ODConv, it still led to an improvement in detection results. Furthermore, the inclusion of both modules resulted in a 2.6% increase in mAP@0.5 compared to the original model.

### 4.3.2 Comparative Experiments

The experimental results indicate that the optimized algorithm achieved a 2.6% improvement in mAP@0.5 compared to the original algorithm, demonstrating that the added modules enhanced the model's ability to detect traffic signs. Figure 4 shows the mAP curve for the YOLOv8_ODY model, which tends to converge around 150 epochs, achieving the best training results within the specified maximum training iterations. Figure 5 provides a comparison of detection results on TT100k before and after algorithm improvement. Panels a and c display the detection images for the unimproved YOLOv8, while panels b and d show recognition images for the optimized model. It can be observed that the improved model achieved a certain improvement in recognition accuracy.

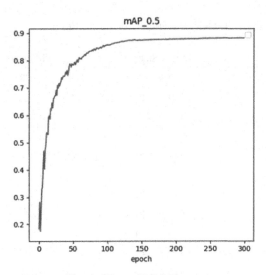

**Fig. 4.** The mAP@0.5 curve

**Fig. 5.** Detection results on TT100k before and after algorithm improvement

To evaluate the improvement, the recognition performance of YOLOv8_ODY was compared with other models on the TT100k dataset through experiments. Table 3 shows the comparison between the improved algorithm and other models, including One-Stage models such as the YOLO series, Retina Net, and SSD, as well as other improved models of YOLO. From the data in the table, it can be seen that the mAP of the YOLOv8_ODY model is as high as 87.7%, generally higher than other One-Stage models, and 1.2% higher than the TRD-YOLO model, demonstrating the effectiveness of the improved model.

**Table 3.** Ablation Experiments Results

| models | Input Size | Map@0.5 |
|---|---|---|
| SSD | 300 × 300 | 0.678 |
| RetinaNet | 640 × 640 | 0.726 |
| YOLOv3 | 416 × 416 | 0.743 |
| YOLOv4 | 640 × 640 | 0.768 |
| YOLOv5 | 640 × 640 | 0.769 |
| YOLOv7 | 640 × 640 | 0.837 |
| Yan et al. [20] | 640 × 640 | 0.835 |
| YOLOX [21] | 640 × 640 | 0.849 |
| YOLOv8 | 640 × 640 | 0.851 |
| TRD-YOLO [22] | 640 × 640 | 0.865 |
| **ours** | **640 × 640** | **0.877** |

# 5  Conclusion

This paper aims to improve the accuracy of traffic sign recognition without increasing the model's complexity. Traffic sign recognition has been a challenge in the field of object detection due to the unique characteristics of its input size and various real-world environmental factors. While previous One-Stage models and other improved models have achieved good detection results in this direction, there is still a demand for improved model accuracy. In this paper, we propose the YOLOv8_ODY model based on YOLOv8, which introduces ODConv in the Backbone to replace C2f. ODConv enhances the model's ability to capture targets by adding complementary attention in four dimensions of the convolution kernel. In the Head, we introduce DyHead to enhance perception of spatial position, spatial scale, and task region. Experimental results show that YOLOv8_ODY achieves an mAP@0.5 of 87.7% without changing the model's depth. This is a significant improvement compared to other One-Stage models and other improved models, demonstrating its valuable applications in traffic sign detection.

# References

1. Wei, H., Yang, X.: Object detection method based on improved one-stage detector. In: 2020 5th International Conference on Smart Grid and Electrical Automation (ICSGEA), pp. 209–212 (2020)
2. Liu, Y., Han, J., Zhang, Q., et al.: Salient object detection via two-stage graphs. IEEE Trans. Circuits Syst. Video Technol. **29**(4), 1023–1037 (2019)
3. Girshick, R., Donahue, J., Darrell, T., Malik, J.: Rich feature hierarchies for accurate object detection and semantic segmentation. In: Proceedings of IEEE Conference on Computer Vision Pattern Recognition, June 2014, pp. 580–587 (2014)
4. Girshick, R.: 'Fast R-CNN. In: Proceedings of IEEE International Conference on Computer Vision (ICCV), June 2015, pp. 1440–1448 (2015)
5. Ren, S., He, K., Girshick, R., Sun, J.: Faster R-CNN: towards real-time object detection with region proposal networks. In: Proceedings of Advanced Neural Information Processing Systems, vol. 28, pp. 91–99 (2015)
6. He, K., Zhang, X., Ren, S., Sun, J.: Spatial pyramid pooling in deep convolutional networks for visual recognition. IEEE Trans. Pattern Anal. Mach. Intell. **37**(9), 1904–1916 (2015)
7. Liu, W., et al.: SSD: single shot multibox detector. In: Leibe, B., Matas, J., Sebe, N., Welling, M. (eds.) Computer Vision – ECCV 2016. ECCV 2016. LNCS, vol. 9905, pp. 21–37. Springer, Cham (2016). https://doi.org/10.1007/978-3-319-46448-0_2
8. Redmon, J., Divvala, S., Girshick, R., Farhadi, A.: You Only Look Once: unified, real-time object detection. In: Proceedings of IEEE Conference on Computer Vision Pattern Recognition (CVPR), June 2016, pp. 779–788 (2016)
9. Cui, L., et al.: MDSSD: multi-scale deconvolutional single shot detector for small objects. arXiv:1805.07009 (2018)
10. Lin, T.Y., Dollár, P., Girshick, R., He, K., Hariharan, B., Belongie, S.: Feature pyramid networks for object detection. In: Proceedings of IEEE Conference on Computer Vision and Pattern Recognition (CVPR) (2017)
11. Liu, S., Qi, L., Qin, H., Shi, J., Jia, J.: Path aggregation network for instance segmentation. In: Proceedings of the IEEE Conference on Computer Vision and Pattern Recognition, Salt Lake City, UT, USA, 18–23 June 2018, pp. 8759–8768 (2018)

12. Belaroussi, R., Tarel, J.-P.: Angle vertex and bisector geometric model for triangular road sign detection. In: Proceedings of Workshop on Applications of Computer Vision (WACV), pp. 1–7, December 2009
13. Fleyeh, H., Biswas, R., Davami, E.: Traffic sign detection based on AdaBoost color segmentation and SVM classification. In: Proceedings of Eurocon, pp. 2005–2010 (2013)
14. Yang, Y., Wu, F.: Real-time traffic sign detection via color probability model and integral channel features. In: Li, S., Liu, C., Wang, Y. (eds.) Proceedings of Chinese Conference on Pattern Recognition, pp. 545–554. Springer, Heidelberg (2014)
15. Zhang, J., Xie, Z., Sun, J., Zou, X., Wang, J.: A cascaded R-CNN with multiscale attention and imbalanced samples for traffic sign detection. IEEE Access **8**, 29742–29754 (2020)
16. Li, C., Zhou, A., Yao, A.: Omni-dimensional dynamic convolution. arXiv preprint arXiv: 2209.07947 (2022)
17. Dai, X., Chen, Y., Xiao, B., et al.: Dynamic head: unifying object detection heads with attentions. In: Proceedings of the IEEE/CVF Conference on Computer Vision and Pattern Recognition, pp. 7373–7382 (2021)
18. Yang, B., Bender, G., Le, Q.V., et al.: CondConv: conditionally parameterized convolutions for efficient inference. In: Advances in Neural Information Processing Systems, vol. 32 (2019)
19. Chen, Y., Dai, X., Liu, M., et al.: Dynamic convolution: attention over convolution kernels. In: Proceedings of the IEEE/CVF Conference on Computer Vision and Pattern Recognition, pp. 11030–11039 (2020)
20. Yan, B., Li, J., Yang, Z., et al.: AIE-YOLO: auxiliary information enhanced YOLO for small object detection. Sensors **22**(21), 8221 (2022)
21. Ge, Z., Liu, S., Wang, F., et al.: YOLOx: exceeding YOLO series in 2021. arXiv 2021. arXiv preprint arXiv:2107.08430 (2021)
22. Chu, J., Zhang, C., Yan, M., et al.: TRD-YOLO: a real-time, high-performance small traffic sign detection algorithm. Sensors **23**(8), 3871 (2023)

# Mask-Based Matching Enhancement
# for Unsupervised Point Cloud Registration

Minghua Jiang, Liyu Ren, Zhaoxiang Chen, Li Liu, and Feng Yu[✉]

Wuhan Textile University, Wuhan, China
{minghuajiang,l_liu,yufeng}@wtu.edu.cn, {renliy,
pclchenzx}@yeah.net

**Abstract.** Partial point cloud registration stands as a pivotal pre-processing stage within computer vision applications, such as robotics, medical imaging, and autonomous driving. Previous feature-based methods rely on the quality of feature extraction to accurately estimate rigid transformations, but non-overlapping regions can easily resist this approach. Enhancing the information quality of overlapping regions and mitigating the side effects of non-overlapping regions in point cloud alignment algorithms hold considerable significance. In order to achieve this objective, we propose an unsupervised mask-based matching enhancement method for overlapping region matching. In our method, we introduce a mask generation module to obtain overlapping information while leveraging EdgeConv to acquire neighborhood information. Subsequently, we integrate this information into the point-wise matching map through the point-wise matching enhancement module, aiming to refine the estimation of point-wise matching, which leads to the generation of a more sophisticated pseudo-target point cloud through establishing more reliable correspondences. Our method demonstrates superior performance relative to existing methods, as evidenced by the experimental results on the ModelNet40, 7Scenes, and ICL-NUIM datasets.

**Keywords:** point cloud registration · over-lapping region matching · mask-based matching enhancement

## 1 Introduction

Point cloud data plays a pivotal role in the realm of robotics, autonomous driving, 3D scene reconstruction [1], simultaneous localization and mapping [2] and contemporary virtual try-on [3] and other related domains [4–12]. The advancement of these realms has also brought forth new challenges and opportunities to the field of point cloud registration [13]. The process of registering point clouds strives to align numerous point clouds captured from various perspectives or temporal moments. The ambition behind point cloud registration is to ascertain the rigid transformation of overlapping domains within the aligned point clouds.

ICP [14] is an extensively used algorithm that facilitates the registration process by iteratively finding correspondences and computing rigid transformations using singular

© The Author(s), under exclusive license to Springer Nature Singapore Pte Ltd. 2025
N. Magnenat Thalmann et al. (Eds.): CASA 2024, CCIS 2374, pp. 13–27, 2025.
https://doi.org/10.1007/978-981-96-2681-6_2

value decomposition (SVD). In similar fashion, FGR [15] extracts FPFH characteristics for swift global enrollment. Nevertheless, these methodologies are susceptible to initial alignment and grapple with partially intersecting point clouds.

Supervised methods developed to address limitations via local and global features for more accurate matches [16–18]. RPM-Net [19] predicts incomplete point correlations through 4D features and Sinkhorn optimization for partial registration [20]. PRNet's iterative framework uses L2-norm keypoints for partial registration [21]. ReAgent [22] introduced reinforcement learning [23] to obtain a sequence of transformations for point clouds.

Additionally, ground truth acquisition is resource-intensive, limiting practicality. Significant efforts focus on advancing unsupervised methods. CEMNet's decision framework enables unsupervised alignment [24]. RIENet iteratively refines matching maps and confidence via correspondences [25]. STORM estimates overlaps from Transformer [6, 26] distributions, achieving good performance on sparsely overlapped clouds. However, existing approaches still have limitations in fully leveraging overlapping information and adequately handling impacts from non-overlapping parts, as overlapping signals cannot be sufficiently exploited and outliers' influences cannot be well alleviated.

In this paper, we propose a novel mask-based matching enhancement method for unsupervised point cloud registration. The method aims to establish an effective point-wise matching map for input point clouds by leveraging overlapping information and fusion spatial information while reducing the negative impact of outliers. Specifically, for a given point cloud pair of unknown relations, we first obtain their spatial features by using EdgeConv, a neural network operation based on GNN [27] that can learn the structural features of each point and its neighboring points. Simultaneously, we propose a mask generation (MG) module to encode global and local fusion features to generate masks containing overlapping information. The neighborhood features and masks are inputted into the point-wise matching enhancement (PME) module. The PME module aims to improve the estimation of the matching relationship between point pairs and generate a more accurate matching map by overlapping information and integrated spatial information. Through this process, we obtain more reliable correspondences and generate more accurate pseudo-point point clouds. Inspired by RIENet [25], we calculate point-wise confidence scores of correspondence by comparing the structural differences between the pseudo-point point clouds and the source point cloud. The key motivation is that the spatial structures of correct matching points are similar, but those of wrong matching points differ significantly. Thus, the geometric structural differences between the source and pseudo-point clouds can serve as an evaluation standard. Finally, we compute a weighted SVD using the confidence scores and correspondences to obtain the rigid transformation. Experimental results show that our method improves the quality and accuracy of point cloud registration in unsupervised tasks.

In summary, our main contributions are as follows:

- We propose an unsupervised mask-based matching enhancement method that incorporates overlapping information and neighborhood information to generate correspondences in the task of incomplete point clouds.

- In the mask generation module, we fuse global and local features to obtain continuous masks with overlapping information. We also utilize a dice loss function to supervise the mask learning of reliable overlapping regions.
- In the point-wise matching enhancement module, we integrate overlapping information and neighborhood information into the matching map to improve point-wise correspondence performance.

## 2  Related Work

### 2.1  Traditional Point Cloud Registration

In point cloud registration [28], traditional methods have been widely used to align input point clouds. One of the commonly employed methods is the Iterative Closest Point (ICP) [14]. ICP iteratively generates point pairs based on spatial distance and estimates the rigid transformation using least-squares [29]. However, ICP has limitations such as susceptibility to local optima and difficulties in differentiating inlier and outlier correspondences. To overcome these limitations, various methods have been proposed to enhance registration performance. These include Generalized-ICP [30], Go-ICP [31], and FGR [15]. Generalized ICP improves algorithm robustness by incorporating a module endowed with inherent ambiguity into the vanilla ICP. Go-ICP looks for ideal solutions inside the SE(3) by combining ICP with the Branch-and-Bound process. FGR utilizes alternate optimization techniques to speed up iterations without relying on the use of RANSAC [32] and nearest-neighbor calculations. These traditional point cloud registration methods are designed to address challenges in the registration process, but they require careful initialization and can present difficulties in falling into local minima or computational efficiency.

### 2.2  Supervised Point Cloud Registration

Due to the excellent feature description capabilities of deep learning, several supervised point cloud registration methods have been designed to overcome poor initialization challenges. PointNetLK [33] integrates the Lucas & Kanade (LK) algorithm into Point-Net [34] to achieve point cloud registration. DCP [35] combines DGCNN [36] for feature extraction and Transformer [37] for learning context information. Its excellent performance on the ModelNet40 [38] dataset proves that learning fusion spatial information can facilitate point cloud registration. IDAM [39] incorporates feature and Euclidean spatial information into the process of pairwise point-matching using a progressive awareness of distances along-side a module for convolving similarity matrices. GeoTransformer [40] encodes distance and angle information between super-points into a Transformer [37] architecture to overcome the challenge of ultra-low overlapping rate. MAC [41] achieves accurate 3D point cloud registration by mining local consensus information in a compatibility graph. RSSR [42] achieves point cloud registration with limited inliers by reconstructing correspondence constraints, allowing the discovery of more potential correspondences. OMNet [43] learns masks to reject points in non-overlapping regions in the partial task, which verifies the importance of overlapping region information for the registration task. In our unsupervised approach, we utilize continuous masks to capture overlapping information for enhancing correspondence, rather than rejecting points for feature extraction in non-overlapping regions. In particular, we encode the spatial fusion features to generate overlapping masks for our unsupervised tasks.

## 2.3 Unsupervised Point Cloud Registration

The challenge of unsupervised networks lies in choosing an evaluation method for aligned results, and various approaches have been put forth to handle this issue. Cycle consistency between pairwise point clouds is used for point matching in techniques like [44–46]. However, cycle consistency cannot be learned directly on partial data. FMR [47] incorporates a decoder branch and optimizes the global feature distance of the inputs. CorrNet3D [48] employs a permutation module to learn point clouds without known corresponding relationships, and performs unsupervised learning by comparing the reconstructed result to the target value. HTMC [49] uses a tolerant blur loss to handle occlusion and applies a differentiable mask to enhance overlapping areas, aiming to establish point correspondences for human registration tasks. In addition, there are deep unsupervised learning-based local descriptors for point cloud correspondence, such as [17, 18, 50]. However, these methods fall short of achieving end-to-end rigid transformations. They rely on a two-step process involving a feature extractor and a geometric matching technique called RANSAC [32]. Moreover, these methods primarily emphasize point-wise feature embedding, which poses challenges in distinguishing points within similarly featured regions. To deal with this problem, our method enhances point-wise matching by learning overlapping masks and neighborhood structure. In addition, we assesses confidence scores for weighted SVD by structural differences.

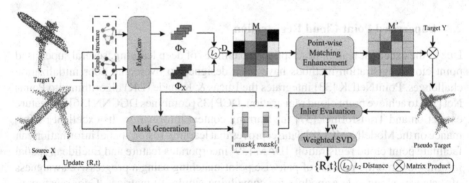

**Fig. 1.** The overall architecture of MMENet.

# 3   Method

In this section, we introduce the Mask-Based Matching Enhancement network (MMENet), a proposed registration method. The structure of MMENet is outlined, followed by a detailed description of how overlap information and neighborhood information are obtained and integrated for point-wise matching. Additionally, a trainingloss function is proposed.

## 3.1   Network Architecture

MMENet is an end-to-endpoint cloud registration network that enhances point-wise matching by leveraging overlap and neighborhood information. The framework of MMENet is depicted in Fig. 1. Specifically, given the source point cloud X and the target point cloud Y, we initially apply a mask generation (MG) module to generate overlapping masks that can describe point-wise overlapping information. Additionally, we extract neighborhood features utilizing EdgeConv. Overlapping masks and point-wise matching map M derived by neighborhood feature distance are delivered into the point-wise matching enhancement (PME) module to obtain an enhanced matching map. Moreover, inspired by RIENet [25] we incorporate an inlier evaluation module to optimize the network. By comparing the differences between the neighborhood features extracted from the source point cloud $Y$ and the pseudo-target point cloud $X'$, we assess the overlapping points and generate a confidence metric denoted as $w$. This similarity-based evaluation facilitates establishing correspondences between the point clouds. Based on the similarity of overlapping point features, a rough rigid transformation matrix containing a rotation matrix $R \in R^{3 \times 3}$ and a translation vector $t \in R^3$ can be obtained through weighted Singular Value Decomposition (SVD).

## 3.2   Mask Generation

In partial-to-partial point cloud matching tasks, particularly in noisy conditions, there exist non-overlapping regions between the input point clouds. Given a source point cloud $X = \{x_i \in R^3 | i = 1, 2, 3, ..., N\}$ and a target point cloud $Y = \{y_i \in R^3 | i = 1, 2, 3, ..., M\}$ where $X$ and $Y$ have an unknown correspondence. To increase the likelihood of correct point pairing in the overlapping regions and reduce the impact of point-wise matching estimation in non-overlapping regions, we integrate global and local features to learn overlapping masks. The masks are obtained by decoding the fusion features, they provide a point-wise description of the overlapping information in the point cloud. The composition of the Mask Generation (MG) module is shown in Fig. 2. To be more specific, the objective of both global and local feature extraction is to become proficient in two functions, $F(\cdot)$ and $f(\cdot)$, that can produce unique global features, $F_X$ and $F_Y$, and local features, $f_X$ and $f_Y$, from the input point clouds $X$ and $Y$. Maintaining the orientation and spatial coordinates of the original input is crucial to estimating the rigid transformation based on the difference between the two global features. Drawing inspiration from PointNet [34], the features of the input X and Y are determined at each iteration using the following equation:

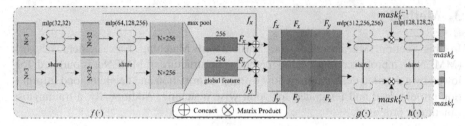

**Fig. 2.** The composition of the MG Module.

$$f_\beta = MLP\{\beta\},$$
$$F_\beta = \max\{f_\beta\}, \beta \in \{X, Y\}, \tag{1}$$

where $f(\cdot)$ represents a multi-layer perceptron (MLP) that receives inputs $X$ and $Y$ and produces point-wise features $f_X$ and $f_Y$. The point-wise features $f_X$ and $f_Y$ are combined using a max-pooling operation, denoted as $max(\cdot)$, capable of handling an arbitrary number of unordered points.

In addition, during each iteration, the global features $F_X$ and $F_Y$ are combined with their respective point features $f_X$ and $f_Y$ by concatenation. These combined features are then fed back into the point-wise features. They are sent to shared MLPs, denoted by $g(\cdot)$, in order to improve the overlapping information within these mixed features. The fusion features are subsequently utilized for partitioning the overlapping regions and estimating rigid transformations. Specifically, we can obtain $mask_X^i$ and $mask_Y^i$ as:

$$mask_X^i = h\Big(g(f_X \oplus F_X \oplus F_Y) \cdot mask_X^{i-1}\Big),$$
$$mask_Y^i = h\Big(g(f_Y \oplus F_Y \oplus F_X) \cdot mask_Y^{i-1}\Big), \tag{2}$$

where the generation network for overlapping, denoted as $h(\cdot)$, is comprised of multiple convolution layers, followed by a softmax layer. The fused point-wise features generated by the function $g(\cdot)$ are defined as $g_X$ and $g_Y$, representing the inputs $X$ and $Y$. The operation $\oplus$ denotes the concatenation of these features. The overlapping mask obtained from the fusion feature decoding contains the overlap confidence of each point in the point cloud, which is used to describe the overlap information.

### 3.3  Point-Wise Matching Enhancement

Point cloud registration methods commonly utilize the single-point feature distance to construct the matching score matrix. However, these methods may encounter difficulties when faced with similar feature points, which can impact the accuracy of the matching scores. To address this limitation, we utilize a point-wise matching enhancement module to enhance neighborhood consistency and overlapping information by considering the neighborhood of the matching points and overlapping masks. The principle is that correctly corresponding point pairs usually exhibit high neighborhood consistency and high overlapping confidence. Conversely, if the neighborhood consistency score is low and the overlap confidence is low, it indicates that there may be an incorrect correspondence. The details of the point-wise matching enhancement module are illustrated in Fig. 3. More specifically, we create a common Edge-Conv from the unaligned input point clouds X and Y during the first neighborhood feature embedding step. The feature representations $\Phi_X \in R^{P \times d}$ and $\Phi_Y \in R^{Q \times d}$ are produced as a con- sequence of this transformation, where d is the dimension of the extracted features. The neighborhood feature $\Phi$ that the EdgeConv produced is stated as follows:

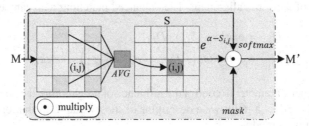

**Fig. 3.** The specifics of the PME module.

$$\Phi = \varphi\{MLP\{concat(x_i, x_i - x_j), \forall j \in P_i\}\}, \tag{3}$$

where *concat* denotes the action of joining the feature embedding and describers of neighbor differences of the vertex, and $P_i$ represents the neighbors j of point i in the graph of edges. The perceptrons with multiple layers (MLPs) that translate the relative feature into a higher-dimensional feature space are indicated by the symbol *MLP*. The aggregation process, max pooling, is represented by $\varphi$.

Following the extraction of features, points in the two input point clouds are associated with their respective feature. The describers of the feature extracted from point $x_i$ and point $y_j$, which are in the input two point clouds, are used to compute the negative distance between their features. This negative feature distance is then normalized using the *softmax* function, resulting in the following expression:

$$M_{i,j} = softmax([-D_{i,1}, \ldots, -D_{i,M}])_j, \tag{4}$$

where $D_{i,j}$ represents the Euclidean distance between the single-point features of point $x_i$ and point $y_j$ as $|\Phi_{X_i} - \Phi_{Y_j}|$. It measures the dissimilarity between the features of these two points in terms of their spatial distance. By using the obtained point-wise matching map, we can calculate the neighborhood-wise scores by taking the average of the correspondence scores of the surrounding points:

$$S_{i,j} = \frac{1}{K} \sum_{X_p \in N_{X_i}} \sum_{Y_q \in N_{Y_j}} M_{i,j}, \tag{5}$$

where $N_{X_i}$ represents the set of k-nearest neighbor points surrounding a particular point $X_i$. The neighborhood score serves as a quantitative measure of the alignment quality between the corresponding point and its surrounding points, specifically in terms of their matching probabilities. It provides an assessment of how effectively the neighboring points conform to the expected correspondence, indicating the degree of agreement in their matching probabilities. The neighborhood score and overlapping confidence serve as valuable tools in distinguishing non-corresponding point pairs. It capitalizes on the observation that genuine correspondences exhibit high neighborhood similarity and overlap confidence, while incorrect correspondences tend to have low values in these regards. By incorporating this information, we optimize the matching map to enhance the accuracy of the correspondences between the point clouds, enabling a more reliable representation of their true alignment. The enhanced matching map can be expressed a

$$
\begin{aligned}
D'_{i,j} &= \exp(\alpha - S_{i,j}) \cdot D_{i,j}, \\
M'_{i,j} &= softmax\left(\left[-D'_{i,1}, \ldots, -D'_{i,M}\right]\right)_j \cdot mask,
\end{aligned}
\tag{6}
$$

where $\alpha$ is a hyper-parameter to control the influence of neighborhood on optimal matching points and *mask* is a point-wise descriptor of the overlap information obtained by the mask generation module.

### 3.4 Loss Function

Due to the efficient rows of the Dice loss function in the segmentation task, we design a similar mask loss to constrain the mask prediction of the network to obtain more reliable overlap information. We encode the target point cloud and the transformed source point cloud after ground truth transformation to obtain $mask_{gt}$. The expression for $L_{mask}$ is as follows:

$$
L_{mask} = 1 - \frac{2 \times mask_{pred} \cdot mask_{gt}}{\left|mask_{pred}\right| + \left|mask_{gt}\right|}
\tag{7}
$$

In implementation, during the operation of our network, we use loss function from RIE and $L_{mask}$ as:

$$
Loss = Loss_{RIE} + \lambda \cdot L_{mask},
\tag{8}
$$

where $\lambda$ acts as a hyper-parameter to control the weight of the used mask loss.

## 4 Experiments

The experimental parameters and the point cloud registration datasets are initially presented in this section. Next, we contrast our method with alternative point cloud methods on different datasets. For a visualization comparison of the registration results, refer to Fig. 4.

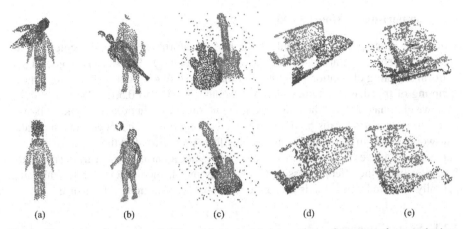

(a)          (b)          (c)          (d)          (e)

**Fig. 4.** The registration results of different datasets. (a)–(e) are the performance of our method on the Same Categories, Unseen Categories, Gaussian Noise, ICL-NUIM, and 7Scenes test datasets.

## 4.1  Experimental Settings

We conduct an evaluation of our method on multiple datasets, including ModelNet40 [38], 7Scenes [51], and ICL-NUIM [52] datasets. There are 12,311 meshed CAD models in 40 categories in the ModelNet40 collection. We use a split of 80% and 20% for testing and training, respectively. This dataset provides a wide variety of items to assess our method's effectiveness. The 7Scenes dataset serves as a widely recognized standard of point cloud alignment assignments in indoor environments. To ensure a comprehensive evaluation of different indoor conditions, we use data sets in training and testing at a approximately ratio of ModelNet40, with a specific number of 278 samples and 53 samples. For the synthetic indoor scene dataset, ICL-NUIM and 7Scenes, we augment the existing dataset and subsequently split it into 1,278 samples for training and 200 samples for testing. This dataset provides additional challenges and variations, enabling a robust assessment of our method's performance in synthetic indoor environments.

We compare our method with traditional approaches, including ICP [14] and FGR [15]. Additionally, it is compared with deep learning methods, such as supervised DCP [35] and IDAM [39], as well as unsupervised CEMNet [24] and RIENet [25]. We use PyTorch to construct our model, and the Adam optimizer is used to optimize the model parameters. 0.001 is the starting learning rate. To train the network for the ModelNet40, we need 75 epochs. As a learning rate decay technique, we double the learning rate by 0.7 at epochs 25 and 50. We employ a similar learning rate decline technique for the interior scenarios. More specifically, for epochs 25, 50, and 75, we multiply the learning rate by 0.7. Using these indoor datasets, the model is trained for a total of 100 epochs. We employ the widely-used assessment metrics of mean absolute error (MAE) and root mean square error (RMSE) in point cloud registration, which offer quantitative metrics to evaluate the precision and caliber of the registration output. For rotation measurement, the root mean square error $RMSE(\mathbf{R})$ and mean absolute error $MAE(\mathbf{R})$ in degrees are utilized, whereas root mean square error $RMSE(\mathbf{t})$ and mean absolute error $MAE(\mathbf{t})$ are used for translation.

## 4.2 Comparison on ModelNet40

Within the training set, a randomly generated transformation matrix is employed to convert each source point cloud $X$ into a target point cloud $Y$. Each axis is subjected to a uniform sampling of rotational degrees ranging from 0 to 45°, and each axis undergoes sampling of translational values within the range of $-0.5$ to 0.5. In line with PRNet [21], we eliminate 25% of the points from input point cloud in order to replicate partial registration scenarios. This partial point cloud data presents challenges and simulates real-world data with incomplete point cloud information. Based on the results in Table 1, our method achieves the lowest error compared to traditional and deep learning methods. It demonstrates the effectiveness and superiority of our method inaccurately aligning partially observed point clouds and achieving robust registration performance.

### 4.2.1 Same Categories

In this experiment, we evaluate the noise-free model's performance on the same categories. We do not apply any further processing to the dataset. Following the fundamental data pre-treatment processes outlined above, we find that our method beats all other methods in terms of registration performance under the same categories condition.

### 4.2.2 Unseen Categories

We assess the noise-free model performance on the unseen categories in this experiment. The first 20 categories are used to train the models, while the next 20 categories are used for testing. The first experiment's data pre-processing procedures were followed. Results show that our method also surpasses all other methods in terms of registration performance under the condition of unseen categories.

### 4.2.3 Gaussian Noise

We train the model on clean ModelNet40 data and add Gaussian noise with a mean ($\mu$) of 0 and a standard deviation ($\sigma$) of 0.5 to the new test set, constraining it within the range of $-1.0$ to 1.0. As demonstrated by the experimental data, our unsupervised model is resistant to noisy circumstances and still produces the best results when compared to previous methods.

## 4.3 Comparison on ICL-NUIM

We also performed a comparative analysis of the indoor synthetic scene for ICL-NUIM. To generate partial data, we repeat the previous data pre-processing method in this experiment, resampling the source point cloud to 2048 points, uniformly sampling along each axis' rotation angle from [0, 45°]; sampling the translation values along each axis from [$-0.5, 0.5$], and finally downsampling the point cloud to 1536 points. The result is shown in the Table 2. The outcomes demonstrate the outstanding performance of our approach in predicting rotation transformation on the ICL-NUIM dataset.

**Table 1.** Comparison on ModelNet40

| Model | Same Categories | | | | Unseen Categories | | | | Gaussian Noise | | | |
|---|---|---|---|---|---|---|---|---|---|---|---|---|
| | RMSE(R) | MAE(R) | RMSE(t) | MAE(t) | RMSE(R) | MAE(R) | RMSE(t) | MAE(t) | RMSE(R) | MAE(R) | RMSE(t) | MAE(t) |
| ICP | 24.8548 | 15.1638 | 0.681640 | 0.316911 | 31.2128 | 19.6756 | 0.262073 | 0.189046 | 25.9254 | 19.0365 | 0.253374 | 0.195481 |
| FGR | 1.5466 | 0.2705 | 0.009386 | 0.001603 | 1.7152 | 0.2568 | 0.005966 | 0.001375 | 9.8759 | 2.5128 | 0.040393 | 0.011635 |
| DCP | 7.5474 | 5.4295 | 0.041318 | 0.031826 | 7.7124 | 5.5485 | 0.053635 | 0.042034 | 9.4405 | 7.4724 | 0.079550 | 0.066277 |
| IDAM | 2.0573 | 0.5708 | 0.010912 | 0.003145 | 1.9489 | 0.7909 | 0.014168 | 0.004691 | 3.7481 | 1.4186 | 0.020614 | 0.009114 |
| CEMNet | 1.6858 | 0.1785 | 0.001008 | 0.000155 | 0.8656 | 0.0786 | 0.001038 | 0.000130 | 2.2361 | 0.3961 | 0.001401 | 0.000786 |
| RIENet | 0.0109 | 0.0022 | 0.000067 | 0.000018 | 0.0614 | 0.0060 | 0.000193 | 0.000040 | 0.0181 | 0.0062 | 0.000101 | 0.000042 |
| **Ours** | **0.0026** | **0.0011** | **0.000023** | **0.000010** | **0.0041** | **0.0008** | **0.000029** | **0.000007** | **0.0071** | **0.0031** | **0.000049** | **0.000022** |

**Table 2.** Comparison on ICL NUIM

| Model | ICL NUIM | | | |
|---|---|---|---|---|
| | RMSE(R) | MAE(R) | RMSE(t) | MAE(t) |
| ICP | 18.7291 | 12.5462 | 0.452297 | 0.226646 |
| FGR | 9.9096 | 2.1239 | 0.303244 | 0.071429 |
| DCP | 5.2724 | 3.6413 | 0.115828 | 0.083564 |
| IDAM | 13.5942 | 7.6176 | 0.438178 | 0.254614 |
| CEMNet | 0.2856 | 0.0674 | **0.000608** | **0.000128** |
| RIENet | 0.0869 | 0.0513 | 0.003141 | 0.002237 |
| Ours | **0.0535** | **0.0417** | 0.002259 | 0.001762 |

**Table 3.** Comparison on 7Scenes

| Model | 7Scene | | | |
|---|---|---|---|---|
| | RMSE(R) | MAE(R) | RMSE(t) | MAE(t) |
| ICP | 31.1673 | 24.6312 | 0.294550 | 0.244384 |
| FGR | 0.5235 | 0.2750 | 0.002357 | 0.001150 |
| DCP | 8.4942 | 5.9854 | 0.027077 | 0.020614 |
| IDAM | 9.9600 | 4.4329 | 0.034253 | 0.183530 |
| CEMNet | 0.0338 | 0.0138 | **0.000058** | **0.000028** |
| RIENet | 0.0276 | 0.0110 | 0.000116 | 0.000064 |
| Ours | **0.0152** | **0.0065** | 0.000063 | 0.000037 |

### 4.4 Comparison on 7Scenes

At the same, we simultaneously resample the source point cloud to 2048 points, rigidly convert the target point cloud, and then downsample the point cloud to 1536 points to do data preprocessing. The result is shown in the Table 3. The experimental findings on the two indoor datasets indicate our method's registration performance in indoor contexts while also confirming its high generalization capabilities.

## 5 Conclusion

We present a novel unsupervised point cloud registration framework that leverages mask-based matching enhancement to improve the accuracy of the matching map. Our method introduces a straightforward mask prediction approach and designs a loss function to train the MG module, thereby acquiring reliable overlapping information. Furthermore, we utilize EdgeConv technology to obtain neighborhood information, which is then integrated into the PME module. This integration results in high-quality matching point pairs and more trustworthy pseudo-target point clouds. Extensive experiments on popular benchmarks demonstrate the effectiveness of our approach. For future work, we plan to evaluate our method on more challenging datasets like 3DMatch [53]. Additionally, the method is sensitive to non-uniform sampling and unstructured noise. We will study how to extend it to more complex point cloud scenarios in future work.

**Acknowledgements.** We thank reviewers and shepherd for their valuable comments and help. This work was supported by national natural science foundation of China (No. 62202346), Hubei key research and development program (No. 2021BAA042), China scholarship council (No. 202208420109), Wuhan applied basic frontier research project (No. 2022013988065212), MIIT's AI Industry Innovation Task unveils flagship projects (Key technologies, equipment, and systems for flexible customized and intelligent manufacturing in the clothing industry), and Hubei science and technology project of safe production special fund (No. SJZX20220908).

# References

1. Zhang, L., Guo, J., Cheng, Z., Xiao, J., Zhang, X.: Efficient pairwise 3-d registration of urban scenes via hybrid structural descriptors. IEEE Trans. Geosci. Remote Sens. **60**, 1–17 (2022)
2. Deschaud, J.-E.: IMLS-SLAM: scan-to-model matching based on 3D data. In: 2018 IEEE International Conference on Robotics and Automation, pp. 2480–2485 (2018)
3. Chenghu, D., Feng, Y., Jiang, M., et al.: VTON-SCFA: a virtual try-on network based on the semantic constraints and flow alignment. IEEE Trans. Multimedia **25**, 777–791 (2023)
4. Guo, J., Xing, X., Quan, W., et al.: Efficient center voting for object detection and 6D pose estimation in 3D point cloud. IEEE Trans. Image Process. **30**, 5072–5084 (2021)
5. Feng, Y., Hua, A., Du, C., et al.: VTON-MP: multi-pose virtual try-on via appearance flow and feature filtering. IEEE Trans. Consum. Electron. **69**, 1101–1113 (2023)
6. Lyu, W., Dong, X., Wong, R., et al.: A multimodal transformer: fusing clinical notes with structured EHR data for interpretable in-hospital mortality prediction. In: AMIA Annual Symposium Proceedings, vol. 2022, p. 719 (2022)
7. Zhang, J., Xiao, Q., Li, L.: Solution space exploration of low-thrust minimum-time trajectory optimization by combining two homotopies. Automatica **148**, 110798 (2023)
8. Feng, Y., Zhang, Y., Li, H., et al.: Phase contour enhancement network for clothing parsing. IEEE Trans. Consum. Electron. **70**, 2784–2793 (2024)
9. Zhou, Y., Li, X., Wang, Q., et al.: Visual in-context learning for large vision-language models. arXiv preprint arXiv:2402.11574 (2024)
10. Feng, Y., Chen, Z., Jiang, M., et al.: Smart clothing system with multiple sensors based on digital twin technology. IEEE Internet Things J. **10**, 6377–6387 (2023)
11. Liao, W., Zhu, R., Ishizaki, T., Li, Y., Jia, Y., Yang, Z.: Can gas consumption data improve the performance of electricity theft detection? IEEE Trans. Ind. Inform. (2024)
12. Yu, F., Yu, C., Tian, Z., et al.: Intelligent wearable system with motion and emotion recognition based on digital twin technology. IEEE Internet Things J. (2024)
13. Agarwal, S., Furukawa, Y., Snavely, N., et al.: Building Rome in a day. Commun. ACM, 105–112 (2011)
14. Besl, P.J., McKay, N.D.: Method for registration of 3-D shapes. In: Sensor Fusion IV: Control Paradigms and Data Structures, vol. 1611, pp. 586–606 (1992)
15. Zhou, Q.-Y., Park, J., Koltun, V.: Fast global registration. In: Computer Vision – ECCV 2016, pp. 766–782 (2016)
16. Choy C., Park, J., Koltun, V.: Fully convolutional geometric features. In: Proceedings of the IEEE/CVF International Conference on Computer Vision, pp. 8958–8966 (2019)
17. Du, J., Wang, R., Cremers, D.: DH3D: deep hierarchical 3D descriptors for robust large-scale 6DoF relocalization. In: Computer Vision, pp. 744–762 (2020)

18. Deng, H., Birdal, T., Ilic, S.: 3D local features for direct pairwise registration. In: Proceedings of the IEEE/CVF Conference on Computer Vision and Pattern Recognition, pp. 3244–3253 (2019)

19. Yew, Z.J., Lee, G.H.: RPM-Net: robust point matching using learned features. In: Proceedings of the IEEE/CVF Conference on Computer Vision and Pattern Recognition, pp. 11824–11833 (2020)

20. Sinkhorn, R.: A relationship between arbitrary positive matrices and doubly stochastic matrices. Ann. Math. Stat. **35**, 876–879 (1964)

21. Wang, Y., Solomon, J.M.: PR-Net: self-supervised learning for partial-to-partial registration. In: Advances in Neural Information Processing Systems, vol. 32, pp. 8812–8824 (2019)

22. Bauer, D., Patten, T., Vincze, M.: Reagent: point cloud registration using imitation and reinforcement learning supplementary material. Recall **40**(60), 80 (2021)

23. Wu, J., Wang, J., Xiao, C., et al.: Preference poisoning attacks on reward model learning. arXiv preprint arXiv:2402.01920 (2024)

24. Jiang, H., Shen, Y., Xie, J., et al.: Sampling network guided cross-entropy method for unsupervised point cloud registration. In: Proceedings of the IEEE/CVF International Conference on Computer Vision, pp. 6128–6137 (2021)

25. Shen, Y., Hui, L., Jiang, H., et al.: Reliable inlier evaluation for unsupervised point cloud registration. In: Proceedings of the AAAI Conference on Artificial Intelligence (2022)

26. Wang, Y., Yan, C., Feng, Y., et al.: STORM: structure-based overlap matching for partial point cloud registration. IEEE Trans. Pattern Anal. Mach. Intell. **45**, 1135–1149 (2023)

27. Liao, W., Zhu, R., Yang, Z., et al.: Electricity theft detection using dynamic graph construction and graph attention network. IEEE Trans. Industr. Inform. (2023)

28. Huang, X., Mei, G., Zhang, J., et al.: A comprehensive survey on point cloud registration. arXiv preprint arXiv:2103.02690 (2021)

29. Arun, K.S., Huang, T.S., Blostein, S.D.: Least-squares fitting of two 3-D point sets. IEEE Trans. Pattern Anal. Mach. Intell. PAMI **9**(5), 698–700 (1987)

30. Segal, A., Haehnel, D., Thrun, S.: Generalized-ICP. In: Robotics: Science and Systems, vol. 2, p. 435 (2009)

31. Yang, J., Li, H., Campbell, D., et al.: Go-ICP: a globally optimal solution to 3D ICP point-set registration. IEEE Trans. Pattern Anal. Mach. Intell. **38**(11), 2241–2254 (2016)

32. Rusu, R.B., Blodow, N., Beetz, M.: Fast point feature histograms (FPFH) for 3D registration. In: 2009 IEEE International Conference on Robotics and Automation, pp. 3212–3217 (2009)

33. Aoki, Y., Goforth, H., Srivatsan, R.A., et al.: Point-NetLK: robust & efficient point cloud registration using PointNet. In: Proceedings of the IEEE/CVF Conference on Computer Vision and Pattern Recognition, pp. 7163–7172 (2019)

34. Qi, C.R., Su, H., Mo, K., et al.: PointNet: deep learning on point sets for 3D classification and segmentation. In: Proceedings of the IEEE Conference on Computer Vision and Pattern Recognition, pp. 652–660 (2017)

35. Wang, Y., Solomon, J.M.: Deep closest point: learning representations for point cloud registration. In: Proceedings of the IEEE/CVF International Conference on Computer Vision, pp. 3523–3532 (2019)

36. Wang, Y., Sun, Y., Liu, Z., et al.: Dynamic graph CNN for learning on point clouds. ACM Trans. Graph. **38**, 1–12 (2019)

37. Vaswani, A., Shazeer, N., Parmar, N., et al.: Attention is all you need. In: Advances in Neural Information Processing Systems, vol. 30 (2017)

38. Wu, Z., Song, S., Khosla, A., et al.: 3D ShapeNets: a deep representation for volumetric shapes. In: Proceedings of the IEEE Conference on Computer Vision and Pattern Recognition, pp. 1912–1920 (2015)

39. Li, J., Zhang, C., Xu, Z., et al.: Iterative distance-aware similarity matrix convolution with mutual-supervised point elimination for efficient point cloud registration. In: Computer Vision, pp. 378–394 (2020)
40. Qin, Z., Yu, H., Wang, C., et al.: Geometric transformer for fast and robust point cloud registration. In: Proceedings of the IEEE/CVF Conference on Computer Vision and Pattern Recognition, pp. 11143–11152 (2022)
41. Zhang, X., Yang, J., Zhang, S., Zhang, Y.: 3D registration with maximal cliques. In: Proceedings of the IEEE/CVF Conference on Computer Vision and Pattern Recognition, pp. 17745–17754 (2023)
42. Yu, F., Chen, Z., Cao, J., et al.: Redundant same sequence point cloud registration. Vis. Comput., 1–12 (2023)
43. Xu, H., Liu, S., Wang, G., et al.: OMNet: learning overlapping mask for partial-to-partial point cloud registration. In: Proceedings of the IEEE/CVF International Conference on Computer Vision, pp. 3132–3141 (2021)
44. Kadam, P., Zhang, M., Liu, S., et al.: Unsupervised point cloud registration via salient points analysis (SPA). In: 2020 IEEE International Conference on Visual Communications and Image Processing, pp. 5–8 (2020)
45. Feng, W., Zhang, J., Cai, H., et al.: Recurrent multi-view alignment network for unsupervised surface registration. In: Proceedings of the IEEE/CVF Conference on Computer Vision and Pattern Recognition, pp. 10297–10307 (2021)
46. Li, X., Wang, L., Fang, Y.: PC-Net: unsupervised point correspondence learning with neural networks. In: 2019 International Conference on 3D Vision, pp. 145–154 (2019)
47. Huang, X., Mei, G., Zhang, J.: Feature-metric registration: a fast semi-supervised approach for robust point cloud registration without correspondences. In: Proceedings of the IEEE/CVF Conference on Computer Vision and Pattern Recognition (2020)
48. Zeng, Y., Qian, Y., Zhu, Z., et al.: Corrnet3D: unsupervised end-to-end learning of dense correspondence for 3D point clouds. In: Proceedings of the IEEE/CVF Conference on Computer Vision and Pattern Recognition, pp. 6052–6061 (2021)
49. Feng, Y., Chen, Z., Liu, L., et al.: HTMC: hierarchical tolerance mask correspondence for human body point cloud registration. PeerJ Comput. Sci. 9, e1724 (2023)
50. Choy, C., Park, J., Koltun, V.: Fully convolutional geometric features. In: Proceedings of the IEEE/CVF International Conference on Computer Vision, pp. 8958–8966 (2019)
51. Shotton, J., Glocker, B., Zach, C., et al.: Scene coordinate regression forests for camera relocalization in RGB-D images. In: Proceedings of the IEEE Conference on Computer Vision and Pattern Recognition, pp. 2930–2937 (2013)
52. Choi, S., Zhou, Q.-Y., Koltun, V.: Robust reconstruction of indoor scenes. In: Proceedings of the IEEE Conference on Computer Vision and Pattern Recognition, pp. 5556–5565 (2015)
53. Zeng, A., Song, S., Nießner, M., et al.: 3DMatch: learning local geometric descriptors from RGB-D reconstructions. In: CVPR (2017)

# Driver Action Recognition Based on Dynamic Adaptive Transformer

Wei Xu[1](✉), Yu Mao[2](✉), Junqi Li[3](✉), Tao Peng[4,5], Cuilan Li[6],
and Yalan Fang[7]

[1] Hangzhou Allsheng Instruments Co., Ltd., Hangzhou, China
xw1129265630@163.com
[2] School of Life Science, Hubei University, Wuhan, China
my@stu.hubu.edu.cn
[3] Hubei Luojia Laboratory, Wuhan, China
wangfuqiong111@gmail.com
[4] Wuhan Textile University, Wuhan, China
[5] Engineering Research Center of Hubei Province of Clothing Information,
Wuhan, China
[6] College of International Business and Economics, WTU, Wuhan, China
[7] Wenhua College, Wuhan, China

**Abstract.** In industrial-grade applications, the efficiency of algorithms
and models takes precedence, ensuring a certain level of performance
while aligning with the specific requirements of the application and the
capabilities of the underlying equipment. In recent years, the Vision
Transformer has been introduced as a powerful approach to significantly
improve recognition accuracy in various tasks. However, it faces challenges concerning portability, as well as high computational and input
requirements. To tackle these issues, a dynamic adaptive transformer
(DAT) has been proposed. This innovative method involves dynamic
parameter pruning, enabling the trained Vision Transformer to adapt
effectively to different tasks. Experimental results demonstrate that the
dynamic adaptive transformer (DAT) is capable of reducing the model's
parameters and Gmac with minimal accuracy loss.

**Keywords:** spatiotemporal attention · computer vision · driver action
recognition · dynamic adaptive network · deep learning

## 1 Introduction

Action recognition pertains to the utilization of computer vision and machine
learning techniques to identify and comprehend human or object actions within
video sequences. It is primarily applied in the domain of video analysis, with the
goal of automatically detecting and classifying various actions or behaviors from
video data. Action recognition has wide-ranging applications in various fields,

---

Y. Mao—Contributed equally to this work.

including Video surveillance, Human-computer interaction, Health and medical applications, and Sports analysis. Among the areas of machine learning is action recognition. Its purpose and significance are to determine the types of actions that the entities in the video do over time. To notify other staff, the driver must make different gestures based on the functioning of the train during driving. Whenever an action recognition algorithm is employed in a drive system, drivers may learn normal actions and detect abnormal behaviors. Action recognition's potential applications in video surveillance, media analysis, and machine vision are also gaining traction. In recent years, action recognition technology has seen significant development in the areas of human-computer interaction, possible routes, human action analysis, and abnormal behavior detection [1–4].

Traditional and deep learning methods are the two kinds of action recognition methods. Manual feature extraction, coding, and classification are used in traditional methods. Traditional methods extract interest points, trajectories, and improved dense trajectories. A point of interest is an area with the largest increase in a particular value during video playback. Trajectories and improved dense trajectories are concepts proposed by Wang et al. [1]. It is a method in use in combination with an action boundary histogram. Traditional methods, on the other hand, have poor applicability and robustness. As a result, this method is time-consuming and has problematic applications in practical problems. In recent years, deep learning has emerged as one of the most essential methods for solving problems in computer vision and other fields. Scholars developed and enhanced DNN following the first deep neural network (DNN) Alexnet [5] was successfully used in the field of image classification. After that, many 2D convolutional neural network (CNN) and 3D CNN [6–9] models were proposed and successfully applied in the field of action recognition, with excellent results. Currently, the mainstream models for action recognition include 2D CNN, 3D CNN, and transformer encoder, with the transformer encoder model gaining the most popularity. Our method is based on the spatio-temporal attention module (Fig. 1). However, the general transformer encoder's frame sequence calculation is redundant, increasing the calculation difficulty and training time. This study advances the DAT model and improves the spatio-temporal attention model. It's a Transformer encoder layout. It improves by about 4% points as compared to Timesformer and other traditional methods.

## 2   Related Work

IDT [10,11] and other early traditional methods are samples. The disadvantage of this method is that it has poor timeliness in processing large datasets and is challenging to apply to applications that have significant real-time requirements. The 2D CNN proposed by Karpath [12] and others did not completely deal with action time domain information. To compensate for this flaw, Simonyan et al.'s [13] dual flow structure is a popular expansion and upgrade. Zeghoud et al.'s [14] approach relies on an innovative spatial normalization technique employed for gesture classification. However, its treatment of temporal aspects

**Fig. 1.** Traditional methods often focus on the overall image (top row). Our method first uses a spatial attention module (second row) to process spatial information and then uses a temporal attention module (bottom row) to obtain more abundant features

remains somewhat constrained. Some [15–17] methods based on the vit [18] model and transformer (multi-head self-attention mechanism, MSA) have been proposed in recent years as a result of the successful use of attention mechanisms in computer vision. The computation involved in these methods, nevertheless, exhibits redundancy. Some patch fragments have little effect on prediction results in the actual computation process, but they increase the number of calculations considerably.

In an industrial-scale task, the paper by Hou et al. [19] used a BP neural network model to classify and recognize basketball movements as an application to the project. Tie et al. [20] applied HOF and FLM and their improved algorithms to a head movement recognition system. Although these models are not novel approaches in academics, they provide some practical ideas for engineers in industrial-scale projects. In this paper, we propose and improve the better explanatory and higher recognition accuracy, Vision Transformer-based driver action recognition model, and successfully apply it in industrial-level projects, which provides certain solutions for subsequent academics and engineers.

Inspired by DynamicViT [21] and AdaptFormermodel [22], this paper proposes a DAT driver action recognition method. The driver action model is improved in this method, and the predictor is used to reduce computational complexity and Gmac to ensure maximum accuracy. Finally, it is successfully applied to the action recognition task. Experiments show that the DAT model outperforms C3D and other methods in both the public and our datasets.

## 3 Dynamic Adaptive Transformer

### 3.1 Overview

Figure 2 depicts the overall framework of our Dynamic Adaptive Transformer. DAT is made up of various modules, including the ones mentioned below. After layering these modules, the whole becomes a Transformer encoder.

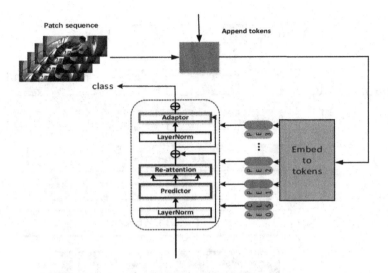

**Fig. 2.** The overall framework of DAT

## 3.2   Predictor

The predictor is the first component, and it may predict and evaluate the input patch sequence, producing a set of pathways with the highest probability for the next attention computation. As shown in Fig. 3 the Predictor module processes the input video patch sequence to produce a lightweight output.

It can dynamically determine which token is to be pruned. A binary mask is generated for each input model to determine which token is to be discarded. $\hat{D}$ is the probability mapping to 0 and 1 using the Softmax function, where 0 means no output and 1 means output. This module can be added to multiple layers. $N$ represents the number of patches.

Map $\hat{D}$ and token $x$ as inputs to MLP to obtain local feature $z^{local}$.

$$z^{local} = \text{MLP}(x) \tag{1}$$

Then obtain the global feature $z^{global}$ with the same formula.

$$z^{global} = \text{aggregate}(\text{MLP}(x), D) \tag{2}$$

The aggregation formula is given by Eq. (3), where $u \in \mathbb{R}$, $C = C/2$ denotes the dimensionality of the input.

$$\text{aggregate}(\hat{D}, u) = \left( \frac{\sum\limits_{i=1}^{N} \hat{D}_i u_i}{\sum\limits_{i=1}^{N} \hat{D}_i} \right) \tag{3}$$

Then the local and global features are spliced, and finally, they are input into MLP to predict which token will be retained or discarded.

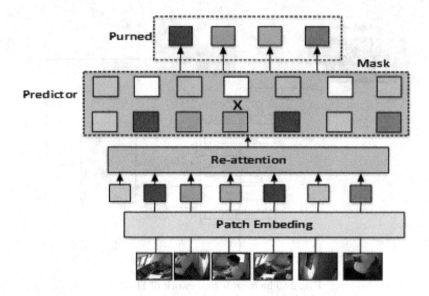

**Fig. 3.** The working principle and flow chart of the predictor

$$z_i = [z_i^{local}, z_i^{global}], 1 \le u \le N \tag{4}$$

$$z' = \text{Softmax}(\text{MLP}(z)) \tag{5}$$

### 3.3   Re-attention

Through layering and residual connection, the re-attention module is composed consisting of a linear projection layer and a Transformer encoder, and each attention layer conducts attention calculation in the adjacent patch. The module calculates the feature and outputs it after MLP.

The specific formula is given by Formula (6) and Formula (7). Where $l = 1, 2....L$ is the number of layers of attention modules, $a = 1, 2....A$ is the number of heads of attention, and $D_h$ is the dimension of heads of attention. $p$ represents the number of patches in $N$ frame images, $t$ represents the current patch from which $F$ frame images, SM represents the SoftMax function.

When the model reaches a specific depth, the accuracy rate is enhanced again by re-attention calculation, which adds no additional overhead compared to self-attention calculation.

$$\alpha_{(p,t)}^{(l,a)^{Spatial}} = \text{SM}(\frac{q_{(p,t)}^{(l,a)^T}}{\sqrt{D_h}} \cdot [\text{k}_{(0,0)}^{(l,a)} \{\text{k}_{(p',t)}^{(l,a)}\}_{p'=1....N}]) \tag{6}$$

$$\alpha_{(p,t)}^{(l,a)^{Temporal}} = \text{SM}(\frac{q_{(p,t)}^{(l,a)^T}}{\sqrt{D_h}} \cdot [\text{k}_{(0,0)}^{(l,a)} \{\text{k}_{(p,t')}^{(l,a)}\}_{t'=1....F}]) \tag{7}$$

## 3.4  Adaptor

Although ViT has had considerable success in the field of computer vision, extending it to video is still difficult. Because of its vast amount of computing and storage, we will be far from reaching our existing hardware conditions if we directly fine-tune it and migrate it to our subway driver action recognition task. To address this problem, a lightweight plug-and-play module is provided, which only adds 5% parameters to the model but increases the original model's accuracy by roughly 2.

The adaptor is comprised of three components: MLP, an activation function, and two trainable modules. MLP and parallel trainable modules aggregate features so that small-scale parameters can be fine-tuned and transferred to the subway driver's action recognition task. Fine-tuned and transferred to the action recognition task of a subway driver. Figure 4 depicts the Adapter's structure. Formulas (6), (7), and (8) are used to do the specific calculation (8).

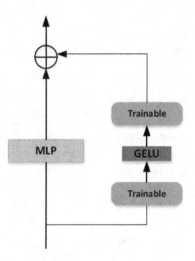

**Fig. 4.** Adaptor structure diagram

First of all, like the traditional Transformer, the attention of token $x_l$ is calculated first, and then the residual connection is performed.

$$x_l = \text{Re-attention}(Q, K, V) = \text{SoftMax}(\frac{QK^T}{\sqrt{d}})V \tag{8}$$

$$x_l' = \text{MLP}(\text{LN}(x_l)) + x_l \tag{9}$$

Secondly, in the trainable modules, we have the feature $x''$ formally via:

$$x_l'' = \text{GELU}(\text{LN}(x_t) \cdot W_{Trainable}) \cdot W_{Trainable'} \tag{10}$$

Finally, both features $x''$ and $x_l$ are fused with $x_l'$ by residual connection.

$$x_l' = MLP(LN(x_l)) + x_l'' + x_l \tag{11}$$

## 4    Experiments

The experimental data is derived from monitoring videos of subway cabs. The data preprocessing involves segmenting five categories of behaviors into small segments ranging from 1 to 5 s. Each segment is then cut into an 8-frames-per-second sequence using a script. To prevent operational issues on our device, we use the Adam optimizer with a batch size set to 8.

There are about 2000 training samples, where the specific information of the dataset is given by Table 1. Car (pointing to the driving screen, It means the driver signals to drive.), Signal (pointing to the signal screen, It means that the driver signals the instructions), Null (no action, It means the driver doesn't make any moves), Double (Car & Signal), and Out are the five types of actions to be recognized (pointing out of the car, It means the driver gestures out the window). As shown in the set of pictures in Fig. 1, there are several displays and a windshield below the driver's hand, both of which are objects the driver is pointing at.

**Table 1.** Details of the dataset

| Action Category/Type | train | Validation | test |
|---|---|---|---|
| null | 195 | 143 | 55 |
| double | 200 | 138 | 51 |
| car | 215 | 130 | 60 |
| out | 206 | 145 | 59 |
| signal | 220 | 148 | 57 |

### 4.1    Experiments Settings

Experiments are used to evaluate the efficacy and feasibility of DAT. It primarily assesses Predictor and Adaptor's ability to improve and migrate model efficiency. Second, it simply assesses the viability of Re-attention in the deep network.

Figure 5 first compare our method to several popular methods in Gmac and Parameters. The size of the legend indicates the value of the horizontal axis intuitively. Furthermore, more specific values are provided in Table 2. Following that, we evaluated the effectiveness of the Re-attention and Self-attention modules as the network depth increased. The experiment Fig. 5(a) discovered that Re-attention can indeed solve the attention collapse problem of our subway driver's action dataset.

Then We selected representatives of 3D CNN and Transformer encoders for an experiment on pruning effects, with results shown in Table 3. Most methods saw improved accuracy, with parameter reduction by about 8%, except for a few. Our model ensures stable accuracy rates while reducing model parameters. Additionally, we compared the Adaptor for cross-model migration. Table 4 shows that the adapter adds only about 10% to the network's parameters, with significantly lower fine-tuning parameters than the Full tuning method, resulting in improved model accuracy.

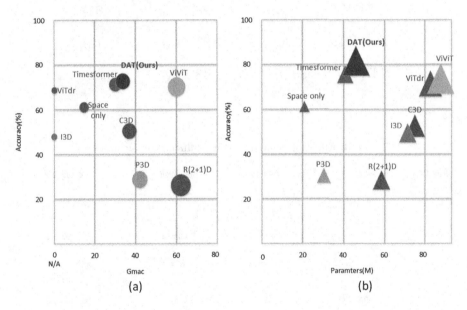

**Fig. 5.** Performance comparison of several methods, in our subway driver datasets: (a) shows the relationship between Gmac and Accuracy, and (b) shows the relationship between parameters and accuracy.

**Table 2.** Detailed data constituting

| Method | GMac | Params | Accuracy |
|---:|---|---|---|
| C3D | 38.67 | 78.02M | 50.17% |
| P3D | 40.81 | 33.18M | 29.28% |
| R(2+1)D | 62.68 | 51.99M | 26.96% |
| Space | 17.45 | 21.90M | 60.17% |
| I3D | N/A | 71.44M | 48.55% |
| Timesformer | 32.08 | 40.82M | 75.51% |
| ViViT | 40.42 | 88.90M | 73.81% |
| ViTdr | N/A | 81.79M | 69.79% |
| DAT(Ours) | 33.57 | 43.14M | 78.33% |

**Table 3.** Effect of pruning and its influence on accuracy

| Method | Pretrain | Predictor(M) | Non-Predictor(M) | Accuracy(%) |
|---|---|---|---|---|
| C3D | ImageNet-1K | 78.02M | 85.11M | 52.26%( ↑ 2.09%) |
| P3D | ImageNet-1K | 33.18M | 35.05M | 31.45%( ↑ 2.17%) |
| R(2+1)D | ImageNet-1K | 51.99M | 55.48M | 30.76%( ↑ 3.8%) |
| I3D | ImageNet-1K | 71.44M | 77.86M | 50.45%( ↑ 1.9%) |
| Timesformer | ImageNet-21K | 40.82M | 43.35M | 76.47%( ↑ 0.96%) |
| ViViT | ImageNet-21K | 88.90M | 94.10M | 72.29%( ↓ 1.52%) |
| ViTdr | ImageNet-21K | 81.79 | 85.36M | 68.51%( ↓ 1.28%) |
| DAT(Ours) | ImageNet-21K | 43.14M | 45.60M | 77.52%( ↓ 0.81%) |

**Table 4.** Influence of Adaptor on model parameters and accuracy

| Method | Adaptor(M) | Non-Adaptor (M) | Tuning Parameter(%) | Accuracy(%) |
|--------|-----------|-----------------|---------------------|-------------|
| C3D | 91.48M | 85.11M | 7.0% | 50.79%( ↑ 0.62%) |
| P3D | 37.11M | 35.05M | 5.6% | 30.71%( ↑ 1.43%) |
| R(2+1)D | 57.68M | 55.48M | 4.0% | 29.22%( ↑ 2.26%) |
| I3D | 82.97M | 77.86M | 6.2% | 47.84%( ↓ 0.71%) |
| Timesformer | 46.77M | 43.35M | 7.4% | 74.94%( ↓ 0.57%) |
| ViViT | 98.23M | 94.10M | 4.3% | 74.06%( ↑ 0.25%) |
| ViTdr | 89.57M | 85.36M | 4.8% | 70.16%( ↑ 0.37%) |
| DAT(Ours) | 47.93M | 45.60M | 5.3% | 79.59%( ↑ 1.26%) |

## 5    Conclusion

In this paper, we apply the DAT model to the task of recognizing subway driver actions. It can dynamically prune the model parameters. At the same time, the Adaptor module increasing the portability. The experiment shows that our method achieves traditional methods in terms of accuracy, parameters, and other indicators, proving its feasibility and effectiveness. We also discovered that the overfitting issue occasionally surfaced at the start of the experiments. This issue was resolved after the datasets was recreated with distinct action features, and we hypothesize that this may be owing to the actions' high repeat rate and shoddy production-however, the precise reason for this has to be established in further research.

## References

1. Planamente, M., et al.: Domain generalization through audio-visual relative norm alignment in first person action recognition. In: Proceedings of the IEEE/CVF Winter Conference on Applications of Computer Vision (2022)
2. Zhang, W., et al.: Collaborative and adversarial network for unsupervised domain adaptation. In: Proceedings of the IEEE Conference on Computer Vision and Pattern Recognition (2018)
3. Wang, F., Liu, J., Gong, W.: WiCAR: WiFi-based in-car activity recognition with multi-adversarial domain adaptation. In: 2019 IEEE/ACM 27th International Symposium on Quality of Service (IWQoS). IEEE (2019)

4. Olabiyi, O., et al.: Driver action prediction using deep (bidirectional) recurrent neural network. arXiv preprint arXiv:1706.02257 (2017)

5. Krizhevsky, A., Sutskever, I., Hinton, G.E.: ImageNet classification with deep convolutional neural networks. Commun. ACM **60**(6), 84–90 (2017)

6. Carreira, J., Zisserman, A.: Quo vadis, action recognition? A new model and the kinetics dataset. In: Proceedings of the IEEE Conference on Computer Vision and Pattern Recognition (2017)

7. Tran, D., et al.: A closer look at spatiotemporal convolutions for action recognition. In: Proceedings of the IEEE Conference on Computer Vision and Pattern Recognition (2018)

8. Xu, P., et al.: Action recognition by improved dense trajectories. J. Syst. Simul. **29**(9), 2053 (2017)

9. Sudhakaran, S., Escalera, S., Lanz, O.: Gate-shift networks for video action recognition. In: Proceedings of the IEEE/CVF Conference on Computer Vision and Pattern Recognition (2020)

10. Wang, H., et al.: Dense trajectories and motion boundary descriptors for action recognition. Int. J. Comput. Vision **103**(1), 60–79 (2013)

11. Wang, H., Schmid, C.: Action recognition with improved trajectories. In: Proceedings of the IEEE International Conference on Computer Vision (2013)

12. Karpathy, A., et al.: Large-scale video classification with convolutional neural networks. In: Proceedings of the IEEE Conference on Computer Vision and Pattern Recognition (2014)

13. Simonyan, K., Zisserman, A.: Two-stream convolutional networks for action recognition in videos. In: Advances in Neural Information Processing Systems, vol. 27 (2014)

14. Zeghoud, S., et al.: Real-time spatial normalization for dynamic gesture classification. Vis. Comput. **38**(4), 1345–1357 (2022)

15. Zhang, X., Cui, Y., Huo, Y.: Deformable patch embedding-based shift module-enhanced transformer for panoramic action recognition. Vis. Comput. **39**(8), 3247–3257 (2023)

16. Ma, W., et al.: PCMG: 3D point cloud human motion generation based on self-attention and transformer. Vis. Comput. **40**(5), 3765–3780 (2024)

17. Diaz-Arias, A., Shin, D.: ConvFormer: parameter reduction in transformer models for 3D human pose estimation by leveraging dynamic multi-headed convolutional attention. Vis. Comput. **40**(4), 2555–2569 (2024)

18. Dosovitskiy, A., et al.: An image is worth 16 × 16 words: transformers for image recognition at scale. arXiv preprint arXiv:2010.11929 (2020)

19. Hou, X., Ji, Q.: Research on the recognition algorithm of basketball technical action based on BP neural system. Sci. Program. **2022** (2022)

20. Hong, T., Li, Y.W., Wang, Z.Y.: Real-time head action recognition based on HOF and ELM. IEICE Trans. Inf. Syst. **102**(1), 206–209 (2019)

21. Rao, Y., et al.: DynamicViT: efficient vision transformers with dynamic token sparsification. Adv. Neural Inf. Process. Syst. **34**, 13937–13949 (2021)

22. Chen, S., et al.: AdaptFormer: adapting vision transformers for scalable visual recognition. arXiv preprint arXiv:2205.13535 (2022)

# SimNET: A Deep Learning Macroscopic Traffic Simulation Model for Signal Controlled Urban Road Network

Jingyao Liu[1,2], Tianlu Mao[1(✉)], Zhaoqi Wang[1], and Huikun Bi[1]

[1] Beijing Key Lab of Mobile Computing and Pervasive Device, Institute of Computing Technology, Chinese Academy of Sciences, Beijing, China
{liujingyao,ltm,zqwang,bihuikun}@ict.ac.cn
[2] University of Chinese Academy of Sciences, Beijing, China

**Abstract.** Modeling traffic in the signal controlled road network is critical to urban traffic simulation and management. However, Existing traffic simulation methods often have difficulty in balancing computational efficiency and simulation accuracy. In this paper, We propose a macroscopic traffic simulation framework for machine learning methods used to simulate traffic flow changes in road networks under signal control. The computational efficiency is ensured by the macroscopic simulation granularity, while the accuracy of the simulation is maintained by extracting the traffic variation patterns through machine learning methods. We design a deep learning simulation model integrated with graph neural networks called SimNET, which accurately mines the macroscopic characteristic changes of traffic flow from data.

We compare SimNET, other state of art deep learning methods for Spatio-temporal problems and a traditional traffic simulation model on real world and generated datasets. Our model demonstrates better accuracy while being more convenient in simulation setup compared to traditional macro models. Furthermore, our model can realistically reproduce some typical traffic phenomena under a signalized road network.

**Keywords:** Traffic Modeling · Urban Traffic Simulation · Graph Neural Networks

## 1 Introduction

Accurate and efficient traffic simulation models have a crucial role in city planning applications. Because of the complexity of traffic flow in urban road networks, microscopic models are generally used for simulation. Microscopic models are simulation models that describe the movement pattern of vehicles. Such methods can reproduce traffic flow phenomena realistically. However, the computational cost of microscopic models increases rapidly with the number of vehicles and the size of the road network, making them difficult to be applied to large scenarios.

N. Magnenat Thalmann et al. (Eds.): CASA 2024, CCIS 2374, pp. 39–56, 2025.
https://doi.org/10.1007/978-981-96-2681-6_4

Macroscopic models have better computational performance so they can be used for traffic simulation and planning in large-scale scenarios. The classical macro models treat the traffic flow as a continuous fluid and describe the variation pattern of the traffic flow. Based on this, many macroscopic simulation models have been proposed to fill the deficiencies in the classical models.

But existing macro models face several serious problems. First, the traffic demand setup procedure is sophisticated. Traffic demand refers to the traffic flow description information such as departure and arrival location, start and end time, etc. In many practical applications, the traffic flow is set up in a demand-route manner. i.e. given a road network, first some entrances and exits are determined, Then the traffic flow and routes from the entrances to the exits are determined. However, Many macroscopic models are difficult to set up the simulation in this way. Those models often needed to set split ratio of vehicles at intersections, specifying the percentage of vehicles that turn left, turn right, and go straight at every intersection, respectively. In the real-world road network, there is a large number of intersections, and the split ratios usually change over time. It is extremely difficult to specify a set of realistic intersection split ratios that dynamically change over time. Manually specified split ratios may produce large errors due to inconsistencies with the real situation.

In addition to the sophisticated simulation setup procedure, the existing macroscopic models are also less accurate compared with microscopic models. Existing macro models are fitted the traffic flow changing pattern through the functions designed by researchers. And there are some crucial parameters in these models and the accuracy of the model depends heavily on these parameters. These parameters are difficult to obtain directly because they vary with road conditions, traffic status, etc.

In recent years, machine learning methods have been widely used in numerous real-world applications. Machine learning methods can fit various characteristics in the data and show excellent accuracy. This can be a possible solution to the problem of low accuracy and over-reliance on the parameters of existing macro models. However, as far as we know, there is no corresponding machine learning model framework in the field of macroscopic traffic simulation.

To address these issues, we propose a macroscopic traffic simulation framework for the machine learning method. By building a suitable machine learning macro traffic simulation model, it is possible to extract changing patterns of traffic flow from data. In this paper, we take the urban traffic simulation problem as a dynamic spatio-temporal problem on a directed graph. Road conditions, traffic flow characteristics, and path selection are identified as inputs to the dynamic directed graph.

Based on this, we design a deep learning macroscopic simulation model based on graph neural networks - SimNET. SimNET could simulate the traffic flow change in the signal controlled network accurately and reproduce some typical traffic phenomena. The main contributions of our work can be summarized as follows:

- We propose a deep learning framework for macroscopic urban traffic simulation. Our designed simulation framework can avoid the problem of cumbersome simulation setup in existing macroscopic simulation models.
- We develop a deep learning algorithm for macroscopic traffic simulation. The input preprocessing module is specially designed in SimNET to handle heterogeneous input information. The temporal preprocessing module and spatial fusion module are also designed to extract temporal and spatial information respectively.
- SimNET has significantly higher simulation accuracy than existing simulation algorithms and other state of art deep learning methods for spatio-temporal problems. It can also reproduce the accumulation and dissipation of the queue and the change of vehicle proportion before the signal realistically.

## 2 Related Work

Urban traffic simulation is a sophisticated problem. One of the reasons is that there are signals and intersections in the urban road network. In this section, we will mainly introduce some related works in urban traffic simulation, especially signal and intersection related.

We can roughly divide existing traffic simulation models into two categories [1]: macroscopic models and microscopic models. Microscopic model aim at describing vehicle moving pattern on the road. The first microscopic model called the car-following model was proposed in [2,3], and many extensions and variations have been further developed since then. However, microscopic models are not commonly used in the simulation of large-scale scenarios, since the computational resources required increase rapidly with the number of vehicles or the size of the road network.

Alternatively, macroscopic models do not model each vehicle but represent the traffic state as average quantities like vehicle density. Due to that, macroscopic models still have irreplaceable advantages for large-scale traffic simulations. One of the most famous macroscopic traffic simulation models is the Lighthill, Whitham and Richards model (LWR model) [4,5]. This model describes dynamically the evolution of vehicle density along a road. Based on that Daganzo et al. proposed the cell transmission model in [6], which is a numerical solution to the differential equations of the LWR model. To provide a realistic simulation of the intersection, [7] use conditional cell to simulate the accumulation and dissipation of vehicles at intersections in oversaturated traffic conditions. Pohlmann et al. [8] defined a new CTM-based Adaptive Traffic Control Systems. It can manage urban road networks with several interconnected signalized intersections. Sumalee et al. proposed a stochastic cell transmission model (SCTM) to simulate traffic flows on networks with stochastic demand and supply [9,10]. Hadfi et al. [11] modified SCTM, and applied it to urban networks.

Apart from CTM and its variants, Coclite et al. [12] coupled the LWR model with a junction model. The dynamics of the junction are modeled with an LP-optimization problem. Lin et al. proposed the BLX model [13,14], in 2012 they developed a macroscopic urban traffic model called S model [15]. It has a lower computational burden and a relatively high degree of accuracy. Lint et al. [16], Liu et al. [17] describe the relationship between vehicles for different congestion regimes on highways.

In recent years, machine learning algorithms, especially deep learning algorithms, have made remarkable progress in the field of spatio-temporal problems. Traffic forecasting is an important one, and it is critical to intelligent transportation systems. And the methods applied in the traffic prediction problem have great implications for traffic simulation because of their similarities. Among the deep learning methods, graph neural networks (GNNs) have become the frontier of deep learning research, showing state-of-the-art performance in various applications [18]. Since road networks can be well expressed by non-Euclidean graph structures, graph neural networks are ideal tools to deal with traffic prediction problems. Li et al. [19] propose to model traffic flow of road network as a diffusion process on a directed graph and introduce *Diffusion Convolutional Recurrent Neural Network* (DCRNN), and achieves 12%–15% improvement over previous methods on two large scale real-world datasets.

Following this paper, many methods have been developed to apply graph neural networks to traffic prediction problems with good results. Mallick et al. [20] used a graph-partitioning method to overcome the limitations of computational and memory bottlenecks when applying DCRNN to large-scale highway networks. Instead of using the empirical spatial graph, Guo et al. [21] learn an optimized graph through a data-driven way in the training phase, Therefore, their method shows high prediction accuracy on specific datasets. Zhao et al. [22] integrated graph convolution network (GCN) and gated recurrent unit (GRU) together for extracting spatial and temporal information, respectively.

With the development of deep learning methods, many complex and specific network structures have been introduced into the field of traffic prediction. Pan et al. [23] proposed a deep-meta-learning-based model, called ST-MetaNet. They used a meta graph attention network to capture diverse spatial correlations, and a meta recurrent neural network to consider diverse temporal correlations. Yu and Yin et al. [24] proposed a multi-scale architecture deep learning method to reveal the temporal and spatial patterns in different scopes. An overview of traffic forecasting methods, which are based on graph neural network in [25]. These methods can provide a lot of inspiration. However, these methods are often difficult to apply directly to traffic simulation, considering that in the field of traffic prediction, the impact of road conditions, signals, and vehicle path selection is not usually considered.

## 3   Model Framework

We divide the road network into nodes and represent the connectivity between nodes by directed edges, which change over time because of signal phase changing, as shown in Fig. 1. The length of each node is determined by the following equation:

$$num = \lfloor \frac{l_r}{l_{exp}} \rfloor$$

$$l = \frac{l_r}{num}$$

In the above equation, $l_r$ denotes the length of the road section, and $l_{exp}$ denotes the expected node length. With such a division, it will ensure that the length of each node is around $l_{exp}$. Then, the road network can be represented by a spatio-temporal dynamic graph, as in the following formula:

$$\mathcal{G}_t = \{\mathcal{V}, \mathcal{E}_t\}$$

Next, we will describe the model inputs and computational flow in detail.

The inputs to the model are defined on the nodes. The distribution of traffic on the road network is represented by the number of vehicles at each node, which we could denote as $\mathbf{n}_t^s$ for node $s$ at time step $t$ called volume features. Each node has some different characteristics, such as length, number of lanes, etc. We call this as node features denote as $\mathbf{nf}_t^s$. Besides, the path choice of vehicles to different exits also affects the vehicle flow distribution, and we call this part as steering features denote as $\mathbf{d}^s$. We use handwritten capital letters to denote the set of features of all nodes. For example, the set of all volume features denotes as $\mathcal{N}_t$. $\mathcal{NF}_t$, $\mathcal{D}$ is the same.

We divide the nodes in the graph into entrance nodes and normal nodes. The number of vehicles at the entrance nodes indicates the number of vehicles entering the road network from there during the current time step. If the set of the number of vehicles of all entrance nodes is denoted as $\mathcal{N}_t^e$, the set of the number of vehicles of all other nodes is denoted as $\mathcal{N}_t^n$, which we called normal nodes, the set of all nodes volume feature is denoted as $\mathcal{N}_t$, They satisfy the following relationships:

$$\mathcal{N}_t = \{\mathcal{N}_t^n, \mathcal{N}_t^e\}$$

Let's next define the volume feature in detail. We identify a fixed number of exists in the road network, and every vehicle in the road network is headed to one of these exits. If the number of exits is $k$, then the volume feature at each node is a $k$-dimensional vector, and the $i$th component represents the number of vehicles in the current node going to the $i$th exits.

To explain the steering feature we need to define the junction nodes in the road network. As shown in the Fig. 2, the graph obtained by connecting each node to all the nodes it can reach in one step without considering traffic lights is defined as the $\mathcal{G}_{all}$. In $\mathcal{G}_{all}$, nodes with the out-degree greater than 1 are defined as junction nodes. The corresponding junction node of a normal node $s$ is the first junction node reachable from that node, which denotes as $J(s)$, and the corresponding junction node of a junction node $j$ is itself, that is $J(j) = j$.

In the road network, especially in junction nodes, vehicles select lanes based on their turn at the next intersection, making the traffic flow movement complex

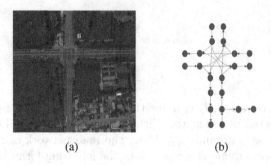

(a)                              (b)

**Fig. 1.** The picture on the right is the original network. Picture on the left shows the nodes after splitting and their connectivity.

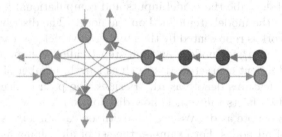

**Fig. 2.** A typical $\mathcal{G}_{all}$ is shown. The orange node is one junction node in $\mathcal{G}_{all}$, and it is the corresponding junction node to the blue nodes and itself.

and difficult to model. Therefore, we designed steering features to represent the relationship between the steering behavior of vehicles at junction nodes and their destination.

As shown in the Fig. 3, we divide the steering features into two parts for node $s$, one part is the steering choice vector $\mathbf{st}^s$ and the other part is the lanes number vector $\mathbf{tl}$.

$\mathbf{st}^s$ is organized as a concatenation of several vectors of one-hot form, which indicates the steering choice for the corresponding junction node heading to different exits.

$$\mathbf{st}^s = st_0^s \oplus st_1^s \oplus \cdots \oplus st_k^s$$
$$st_i^s = [\mathbb{I}\{p(left)\}, \mathbb{I}\{p(right)\}, \mathbb{I}\{p(straight)\}]^T$$

In the above equation $p(dir)$ is a proposition with the meaning that "steer to $dir$ at $J(s)$ when heading to exit $i$". And $\mathbb{I}\{\cdot\}$ is the indicator function.

Lanes number vector $tl$ is the number of corresponding lanes for the corresponding junction node heading to different exits. If we use $tl_i^s$ to denote the number of lanes heading to exit $i$ at $J(s)$, $\mathbf{tl}^s$ can be expressed as:

$$\mathbf{tl}^s = [tl_0^s, tl_1^s, \cdots, tl_k^s]$$

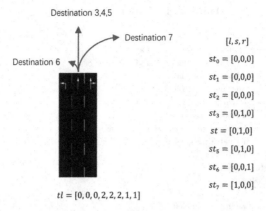

**Fig. 3.** At a junction node, to get to exit nodes 3,4,5 from the nodes in the figure, you need to go straight, to exit node 6, you need to turn left, and to exit node 7, you need to turn right at the next intersection. The corresponding values of **tl** and **st** are shown in the figure.

The steering features allow the microscopic vehicle steering behavior to be reflected on the macroscopic traffic flow level. This is the major difference between our model and the traditional macroscopic model.

The node features are some features of the node at the current time, which are related only to itself and signal phases, including length, number of lanes, Passable time, etc.

The definitions of all the input variables in the paper can be found in Table 1.

Based on the above inputs, one step of our model during the simulation can be formalized as:

$$n_{t-1}, n\mathcal{F}_t, \mathcal{D} \xrightarrow[m]{\mathcal{G}_t} n_t^n$$

The node features are constantly changing over time, so an update step is required before each step of the model simulation:

$$n\mathcal{F}_{t-1} \xrightarrow{\mathcal{G}_t} n\mathcal{F}_t$$

$$n_{t-1} = \{n_{t-1}^n, n_{t-1}^e\}$$

$n_t^e$ in the above equation is the specified value to indicate the number of vehicles entering the road network in each time step, while $n_t^n$ is the calculated value, and it is the result of the model simulation in the previous time step.

As we can see from the previous description, the role of the model is to calculate the volume features of all normal nodes at the current time step based on steering features, node features, and volume features of all nodes from the previous time step, in the current structure of the road network.

**Table 1.** Definition of variables

| variables | definition | notes |
|---|---|---|
| $J(s)$ | The corresponding junction node of $s$ | |
| $n_t^{s,i}$ | The number of vehicles in node $s$ heading to exit $i$ | |
| $tl_i^s$ | Number of lanes to exit $i$ in $J(s)$ | |
| $d_i^s$ | Steering direction to exit $i$ in $J(s)$ | |
| $\mathbf{n}_t^s = [n_t^{s,0}, ..., n_t^{s,k}]$ | Number of vehicles in node $s$ at time $t$ | Volume Feature |
| $\mathbf{tl}^s = [tl_0^s, ..., tl_k^s]$ | Number of lanes to each exits of $J(s)$ | Steering Feature $\mathbf{d}^s = \mathbf{st}^s \oplus \mathbf{tl}^s$ |
| $\mathbf{st}^s = [st_0^s, ..., st_k^s]$ | Steering direction to each exits of $J(s)$, in one-hot encoding form | |
| $tg_t^s$ | Time to the end of the green light | Node Feature $\mathbf{nf}_t$ |
| $tr_t^s$ | Time to the end of red light | |
| $l^s$ | Length of node $s$ | |
| $lane^s$ | Lane number of node $s$ | |
| $isEnd^s$ | is node $s$ an end node | |
| $isJunc^s$ | is node $s$ an intersection node | |
| $x_t^s = [\mathbf{n}_t^s, \mathbf{tl}^s, \mathbf{d}^s, \mathbf{nf}_t^s]$ | input at node $s$ time step $t$ | |
| $\mathcal{D}$ | The set of steering features of all nodes | |
| $n\mathcal{F}_t$ | The set of node features of all nodes | |
| $n^n$ | The set of volume features of all normal nodes | |
| $n^e$ | The set of volume features of all entrance nodes | |

# 4   Model Structure

SimNET could be seen as a state machine. For each step in simulation, SimNET maintains a state vector $h_t^s$ for node $s$ at time $t$. The state vector here does not have a specific physical meaning but is the spatio-temporal information extracted by the machine learning algorithm for that node.

Based on $h_{t-1}^s$, $h_{t-1}^i$ for $i \in \mathcal{K}_s$ and $x_t^s$. $\mathcal{K}_s$ denotes the set of nodes connected to or connected by $s$. After that, SimNET could predict $n_{t+1}^s$ through a multi-layer perception(MLP). During the simulation, $\mathbf{d}^s$ do not change with time, and $\mathbf{nf}_t$ changes periodically with signal. Therefore, as shown in Fig. 4, the overall computational flow of our model at node $s$ could be formalized as:

$$h_t^s = \mathcal{SE}(H_{t-1}^s, n_{t-1}^s, d^s, nf_{t-1}^s)$$

$$n_t = MLP(h_t^s)$$

$$nf_t^s \overset{\mathcal{G}_t}{\leftarrow} nf_{t-1}^s$$

In the above equation $\mathcal{SE}$ is the state estimation function, and the accuracy of our model relies on it. The state estimation needs to take into account the information of its previous state, as well as the information of the nodes connected to it. Besides, the pre-processing process of inputs is also essential, since the inputs are heterogeneous.

Therefore, we design three main components in the state estimation: spatial fusion module, input pre-processing module, and temporal processing module. The overall structure is as shown in Fig. 5.

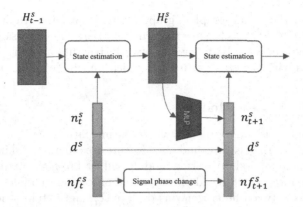

**Fig. 4.** The computational flow of SimNET on a node s at time step t. The $H_{t-1}{}^s$ in the picture indicates the combination of $h_{t-1}^s$ and $h_{t-1}^i$ for $i \in \mathcal{K}_s$.

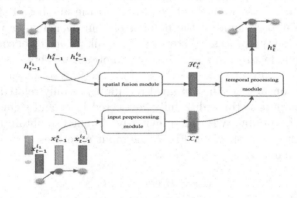

**Fig. 5.** Overall computing procedure of state estimation in SimNET.

## 4.1  Spatial Fusion Module

The spatial state fusion module fuses the state of node $s$ and the state $h$ of its neighboring nodes $i, i \in \mathcal{K}_s$ to obtain the spatial information $\mathcal{H}_t^s$ based on the current graph $\mathcal{G}_t$. Since the upstream and downstream nodes have completely different effects on the current node, we use two separate graph convolution networks with the same structure and different parameters in this module, as shown in Fig. 6. The spatial information is obtained by concatenating the outputs of these two networks.

We can formally express the computational flow of the spatial information fusion module as:

$$h_{\text{forward}} = \mathcal{G}_t *_g H$$
$$h_{\text{backward}} = \mathcal{G}_t^{\text{reverse}} *_g H \qquad (1)$$
$$\mathcal{H}_t^s = \left[ h_{\text{forward}}^T, h_{\text{backward}}^T \right]^T$$

$\mathcal{G}_{t}^{\text{reverse}}$ denotes the inverse graph of graph $\mathcal{G}_t$, $*_g$ denotes the graph convolution operation, and $H \in \mathbb{R}^{N \times c}$ is the matrix formed by the state vectors of nodes. The above structure is also the basic neural network structure used in our model for processing data with the graph structure, which we will denote as $BiGCN_{\mathcal{G}}(\cdot)$.

## 4.2  Input Preprocess Module

The model input $x_t^s$ is heterogeneous, where the magnitudes and meanings of the volume feature, steering feature, and node feature are different. Taking it directly as input into the temporal processing module will lead to high complexity of the problem. Therefore, we designed the input preprocessing module to represent the interactions between heterogeneous data in $\mathcal{X}_t^s$ and obtain a homogeneous feature vector after processing.

The role of both steering features and node features is reflected in the number of vehicles feature in various ways, for example, the number of lanes and node length limit a maximum number of vehicles, and the number of steering lanes determines the upper bound of the number of vehicles going to a certain exit node. Therefore our preprocessing step mimics similar steps by encoding steering features and node features in a suitable way to obtain weights.

$d$ are closely related to the road network structure, so we encode them by a $BiGCN$ and concatenate the obtained results. $nf$ is only related to the node itself, so we compute it through a fully connected layer and sigmoid function, then element-wise product with the previously obtained to obtain the final pre-processing result $x_t^s$. As shown in Fig. 7, the input preprocessing module can be represented formally as:

$$\alpha_{st} = BiGCN_{\mathcal{G}_t}(\boldsymbol{st})$$
$$\alpha_{tl} = BiGCN_{\mathcal{G}_t}(\boldsymbol{tl})$$
$$a_d = \text{softmax}\,(\alpha_d)$$
$$a_{tl} = \text{softmax}\,(\alpha_{tl})$$
$$g = \text{sigmoid}(\text{MLP}(\boldsymbol{nf}_t))$$
$$x_t^s = \text{Concat}\,(a_{tl} \odot \boldsymbol{n}_t, a_d \odot \boldsymbol{n}_t) \odot g$$

## 4.3  Temporal Processing Module

The temporal processing module is a recurrent neural network, which is used to calculate $h_t^s$ using the output of the spatial information fusion module $\mathcal{H}_t^s$ as the hidden state and the output of the input preprocessing module $\mathcal{X}_t^s$ as the input. In this paper we use long and short term memory networks (LSTM) as time processing modules. The numbers of vehicles heading to each end node $n_{t+1}^s$ could been predicted through a fully connected layer from $h_t^s$.

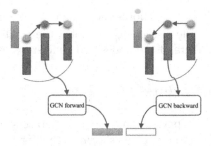

**Fig. 6.** Structure of BiGCN.

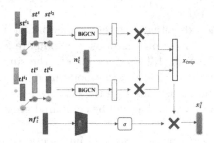

**Fig. 7.** Structure of input preprocess module.

## 4.4  Loss Function and Metrics

There are two terms in the loss function used to train the model: mean square error (MSE) between the actual and predicted values of every component in $v_t^s$, which reflects the model's prediction of the proportion of the vehicles heading to different exit nodes; the other one is MSE between the actual and predicted values for the sum of all components in $v_t^s$. We denote the model predicted result of $i$th of $v_t^s$ as $\hat{v}_i$ and the ground truth as $v_i$, thus the loss function of node $s$ at time step $t$ can be formalized as:

$$\mathcal{L}_{s,t} = \alpha \mathcal{L}_{s,t}^{total} + \beta \mathcal{L}_{s,t}^{component}$$

$$\mathcal{L}_{s,t}^{component} = \sum (v_i - \hat{v}_i)^2$$

$$\mathcal{L}_{s,t}^{total} = \left(\sum v_i - \sum \hat{v}_i\right)^2$$

The $\alpha$ and $\beta$ in the above equation are used to control the weights of the two terms in the loss function. During the training process, we gradually increase $\alpha$ and decrease $\beta$ to 0.

In this paper, we take the mean square error of all nodes in the simulation process as a quantitative indicator of model accuracy as follows:

$$errors = \frac{\sum_n \sum_t (v_{n,t}^i - \hat{v}_{n,t}^i)^2}{T * I}$$

In the above equation, $v_{n,t}^i$ denotes the number of vehicles at the node $n$ at time $t$ heading to exit node $i$, then $\hat{v}_{n,t}^i$ denotes the predicted value of $v_{n,t}^i$. $I$ and $T$ are the total numbers of the nodes and time steps, respectively.

# 5   Experimental Results

We validated the model's performance on two datasets: one generated using SUMO on a simulated road network as shown in the Fig. 9, and the other on the "PermissiveLeftTurnPhasing" scenario in the CitySim dataset [26]. SUMO can generate diverse traffic scenarios, which we categorized into several scenes based on traffic density as in Table 2.

To demonstrate the advantages of the framework and model we designed over those traditional macroscopic methods, we compare SimNET with typical traditional methods, S model [13]. Besides, due to the similarity in the form of data organization, some deep learning methods used for traffic prediction are also used for comparison to demonstrate the effectiveness of our model. In this paper, the deep learning models that will be compared are STGAT [26], STGCN [27], Gman [28].

S model takes the segment between two intersections as a simulation unit, which called "link". Therefore, we directly select the error of link level for comparison. In addition, the simulation time step in S model is the same length as the traffic lights cycle time. And to accommodate this we down sample the training and testing data, i.e. the average number of vehicles at all time steps within a signal cycle is used as the number of vehicles in the link at that time.

## 5.1   Comparison with Existing Methods

Table 2. Mean squared errors of different methods

|  | SimNET | S model | STGAT | STGCN | GMAN |
|---|---|---|---|---|---|
| Low density | **7.01** | 11.4 | 9.68 | 9.41 | 51.82 |
| Medium density 1 | **2.89** | 13.26 | 7.77 | 16.22 | 66.37 |
| Medium density 2 | **8.74** | 15.11 | 17.74 | 15.37 | 118.04 |
| High density | **12.41** | 22.13 | 30.24 | 54.41 | 77.92 |
| SUMO-average | **7.76** | 15.47 | 16.11 | 23.85 | 78.54 |
| CitySim | **8.23** | 10.32 | 15.33 | 43.21 | 123.19 |

The mean squared errors of the different methods are shown in Table 2. It shows that the error of SimNET is lower than that of the S model. More importantly, the traditional model relies heavily on the proportion of splits at intersections. We compared the results of simulations using calibrated vehicle split

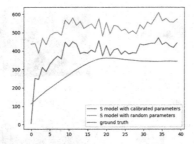

**Fig. 8.** Simulation result of S model with different parameters.

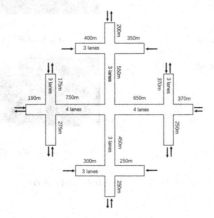

**Fig. 9.** network structure.

ratios with those using uncalibrated vehicle split ratios as shown in Fig. 8. As can be seen from the picture, uncalibrated parameters can produce significant errors, which can be fatal in many applications. For example, when we want to simulate an emergency evacuation, it is difficult to calibrate or specify the split ratio in advance. Other discrete macroscopic models have similar problems.

Next, we compare it with other deep learning methods. As we can see in the Table 2 the error of SimNET is significantly smaller than that of the other deep learning methods.

The error of STGCN is large, which may be since the timing processing in it relies on a fixed-length time window. And at some nodes before the signal, the time window to be referred to keeps changing depending on the congestion. Therefore a fixed time window is difficult to cope with such a simulation. For GMAN, it is a model based entirely on attention mechanisms. The absence of any input of graph structure means that the training results on a specific dataset cannot be applied to other road networks. Also, more complex models require more balanced data, which leads to the fact that models trained on the same data give almost no reliable results in long-time simulations. Therefore it cannot be directly applied in simulation at all.

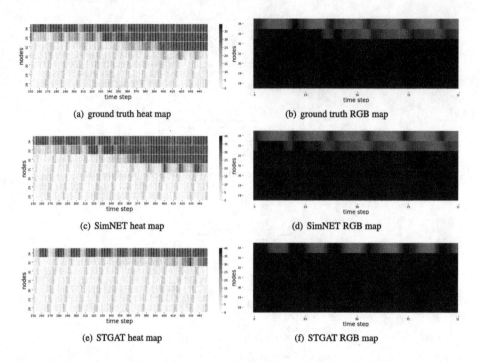

**Fig. 10.** RGB map and heat map of vehicle distribution over time on a road segment

Next, we selected the STGAT for visual comparison to show the advantages of our model, since it has relatively better numerical results. According to the left column in Fig. 10 we can see that the results of SimNET simulation are more similar to ground truth, indicating that it could more accurately simulate the accumulation of vehicle queues. Please refer to the multimedia appendix for videos on the variation of vehicle density within the whole road network in the simulation results of different methods.

In addition to the total number of vehicles within each node, the percentage of vehicles turning within each node is also an important detail. To visualize the vehicle split ratio for the model simulation, we designed a color map that uses RGB values to represent the proportion of traffic turning on the road.

We use $v_l$ to denote the number of vehicles turning left at the next intersection, and similarly $v_r, v_s$. In practice, these variables take values in the range of 0–70. Therefore we use the following formula to calculate the RGB value of a node during simulation.

$$R, G, B = 16\sqrt{\frac{256v_l}{70}}, 16\sqrt{\frac{256v_s}{70}}, 16\sqrt{\frac{256v_r}{70}}$$

As can be seen in the right column in Fig. 10, SimNET can produce more accurate split ratio than other deep learning methods. This is important for long time, large scale road network simulation. Error in the split ratio at one intersection can have a knock-on effect at multiple intersections later on, resulting in a distorted simulation. Therefore, a model that can simulate the split ratio more accurately can be better adapted to the simulation of larger networks.

**Table 3.** Computing time

| Total length | 15 km | 20 km | 30 km | 40 km |
|---|---|---|---|---|
| our model | 1.63 s | 1.65 s | 1.68 s | 1.72 s |
| S model | 0.32 s | 0.35 s | 0.41 s | 0.47 s |
| micro model | 751.22 s | 1051.4 s | 1436.91 s | 1834.52 s |

Finally, let us focus on the computational time consumption of the following different methods. As can be seen from Table 3, the calculation time of the model increases slightly with the increase of the road network size. The simulation time of 5000 s within a road network with a total length of 50 km does not exceed 2 s. It can be applied to traffic simulation planning problems in large-scale scenarios.

## 5.2 Generalizability Validation

We will validate the Generalization of SimNET in the following two aspects: a ultra-high-density scenario that does not appear in the training dataset, and another one with a different road network topology.

We first tested the Generalization of our model in a scenario where the overall road network density is much higher. In this scenario, the number of vehicles in the same road network is about 30–40% higher than the highest density in the training dataset, which we call the ultra-high density dataset. This means that there are more congested nodes in the network and longer queues of vehicles in front of intersections. We compared the mean error of our model and STGAT on the ultra-high density dataset in Table 4. We also selected the relatively accurate model, STGAT, as a comparison.

**Table 4.** Mean error on different dataset

| | SimNET | STGAT |
|---|---|---|
| high density dataset | 12.41 | 30.24 |
| test dataset average | 7.76 | 16.11 |
| ultra-high dataset | 10.01 | 47.06 |
| different topology dataset | 14.11 | 17.23 |

From the table, we can see that the error of our model in the ultra-high density data set is slightly higher than the average error of the previous test datasets but lower than the error of the high density dataset, indicating that the overall error variation is acceptable within a small range.

Further, We tested our model on the dataset collected on another road network with the topology, the error is also shown in Table 4. From the above experiments, we can see that SimNET has a certain generalization performance.

## 6  Conclusion

In this paper, we propose a machine learning framework for the simulation of signal controlled traffic flow. In this framework, the signal controlled road network is modeled by a directed graph, the topology of which changes with time. The road conditions, path selection, and the number of vehicles are also described by the inputs of the nodes. In this framework, the traffic flow movement patterns contained in the data can be extracted by suitable machine learning algorithms. It can also avoid the drawbacks of traditional macroscopic methods that need to specify intersection split ratios.

Based on this framework, we develop a deep learning based traffic simulation model. We use bidirectional graph convolutional network components to extract the features of the forward and backward nodes in the graph separately. A specially designed input preprocessing module is used to embed the heterogeneous data in the input. On the data set generated by SUMO, our model can simulate more accurately compared to other deep learning models, while reproducing some typical traffic phenomena.

Our approach still has some limitations. Firstly the model cannot simulate a scenario where there are multiple paths between a pair of entrances and exits. Secondly, the model does not consider the scenario where multiple nodes converge to a single node. The competition between nodes needs to be considered in such a scenario, but it is not reflected in the model. Our future work will be focused on these problems.

## References

1. Chao, Q., et al.: A survey on visual traffic simulation: models, evaluations, and applications in autonomous driving. Comput. Graph. Forum **39**, 287–308 (2020)
2. Pipes, L.A.: An operational analysis of traffic dynamics. J. Appl. Phys. **24**(3), 274–281 (1953)
3. Chandler, R.E., Herman, R., Montroll, E.W.: Traffic dynamics: studies in car following. Oper. Res. **6**(2), 165–184 (1958)
4. Lighthill, M.J., Whitham, G.B.: On kinematic waves II. A theory of traffic flow on long crowded roads. Proc. R. Soc. London. Ser. A. Math. Phys. Sci. **229**(1178), 317–345 (1955)
5. Richards, P.I.: Shock waves on the highway. Oper. Res. **4**(1), 42–51 (1956)
6. Daganzo, C.F.: The cell transmission model: a dynamic representation of highway traffic consistent with the hydrodynamic theory. Transp. Res. Part B: Methodol. **28**(4), 269–287 (1994)

7. Wang, P.: Conditional cell transmission model for two-way arterials in oversaturated conditions. Ph.D. thesis, University of Alabama Libraries (2010)
8. Pohlmann, T., Friedrich, B.: Online control of signalized networks using the cell transmission model. In: 13th International IEEE Conference on Intelligent Transportation Systems, pp. 1–6. IEEE (2010)
9. Sumalee, A., Zhong, R., Pan, T., Szeto, W.: Stochastic cell transmission model (SCTM): a stochastic dynamic traffic model for traffic state surveillance and assignment. Transp. Res. Part B: Methodol. **45**(3), 507–533 (2011)
10. Zhong, R., Sumalee, A., Pan, T., Lam, W.: Stochastic cell transmission model for traffic network with demand and supply uncertainties. Transportmetrica A: Transp. Sci. **9**(7), 567–602 (2013)
11. Hadfi, R., Tokuda, S., Ito, T.: Traffic simulation in urban networks using stochastic cell transmission model. Comput. Intell. **33**(4), 826–842 (2017)
12. Coclite, G.M., Garavello, M., Piccoli, B.: Traffic flow on a road network. SIAM J. Math. Anal. **36**(6), 1862–1886 (2005)
13. Lin, S., Xi, Y.: An efficient model for urban traffic network control. IFAC Proceedings Volumes **41**(2), 14066–14071 (2008)
14. Lin, S., De Schutter, B., Xi, Y., Hellendoorn, J.: A simplified macroscopic urban traffic network model for model-based predictive control. IFAC Proceedings Volumes **42**(15), 286–291 (2009)
15. Lin, S., De Schutter, B., Xi, Y., Hellendoorn, H.: Efficient network-wide model-based predictive control for urban traffic networks. Transp. Res. Part C: Emerg. Technol. **24**, 122–140 (2012)
16. Van Lint, J., Hoogendoorn, S.P., Schreuder, M.: Fastlane: new multiclass first-order traffic flow model. Transp. Res. Rec. **2088**(1), 177–187 (2008)
17. Liu, S., Hellendoorn, H., De Schutter, B.: Model predictive control for freeway networks based on multi-class traffic flow and emission models. IEEE Trans. Intell. Transp. Syst. **18**(2), 306–320 (2016)
18. Wu, Z., Pan, S., Chen, F., Long, G., Zhang, C., Philip, S.Y.: A comprehensive survey on graph neural networks. IEEE Trans. Neural Netw. Learn. Syst. **32**(1), 4–24 (2020)
19. Li, Y., Yu, R., Shahabi, C., Liu, Y.: Diffusion convolutional recurrent neural network: data-driven traffic forecasting. arXiv preprint arXiv:1707.01926 (2017)
20. Mallick, T., Balaprakash, P., Rask, E., Macfarlane, J.: Graph-partitioning-based diffusion convolutional recurrent neural network for large-scale traffic forecasting. Transp. Res. Rec. **2674**(9), 473–488 (2020)
21. Guo, K., et al.: Optimized graph convolution recurrent neural network for traffic prediction. IEEE Trans. Intell. Transp. Syst. **22**(2), 1138–1149 (2020)
22. Zhao, L., et al.: T-GCN: a temporal graph convolutional network for traffic prediction. IEEE Trans. Intell. Transp. Syst. **21**(9), 3848–3858 (2019)
23. Pan, Z., Liang, Y., Wang, W., Yu, Y., Zheng, Y., Zhang, J.: Urban traffic prediction from spatio-temporal data using deep meta learning. In: Proceedings of the 25th ACM SIGKDD International Conference on Knowledge Discovery & Data Mining, pp. 1720–1730 (2019)
24. Yu, B., Yin, H., Zhu, Z.: ST-UNet: a spatio-temporal U-Network for graph-structured time series modeling. arXiv preprint arXiv:1903.05631 (2019)
25. Jiang, W., Luo, J.: Graph neural network for traffic forecasting: a survey. arXiv preprint arXiv:2101.11174 (2021)
26. Huang, Y., Bi, H., Li, Z., Mao, T., Wang, Z.: STGAT: modeling spatial-temporal interactions for human trajectory prediction. In: Proceedings of the IEEE/CVF International Conference on Computer Vision, pp. 6272–6281 (2019)

27. Yu, B., Yin, H., Zhu, Z.: Spatio-temporal graph convolutional networks: a deep learning framework for traffic forecasting. arXiv preprint arXiv:1709.04875 (2017)
28. Zheng, C., Fan, X., Wang, C., Qi, J.: GMAN: a graph multi-attention network for traffic prediction. In: Proceedings of the AAAI Conference on Artificial Intelligence, vol. 34, pp. 1234–1241 (2020)

# UAV-LMDN: Lightweight Multi-scale Small Object Detection Network for Unmanned Aerial Vehicle Perspective

Li Liu, Long Chen, Feng Yu$^{(\boxtimes)}$, Tao Peng, Xinrong Hu, and Minghua Jiang

Wuhan Textile University, Wuhan, China
{l_liu,yufeng,pt,hxr,minghuajiang}@wtu.edu.cn, chencipher@yeah.net

**Abstract.** Object detection is crucial in various Unmanned Aerial Vehicle (UAV) applications, including security monitoring, search and rescue operations, and military surveillance. However, objects observed from the drone view frequently exhibit the characteristics of small size and complex shapes. Current small object detection methods often encounter issues of missed detections and false positives. In this work, we propose a lightweight multi-scale small object detection network for UAV perspective (UAV-LMDN) to enhance the detection accuracy of small objects while reducing the model's parameters. Firstly, we propose a lightweight multi-scale detection head structure, enabling the detection of objects with smaller pixel sizes and reducing the network parameters by 1) adding a small object detection head that integrates shallow feature layers and 2) removing the large object detection head and its associated network layers. Secondly, we introduce the efficient channel attention module at the neck of the network, enhancing the ability to capture key details for small objects. Experimental results demonstrate that our method achieves a 2.9% improvement in mean Average Precision (mAP) on the VisDrone dataset and a 5.1% improvement on the TinyPerson dataset. Furthermore, our method reduces the parameters by 33.5% compared to the baseline method.

**Keywords:** small object detection · unmanned aerial vehicle · detection head structure · attention mechanism

## 1 Introduction

Object detection is a critical research field in UAV image processing, with extensive applications in domains such as environmental monitoring [1], transportation management [2], disaster response [3], and other related areas [4–10]. Object detection methods for the UAV perspective make significant progress with the widespread application of UAV technology and the continuous evolution of deep learning techniques [11–16].

For instance, in UAV search and rescue missions, the high perspective of the images captured by the UAV results in smaller object sizes, making object

N. Magnenat Thalmann et al. (Eds.): CASA 2024, CCIS 2374, pp. 57–71, 2025.
https://doi.org/10.1007/978-981-96-2681-6_5

detection tasks more challenging [17]. According to existing academic definitions, small objects can be categorized into two main types. In the first type, relative scale-based definition, the features of small objects lie within a relative area range of 0.08% to 0.58% [18]. The second type, referred to as the absolute size-based, defines small objects with a size smaller than 32 pixels × 32 pixels [19].

Data augmentation methods [20] overcome the limitation of low resolution in small objects by applying image scaling and concatenation techniques. However, this approach also introduces an increase in computational cost. Generative Adversarial Networks (GAN) [21] enhance detection accuracy by restoring blurry small objects into clear high-resolution objects. However, GAN is challenging to train, and achieving a better balance between the generator and discriminator is difficult.

Furthermore, due to the need for fast response and real-time operations, the UAV object detection often faces limitations in terms of computational resources and storage capacity [22]. Current research often encounters the challenge of simultaneously improving the detection accuracy of small objects while lightweighting the model. To address these challenges, we propose a lightweight multi-scale object detection network specifically designed to handle small object detection from the UAV perspective.

Firstly, a lightweight multi-scale detection head structure called LMS is proposed to capture feature information of small-sized objects and remove redundant network layers. Specifically, this structure adds a small object detection head that integrates shallow feature layers. This leads to an improved learning capability of the network for small object features. Simultaneously, we effectively reduce the number of network parameters by removing the large object detection head and unnecessary network layers. Secondly, by introducing the Efficient Channel Attention (ECA) [23] at the network's neck, we enable precise capture of key details in small object detection.

In summary, we propose a lightweight multi-scale small object detection network for UAV perspective, called UAV-LMDN. Experiments demonstrate significant improvements achieved by our method on the VisDrone and TinyPerson datasets. This paper makes the following key contributions.

- We employ the LMS detection head structure, which increases the accuracy of small object detection while reducing network parameters.
- We introduce the ECA module into the neck of the network to enhance its ability to accurately capture key details when dealing with small objects.
- The LMS achieves a 2.5% improvement in mAP on the VisDrone dataset and a 2.6% improvement on the TinyPerson dataset. Moreover, it reduces the parameters by 33.5% compared to the baseline method. The ECA module achieves a 0.4% improvement in mAP on the VisDrone dataset and a 2.5% improvement on the TinyPerson dataset.

The remaining content of the article is structured as follows: Sect. 2 provides a comprehensive review of general object detection algorithms and specific methodsdedicated to small object detection. Section 3 provides a detailed introduction to our proposed UAV-LMDN framework. Section 4 is dedicated to presenting and analyzing the experimental findings, while Sect. 5 concludes the contributions of our proposed method.

## 2   Related Work

### 2.1   General Object Detection Algorithms

In the field of computer vision, object detection algorithms hold great significance as they employ convolutional neural networks to extract features from images. These algorithms are commonly classified into two main categories: anchor-based and anchor-free object detection algorithms [24].

Anchor-based object detection algorithms employ pre-defined anchor boxes to detect objects in images. These anchor boxes are generated at multiple scales and aspect ratios to encompass potential object sizes and shapes. They are then utilized by a convolutional neural network for classification and regression tasks. Anchor-based methods can be further categorized into two types: one-stage and two-stage algorithms. One-stage object detection algorithms perform object localization and classification in a single forward pass of the convolutional neural network, eliminating the need for a separate region proposal step. One-stage algorithms are characterized by their simplicity and efficiency, such as YOLOv1 [25], YOLOv2 [26], YOLOv3 [27], YOLOv4 [28], YOLOv5 [29], YOLOv6 [30], YOLOv7 [31], SSD [32], and RetinaNet [33]. They perform object detection on the entire image through dense predictions, making them suitable for scenarios with high real-time requirements. Two-stage anchor-based object detection algorithms follow a two-step process. Firstly, they generate candidate boxes that potentially contain objects of interest. Subsequently, these candidate boxes are classified and refined through regression to obtain accurate object detections. In the first stage, commonly referred to as the Region Proposal Network (RPN), is responsible for generating selective candidate boxes that have the potential to contain objects of interest. In the second stage, the candidate boxes are then fed into subsequent classification and regression networks for further processing. Prominent examples of these algorithms include Faster R-CNN [34] and Mask R-CNN [35].

Relatively, anchor-free object detection algorithms do not utilize pre-defined anchor boxes as a basis for detecting objects. Instead, they directly use convolutional neural networks to output the position and class information of objects without the need for additional regression steps. Anchor-free algorithms often achieve this by either generating a fixed number of bounding boxes at each position in the image or using dense predictions. Common anchor-free algorithms include CenterNet [36], Cornernet [37], FCOS [38], and YOLOv8 [39]. General object detection algorithms are generally effective for detecting medium to large-sized objects, but their performance is not ideal when it comes to detecting small objects.

## 2.2  Small Object Detection Algorithms

Recognizing the challenges posed by detecting small objects in images, researchers are proposing various algorithms specifically designed to tackle this task.

OFFR [40] effectively improves the performance of small object detection in intelligent transportation scenes by leveraging object feedback, introducing the SOIoU loss function, and incorporating the SOPANet for feature information retention. DTMSI-Net [41] leverages the fusion of physical simulation images and neural network features. This fusion enables DTMSI-Net to achieve superior detection accuracy and stability when compared to existing methods. NACAD [42] incorporates a noise-adaptive module to leverage positive-incentive noise, a context-aware module to enhance object features, and a position-refined module to reduce interference from pure noise. IS-YOLOv5 [43] incorporates architectural changes, including attention-based dilated CSP blocks and various proposed modules, to enhance detection accuracy and speed. UAV-FDN [44] effectively detects wildfires in real time while addressing challenges such as diverse smoke and fire appearances and interference from similar objects. ALFPN [45] incorporates adaptive feature inspection and a context-aligned supervisor to address the limitations of traditional feature fusion methods. DKT-Net [46] enhances feature attention through dual-K integration and utilizes 2D and 1D convolutions to capture local details and reduce network complexity. AD-RCNN [47] enhances region proposals, extracts region features using visual attention mechanisms [48], and refines detection results through an adaptive dynamic training module. However, existing approaches do not pursue a balance between detection performance and detection accuracy. In our proposed UAV-LMDN framework, we have successfully achieved significant improvements in small object detection accuracy while simultaneously reducing the network's parameters. This advancement contributes to more reliable and efficient operations in real-world scenarios.

## 3  Method

This paper takes YOLOv8s as the baseline model and incorporates two key components: the Lightweight Multi-Scale (LMS) detection head structure and the Efficient Channel Attention (ECA) module. In the following sections, we present an outline of the network's overall architecture. Then, we describe the two key components in detail.

### 3.1  UAV-LMDN Network Architecture

Figure 1 illustrates the architecture of the UAV-LMDN network, which includes modules such as input image, Conv, C2f, SPPF, ECA, LMS, and output image. The fundamental components of UAV-LMDN include the Conv module, the SPPF module, and the C2F module. The Conv module consists of a $3 \times 3$ convolutional layer, a Batch Normalization layer, and a SiLU activation function.

This configuration contributes to better feature extraction and faster convergence in the network. The SPPF (Spatial Pyramid Pooling Fusion) module handles variable-sized inputs and generates fixed-length feature representations by capturing multi-scale features through spatial pyramid pooling operations while preserving spatial information. The C2F module draws inspiration from the C3 module. It enables a lightweight implementation within UAV-LMDN based on the YOLOv8 framework while achieving optimal performance. Contact refers to feature concatenation, where feature maps of different scales are merged, allowing the network to obtain richer semantic information. These components collectively contribute to the overall performance of UAV-LMDN.

To make up for the shortcomings of the original YOLOv8 network structure in small object detection, UAV-LMDN introduces the LMS detection head structure and the ECA module. The specific improvement strategies are as follows: 1) UAV-LMDN enhances the model's detection capability for small objects by adding a small detection head, 2) UAV-LMDN removes the large object detection head and its related feature extraction and fusion layer. This helps streamline the model architecture while maintaining effective detection performance, and 3) UAV-LMDN effectively captures detailed features of small objects during the feature extraction process by introducing the ECA module. By incorporating the LMS detection head structure and the ECA module, UAV-LMDN overcomes the limitations of the original YOLOv8 network and reduces the parameters of the model while improving detection accuracy.

## 3.2    LMS Detection Head Structure

The LMS detection head structure consists of two essential components. The first part involves adding a small detection head that fusion with shallow feature layers. This small detection head is responsible for detecting smaller objects at the pixel level. The second part involves removing the large object detection head and the corresponding network layers, resulting in a reduction in network parameters without compromising detection accuracy.

### 3.2.1    Multi-scale Detection Head

This paper focus on detecting objects from the perspective of the UAV. When using drones to capture images, the objects in the images are typically small compared to the overall image size. In the original structure of YOLOv8, the backbone network consists of five feature extraction layers, namely P1–P5. After concatenating the feature maps of P3 and P4 with the neck network, the output feature map size becomes $80 \times 80 \times 256$. This feature map is then fed into the original small object detection head, which is designed to detect objects as small as $8 \times 8$ pixels. However, the feature information of small objects tends to be concentrated in the shallow layers. This is because the shallow layers have larger feature maps, allowing them to retain more detailed information. As the network goes deeper, the fine-grained details of small objects are gradually lost.

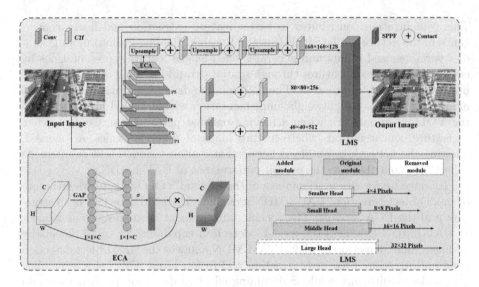

**Fig. 1.** The structure diagram of UAV-LMDN.

To address this issue, we introduce an additional small object detection head that incorporates the fusion of shallow feature layers. Specifically, we continue upsampling in the neck module. By performing upsampling, we enlarge the feature map size to twice its original dimensions, resulting in a size of $160 \times 160 \times 128$. Subsequently, we combine the upsampled feature map with the feature map extracted from P2 by concatenating them together. Subsequently, the concatenated feature map undergoes processing by a C2F module. The resulting feature map is subsequently fed into the newly introduced small object detection head in UAV-LMDN, enabling the detection of objects as small as $4 \times 4$ pixels. The addition of this specialized detection head enables the network to effectively identify and classify objects with reduced pixel sizes. This enhancement significantly improves the network's ability to capture and analyze fine-grained details, making it more suitable for detecting small objects in UAV-captured images.

### 3.2.2    Lightweight Detection Head

The incorporation of small object detection heads has effectively resolved the challenge of inadequate detection accuracy for small objects. However, In the case of images captured by drones, the majority of objects tend to be small, making large detection heads redundant in small object scenarios.

As a result, the original YOLOv8 structure, which includes a detection head designed for larger objects, is considered redundant for drone detection tasks. To reduce network parameters and improve practical feasibility, we have decided to remove the original detection head for larger objects, along with its associated network layers. By implementing this modification, we streamline the architecture and reduce the parameters, rendering it highly suitable for UAV object detection tasks.

Specifically, we remove the original large detection head that produces an output feature map size of $20 \times 20 \times 512$. Along with it, we have also eliminated the associated Conv modules, Concat modules, and the C2F module. These components are responsible for processing and capturing features related to larger objects. By removing them, we significantly reduce the network parameters and streamline the architecture. This modification improves the efficiency and feasibility of the network for UAV object detection tasks.

### 3.3  ECA Module

We introduce the ECA module to enhance the detection capability of small objects. The ECA module in UAV-LMDN takes the feature maps that are extracted by a feature extraction network as its input.

As shown in the bottom left corner of Fig. 1, the ECA module performs global average pooling (GAP) to obtain global features, which are then mapped to a lower dimension using a fully connected layer. Through the utilization of a sigmoid activation function, the ECA module generates attention weights that indicate the significance of each channel in the input feature maps. The attention weights produced by the ECA module are applied element-wise to the original feature maps, resulting in a multiplication process that amplifies informative channels while reducing the impact of less relevant ones. The output is enhanced feature maps that prioritize small object-related information. Integrating the ECA module into the UAV-LMDN to enhance detection performance, particularly for small objects within UAV scenarios.

Specifically, we incorporated the ECA module in two specific locations, both before and after the SPPF module. This configuration allows the ECA module to capture and enhance relevant features at different stages of the network. By placing the ECA module before the SPPF module, we enable it to capture more discriminative information from the input features. On the other hand, inserting the ECA module after the SPPF module helps refine the fused feature representations and further improve the discriminative power of the network. This combination of ECA module integration before and after the SPPF module contributes to enhanced feature learning and promotes better object detection performance.

## 4  Experiments

In this section, we initially present an introduction to the dataset utilized in our experiment, as well as the evaluation metrics used to assess performance. Subsequently, a series of comparative experiments are conducted using the UAV Image Dataset to assess the performance of the proposed method in comparison to other object detection algorithms. In continuation, ablation experiments are performed to assess the impact and efficacy of the proposed improvements (Fig. 2).

### 4.1  Experimental Environment and Datasets

The experimental environment is configured with the following specifications: The system version is Windows 11 64-bit, equipped with a 10th generation Intel Core i7 10700KF processor and an NVIDIA GeForce RTX 3070 8 GB GPU. The system relies on Python 3.9.13, numpy 1.21.5, torchvision 0.12.0+cu113, and torch 1.11.0+cu113. We configure the batch size to be 4 and utilize 8 workers for parallel processing. The training process spans 300 epochs, with a fixed learning rate of 0.01.

The proposed method is evaluated using the VisDrone [49] UAV image dataset. The images in this dataset encompass a wide range of weather and lighting conditions commonly encountered in various scenarios. The dataset's image size is from 480 × 360 to 2000 × 1500. VisDrone dataset consists of 10 object categories, including pedestrians, people, bicycles, cars, vans, trucks, tricycles, awning-tricycle, buses, and motors. The dataset comprises 6,471 training images, 548 validation images, and 1,610 testing images.

TinyPerson [50] is a public dataset with a maritime rescue background. In the TinyPerson dataset, the resolution of people in maritime and beach scenes is relatively low. The dataset categorizes people into two classes: "sea person" and "earth person". It consists of 1,049 training images, 300 validation images, and 150 testing images. The TinyPerson dataset effectively supplements existing datasets in terms of diversity, as it includes more complex poses of people.

### 4.2  Evaluation Indicators

This paper adopts four metrics, namely precision, recall, F1 score, and mean Average Precision (mAP), to evaluate the model's accuracy. These metrics provide comprehensive and objective measures for assessing the performance of the proposed approach. In addition, Parameters are used as a performance metric to evaluate the parameter quantity of the model.

The formulas for precision (P), recall (R), and F1 score are the following:

$$P = \frac{TP}{(TP + FP)} \tag{1}$$

$$R = \frac{TP}{(TP + FN)} \tag{2}$$

$$F1 = \frac{2 \times (P \times R)}{(P + R)} \tag{3}$$

In object detection evaluation, TP represents the number of accurately predicted bounding boxes that match with ground truth boxes. FP represents the number of falsely identified positive samples, where the predicted bounding boxes do not correspond to any ground truth boxes. FN represents the number of missed objects, where the ground truth boxes are not detected by the model.

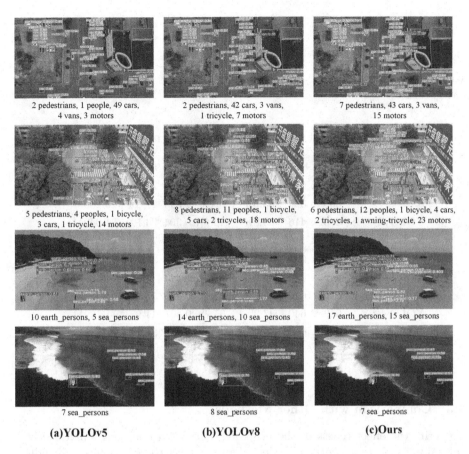

| 2 pedestrians, 1 people, 49 cars, 4 vans, 3 motors | 2 pedestrians, 42 cars, 3 vans, 1 tricycle, 7 motors | 7 pedestrians, 43 cars, 3 vans, 15 motors |
| 5 pedestrians, 4 peoples, 1 bicycle, 3 cars, 1 tricycle, 14 motors | 8 pedestrians, 11 peoples, 1 bicycle, 5 cars, 2 tricycles, 18 motors | 6 pedestrians, 12 peoples, 1 bicycle, 4 cars, 2 tricycles, 1 awning-tricycle, 23 motors |
| 10 earth_persons, 5 sea_persons | 14 earth_persons, 10 sea_persons | 17 earth_persons, 15 sea_persons |
| 7 sea_persons | 8 sea_persons | 7 sea_persons |
| **(a)YOLOv5** | **(b)YOLOv8** | **(c)Ours** |

**Fig. 2.** The results of compare experimental. (a)–(c) are the results of YOLOv5, YOLOv8, and ours on the Visdrone dataset and TinyPerson dataset respectively. The red box indicates the locations where other networks have false positives. (Color figure online)

The mAP metric is a comprehensive evaluation measure that takes into account both precision and recall. It provides a holistic assessment of the model's performance by considering the trade-off between precision and recall. To calculate the mAP, the Average Precision (AP) is determined at fixed Intersection Over Union (IOU) thresholds for each object category. These AP values are then averaged across all categories. The mAP value is obtained by computing the area under the precision-recall (P-R) curve for each category. mAP50 refers to the mean average precision at an IOU threshold of 0.5. In this curve, precision is plotted on the X-axis, while recall is plotted on the Y-axis. The following formulas are used to calculate AP and mAP:

$$AP = \int_0^1 P(r)\, dr \tag{4}$$

$$mAP = \frac{\sum_{i=1}^{C} AP_i}{(C)} \qquad (5)$$

where p(r) represents the P-R curve and C represents the number of detection categories.

**Table 1.** Experimental results of different modules on VisDrone dataset.

| Model | Input Shape | Precision | Recall | F1 | mAP50 | Parameters |
|-------|-------------|-----------|--------|-----|-------|------------|
| Faster R-CNN | 600 × 600 | 43.1% | 23.2% | 0.302 | 20.7% | 137.099M |
| SSD | 300 × 300 | 55.5% | 5.1% | 0.093 | 11.0% | 26.285M |
| YOLOv3 | 416 × 416 | 65.8% | 19.8% | 0.304 | 23.7% | 61.949M |
| YOLOv4-tiny | 416 × 416 | 46.9% | 7.2% | 0.125 | 7.9% | 6.057M |
| YOLOv5s | 640 × 640 | 39.8% | 31.6% | 0.352 | 28.7% | 7.037M |
| YOLOv5s-LMS | 640 × 640 | 43.3% | 34.4% | 0.383 | 32% | **5.388M** |
| YOLOv7-tiny | 640 × 640 | 44.7% | 33.8% | 0.385 | 31% | 6.032M |
| YOLOv8s | 640 × 640 | 47.3% | 35.7% | 0.407 | 34% | 11.129M |
| Ours | 640 × 640 | 49.8% | 37.4% | **0.427** | **36.9%** | 7.403M |

### 4.3  Comparison with Other Methods

To verify the effectiveness of the proposed method in detecting small objects, several well-known networks are selected for comparative experiments, including Faster R-CNN [34], SSD [32], YOLOv3 [27], YOLOv4-tiny [28], YOLOv5s [29], YOLOv7-tiny [31], and YOLOv8s [39]. We choose the VisDrone dataset for comparative experiments because it covers diverse scenarios, includes multiple object categories, and provides a large-scale testing dataset. The results obtained from these experiments are summarized and presented in Table 1.

Faster R-CNN is a two-stage object detection algorithm, it uses the Region Proposal Network (RPN) to select candidate regions from extracted features. These regions are then used for object detection. However, It has a high parameter count of 137.099M, which increases computational requirements.

For the SSD algorithm, although its accuracy is better than Faster R-CNN and significant reduction in parameters, its recall rate is relatively low, resulting in a low mAP50 of only 11%.

The YOLOv4-tiny algorithm is a lightweight version of yolov4. However, its lower recall rate results in a suboptimal mAP performance. Nevertheless, it achieves a significant reduction in parameter count compared to previous models.

Both the YOLOv5s and YOLOv7-tiny algorithms achieve impressive detection results with relatively fewer parameters. Specifically, YOLOv5s achieves an mAP50 of 28.7% with 7.037M parameters, while YOLOv7-tiny achieves an mAP50 of 31% with 6.032M parameters. However, there remains room for improvement in terms of detection accuracy.

While the YOLOv8s algorithm achieves an mAP50 of 34% with 11.129M parameters, there is still space for improvement in terms of mAP and lightweight network design.

The proposed method effectively combines the LMS detection head structure and incorporates the ECA module to enhance the network's ability to capture detailed feature information. Through a comparison with the original YOLOv8s algorithm, the proposed method achieves a significant 2.9% improvement in mAP50 while simultaneously reducing the number of model parameters.

To validate the effectiveness of our proposed method, the LMS detection head structure is incorporated into the YOLOv5s algorithm, resulting in a modified version called YOLOv5s-LMS. The experimental results demonstrate a 3.3% improvement in mAP50, along with a reduction in parameter count by 1.649M.

Our method achieves the best performance in terms of detection accuracy, with an F1 score of 0.427 and an mAP50 of 36.9%. Additionally, we have reduced the parameter count to 7.403M. Although our parameter count is 1.371M higher than YOLOv7-tiny, our mAP50 is 5.9% higher than theirs. Taking into account both detection accuracy and parameters, our method demonstrates the best overall performance.

### 4.4   Ablation Experiments

The experiments also aim to demonstrate the benefits of the LMS detection head structure utilized in this research. Particularly, the LMS detection head structure is integrated with the ECA module, and the outcomes of these experiments are showcased in Table 2.

**Table 2.** The results of ablation experiment

| Dataset | Network | Precision | Recall | F1 | mAP50 | Parameters |
|---------|---------|-----------|--------|-----|-------|------------|
| VisDrone | Baseline | 47.3% | 35.7% | 0.407 | 34% | 11.129M |
| | Baseline + LMS | 48.6% | 37.5% | 0.423 | 36.5% | 7.403M |
| | Baseline + LMS + ECA | 49.8% | 37.4% | 0.427 | **36.9%** | **7.403M** |
| TinyPerson | Baseline | 44.9% | 23.2% | 0.306 | 22.7% | 11.126M |
| | Baseline + LMS | 41.6% | 27.8% | 0.333 | 25.3% | 7.401M |
| | Baseline + LMS + ECA | 46.6% | 27.5% | 0.346 | **27.8%** | **7.401M** |

Through the utilization of the LMS detection head structure, notable advancements in mAP50 and reduction in model parameters are achieved. The experimental results clearly demonstrate that the adoption of the LMS detection head structure not only enhances the mAP50 of the VisDrone dataset and

TinyPerson dataset by 2.5% and 2.6% respectively but also reduces the parameter count by one-third. These findings highlight the effectiveness of the LMS detection head structure in striking a balance between improved performance and model efficiency.

To assess the effectiveness of the ECA module, we integrate it into the baseline model alongside the LMS detection head structure. This joint integration allows us to evaluate the impact of the ECA module on the overall performance and capabilities of the model. The results demonstrate improvements in precision on the VisDrone dataset and a 0.4% increase in mAP50. Additionally, on the TinyPerson dataset, the mAP50 is boosted by 2.5% with the addition of the ECA module. Furthermore, due to the nature of the ECA module, it does not require input channel dimensions, resulting in minimal impact on the overall parameters. These experiments indicate that integrating the ECA module enhances detection performance.

## 5   Conclusion

In this paper, we propose a lightweight multi-scale small object detection network for the UAV perspective, called UAV-LMDN, which consists of two carefully crafted modules. Firstly, to tackle the challenges of detecting objects with small pixel sizes and to reduce the computational load of the model, we propose a lightweight multi-scale detection head structure. This enables the network to detect objects with even smaller pixel sizes and effectively reduces the network parameters. Secondly, the ECA module amplifies important feature channels by adaptively weighting each channel, thereby enhancing the network's feature extraction capabilities for small objects. Extensive experiments are conducted on two public datasets involving small objects such as pedestrians, cars, earth persons, and sea persons. These experiments demonstrate that our proposed UAV-LMDN significantly improves detection performance while effectively reducing the parameter count, striking a better balance between the two aspects.

**Acknowledgements.** We thank reviewers for their valuable comments and help. This work is funded in part by national natural science foundation of China (No. 62202346), China scholarship council (No. 202208420109), Wuhan applied basic frontier research project (No. 2022013988065212), Educational Commission of Hubei Province of China (NO. D20211701), and Hubei science and technology project of safe production special fund (No. SJZX20220908).

## References

1. Liu, K., Zheng, J.: UAV trajectory optimization for time-constrained data collection in UAV-enabled environmental monitoring systems. IEEE Internet Things J. **9**(23), 24300–24314 (2022)
2. Al-Hilo, A., Samir, M., Assi, C., et al.: UAV-assisted content delivery in intelligent transportation systems-joint trajectory planning and cache management. IEEE Trans. Intell. Transp. Syst. **22**(8), 5155–5167 (2020)

3. Wan, Y., Zhong, Y., Ma, A., et al.: An accurate UAV 3-D path planning method for disaster emergency response based on an improved multiobjective swarm intelligence algorithm. IEEE Trans. Cybern. **53**(4), 2658–2671 (2022)

4. Yu, F., Chen, Z., Cao, J., et al.: Redundant same sequence point cloud registration. Vis. Comput., 1–12 (2023)

5. Wu, J., Vorobeychik, Y.: Robust deep reinforcement learning through bootstrapped opportunistic curriculum. In: International Conference on Machine Learning, pp. 24177–24211. PMLR (2022)

6. Yu, F., et al.: VTON-MP: multi-pose virtual try-on via appearance flow and feature filtering. IEEE Trans. Consum. Electron. **69**(4), 1101–1113 (2023)

7. Chen, W., Shen, Z., Pan, Y., Tan, K., Wang, C.: Applying machine learning algorithm to optimize personalized education recommendation system. J. Theory Pract. Eng. Sci. **4**(01), 101–108 (2024)

8. Chenghu, D., Feng, Yu., Jiang, M., et al.: VTON-SCFA: a virtual try-on network based on the semantic constraints and flow alignment. IEEE Trans. Multimedia **25**, 777–791 (2022)

9. Liao, W., Zhu, R., Ishizaki, T., Li, Y., Jia, Y., Yang, Z.: Can gas consumption data improve the performance of electricity theft detection? IEEE Trans. Ind. Inform. **20**(6), 8453–8465 (2024)

10. Feng, Yu., Chen, Z., Jiang, M., et al.: Smart clothing system with multiple sensors based on digital twin technology. IEEE Internet Things J. **10**(7), 6377–6387 (2022)

11. Ye, T., Qin, W., Li, Y., et al.: Dense and small object detection in UAV-vision based on a global-local feature enhanced network. IEEE Trans. Instrum. Meas. **71**, 1–13 (2022)

12. Jing, R., Zhang, W., Liu, Y., et al.: An effective method for small object detection in low-resolution images. Eng. Appl. Artif. Intell. **127**, 107206 (2024)

13. Yu, F., et al.: Intelligent wearable system with motion and emotion recognition based on digital twin technology. IEEE Internet Things J. **11**(15), 26314–26328 (2024)

14. Feng, Yu., Zhang, Y., Li, H., ChengHu, D., Liu, L., Jiang, M.: Phase contour enhancement network for clothing parsing. IEEE Trans. Consum. Electron. **70**(1), 2784–2793 (2024)

15. Pan, B., Li, C., Che, H., Leung, M.-F., Yu, K.: Low-rank tensor regularized graph fuzzy learning for multi-view data processing. IEEE Trans. Consum. Electron. **70**(1), 2925–2938 (2023)

16. Zhou, Y., Li, X., Wang, Q., Shen, J.: Visual in-context learning for large vision-language models. arXiv preprint arXiv:2402.11574 (2024)

17. Paulin, G., Sambolek, S., Ivasic-Kos, M.: Application of raycast method for person geolocalization and distance determination using UAV images in real-world land search and rescue scenarios. Expert Syst. Appl. **237**, 121495 (2024)

18. Chen, C., Liu, M.-Y., Tuzel, O., et al.: R-CNN for small object detection. In: Lai, S.H., Lepetit, V., Nishino, K., Sato, Y. (eds.) Computer Vision–ACCV 2016: 13th Asian Conference on Computer Vision, Taipei, Taiwan, 20–24 November 2016, Revised Selected Papers, Part V 13, pp. 214–230. Springer, Cham (2017). https://doi.org/10.1007/978-3-319-54193-8_14

19. Lin, T.-Y., Maire, M., Belongie, S., et al.: Microsoft COCO: common objects in context. In: Fleet, D., Pajdla, T., Schiele, B., Tuytelaars, T. (eds.) Computer Vision–ECCV 2014: 13th European Conference, Zurich, Switzerland, 6–12 September 2014, Proceedings, Part V 13, pp. 740–755. Springer, Cham (2014). https://doi.org/10.1007/978-3-319-10602-1_48

20. Zoph, B., Cubuk, E.D., Ghiasi, G., et al.: Learning data augmentation strategies for object detection. In: Vedaldi, A., Bischof, H., Brox, T., Frahm, J.M. (eds.) Computer Vision–ECCV 2020: 16th European Conference, Glasgow, UK, 23–28 August 2020, Proceedings, Part XXVII 16, pp. 566–583. Springer, Cham (2020). https://doi.org/10.1007/978-3-030-58583-9_34

21. Bosquet, B., Cores, D., Seidenari, L., et al.: A full data augmentation pipeline for small object detection based on generative adversarial networks. Pattern Recogn. **133**, 108998 (2023)

22. Yao, F., Wang, S., Ding, L., et al.: Lightweight network learning with zero-shot neural architecture search for UAV images. Knowl.-Based Syst. **260**, 110142 (2023)

23. Wang, Q., Wu, B., Zhu, P., et al.: ECA-Net: efficient channel attention for deep convolutional neural networks. In: Proceedings of the IEEE/CVF Conference on Computer Vision and Pattern Recognition, pp. 11534–11542 (2020)

24. Zou, Z., Chen, K., Shi, Z., et al.: Object detection in 20 years: a survey. Proc. IEEE **111**(3), 257–276 (2023)

25. Redmon, J., Divvala, S., Girshick, R., et al.: You Only Look Once: unified, real-time object detection. In: Proceedings of the IEEE Conference on Computer Vision and Pattern Recognition, pp. 779–788 (2016)

26. Redmon, J., Farhadi, A.: YOLO9000: better, faster, stronger. In: Proceedings of the IEEE Conference on Computer Vision and Pattern Recognition, pp. 7263–7271 (2017)

27. Redmon, J., Farhadi, A.: YOLOv3: an incremental improvement. arXiv preprint arXiv:1804.02767 (2018)

28. Bochkovskiy, A., Wang, C.-Y., Liao, H.-Y.M.: YOLOv4: optimal speed and accuracy of object detection. arXiv preprint arXiv:2004.10934 (2020)

29. Ultralytics. YOLOv5: Open-source object detection (2020). https://github.com/ultralytics/yolov5

30. Li, C., Li, L., Jiang, H., et al.: YOLOv6: a single-stage object detection framework for industrial applications. arXiv preprint arXiv:2209.02976 (2022)

31. Wang, C.-Y., Bochkovskiy, A., Liao, H.-Y.M.: YOLOv7: trainable bag-of-freebies sets new state-of-the-art for real-time object detectors. In: Proceedings of the IEEE/CVF Conference on Computer Vision and Pattern Recognition, pp. 7464–7475 (2023)

32. Liu, W., Anguelov, D., Erhan, D., et al.: SSD: single shot multibox detector. In: Leibe, B., Matas, J., Sebe, N., Welling, M. (eds.) Computer Vision–ECCV 2016: 14th European Conference, Amsterdam, The Netherlands, 11–14 October 2016, Proceedings, Part I 14, pp. 21–37. Springer, Cham (2016). https://doi.org/10.1007/978-3-319-46448-0_2

33. Lin, T.-Y., Goyal, P., Girshick, R., et al.: Focal loss for dense object detection. In: Proceedings of the IEEE International Conference on Computer Vision, pp. 2980–2988 (2017)

34. Ren, S., He, K., Girshick, R., et al.: Faster R-CNN: towards real-time object detection with region proposal networks. IEEE Trans. Pattern Anal. Mach. Intell. **28**(8) (2015)

35. He, K., Gkioxari, G., Dollár, P., et al.: Mask R-CNN. In: Proceedings of the IEEE International Conference on Computer Vision, pp. 2961–2969 (2017)

36. Zhou, X., Wang, D., Krähenbühl, P.: Objects as points. arXiv preprint arXiv:1904.07850 (2019)

37. Law, H., Deng, J.: CornerNet: detecting objects as paired keypoints. In: Ferrari, V., Hebert, M., Sminchisescu, C., Weiss, Y. (eds.) Computer Vision – ECCV 2018.

LNCS, vol. 11218, pp. 765–781. Springer, Cham (2018). https://doi.org/10.1007/978-3-030-01264-9_45

38. Tian, Z., Shen, C., Chen, H., et al.: FCOS: fully convolutional one-stage object detection. In: Proceedings of the IEEE/CVF International Conference on Computer Vision, pp. 9627–9636 (2019)

39. Ultralytics. YOLOv8: Open-source object detection (2023). https://github.com/ultralytics/ultralytics

40. Tian, D., Han, Y., Wang, S.: Object feedback and feature information retention for small object detection in intelligent transportation scenes. Expert Syst. Appl. **238**, 121811 (2024)

41. Cao, Y., Guo, L., Xiong, F., Kuang, L., Han, X.: Physical-simulation-based dynamic template matching method for remote sensing small object detection. IEEE Trans. Geosci. Remote Sens. **62**, 1–14 (2023)

42. Yuan, Y., Zhao, Y., Ma, D.: NACAD: a noise-adaptive context-aware detector for remote sensing small objects. IEEE Trans. Geosci. Remote Sens. **61**, 1–13 (2023)

43. Mahaur, B., Mishra, K.K., Kumar, A.: An improved lightweight small object detection framework applied to real-time autonomous driving. Expert Syst. Appl. **234**, 121036 (2023)

44. Jiang, M., Wang, Y., Yu, F., et al.: UAV-FDN: forest-fire detection network for unmanned aerial vehicle perspective. J. Intell. Fuzzy Syst. (Preprint), 1–16 (2023)

45. Chen, H., Wang, Q., Ruan, W., et al.: ALFPN: adaptive learning feature pyramid network for small object detection. Int. J. Intell. Syst. **2023** (2023)

46. Shoukun, X., Jianan, G., Hua, Y., et al.: DKTNet: dual-key transformer network for small object detection. Neurocomputing **525**, 29–41 (2023)

47. Zhonghong, O., Wang, Z., Xiao, F., et al.: AD-RCNN: adaptive dynamic neural network for small object detection. IEEE Internet Things J. **10**(5), 4226–4238 (2022)

48. Lyu, W., Zheng, S., Ma, T., Chen, C.: A study of the attention abnormality in trojaned BERTs. arXiv preprint arXiv:2205.08305 (2022)

49. VisDrone Dataset: Object detection in UAV images. https://github.com/VisDrone/VisDrone-Dataset

50. TinyPerson Dataset: Maritime rescue background. https://www.cvmart.net/dataSets/detail?tabType=1&currentPage=7&pageSize=12&id=364&utm_campaign=zywang&utm_source=social&utm_medium=gongzhonghao

# LRDN: Lightweight Risk Detection Network for Power System Operations

Li Liu, Yukun Chen, Feng Yu$^{(\boxtimes)}$, Tao Peng, Xinrong Hu, and Minghua Jiang

Wuhan Textile University, Wuhan, China
{l_liu,yufeng,pt,hxr,minghuajiang}@wtu.edu.cn

**Abstract.** Accidents often occur in the electric power operation sites due to workers not wearing safety equipment. Existing risk detection algorithms primarily focus on improving detection accuracy, however, it ignore the memory and computational costs, making them unsuitable for resource-constrained devices. Therefore, this paper proposes a lightweight network LRDN to detect whether personnel at power operation sites are wearing safety equipment correctly. It can be integrated into the system, suitable for portable intelligent terminal devices, and effectively reduce risks.

To reduce model parameters and computational complexity while enhancing feature extraction and fusion, lightweight convolution and feature enhancement modules are introduced into the backbone and neck of the network. To alleviate the gradient vanishing problem and balance computational efficiency with model performance, inverted residual is introduced. Subsequently, in order to further improve the model's ability to express input features while ensuring the lightweight of the model, and enhancing its performance and generalization ability, the Efficient Channel and Spatial Attention (ECSA) module is introduced. Experimental results show that our method achieves a mean Average Precision (mAP) of 94.91%, F1-score of 0.93. Without compromising model performance, the method reduces Floating Point Operations Per Second (FLOPs) by 29.3%, parameters by 40.9%, and model size by 39.8%. The detection efficiency of LRDN is superior to existing methods.

**Keywords:** power operation · risk detection · lightweight network · terminal devices

## 1 Introduction

In recent years, research on artificial intelligence has gradually been applied to our daily life [1]. Safety equipment is vitally important for workers in the power field, but many work- ers choose not to wear it due to the lack of comfort, which will endanger the life safety of workers [2], in the power field, real-time risk detection and prevention becomes increasingly important [3]. When a temporary incident oc- curs, the safety risk prevention and control of electric power operations mainly adopts manual inspection, which is costly and inefficient. The means based on video surveillance improves the risk prevention and control ability, but cannot realize real-time detection of risk behaviors

© The Author(s), under exclusive license to Springer Nature Singapore Pte Ltd. 2025
N. Magnenat Thalmann et al. (Eds.): CASA 2024, CCIS 2374, pp. 72–85, 2025.
https://doi.org/10.1007/978-981-96-2681-6_6

[4]. Recently, the development of computer vision and deep learning technology has made intelligent identification technology for smart worksites mainstream [5].

As an important part of computer vision, object detection technology has always been a research hotspot [6], widely used in electric power operations [7], video surveillance [8], smart clothing [9], virtual fitting [10, 11] and digital twin [12]. It is also commonly applied in other deep learning related fields [13–16], which can be divided into traditional object detection algorithm, region proposal-based object detection algorithm and regression-based object detection algorithm [17]. As the depth of Convolutional Neural Networks (CNN) [18] from shallow LeNet-5 [19] and AlexNet [20] to deep GoogleNet [21] networks continues to improve, the performance of object detection is also improving. However, these networks have larger model size and computational complexity, and higher hardware requirements on devices, resulting in higher computing costs and energy consumption, and are not suitable for platforms with limited storage and computing resources that require real-time detection, such as terminal devices [22].

In view of the emergencies in the power work site, conventional equipment cannot meet the real-time requirements, how to reduce the parameters of the model and accelerate the inference while ensuring performance is a difficult problem. Therefore, it has become an opportunity to study a lightweight risk detection network for portable terminal devices. However, the common lightweight networks have limited ability to deal with complex features, and their accuracy is not as high as that of traditional net- works in real-time detection. Focusing on the characteristics of lightweight network model, such as small model size, low computational complexity and fast inference speed, this paper proposes a lightweight LRDN, which is used to detect whether workers in the power operation sites are wearing safety equipment correctly, so as to effectively reduce the risk. Firstly, lightweight GhostConv [23] and C2fGhost modules are used in the design of backbone to reduce the number of parameters required for feature extraction and improve the inference speed. Lightweight DWConv [24] and C2fGhost modules are used in the design of neck. Improve the feature fusion effect and reduce the computational complexity, the above two steps realize the lightweight of the network. Then, in order to alleviate the problem of gradient disappearance and balance computational efficiency and model performance, inverted residual [25] is introduced. Finally, a novel ECSA module is proposed to improve the expression ability of the network for input features and further improve the effectiveness of feature extraction and feature fusion. The implementation improves the performance and generalization ability of the model, and accelerates the inference speed under the premise of ensuring the lightweight and computational efficiency of the model.

The experimental results indicate superior detection performance in safety equipment in power operation scenarios compared to existing methods. Additionally, the model has a smaller size and shorter inference time. The main contributions of this paper are as follows:

- An efficient lightweight network architecture is designed by stacking lightweight convolutions and modules, and combining the feature pyramid, classification and regression prediction components.
- The inverted residual is introduced to alleviate the problem of gradient disappearance and balance the computational efficiency and model performance.

- The ECSA module is introduced to improve the performance and generalization ability of the model, so as to better adapt to the complex environment and changing situation in the power operation scenarios.

## 2 Related Work

### 2.1 Detection of Risk

The power operation site is a high-risk workplace, and the illegal operation will bring serious threats to the safety of relevant personnel. Therefore, it is necessary to improve the supervision efficiency of electric power operations.

By introducing the Attention-Guided Multi-Task Convolutional Neural Network (AGMNet) for detecting power line components in aerial images, the challenges brought by complex backgrounds and drone shooting perspectives are solved [26]. By making the YOLOv4 algorithm lightweight and combining the innovative bidirectional feature fusion network and loss function, the real-time risk detection is realized on edge computing devices, solving the minority problem of limited capacity and computing power of AI chips on the edge [27]. By adding detection heads and using BiFPN for feature fusion, the Convolutional Block Attention Module (CBAM) [28] is introduced to improve the YOLOv5 algorithm, which achieves good detection results in the illegal identification experiments of power grid on six types of self-made power operation dataset [29]. By introducing the Combine Attention Partial Network (CAPN) into the CNN and combining transfer learning and attention mechanism, a real-time glove detection algorithm is proposed to solve the problem of safety accidents caused by workers not wearing safety gloves correctly in the electric power operation scenarios [30]. By using ultra-lightweight backbone for feature extraction, combined with adaptive feature fusion path aggregation network, multi-scale feature fusion is efficiently realized, which can quickly identify abnormal transmission line targets, solving the problems of traditional models and multi-scale object detection [31].

However, the current risk detection methods for power operations still have some limitations. When an emergency occurs, conventional devices are inconvenient to use, and the storage and computing resources of portable terminal devices are limited. Although some networks have high detection accuracy, the volume and computing complexity of the model bring a great burden on the devices and are not applicable. Our method proposes a lightweight network research for power operations, which can achieve efficient and real-time risk detection.

### 2.2 Lightweight Object Detection Algorithm

With the development of deep learning technology, neural network models have achieved better performance. However, this progress has led some issues such as deeper model architecture, more parameters, and slower inference speed. Therefore, it is necessary to pursue model lightweighting to achieve efficient and real-time detection on portable intelligent terminal devices.

Lightweight networks refers to neural network models with smaller model size, lower computational complexity, and smaller memory footprint compared to traditional deep learning networks. This type of networks are suitable for devices with limited storage and computing resources [32]. SqueezeNet [33] reduces the parameters by replacing part of the 3 × 3 convolution with 1 × 1 convolution. MobileNet [34] uses depth-separable convolution for feature extraction, making the network more efficient and convenient to be applied on mobile devices. After the optimization, MobileNet V2 [25] introduces linear bottleneck and inverted residual structure, further improving the accuracy while reducing the model volume. MobileNet V3 [35] inherits the practical skills of v1 and v2, and further improves the performance by adding SE attention mechanism and using new activation functions. ShuffleNet [36] uses group convolution and channel shuffle to achieve feature fusion between different convolution groups. EfficientNet [37] proposes a composite scaling method to achieve more efficient model design by balancing the depth, width, and resolution of the network. GhostNet [38] removes redundant feature map information at a small cost by applying a series of linear transformations, and uses fewer parameters to generate more feature maps.

Although the above methods can be used to construct lightweight object detection network architectures, in some cases, the performance of these networks may not meet the requirements, especially in power operation scenarios where they may perform poorly. Our method significantly reduces the size and computational complexity of the model while ensuring network performance. This improvement not only improves inference speed, but also makes the model more suitable for intelligent terminal devices with limited storage and computing resources. Moreover, this optimization also enables our model to run more efficiently and perform well in various environments.

## 3   Method

This paper introduces a lightweight risk detection network that employs intelligent recognition technology to assess the safety equipment compliance of personnel in power operation scenarios. The proposed network offers an effective solution for devices with limited storage and computing resources.

### 3.1   LRDN Network Overview

Focusing on the characteristics of small model size, low computational complexity, and fast inference speed, this paper proposes a lightweight LRDN by enhancing the YOLOv8. The network framework is shown in Fig. 1. Through the use of lightweight convolutions and modules, as well as the introduction of inverted residual and ECSA module, the model's size and computational complexity are significantly reduced without compromising performance. Additionally, the inference speed is accelerated. The LRDN primarily consists of five parts: input, backbone, neck, head, and output.

The input and output parts involve the model's data input and result output. After images preprocessing, the input section takes the images as input and passes them to the backbone for further processing. The output section primarily outputs the results processed by the head, which includes the coordinates of the object box, class labels, and confidence scores. This result enables efficient and real-time discrimination of power operation risks.

In the backbone of the network, after the first convolution, one layer of GhostConv and C2fGhost modules is stacked to extract features and enhance feature representation. Following this, an inverted residual is added. Behind this module, three additional layers of GhostConv and C2fGhost modules are stacked to achieve deeper feature extraction and enhancement, capturing features of different scales. The last two layers of the backbone consist of Spatial Pyramid Pooling Fusion (SPPF) [39] and ECSA module. The SPPF module enhances operational speed by using a cascade of three small-sized pooling kernels. This accelerates processing speed while preserving the functionality of fusing feature maps from diverse sensory domains. It combines the output of each layer, facilitating multi-scale fusion and reducing computational complexity. The ECSA module enhances the model's expressive capability and the perception ability of multi-scale objects, allowing the network to focus on more critical information and thereby improving risk detection performance.

In the neck of the network, it is mainly composed of components such as DWConv, C2fGhost, Concat, and Upsample layers. Drawing inspiration from and optimizing the design philosophy of PAN-FPN, the Feature Pyramid Network (FPN) [40] is utilized to extract features from images of different scales, while the Path Aggregation Network (PAN) is employed to aggregate these features across different layers of the network. After feature extraction by the backbone, the neck of the LRDN plays a crucial role in feature fusion. The DWConv is used for dimensionality reduction, aiding in the transfer and integration of information across different layers. The Upsample operation adjusts the scale and resolution of feature maps, enlarging low-resolution feature maps to the same size as high-resolution feature maps. Subsequently, Concat operations combine detailed features from lower levels with semantic features from higher levels, enhancing the model's accuracy in detecting multi-scale objects and obtaining a more comprehensive and rich feature representation.

Following this, C2fGhost is used again for feature enhancement. Through four Concat operations at different levels, LRDN effectively extracts and merges features of different scales, improving the performance and robustness of object detection. Additionally, an ECSA module is added after the second C2fGhost module, enhancing the model's perception of multi-scale object. This allows the model to achieve more accurate detection results in complex scenarios.

In the head of the network, it receives the out- put of three different scales of feature maps processed by the neck. These feature maps are then input into separate decoupled heads for predictions. Due to the potential bias in traditional IoU evaluation, our method employs the Weighted Intersection over Union (WIOU) loss function in the regression branch of the detection head. The calculation formula is as follows:

$$WIOU = \frac{\sum_{i=1}^{n} w_i IOU(b_i, g_i)}{\sum_{i=1}^{n} w_i} \tag{1}$$

where n represents the number of object boxes, $b_i$ represents the coordinates of the i-th object box, $g_i$ represents the coordinates of the actual annotation box of the i-th object, $IOU(b_i, g_i)$ represents the IoU value between the i-th object box and the actual annotation box, and $w_i$ repre- sents the weight value.

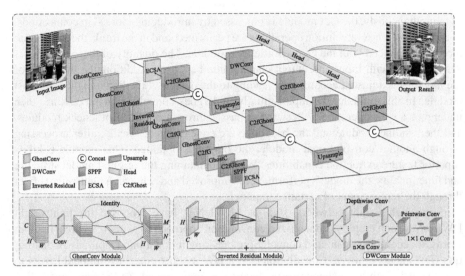

**Fig. 1.** The network architecture of the LRDN.

After processing through the regression and classification heads, the final step involves using the Non-Maximum Suppression (NMS) [41] method to eliminate redundant boxes. This process retains object boxes with high confidence levels. The post-processed results are then output through the output part, representing the final detection results.

## 3.2 Network Lightweight

In order to make the model suitable for portable intelligent terminal devices, this paper focuses on network lightweight research. The general method for feature extraction involves using multiple convolutional kernels to perform convolutional mapping operations on all channels of the input feature map. In deep networks, stacking numerous convolutional layers can capture rich feature information but also results in a lot of redundant information, requiring a large number of parameters and computations. Therefore, inspired by the GhostNet, a novel and effective GhostConv is utilized to separately extract rich features and redundant features to enhance model efficiency. Initially, a small number of convolutional kernels are used to extract features from the input feature map. Subsequently, this subset of feature maps undergoes a more cost-effective linear transformation operation, and finally, the Concat operation is applied to generate the final feature map. The Ghost module is plug-and-play, easily substituting conventional convolutions to achieve an excellent backbone network structure. Therefore, when performing feature extraction, the ordinary convolutions in the backbone network are replaced with GhostConv, this method aims to effectively reduce the number of parameters, lower the demand for computational and improve inference speed while maintaining model performance. Here, the GhostConv uses 3×3 convolution kernels with a stride of 2 and padding of 1.

Simultaneously, the C2f module is processed by introducing more skip connections. In the branches, no convolution operations are performed, and in the trunk, the Bottleneck module is replaced with the GhostBottleneck module. The quantity of these modules is denoted as n, with input and output channel numbers as c. Additionally, the depth of the modules is adjusted accordingly, leading to the design of the lightweight C2fGhost module. In this module, the input initially undergoes convolutional processing, then undergoes a split operation. Afterward, it passes through n GhostBottleneck modules, and the residual module and the backbone are concatenated. Finally, after processing through another convolutional module, the output is obtained. This module exhibits superior feature extraction capabilities. While maintaining the original model structure and functionality, the model's performance is improved and achieves a lightweight effect through the replacement of certain components.

Some lightweight networks, such as MobileNet, have proposed the lightweight DWConv, which employs a factorized convolution approach to extract features. In other words, it decomposes standard convolution, breaking it down into Depthwise Convolution (DW) and Pointwise Convolution (PW). DW assigns one convolutional kernel to one channel, with each channel convolved by a single kernel. After generating a feature map using DW, the number of channels remains unchanged. Following this, PW is used to perform a weighted combination in the depth direction on the previous feature map, generating a new feature map. Compared to regular convolution, DWConv offers advantages like fewer parameters and lower computation requirements. By using DWConv, feature extraction efficiency can be improved, achieving results comparable to traditional convolution with fewer parameters and computations.

The inverted residual is a commonly used module in lightweight convolutional neural networks designed to enhance model efficiency and performance. To address the issue of gradient vanishing and strike a balance between computational efficiency and model performance, the inverted residual is introduced into the backbone. Its core idea is to modify the traditional residual block to adapt to the characteristics of lightweight networks. In a traditional Residual Block, the input feature map undergoes a series of convolution operations and is then added to the original input to obtain the output. In contrast, in the inverted residual, the input feature map is first subjected to a lightweight expand convolution, followed by a depthwise convolution, significantly reducing the computational cost. This approach achieves efficient feature extraction in lightweight networks. Subsequently, a pointwise convolution reduces the number of channels, and non-linear transformations can be introduced to enhance the network's expressive power. Finally, the output is obtained by adding the result to the original input feature map. This module is initially introduced by MobileNetV2 and has since been widely adopted in subsequent networks.

## 3.3 ECSA Attention Mechanism

Introducing attention mechanisms into object detection networks can enhance the model's attention to important information, thereby more effectively extracting key details while ignoring less relevant information. Common attention mechanisms based on convolutional neural networks, such as Squeeze-and-Excitation Network (SENet) [42], Shuffle Attention (SA) [43], Efficient Channel Attention (ECA) [44], often focus on channel-wise analysis, limiting consideration to the interactions among feature map channels. Multi-scale Efficient Transformer Attention (META) [45] excels in handling information at different scales but requires more computational resources [46], making it unsuitable for portable devices. The CBAM module is proposed to execute attention mechanisms in both channel and spatial dimensions, enhancing the processing capabilities for complex scenes and multi-scale objects. However, further improvements are still needed for optimal effectiveness.

Due to the possibility of missing contextual information caused by using FPN in the neck section, this paper enhances the ECA module and designs a novel ECSA module, as shown in Fig. 2. The ECSA module is introduced in the backbone and neck to compensate it. This module introduces two dimensions: channel attention and spatial attention, achieving a sequential attention structure from channel to spatial. When using the ECSA module, in the first part, the input feature map undergoes global average pooling, followed by a 1×1 convolutional layer to facilitate inter-channel information interaction while avoiding dimension reduction. Subsequently, an adaptive one-dimensional convolutional kernel size is calculated based on the number of channels in the feature map, the calculation formula is as follows:

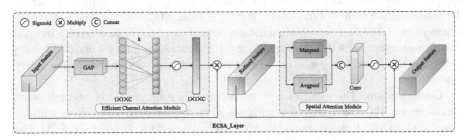

**Fig. 2.** The composition of the ECSA Module.

$$k = \psi(C) = \left| \frac{log_2(C)}{\gamma} + \frac{b}{\gamma} \right|_{odd} \tag{2}$$

where k represents the coverage range for local inter-channel interactions, C represents the channel dimension, |t|odd represents the odd number closest to t. In this paper, all experiments are set with $\gamma = 2$ and b = 1.

This kernel size is then used in a one-dimensional convolution operation to obtain weights for each channel of the corresponding feature map. Finally, the weights obtained after normalization through the Sigmoid activation function are multiplied channel-wise with the original input feature map, generating the weighted feature map. The second part involves spatial domain processing of the output feature map from the channel attention mechanism. Initially, max pooling and average pooling are applied to the input feature map along the channel dimension, and the pooled feature maps are stacked. Subsequently, a 3 × 3 convolutional kernel is employed to fuse channel information. Lastly, the result of the convolution is normalized through the Sigmoid function to obtain spatial weights for the feature map. Then multiply these normalized spatial weights with the input feature maps of the spatial attention mechanism, resulting in the final weighted feature map.

In the ECSA module, Channel attention deals with the allocation relationships of feature map channels. Spatial attention enables the network to focus more on pixel regions in the image that play a decisive role while ignoring irrelevant areas. The simultaneous allocation of attention mechanism to two dimensions enhanced the model's ability to express input data and understand multi-scale features. Furthermore, the ECSA module involves only a small number of parameters, yet it yields significant effects.

## 4    Experiments

### 4.1    Experimental Setup

**Dataset:** Due to the scarcity of dataset in the field of power operation, coupled with the complexity and variability of on-site environments, we conduct extensive data collection in power operation sites. Building upon initial manual screening, we ingeniously apply data augmentation techniques for further processing. This approach enhances the generalization ability of the model, making it more adaptable to actual application requirements. Therefore, we obtain a dataset consisting of 5,750 high-quality images. The dataset comprises 4,025 training images, 1,150 validation images, and 575 testing images, with labeled categories including safety helmets, work uniforms, and safety gloves.

**Configuration:** The experimental environment is configured with the following specifications: The system version is windows 10 64-bit, equipped with 13th Gen Intel® CoreTM i7-13700KF processor and an NVIDIA GeForce RTX 4070Ti 8 GB GPU. The system relies on CUDA 11.3, cuDNN 8302, python 3.8, pytorch 1.21.1. The batch size is set to 64 and the number of processors is set to 4.

**Evaluating Indicators:** In object detection tasks, it is imperative to consider both the precision rate (P) and recall rate (R). Based on this, an indicator called average precision (AP) is introduced to assess the performance of object detection algorithms. The precision-recall (PR) curve describes the precision and recall values based on the variation of confidence level thresholds. Conceptually, AP is the area under the PR curve. The relevant calculation formulas are as follows:

$$Precision = \frac{TP}{TP + FP} \tag{3}$$

$$Recall = \frac{TP}{TP + FN} \tag{4}$$

$$AP = \int_0^1 P(R) \tag{5}$$

where True Positive (TP) represents the number of positive class samples correctly predicted by the model as positive class, False Positive (FP) represents the number of

**Table 1.** The Comparison of different network.

|  | Precision | Recall | F1 | mAP | FLOPs | Parameters | Model Size |
|---|---|---|---|---|---|---|---|
| EfficientDet | 94.21% | 72.40% | 0.82 | 83.20% | 4.8G | 3.82M | 15.42 MB |
| YOLOv4-tiny | 93.63% | 85.34% | 0.89 | 89.74% | 6.8G | 5.87M | 23.03 MB |
| YOLOv5n | 95.77% | 84.40% | 0.90 | 89.32% | 4.1G | 1.76M | 3.78 MB |
| YOLOv5-lite | 93.16% | 82.75% | 0.88 | 86.89% | 2.6G | 0.72M | 1.63 MB |
| YOLOX-tiny | 95.34% | 90.66% | 0.93 | 94.33% | 15.2G | 5.03M | 19.89 MB |
| YOLOv7-tiny | 95.99% | 92.87% | 0.94 | 94.67% | 13.2G | 6.01M | 23.68 MB |
| YOLOv8n | 95.70% | 89.82% | 0.93 | 94.29% | 8.2G | 3.01M | 6.30 MB |
| LRDN(ours) | 96.79% | 89.69% | 0.93 | 94.91% | 5.8G | 1.78M | 3.79 MB |

negative class samples incorrectly predicted by the model as positive class, and False Negative (FN) represents the number of positive class samples incorrectly predicted by the model as negative class.

In the experiment, the mean average precision (mAP) of detecting all categories is commonly used as the ultimate metric for evaluating the performance of detection algorithms. The calculation formula is as follows:

$$mAP = \frac{1}{n} \sum_{i=1}^{n} AP_i \qquad (6)$$

When dealing with multiple categories, the performance difference of the model can be evaluated by comparing the F1 score, and the calculation formula is as follows:

$$F1 = \frac{2 \times Precision \times Recall}{Precision + Recall} \qquad (7)$$

In this paper, additional evaluation indicators include model size, parameters and FLOPs. Model size is employed to measure the size of the model, parameters and FLOPs are utilized to measure the complexity and computational requirements of the model.

## 4.2 Comparison of Different Networks

In order to verify the effectiveness of the lightweight LRDN proposed in this paper in detecting safety equipment, such as safety helmets, work clothes, and safety gloves, algorithm comparison experiments are conducted on self-built dataset. The experimental results obtained on the same dataset and experimental environment are shown in Table 1 above.

From the table, it can be seen that YOLOX-tiny and YOLOv7-tiny have better detection performance, but the model size is too large and not suitable for portable terminal devices. EfficientDet and YOLOv4-tiny have average detection performance, and the model size is also large and not suitable. Although YOLOv5n and YOLOv5-lite have advantages in parameters, FLOPs, and model size, their detection performance is not good enough. Compared to the previous networks, YOLOv8n performs better, but the LRDN proposed in this paper has better performance than YOLOv8n. Experimental results show that LRDN achieves precision of 96.79%, recall of 89.69%, mAP of 94.91% and F1-score of 0.93. Without compromising model performance, FLOPs is reduced by 29.3%, parameters is reduced by 40.9%, and model size is reduced by 39.8%. When considering the lightweight versions of various classical networks and comprehensively analyzing the model's computational complexity, parameters and actual detection performance, it can be seen that LRDN outperforms these methods.

**Table 2.** The Ablation study.

| baseline | LightWeight | Inverted Residual | ECSA | Precision | Recall | F1 | mAP | FLOPs | Parameters | Model Size |
|---|---|---|---|---|---|---|---|---|---|---|
| ✓ | | | | 95.70% | 89.82% | 0.93 | 94.29% | 8.2G | 3.01M | 6.30 MB |
| ✓ | ✓ | | | 94.35% | 89.03% | 0.92 | 93.33% | 5.3G | 1.73M | 3.67 MB |
| ✓ | ✓ | ✓ | | 95.03% | 88.51% | 0.92 | 93.74% | 5.7G | 1.74M | 3.72 MB |
| ✓ | ✓ | | ✓ | 95.59% | 88.58% | 092 | 93.68% | 5.3G | 1.73M | 3.68MB |
| ✓ | ✓ | ✓ | ✓ | 96.79% | 89.68% | 0.93 | 94.91% | 5.8G | 1.78M | 3.79MB |

### 4.3 Ablation Study

To comprehensively evaluate the proposed LRDN in this paper and understand the impact of each improvement on the overall model performance, an ablation study is conducted. It can be seen from the Table 2 that both the performance and efficiency of the original model show a significant improvement. Specifically, the YOLOv8n model is first lightweighted, resulting in significant reduction in FLOPs, parameters and model size. Furthermore, building upon the initial lightweighting of the model, inverted residual and ECSA module are separately added for optimization. For the former, adding inverted residual in the backbone increases mAP by 0.41% while ensuring model lightweightness. For the latter, incorporating the ECSA module near the feature fusion module improves mAP by 0.35% while maintaining model lightweightness. Finally, simultaneous addition of inverted residual and ECSA modules leads to a noticeable enhancement in both model performance and efficiency. The model achieves efficient and accurate real-time detection of safety equipment, ensuring the safety of workers in the power operation sites.

## 5   Conclusion

This paper focuses on the characteristics of lightweight network models, such as small model size, low computational complexity, and fast inference speed. It proposes an efficient and lightweight network LRDN for the detection of safety equipment, effectively preventing risks in the field of power operations. Firstly, the real dataset is built to solve the complex environment and the changing status of the workers in the power operation sites. Secondly, inspired by the design principles of the YOLOv8n network, the paper combines lighter GhostConv and C2fGhost modules in the backbone to reduce model parameters while ensuring predictive accuracy. Then, DWConv and C2fGhost modules are introduced into the neck to further accelerate feature fusion and reduce computational complexity. Subsequently, a balanced introduction of inverted residual and ECSA module is employed to enhance the effectiveness of feature extraction and fusion, achieving improved performance and generalization capabilities while ensuring model lightweightness and computational efficiency. Experimental results demonstrate that LRDN outperforms the existing methods in detection performance in power operation sites, with smaller model size and shorter inference time.

In future research, we will investigate how to effectively combine pruning, quantization, and knowledge distillation techniques to further reduce the size of LRDN models and accelerate inference. In addition, although LRDN performs well in the field of power operations, its universality still needs to be improved. In the future, we will expand and optimize it for different safety equipment and work scenarios to ensure that the model can accurately detect potential safety hazards. At the same time, we will also explore how to integrate the LRDN model with existing safety monitoring systems or construction site management platforms to achieve real-time monitoring and early warning, further improving workplace safety and efficiency. Through these efforts, the LRDN will become more universal and practical, providing more reliable security and intelligent monitoring solutions for various industries.

**Acknowledgements.** This work was supported by national natural science foundation of China (No. 62202346), Hubei key research and development program (No. 2021BAA042), China scholarship council (No. 202208420109), Wuhan applied basic frontier research project (No. 2022013988065212), MIIT's AI Industry Innovation Task unveils flagship projects (Key technologies, equipment, and systems for flexible customized and intelligent manufacturing in the clothing industry), and Hubei science and technology project of safe production special fund (No. SJZX20220908).

# References

1. Zhang, C., Lu, Y.: Study on artificial intelligence: the state of the art and future prospects. J. Ind. Inf. Integr. (23-), 23 (2021)
2. Pearton, S.J., Abernathy, C.R., Norton, D.P., et al.: Advances in wide bandgap materials for semiconductor spintronics. Mater. Sci. Eng. R Rep. **40**(4), 137–168 (2003)
3. Langeroudi, A.S.G., Sedaghat, M., Pirpoor, S., et al.: Risk-based optimal operation of power, heat and hydrogen-based microgrid considering a plug-in electric vehicle. Int. J. Hydrogen Energy **46**(58), 30031–30047 (2021)
4. Jiao, L., Zhang, R., Liu, F., et al.: New generation deep learning for video object detection: a survey. IEEE Trans. Neural Netw. Learn. Syst. **33**(8), 3195–3215 (2021)
5. Janai, J., Guney, F., Behl, A., et al.: Computer vision for autonomous vehicles: problems, datasets and state of the art. Found. Trends® Comput. Graph. Vis. **12**(1–3), 1–308 (2020)
6. Zou, Z., Chen, K., Shi, Z., et al.: Object detection in 20 years: a survey. In: Proceedings of the IEEE (2023)

7. Ibrahim, M.S., Dong, W., Yang, Q.: Machine learning driven smart electric power systems: current trends and new perspectives. Appl. Energy **272**, 115237 (2020)
8. Mabrouk, A.B., Zagrouba, E.: Abnormal behavior recognition for intelligent video surveillance systems: a review. Expert Syst. Appl. **91**, 480–491 (2018)
9. Feng, Y., Chen, Z., Jiang, M., Tian, Z., Peng, T., Hu, X.: Smart clothing system with multiple sensors based on digital twin technology. IEEE Internet Things J. **10**(7), 6377–6387 (2023)
10. Chenghu, D., et al.: VTON-SCFA: a virtual try-on network based on the semantic constraints and flow alignment. IEEE Trans. Multimedia **25**, 777–791 (2023)
11. Feng, Y., Hua, A., Du, C., et al.: VTON-MP: multi-pose virtual try-on via appearance flow and feature filtering. IEEE Trans. Consum. Electron. **69**(4), 1101–1113 (2023)
12. Yu, F., Yu, C., Tian, Z., et al.: Intelligent wearable system with motion and emotion recognition based on digital twin technology. IEEE Internet Things J. **11**, 26314–26328 (2024)
13. Liao, W., Zhu, R., Ishizaki, T., et al.: Can gas consumption data improve the performance of electricity theft detection? IEEE Trans. Ind. Inform. **20**, 8453–8465 (2024)
14. Wu, J., Vorobeychik, Y.: Robust deep reinforcement learning through bootstrapped opportunistic curriculum. In: International Conference on Machine Learning, vol. 162, pp. 24177–24211. PMLR (2022)
15. Pan, B., Li, C., Che, H., Leung, M.-F., Yu, K.: Low-rank tensor regularized graph fuzzy learning for multi-view data processing. IEEE Trans. Consum. Electron. **70**, 2925–2938 (2023)
16. Hershcovich, D., Aizenbud, Z., Choshen, L., et al.: SemEval-2019 task 1: cross-lingual semantic parsing with UCCA. arXiv preprint arXiv:1903.02953 (2019)
17. Zou, Z., Chen, K., Shi, Z., et al.: Object detection in 20 years: a survey. Proc. IEEE **111**(3), 257–276 (2023)
18. Cong, I., Choi, S., Lukin, M.D.: Quantum convolutional neural networks. Nat. Phys. **15**(12), 1273–1278 (2019)
19. Zhu, Y., Li, G., Wang, R., et al.: Intelligent fault diagnosis of hydraulic piston pump combining improved LeNet-5 and PSO hyperparameter optimization. Appl. Acoust. **183**, 108336 (2021)
20. Hosny, K.M., Kassem, M.A., Fouad, M.M.: Classification of skin lesions into seven classes using transfer learning with alexnet. J. Digit. Imaging **33**, 1325–1334 (2020)
21. Tang, P., Wang, H., Kwong, S.: G-MS2F: GoogleNet based multi-stage feature fusion of deep CNN for scene recognition. Neurocomputing **225**, 188–197 (2017)
22. Cui, L., Qu, Y., Xie, G., et al.: Security and privacy-enhanced federated learning for anomaly detection in IoT infrastructures. IEEE Trans. Industr. Inform. **18**(5), 3492–3500 (2021)
23. Cao, J., Bao, W., Shang, H., et al.: GCL-YOLO: a GhostConv-based lightweight YOLO network for UAV small object detection. Remote Sens. **15**(20), 4932 (2023)
24. Khan, Z.Y., Niu, Z.: CNN with depthwise separable convolutions and combined kernels for rating prediction. Expert Syst. Appl. **170**, 114528 (2021)
25. Li, Y., Zhang, D., Lee, D.-J.: IIRNet: a lightweight deep neural network using intensely inverted residuals for image recognition. Image Vis. Comput. **92**, 103819 (2019)
26. Zhang, H., Liuchen, W., Chen, Y., et al.: Attention-guided multitask convolutional neural network for power line parts detection. IEEE Trans. Instrum. Meas. **71**, 1–13 (2022)
27. Li, Q., Zhao, F., Xu, Z., et al.: Improved YOLOv4 algorithm for safety management of on-site power system work. Energy Rep. **8**, 739–746 (2022)
28. Liu, Z., Juan, D., Wang, M., et al.: ADCM: attention dropout convolutional module. Neurocomputing **394**, 95–104 (2020)
29. Zhu, W., Shu, Y., Liu, S.: Power grid field violation recognition algorithm based on enhanced yolov5. J. Phys. Conf. Ser. **2209**, 012033 (2022)
30. Feng, Y., Zhu, J., Chen, Y., Liu, S., Jiang, M.: CAPN: a combine attention partial network for glove detection. PeerJ Comput. Sci. **9**, e1558 (2023)

31. Zhang, J., Wang, J., Zhang, S.: An ultra-lightweight and ultra-fast abnormal target identification network for transmission line. IEEE Sens. J. **21**(20), 23325–23334 (2021)
32. Lan, R., Sun, L., Liu, Z., et al.: MadNet: a fast and lightweight network for single-image super resolution. IEEE Trans. Cybern. **51**(3), 1443–1453 (2020)
33. Liyuan, S., Ma, L., Qin, N., et al.: Fault diagnosis of high-speed train bogie by residual-squeeze net. IEEE Trans. Industr. Inf. **15**(7), 3856–3863 (2019)
34. Kulkarni, U., Meena, S.M., Gurlahosur, S.V., Bhogar, G.: Quantization friendly mobilenet (Qf-MobileNet) architecture for vision based applications on embedded platforms. Neural Netw. **136**, 28–39 (2021)
35. Huang, X., Yang, R., Wang, Q., et al.: A novel method for real-time ATR system of AUV based on attention-MobileNetV3 network and pixel correction algorithm. Ocean Eng. **270**, 113403 (2023)
36. Chen, Z., Yang, J., Chen, L., Jiao, H.: Garbage classification system based on improved shufflenet v2. Resour. Conserv. Recycl. **178**, 106090 (2022)
37. Marques, G. and Agarwal, D.: Automated medical diagnosis of Covid-19 through EfficientNet convolutional neural network. Appl. Soft Comput. **96**, 106691 (2020)
38. Paoletti, M.E., Haut, J.M., Pereira, N.S., et al.: GhostNet for hyperspectral image classification. IEEE Trans. Geosci. Remote Sens. **59**(12), 10378–10393 (2021)
39. Tang, H., Liang, S., Yao, D., Qiao, Y.: A visual defect detection for optics lens based on the YOLOv5- C3CA-SPPF network model. Opt. Express **31**(2), 2628–2643 (2023)
40. Zhao, G., Ge, W., Yu, Y.: GraphFPN: graph feature pyramid network for object detection. In: Proceedings of the IEEE/CVF International Conference on Computer Vision, pp. 2763–2772 (2021)
41. Song, Y., Pan, Q.-K., Gao, L., et al.: Improved non-maximum suppression for object detection using harmony search algorithm - sciencedirect. Appl. Soft Comput. **81**, 105478 (2019)
42. Jin, X., Xie, Y., Wei, X., et al.: Delving deep into spatial pooling for squeeze-and-excitation networks. Pattern Recogn. **121**, 108159 (2022)
43. Yang, K., Chang, S., Tian, Z., et al.: Automatic polyp detection and segmentation using shuffle efficient channel attention network. Alexandria Eng. J. **61**, 917–926 (2021)
44. Wang, Q., Wu, B., Zhu, P., et al.: ECA-Net: efficient channel attention for deep convolutional neural networks. In: Proceedings of the IEEE/CVF Conference on Computer Vision and Pattern Recognition, pp. 11534–11542 (2020)
45. Han, K., Wang, Y., Chen, H., et al.: A survey on vision transformer. IEEE Trans. Pattern Anal. Mach. Intell. **45**(1), 87–110 (2022)
46. Wu, H., Zhao, Z., Wang, Z.: META-Unet: multi-scale efficient transformer attention Unet for fast and high-accuracy polyp segmentation. IEEE Trans. Autom. Sci. Eng. **21**, 4117–4128 (2023)

# Personalized Federated Learning by Model Pruning via Batch Normalization Layers

Annan Wang[1] and Bencan Gong[2(✉)]

[1] Hubei Key Laboratory of Intelligent Vision Monitoring for Hydropower Engineering,
Three Gorges University, Yichang, China
[2] College of Computer and Information Technology, Three Gorges University, Yichang, China
gonbc@sina.com

**Abstract.** Due to the privacy preserving capabilities, federated learning (FL) has emerged as an efficient decentralized deep learning paradigm. Traditional FL attempts to learn a single global model with the cooperation of many clients under the coordination of a central server. However, learning a single global model cannot achieve satisfactory model accuracy for all clients joining in FL on heterogeneous data. In addition, in the process of collaborative learning of the global model among a large number of clients, massive data exchange between the clients and server results in high communication cost, which is unlikely to be affordable for resource constrained mobile devices or Internet of Things (IoT) devices. Therefore, we propose a novel Personalized Federated Learning by Model Pruning (PFLMP) which uses batch-normalization (BN) layers of clients to personalize the global model to solve the challenge that arise with data heterogeneity across clients, and uses BN layers of server to prune the global model to reduce the communication cost. Extensive experiments show that PFLMP outperforms current state-of-the-art personalized algorithms and pruning algorithms in FL in terms of the model accuracy and the communication overheads.

**Keywords:** personalized federated learning · model pruning · batch normalization layers · heterogeneous data

## 1 Introduction

With the rapid development of data-driven intelligent applications, deep learning has been widely used in many fields, such as computer vision, intelligent transportation, smart finance, medical health, and natural language processing [1]. However, the centralized deep learning system needs to collect a large amount of training data from mobile phones, IoT devices, or social networks. Concerns about data privacy lead to users being unwilling to provide their potentially sensitive data to the server for model training. Federated learning [2] emerged as an efficient distributed deep learning paradigm, which can not only handle privacy issues but also efficiently optimize models. Federated learning has been applied in a wide range of application scenarios such as healthcare, financial services, intelligent transportation, and the Internet of Things [3].

In FL, each client downloads a global model from the server, and then uses the its private data to train the global model and uploads the trained model parameters to the server. The server aggregates model parameters collected by many clients and obtains a new global model, and then sends it to clients. FL can build the global model by exchanging local model parameters from clients and ensure that sensitive data of clients does not leave the local device to protect data privacy. FL has been successfully adopted for distributed training and inference of large-scale deep neural networks. However, in the practical applications, FL still faces two fundamental challenges:

(1) Low model accuracy on heterogeneous data: The collected data from different client devices might be non-Independent Identically Distributed (non-IID) data [4], such as uneven data distribution, label drift, feature drift, and feature preference drift, thus training a single global model for all clients might significantly reduce the accuracy and convergence of model [5].
(2) High communication and computing cost: Deep neural networks are characterized by an extremely large number of parameters, which yields significant challenge in exchanging these parameters among distributed nodes and managing the memory. For example, a 152-layer ResNet network model has more than 60 million parameters and requires more than 20 Giga float-point-operations when inferencing an image with resolution $224 \times 224$ [6]. Evidently, resource constrained intelligent devices, such as mobile phones, wearables or IoT devices, cannot afford so high communication and computing cost due to their limited communication bandwidth and computing power.

For the first problem, the personalization of the global model is the key to solving the challenge that arise with data heterogeneity across clients. Personalized FL [7, 8] allows each client to train a personalized model to focus on its non-IID data distribution. Personalized FL aims to minimize the impact of heterogeneous data and enable each client to get as much help as possible from other clients. In personalized FL, an important issue is determining which parameters of the client should be localized to decrease the impact of heterogeneous data or be shared with other clients to get help. Current mainstream methods are to localize layers that are sensitive to heterogeneous data to decrease the negative impact of collaboration, and share other layers. For example, FedRep [9] personalizes the classifier layers, while FedBN [10] and MTFL [11] personalize the BN layers.

For the second problem, model pruning is an effective technique commonly used in distributed learning, which reduces a great burden on distributed computing nodes when exchanging model parameters during training. Long et al. [12] proposed a novel FL framework which combines dynamic model pruning with error feedback to eliminate redundant information exchange and uses incremental regularization to achieve extreme sparsity of models. In order to reduce the computation, storage, and communication cost and accelerate the FL training process, Xu et al. [13] proposed a new efficient FL framework which is composed of structured pruning, weight quantization and selective updating.

Personalized FL reduces the impact of non-IID data among clients by allowing each client to train a personalized model when collaborating with others. Model pruning decreases the complexity of neural network model. But these existing researches only focus on one of the two technologies of model personalization or model pruning. We combine the two technologies via BN layers and propose a novel personalized federated learning by model pruning. Our key contributions are summarized as follows:

(1) We propose PFLMP algorithm which uses BN layers of clients to personalize the global model to improve model accuracy. After the training of clients is completed, the BN layer parameters are saved locally. When the client receives the aggregated global model from the server, the locally saved BN layer parameters are used to replace the corresponding parameters in the global model to achieve personalization.

(2) We use BN layer parameters of server to prune the global model to reduce the model size and the communication cost. PFLMP algorithm imposes L1 regularization on the scaling factors in BN layers, which pushes the values of BN scaling factors in insignificant channels towards zero to facilitate the model pruning. After global model aggregation, the BN scaling factors are sorted, and unimportant channels are pruned according to the BN scaling factors. After pruning, the resulting model will be more compact in terms of communication cost, runtime memory, and computing time compared to the initial model.

(3) We conduct extensive experiments on CIFAR10 dataset. The results show that PFLMP is able to significantly improve the model accuracy and reduce the communication overheads compared to other state-of-the-art personalized algorithms and pruning algorithms in FL.

## 2 Related Work

### 2.1 Personalized Federated Learning

Personalized FL is an effective method to solve non-IID problem. The main purpose of personalized FL is to enable personalized models to benefit from collaboration between clients while reducing the impact of non-IID. Among the current excellent personalized FL algorithms, parameter decoupling and personalized aggregation are two typical algorithms.

**Parameter decoupling** localizes layers that are sensitive to non-IID data, while globally sharing other layers. GPFL [14] proposes a novel personalized FL framework to achieve both collaborative learning and individualized goals, which learns the global feature information through the trainable global category embedding layer, and learns personalized feature information through personalized tasks. Fed-RoD [15] trains a generic feature extractor with a consistent objective to extract global feature information for the global objective and constructs a personalized predictor to minimize each client's empirical risk based on the generic predictor. But it cannot extract personalized feature information for each client's personalized tasks. FedRep [9] only leverages local data to train the model to learn a global low-dimensional representation and enable each client to generate a personalized low-dimensional classifier. But it is not beneficial for collaborative learning because of losing some global information during local training. Per-FedAvg [16] uses meta learning to find an initial shared model and allows clients to quickly adapt to local datasets with only one or a few steps of gradient descent. However, the aggregated trend cannot meet each client's model update trend. In Ditto [17], the personalized model can benefit from the global parameter guidance. However, it ignores to extract the global and personalized feature information. pFedMe [18] proposes a new bi-level optimization algorithm by using the Moreau envelope as clients' regularized loss functions, which helps decouple optimizing personalized models from learning the global model. To improve the tolerance to heterogeneity, FedProto [19] uses the abstract class prototypes instead of the gradients to guide personalized feature extraction, which aggregates the local prototypes collected from each client, and then sends the global prototypes back to each client to train local models. However, poor global prototypes may mislead feature extraction. These algorithms can effectively alleviate the negative impact of non-IID by adapting local layers. However, in these algorithms, the localization layer ignores collaboration with other layers, which results in poor performance in complicated non-IID circumstances.

**Personalized aggregation** allows clients with homologous data distributions to collaborate to mitigate the effect of non-IID data. FedAMP [20] proposes a new joint attention information transmission method, which implements a message passing mechanism by carefully passing the personalized model of each client as a message to a personalized cloud model with similar model parameters, and allows similar models to aggregate with larger weights. Seo et al. [21] designed effective functions to estimate the utility of non-IID data, cost of computational resource, and cost of data generation, and proposed a resource-efficient method to minimize cost through an auction approach and mitigate quality degradation through data sharing. FedFomo [22] evaluates the degree of similarity in data distribution through model validation sets on each client. Give a higher aggregation weight to a model with better performance. CAPFL [23] introduces the global model as a latent variable to increase the joint distribution of clients' parameters and capture the common trends of different clients. APPLE [24] adaptively learns a unique set of local weights on each client to guide personalized model aggregation, which allows personalized models to make more use of beneficial core models while suppressing potentially harmful core models. However, finding clients with similar data distributions for collaboration is a challenge, especially when there are significant differences in data distribution on the clients.

In short, current personalized FL algorithms only consider the impact of partial factors on collaboration and lack consideration for communication costs and clients' resource limitations, which cannot adapt to various complex network scenarios.

## 2.2  Model Pruning

Although the model of large-scale deep neural networks has strong expressive power, it requires high computing and storage capabilities, which makes it difficult to apply to resource constrained mobile devices. To solve the problem, many model pruning algorithms have been proposed. Model pruning removes redundant parameters based on their importance while maintaining network accuracy, which can be categorized as structured pruning and unstructured pruning.

**Structured Pruning:** Yu et al. [25] proposed an adaptive dynamic pruning method for federated learning, which can evaluate the importance of model parameters based on the training samples to dynamically slim the model, and only retain the gradients of significant parameters during backpropagation. Jiang et al. [26] proposed the Complement Sparsification (CS) pruning mechanism. In each round, CS creates a global sparse model, while the client creates a local sparse model with weights trimmed from the global model to capture local trends. These two types of complementary sparse models are aggregated into a dense model which is subsequently trimmed during the iteration process. PQSU [13] consists of three parts: structured pruning, weight quantization, and selective updating, which work together to decrease the cost of computing, storage, and communication.

**Unstructured Pruning:** PruneFL [27] includes adaptive initial pruning at a selected client and further distributed parameter pruning as part of FL procedure. The model size is adapted during this process to find the best model parameter set that learns the "fastest". Wu et al. [28] proposed an efficient joint training framework based on model pruning, which dynamically selects convolutional kernels before releasing the global model, prunes the current optimal subnet, and then sends the compressed model to all clients for training.

Although these pruning works achieve model compression and save computational and communication costs, there is still a problem of low model accuracy when client data is heterogeneous. Therefore, it is necessary to combine pruning algorithm with personalized algorithm to improve model accuracy while compressing the model.

## 3  PFLMP

### 3.1  System Architecture

Figure 1 shows a high-level overview of how PFLMP operates in application. More detailed description of optimization on client and server is given in the later subsections. PFLMP uses the client-server framework, where the client is responsible for model training and personalization, while the server is responsible for model aggregation and pruning. First, the server generates a global model and initializes it, then selects all or a subset of all clients from the client database, and performs the following steps in each round:

Step 1: The server sends the global model to all clients, and all clients receive and save the global model.

Step 2: If the current round is not the first round, the client replaces the corresponding BN layer parameters in the global model with locally saved BN layer parameters. Otherwise, do nothing, because there were no locally saved BN layer parameters yet in the first round.

Step 3: Each client performs local training using its own datasets and get the local model.

Step 4: Each client saves the BN layer parameters from the local model for use in the next round.

Step 5: Each client uploads its local model parameters to the server.

Step 6: After the server receives the models uploaded by the clients, it will aggregate all received models to generate a single global model.

Step 7: If the current round is equal to the pre-set pruning round, the global model is pruned to generate a compact global model. Otherwise, do nothing.

After completing the above steps, a new round starts. In each client, PFLMP utilizes locally saved BN layer parameters to achieve personalization and improve the accuracy of the model on non-IID datasets. In server, BN layer parameters are used to prune the aggregated global model to reduce communication and computational cost.

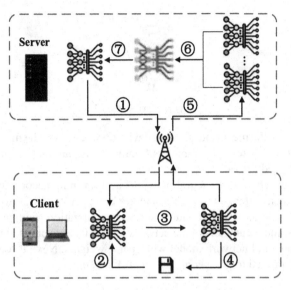

**Fig. 1.** System architecture

## 3.2 PFLMP Pruning

Suppose the $K$ clients are indexed by $k$, and the $k$th client owns its local private dataset $D_k = \left\{ \left( x_k^i, y_k^i \right) \right\}_{i=1}^{N_k}$, where $y_k^i \in C = \{1, 2, \cdots, c\}$. On the $k$th client, $N_k$ is the total number of samples, and $\left\{ N_k^1, \cdots, N_k^c \right\}$ is the number of samples for each class. The whole dataset with $N$ samples is denoted as $D = D_1 \cup \cdots \cup D_K$. In neural networks, convolutional layers and BN layers are widely used. Reducing the number of channels in the convolutional layer can effectively decrease the number of network parameters, accelerate the inference speed of the model, and lower the communication overhead of FL. In the BN layer, a scaling factor $\gamma$ corresponds to a channel, which represents the degree of activation of the channel. BN layer uses minibatch statistics to normalize the internal activation. Let $x$ and $y$ be the input and output of a BN layer, $B = \{x_1, \cdots, x_n\}$ denotes the current minibatch, BN layer can perform the following transformation:

$$\mu_B = \frac{1}{n} \sum_{i=1}^{n} x_i \tag{1}$$

$$\sigma_B^2 = \frac{1}{n} \sum_{i=1}^{n} (x_i - \mu_B)^2 \tag{2}$$

$$\hat{x}_i = \frac{x_i - \mu_B}{\sqrt{\sigma_B^2 + \varepsilon}} \tag{3}$$

$$y_i = \gamma_i \hat{x}_i + \beta_i \tag{4}$$

where $\mu_B$ and $\delta_B$ are the mean and standard deviation values over the minibatch $B$, $\gamma_i$ and $\beta_i$ are trainable transformation parameters (scaling factor and bias) which can linearly transform normalized activations to any scales.

Figure 2 shows changes in neural networks after pruning according to the scaling factors in BN layer. After pruning, we obtain a compact neural network model. For the convenience of pruning, we conduct sparse regularization training on the scaling factors to make some parameters of the network tend to be zero or equal to zero, thereby obtaining a deep neural network model with sparse weights. Next, those channels with small factors are pruned to get a compact network model.

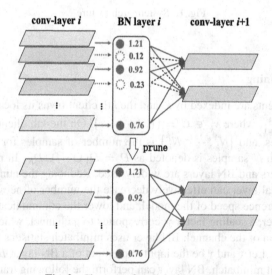

**Fig. 2.** Changes of model after pruning

After adding sparse regularization training, the loss function on the client $k$ can be expressed as:

$$L_k(w_k) = \frac{1}{|D_k|} \sum_{(x_k^i, y_k^i) \in D_k} l\left(x_k^i, y_k^i; w_k\right)$$

$$+\alpha \sum_{\gamma \in bn_k} f(\gamma) \tag{5}$$

where $l(\cdot)$ denotes the loss function on training samples $(x_k^i, y_k^i)$, e.g., cross-entropy loss, and $w_k$ is the set of local model parameters on the client $k$. $|D_k|$ is the number of training samples on the client $k$. The first sum-term is the normal training loss of a deep neural network, $f(\cdot)$ is a sparsity-induced penalty on the scaling factors, $\alpha$ is used to balance the two terms, and $bn_k$ is the set of the scaling factors in BN layers. L1-norm on neural networks is widely used to achieve sparsity, therefore we choose $f(s) = |s|$. During the training, the partial derivative of $f(s)$ over $s$ is given by:

$$\frac{\partial f(s)}{\partial(s)} = sign(s) \tag{6}$$

where $sign(\cdot)$ is a sign function that judges the sign of $s$. When s > 0, s = 0, and s < 0, the values of the function are 1, 0, and $-1$ respectively. Sub-gradient descent is used as the optimization method for the L1-norm penalty term. In addition to normal training updates, BN layer parameters also need L1-norm updates.

Pruning a channel essentially corresponds to deleting all the incoming and outgoing connections of the channel. Because the scaling factors in BN layers are jointly trained with the network weights, they can act as the agents for channel selection. PFLMP can automatically identity unimportant channels according to the scaling factors, and safely remove them without greatly affecting the network performance.

## 3.3  PFLMP Personalization

In heterogeneous FL, participating clients are critically not restricted to single distribution of the local training data, and prior we do not know anything about these distributions. The distribution of the training data on the client $k$ is denoted as $p_k(x_k, y_k)$. non-IID refers to $p_i(x_i, y_i) \neq p_j(x_j, y_j)$ for different client $i$ and $j$. The objective of the client $k$ is:

$$minL_k(w_k) \tag{7}$$

For all clients, the optimal objective can be expressed as:

$$\{\hat{w}_1, \cdots, \hat{w}_k\} = argminF(L_1, \cdots, L_K) \tag{8}$$

$$F(L_1, \cdots, L_K) = \sum_{k=1}^{K} \frac{|D_k|}{|D|} L_k(w_k) \qquad (9)$$

where $\hat{w}_k$ is local model parameters on the client $k$ after model aggregation and model pruning. $|\hat{w}_k| = r|w_k|$, where $r$ is pruning rate of model.

Figure 3 shows composition of a neural network model in PFLMP. After each convolutional (Conv) layer, there is a BN layer and a max pooling layer. After the first fully-connected (FC) layer, there is a BN layer.

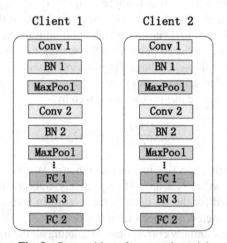

**Fig. 3.** Composition of a network model

Each client shares the global model parameters in convolutional layers and fully-connected layers, and saves its private BN layer parameters. After the client downloads the global model, it replaces the corresponding BN layer parameters in the global model with its private BN layer parameters, then begins local training. After local training, each client saves the BN layer parameters of the local model for use in the next round. With the help of the BN layer, the client achieves personalization of the local model and improves model accuracy. PFLMP is based on the client-server framework, and each round is initiated by the server, as shown in Algorithm 1.

---

**Algorithm 1: PFLMP.**

**Input:**
$B$: Local minibatch size
$T$: Number of global rounds
$E$: Number of local epochs
$K$: Total number of clients
$R$: Proportion of clients participating in FL
$\eta$: Learning rate
$r$: Pruning rate
$\tau$: Number of pre-set pruning round
**Output:**
$w^k$: Personalized model after pruning for each client $k$
**Server executes:**
1: Initialize the global model $w_0$ and
    $mask \in \{0,1\}^m$
2: For each round $t = 0, \dots, T - 1$ do
3:    $n \leftarrow max(K \cdot R, 1)$
4:    $S_t \leftarrow set\ of\ n\ selected$ clients
5:    For each client $k \in S_t$ in parallel do
6:       $w_{t+1}^k \leftarrow ClientDo(t, k, w_t, mask)$
7:       $m_t \leftarrow \sum_{k \in S_t} |D_k|$
8:       $w_{t+1} \leftarrow \sum_{k \in S_t} \frac{|D_k|}{m_t} w_{t+1}^k$
9:    End for
10:   If $t == \tau$ do   //Perform pruning
11:      Sort the scaling factors in $bn_{t+1}$
12:      $n \leftarrow r \cdot |bn_{t+1}|$
13:      Prune $n$ smallest BN layer parameters
and their corresponding channels in $w_{t+1}$
14:      Generate $mask$
15:   Else do
16:      $mask = [1,1,\dots,1]$
17:   End if
18: End for
**Client executes** $ClientDo(t, k, w_t, mask)$:
19: Download global model $w_t$ from server
20: If $t \neq 0$ do
21:    $bn_k \leftarrow bn_k \odot mask$
22:    Delete parameters with value 0 in $bn_k$
23:    Replace the corresponding parameters
in $w_t$ with $bn_k$

---

24:  End for
25: End if
26: Split local dataset $D_k$ into batches $B$
27: For each epoch $j = 0, ..., E - 1$ do
28:   For each batch $b \in B$ do
29:     $w_t \leftarrow w_t - \eta \nabla L(w_t; b)$
30:       For $i \in I$ do $//I$ is the set of indexes of
BN layer parameters
31:         $w_t(i) \leftarrow w_t(i) + \alpha \cdot sign(w_t(i))$
32:       End for
33:   End for
34: End for
35: Save $bn_k$ in $w_t$
36: Return $w_t$ to server

Line 1: The initial value of $w_0$ is a set of random numbers. $mask \in \{0, 1\}^m$ denotes a vector, and $m$ is the total number of scaling factors in BN layers. The value of $mask_i$ indicates whether the connection $i$ is pruned ($mask_i = 0$) in BN layers or not pruned ($mask_i = 1$). The initial value of $mask$ is all 1. Lines 3–4: Randomly select some clients from all clients to participate in federated learning based on a pre-set proportion $R$. Lines 6–8: Server collects the network models uploaded by all clients and aggregate them. Line 10: Determines whether pruning is performed in this round. Line 11: Sort the scaling factors in BN layers in ascending order. Line 12: Calculate the number of channels to be pruned based on the pre-set pruning ratio $r$. Line 13: Prune the $n$ smallest BN layer parameters and their corresponding channels in the global model. Line 14: Generate $mask$. If the $i$-th parameter in BN layers is pruned, the value of $mask_i$ is set 0, otherwise it is 1. Lines 15–16: If pruning is not performed in this round, the value of $mask$ is set to all 1.

Lines 20–25: If this round is not the first round, in line 21, set the local BN layer parameters that should be pruned to 0, and $\odot$ denotes the elementwise product. In line 22, delete local BN layer parameters with value 0. In line 23, the corresponding BN layer parameters in the global model are replaced with local BN layer parameters to achieve personalization. If this round is the first round, since the BN layer parameters have not been saved locally, they don't need to be replaced. Line 27: Perform local iterative training. Line 29: Execute the random gradient descent algorithm and update the model parameters. Lines 30–32: Perform L1 regular updates on the BN layer parameters to achieve sparsity. Line 35: Save the local BN layer parameters for use in the next round.

To better analyse the influence of the BN layer on the overall training accuracy, we consider a simple deep neural network consisting of dense layers followed by BN layer. The activations of the first dense layer can be modelled as:

$$y_i \triangleq [W_0 X + b_0]_i \tag{10}$$

$$y_i \sim N(\mathbb{E}[y_i], Var[y_i]) \tag{11}$$

where $\mathbb{E}[y_i]$ and $Var[y_i]$ are the mean and variance, $W_0$ and $b_0$ are weights and biases, and $X$ is the dataset of the client. After local training, the BN layer of the client is updated. Supposing $\mu_i \approx \mathbb{E}[y_i]$ and $\sigma_i^2 \approx Var[y_i]$, the BN layer is calculated as follows:

$$\hat{x}_i \triangleq \frac{y_i - \mu_i}{\sigma_i} \tag{12}$$

$$\hat{x}_i \sim N(0, 1) \tag{13}$$

$$BN(\hat{x}_i) \sim N\left(\beta_i, \gamma_i^2\right) \tag{14}$$

where $\beta_i$ and $\gamma_i^2$ are learning parameters in BN layer. After the client downloads the aggregated global model from the server, the weights and biases of the first layer on the client become $\overline{W}_0$ and $\overline{b}_0$, and the activations of the first dense layer can be modelled as:

$$\overline{y}_i \triangleq \left[\overline{W}_0 X + \overline{b}_0\right]_i \tag{15}$$

$$\overline{y}_i \sim N\left(\mathbb{E}[\overline{y}_i], Var[\overline{y}_i]\right) \tag{16}$$

Assuming $\Delta\mu_i = \mathbb{E}[\overline{y}_i] - \mathbb{E}[y_i]$, $\Delta\sigma^2 = Var[\overline{y}_i] - Var[y_i]$, then the output of BN layer in PFLMP is:

$$\hat{\overline{x}} \sim N\left(\frac{\Delta\mu_i}{\sigma_i}, 1 + \frac{\Delta\sigma_i^2}{\sigma_i^2}\right) \tag{17}$$

$$BN\left(\hat{\overline{x}}\right) \sim N\left(\gamma\frac{\Delta\mu_i}{\sigma_i} + \beta_i, \gamma_i^2\left(1 + \frac{\Delta\sigma_i^2}{\sigma_i^2}\right)\right) \tag{18}$$

If the BN layer of the global model is not replaced by the locally saved BN layer, the client will use BN values $(\overline{\mu}, \overline{\sigma}, \overline{\beta}, \overline{\gamma})$ in the global model, and the output of BN layer is:

$$\hat{\overline{x}} \sim N\left(\frac{\mu_i + \Delta\mu_i - \overline{\mu}_i}{\overline{\sigma}_i}, \frac{\sigma_i^2 + \Delta\sigma_i^2}{\overline{\sigma}_i^2}\right) \tag{19}$$

$$\overline{BN}\left(\hat{\overline{x}}\right) \sim N\left(\begin{matrix} \overline{\gamma}\left(\frac{\mu_i+\Delta\mu_i-\overline{\mu}_i}{\overline{\sigma}_i}\right) + \overline{\beta}_i, \\ \overline{\gamma}_i^2\left(\frac{\sigma_i^2+\Delta\sigma_i^2}{\overline{\sigma}_i^2}\right) \end{matrix}\right) \tag{20}$$

PFLMP has smaller differences in mean and variance before and after server aggregation than FL:

$$\left|\gamma\frac{\Delta\mu_i}{\sigma_i}\right| < \left|\beta_i - \overline{\gamma}\left(\frac{\mu_i + \Delta\mu_i - \overline{\mu}_i}{\overline{\sigma}_i}\right) - \overline{\beta}_i\right| \tag{21}$$

$$\left|\gamma_i^2\frac{\Delta\sigma_i^2}{\sigma_i^2}\right| < \left|\gamma_i^2 - \overline{\gamma}_i^2\left(\frac{\sigma_i^2 + \Delta\sigma_i^2}{\overline{\sigma}_i^2}\right)\right| \tag{22}$$

PFLMP makes the output of the deep neural networks closer to the values before aggregation, thus it has higher accuracy than FL.

# 4 Experiments

## 4.1 Experimental Parameters Set

To verify the effectiveness of PFLMP and the influence of relevant parameters on the model accuracy of PFLMP, we conduct extensive experiments and compare PFLMP with PQSU [13], Fedavg [2], pfedMe [18], and CAPFL [23]. PFLMP trains deep learning models using the PyTorch 1.7.0 deep learning framework and CIFAR10 dataset.

Experimental parameter settings are shown in Table 1. Convolutional neural network has two $3 \times 3$ convolutional layers with 256 filters, and each convolutional layer is followed by BN layer, ReLU and $2 \times 2$ max pooling layer; one fully connected layer with 128 neurons, followed by BN layer and ReLU; and one softmax output layer. To generate non-IID client data, PFLMP uses the popular approach from [11]: we sort the training and testing data by label, split them into $2K$ shards, and randomly allocate several shards to each client. In each client, the classes in training dataset are the same as those in the test dataset. This splitting ensures that each client's data has strong statistical heterogeneity, thus meeting the condition of strongly non-IID distribution across clients.

**Table 1.** Experimental parameters

| Parameter | Value |
|---|---|
| $B$: Local minibatch size | 20 |
| $T$: Number of global rounds | 200 |
| $E$: Number of local epochs | 2 |
| $K$: Total number of clients | 100, 200, 400 |
| $R$: Proportion of clients participating in FL | 0.5, 1 |
| $\eta$: Learning rate | 0.1 |
| $r$: Pruning rate | 0.1–0.8 |
| $\tau$: Number of pruning round | 2 |

## 4.2 Pruning Experiment of PFLMP

In order to investigate the impact of different pruning times on the model accuracy, we set the pruning time to the 2nd, 10th, 20th, and 30th rounds respectively, and the model accuracy for CIFAR10 is shown in Fig. 4.

When the model is pruned, the model accuracy will sharply decrease, but as the model continues to be trained, the model accuracy will quickly recover. When the model training is completed, the model accuracies are almost the same for four different pruning times. Due to the earlier the pruning timing, the lower the communication overhead of the network, therefore, in subsequent experiments, the pruning timing is set to the second round. Figure 5 shows that the model accuracies of PFLMP under different pruning rates for CIFAR10.

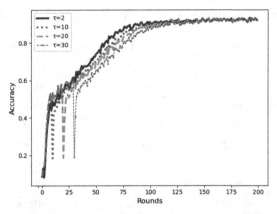

**Fig. 4.** Impact of pruning timing on the model accuracy of PFLMP

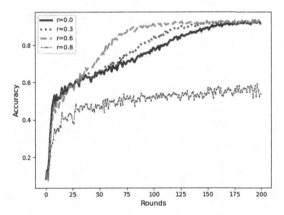

**Fig. 5.** Model accuracies of PFLMP under different pruning rates

When the pruning rates are 0, 0.3, and 0.6, the final model accuracies of PFLMP are almost the same. But when the pruning rate is 0.8, the model accuracy decreases significantly.

To evaluate the pruning performance of PFLMP, PFLMP is compared with the pruning algorithm PQSU, and the results for CIFAR 10 are shown in Table 2. At different pruning rates, the model accuracies of PFLMP are much higher than those of PQSU. When the pruning rate is 10%, the model accuracy of PFLMP is 36.1% higher than that of PQSU. When the pruning rate is 70%, the model accuracy of PFLMP still has 91.2%, and is 38.0% higher than that of PQSU. Figure 6 shows the comparison of model accuracies between PFLMP and PQSU at different pruning rates. PFLMP performs better than PQSU, because PQSU only considers model pruning without considering model personalization.

**Table 2.** Accuracy comparison of different pruning algorithms

| Pruning rate | PQSU | PFLMP | Exceeding rate |
|---|---|---|---|
| 10% | 68.4 | 93.1 | 36.1% |
| 20% | 67.4 | 92.8 | 37.7% |
| 30% | 67.5 | 93.1 | 37.9% |
| 40% | 67.6 | 93.7 | 38.6% |
| 50% | 66.8 | 93.5 | 40.0% |
| 60% | 66.7 | 93.3 | 39.8% |
| 70% | 66.1 | 91.2 | 38.0% |
| 80% | 53.2 | 59.0 | 10.9% |

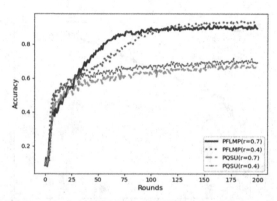

**Fig. 6.** Model accuracies of PFLMP and PQSU under different pruning rates

### 4.3 Personalization Experiment of PFLMP

To evaluate the performance of PFLMP personalization, PFLMP is compared with Fedavg, pfedMe, and CAPFL. When the number of clients $W = 100$ and 200, and the client participation rates $C = 0.5$ and 1, the experimental results of the four algorithms are shown in Fig. 7. Under different parameters, the model accuracy of PFLMP is higher than that of the other three algorithms.

Fedavg has the lowest accuracy because it does not personalize the model. Although pfedMe and CAPFL consider personalization, the performance of their personalization algorithms is lower than PFLMP. Table 3 shows that comparison of the highest accuracy of different algorithms.

Under different parameters, the model accuracy of PFLMP is higher than that of the other three algorithms. When the number of clients $W = 100$ and the client participation rate $C = 0.5$, The model accuracy of PFLMP is 33.0%, 5.6%, and 24.2% higher than that of Fedavg, pfedMe, and CAPFL, respectively. PFLMP has excellent performance due to the use of personalized algorithm based on the BN layers.

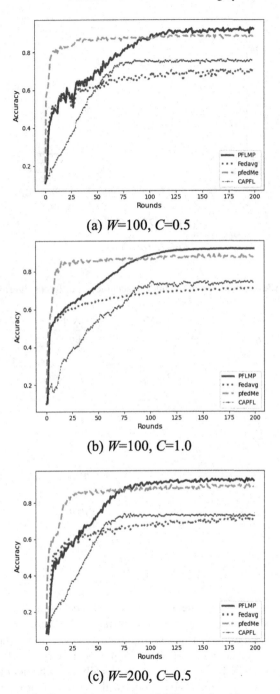

(a) $W$=100, $C$=0.5

(b) $W$=100, $C$=1.0

(c) $W$=200, $C$=0.5

**Fig. 7.** Model accuracies of different algorithms

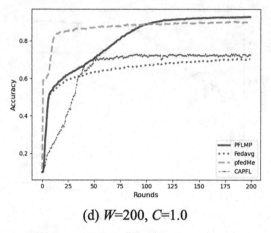

(d) *W*=200, *C*=1.0

**Fig. 7.** (*continued*)

**Table 3.** Comparison of the highest accuracy of different algorithms

| Parameters | Fedavg | pfedMe | CAPFL | PFLMP |
|---|---|---|---|---|
| W = 100<br>C = 0.5 | 69.8 | 87.9 | 74.7 | 92.8 |
| W = 200<br>C = 0.5 | 69.2 | 88.4 | 72.9 | 93.3 |
| W = 100<br>C = 1.0 | 71.1 | 88.9 | 76.1 | 92.0 |
| W = 200<br>C = 1.0 | 70.4 | 89.6 | 73.9 | 92.6 |
| W = 400<br>C = 0.5 | 69.8 | 81.6 | 71.9 | 88.9 |
| W = 400<br>C = 1.0 | 68.9 | 82.0 | 70.9 | 88.0 |

## 5  Conclusions

In the scenario of heterogeneous client data, we design a personalized federated learning algorithm using model pruning based on BN layers. PFLMP sorts the BN layer parameters of the model in server and prunes unimportant parameters to compress the size of the model and reduce the computational and communication costs. After each round of training, PFLMP saves the BN layer parameters locally in each client and replaces the corresponding parameters of the global model with them to improve model accuracy. The experimental results show that PFLMP performs better than the federated average algorithm Fedavg, pruning algorithm PQSU, and personalized algorithms pfedMe and CAPFL.

**Acknowledgements.** This work is supported by the National Natural Science Foundation of China (No. 62172255).

# References

1. Naseem, U., Razzak, I., Khan, S.K., Prasad, M.: Comprehensive survey on word representation models: from classical to state-of-the-art word representation language models. ACM Trans. Asian Low-Resour. Lang. Inf. Process. **20**(5), 1–35 (2021)
2. McMahan, B., Moore, E., Ramage, D., Arcas, B.A.: Communication-efficient learning of deep networks from decentralized data. In: International Conference on Artificial Intelligence and Statistics (AISTATS), pp. 1273–1282 (2017)
3. Lim, W.Y.B., et al.: Federated learning in mobile edge networks: a comprehensive survey. IEEE Commun. Surv. Tutor. **22**(3), 2031–2063 (2020)
4. Karimireddy, S.P., Kale, S., Mohri, M., Reddi, S.J., Stich, S.U., Suresh, A.T.: SCAF-FOLD: stochastic controlled averaging for federated learning. In: International Conference on Machine Learning (ICML), pp. 5132–5143 (2020)
5. Zhang, J., et al.: Adaptive federated learning on non-IID data with resource constraint. IEEE Trans. Comput. **71**(7), 1655–1667 (2022)
6. Liu, Z., Li, J., Shen, Z., Huang, G., Yan, S., Zhang, C.: Learning efficient convolutional networks through network slimming. In: IEEE International Conference on Computer Vision (ICCV) (2017)
7. Li, Q., Diao, Y., Chen, Q., He, B.: Federated learning on non-IID data silos: an experimental study. In: IEEE the 38th International Conference on Data Engineering, pp. 965–978 (2022)
8. Li, L., Zhan, D., Li, X.: Aligning model outputs for class imbalanced non-IID federated learning. Mach. Learn. 1–24 (2022)
9. Collins, L., Hassani, H., Mokhtari, A., Shakkottai, S.: Exploiting shared representations for personalized federated learning. arXiv preprint arXiv:2102.07078 (2021)
10. Li, X., Jiang, M., Zhang, X., Kamp, M., Dou, Q.: FedBN: federated learning on non-IID features via local batch normalization. In: International Conference on Learning Representations (2021)
11. Mills, J., Hu, J., Min, G.: Multi-task federated learning for personalised deep neural networks in edge computing. IEEE Trans. Parallel Distrib. Syst. **33**(3), 630–641 (2021)
12. Long, Q., Anagnostopoulos, C., Parambath, S.P., Bi, D.: FedDIP: federated learning with extreme dynamic pruning and incremental regularization. arXiv preprint arXiv:2309.06805 (2023)
13. Xu, W., Fang, W., Ding, Y., Zou, M., Xiong, N.: Accelerating federated learning for IoT in big data analytics with pruning, quantization and selective updating. IEEE Access **9**, 38457–38466 (2021)
14. Zhang, J., et al.: GPFL: simultaneously learning global and personalized feature information for personalized federated learning. In: International Conference on Computer Vision (ICCV), pp. 5041–5051 (2023)
15. Chen, H., Chao, W.: On bridging generic and personalized federated learning for image classification. In: International Conference on Learning Representations (ICLR), pp. 1–32 (2022)
16. Fallah, A., Mokhtari, A., Ozdaglar, A.: Personalized federated learning with theoretical guarantees: a model-agnostic meta-learning approach. In: Proceedings of Advances in Neural Information Processing Systems, vol. 33, pp. 3557–3568 (2020)
17. Li, T., Hu, S., Beirami, A., Smith, V.: Ditto: fair and robust federated learning through personalization. In: International Conference on Machine Learning, pp. 6357–6368 (2021)

18. Dinh, C.T., Tran, N.H., Nguyen, T.D.: Personalized federated learning with Moreau envelopes. In: Conference on Neural Information Processing Systems (NeurIPS) (2020)

19. Tan, Y., et al.: FedProto: federated prototype learning across heterogeneous clients. In: AAAI Conference on Artificial Intelligence (2022)

20. Huang, Y., et al.: Personalized cross-silo federated learning on non-IID data. In: AAAI Conference on Artificial Intelligence (2021)

21. Seo, E., Niyato, D., Elmroth, E.: Resource-efficient federated learning with non-IID data: an auction theoretic approach. IEEE Internet Things J. 9(24), 25506–25524 (2022)

22. Zhang, M., Sapra, K., Fidler, S., Yeung, S., Alvarez, J.M.: Personalized federated learning with first order model optimization. In: International Conference on Learning Representations (2021)

23. Zhu, J., Ma, X., Blaschko, M.B.: Confidence-aware personalized federated learning via variational expectation maximization. In: IEEE/CVF Conference on Computer Vision and Pattern Recognition (CVPR), pp. 24542–24551 (2023)

24. Luo, J., Wu, S.: Adapt to adaptation: learning personalization for cross-silo federated learning. In: International Joint Conference on Artificial Intelligence (IJCAI), pp. 2166–2173 (2022)

25. Yu, S., Nguyen, P., Anwar, A., Jannesari, A.: Heterogeneous federated learning using dynamic model pruning and adaptive gradient. In: IEEE/ACM International Symposium on Cluster, Cloud and Internet Computing (CCGrid), pp. 322–330 (2023)

26. Jiang, X., Borcea, C.: Complement sparsification: low-overhead model pruning for federated learning. In: AAAI Conference on Artificial Intelligence, vol. 37, pp. 8087–8095 (2023)

27. Jiang, Y., et al.: Model pruning enables efficient federated learning on edge devices. IEEE Trans. Neural Netw. Learn. Syst., pp. 1–13 (2022)

28. Wu, T., Song, C., Zeng, P.: Efficient federated learning on resource-constrained edge devices based on model pruning. Complex Intell. Syst., 1–15 (2023)

# IT-HMDM: Invertible Transformer for Human Motion Diffusion Model

Jiashuang Zhou and Xiaoqin Du[✉]

School of Computer Science and Artificial Intelligence, Wuhan Textile University, Wuhan, China
2115363027@mail.wtu.edu.cn, xiaoqindu@wtu.edu.cn

**Abstract.** Generating realistic and natural human motions has been a challenging task. Despite decades of research on modeling human motions, synthesizing realistic and natural sequences remains extremely challenging. In this paper, we propose an invertible Transformer for human motions with diffusion model (IT-HMDM). The model takes into account the input text lexicality and uses lexical encoding to enhance the feature capturing in hidden space. It also uses bijective affine transformation and logarithmic determinant regular terms to reduce information loss during the encoding process. We also use an improved grouping attention mechanism for semantic injection in order to reduce computation complexity and provide better model performance. The experimental results prove the validation of our model. When tested on the HumanML3D datasets, our model improves over MDM in R Precision (top 3), FID, and Multimodal Dist by 5%, 27.6%, and 6%, respectively.

**Keywords:** Invertible Transformer · Diffusion model · Motion Synthesis

## 1 Introduction

Realistic and natural human motion generation is the main aim in various industries such as gaming and movies. In recent years, more and more researchers are investing in the field of text-driven motion generation [1–5]. Text-driven motion generation allows for the creation of semantically informed human motion from the input text, resulting in cost savings and a wide range of possible potential applications.

There are some motion generation methods such as VAE-based [2, 3], GAN-based [4], Normalizing Flows Model based [5], Diffusion Model based [6], and hybrid models based [7] methods. The expressive power of those model is more and more powerful. The motion generation methods can be categorized into those based on joint embedding and those based on conditional generation. For the joint embedding encoding [7, 8], it is important to align the text feature space and motion feature space, and the decoder's input can be one of the two features in general. For the conditional generation [2, 3, 6], the text features need to be fused with the motion features, and the decoder's input can be a combination of features. In this paper, we focus on a condition-based diffusion model with Transformer.

© The Author(s), under exclusive license to Springer Nature Singapore Pte Ltd. 2025
N. Magnenat Thalmann et al. (Eds.): CASA 2024, CCIS 2374, pp. 105–117, 2025.
https://doi.org/10.1007/978-981-96-2681-6_8

JL2P [8] is a method that uses joint embedding to ensure consistency between text and motion feature spaces. The two-stream encoder-decoder model ACTOR developed by Ghosh et al. [7] jointly encodes text and motion feature spaces. However, the two methods have difficulty in training the joint embedding space when insufficient text-motion semantic information in train datasets. MotionCLIP [9] was the first to apply CLIP [10] to text-driven motion generation, injecting the semantics of the big model directly into the text space through conditional generation, enabling the model to have zero-shot generation ability. Since then, based on the CLIP [10] model, AvatarCLIP [11] and other models [12] have been developed. Although a large language model is of better text encoding ability, verbs and adverbs which are often related to motions and trajectories are not used effectively in those methods. In this paper, we mix lexical encoding in the text feature vector to make it more powerful.

The normalizing flows model [13] has inspired a mapping technique that can transform simple probability distributions into arbitrary distributions through a series of invertible transformations. MoGlow [5] is the first to utilize flow modeling in motion synthesis. By combining the Glow [14] with LSTM, the model can capture the dependencies between long sequences of frames and thus generate high-quality motions that get close to the ground truth. In normalizing flows model, lossless coding is a result of the logarithmic determinant term in the Change of Variables Theorem [15], which makes the generative method stronger. In this paper, we also aim to apply the logarithmic determinant term to Transformer for improving the quality of motion generation.

Stable Diffusion [16] shows remarkable performance in image generation, which has resulted in a surge of interest from researchers in diffusion model field. MDM (Motion Diffusion Model) [6] utilizes diffusion models to directly predict the input motion itself, instead of progressively denoising [17]. Moreover, MDM [6] takes physical losses into account to effectively reduce motion artifacts and achieves state-of-the-art (SOTA) performance on text-to-motion tasks. Leveraging the expressive ability of the diffusion model, our study is also conducted under this framework. The proposed invertible Transformer uses lexical coding, a grouping attention mechanism, and log-decimal regular terms to enhance signal prediction ability.

In this paper, we introduce the invertible Transformer model for human motion diffusion. We address the issue of different lexical properties affecting the generated motion in the input text by employing lexical positional coding to extract key features of the text. To further improve accuracy and tackle the problem of large information loss in the encoding process, we use invertible linear encoding and logarithmic determinant regular terms. However, the logarithmic determinant regular terms require a large amount of computation, hence we propose an improved grouping attention mechanism that reduces computation without dropping down the model's performance through semantic injection. Our experiments demonstrate that our proposed method is effective and reliable, and outperforms the SOTA in most of the metrics. The motion visualizations are also shown.

## 2  Methods

### 2.1  Invertible Transformer

Our invertible Transformer uses the bijective affine transformation as a key module and uses the logarithmic determinant as a regular term for reducing information loss during the encoding process and producing better-generated motions. The structure of the invertible Transformer is shown in Fig. 1. Compared with the standard Transformer [18], the invertible Transformer takes into account the influence of different lexical properties on the input text and combines lexical encoding with positional encoding for better model performance. However, there are a larger amount of computation due to the use of the logarithmic determinant regular term. In order to alleviate this problem, we use the improved group attention mechanism, which reduces the amount of computation and also effectively suppresses the phenomenon of overfitting.

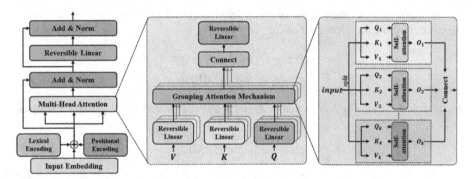

**Fig. 1.** The invertible Transformer

### 2.1.1  Lexical Embedding

In the input text example "Take four steps forward", the "Take" word means human action, the words "four steps" and "forward" depicts the trajectory. It shows that, in text-controlled human motion generation tasks, lexicality plays a crucial role in the encoding process, and different lexical properties have important effects on the generation process. To take the rich lexical and semantic information in input text, lexical embedding module is considered to be introduced. In this paper, our model uses lexical embedding as a supplement to general word embedding (such as BERT [19], CLIP [10], etc.). They both use the same CLIP [10]. This structure has two advantages: (1) both lexical embedding and word embedding share the same vector representation, and can sufficiently utilize the semantic information depicted by the lexicality in a word; (2) the use of CLIP [10] can effectively avoid the problem of insufficient semantic information by training datasets, and the large language model can be effectively applied to the embedding vectors.

## 2.1.2 Logarithmic Determinant Regular Terms

Let us first recall the Change of Variables Theorem. Let $u$ is a $D$-dimensional vector of real numbers that can be transformed by a transformation function $T$ (e.g., a neural network) to obtain a new variable $x$. Define the joint probability distribution of $x = \{x^i\}_{i=1}^N$ to be $p_x(x)$ and the joint probability distribution of $u = \{u^i\}_{i=1}^N$ to be $p_u(u)$, and the transformation process can be expressed as follows:

$$x = T(u) \tag{1}$$

In addition, the transformation function must meet three conditions:

1. The transformation function $T$ must be invertible;
2. The transformation function $T$ and the invertible transformation function $T^{-1}$ must be differentiable;
3. Both $u$ and $x$ must have the same dimension.

By applying the Change of Variables Theorem [15] under the given conditions above, we can determine the probability of $x$:

$$\begin{aligned} p_x(x) &= p_u(u)|\det(J_T(u))|^{-1} \\ &= p_u(u)|\det(J_{T^{-1}}(u))| \end{aligned} \tag{2}$$

where $u = T^{-1}(x)$. The Jacobi matrix $J_T(u)$ is a $D \times D$ matrix of all partial derivatives of $T$:

$$J_T(u) = \begin{bmatrix} \frac{\partial T_1}{\partial u_1} & \cdots & \frac{\partial T_1}{\partial u_D} \\ \vdots & \ddots & \vdots \\ \frac{\partial T_D}{\partial u_1} & \cdots & \frac{\partial T_D}{\partial u_D} \end{bmatrix} \tag{3}$$

From an information theory perspective, the amount of information in two variables satisfies the following relationship before and after transformation:

$$H(x) = H(u) + E\big(\log \det(J_{T^{-1}}(u))\big) \tag{4}$$

The invertible transformation reduces the volume of information of the two variables between $x$ and $u$ by $E\big(\log \det(J_{T^{-1}}(u))\big)$.

The invertibility of the affine layer is achieved through the constraint of the same dimension for input and output. This means that the dimensionality of the text embedding vector, the multi-headed self-attention embedding vector, and the final output feature vector are set to the same value. The invertible affine layer is used to replace the original affine layer from the standard Transform [18].

When dealing with invertible transformations, the amount of information lost during encoding can be measured and expressed as a logarithmic determinant value. Therefore, to prevent excessive loss of information in the variables before and after encoding by the Transformer, we add an information loss term as a regular term expressed by the logarithmic determinant directly into the loss function.

1. **For the invertible linear layer**: let the weight of the invertible linear layer $W$, the bias $b$, the input $x$, and the output $y$. The forward computation process is $y = W^T x + b$, and the information loss of the current layer is $\log detJ_{T^{-1}}(x) = log|det(W)|$.
2. **For the residual module**: suppose the input is $x$, the computation process is denoted as $T$, the final output is $x + T(x)$, and the information loss is $log|detJ_{T^{-1}}(x) + I|$. And the constant term has no effect on the optimization objective function, so it can be ignored.
3. **For the multi-head self-attention mechanisms**: There are no additional parameters introduced, one input corresponds to a unique output, and there is no information loss between the two variables before and after.

For a complete invertible Transformer Encoder with three invertible linear layers, two residual modules and one multi-head self-attention module in Fig. 1, it may be useful to set the whole neural network to have $K$ invertible Transformer Encoders, and then the logarithmic determinant regular term is computed as:

$$\mathcal{L}_{ld} = \sum_{i=1}^{K} \sum_{j=1}^{3} \log|det(W_{ij}) + \mathcal{E}| \tag{5}$$

In this context, $W_{ij}$ represents the weight of the $i$ invertible Transformer Encoder and the $j$ invertible linear layer. The $\mathcal{E}$ is a small constant used to prevent computational errors arising from the calculation of $det(W_{ij}) = 0$. By minimizing the logarithmic determinant regular term, the determinant of the model parameters can be limited to a small range. This helps to reduce the model complexity, suppress the overfit, and improve the model stability.

### 2.1.3 The Grouping Attention Mechanism

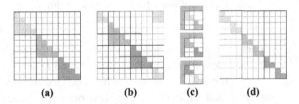

(a)          (b)          (c)          (d)

**Fig. 2.** The grouping attention mechanism

The logarithmic determinant regular term can be computationally expensive when the dimension of the input hidden variable is big. Meanwhile, using too small a hidden variable can result in significant information loss during the coding and decoding process. To ensure that the generated motions are realistic and reliable, we use a hidden variable length of 512 and introduce the grouping attention mechanism. This module splits the complete feature into different attention heads in different groups, thereby reducing both computational costs and memory overheads.

As shown in Fig. 2, the grouping attention mechanism in the Transformer can handle long sequences more efficiently. However, it should be noted that this mechanism introduces certain information loss because the positions between different groups cannot directly pay attention to each other. To address this issue, we take inspiration from Swin-Transformer [20] and use the shifted window operation to enhance the flow of information between different groups. Additionally, we add conditional encoding before each group to enhance feature fusion.

The paper outlines the process of the grouping attention mechanism in four steps, as shown in Fig. 2(a)–(d). Figure 2 (a) shows the result after taking the lower triangular matrix and after grouping. This leads to the resulting Fig. 2(b) after a shifted window operation. In Fig. 2(c), conditional encoding is added for each grouping before computing the attention matrix. Here, the conditional encoding refers to text encoding. The computed results from Fig. 2(c) are then spliced to obtain the final self-attention matrix, shown in Fig. 2(d) after a reverse-shifted window operation.

## 2.2 Invertible Transformer for Human Motion Diffusion Model

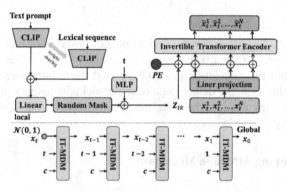

**Fig. 3.** The invertible Transformer for human motion diffusion model

Our goal is to generate human motions $x^1, x^2, \ldots, x^N$ of length $N$ given a text prompt, where $x^i \in \mathcal{R}^{J \times D}$, $J$ denotes the number of joints and $D$ denotes the representation of each node. Locally, the lexical sequence is first encoded using CLIP and linear layer encoding and then is added with the encoded Text prompt. The result obtained is mapped linearly to get the initial condition encoding. The initial conditional encoding after random masking is added to the output by the MLP inputted by the time step $t$, and finally together with the encoded motion sequences to the invertible Transformer Encoder as input to complete the one-shot prediction. The whole framework is called IT-HMDM. Globally, IT-HMDM progressively predicted the human motion $x^1, x^2, \ldots, x^N$ under the control of the conditional encoding as the time step increases, and ultimately generates the human motions $\hat{x}^1, \hat{x}^2, \ldots, \hat{x}^N$. The overall data flow diagram is shown in Fig. 3, with the top figure showing the local data flow and the bottom figure showing the global data flow.

## 2.3 Loss Function

### 2.3.1 Sampling Loss Function

The diffusion process is to continuously add Gaussian noise to the original signal so that the final signal also exhibits the characteristics of Gaussian distribution. And the denoising process is the process of continuously removing the noise from the random Gaussian noise so that it can be restored to get the original signal. Both the noising process and the denoising process are Markov stochastic processes, and the signal of the two consecutive stages satisfy the following law:

$$q(x_t|x_{t-1}) = N\left(\sqrt{\alpha_t}x_{t-1}, (1 - \alpha_t)I\right) \tag{6}$$

where $x_t = \{x_t^i\}_{i=1}^N$, $\mathcal{N}(\mu, \Sigma)$ denotes a Gaussian distribution with mean $\mu$ and covariance $\Sigma$, $I$ denotes the unit matrix, $\alpha_t$ is a hyperparameter, and $\alpha_t \in (0, 1)$. The sampling process is denoted as $\hat{x}_0 = G(x_t, t, c)$, indicating that IT-HMDM sampling is inputted with the motion $x_t$, the conditional encoding $c$, and the timestep $t$. To generate a human motion as close as the ground truth, the sampling loss is denoted as in Ho et al.:

$$\mathcal{L}_s = E_{x_0 \sim q(x_0|t,c)}\left[\|x_0 - G(x_t, t, c)\|_2^2\right] \tag{7}$$

### 2.3.2 Physical Loss

To prevent artifacts, it is desired that the model generate natural and coherent motion. We force physical losses [21] in the loss function, including motion loss, foot loss [22], and velocity loss [21].

**Motion Loss:** In our experiments, we predict the rotation angle of each joint point, and $FK(*)$ can convert the rotation matrix to the corresponding joint point positions (coordinates). The motion loss minimizes the coordinate difference of each joint point between the generated motion and the real motion, thus forcing the two motions to be similar.

$$\mathcal{L}_m = \frac{1}{N} \sum_{i=1}^N \left\| FK\left(x_0^i\right) - FK\left(\hat{x}_0^i\right) \right\|_2^2 \tag{8}$$

**Foot Loss:** $f_i \in \{0, 1\}^J$ indicates whether the foot touches the ground in each frame. The foot loss is essentially a reconstruction loss for the foot, by which motion artifacts can be effectively reduced.

$$\mathcal{L}_f = \frac{1}{N} \sum_{i=1}^{N-1} \left\| FK\left(\hat{x}_0^{i+1}\right) - FK\left(\hat{x}_0^i\right) * f_i \right\|_2^2 \tag{9}$$

**Angular Velocity Loss:** The angular velocity loss is essentially the reconstruction loss of the motion on the temporal dimension. The amount of change in the angle of the same node in two consecutive frames can be expressed as the angular velocity. The

a man dances by himself using both arms and legs.

a person uses the left arm to demonstrate throwing an object in front of them

**Fig. 4.** Motion visualization results

angular velocity loss expressed by the mean square error forces the generated motion as close as the ground truth, indirectly improving the generated motion's realisticity.

$$\mathcal{L}_a = \frac{1}{N-1} \sum_{i=1}^{N-1} \|a_i - \hat{a}_i\|_2^2 \tag{10}$$

where $a_i = x_0^{i+1} - x_0^i$ represents the angular velocity at moment $i$.

### 2.3.3  Total Loss

The final loss consists of the sampling loss, the physical loss, and the logarithmic determinant regular term. It is denoted as:

$$L = \lambda_s \mathcal{L}_s + \lambda_m \mathcal{L}_m + \lambda_f \mathcal{L}_f + \lambda_a \mathcal{L}_a + \lambda_{ld} \mathcal{L}_{ld} \tag{11}$$

In our experiment, $\lambda_{ld} = 0.001$. The other hyperparameters are the same as MDM's experimentation.

## 3  Experiments

### 3.1  Quantitative Experimental Results

The KIT dataset was introduced by Plappert et al. [24] and contains 3911 data samples along with 6353 text annotations. On the other hand, HumanML3D is a newer dataset that has been reorganized and text annotated by Guo et al. [25], containing 14616 motions with 44970 text descriptions.

To evaluate our model, we compare it with JL2P [8], Text2Gesture [23], and MDM [6], and use the metrics suggested by Tevet et al. Our proposed model outperforms the SOTA techniques, with significant improvements in R Precision (top 3) and FID metrics, as shown in Tables 1 and 2.

When tested on the HumanML3D dataset, although it does not completely outperform the existing models, our model improves over MDM in R-accuracy (top 3), FID, and multimodal distribution by 5%, 27.6%, and 6%, respectively. On the KIT dataset, our model is optimal on all metrics.

## 3.2 Generated Motion Visualizations

The results of visualizing the generated motions are presented in Fig. 4. The figure shows the outcome obtained by inputting the text "a man dances by himself using both arms and legs." The man in the figure follows the semantic information of selecting, waving, and jumping with semantic information consistent in the input text. Moreover, Fig. 4 illustrates the motions generated by the text "a person uses the left arm to demonstrate throwing an object in front of them." In this case, the person completes the motion from lifting the right arm to the left arm to throw quickly. The generated motion is realistic, and natural, and obeys the law of human motion. Overall, the visualized motion results are consistent with the semantic information in the input text and are of good quality.

**Table 1.** Quantitative results on the HumanML3D test set.

| Method | R Precision (top 3) | FID | Multimodal Dist | Diversity |
|---|---|---|---|---|
| Real† | $0.779^{\pm0.002}$ | $0.002^{\pm0.000}$ | $2.974^{\pm0.012}$ | $9.503^{\pm0.065}$ |
| Real* | $0.778^{\pm0.004}$ | $0.002^{\pm0.000}$ | $2.961^{\pm0.017}$ | $9.401^{\pm0.931}$ |
| JL2P | $0.486^{\pm0.002}$ | $11.02^{\pm0.046}$ | $5.296^{\pm0.030}$ | $7.760^{\pm0.058}$ |
| Text2Gesture | $0.345^{\pm0.002}$ | $1.067^{\pm0.002}$ | $6.030^{\pm0.030}$ | $6.409^{\pm0.071}$ |
| MDM | $0.645^{\pm0.005}$ | $0.544^{\pm0.051}$ | $5.566^{\pm0.020}$ | $9.559^{\pm0.072}$ |
| ours | $0.682^{\pm0.002}$ | $0.393^{\pm0.035}$ | $5.151^{\pm0.010}$ | $9.686^{\pm0.089}$ |

The metrics tested from the test set are denoted by both † and *. However, † is consistent with the results of the MDM experiments, while * denotes the results of the experiments tested on our machine. The meaning of the latter is the same as the former.

## 3.3 Ablation Experiment

### 3.3.1 Different Numbers of Groups

Different numbers of groups can have varying effects on the results of the grouping attention mechanism. In this experiment, we used 2 groups (att_2), 3 groups (att_3), and 4 groups (att_4) respectively on the HumanML3D dataset. We set the multi-head attention mechanism of the Transformer to 8 and find that the best performance was

**Table 2.** Quantitative results on the KIT test set.

| Method | R Precision (top 3) | FID | Multimodal Dist | Diversity |
|---|---|---|---|---|
| Real† | $0.797^{\pm0.006}$ | $0.002^{\pm0.004}$ | $2.788^{\pm0.012}$ | $11.08^{\pm0.097}$ |
| Real* | $0.778^{\pm0.004}$ | $0.031^{\pm0.002}$ | $2.763^{\pm0.017}$ | $11.057^{\pm0.931}$ |
| JL2P | $0.483^{\pm0.005}$ | $6.545^{\pm0.072}$ | $5.147^{\pm0.030}$ | $9.073^{\pm.0100}$ |
| Text2Gesture | $0.338^{\pm0.005}$ | $12.12^{\pm0.185}$ | $6.964^{\pm0.030}$ | $9.334^{\pm0.079}$ |
| MDM | $0.396^{\pm0.004}$ | $0.497^{\pm0.109}$ | $9.191^{\pm0.020}$ | $10.847^{\pm0.109}$ |
| ours | $0.412^{\pm0.004}$ | $0.467^{\pm0.030}$ | $9.767^{\pm0.010}$ | $11.014^{\pm0.067}$ |

achieved with 4 groups. Grouping the hidden features make it dependent only on the previous frames and reduce the impact of subsequent frames. However, too few groupings ($n = 2$) can lead to the overfit of the model on the training data, also resulting in poor performance on the test set.

### 3.3.2 Lexical Encoding and Positional Encoding

In our experiment, we compared three different configurations of the HumanML3D dataset, to analyze the effectiveness of positional encoding and lexical encoding. We examine the only use of positional encoding (without lexical encoding, w/o LE), only lexical encoding (without positional encoding, w/o LP), and both. Our results suggest that the both use leads to the best performance, indicating that the lexical properties have positive effects on the generated motions. Additionally, our results show that the model hardly works without positional encoding. This is obvious that the lexical features with different positions have different impacts on generated motion.

### 3.3.3 Modular Ablation

To verify whether the proposed modules in our model works, the grouping attention mechanism (GA), conditional coding (CC), and logarithmic determinant regular term (LogDet) are progressively added. The experimental results obtained for the three different settings of the model on the HumanML3D dataset are presented in the table below. The experiments demonstrate that all three contributions all have a positive impact on the model. Among them, the logarithmic determinant regular term has the most significant improvement in all four metrics, indicating that the logarithmic determinant regular term plays the most important role (Tables 3, 4 and 5).

## 4   Discussion

In our paper, we have developed a diffusion model for generating human motions based on text input. We have used an invertible Transformer on the denoising procession. First, we extract keywords based on different properties of the text using lexical coding, which has positive impacts when combined with positional embedding on the generated

**Table 3.** Ablation experiment result about different numbers of groups on the HumanML3D test set.

| Method | R Precision (top 3) | FID | Multimodal Dist | Diversity |
|---|---|---|---|---|
| Real* | $0.778^{\pm0.004}$ | $0.002^{\pm0.000}$ | $2.961^{\pm0.017}$ | $9.401^{\pm0.931}$ |
| att_2 | $0.655^{\pm0.006}$ | $0.448^{\pm0.072}$ | $5.452^{\pm0.028}$ | $9.641^{\pm0.093}$ |
| att_3 | $0.663^{\pm0.005}$ | $0.435^{\pm0.185}$ | $5.215^{\pm0.026}$ | $9.744^{\pm0.081}$ |
| att_4 | $0.682^{\pm0.002}$ | $0.393^{\pm0.035}$ | $5.151^{\pm0.010}$ | $9.686^{\pm0.089}$ |

**Table 4.** Ablation experiment result about lexical encoding and positional encoding on the HumanML3D test set.

| Method | R Precision (top 3) | FID | Multimodal Dist | Diversity |
|---|---|---|---|---|
| Real* | $0.778^{\pm0.004}$ | $0.002^{\pm0.000}$ | $2.961^{\pm0.017}$ | $9.401^{\pm0.931}$ |
| att_4 | $0.682^{\pm0.002}$ | $0.393^{\pm0.035}$ | $5.151^{\pm0.010}$ | $9.686^{\pm0.089}$ |
| att_4 w/o PE | $0.142^{\pm0.004}$ | $51.69^{\pm0.010}$ | $9.860^{\pm0.046}$ | $2.641^{\pm0.039}$ |
| att_4 w/o LE | $0.658^{\pm0.002}$ | $0.425^{\pm0.041}$ | $5.265^{\pm0.032}$ | $9.614^{\pm0.068}$ |

**Table 5.** Ablation experiment result about different modular on the HumanML3D test set.

| Method | | | R Precision (top 3) | FID | Multimodal Dist | Diversity |
|---|---|---|---|---|---|---|
| Real* | | | $0.778^{\pm0.004}$ | $0.002^{\pm0.000}$ | $2.961^{\pm0.006}$ | $9.401^{\pm0.931}$ |
| GA | CC | LogDet | – | – | – | – |
| × | × | × | $0.638^{\pm0.005}$ | $0.488^{\pm0.039}$ | $5.452^{\pm0.028}$ | $9.767^{\pm0.089}$ |
| √ | × | × | $0.666^{\pm0.004}$ | $0.487^{\pm0.037}$ | $5.263^{\pm0.027}$ | $9.642^{\pm0.093}$ |
| √ | √ | × | $0.670^{\pm0.005}$ | $0.452^{\pm0.035}$ | $5.219^{\pm0.026}$ | $9.730^{\pm0.080}$ |
| √ | √ | √ | $0.6826^{\pm0.002}$ | $0.393^{\pm0.035}$ | $5.151^{\pm0.026}$ | $9.685^{\pm0.089}$ |

motions. We then use the Change of Variables Theorem to minimize the information loss during the denoising process by utilizing invertible affine transformations and logarithmic determinant regular terms. To reduce the computational burden of computing the logarithmic determinant regular term, we incorporate a grouping attention mechanism to enable information exchange between different groups. Additionally, we use the shifted window operation and conditional coding to facilitate this operation.

In our experiments, the model proposed in this paper outperforms over the baseline. In ablation experiments, we conclude the positive effects of our proposed modules. The experimental results demonstrate that our model can synthesize realistic and natural human motions.

# References

1. Zhang, M., et al.: MotionDiffuse: text-driven human motion generation with diffusion model. arXiv preprint arXiv:2208.15001 (2022)
2. Petrovich, M., Black, M.J., Varol, G.: TEMOS: generating diverse human motions from textual descriptions. In: European Conference on Computer Vision, pp. 480–497. Springer, Cham (2022)
3. Athanasiou, N., Petrovich, M., Black, M.J., Varol, G.: Teach: temporal action composition for 3D humans. In: 2022 International Conference on 3D Vision (3DV), pp. 414–423. IEEE (2022)
4. Xu, L., et al.: ActFormer: a GAN-based transformer towards general action-conditioned 3D human motion generation. In: Proceedings of the IEEE/CVF International Conference on Computer Vision, pp. 2228–2238 (2023)
5. Henter, G.E., Alexanderson, S., Beskow, J.: MoGlow: probabilistic and controllable motion synthesis using normalising flows. ACM Trans. Graph. (TOG) **39**(6), 1–14 (2020)
6. Tevet, G., Raab, S., Gordon, B., Shafir, Y., Cohen-or, D., Bermano, A.H.: Human motion diffusion model. In: The Eleventh International Conference on Learning Representations (2023)
7. Ghosh, A., Cheema, N., Oguz, C., Theobalt, C., Slusallek, P.: Synthesis of compositional animations from textual descriptions. In: Proceedings of the IEEE/CVF International Conference on Computer Vision, pp. 1396–1406 (2021)
8. Ahuja, C., Morency, L.-P.: Language2Pose: natural language grounded pose forecasting. In: 2019 International Conference on 3D Vision (3DV), pp. 719–728. IEEE (2019)
9. Tevet, G., Gordon, B., Hertz, A., Bermano, A.H., CohenOr, D.: MotionClip: exposing human motion generation to clip space. In: European Conference on Computer Vision, pp. 358–374. Springer, Cham (2022)
10. Radford, A., et al.: Learning transferable visual models from natural language supervision. In: International Conference on Machine Learning, pp. 8748–8763. PMLR (2021)
11. Hong, F., Zhang, M., Pan, L., Cai, Z., Yang, L., Liu, Z: AvatarClip: zeroshot text-driven generation and animation of 3D avatars. arXiv preprint arXiv:2205.08535 (2022)
12. Youwang, K., Ji-Yeon, K., Oh, T.: Clip-actor: text-driven recommendation and stylization for animating human meshes. In: European Conference on Computer Vision, pp. 173–191. Springer, Cham (2022)
13. Papamakarios, G., Nalisnick, E., Rezende, D.J., Mohamed, S., Lakshminarayanan, B.: Normalizing flows for probabilistic modeling and inference. J. Mach. Learn. Res. **22**(1), 2617–2680 (2021)
14. Kingma, D.P., Dhariwal, P.: Glow: generative flow with invertible $1 \times 1$ convolutions. In: Advances in Neural Information Processing Systems, vol. 31 (2018)
15. Shapiro, V.L.: Book review: Walter Rudin, real and complex analysis (1968)
16. Rombach, R., Blattmann, A., Lorenz, D., Esser, P., Ommer, B.: High-resolution image synthesis with latent diffusion models. In: Proceedings of the IEEE/CVF Conference on Computer Vision and Pattern Recognition, pp. 10684–10695 (2022)
17. Ho, J., Jain, A., Abbeel, P.: Denoising diffusion probabilistic models. Adv. Neural. Inf. Process. Syst. **33**, 6840–6851 (2020)
18. Vaswani, A., et al.: Attention is all you need. In: Advances in Neural Information Processing Systems, vol. 30 (2017)
19. Devlin, J., Chang, M.-W., Lee, K., Toutanova, K.: BERT: pre-training of deep bidirectional transformers for language understanding. arXiv preprint arXiv:1810.04805 (2018)
20. Liu, Z., et al.: Swin transformer: hierarchical vision transformer using shifted windows. In: Proceedings of the IEEE/CVF International Conference on Computer Vision, pp. 10012–10022 (2021)

21. Petrovich, M., Black, M.J., Varol, G.: Action-conditioned 3D human motion synthesis with transformer VAE. In: Proceedings of the IEEE/CVF International Conference on Computer Vision, pp. 10985–10995 (2021)

22. Shi, M., et al.: MotioNet: 3D human motion reconstruction from monocular video with skeleton consistency. ACM Trans. Graph. (TOG) **40**(1), 1–15 (2020)

23. Bhattacharya, U., Rewkowski, N., Banerjee, A., Guhan, P., Bera, A., Manocha, D.: Text2Gestures: a transformer-based network for generating emotive body gestures for virtual agents. In: 2021 IEEE Virtual Reality and 3D User Interfaces (VR), pp. 1–10. IEEE (2021)

24. Plappert, M., Mandery, C., Asfour, T.: The kit motion language dataset. Big Data **4**(4), 236–252 (2016)

25. Guo, C., et al.: Generating diverse and natural 3D human motions from text. In: Proceedings of the IEEE/CVF Conference on Computer Vision and Pattern Recognition, pp. 5152–5161 (2022)

# Fashion Image Retrieval Based on Multimodal Features Enhancement and Fusion

Yingjin Li[1,2], Shufan He[1,2], Zhaojing Wang[1,2(✉)], Jin Huang[1,2(✉)], Xinrong Hu[1,2], and Li Li[1,2]

[1] School of Computer Science and Artificial Intelligence, Wuhan Textile University, Wuhan, China
{zjwang,hxr,li}@wtu.edu.cn, derick0320@foxmail.com
[2] Engineering Research Center of Hubei Province for Clothing Information, Wuhan, China

**Abstract.** Fashion image retrieval (FIR) is of great interest due to its potential to enhance the convenience of online shopping. The exponential increase in online clothing image data has led to a corresponding rise in similar style data, challenging the accuracy of traditional FIR methods. To address this, we present a novel FIR framework leveraging the multimodal features enhancement and fusion model with SE-ConvNeXt-Text. In our approach, the feature extraction part of the ConvNeXt network serves as the image feature extraction module, with the addition of the Squeeze-and-Excitation (SE) attention mechanism to address insufficient feature extraction for similar styles. The text feature processing module is constructed to supplement image features by extracting text information on the image. Our method effectively fuses multimodal information from images and texts through a designed contrastive learning module, ensuring the accuracy of FIR. To validate the efficacy of our approach, we conducted experiments on two sub-tasks (In-Shop and Extended In-Shop dataset). The results demonstrate an average improvement of 3.76% and 3.51% in accuracy and precision compared to the state-of-art methods.

**Keywords:** image retrieval · fashion image · attention model · multimodal features

## 1 Introduction

In the modern era of e-commerce, clothing shopping has become a crucial component of the consumer shopping experience. However, faced with a diverse array of styles that often bear minimal differences, it's often challenging for consumers to find their ideal fit based solely on textual descriptions online [1]. In this case, consumers can more accurately find the style they want through clothing image search. Consequently, the image retrieval technology plays a pivotal role in the online clothing shopping process for consumers.

N. Magnenat Thalmann et al. (Eds.): CASA 2024, CCIS 2374, pp. 118–131, 2025.
https://doi.org/10.1007/978-981-96-2681-6_9

The development of FIR technology has undergone several pivotal stages. Initially, traditional image retrieval methods were employed, relying on traditional features such as color, texture, or shape [2]. However, these methods have certain limitations when deal with complex clothing images. With the rise of deep learning, models such as convolutional neural networks (CNN) were introduced [3], which enhanced the accuracy of identifying clothing images, excelling in retrieving clothing similar to provided images. However, the retrieval accuracy of similar style clothing with similar style and pattern is not satisfactory. Especially in the case of processing the text in the picture, the traditional FIR method recognizes the text in the picture as image features, rather than processing the semantic information of the text in the picture.

To address the issues, this study proposes an optimization scheme based on the ConvNeXt [4], named Multimodal Features Enhancement and Fusion Model with ConvNeXt (MFEFMC). The ConvNeXt model, rooted in the Transformer [5] philosophy, exhibits commendable recognition performance while preserving CNN characteristics. To this model, we integrate the SE attention mechanism [6] and text encoder. We extract image features from the ConvNeXt output and text features from the output of the text encoder [7]. These features are then subjected to a training process utilizing contrastive learning [8].

The following points summarize the key contributions of our work:

- Multimodal features enhancement and fusion model that aligns text with images is developed to enhance the recognition efficacy for images accompanied by text.
- The contrastive learning method is designed for training, enabling the model to better understand the relationship between image features and text features.
- The proposed method has higher image retrieval accuracy than the state-of-the-art methods in fashion image retrieval, particularly in the processing of the images accompanied by text.

The structure of this article is as follows: Sect. 2 provides a review of the related work. Our proposed method is detailed in Sect. 3. Section 4 outlines the implementation specifics of our experiments. Finally, in Sect. 5, we present our conclusions drawn from the results of our study.

## 2  Related Work

With the advancement of image processing technology and the continuous expansion of image datasets, extensive research has been conducted on image retrieval networks [9–12]. Numerous FIR methods have been proposed to address the evolving challenges in this domain [13–16]. Typically, image retrieval models are constructed by removing the last fully connected layer of a pre-trained classification model. Retrieval is then accomplished through vector similarity assessment, involving the extraction of feature vectors from the penultimate layer of the network. The search for the most similar images is subsequently conducted based

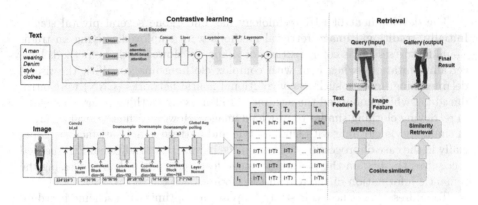

**Fig. 1.** The whole framework of the proposed method. On the left is the training part of MFEFMC. It is divided into two modules: Text feature processing module and Image feature processing module. Input pictures and corresponding text information, and then carry out contrastive learning training. On the right is the retrieval part. After extracting the feature vector from the query, the model retrieves the gallery by calculating the cosine similarity.

on these feature vectors, thereby facilitating the retrieval of visually analogous images [17].

On the model structure of the above retrieval, the model can be adjusted to achieve unexpected results in some fields. In the field of FIR, image retrieval models become more targeted. Here are three representative methods commonly employed in the field of fashion image retrieval:

The Dual Attention Composition Network [18] integrates spatial and channel attention to capture fine-grained image-text alignment, followed by corresponding affine transformations to satisfy multimodal combinations. This method is capable of learning more representative features, thereby enhancing the performance of attribute-manipulated FIR. However, it requires a significant amount of domain knowledge and the quality of the model largely depends on manually engineered features [19]. Furthermore, the model's recommendations are based solely on the user's existing interests, indicating a limited ability to expand upon these interests.

The Multi-Granular Alignment (MGA) method [20] leverages both global and fine-grained features. It designs a Fine-Granular Aggregator (FGA) to capture and aggregate detailed patterns and proposes an Attention-based Token Alignment (ATA) to align image features at the multi-granular level in a coarse-to-fine manner. This method can capture more detailed information, thereby improving the accuracy of FIR. However, despite the excellent performance achieved by multi-stream deep architectures, a key limitation of this method is that the feature extraction of different modalities is performed separately rather than leveraging the features of both modalities together.

The Multi-Turn FIR via Cascaded Memory [21] focuses on a real-world setting where users can iteratively provide information to refine retrieval results until they find an item that fits all their requirements. This method can better meet the personalized needs of users, thereby improving user experience. However, evaluation primarily relies on specific datasets such as Multi-turn FashionIQ which may limit its performance in other datasets or practical applications. Additionally, this method may require large computational resources and time to process and learn information from all past dialogue turns.

The domain of FIR has witnessed substantial progress with the advent of diverse innovative methodologies. Each approach, be it the Dual Attention Composition Network, the Multi-Granular Alignment method, or the Multi-Turn FIR via Cascaded Memory, offers unique advantages to tackle specific challenges inherent in the field. Nevertheless, these methods also present their own set of constraints, which necessitate further exploration and research.

## 3   Method

In the FIR field, existing methods, despite their success, struggle with precise feature extraction from images and often overlook textual information. This study addresses these limitations by integrating the SE attention mechanism and a text encoder into the ConvNeXt model. The resulting multimodal model, MFEFMC, excels in handling clothing images with text, leveraging the strengths of both Transformer concepts and CNN models.

In this section, we introduce the implementation method of the above model in detail. As shown in Fig. 1, the structure of the model consists of two main parts: image encoding and text encoding. In the implementation process, we first extract features from images and texts, and then train the model using contrastive learning to achieve a multimodal model that fuses text and images. This improvement not only improves the recognition performance of text-bearing images, but also provides strong support for practical applications in related fields.

### 3.1   Image Feature Processing Module

Given the significant characteristics of clothing image features, such as the similarity of clothing contours, we introduce the SE attention mechanism after each module of the ConvNeXt network to enhance the ability of ConvNeXt to capture key region information. The SE attention mechanism re-adjusts the weights between feature channels to better capture the global information of input data. The structural diagram of the SE attention mechanism is shown in Fig. 3 [6]. During the Squeeze, a global pooling operation is employed, transforming the feature map of size $H \times W \times C$ along the channel direction into a $1 \times 1 \times 1$ feature. This is akin to the process depicted in Fig. 3, where the $\mathbf{F}_{sq}$ process transforms each two-dimensional feature map into a real number $z_c$ with a comprehensive

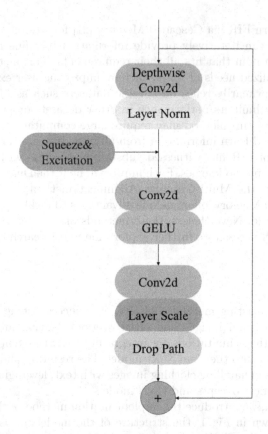

**Fig. 2.** ConvNeXt-Block structure with the integrated SE attention mechanism.

convolutional receptive field. The $z_c$ is calculated as follows:

$$z_c = \mathbf{F}_{sq}(\mathbf{u}_c) = \frac{1}{H \times W} \sum_{i=1}^{H} \sum_{j=1}^{W} u_c(i, j) \tag{1}$$

where $H$, $W$ are the height and width of the input characteristic graph, and $u_c(i, j)$ is the eigenvalue at $i, j$ position.

The operation $\mathbf{F}_{ex}(\mathbf{z}, \mathbf{W})$ of the Excitation process is to capture the internal dependence parameter of the channel through two full connection layers to obtain the clipping coefficient of the characteristic channel as follows:

$$\mathbf{s} = \mathbf{F}_{ex}(\mathbf{z}, \mathbf{W}) = \sigma(g(\mathbf{z}, \mathbf{W})) = \sigma(\mathbf{W}_2 \delta(\mathbf{W}_1 \mathbf{z})) \tag{2}$$

where $\mathbf{W}_1$ and $\mathbf{W}_2$ represent the learning parameters of two fully connected layers, $\delta$ represents the *Relu* function, $\sigma$ represents the *Sigmoid* function, and $\mathbf{z}$ is the $1 \times 1 \times C$ feature vector calculated in the previous step.

Finally, adjust the weight, regard s as the importance of each channel, and use $\mathbf{F}_{scale}(\mathbf{u}_c, s_c)$ to weight each channel onto the previous feature map to complete the calculation of attention mechanism in the channel dimension as follows:

$$\mathbf{F}_{scale}(\mathbf{u}_c, s_c) = s_c \cdot \mathbf{u}_c \tag{3}$$

where $s_c$ is the clipping coefficient of channel $C$ and $\mathbf{u}_c$ is the characteristic diagram of channel $C$.

This mechanism helps the network to more accurately identify complex clothing images, focusing its attention on areas that highlight key details of the clothing, thereby improving the efficiency of feature extraction and ultimately optimizing retrieval performance. Specifically, because each block of ConvNeXt [4] adopts an inverted bottleneck layer architecture with large middle and small ends, we add the channel attention mechanism after the deep separable convolutional layer. This location selection improves performance while increasing the amount of parameters by a small amount. The ConvNeXt-Block structure with SE attention mechanism is shown in Fig. 2.

### 3.2 Text Feature Processing Module

In order to improve the retrieval performance of networks when processing images containing text, extracting text features is particularly important. In this study, we designed a text feature extraction module that is parallel to the image feature processing module to jointly provide accurate feature representations for subsequent retrieval tasks.

The core of this module is a transformer-based text encoder. When receiving input text information, the encoder first processes the text and converts the original text sequence into a series of vector representations through its internal self-attention mechanism and position encoding. These vectors not only preserve the information of the original text, but also further capture the semantic information in the text by calculating the attention weights between each word and other words. Afterwards, these vectors are passed to a feedforward neural network sublayer. This sublayer performs nonlinear transformations on these vectors to further extract features from the text. The structure of the module is shown in Fig. 1.

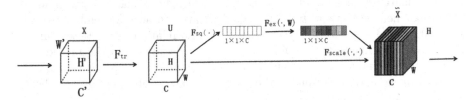

**Fig. 3.** Squeeze-and-Excitation Attention Mechanism (The figure is derived from the article titled "Squeeze-and-Excitation Networks") [6]

### 3.3   Contrastive Learning Module

ConvNeXt network is a native classification network. In order to extract image features so as to realize the comparative learning between image features and text features, we removed the last full connection layer of ConvNeXt, so that the input image features can be converted into the feature direction that can be used to calculate the comparison through ConvNeXt. At the same time, the transformer text encoder is used to output the corresponding text features.

For the features extracted from images and texts, we use a contrastive learning method for model training. As shown in Fig. 1, where $I_j$ represents the $j$th image feature extracted, $T_k$ represents the $k$th text feature extracted, and $N$ represents the total number of features. We define the image-text pairs on the diagonal of the feature matrix as positive samples, while the other pairs are negative samples. At the same time, we choose the cross-entropy loss function as the loss function for contrastive learning as following:

$$L_i = -\frac{1}{N} \sum_{i=1}^{N} \sum_{j=1}^{C} y_{m_{ij}} \log(p_{ij}) \tag{4}$$

where $y_{m_{ij}}$ represents whether the label in the image is correctly classified, and $p_{i,j}$ represents the cosine similarity between each image-text pair. Similarly, the loss calculation formula for text feature is:

$$L_t = -\frac{1}{N} \sum_{i=1}^{N} \sum_{j=1}^{C} y_{t_{ij}} \log(p_{ij}) \tag{5}$$

where $y_{t_{ij}}$ represents the label of whether the text is correctly classified. The final loss calculation formula for the text-image pair is:

$$L = \frac{L_i + L_t}{2} \tag{6}$$

### 3.4   Image Retrieval

First, image and text are mapped to the same representation space to achieve unified modeling. This ensures that similar images and texts have similar representations in the shared embedding space. By maximizing the similarity between correctly matched images and texts and minimizing the similarity between incorrectly matched images and texts, the model learns an accurate embedded representation and accurately captures the semantic relationship between images and texts. This makes the model more accurately understand the relationship between image and text, so as to improve the modeling ability of the relationship between image and text. Finally, the retrieval image is obtained by calculating the cosine similarity between images:

$$Similarity = \frac{\sum\limits_{i=1}^{n} (\mathbf{x}_i \times \mathbf{y}_i)}{\sqrt{\sum\limits_{i=1}^{n} (\mathbf{x}_i)^2} \times \sqrt{\sum\limits_{i=1}^{n} (\mathbf{y}_i)^2}} \tag{7}$$

where $\mathbf{x}$ represents the eigenvector of query, $\mathbf{y}$ represents the eigenvector of Gallery and $n$ represents $n$ dimensions of the eigenvector.

## 4 Experiments

### 4.1 Datasets

We trained the model on the In-Shop subset of the publicly available DeepFashion clothing image dataset (Dataset 1) [22]. The In-Shop subset is a collection of seller's show images, with multiple seller's show photos of each product from different angles. According to the clear definition of the dataset, we divided it into a training set, a query set, and an gallery set. There are 25,891 images for model training. The query set contains 14,213 query images, while the gallery set contains 12,608 images.

In order to verify the effectiveness of the method proposed in this paper in the case of images with text, we have generated a new dataset (Dataset 2) based on the In-Shop dataset. The specific generation process is to add the text of the overall style of clothing of each item category to the image of each item category. In view of the weak semantics of the picture labels attached to the dataset, we add matching text information to the model with text encoder according to the characteristics of each picture for training. For example, for Fig. 4, the text information we added is: "A man wears Shirts-Polo style clothes".

**Fig. 4.** A man wearing Shirts-Polos style clothes

### 4.2 Implementation Details

We use two A100-SXM4-80GB graphics cards for model training. Initially, we trained the original ConvNeXt on Dataset 1 using a batch size of 32 for 100 epochs. Subsequently, we trained models with and without the SE attention mechanism, as well as the proposed MFEMC, on the same dataset with the same training parameters. Other comparative models, including ResNet50 [23], SE-ResNet50 [6], ResNeXt [24], and Swin-Transformer [25], were also trained on this dataset.

For the model without adding a text encoder, we only use the Dataset 2 images for training. For the model with adding a text encoder, we add corresponding text information to each input image to achieve contrastive learning between image and text. Then we use the trained model to extract feature vectors from the query set images, and calculate the Euclidean distance between feature vectors to compare the similarity of different image features. Finally, we output the images in the queried image set in descending order of similarity.

### 4.3   Evaluation Criterion

To evaluate the retrieval performance, we compare the labels of the images to be retrieved with the labels of each image in the retrieval results. If the labels are consistent, we consider the image retrieval successful. Through the results of different models, we can calculate their precision and accuracy. By comparing the precision and accuracy, we can determine the effectiveness of different models. Take $T$ as the number of successful searches, $N$ as the total number of searches

**Table 1.** Accuracy of different models in Dataset 1 retrieval results

| Model | A@1 | A@2 | A@4 | A@8 |
|---|---|---|---|---|
| ResNet50 | 88.47% | 92.84% | 95.62% | 97.93% |
| SE-ResNet50 | 89.13% | 93.22% | 95.79% | 98.07% |
| ResNeXt | 88.74% | 93.15% | 96.42% | 97.02% |
| Swin-Transfomer | 91.96% | 94.39% | 96.92% | 98.11% |
| ConvNeXt | 92.62% | 96.54% | 98.33% | 99.21% |
| ConvNeXt-Text | 92.53% | 96.42% | 98.17% | 99.06% |
| SE-ConvNeXt | **93.82%** | **96.87%** | **98.52%** | 99.23% |
| SE-ConvNeXt-Text | 93.57% | 96.23% | 98.36% | **99.27%** |

**Table 2.** Precision of different models in Dataset 1 retrieval results

| Model | P@1 | P@2 | P@4 | P@8 |
|---|---|---|---|---|
| ResNet50 | 88.47% | 78.93% | 55.42% | 35.73% |
| SE-ResNet50 | 89.13% | 79.69% | 57.53% | 36.32% |
| ResNeXt | 88.74% | 79.49% | 56.13% | 37.12% |
| Swin-Transfomer | 91.96% | 81.74% | 58.26% | 38.09% |
| ConvNeXt | 92.62% | 81.55% | 58.83% | 38.12% |
| ConvNeXt-Text | 92.53% | 81.27% | 57.46% | 37.59% |
| SE-ConvNeXt | **93.82%** | **81.82%** | 58.59% | 37.47% |
| SE-ConvNeXt-Text | 93.57% | 81.79% | **58.66%** | **38.34%** |

in the experiment, and $P$ as the number of images with different items in the search results and the images to be retrieved. The accuracy rate is calculated as follows:

$$Accuracy = \frac{T}{N} \times 100\% \tag{8}$$

The precision rate is calculated as follows:

$$Precision = \frac{T}{P+T} \times 100\% \tag{9}$$

### 4.4    Experimental Results

#### 4.4.1    Original In-shop Dataset

Through the training of the models in Sect. 4.2, we obtained the accuracy of different models on the Dataset 1, as shown in Table 1, and the precision, as shown in Table 2, where @$k$ represents the first $k$ pictures, the best results are in bold.

By analyzing the data in Table 1 and Table 2, we find that ConvNeXt model is superior to other models in accuracy and precision, which are 1.53% and 1.49% higher on average. Furthermore, when SE attention mechanism was introduced into ConvNeXt model, the accuracy and precision were improved by 0.44% and 0.14%, respectively. Among them, when the K value is 1, the improvement effect is the most significant, reaching 1.2%. This shows that SE attention mechanism is helpful for ConvNeXt model to better learn and extract the clothing features in the image, so as to significantly improve the retrieval accuracy and precision.

Subsequently, we evaluated the effects of incorporating a text encoder into ConvNeXt. Results indicate that on the Dataset 1, the addition of a text encoder to ConvNeXt resulted in an impact of less than 0.3% on both the model's accuracy and precision. Given the variability in model outcomes, this impact is deemed negligible. This is primarily due to the absence of textual information within the Dataset 1, which impedes the extraction of semantic features, thereby limiting the enhancement potential of incorporating a text encoder into the model.

**Table 3.** Accuracy of different models in Dataset 2 retrieval results

| Model | A@1 | A@2 | A@4 | A@8 |
|---|---|---|---|---|
| ResNet50 | 83.29% | 88.57% | 91.03% | 94.28% |
| SE-ResNet50 | 83.95% | 89.17% | 91.67% | 94.55% |
| ResNeXt | 83.63% | 88.94% | 91.29% | 94.47% |
| Swin-Transfomer | 86.32% | 89.46% | 92.37% | 95.74% |
| ConvNeXt | 87.16% | 90.33% | 92.54% | 96.27% |
| ConvNeXt-Text | 89.66% | 92.53% | 95.83% | 97.54% |
| SE-ConvNeXt | 89.65% | 91.07% | 93.37% | 96.43% |
| SE-ConvNeXt-Text | **90.25%** | **93.14%** | **95.87%** | **98.45%** |

**Table 4.** Precision of different models in Dataset 2 retrieval results

| Model | P@1 | P@2 | P@4 | P@8 |
|---|---|---|---|---|
| ResNet50 | 83.29% | 75.94% | 52.26% | 31.47% |
| SE-ResNet50 | 83.95% | 76.44% | 53.07% | 32.16% |
| ResNeXt | 83.63% | 76.42% | 52.16% | 31.97% |
| Swin-Transfomer | 86.32% | 78.46% | 56.18% | 35.63% |
| ConvNeXt | 87.16% | 77.63% | 53.23% | 32.12% |
| ConvNeXt-Text | 89.66% | 79.56% | 56.40% | 35.57% |
| SE-ConvNeXt | 89.65% | 78.54% | 55.43% | 33.26% |
| SE-ConvNeXt-Text | **90.25%** | **80.76%** | **56.73%** | **36.83%** |

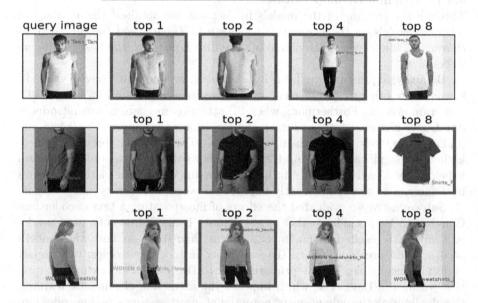

**Fig. 5.** Image retrieval example of SE-ConvNeXt-Text. The picture marked with green box is the correct retrieval, otherwise it is the incorrect retrieval. (Color figure online)

### 4.4.2   Extended In-shop Dataset

To make the experimental results more complete and more suitable for the situation of text on clothes in real life, we used the Dataset 2 to retrain the model in Sect. 4.2, and obtained the accuracy rates of different models on the modified In-Shop dataset, as shown in Table 3, and the precision rates, as shown in Table 4.

By analyzing the data in Table 3 and Table 4, we found that when using the Dataset 2, the retrieval accuracy and precision of ResNet50, SE-ResNet50, ResNeXt, Swin-Transfomer, ConvNeXt, and SE-ConvNeXt decreased by about 5% on average compared to the previous dataset without added text. This is mainly because after adding text to the image, the above models mistakenly

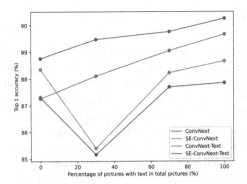

**Fig. 6.** $A@1$ changes of models

treat the text as image features for retrieval, leading to misleading retrieval of model features.

Unlike these models, the proposed SE-ConvNeXt-Text have text encoders that extract text information from images during feature extraction. By analyzing the semantics of the text information, it can perform image retrieval more accurately. The accuracy rate increased by 3.32% on average, and the precision rate increased by 3.37% on average An example of image retrieval using Multimodal Features Enhancement and Fusion Model with SE-ConvNeXt-Text is shown in Fig. 5. This finding highlights the superior performance of models that use text encoders for image retrieval tasks compared to models that only consider image features when processing images containing text information.

## 4.5   Discussion on Parameters

To further investigate the impact of the ratio of image-text pairs in the training set on the retrieval accuracy and precision of models based on ConvNeXt, we gradually increased the ratio of text-image pairs in the dataset. Subsequently, we trained models including ConvNeXt, ConvNeXt-Text, SE-ConvNeXt, and SE-ConvNeXt-Text, and recorded their retrieval accuracy and precision at different ratios. The $A@1$ changes of the models are shown in Fig. 6.

By analyzing the results in Fig. 6, we can draw the following conclusion: when adding a small amount of text to the image, the text will interfere with the retrieval accuracy of the model without text encoder. However, for the model with text encoder, the retrieval accuracy is significantly improved. With the increase of the proportion of pictures with text added, the retrieval accuracy of the model with text encoder is gradually improved, while the accuracy of the model without text encoder tends to be the level when no text is added. When the image proportion of the added text is large enough, other models can learn the characteristic information of the text in the image, rather than the semantic information of the text, so as to reduce the interference caused by adding text to a certain extent. Therefore, we conclude that the modified dataset is valid in proving the effectiveness of adding text encoders to text.

# 5    Conclusion and Future Work

In this study, a multimodal features enhancement and fusion framework for FIR is developed. This framework integrates the SE attention mechanism into ConvNeXt, enhancing the model's ability to extract channel features from images, while also effectively enriching the textual features through the incorporation of a text encoder. The experimental results demonstrate that our approach surpasses all baselines and state-of-the-art models. Notably, as the proportion of text-containing images in the dataset increases, a significant upward trend in the model's retrieval accuracy is observed. In future work, we plan to further explore the SE attention mechanisms and assess the adaptability of text encoders on datasets from diverse domains to validate their universality and generalizability.

# References

1. Li, W., Duan, L., Xu, D., Tsang, I.W.-H.: Text-based image retrieval using progressive multi-instance learning. In: 2011 International Conference on Computer Vision, pp. 2049–2055. IEEE (2011)
2. Gudivada, V.N., Raghavan, V.V.: Content based image retrieval systems. Computer **28**(9), 18–22 (1995)
3. LeCun, Y., Bottou, L., Bengio, Y., Haffner, P.: Gradient-based learning applied to document recognition. Proc. IEEE **86**(11), 2278–2324 (1998)
4. Liu, Z., Mao, H., Wu, C.-Y., Feichtenhofer, C., Darrell, T., Xie, S.: A convnet for the 2020s. In: Proceedings of the IEEE/CVF Conference on Computer Vision and Pattern Recognition, pp. 11976–11986 (2022)
5. Vaswani, A., et al.: Attention is all you need. Adv. Neural Inform. Process. Syst. **30** (2017)
6. Hu, J., Shen, L., Sun, G.: Squeeze-and-excitation networks. In: Proceedings of the IEEE Conference on Computer Vision and Pattern Recognition, pp. 7132–7141 (2018)
7. Dosovitskiy, A., et al.: An image is worth 16x16 words: transformers for image recognition at scale. arXiv preprint arXiv: 2010.11929 (2020)
8. Hjelm, R.D., et al.: Learning deep representations by mutual information estimation and maximization. arXiv preprint arXiv: 1808.06670 (2018)
9. Yan, C., Gong, B., Wei, Y., Gao, Y.: Deep multi-view enhancement hashing for image retrieval. IEEE Trans. Pattern Anal. Mach. Intell. **43**(4), 1445–1451 (2020)
10. He, J., Dong, C., Qiao, Yu.: Interactive multi-dimension modulation with dynamic controllable residual learning for image restoration. In: Vedaldi, A., Bischof, H., Brox, T., Frahm, J.-M. (eds.) ECCV 2020. LNCS, vol. 12365, pp. 53–68. Springer, Cham (2020). https://doi.org/10.1007/978-3-030-58565-5_4
11. Li, Y., Ma, J., Zhang, Y.: Image retrieval from remote sensing big data: a survey. Inform, Fusion **67**, 94–115 (2021)
12. El-Nouby, A., Neverova, N., Laptev, I., Jégou, H.: Training vision transformers for image retrieval. arXiv preprint arXiv: 2102.05644 (2021)
13. Haibo, S., Wang, P., Liu, L., Li, H., Li, Z., Zhang, Y.: Where to look and how to describe: fashion image retrieval with an attentional heterogeneous bilinear network. IEEE Trans. Circuits Syst. Video Technol. **31**(8), 3254–3265 (2020)

14. Goenka, S., et al.: Fashionvlp: vision language transformer for fashion retrieval with feedback. In: Proceedings of the IEEE/CVF Conference on Computer Vision and Pattern Recognition, pp. 14105–14115 (2022)

15. Wu, H., et al.: Fashion iq: a new dataset towards retrieving images by natural language feedback. In: Proceedings of the IEEE/CVF Conference on Computer Vision and Pattern Recognition, pp. 11307–11317 (2021)

16. Lang, Y., He, Y., Yang, F., Dong, J., Xue, H.: Which is plagiarism: fashion image retrieval based on regional representation for design protection. In: Proceedings of the IEEE/CVF Conference on Computer Vision and Pattern Recognition, pp. 2595–2604 (2020)

17. Hosseinzadeh, M., Wang, Y.: Composed query image retrieval using locally bounded features. In: Proceedings of the IEEE/CVF Conference on Computer Vision and Pattern Recognition, pp. 3596–3605 (2020)

18. Wan, Y., Zou, G., Yan, C., Zhang, B.: Dual attention composition network for fashion image retrieval with attribute manipulation. Neural Comput. Appl. **35**(8), 5889–5902 (2023)

19. Mohla, S., Pande, S., Banerjee, B., Chaudhuri, S.: Fusatnet: dual attention based spectrospatial multimodal fusion network for hyperspectral and lidar classification. In: Proceedings of the IEEE/CVF Conference on Computer Vision and Pattern Recognition Workshops, pp. 92–93 (2020)

20. Zhu, J., Huang, H., Deng, Q.: Fashion image retrieval with multi-granular alignment. arXiv preprint arXiv: 2302.08902 (2023)

21. Pal, A., et al.: Fashionntm: multi-turn fashion image retrieval via cascaded memory. In: Proceedings of the IEEE/CVF International Conference on Computer Vision, pp. 11323–11334 (2023)

22. Qiu, S., Wang, X., Liu, Z., Luo, P., Tang, X.: Deepfashion: powering robust clothes recognition and retrieval with rich annotations. In: Proceedings of IEEE Conference on Computer Vision and Pattern Recognition (CVPR) (2016)

23. He, K., Zhang, X., Ren, S., Sun, J.: Deep residual learning for image recognition. In: Proceedings of the IEEE Conference on Computer Vision and Pattern Recognition, pp. 770–778 (2016)

24. Xie, S., Girshick, R., Dollár, P., Tu, Z., He, K.: Aggregated residual transformations for deep neural networks. In: Proceedings of the IEEE Conference on Computer Vision and Pattern Recognition, pp. 1492–1500, (2017)

25. Liu, Z., et al.: Swin transformer: hierarchical vision transformer using shifted windows. In: Proceedings of the IEEE/CVF International Conference on Computer Vision, pp. 10012–10022 (2021)

# Syntactic Enhanced Multi-channel Graph Convolutional Networks for Aspect-Based Sentiment Analysis

Yuhang Ding[✉] and Jianyu Gao

School of Computer Science and Artificial Intelligence, Wuhan Textile University,
Wuhan 430070, China
2215063019@mail.wtu.edu.cn

**Abstract.** Aspect-based sentiment analysis (ABSA) focuses on accurately classifying the sentiment polarity of various aspects within a sentence. In recent years, graph convolutional networks leveraging syntactic dependency trees have gained popularity in ABSA tasks due to their exceptional ability to capture syntactic structures. However, the challenge lies in effectively integrating both syntactic and semantic information without introducing excessive noise interference. This paper addresses this issue by proposing a novel syntax-enhanced multi-channel graph convolutional network model for ABSA. To enhance the model's understanding of grammatical structures, we have devised a multi-channel graph structure. This structure employs syntactic dependency types, positional information, and tree-based distances as adjacency matrices in various channel graphs to represent different types of relationships between words. Additionally, to accurately capture aspect-related information, we've incorporated an aspect attention module, complemented by a mask matrix to filter out non-aspect word features. Our experimental results, based on three benchmark datasets, demonstrate that our proposed model outperforms existing approaches, achieving the highest level of performance.

**Keywords:** sentiment analysis · graph convolution network · aspect-based sentiment analysis · aspect-aware attention

## 1 Introduction

Sentiment analysis is a crucial area within natural language processing [1, 2]. In our modern digital era, vast quantities of textual data continually emerge, including social media posts, product reviews, news articles, and user feedback. These textual data encapsulate people's emotions and sentiments, holding significant value for individuals, organizations, and society at large [3]. By discerning and comprehending the emotions, moods, and attitudes expressed in text or speech, companies can gain insights into consumer needs, enhance products and services, and boost customer satisfaction. Similarly, the healthcare sector can utilize sentiment analysis to assess patients' emotional well-being, enabling more personalized treatment and support, among other benefits. Sentiment analysis can be categorized into three levels: document level, sentence level, and aspect level [4]. Unlike traditional document and sentence-level sentiment analysis, aspect-level sentiment analysis (ABSA) is geared towards identifying specific aspects within sentences and evaluating emotional polarity [5]. As depicted in Fig. 1, for instance, in the given sentence, the aspects are "appetizers" and "service," with the corresponding emotion words being "ok" and "slow," carrying positive and negative emotional polarities, respectively.

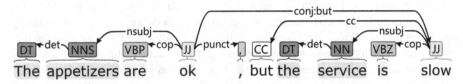

**Fig. 1.** An example sentence with its dependency tree

Aspect-level sentiment analysis represents a more more fine-grained approach to sentiment analysis, focusing on the determination of sentiment polarity specific to particular aspects. In earlier sentiment analysis tasks, manual feature engineering was the norm, involving methods such as sentiment dictionaries, word frequency statistics, and others [6, 7]. Nonetheless, these handcrafted rules proved to be inefficient and incapable of comprehensively capturing the contextual information within sentences. With the advancement of deep learning, many studies have applied neural networks to various natural language processing tasks, including recurrent neural networks (RNN), convolutional neural networks (CNN), and long short-term memory networks (LSTM) [8]-[10]. While these methods excel at extracting contextual information from the source text, they face challenges in effectively identifying designated aspects and the intricate word dependencies within sentences when it comes to aspect sentiment analysis. In response to these challenges, some researchers have employed dependency trees to model sentences using syntactic information, thereby better capturing the interactions between aspects and viewpoints within the text [11]. For instance, Yin et al. introduced a tree-structured latent variable model for semi-supervised semantic analysis, aimed at learning aspect feature representations [12]. Tai et al. proposed a tree structure model to enhance the contextual information within bidirectional long short-term memory networks [13]. These approaches have achieved significant success.

More recent studies have explored the use of graph neural networks to amalgamate syntactic structure and semantic information in sentences. Jiang et al. [14] and Yu et al. [15] employed syntactic trees as inputs for graph convolutional networks to learn syntactic structures. Xu et al. [16] introduced a hybrid graph convolutional network for parsing sentence structure. Nonetheless, these graph-based methods still exhibit certain limitations. Existing GCN-based methods predominantly focus on neighbor nodes' information and might not harness the full potential of syntactic structure and semantic features. Moreover, the accuracy of the syntactic tree obtained is sometimes compromised due to the imperfections of syntax parsing tools, rendering it infeasible to solely rely on the syntactic structure of the dependency tree. Furthermore, the adjacency matrix used in graph-based models is limited to binary values (1 and 0), which results in the loss of information conveyed by different dependencies. For instance, as depicted in Fig. 1, the term "slow" related to the viewpoint demonstrates dependencies with both the predicate "is" and the aspect word "service." However, these two dependencies should not carry equal weight, opinion terms should have a higher weight.

To address these issues, we propose a Syntactic Enhanced Multi-Channel Convolutional Graph Model (SEMCGCN). Our approach comprises the following key steps: First, SEMCGCN begins by acquiring the contextual representation and sentence features. Second, SEMGCN utilizes words and critical relationship tensors as nodes and edges, respectively, to transform the sentence into a multi-channel graph. To fully leverage the sentence's syntactic features, we differentiate between syntactic dependency type, location information, and tree-based distance, designating them as edges in distinct channel graphs. In order to make full use of the syntactic features of the sentence, this article separates the syntax Dependence type, location information, and tree-based distance as edges of different channel graphs. Third, to glean semantic information pertaining to specific aspects, we introduce an aspect attention module. This module focuses on learning the semantic attributes of aspects and integrates them into the adjacency matrix of the graph convolution, thereby enhancing the model's capacity to grasp specific aspect-related information. Finally, a fusion module is employed to combine aspect information with syntactic and contextual information generated by the graph convolution layer.

The primary contributions of our work are as follows:

- We present SEMCGCN, a semantically enhanced multi-channel convolutional graph model, which effectively combines semantic and syntactic information. SEMCGCN excels at proficiently identifying aspect-related information for ABSA.
- We introduce a novel method for fully harnessing the syntactic structural aspects of sentences, encompassing syntactic dependency type, location data, and tree-based distance. To enhance the recognition of specific aspects, we introduce an aspect-aware attention module adept at capturing the semantic attributes of aspects.
- We conducted experiments using three datasets, including SemEval 2014 and Twitter, which validate the effectiveness of the model in ABSA.

## 2  Related Work

With the proven success of the attention mechanism in the field of natural language processing, recent research has focused on utilizing this mechanism to learn the interaction between aspects and context. Wang et al. [17] introduced a bidirectional LSTM neural network that leverages the attention mechanism, combining sentence-level and word-level attention to capture sentence representations at varying granular levels. Chen et al. [18] designed a multi-layer attention time series network to ascertain the emotional polarity of specific aspects. Ma et al. [19] employed an interactive attention network to model and generate representations of targets and contexts. Recognizing that the attention mechanism may not adequately capture distance characteristics in sentences of different lengths, Li et al. [20] integrated position coding into the attention module, thereby utilizing relative position information of sentences.

With the development of graph neural networks, graph-based networks such as graph convolutional neural networks and graph attention networks are widely used in ABSA tasks. These approaches structurally represent word features and capture rich semantic information in text by modeling words as nodes and relationships between words as edges. Wu et al. [21] introduced a phrase dependency graph attention network that aggregates directed dependency edges and phrase information. Liang et al. [22] proposed a grammatical perceptual attention network to learn intra- and inter-context emotional information. Zhou et al. [23] developed a multi-channel graph attention network that employs a two-layer dynamic fusion mechanism to adaptively adjust the fusion weights of different channels. Some studies have harnessed graph convolutional networks to effectively learn aspect representations based on dependency trees, establishing relationships between aspects and opinion words [24, 25]. Liu et al. [26] introduced a double-gated graph convolution network, using gated units to enhance the learning of specific aspects by aggregating node information input by GCN. In order to fully utilize syntactic structure information, Dai et al. [27] designed a syntactic graph convolutional network to capture aspect-sentiment pairs. Li et al. [28] created a dual-graph convolutional network to learn syntactic structure and semantic features separately, introducing orthogonal and differential regularizers to minimize errors. Zhang et al. [29] enhanced the node representation of graph convolutional networks by incorporating syntax mask matrices. Additionally, some studies have improved graph-based neural networks for ABSA tasks by incorporating external knowledge. Lu et al. [30] connected aspect information to a knowledge graph and used knowledge graph embedding to encode common sense knowledge of entities. Gu et al. [31] introduced an external emotion dictionary and constructed an emotion score matrix to enhance the weight of emotion words, compensating to some extent for the inability of syntactic dependency trees to capture edge labels. Wu et al. [32] combined domain knowledge based on syntactic structure and dependency tags to accurately capture the emotional polarity of a specific domain. These experiments have demonstrated the ability of graph-based neural networks to enhance model performance in ABSA tasks.

## 3  Methodology

The comprehensive architecture of SEMCGCN is depicted in Fig. 2. The model is structured into distinct components, including the input and encoding layers, syntactic enhancement layers, multi-channel graph convolution layers, fusion layers, and prediction output layers. Each of these sections will be elucidated in detail in the subsequent discussion.

### 3.1  Encoding Layer

Given a sentence $s = \{w_1, w_2, \ldots, w_n\}$ and aspect terms $a = \{a_1, a_2, \ldots, a_n\}$, where A is a subset of $s$. we employ BERT as a sentence encoder to extract hidden context representation [33], In this approach, we use "*[CLS] sentence [SEP] aspect [SEP]*" as the input format. Subsequently, the sentence is transformed into a vector representation.

### 3.2  Syntactic Enhanced Layer

Once the vector representation of the sentence is obtained, the self-attention mechanism is applied to establish semantic correlations between words. This involves constructing

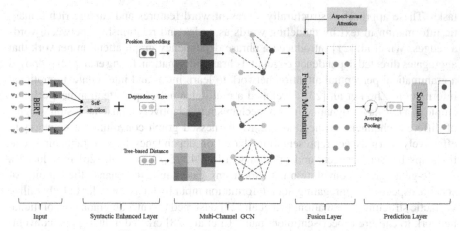

**Fig. 2.** The overall architecture of SEMCGCN

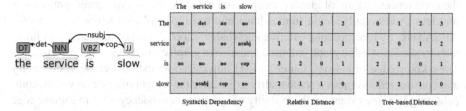

**Fig. 3.** An example of three Syntactic features

the query matrix and key matrix, and the calculation of attention scores is illustrated as follows. Here, $W^Q \in \mathbb{R}^{d \times d}$ and $W^K \in \mathbb{R}^{d \times d}$ are trainable matrices, Q and K are equal to H produced by the encoding layer.

$$A_s = \frac{QW^Q \times (KW^K)^T}{\sqrt{d}} \quad (1)$$

In order to comprehensively capture the syntactic structure of sentences and enhance SEMCGCN, this paper introduces three distinct grammatical features: relative position distance, tree-based distance, and dependency type. The process begins by employing a dependency parser to construct the dependency tree, which takes the form of an undirected graph, with each token serving as a node on this graph. To calculate the distance based on this dependency tree, we define the distance between nodes $v_x$ and $v_y$ as $d(v_x, v_y)$. Given that there can be multiple paths between node $x$ and $y$, we designate the shortest path distance as $D$. Additionally, we utilize the dependency parser to extract dependencies between entity words and other words, assigning labels to each dependency. To facilitate computation, this paper introduces a relationship mapping table to translate word dependencies into corresponding numerical values. Initially, three adjacency matrices $A_p, A_l$, and $A_r$ are initialized randomly, corresponding to the three features mentioned above. Subsequently, the syntactic features of the input sentence are extracted and the matrices are updated, as illustrated in Fig. 3. Ultimately, each feature representation is combined with the attention scores to produce a sentence representation that encompasses a wealth of syntactic and semantic information. The relevant formulas are provided as follows:

$$\widetilde{A_p} = |i - j| \tag{2}$$

$$D(x, y) = \min(v_x, v_y) \tag{3}$$

$$A_i = softmax(A_s + \widetilde{A_j})(j = p, t, r) \tag{4}$$

### 3.3 Multi-channel Graph Convolution Layer

The multi-channel graph convolution layer aggregates the relevant information of nodes and edges in the graph through convolution operations. The formula is as follows:

$$h_i^l = \sigma\left(\sum_{j=1}^{n} A_{ij} W^l h_j^{l-1} + b^l\right) \tag{5}$$

where $h_j^{l-1}$ is the $j$-th node representation of the $l$-th layer, and $h^l$ is the output of the $l$-th layer. $A_{ij}$ represents the relationship between each node. In this context, it signifies the relative position between words, the tree-based distance, and the dependencies between words. $h^0$ is the context representation output by the coding layer. $W^l$ and $b^l$ are the linear transformation matrix and bias term of each layer, both of which are learnable parameters. $\sigma$ is a nonlinear function. The above operation is performed for each channel, and the output of the final layer is expressed as $H = \{h_1, h_2, \ldots, h_n\}$. To preserve most of the syntactic structural features and facilitate information exchange between channels, we interconnect the outputs of multiple channels from the graph convolution layer, each of which is mapped to different vector spaces. Finally, following multi-layer processing, we arrive at the output for each channel, which encapsulates grammatical representations of sentences. $\oplus$ means concatenating the tensors, $W_c$ and $b_c$ are learnable parameters.

$$x_i = H_p \oplus H_t \oplus H_r \tag{6}$$

$$H_c = relu(W_c x_i + b_c) \tag{7}$$

### 3.4 Aspect-Aware Attention

In this paper, a fine-grained attention module is introduced to enhance its suitability for aspect-level sentiment analysis tasks. This module employs aspect terms as query matrices for learning the semantic features of specific aspects. The process begins by mapping the aspect representation obtained from the encoding layer to a different vector space. After calculating the aspect perception score, a mask matrix is applied to filter out noise unrelated to aspect information. The relevant formula is as follows:

$$A_s = tanh\left(H_p W_p \times \left(H_q W_q\right)^T + b\right) \tag{8}$$

$$M_{ij} = \begin{cases} 0, w_i, w_j \in a \\ -\infty, otherwise \end{cases} \tag{9}$$

$$H_m = softmax\left(A_s + M_{ij}\right) \tag{10}$$

where $H_p$ and $H_q$ are both from the output of the coding layer, $W_p \in \mathbb{R}^{d \times d}$ and $W_q \in \mathbb{R}^{d \times d}$ are learnable weights, $w_i$ and $w_j$ respectively represent the $i$-th and $j$-th word, and $a$ represents a specific aspect collection. The equation operates by evaluating whether the $i$-th word is an aspect word, determining whether to retain or exclude the feature vector of the word. Following a weighted summation, the output is passed through a softmax layer to produce the aspect representation of the sentence.

### 3.5  Fusion and Prediction Layer

After obtaining the final node representations of different channel graphs, aggregate the aspect representations of the sentences to obtain aspect information, and use average pooling to retain most of the hidden information.

$$H_i = H_c + H_m \tag{11}$$

$$H = f(H_1, H_2, \ldots, H_n) \tag{12}$$

where $H_i$ represents the characteristics of all nodes of the $i$-th channel, and $f(\cdot)$ represents the average pooling function. After obtaining the sentence representation of the syntactically enhanced fusion information, $H$ is sent to the linear layer and the final result distribution is obtained through the softmax function.

$$p(a) = softmax\left(W_q H + b_q\right) \tag{13}$$

where $W_q$ and $b_q$ are learnable weights and bias terms respectively.

**Table 1.** Statistics of evaluation datasets

| Dataset | Positive | | Negative | | Neural | |
|---|---|---|---|---|---|---|
| | Train | Test | Train | Test | Train | Test |
| Res14 | 2164 | 727 | 807 | 196 | 637 | 196 |
| Lap14 | 976 | 337 | 851 | 128 | 455 | 167 |
| Twitter | 1507 | 172 | 1528 | 169 | 3016 | 336 |

## 3.6 Model Training

We use the standard cross-entropy loss function as the objective function of this article:

$$Loss = - \sum_{(s,a)\epsilon D} \sum_{c\epsilon C} logp(a) + \lambda \|\Theta\| \tag{14}$$

where $D$ contains all sentences and corresponding aspects in the data set, and $C$ is the set of all emotional polarity categories. $\Theta$ represents the training parameters of the model.

# 4 Experiments

## 4.1 Datasets

Our experiments were carried out on three publicly available datasets: Restaurant, Laptop, and Twitter. These datasets are widely recognized benchmarks for aspect-level sentiment analysis tasks. Specifically, the Restaurant and Laptop datasets are sourced from SemEval 2014 Task 4 [34], while the Twitter dataset is obtained from Dong et al. [8]. As outlined in Table 1, each review within these datasets is categorized as positive, negative, or neutral.

## 4.2 Experiment Settings

We use the BERT-base-uncased version as the sentence encoder, Adam as the optimizer to optimize each parameter, the learning rate is set to $2*10-5$, the dropout rate is set to 0.3, and the hidden layer dimension is 768. All sentences were parsed using the Stanfordcorenlp tool.[1] For the graph convolution layer, the learning rate is set to 0.002, the dropout rate is 0.1, and the hidden layer dimension is 300. The epoch and batch sizes of SEMCGCN are 15 and 16 respectively. In addition, we used NVIDIA GeForce RTX 3080 GPU to conduct experiments and averaged the experimental results of 5 different random number seeds as the final result.

## 4.3 Baseline Models

To verify the effectiveness of the proposed model, we compare it with state-of-the-art models on three benchmark datasets.

- BERT utilizes a bidirectional encoder to learn sentence features and classify them in downstream tasks [33].
- CDT uses graph convolutional networks to learn information on sentence dependency trees [35].
- ASGCN uses syntactic information and word dependencies to build a graph convolutional network on the dependency tree of sentences [36].
- R-GAT uses relational GAT to encode the proposed aspect-oriented dependency tree [37].

---

[1] https://stanfordnlp.github.io/CoreNLP/.

- DGEDT proposes a double transformer network that relies on graph augmentation to learn graph-based representations [38].
- BiGCN uses a two-layer graph structure to aggregate word co-occurrence information and dependency relationships [39].
- T-GCN uses graph and attention integration to comprehensively learn the contextual information of different GCN layers [40].
- DualGCN proposes a dual-graph convolutional network to learn grammatical knowledge and semantic information simultaneously [28].
- C3DA uses a generative pre-trained model to generate the aspect and polarity of a given sentence from two channels respectively [41].
- AG-VSR uses graph convolution to fuse dependency tree information and common sense knowledge information [42].
- Sentic GCN enhances the dependency graph of sentences by integrating the emotional knowledge of SenticNet [43].
- SSK-GAT proposes a graph attention network that considers syntactic and semantic information and introduces relevant emotional information in terms of emotional knowledge base enhancement [44].
- KDGN proposes a dependency graph network to combine domain knowledge, dependency labels, and syntax paths [32].

### 4.4 Results and Analysis

We conducted a comparative analysis between SEMCGCN and previous approaches, and the results are summarized in Table 2. Our evaluation metrics include accuracy and macro-averaged F1 scores, with the experimental findings showcasing that our model outperforms existing methods. Many GCN-based models have traditionally focused on constructing syntactic dependency trees to effectively leverage the syntactic structure of sentences and capture dependency relationships between aspect words and opinion words over an extended period. In contrast, GAT models may not optimally utilize grammatical information. Compared to dependency tree based GCN models like ASGCN and T-GCN, our model benefits from both syntactic structures and semantic insights from aspect attention. Consequently, it fully utilizes sentence information in contrast to models that rely solely on a single syntax graph. BiGCN and DualGCN leverage dual-graph structures to simultaneously learn both grammatical and semantic knowledge. However, they do not specifically enhance aspect features, resulting in limitations in distinguishing between dependencies related to aspect words and viewpoint terms versus dependencies among other words. In comparison to GCN-based models, SEMCGCN demonstrates an average accuracy improvement of 2.93%, 3.48%, and 2.72% on the three datasets, along with an average F1-score increase of 4.64%, 4.09%, and 2.81%. While models like AG-VSR, SSK-GAT, and KDGN enhance graph convolution by introducing external knowledge, the inclusion of external knowledge can introduce noise interference, which may not be conducive to further performance enhancement. Furthermore, we observed that employing BERT as a sentence encoder significantly enhances model performance. This observation underscores that large language models are capable of obtaining superior sentence representations compared to bidirectional long short-term memory models.

## 4.5  Ablation Study

To assess the effectiveness of each component of our proposed SEMCGCN, we conducted an ablation experiment, and the results are presented in Table 3. In this table, "w/o" denotes "without." It's evident from the table that removing the self-attention module, dependency tree, location information, and aspect attention module results in a decrease in model accuracy and F1 values. Among these omissions, the most significant drop in accuracy occurs when the aspect attention module is removed, decreasing by 2.31%, 1.27%, and 1.95% respectively. This is because the model loses the capability to discern specific aspect semantics when the aspect attention module is omitted. Furthermore, the removal of the self-attention module leads to a reduction in global semantic awareness in SEMCGCN, hampering the model's ability to capture global information adequately. Eliminating the dependency tree prevents the model from utilizing syntactic structural information because dependency trees are essential for learning word dependencies. Interestingly, the absence of location information has little effect on the Restaurant and Twitter datasets but results in a 1.04% and 1.23% drop in accuracy on the Laptop dataset. This discrepancy is due to the relatively small amount of data in the Laptop dataset, where location encoding can provide valuable additional information. It is particularly beneficial for improving model accuracy and F1 values when data is scarce.

**Table 2.**  Experimental results on three benchmark datasets

| Models | Restaurant | | Laptop | | Twitter | |
|---|---|---|---|---|---|---|
| | Accuracy | Macro-F1 | Accuracy | Macro-F1 | Accuracy | Macro-F1 |
| BERT [33] | $83.62^{\dagger}$ | $78.28^{\dagger}$ | $77.58^{\dagger}$ | $72.38^{\dagger}$ | $75.28^{\dagger}$ | $74.11^{\dagger}$ |
| CDT [35] | 82.30 | 74.02 | 77.19 | 72.99 | 74.66 | 73.66 |
| ASGCN [36] | 80.77 | 72.02 | 75.55 | 71.05 | 72.15 | 70.40 |
| R-GAT + BERT [37] | 86.60 | 81.35 | 78.21 | 74.07 | 76.15 | 74.88 |
| DGEDT + BERT [38] | 86.30 | 80.00 | 79.80 | 75.60 | 77.90 | 75.40 |
| BiGCN [39] | 81.97 | 73.48 | 74.59 | 71.84 | 74.16 | 73.35 |
| T-GCN + BERT [40] | 86.16 | 79.95 | 80.88 | 77.03 | 76.45 | 75.25 |
| DualGCN [28] | 84.27 | 78.08 | 78.48 | 74.74 | 75.92 | 74.29 |
| C3DA + BERT [41] | 86,93 | 81.23 | 80.61 | 77.11 | $76.66\natural$ | $75.79\natural$ |
| AG-VSR + BERT [42] | 86.34 | 80.88 | 79.92 | 75.85 | 76.45 | 75.04 |
| SenticGCN [43] | $86.94^{\dagger}$ | $81.62^{\dagger}$ | $81.35^{\dagger}$ | $77.90^{\dagger}$ | $76.22^{\dagger}$ | $74.90^{\dagger}$ |
| SSK-GAT [44] | **87.41** | 81.65 | 80.25 | 75.85 | 75.72 | 74.44 |
| KDGN [32] | 87.01 | **81.94** | 81.32 | 77.59 | 77.64 | 75.55 |
| Our SEMCGCN | 86.95 | 81.67 | **81.65** | **78.60** | **77.70** | **76.45** |

The results with "$\dagger$" are retrieved from [32], the results with "$\natural$" are based on open source codes, and others are retrieved from the original papers.

**Table 3.** Experimental results on three benchmark datasets

| Model | Restaurant | | Laptop | | Twitter | |
|---|---|---|---|---|---|---|
| | Accuracy | Macro-F1 | Accuracy | Macro-F1 | Accuracy | Macro-F1 |
| SEMCGCN | **86.95** | **81.67** | **81.65** | **78.60** | **77.70** | **76.45** |
| w/o self-attention | 85.16 | 79.41 | 80.54 | 76.93 | 76.51 | 74.35 |
| w/o dependency tree | 85.90 | 80.73 | 80.32 | 76.56 | 76.81 | 75.52 |
| w/o relative position | 86.03 | 81.09 | 80.61 | 77.37 | 76.58 | 76.23 |
| w/o aspect attention | 84.64 | 79.22 | 79.78 | 77.48 | 75.75 | 75.47 |

### 4.6 Case Study

We selected specific examples from the dataset to assess whether SEMCGCN effectively leverages both syntactic and semantic information to accurately identify aspect items and classify them. In Table 4, we compare SEMCGCN with ASGCN, CDT, and Sentic GCN, and the results are presented in the table. In this table, P, O, and N respectively denote the emotional polarity categories of positive, neutral, and negative. In the first example, "The staff should be a bit more friendly," and the second example, "Food was decent, but not great," all models correctly predict the sentiment, highlighting the capability of graph neural networks constructed based on dependencies. These models effectively capture aspect items and viewpoints, avoiding misclassification solely based on the attention mechanism, as seen with the term "friendly." However, in Example 3, for the aspect item "Microsoft Windows," ASGCN and CDT make an incorrect judgment, attributing a dependency to "not hard," leading to misclassification. Sentic GCN, which integrates external knowledge, enhances the identification of aspect-view term pairs and achieves accurate classification. In the final example, the other three models are influenced by "big and "nice," leading them to identify the two aspects, "storage" and "screen," as having positive emotions. In contrast, SEMCGCN employs the aspect attention module to mask out extraneous information, focusing solely on aspect items. This approach minimizes the interference of noise and results in accurate classification.

**Table 4.** Experimental results on three benchmark datasets

| Review | ASGCN | CDT | Sentic GCN | SEMCGCN | Label |
|---|---|---|---|---|---|
| 1 The staff should be a bit more friendly | (N) | (N) | (N) | (N) | (N) |
| 2 **Food** was decent, but not great | (P,N) | (P,N) | (P,N) | (P,N) | (P,N) |
| 3 The **Mountain Lion OS** is not hard to figure out if you are familiar with **Microsoft Windows** | (P,P) | (P,P) | (P,O) | (P,O) | (P,O) |
| 4 I needed a laptop with big **storage**, a nice **screen** and fast so I can photoshop without any problem | (P,P) | (P,P) | (P,P) | (O,O) | (O,O) |

## 5 Conclusion

In this paper, we introduce a syntactic enhanced multi-channel convolutional graph network that not only combines semantic information and syntactic structure but also accounts for specific aspect information. The model comprises five key components. To begin, we utilize the sentence encoder BERT to obtain the initial output and conduct self-attention calculations to extract global semantic information. To fully leverage syntactic structural features, we incorporate syntactic dependency types, positional data, and tree-based distances as adjacency matrices for various channel graphs, facilitating the modeling of distinct word relationships. Subsequently, an aspect attention module is designed to acquire specific aspect representations and eliminate noise through the use of a mask matrix. Finally, we merge this aspect information with the node representation obtained through weighted averaging after multi-channel graph pooling and derive the classification results through softmax. Extensive experiments were carried out on three widely used datasets: Restaurant, Laptop, and Twitter, confirming the efficacy of our proposed model.

## References

1. Birjali, M., Kasri, M., Beni-Hssane, A.: A comprehensive survey on sentiment analysis: approaches, challenges and trends. Knowl.-Based Syst. **226**, 107134 (2021)
2. Zhang, W., Li, X., Deng, Y., Bing, L., Lam, W.: A survey on aspect-based sentiment analysis: tasks, methods, and challenges. IEEE Trans. Knowl. Data Eng. **01**, 1–20 (2022)
3. Wang, J., Tong, W., Yu, H., et al.: Mining multi-aspect reflection of news events in twitter: Discovery, linking and presentation. In: Proceedings of the 2015 IEEE International Conference on Data Mining, pp 429–438 (2015)
4. Nazir, A., Rao, Y., Wu, L., Sun, L.: Issues and challenges of aspect-based sentiment analysis: a comprehensive survey. IEEE Trans. Affect. Comput. **13**(2), 845–863 (2020)
5. Kiritchenko, S., Zhu, X., Cherry, C., Mohammad, S.: Detecting aspects and sentiment in customer reviews. In Proceedings of the 8th International Workshop on Semantic Evaluation (SemEval), pp 437–442 (2014)
6. Hu, M., Liu, B.: Mining opinion features in customer reviews. In: Proceedings of the 19th National Conference on Artifical Intelligence, pp. 755–760 (2004)
7. Schouten, K., Frasincar, F.: Survey on aspect-level sentiment analysis. IEEE Trans. Knowl. Data Eng. **28**(3), 813–830 (2015)
8. Dong, L., Wei, F., Tan, C., Tang, D., Zhou, M., Xu, K.: Adaptive recursive neural network for target-dependent Twitter sentiment classification. In: ACL, vol. 2., pp. 49–54. The Association for Computer Linguistics (2014)
9. Fan, C., Gao, Q., Du, J., Gui, L., Xu, R., Wong, K.F.: Convolution-based memory network for aspect-based sentiment analysis. In: The 41st International ACM SIGIR Conference on Research & Development in Information Retrieval, pp 1161–1164 (2018)
10. Ma, Y., Peng, H., Khan, T., Cambria, E., Hussain, A.: Sentic LSTM: a hybrid network for targeted aspect-based sentiment analysis. Cogn. Comput. **10**(4), 639–650 (2018)
11. Chen, C., Teng, Z., Wang, Z., Zhang, Y.: Discrete opinion tree induction for aspect-based sentiment analysis. In: Proceedings of the 60th Annual Meeting of the Association for Computational Linguistics (Volume 1: Long Papers), pp 2051–2064 (2022)
12. Yin, P., Zhou, C., He, J., Neubig, G.: StructVAE: tree-structured latent variable models for semi-supervised semantic parsing. In: Proceedings of the 56th Annual Meeting of the Association for Computational Linguistics (Volume 1: Long Papers), pp 754–765 (2018)

13. Tai, K.S., Socher, R., Manning, C.D.: Improved semantic representations from tree-structured long short-term memory networks. In: Proceedings of the Association for Computer Linguistics 2015, pp. 1556–1566 (2015)
14. Jiang, B., Xu, G., Liu, P.: Aspect-level sentiment classification via location enhanced aspect-merged graph convolutional networks. J. Supercomput., 1–26 (2023)
15. Yu, B., Zhang, S.: A novel weight-oriented graph convolutional network for aspect-based sentiment analysis. J. Supercomput. **79**(1), 947–972 (2023)
16. Xu, L., Pang, X., Wu, J., Cai, M., Peng, J.: Learn from structural scope: Improving aspect-level sentiment analysis with hybrid graph convolutional networks. Neurocomputing **518**, 373–383 (2023)
17. Wang, J., et al.: Aspect sentiment classification with both word-level and clause-level attention networks. In IJCAI **2018**, 4439–4445 (2018)
18. Chen, P., Sun, Z., Bing, L., Yang, W.: Recurrent attention network on memory for aspect sentiment analysis. In: Proceedings of the 2017 Conference on Empirical Methods in Natural Language Processing, pp 452–461 (2017)
19. Ma, D., Li, S., Zhang, X., Wang, H.: Interactive attention networks for aspect-level sentiment classification. In: Proceedings of the 26th International Joint Conference on Artificial Intelligence, pp. 4068–4074 (2017)
20. Li, L., Liu, Y., Zhou, A.: Hierarchical attention based position-aware network for aspect-level sentiment analysis. In: Proceedings of the 22nd Conference on Computational Natural Language Learning, Association for Computational Linguistics, pp. 181–189 (2018)
21. Wu, H., Zhang, Z., Shi, S., Wu, Q., Song, H.: Phrase dependency relational graph attention network for aspect-based sentiment analysis. Knowl.-Based Syst. **236**, 107736 (2022)
22. Liang, S., Wei, W., Mao, X.L., Wang, F., He, Z.: BiSyn-GAT+: Bi-syntax aware graph attention network for aspect-based sentiment analysis. In: Findings of the Association for Computational Linguistics, pp. 1835–1848 (2022)
23. Zhou, X., Zhang, T., Cheng, C., Song, S.: Dynamic multichannel fusion mechanism based on a graph attention network and BERT for aspect-based sentiment classification. Appl. Intell. **53**(6), 6800–6813 (2023)
24. Ma, Y., Song, R., Gu, X., Shen, Q., Xu, H.: Multiple graph convolutional networks for aspect-based sentiment analysis. Appl. Intell. **53**(10), 12985–12998 (2023)
25. Chen, H., Zhai, Z., Feng, F., Li, R., Wang, X.: Enhanced multi-channel graph convolutional network for aspect sentiment triplet extraction. In: Proceedings of the 60th Annual Meeting of the Association for Computational Linguistics (Volume 1: Long Papers), pp. 2974–2985 (2022)
26. Liu, H., Wu, Y., Li, Q., et al.: Enhancing aspect-based sentiment analysis using a dual-gated graph convolutional network via contextual affective knowledge. Neurocomputing **553**, 126526 (2023)
27. Dai, A., Hu, X., Nie, J., Chen, J.: Learning from word semantics to sentence syntax by graph convolutional networks for aspect-based sentiment analysis. Inter. J. Data Sci. Analy. **14**(1), 17–26 (2022)
28. Li, R., Chen, H., Feng, F., Ma, Z., Wang, X., Hovy, E.: Dual graph convolutional networks for aspect-based sentiment analysis. In: Proceedings of the 59th Annual Meeting of the Association for Computational Linguistics and the 11th International Joint Conference on Natural Language Processing (Volume 1: Long Papers), pp. 6319–6329 (2021)
29. Zhang, Z., Zhou, Z., Wang, Y.: SSEGCN: Syntactic and semantic enhanced graph convolutional network for aspect-based sentiment analysis. In: Proceedings of the 2022 Conference of the North American Chapter of the Association for Computational Linguistics: Human Language Technologies, pp. 4916–4925 (2022)
30. Lu, G., Yu, H., Yan, Z., Xue, Y.: Commonsense knowledge graph-based adapter for aspect-level sentiment classification. Neurocomputing **534**, 67–76 (2023)

31. Gu, T., Zhao, H., He, Z., Li, M., Ying, D.: Integrating external knowledge into aspect-based sentiment analysis using graph neural network. Knowl.-Based Syst. **259**, 110025 (2023)
32. Wu, H., Huang, C., Deng, S.: Improving aspect-based sentiment analysis with knowledge-aware dependency graph network. Information Fusion **92**, 289–299 (2023)
33. Devlin, J., Chang, M.W., Lee, K., Toutanova, K.: BERT: pre-training of deep bidirectional transformers for language understanding. In Proceedings of the 2019 Conference of the North American Chapter of the Association for Computational Linguistics: Human Language Technologies, Volume 1 (Long and Short Papers), pp. 4171–4186 (2019)
34. Pontiki, M., Galanis, D., Pavlopoulos, J., Papageorgiou, H., Androutsopoulos, I., Manandhar, S.: SemEval-2014 task 4: Aspect based sentiment analysis. In: Proceedings of the 8th International Workshop on Semantic Evaluation (SemEval 2014), pp. 27–35 (2014)
35. Sun, K., Zhang, R., Mensah, S., Mao, Y., Liu, X.: Aspect-level sentiment analysis via convolution over dependency tree. In: Proceedings of the 2019 Conference on Empirical Methods in Natural Language Processing and the 9th International Joint Conference on Natural Language Processing (EMNLP-IJCNLP), pp. 5679–5688 (2019)
36. Zhang, C., Li, Q., Song, D.: Aspect-based sentiment classification with aspect-specific graph convolutional networks. In: Proceedings of the 2019 Conference on Empirical Methods in Natural Language Processing and the 9th International Joint Conference on Natural Language Processing (EMNLP-IJCNLP), pp. 4568–4578 (2019)
37. Wang, K., Shen, W., Yang, Y., Quan, X., Wang, R.:   Relational graph attention network for aspect-based sentiment analysis. In: Proceedings of the 58th Annual Meeting of the Association for Computational Linguistics, Association for Computational Linguistics, pp. 3229–3238 (2020)
38. Tang, H., Ji, D., Li, C., Zhou, Q.: Dependency graph enhanced dual-transformer structure for aspect-based sentiment classification. In: Proceedings of the 58th Annual Meeting of the Association for Computational Linguistics, pp. 6578–6588
39. Zhang, M., Qian, T.: Convolution over hierarchical syntactic and lexical graphs for aspect level sentiment analysis. In Proceedings of the 2020 Conference on Empirical Methods in Natural Language Processing (EMNLP), pp. 3540–3549 (2020)
40. Tian, Y., Chen, G., Song, Y.: Aspect-based sentiment analysis with type-aware graph convolutional networks and layer ensemble. In: Proceedings of the 2021 Conference of the North American Chapter of the Association for Computational Linguistics: Human Language Technologies, pp 2910–2922 (2021)
41. Wang, B., Ding, L., Zhong, Q., Li, X., Tao, D.: A Contrastive Cross-Channel Data Augmentation Framework for Aspect-Based Sentiment Analysis. In: Proceedings of the 29th International Conference on Computational Linguistics, pp. 6691–6704 (2022)
42. Feng, S., Wang, B., Yang, Z., Ouyang, J.: Aspect-based sentiment analysis with attention-assisted graph and variational sentence representation. Knowl.-Based Syst. **258**, 109975 (2022)
43. Liang, B., Su, H., Gui, L., Cambria, E., Xu, R.: Aspect-based sentiment analysis via affective knowledge enhanced graph convolutional networks. Knowl.-Based Syst..-Based Syst. **235**, 107643 (2022)
44. Zhang, S., Gong, H., She, L.:   An aspect sentiment classification model for graph attention networks incorporating syntactic, semantic, and knowledge. Knowl.-Based Syst. 110662 (2023)

# Intelligent Helmet with Hazardous Area Detection Based on Digital Twin Technology

Jiajie Liu, Feng Yu$^{(\boxtimes)}$, Li Liu, and Minghua Jiang

Wuhan Textile University, Wuhan, China
liujiajielunwen@yeah.net, {yufeng,l_liu,minghuajiang}@wtu.edu.cn

**Abstract.** In recent years, in the construction industry, there have been frequent incidents of people mistakenly entering hazardous areas, resulting in loss of life and property. Existing intelligent wearable devices are unable to accurately identify and provide real-time monitoring and alerts for hazardous areas, and they are also unable to monitor hazardous areas using a virtual 3D visualization platform. To address these issues, this paper proposes a novel intelligent helmet system with 3D real-time monitoring and alerting capabilities. The system uses a miniature camera to collect information about the surrounding environment, uses a speaker to sound an alarm, and provides real-time feedback to the user. In order to accurately classify and identify hazardous areas, we have improved the YOLOv8 network by adding a small target detection enhancement module(STDEM), which improves the overall performance of the model and its ability to detect distant hazardous area signage. In order to establish the connection between the real world and the virtual world, we construct a digital twin(DT) platform with the help of DT technology to achieve 3D real-time monitoring and information interaction. Experimental results show that our method achieves a mean average precision(mAP) of 93.1% on the self-constructed hazardous area signage dataset. Based on DT and intelligent wearable technology, the system achieves accurate detection of hazardous area signage and information interaction between the real and virtual worlds, which has a wide range of applications in the safety and industrial fields.

**Keywords:** digital twin · intelligent helmet system · hazardous areas · YOLOv8

## 1 Introduction

Intelligent helmet is a popular research object in the field of intelligent wearable. The technology provides detection, monitoring and other functions to the user by combining various types of sensors, communication devices, and artificial intelligence with the helmet [1]. Intelligent helmets use sensors such as miniature cameras, heart rate sensors and brain wave sensors to collect data, and

© The Author(s), under exclusive license to Springer Nature Singapore Pte Ltd. 2025
N. Magnenat Thalmann et al. (Eds.): CASA 2024, CCIS 2374, pp. 146–159, 2025.
https://doi.org/10.1007/978-981-96-2681-6_11

analyze and process the data. In recent years, with the continuous development of sensors, communication devices, and artificial intelligence technology, intelligent helmets play an important role in various fields. For instance, in the transportation field, intelligent helmets can perform risk assessments on the safety of cyclists and ensure their safety [2]. In the healthcare field, patients wearing intelligent helmets can effectively identify and detect strokes to ensure they are quickly diagnosed and receive the most effective treatment [3].

However, in the prior art, most intelligent wearable systems have some shortcomings in hazardous area detection. For example, the sensors currently used in most intelligent wearable systems are expensive and difficult to wear [4], which limits their large-scale application in various fields. In terms of algorithms, the commonly used hazardous area detection algorithms for wearable devices have low mAP and are difficult to apply in real-world situations [5]. In addition, the information collected by wearable systems for hazardous area detection is complex and is usually presented in the form of text. however, the effect of this presentation is limited. Especially for some specific hazardous areas, a more intuitive 3D display is needed for visualization [6].

Aiming at the problem of low mAP of intelligent wearable systems in hazardous area detection and lack of 3D display visualization requirements, this paper proposes a DT based intelligent helmet system. We take the helmet as the main body, which enables it to be widely used in various scenarios and reduces the limitations of hazardous area detection. At the same time, our system employs an improved YOLOv8 network for higher mAP hazardous area detection, which better safeguards the wearer's safety. In addition, the system introduces DT technology, builds a DT platform, and can generate a DT model of the surrounding environment for display. When a hazardous area is found, the system will provide timely feedback to the user, providing a safe and reliable intelligent helmet system. The main contributions of this paper are as follows:

- We propose a novel and complete intelligent helmet system with hazardous area detection. It integrates hardware devices such as miniature cameras and speakers for collecting information about the user's surroundings. Through our established DT platform, the system is able to display the current environment in real time and provide feedback to the user using DT technology [7].
- We propose a signage dataset that can be used for hazardous area detection, which contains warning signs, number signs, prohibited signs, cue signs, and protective fences, totaling about 2,000 images.
- We use a deep learning algorithm to identify hazardous areas and improve YOLOv8 by adding a STDEM, which allows the network to pay more attention to the detection of small targets and improves the detection effect, as well as by applying the Focal-SIoU loss function, which allows for better balancing of the weights of positive and negative samples during the training process and improves the accuracy of the target frame regression.

The rest of the paper is as follows: Sect. 2 introduces and summarizes the state of the art and research related to the intelligent helmet system proposed in this paper. Section 3 describes in detail the system structure and algorithms proposed in this paper. Section 4 verifies the accuracy of hazardous area detection and the reliability of the DT platform in the intelligent helmet system through experiments. The last section summarizes the whole system and looks into the future.

## 2    Related Work

### 2.1    Hazard Detection Based on Wearable Devices

Hazard detection has always been a key concern in the field of safety. Currently, most wearable devices are mainly used to monitor human body metrics to determine the user's safety status. These devices collect various metrics from the user's body, such as heart rate, blood oxygen, and brain waves, and then process this data through natural language processing algorithms [8] to achieve the function of safety monitoring [9]. However, research on wearable systems is not limited to this. One such application is the classification of uncountable and countable activities through the use of smartphones and accelerometer sensors, and the system has a wide range of applications in fitness tracking, bad habit detection, and healthcare, greatly improving the preventive nature of hazard detection [10]. Wearable systems can be used not only for prevention but also for patient monitoring. One such application is the continuous monitoring of vital signs and improved patient safety using two wearable devices, ViSi Mobile (VM) and HealthPatch (HP) [11]. Wearable systems are also used in transportation. One application is the embedding of multi-channel audio sensors in headphones to detect and locate cars from noise and issue warnings. This has significantly reduced the incidence of traffic accidents [12]. Wearable devices still face difficulties in many aspects. One difficulty is that with the development of wearable devices that provide real-time information about the human body and human-computer interaction, there are still significant barriers to providing green and sustainable energy technologies as a power source [13].

Traditional hazard monitoring is identified manually. One survey invited 61 subjects to assess their level of risk and to estimate the probability and severity of a possible accident [14]. The results show that construction supervisors with many years of experience were not able to identify all hazards in the work environment and that their method of assessing risk levels differed in significant ways from most formal safety risk assessment methods [15]. Therefore, hazard monitoring using highly accurate wearable devices is currently the most effective solution. In addition, hazard monitoring can prevent hazards by monitoring external objects [16]. In this paper, a miniature camera and speaker are embedded in a helmet so that workers do not need to wear other hazard detection devices. The helmet is made to not only have a protective function but also be able to detect hazardous environments, which reduces the burden on the operator. It also optimizes the detection ability of small targets through improved algorithms, which significantly improves the detection ability of hazardous environments while ensuring the convenience of the helmet. This technology has potential for practical application. In this paper, a miniature camera and speaker are embedded in a helmet so that workers do not need to wear other hazard detection devices. The helmet is made to not only have a protective function but also be able to detect hazardous environments, which reduces the burden on the operator. It also optimizes the detection ability of small targets through improved algorithms, which significantly improves the detection ability of hazardous environments while ensuring the convenience of the helmet. This technology has potential for practical application.

## 2.2  Digital Twin Technology

3D human-computer interaction is an important research area, mainly applied in the fields of games and visualization, to realize the interaction between the real world and the virtual world.

DT technology is a technology that combines a digital representation of a real-world entity or system with its actual physical form. It creates an accurate digital model that simulates and predicts the behavior, performance, and operational state of an entity or system through the use of technologies such as sensors, simulation models, real-time data, and artificial intelligence. DT technology can be applied in a variety of fields [17], including industrial manufacturing [18], energy management, healthcare, and more. One of the applications is a quantitative green performance evaluation of industrial information integration system-driven smart manufacturing (GPEoSM) using DT technology, and the results show that the DT-driven GPEoSM framework is effective and enhances the green performance evaluation of smart manufacturing [19]. In the industrial domain. One of these applications is the construction of a DT model of a damaged structure, which employs a discrete physical computational model to investigate several damage scenarios to support real-time engineering decisions [20]. In the field of manufacturing. One such application is the utilization of an overarching Knowledge-Driven DT Manufacturing Cell (KDTMC) [21] framework for smart manufacturing that can support autonomous manufacturing through intelligent sensing, simulation, understanding, prediction, optimization, and control strategies [22]. In this paper, a DT platform is created with the help of DT technology, which establishes a link between the real world and the virtual world, enabling real-time monitoring and information interaction. The DT technology can more concretely represent the hazardous environments encountered by workers, which helps to help workers make quick decisions in dangerous situations.

## 3   Method

In order to facilitate the application of hazardous area detection into practice, we designed a new intelligent helmet system with a helmet as the main body. The DT based system framework of the intelligent helmet system is shown in Fig. 1. The system consists of a data acquisition module, a data analysis module, and a digital twin module. In the data acquisition module, the environmental information around the user can be acquired in real time and transmitted to

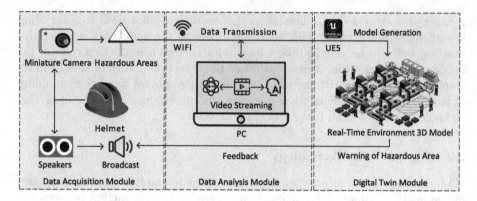

**Fig. 1.** The intelligent helmet system uses a miniature camera to collect environmental data from the user's surroundings, transmits the video streaming data to the PC via WIFI, and analyzes it using deep learning algorithms. Subsequently, the system uses UE5 to generate a 3D model in the virtual world based on the analysis. Finally, the system provides feedback to the user through speakers.

the data analysis module for hazardous area detection via a wireless network. At the same time, the detection results can also be transmitted wirelessly to the digital twin module for real-time display and interaction with the user through the speaker. The system applies intelligent wearable technology and DT technology to provide an intelligent helmet system with 3D visualization and strong interactivity [1].

### 3.1   Data Acquisition Module

The role of the data acquisition module proposed in this paper in an intelligent helmet system is to collect information about the user's surroundings. It transmits the data to a local client via a wireless network and analyzes it in the data analysis module. This data supports the subsequent real-time presentation of the DT. The module mainly uses a micro-camera and a speaker as hardware devices; the miniature camera is used to collect data from the surrounding environment, while the speaker interacts with the user in real time.

A miniature camera is a miniaturized camera device that is usually small and lightweight, making it easy to carry and install [23]. It is equipped with a high-definition image capture function and can record and transmit real-time images. Due to its compact size, a miniature camera can be easily installed in an intelligent helmet. It utilizes a high-sensitivity sensor with the ability to shoot in low-light environments, providing clear images in darker environments and thus improving the accuracy of hazard detection. Given the compact and portable, high-definition, and multifunctional characteristics of the miniature camera, it is placed on top of theintelligent helmet to be used as a data collector. This paper also proposes that the intelligent helmet system utilize speakers to play prompting speech to interact with the user. These speakers also have recording capability. The miniature camera and speakers are connected to the Raspberry Pi through a USB port and powered by a Li-ion battery [24].

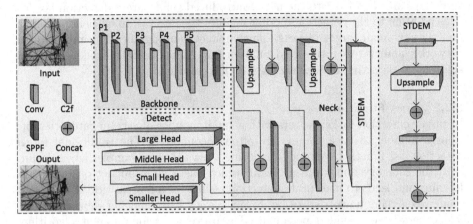

**Fig. 2.** The improved YOLOv8 adds STDEM to the initial YOLOv8 structure, which consists of two C2F modules, one Upsample module, one Conv module, and two Concat modules. A small target detection header is added to the detection header part.

## 3.2    Data Analysis Module

This module focuses on analyzing the environmental information collected by the data acquisition module for hazardous area detection. The results of this analysis pave the way for the subsequent 3D presentation of the digital twin module. We improved the initial YOLOv8 network by adding a STDEM to improve the detection of small signage. The specific network structure is shown in Fig. 2. To address the sample imbalance and bounding box overlap issues, we introduced the Focal-SIoU loss function. Specific schemes for these two steps are provided below.

### 3.2.1    Small Target Detection Enhancement Module

One of the reasons why YOLO small target detection is not effective is that, due to the small size of the small target samples and the large downsampling multiplier of YOLOv8, it is difficult for the deeper feature maps to learn the feature information of the small targets. Therefore, we propose the method of adding a STDEM, the shallower feature maps and the deeper feature maps are spliced and then detected. By introducing the STDEM, the network can be made to pay more attention to the detection of small targets, thus improving the detection effect.

In this paper, we improve the YOLOv8 model by introducing STDEM. Specifically, STDEM incorporates a new feature layer that we continue to upsample in the Neck module. We introduce STDEM into the neck layer, where the upsampled feature maps are connected to the feature maps extracted from P2. The connected feature maps are then processed by the C2F module. The obtained feature maps are then fed into the newly introduced small target detection header. This addition to the detection module enables the network to efficiently identify and classify small target objects. This enhancement significantly improves the network's ability to capture and analyze fine-grained details, making it more suitable for detecting distant signage in video streams.

### 3.2.2    Loss Function

In target detection tasks, targets with a small number of certain categories and a large number of backgrounds are often encountered. The traditional target detection loss function is prone to ignoring a few category samples when dealing with the category imbalance problem, which has a large impact on the model learning and leads to inaccurate detection results for a few categories of targets. Some researchers have tried to improve accuracy by enhancing robustness [25], and others have provided personalized improvements for different algorithms [26]. In order to solve the serious sample imbalance and bounding box overlap problems, this paper introduces the Focal-SIoU loss function, which combines the two parts of Focal Loss and SIoU. This loss function is designed to alleviate the sample imbalance problem, improve the accuracy of target box position prediction, and pay more attention to the learning of samples with higher difficulty [27].

Focal Loss is a commonly used loss function that is particularly suitable for dealing with problems where sample balancing is difficult [28]. The formula for Focal Loss is as follows:

$$FL(p_t) = -\alpha_t (1 - p_t)^\gamma log(p_t) \tag{1}$$

where $p_t$ is the model's categorical prediction probability, $\alpha_t$ the model's categorical prediction probability, and $\gamma$ is an adjustment factor. $log(p_t)$ denotes the standard cross-entropy loss function when the prediction is correct, which partially ensures that the model correctly categorizes the ones with a high probability. $(1 - p_t)_\gamma$ is the adjustment factor introduced to adjust the weight of the samples with a low probability of prediction. $\alpha_t$ is the weight factor for each sample, which is used for further adjusting the weight of the samples.

The SIoU loss function improves the IoU to address the problem of inconsistent target scales [29]. When the target scale varies greatly, the traditional IoU calculation may lead to inaccurate loss functions. To solve this problem, SIoU introduces a scale factor to improve its robustness. When dealing with the task of target detection on different scales, the use of the SIoU loss function can accurately measure the degree of overlap between the predicted bounding box and the real bounding box, thus improving the accuracy of target detection. The formula for SIoU is as follows:

$$SIoULoss = \frac{I}{U + S} \tag{2}$$

$$S = \frac{|w_d - w_g|}{w_g} + \frac{|h_d - h_g|}{h_g} \tag{3}$$

where I is the intersection area of the detection frame and the real frame, U is the concatenation area of the detection frame and the real frame, and S refers to the proportional difference between the length and width of the detection frame and the real frame. $w_d$ and $h_d$ refer to the width and height of the detection frame, respectively, and $w_g$ and $h_g$ refer to the width and height of the real frame, respectively.

### 3.3   Digital Twin Module

DT technology is an innovative technology that combines real-world entities with their digital representations [30]. It builds a virtual model corresponding to the entity by collecting, integrating, and analyzing various data about the real entity in real time, so as to realize the simulation, optimization, and prediction of the entity.

Therefore, we built the DT module on the UE5 platform. It is a 3D model according to the real scene, taking into account a variety of factors such as lighting, material, texture, etc., and realized by the rendering system of Unreal Engine to generate the corresponding virtual world model. The DT platform receives the analysis results from the data analysis module and displays the corresponding information on the DT platform in real-time. Real-time interaction with the user is carried out through the speaker, and if hazardous area signage is detected, a hazard alert will be sent to the user through the speaker to remind them that they are about to enter a hazardous area. At the same time, the speaker also has a recording function. When the user presses the recording button on the speaker, the system will start recording and transmit its recording results to the DT platform to complete the information interaction function. The DT platform provides a 3D user interaction interface, allowing users to observe and manipulate 3D models directly in the real world, resulting in a more vivid and realistic interaction experience [31].

## 4   Experiments

In this section, we first describe the experimental setting and the dataset used. We then conduct a series of comparative experiments on the dataset to highlight the high mAP achieved by our method in detecting hazardous area signage, followed by ablation experiments to assess the impact and effectiveness of the proposed improvements. Finally, we present a demonstration of the effects presented by the DT platform, reflecting the interactivity between the real and virtual worlds.

**Table 1.** Experimental results of different modules.

| Model | mAP | Recall | Precision | F1 |
|---|---|---|---|---|
| Yolov5 | 89.8% | 86.7% | 89.8% | 88.2% |
| Yolov7 | 85.2% | 81.7% | 87.1% | 84.3% |
| YolovX | 88.5% | 85.9% | 82.5% | 84.1% |
| Yolov8 | 90.9% | 83.8% | **92.6%** | 87.9% |
| Yolov8-EIoU | 91.0% | 84.5% | 92.2% | 88.2% |
| Yolov8-Focal-EIoU | 91.2% | 86.6% | 89.3% | 87.9% |
| Yolov8-Focal-SIoU | 91.6% | 84.7% | 91.0% | 87.7% |
| Ours | **93.1%** | **88.6%** | 88.8% | **88.7%** |

**Table 2.** The results of ablation experiment.

| Network | mAP | Recall | Precision | F1 |
|---|---|---|---|---|
| Baseline | 90.9% | 83.8% | **92.6%** | 87.9% |
| Baseline + STDEM | 92.2% | 88.1% | 89.4% | 88.7% |
| Baseline + Focal-SIoU | 91.6% | 84.7% | 91.0% | 87.7% |
| Baseline + STDEM + Focal-SIoU | **93.1%** | **88.6%** | 88.8% | **88.7%** |

### 4.1 Experimental Environment And Datasets

The intelligent helmet system proposed in this paper is equipped with a minia-ture camera, speaker, and Raspberry Pi 4B. The Raspberry Pi is using Python version 3.7 for displaying on a 3D display on the DT platform. In the exper-iment, the PC and Raspberry Pi are connected through the same WIFI, and various information is transferred to the PC through socket communication [32]. The 3D model display platform uses UE5 engine version 5.1.1. The experimental platform system used to train the deep learning models is 64-bit Windows 11 with a 10th generation Intel Core i5 12600KF processor and an NVIDIA GeForce RTX 3050 8GB GPU. We use a self-built dataset of hazardous area signage. For training, the dataset contains five objects, which include warning signs, marking signs, prohibited signs, hint signs, and protective fences, totaling about 2,000 images [33].

### 4.2 Experimental Results

The main objective of this paper is to propose an intelligent helmet system that combines intelligent wearable technology and DT technology to detect and alert hazardous areas. One of the key points is to ensure a high level of model accuracy. In order to address the problem of hazardous area detection, this paper uses four metrics-accuracy, recall, F1 score, and mAP (mean average precision)-to evaluate the accuracy of the model [34]. Next, we will compare them with other models and perform ablation experiments.

### 4.2.1   Comparison With Other Methods

In order to verify the effectiveness of our proposed method for hazardous area signage detection, we conducted comparative experiments. We select several well-known network models, including YOLOv5, YOLOv7, YOLOvX, Yolov8-EIoU, Yolov8-SIoU, Yolov8-Focal-EIoU, Yolov8-Focal-SIoU, and the initial model of YOLOv8 with different loss functions. The experimental results are summarized in Table 1 below.

For YOLOv5, YOLOv7, and YOLOvX models, they are lower than the YOLOv8 model in terms of mAP, precision, and F1 metrics, so for that experiment, we chose to improve on YOLOv8. We also compared several loss functions commonly used for YOLOv8 modeling and found that our method works better than others on the initial model. Experimental results show that our method is more reliable for hazardous area detection and improves the safety of workers' operations.

(a) Real Hazardous Area                              (b) 3D Hazardous Area

**Fig. 3.** A connection between real hazardous areas and 3D hazardous areas is created using DT technology, alerting to hazardous areas on the digital twin platform.

### 4.2.2   Ablation Experiments

The experiments were designed to demonstrate the benefits of using STDEM and the Focal-SIoU loss function in this study. The results of the experiments are shown in Table 2, where the use of STDEM improves the mAP of the original YOLOv8 algorithm. In order to evaluate the effectiveness of the Focal-SIoU loss function, we integrate it into the baseline model along with STDEM. This joint integration allows us to assess the impact of Focal-SIoU on several properties and capabilities of the model. The results show that the incorporation of the Focal-SIoU loss function improves both the mAP and recall of the detection results of the hazardous area identification dataset compared to the initial YOLOv8 model, with an improvement of 1.7% in mAP and 0.9% in recall. Overall, the improved model improves the mAP by 2.2%, the recall by 4.8%, and the F1 score by 0.8% compared to the initial YOLOv8 model, which indicates that the overall performance and accuracy of the hazardous area detection algorithm have been improved, which is very useful for practical applications.

### 4.3 Digital Twin Visualization Display

Based on the experimental environment, we use the virtual engine UE5 to create a virtual world model corresponding to the real world. In Fig. 3, we demonstrate the DT interaction function of the intelligent helmet system in the DT. In the real world, the user wears an intelligent helmet and detects hazardous area markers using a miniature camera on the helmet. At the same time, the hazardous area markers in the virtual scene are detected in a realistic virtual scene, and a hazard alert is issued in the virtual scene. The system achieves timeliness and accuracy of detection through improved YOLOv8 network algorithms, resulting in a smooth interaction function. Compared with traditional 3D interactive systems, the virtual world applied by the DT gives a more immersive feeling. Users can observe the virtual world from the first viewpoint and be fully immersed in the scene. On the DT platform, hazardous area alerts can be displayed, and voice interaction can be carried out using speakers. Overall, the intelligent helmet system breaks the limitations of traditional 3D motion interaction systems and greatly enhances the user's sense of immersion and the naturalness of the interaction, providing a more realistic, smooth, and captivating 3D virtual experience. The DT system in this paper requires virtual-world modeling of hazardous areas. By scaling down, the modeling resource requirements can be reduced. However, for hazardous areas that are very large and complex, the virtual world modeling resources required are relatively large. In the future, we will conduct research on this type of special scenario to improve the system's ability to generalize applications.

## 5   Conclusion

In this paper, a new intelligent wearable system with a hazardous area detection function is proposed. The system utilizes intelligent wearable technology and DT technology to construct a complete intelligent helmet system that realizes high-MAP hazardous area detection, voice interaction functions and 3D visualization interaction functions. The system mainly consists of a data acquisition module, a data analysis module, and a digital twin module. The data acquisition module is equipped with a miniature camera and a speaker, which are used to collect information about the environment around the user and realize the interaction function. The data analysis module analyzes the collected environmental information through deep learning to accurately identify the hazardous area signage. The digital twin module displays the analysis results in real time on the DT platform. When a hazardous area occurs, the system immediately sends an alarm to the user through the speaker and interacts with the user by voice to ensure the user's safety. The experimental results show that the system realizes high MAP hazardous area detection and successfully realizes the information interaction between the real world and the virtual world, which solves the current problems of low hazardous area detection and the inability of wearable systems to establish connections with the virtual world. In the future, we hope to continue to optimize the system and improve its functionality and comfort for application in various fields.

**Acknowledgements.** This work was supported by national natural science foundation of China (No. 62202346), Hubei key research and development program (No.2021BAA042), China scholarship council (No.202208420109), Wuhan applied basic frontier research project (No. 2022013988065212), MIIT's AI Industry Innovation Task unveils flagship projects (Key technologies, equipment, and systems for flexible customized and intelligent manufacturing in the clothing industry), and Hubei science and technology project of safe production special fund (No. SJZX20220908).

# References

1. Feng, Y., Chen, Z., Jiang, M., Tian, Z., Peng, T., Xinrong, H.: Smart clothing system with multiple sensors based on digital twin technology. IEEE Internet Things J. **10**(7), 6377–6387 (2023)
2. Sinha, S., Teli, E., Tasnin, W.: An IoT-based automated smart helmet. In: Karrupusamy, P., Balas, V.E., Shi, Y. (eds.) Sustainable Communication Networks and Application. LNDECT, vol. 93, pp. 371–384. Springer, Singapore (2022). https://doi.org/10.1007/978-981-16-6605-6_27
3. Bisio, I., Fedeli, A., Garibotto, C., Lavagetto, F., Pastorino, M., Randazzo, A.: Two ways for early detection of a stroke through a wearable smart helmet: signal processing vs. electromagnetism. IEEE Wireless Commun. **28**(3), 22–27 (2021)
4. Yin, R., Wang, D., Zhao, S., Lou, Z., Shen, G.: Wearable sensors-enabled human-machine interaction systems: from design to application. Adv. Func. Mater. **31**(11), 2008936 (2021)
5. Liao, P.-C., Sun, X., Zhang, D.: A multimodal study to measure the cognitive demands of hazard recognition in construction workplaces. Saf. Sci. **133**, 105010 (2021)
6. Yan, X., Zhang, H., Li, H.: Computer vision-based recognition of 3d relationship between construction entities for monitoring struck-by accidents. Comput.-Aided Civil Infrastructure Eng. **35**(9), 1023–1038 (2020)
7. Tao, F., Xiao, B., Qi, Q., Cheng, J., Ji, P.: Digital twin modeling. J. Manuf. Syst. **64**, 372–389 (2022)
8. Lyu, W., Zheng, S., Ling, H., Chen, C.: Backdoor attacks against transformers with attention enhancement. In: ICLR 2023 Workshop on Backdoor Attacks and Defenses in Machine Learning (2023)
9. Yu, F., et al.: Intelligent wearable system with motion and emotion recognition based on digital twin technology. IEEE Internet of Things J. **11**(15), 26314–26328 (2024)
10. Jianchao, L., Zheng, X., Sheng, M., Jin, J., Shui, Yu.: Efficient human activity recognition using a single wearable sensor. IEEE Internet Things J. **7**(11), 11137–11146 (2020)

11. Weenk, M., Bredie, S.J., Koeneman, M., Hesselink, G., van Goor, H., van de Belt, T.: Continuous monitoring of vital signs in the general ward using wearable devices: randomized controlled trial. J. Med. Internet Res. **22**(6), 15471 (2020)

12. Xia, S., et al.: Improving pedestrian safety in cities using intelligent wearable systems. IEEE Internet of Things J. **6**(5), 7497–7514 (2019)

13. Gao, M., et al.: Power generation for wearable systems. Energy Environ. Sci. **14**(4), 2114–2157 (2021)

14. Perlman, A., Sacks, R., Barak, R.: Hazard recognition and risk perception in construction. Saf. Sci. **64**, 22–31 (2014)

15. Liao, W., Zhu, R., Ishizaki, T., Li, Y., Jia, Y., Yang, Z.: Can gas consumption data improve the performance of electricity theft detection? IEEE Trans. Indust. Inform. **20**(6), 8453–8465 (2024)

16. Feng, Yu., Zhu, J., Chen, Y., Liu, S., Jiang, M.: Capn: a combine attention partial network for glove detection. PeerJ Comput. Sci. **9**, e1558 (2023)

17. Semeraro, C., Lezoche, M., Panetto, H., Dassisti, M.: Digital twin paradigm: a systematic literature review. Comput. Ind. **130**, 103469 (2021)

18. Feng, Yu., Hua, A., Chenghu, D., Jiang, M., Wei, X., Peng, T., Lijun, X., Xinrong, H.: Vton-mp: multi-pose virtual try-on via appearance flow and feature filtering. IEEE Trans. Consum. Electron. **69**(4), 1101–1113 (2023)

19. Li, L., Lei, B., Mao, C.: Digital twin in smart manufacturing. J. Ind. Inf. Integr. **26**, 100289 (2022)

20. Ritto, T.G., Rochinha, F.A.: Digital twin, physics-based model, and machine learning applied to damage detection in structures. Mech. Syst. Signal Process. **155**, 107614 (2021)

21. Zhou, G., Zhang, C., Li, Z., Ding, K., Wang, C.: Knowledge-driven digital twin manufacturing cell towards intelligent manufacturing. Int. J. Prod. Res. **58**(4), 1034–1051 (2020)

22. Chenghu, D., et al.: Vton-scfa: a virtual try-on network based on the semantic constraints and flow alignment. IEEE Trans. Multimedia **25**, 777–791 (2023)

23. Huang, J., Zhang, H., Wang, L., Zhang, Z., Zhao, C.: Improved yolov3 model for miniature camera detection. Optics Laser Technol. **142**, 107133 (2021)

24. Jolles, J.W.: Broad-scale applications of the raspberry pi: a review and guide for biologists. Methods Ecol. Evolution **12**(9), 1562–1579 (2021)

25. Wu, J., Vorobeychik, Y.: Robust deep reinforcement learning through bootstrapped opportunistic curriculum. In: International Conference on Machine Learning, pp. 24177–24211. PMLR (2022)

26. Wu, J., Wang, J., Xiao, C., Wang, C., Zhang, N., Vorobeychik, H.: Preference poisoning attacks on reward model learning. arXiv preprint arXiv: 2402.01920 (2024)

27. Che, H., Pan, B., Leung, M.-F., Cao, Y., Yan, Z.: Tensor factorization with sparse and graph regularization for fake news detection on social networks. IEEE Trans. Comput. Soc. Syst. **11**(4), 4888–4898 (2024)

28. Zhang, Y.-F., Ren, W., Zhang, Z., Jia, Z., Wang, L., Tan, T.: Focal and efficient iou loss for accurate bounding box regression. Neurocomputing **506**, 146–157 (2022)

29. Peng, H., Shiqi, Yu.: A systematic iou-related method: beyond simplified regression for better localization. IEEE Trans. Image Process. **30**, 5032–5044 (2021)

30. Jiang, H., Qin, S., Jianlin, F., Zhang, J., Ding, G.: How to model and implement connections between physical and virtual models for digital twin application. J. Manuf. Syst. **58**, 36–51 (2021)

31. Lehtola, V.V., et al.: Digital twin of a city: review of technology serving city needs. Inter. J. Appli. Earth Observation Geoinform. 102915 (2022)

32. Izagirre, U., Andonegui, I., Landa-Torres, I., Zurutuza, U.: A practical and synchronized data acquisition network architecture for industrial robot predictive maintenance in manufacturing assembly lines. Robot. Comput.-Integrated Manufact. **74**, 102287 (2022)
33. Liao, W., et al.: Simple data augmentation tricks for boosting performance on electricity theft detection tasks. IEEE Trans. Industry Appli. **59**(4), 4846–4858 (2023)
34. Bazame, H.C., Molin, J.P., Althoff, D., Martello, M.: Detection, classification, and mapping of coffee fruits during harvest with computer vision. Comput. Electr. Agricult. **183**, 106066 (2021)

# An Evaluation of a Simulation System for Visitors in Exhibit Halls

Cheng-Hao Hung[1], Sai-Keung Wong[1]($\boxtimes$), Shu-Chi Yang[1], and I-Cheng Yeh[2]

[1] National Yang Ming Chiao Tung University, Hsinchu, Taiwan
cswingo@nycu.edu.tw
[2] Yuan Ze University, Taoyuan, Taiwan

**Abstract.** Simulation systems for simulating visitors in exhibition halls are widely adopted for users to have a good experience in viewing valuable exhibits but also provide designers to find the appropriate layout for installing exhibits. In addition, such simulation systems provide opportunities for educational and gaming purposes by casual visitors. In this study, we implemented a visitor simulation system that animated virtual visitors in virtual small-scale exhibit halls in three-dimensional space. We recruited 32 participants in a user study to investigate how users evaluated the system in some essential aspects, such as interaction interface, visitor animation, and overall simulation results that were presented in charts (e.g., heat map of visitors' trajectories and visitors' walking speed, visitor transfer between exhibits, and distribution of visitors staying around exhibits). The results showed that presenting visitor behavior through 3D animations helped users recognize visitor behaviors. Editing exhibits with bimanual operation was better in terms of efficiency. Intuitive charts of simulation results helped users understand and evaluate whether the virtual visitors achieved expected overall activities.

**Keywords:** Visitor Simulation System · Animation · User Evaluation

## 1 Introduction

Visitor simulation systems enable users to design layouts of exhibit objects and investigate user experience in exhibit halls. A visitor simulation system is complex because it consists of a large number of variables and complex user interfaces, such as the number of visitors, visitor types, visitor behaviours, exhibit object influences, exhibit object sizes, exhibit hall structures, and simulation results (e.g. exhibit hall space utilisation, visitor visit duration, and visitor walking speed). Visitor simulations provide curators with a low-cost method to simulate visitor behaviors [1,2] and evaluate how well visitors move around in exhibit environments [3]. Visitors have different behaviors in museums according to their visiting habits [4] and surrounding environments [5]. Previous studies have analyzed the visitor behaviors, such as the relationship between the visitors and the exhibit objects [6], the relationship between the visitors and the exhibition hall

© The Author(s), under exclusive license to Springer Nature Singapore Pte Ltd. 2025
N. Magnenat Thalmann et al. (Eds.): CASA 2024, CCIS 2374, pp. 160–176, 2025.
https://doi.org/10.1007/978-981-96-2681-6_12

size [7], and the visitor movement patterns [8,9]. Museum curators study visitor behaviours to find optimal solutions for designing layouts for exhibit objects and improving the overall visitor experience. Visualization of the simulation results helps curators quickly understand and summarize the results [8,10–12]. Some studies simulated visitors as grid cells, 2D circles, or simple primitive 3D models to show how visitors navigate in exhibition halls [3,13]. Although such representations of visitors are efficient for computation, they are not intuitive enough to understand well what the visitors are doing. Animation is the method of presenting the results of the simulation in a lively way [14,15]. The variety of animations increased the realism for the users [16].

Research has been carried out to explore designers' views on the opportunities and challenges of using visitor simulation in exhibition design [17]. In addition to professional applications, visitor simulations are also used for educational and gaming purposes. With the proliferation of museum websites for visitors [18], there is an opportunity for these visitors to get involved in designing their own virtual museums. Casual visitors interested in curatorial work can use the visitor simulation systems to gain a preliminary understanding of the field of curation. In this study, we implemented a visitor simulation system that simulates visitors with various behaviors and produces animation of the visitors in small-scaled exhibit halls in a three-dimensional space. It allows users to design the layout of exhibition objects, simulate visitors navigating through exhibition halls, animate visitors and produce overall simulation results. Our major contributions are as follows. We investigated the extent to which casual users evaluated the visitor simulation system in several essential aspects. We focused on the visitor animation, interaction interface, and overall simulation results. We recruited 32 participants to evaluate: (1) the quality of the visitor animations and the extent to which the animations helped to understand visitor behaviour; (2) the efficiency of editing exhibit objects in two conditions: bimanual and unimanual; (3) the extent to which the charts helped to evaluate the simulation results and adjust the layouts of the exhibit objects; and (4) the user experience of the system. The results of the user study gave us insights into how to improve visitor simulation systems for general users.

## 2   Related Work

**Visitor Behaviors.** Museum curators analyze visitor behaviors to understand visitor movement flows and how visitors watch exhibit objects. Kuhnapfel et al. found that the closer visitors were to an artwork, the more interesting and meaningful they rated it [19]; and they also felt more stimulated and insightful. Serrell pointed out that the patterns of visitor behaviors in many exhibit sites included most visitors visiting less than half of the exhibits, and visitors spending less time per unit area in large exhibition halls [20]. However, visitors preferred to watch larger exhibit objects than smaller ones [21]. Bitgood et al. indicated that visual competition between exhibit objects reduced the likelihood of stopping, and that viewing time was positively correlated with the exhibit object size and visibility [22]. Yoshimura et al. tracked the visitors with Bluetooth to realize the visitor movement flow and apply an appropriate solution to the "hyper congestion" problem [23]. Their analysis showed that the difference between the visiting styles of short-stay and long-stay visitors was not significant. Both types of visitors visited a similar number of key exhibits, but the long-stay visitors tended to do so more extensively.

**Visitor Simulation Systems.** Alessandro et al. investigated the carrying capacity of the museum by conducting visitor simulations in different crowding levels [24]. Their result revealed that the optimal average flow of incoming visitors (20 visitors/min) had the maximum visitor satisfaction. Visitor simulations provide curators with a cost-effective way to evaluate the interior design and observe visitor behaviors. Güler recruited designers to explore the opportunities and challenges of modeling and implementing simulations in the context of exhibition design and the design process [17]. The results indicated that designers acknowledged the usefulness of the system in three aspects: as a learning tool, as an assessment tool, and as a communication tool. The challenges of the system were primarily related to the lack of presence, accessibility, and integration.

## 3   Research Questions

We presented visitor behaviours through animation to show what the virtual visitors were doing. Users viewed the simulation result to understand the visitors' behaviours. Therefore, we wanted to examine the usefulness of the animations in understanding visitor behaviors and how users rated the quality of the animations. Furthermore, the system enabled users to use the keyboard and mouse to modify the arrangement of the exhibit objects. We designed two methods to edit the exhibit objects. One was the bimanual operation, and the other one was the unimanual operation. We wanted to investigate the difference in efficiency between the two edit modes. Additionally, we provided the simulation result charts for users to evaluate the results in different scene layouts of exhibit objects. Users analyzed the charts and adjusted the exhibit objects to achieve a predefined simulation outcome. The users rated the usefulness of the charts after they evaluated the simulation results and adjusted the layout. Therefore, we answered the following three research questions:

**RQ1:** To what extent do the visitors with head and body motion, and visitor animation help users understand how the visitors behave?

**RQ2:** To what extent do the simulation result charts help users adjust a virtual exhibit hall layout?

**RQ3:** To what extent do the two edit modes affect the efficiency of designing a virtual exhibit hall layout?

For **RQ1**, the visitor animations include watching exhibit objects, walking, and gathering and separating around the exhibit objects. Previous studies have shown that the variety of the animations made the simulation more realistic [16], that the presentation of detailed behavior had a significant impact on the visual quality of crowd animations [15], and that the highest quality animations were the least distracting [25]. However, it is unclear whether animations are helpful for users interpreting how the visitors are doing in exhibit halls. For **RQ2**, our system produces a variety of charts that summarize the simulation results of visitors (see Sect. 4). The users can analyze the charts to adjust the arrangement of the exhibit objects to improve virtual visitors' satisfaction. For **RQ3**, the two Edit Modes are developed based on the keyboard and mouse for users to modify the exhibit objects (see Sect. 4). Previous studies have compared the difference between unimanual and bimanual computer interaction. The bimanual interface outperformed the unimanual interface in indirect techniques but the unimanual interface outperformed the bimanual interface in direct techniques [26]. The interface bimanual performance was better than the unimanual performance in the task of matching a response curve to a target curve [27]. In our system, users need to place exhibit objects in specific locations and adjust their orientations. We would like to know which Edit Mode users prefer and the efficiency of the two modes.

## 4   System Overview

The virtual environment was constructed based on the floor plans provided by the National Museum of Marine Science and Technology (NMMST). We analyzed the surveillance videos provided by NMMST to extract the attributes of exhibits and visitors in three exhibit halls whose dimensions were inside $[10, 20]^2 m^2$. There were up to ten exhibits. The small exhibit halls correspond to a local region of a larger exhibition hall, allowing users to quickly get an idea of the whole simulation. The attributes of exhibit objects included maximum capacity, staying time, the best viewing direction, chosen probability for viewing exhibits, and probability for revisiting exhibit objects. The attributes of visitors included the percentage of adults, walking speed, desired viewing list of exhibit objects, transition probability of the "stop-and-go" behavior, desire to gather, and transition probability of gathering behavior (e.g., the probability of joining another group and staying in the same group). To edit these settings, the system provides buttons to specify each of the attributes. Furthermore, there are predefined camera positions for the users to quickly view the specific regions of an exhibit hall. Figure 1 shows the system user interface developed in Unity. Users

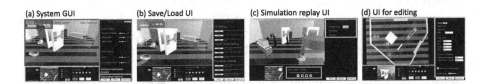

(a) System GUI        (b) Save/Load UI        (c) Simulation replay UI        (d) UI for editing

**Fig. 1.** System User Interface.

can use the interface for simulation replay to quickly review how the visitors behave.

**Table 1.** Operations of Edit Modes

| Operations | Edit Mode One | Edit Mode Two |
|---|---|---|
| Select exhibits | Click left mouse button | Click left mouse button |
| Move exhibits | Hold and drag left mouse button | Hold and drag right mouse button |
| Teleport exhibits | Click right mouse button | Click right mouse button |
| Rotate exhibits in clockwise | Hold Key E | Scroll mouse wheel forward |
| Rotate exhibits in counterclockwise | Hold Key Q | Scroll mouse wheel backward |
| Confirm | Click left mouse on the plane | Click left mouse button twice |

The simulation is based on the premise that visitors know the exhibition halls well in advance. Therefore, visitors have a list of desired exhibit objects to visit. Inspired by crowd simulation frameworks [28,29], we design the influence maps to represent the attractiveness of the exhibit objects and the visitors. An exhibit influence map includes the following items: (1) occupancy, (2) estimated time spent at the exhibits, (3) popularity level, (4) visitor preference for viewing exhibits, and (5) the number of visitors that are near the best viewing positions. A visitor influence map includes (1) the desire to follow the crowd, (2) the estimated time spent with visitors, (3) the desire to gather with other visitors, and (4) the desire to follow a particular type of visitors (e.g., adult or child). The system adopts the influence maps of the visitors to drive the visitors to perform actions. The visitors make decisions to visit the exhibit objects based on their attractiveness. The visit time for the visitors is around 3 min in an exhibit hall.

To represent the behavior of watching the exhibit objects, the visitors' heads are simulated to move properly as they look at the exhibit objects. We use Unity Animation Rigging to control the body orientation and to associate the visitors' heads with viewing points. The viewing points are prepared beforehand to guide the visitors' viewing focus on exhibit objects (e.g., staring time and viewing transitions). The visitors gaze at the viewing points, and so they watch naturally different parts of the exhibit objects (Fig. 2).

To evaluate the simulation results in different layouts of exhibit objects, we design two Edit Modes to modify exhibits and seven charts. Edit Mode One is a bimanual operation, and Edit Mode Two is a unimanual operation (Table 1). In Edit Mode One, a user uses two hands to perform operations (i.e. one hand uses the keyboard and the other uses the mouse). In Edit Mode Two, a user uses one hand as all operations are tied to the mouse. Furthermore, in Edit Mode Two, when users modify an exhibit object, the system generates a

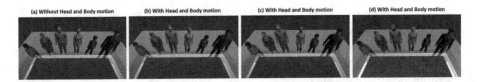

**Fig. 2.** Virtual visitors with and without motion in the same scene. (a) Visitors without head and body motion, looking straight ahead. (b)(c)(d) Visitors with head and body motion, gazing at different parts of the exhibit.

cloned exhibit object (i.e. the exhibit is duplicated). The cloned exhibit object acts as a reference, allowing users to observe how much it has changed from the original exhibit object (Fig. 3). After users have approved the changes, the original exhibit object disappears.

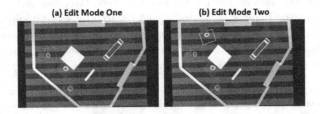

**Fig. 3.** The screenshots of editing an exhibit object in two Edit Modes. The red and cyan rectangles indicate the original and cloned exhibit objects, respectively. Users edit the cloned exhibit object. After editing, the users confirm the change, and then the original exhibit object disappears. (Color figure online)

We developed a Python program to display charts in a website dashboard. Figure 4 shows the layout of an exhibit and the charts. The purposes of the charts are as follows:

1. **Trajectory Heat Map:** The frequency of passing through regions. It shows the places where visitors frequently pass by or which are not used.
2. **Walking Speed Heat Map:** The average walking speed of visitors in regions. It shows the locations where visitors are moving slower or faster.
3. **Visitor Satisfaction:** "Visitor satisfaction" $\nu$ is the completion percentage of the visitor's desired viewing exhibit list. Formally, we have $\nu = \frac{d}{D}$, where $d$ is the number of exhibits that have been visited, and $D$ is the number of exhibits in the list. We adopt a Pareto chart to show "visitor satisfaction".
4. **Time Distribution of Visitor Action States:** The duration of visitors performing an action state. There are three action states. "Go": Visitors are walking to target exhibit objects; "Close": They are near an exhibit object; "At": They are looking at an exhibit object.
5. **Visit Time Distribution in Each Exhibit:** The amount of time visitors spent in each exhibit object.

6. **Real Time Distribution of Visitors in Exhibits:** The number of visitors staying around each exhibit object per second.
7. **Visitor Transfer Between Exhibits:** The visitor transfer distribution between exhibit objects. It shows the number of visitors moving from one exhibit object to another.

## 5    Experiment Simulation

### 5.1    Experiment Design

We designed three tasks and a user experience evaluation in our experiment to evaluate the visitor simulation system.

**Task One.** The purposes of Task One were to evaluate the naturalness of the visitor behaviors (i.e., animations) and to investigate the extent to which the animations helped observe how the visitors behaved. We produced 16 video clips that showed visitor behaviors, including (A) watching exhibit objects (5 clips with head and body motion, and 5 clips without head and body motion), (B) walking animation (3 clips), and (C) visitor gathering and separating animation (3 clips). The average length of the video clips was 30 s.

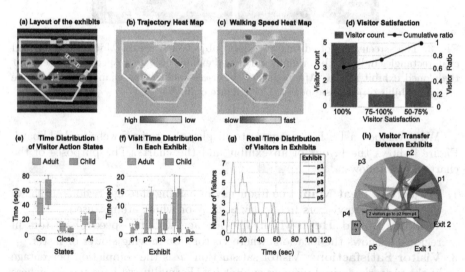

**Fig. 4.** Layout of exhibit objects and all charts. (a) Layout. (b,c) Heat maps. (d) Pareto chart. (e,f) Box plots. (g) Curve graph. (h) Chord diagram. Each color represents an exhibit object or an exit. The chord illustrates the transfer situation, i.e., the number of visitors going from A to B (A and B are the exhibit objects or the exits). The size of the chord is positively correlated with the number of visitors. When the user moves the mouse over the chart, a dialog box displays the information. The dialog box over the boundary of the circle shows the name of the exhibit object and the number of visitors going to other exhibits or the exits from the exhibit. For example, seven visitors leave "p4" and go to other locations.

**Task Two.** The purpose of Task Two was to evaluate the efficiency of the two Edit Modes. The participants were asked to use the two Edit Modes to adjust the exhibit objects to predefined positions and orientations (i.e., the yaw angles). There were a total of ten trials (five scenes x two Edit Modes). The objectives of the first two scenes were to adjust the position and orientation of an exhibit object, respectively. In the remaining three scenes, there were multiple exhibit objects and the goal was to adjust their positions and orientations. We investigated the difference in efficiency between bimanual and unimanual operations. We also wanted to find out which interface was preferred by the participants.

**Task Three.** Data visualisation helps people understand the simulation results intuitively. We implemented the charts that were essential for visualizing the overall visitor behaviors. The purpose of Task Three was to evaluate the extent to which charts helped adjust the layout of exhibit objects. In the experiment, the system parameters were given. Initially, there were eight visitors and "visitor Satisfaction" of five visitors was 100%. The experimental procedure of Task Three was as followed: (1) the participants analyzed a poor simulation result based on the charts, (2) adjusted the exhibition layout, (3) ran a simulation, and (4) the system generated the entire simulation result and charts. The users repeated the procedure to finish the task. The goal was to increase the number of visitors with 100% "Visitor Satisfaction" in the new result.

Regarding Tasks One, Two and Three, participants answered the following questions based on a seven-point Likert scale (1 = strongly disagree, 4 = neutral, 7 = strongly agree):

Q1.1 (Task One): Do you agree that the behavior of the visitors is natural? The participants answer this question for every video clip.

Q1.2 (Task One): Do you agree that the animations can help you understand how visitors behave in exhibit halls?

Q2.1 (Task Two): Do you agree that it is easy to move and rotate an exhibit object at the same time in Edit Mode One?

Q2.2 (Task Two): Do you agree that it is easy to move and rotate an exhibit object at the same time in Edit Mode Two?

Q2.3 (Task Two): Do you agree that it is helpful to edit an exhibit object with the cloned exhibit object as a reference in Edit Mode Two?

Q3 (Task Three): Do you agree that the chart can serve as an important reference for editing the exhibit hall layout? The participants answer this question for every chart.

To evaluate the user experience of users, we designed ten questions of a questionnaire based on SUS (System Usability Scale) and software evaluation [30–33]. The questions were about the simulation display, system interface, editing operations, and the dashboard (Table 3).

## 5.2 Participants

32 participants were recruited in the user study (Female = 16, Male = 16, Age Mean = 24.88, SD = 5.25, Age = 20–40). All of them had a college education degree or higher. None of them were professional curators. This study was

approved by the Institutional Review Board (IRB). As our study was a within-subjects study for Task One and Task Two, we adopted the Latin square arrangement for the participants.

### 5.3   User Study Procedure

The experimental procedure was as follows. (1) The experiment coordinator explained the experiment to the participants and obtained their signed consent form. (2) They filled out the pre-experiment questionnaire about demographics and experience related to curation work. (3) In the main experiment session, they had to complete three tasks and then evaluate user experience of the system. (4) After that, a post-experiment interview with the participants was conducted. (5) Finally, the participants were debriefed.

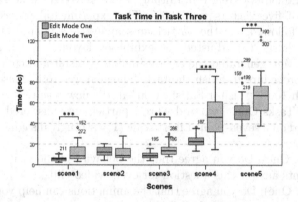

**Fig. 5.** Box plot comparisons for task time between the two edit modes in Task Three.

## 6   Analysis Procedure

The subjective measures included the questions based on a 7-point Likert scale in each task, which were ordinal data. We did not deal with outliers in the ordinal data because of the limited range of scores. We asked the participants about why they gave extreme values in the interview. For ordinal data, we calculated the mean ($M$), standard deviation ($SD$), median ($Mdn$), and interquartile range of the data ($IQR$). In Task Two, the objective measures included participants' task time on the five trials in the two editing mode conditions, which were continuous data. For continuous data, we dealt with outliers because some participants took too long time to complete the tests. We detected outliers using the SPSS software and replaced them with the median value. We used the Shapiro-Wilk test to check all data in each test and found that all the tests did not follow the normal distribution. Therefore, we used the Wilcoxon signed rank test to compare the continuous data in the two edit mode conditions.

# 7   Results of Tasks

## 7.1   Results for Task One: Evaluation of Animation Quality

The evaluation of the animation quality has three parts: (A) watching exhibit objects, (B) walking animation, and (C) gathering and separating animation.

**(A) Watching exhibit objects.** There were two conditions: with and without head and body motion. A Wilcoxon signed rank test indicated that there was a main effect on the head and body motion of visitors, $Z = -4.865, p = 0.000$. The rating of the visitors with head and body motion was ($M = 4.894, SD = 1.295, Mdn = 5.000, IQR = 1.500$) significantly higher than that of the visitors without head and body motion ($M = 2.425, SD = 1.086, Mdn = 2.300, IQR = 1.700$) (Fig. 5(a)). Eight participants commented positively on the naturalness of the visitors with head and body motion while they swayed and looked at different parts of the exhibit objects. However, five participants mentioned that the body sway animation was not obvious to watch and the head-turning speed was too slow.

**(B) Walking animation.** The rating was ($M = 4.312, SD = 0.982, Mdn = 4.333, IQR = 1.333$). Five participants gave positive comments that the visitors chose reasonable paths in navigating the environment to watch exhibits. However, five participants felt that the visitors were too close to each other when they met.

**(C) Gathering and separating animation.** The rating was ($M = 4.750, SD = 0.905, Mdn = 4.667, IQR = 1.083$). Five participants commented that the mechanism for grouping visitors was reasonable. However, four participants felt that it was not rigorous enough to judge the group of visitors based on the area they were in. Three participants suggested that it was necessary to use the visitors' forward direction or the exhibit objects they were currently looking at as a basis for judging the behaviors of the visitors.

Overall, the participants felt that adding the behavioural animations would help to present visitors in a more detailed way ($M = 5.500, SD = 1.173, Mdn = 6.000, IQR = 1.000$).

## 7.2   Results for Task Two: Evaluation of Edit Modes

26 participants (81.25%, 26/32) preferred to use Edit Mode One. They found it intuitive to use one hand to control the position of the objects and the other hand to control their orientation. They had two reasons for not liking Edit Mode Two: (A) the mode of operation was different from their habits of using the mouse and their cognition (11 participants). For example, they would like the *move* command assigned to the left mouse button; and (B) it was too tedious to rotate multiple exhibit objects with the scroll wheel (seven participants). However, in Edit Mode One, it was required only holding down a button for rotating the exhibit objects. On the contrary, the other six participants preferred Edit Mode Two for the following two reasons: (A) it was more comfortable to edit the position and orientation of the exhibit objects with one hand (three

participants); and (B) they could control the speed at which they wanted to change the orientation of the exhibits by using a scroll wheel (two participants).

In Edit Mode Two, participants had to adapt an exhibit object to a pre-defined setting. In this way, the exhibit object was cloned and two identical exhibit objects were displayed. The cloned exhibit object was the target exhibit (rendered in transparency) and another exhibit was the reference (rendered in solid). In response to the question: *"Do you agree that it is helpful to edit an exhibit object with the cloned exhibit object as a reference in Edit Mode Two?"*, the score was ($M = 4.719, SD = 1.566, Mdn = 5.000, IQR = 2.250$). However, four participants (P5, P8, P27, P30) felt that the cloned exhibit object made the screen too cluttered (Fig. 3).

Regarding the task time in the two editing modes, Wilcoxon signed rank tests (Table 2 showed that there was a main effect on the task time between the two Edit Modes (Fig. 5(b)). $Z$ score was calculated by subtracting the task time (sec) in Edit Mode Two from the task time in Edit Mode One (b: Based on positive ranks. c: Based on negative ranks.). Except for the trial in Scene Two, the task time in Edit Mode One was significantly higher than that in Edit Mode Two in the other four scenes. In response to the question "Do you agree that it is easy to move and rotate an exhibit object at the same time?", the result showed that Edit Mode One ($M = 5.812, SD = 1.261, Mdn = 6.000, IQR = 2.000$) was preferred by the participants over Edit Mode Two ($M = 3.531, SD = 1.639, Mdn = 3.000, IQR = 3.000$). It was worth noting that in Scene Two, the goal was to adjust the orientation of an exhibit. In Edit Mode Two, the participants could rotate the mouse wheel quickly to adjust the exhibit object. But in Edit Mode One, the users had to hold down the key 'Q' or 'E' to rotate the exhibit object at a predefined rotation speed. But in Scenes Three, Four, and Five, the users had to adjust the positions and orientations of the exhibit objects. The result revealed that using one hand to perform both operations in Edit Mode Two was not efficient, as compared to using both hands to perform such operations.

**Table 2.** Wilcoxon signed ranked tests for comparison between the two edit modes in Task Two.

| | Scene One | Scene Two | Scene Three | Scene Four | Scene Five |
|---|---|---|---|---|---|
| Z score | -4.095[b] | -1.533[c] | -4.031[b] | -4.637[b] | -4.039[b] |
| Asymp. Sig. (2-tailed) | .000 | .125 | .000 | .000 | .000 |

## 7.3    Results for Task Three: Evaluation of Charts

27 participants (84.4%, 27/32) achieved the goal that all the visitors' "Visitor Satisfaction" was 100%. In response to "Do you agree that the chart can serve as an important reference for editing the exhibit hall layout?", the heat maps of

**Table 3.** The results of system evaluation. The questions are on a 7-point Likert scale.

| Questions | M | SD | Mdn | IQR |
|---|---|---|---|---|
| 1. It is easy to observe the visitors' group. | 5.219 | 1.293 | 5.000 | 2.000 |
| 2. I think the number of cameras in the exhibition hall is sufficient. | 5.969 | .809 | 6.000 | 2.000 |
| 3. I think the display window is big enough to watch. | 5.750 | 1.173 | 6.000 | 2.000 |
| 4. It is easy to select the visitor or exhibit to display information. | 5.188 | 1.285 | 5.000 | 2.000 |
| 5. I think the interface of the system is complex. | 4.438 | 1.540 | 4.500 | 3.000 |
| 6. It is easy to start the visitor behavior simulation. | 5.688 | 1.073 | 6.000 | 1.250 |
| 7. It is easy to find a specific function in the system interface. | 5.062 | 1.248 | 5.000 | 2.000 |
| 8. It is easy to edit the layout of the exhibition. | 6.156 | 1.003 | 6.000 | 1.000 |
| 9. It is easy to get charts of simulation result. | 5.938 | 1.059 | 6.000 | 2.000 |
| 10. It is easy to compare the simulation result with others. | 6.375 | .820 | 7.000 | 1.000 |
| 11. All | 5.578 | .685 | 5.500 | .925 |

*Trajectory* ($M = 5.812, SD = 0.982, Mdn = 6.000, IQR = 2.000$) and *Walking Speed* ($M = 5.875, SD = 1.340, Mdn = 6.000, IQR = 2.000$) were more intuitive than the other charts when it came to adjusting the halls. Eight participants commented that they could simply apply the two heat maps to assess space utilisation and observed visitor walking speeds to adjust the layout of the exhibit objects.

The rating of the *Visitor Satisfaction* chart was ($M = 5.844, SD = 1.003, Mdn = 6.000, IQR = 2.000$). Four participants (P5, P10, P23, P30) considered the chart to be the most important and intuitive indicator of whether the exhibit hall layout was well designed.

The rating of the *Distribution of Visiting Time in Each Exhibit* chart was ($M = 5.469, SD = 1.369, Mdn = 6.000, IQR = 1.250$). 12 participants thought that knowing the distribution of visiting time in each exhibit would allow them to prioritize the placement of exhibits with longer visiting durations.

The rating of the *Transfer Probability Between Exhibits* chart was ($M = 4.875, SD = 1.672, Mdn = 5.000, IQR = 2.250$). Seven participants stated that they found it difficult to fully understand the concept of the chart because it was too technical. However, one participant (P15) said that the chart helped plan visiting routes.

The rating of the *Real-time Distribution of Visitors in Exhibits* chart was ($M = 4.875, SD = 1.495, Mdn = 5.000, IQR = 2.250$). One participant (P2) mentioned that there were casual visitors in real life, e.g., the visitors who did not spend much time watching exhibits. Thus, the chart was not an important reference for designing an exhibition layout.

The rating of the *Time Distribution of Visitor Action States* chart was ($M = 4.812, SD = 1.285, Mdn = 5.000, IQR = 2.000$). Two participants (P1, P31) suggested that the chart had no reference value because visitors might choose to move to other exhibits because the target exhibit was too crowded. Thus they would come back to view it later. As a result, this could increase the visitors' dwell time. Two participants (P10, P26) thought that the chart could be used to evaluate the effectiveness of the exhibition hall design, especially to avoid excessive visitor movement time.

## 7.4    Results for System Evaluation

Table 3 shows the results of the system evaluation. In general, the system received a positive feedback. The participants commented on the questions about the simulation display as follows (Question One to Question Four). One participant (P26) recommended that we should mark the positions of the cameras because identifying the position of the camera was a waste of time during the simulation. Four participants (P3, P7, P21, P27) mentioned that they had to change the camera view to select the visitors because the exhibits blocked the way to select the visitors, which was inconvenient.

## 8    Discussion and Limitations

### 8.1    Response to Research Question RQ1

In response to the question **RQ1**: *"To what extent do the visitors with head and body motion, and visitor animation help users understand how the visitors behave?*, we found evidence that the head and body motion and visitor animation helped users figure out how visitors behaved. 30 participants felt that the 3D presentation of visitor behaviours helped them to understand the simulation. Four participants (P11, P13, P18, P25) said that the visualisation of the simulation helped them to imagine the real situation. One participant (P14) said that showing the visitor animation was necessary because everyone had different opinions about the results shown in the charts, but the animation showed the real situation and what the visitors were doing.

Our results in Task One were consistent with the existing findings that animations and detailed character behaviours made the simulation realistic [16]. Of all the types of animation, the animation in which the visitors watched the exhibits with head and body motion received the highest average score ($M = 4.894$). Presenting visitor behaviors through animation helped participants understand what the visitors behaved. The more animations, such as interaction with other visitors and interaction with exhibits, the more lifelike the simulation became. Although the average score of all the animations was above four, none exceeded five. We might encounter the Uncanny Valley effect on the virtual visitors [34]. To improve the quality of the animations, we should make the virtual human models and animations more sophisticated based on what the virtual humans are doing.

### 8.2    Response to Research Question RQ2

In response to the question **RQ2:** *"To what extent do the simulation result charts help users adjust a virtual exhibit hall layout?"*, we found evidence that the charts helped users design a virtual exhibition hall layout. The participants (24/32) thought that the visualization of simulation results helped users comprehend the simulation quickly and intuitively, and knew how to modify the layout.

We found that intuitive charts (e.g. heat maps of trajectory and walking speed) and charts with simple statistics (e.g. *Visitor Satisfaction* and *Visit Time Distribution in Each Exhibit*) received higher scores than other charts. When the participants saw these charts, they quickly understood the simulation result. However, the charts, such as *Time Distribution of Visitor Action States* and *Visitor Transfer Between Exhibits*, did not give the participants direct information to understand the simulation result. Therefore, we should choose charts that present the simulation result coupled with the exhibition hall layouts. For example, the system shows the chord diagram to represent the transfer situation between the exhibit objects. However, the chord diagram is not intuitive because it is detached from the exhibition floor plan; and labels are used to represent the objects. Therefore, it would be better to directly show arrows that represent the transfer situation between exhibits in the bird view of the environment; and the colours of the arrows indicate the frequency of the paths [10] on a single figure.

### 8.3   Response to Research Question RQ3

In response to the question **RQ3:** *"To what extent do the two edit modes affect the efficiency of designing a virtual exhibit hall layout?"*, we found evidence that the efficiency of Edit Mode One was significantly higher than the efficiency of Edit Mode Two in four out of five test cases. According to the participants' feedback, most of them thought that Edit Mode One was more convenient than Edit Mode Two because the operation of Edit Mode One was similar to their operation habits. The participants commented that Edit Mode One was more intuitive than Edit Mode Two.

### 8.4   Limitations

The system has limitations. Visitors made decisions based on the influence map, i.e., they moved toward the most attractive exhibit or visitor. However, we did not consider the visitors' exploration styles. In the literature, the visitors' exploration styles can be categorized into four animals, including ants, fish, butterflies, and grasshoppers [4]. For example, ants represent visitors who look at almost all the exhibit objects and follow specific paths, and fish represent visitors who avoid detailed exhibit information and prefer to view the exhibits from a distance. In this study, we implemented a visitor simulation system that supported a variety of features and displayed the simulation results as charts. The user study evaluated a limited subset of the features supported by our system. We did not consider tools for arranging exhibit objects to meet user expectations. In the future, we would like to develop editing tools and evaluate how users will apply the tools to finish exhibition layouts in large exhibition halls.

## 9   Conclusion

We investigated to what extent casual users evaluated a visitor simulation system in three essential aspects. The participants evaluated the animations, Edit

Modes, the simulation charts. Our results showed that presenting visitor behavior through animations in 3D helped users understand the simulation. Most of the participants preferred to use the bimanual operation to edit the exhibits because the operation was similar to their operating habits. The simulation result charts helped the participants understand and evaluate the simulation. The participants preferred charts that displayed intuitive information, such as "Trajectory Heat Map", "Walking Speed Heat Map", and "Visitor Satisfaction". The charts gave them ideas for adjusting the layout. However, we received polarised opinions about the complexity of the system interface, which consisted of too many buttons associated with different features. Some participants thought they could control more elements, but others felt overwhelmed when using the system for the first time. This research was supported by the National Science and Technology Council of the R.O.C. under grant no. NSTC 112-2221-E-A49-118.

# References

1. Guler, K.: Simulating Visitor Behavior. Cambridge Scholar Publishing (2016)
2. Solmaz, G., Akbaş, M.I., Turgut, D.: Modeling visitor movement in theme parks. In: 37th Annual IEEE Conference on Local Computer Networks, pp. 36–43 (2012)
3. Güler, O.K.: A simulation application for visitor circulation in exhibition environments. PhD thesis, Bilkent Universitesi (Turkey) (2009)
4. Véron, E., Levasseur, M.: Ethnographie de l'exposition: l'espace, le corps et le sens. Bibliothèque publique d'information du Centre Pompidou (1989)
5. Goulding, C.: The museum environment and the visitor experience. Eur. J. Mark. **34**(3/4), 261–278 (2000)
6. Iio, T., Satake, S., Kanda, T., Hayashi, K., Ferreri, F., Hagita, N.: Human-like guide robot that proactively explains exhibits. Int. J. Soc. Robot. **12**, 549–566 (2020)
7. Trunfio, M., Lucia, M.D., Campana, S., Magnelli, A.: Innovating the cultural heritage museum service model through virtual reality and augmented reality: The effects on the overall visitor experience and satisfaction. J. Heritage Tourism **17**(1), 1–19 (2022)
8. Lanir, J., Kuflik, T., Sheidin, J., Yavin, N., Leiderman, K., Segal, M.: Visualizing museum visitors' behavior: where do they go and what do they do there? Pers. Ubiquit. Comput. **21**, 313–326 (2017)
9. Centorrino, P., Corbetta, A., Cristiani, E., Onofri, E.: Managing crowded museums: visitors flow measurement, analysis, modeling, and optimization. J. Comput. Sci. **53**, 101357 (2021)
10. Strohmaier, R., Sprung, G., Nischelwitzer, A., Schadenbauer, S.: Using visitor-flow visualization to improve visitor experience in museums and exhibitions. Museums Web, 1–15 (2015)
11. Lanir, J., Bak, P., Kuflik, T.: Visualizing proximity-based spatiotemporal behavior of museum visitors using tangram diagrams. Comput. Graph. Forum **33**, 261–270 (2014)
12. Martella, C., Miraglia, A., Frost, J., Cattani, M., van Steen, M.: Visualizing, clustering, and predicting the behavior of museum visitors. Pervasive Mob. Comput. **38**, 430–443 (2017)

13. Cheng, S.-T., Chen, Y.-J., Horng, G.-J., Wang, C.-H.: Using cellular automata to reduce congestion for tourist navigation systems in mobile environments. Wireless Pers. Commun. **73**, 441–461 (2013)
14. Zhou, S., et al.: Crowd modeling and simulation technologies. ACM Trans. Model. Comput. Simulat. (TOMACS) **20**(4), 1–35 (2010)
15. Hoyet, L., Olivier, A.-H., Kulpa, R., Pettré, J.: Perceptual effect of shoulder motions on crowd animations. ACM Trans. Graph. (TOG) **35**(4), 1–10 (2016)
16. Elena Molina, Alejandro Ríos, and Nuria Pelechano. The impact of animations in the perception of a simulated crowd. In *Advances in Computer Graphics: 38th Computer Graphics International Conference*, pages 25–38. Springer, 2021
17. Güler, K.: Utilizing visitor simulations in exhibition design process: Evaluating designers' perspectives. Journal of Simulation **16**(6), 645–658 (2022)
18. David Walsh, Mark M Hall, Paul Clough, and Jonathan Foster. Characterising online museum users: a study of the national museums liverpool museum website. *International Journal on Digital Libraries*, 21(1):75–87, 2020
19. Kühnapfel, C., et al.: How do we move in front of art? how does this relate to art experience? linking movement, eye tracking, emotion, and evaluations in a gallery-like setting. Empir. Stud. Arts **42**(1), 86–146 (2024)
20. Serrell, B.: Paying attention: the duration and allocation of visitors' time in museum exhibitions. Curator Museum J. **40**, 108–113 (2010)
21. Zıraman, A.T., Imamoğlu, C.: Visitor attention in exhibitions: the impact of exhibit objects' ordinal position, relative size, and proximity to larger objects. Environ. Behav. **52**(4), 343–370 (2020)
22. Bitgood, S., Patterson, D., Benefield, A.: Exhibit design and visitor behavior: Empirical relationships. Environ. Behav. **20**(4), 474–491 (1988)
23. Yoshimura, Y., et al.: An analysis of visitors' behavior in the louvre museum: a study using bluetooth data. Environ. Planning B Planning Design **41**, 1113–1131 (2014)
24. Pluchino, A., Garofalo, C., Inturri, G., Rapisarda, A., Ignaccolo, M.: Agent-based simulation of pedestrian behaviour in closed spaces: a museum case study. J. Artif. Soc. Soc. Simul. **17**(1), 16 (2014)
25. Parmar, D., Olafsson, S., Utami, D., Murali, P., Bickmore, T.: Designing empathic virtual agents: manipulating animation, voice, rendering, and empathy to create persuasive agents. Auton. Agent. Multi-Agent Syst. **36**(1), 17 (2022)
26. Barnert, W.C.: A comparison of one-handed and two-handed direct and indirect computer interaction. Technical report, Tufts University (2005)
27. Owen, R., Kurtenbach, G., Fitzmaurice, G., Baudel, T., Buxton, W.: When it gets more difficult, use both hands - exploring bimanual curve manipulation, pp. 17–24 (2005)
28. Krontiris, A., Bekris, K.E., Kapadia, M.: Acumen: activity-centric crowd authoring using influence maps. In: Proceedings of the 29th International Conference on Computer Animation and Social Agents, pp. 61–69 (2016)
29. Yang, S., Li, T., Gong, X., Peng, B., Jie, H.: A review on crowd simulation and modeling. Graph. Models **111**, 101081 (2020)
30. Brooke, J.: Sus: a quick and dirty usability scale. Usability Eval. Ind. **189**, 11 (1995)
31. Karat, J.: User-centered software evaluation methodologies. In: Handbook Of Human-computer Interaction, pp. 689–704. Elsevier (1997)
32. Verma, R., Gupta, A., Singh, K.: Simulation software evaluation and selection: a comprehensive framework. J. Autom. Syst. Eng. **2**, 221–234 (2008)

33. Gediga, G., Hamborg, K.-C., Düntsch, I.: Evaluation of software systems. Encyclop. Comput. Sci. Technol. **45**, 127–153 (2002)
34. Bouwer, W., Human, F.: The impact of the uncanny valley effect on the perception of animated three-dimensional humanlike characters. Comput. Games J. **6**, 185–203 (2017)

# Foley Agent: Automatic Sound Design and Mixing Agent for Silent Videos Driven by LLMs

Kun Lin and Shiguang Liu[✉]

Tianjin University, Tianjin, China
{linkun,lsg}@tju.edu.cn

**Abstract.** The current movie sound effect dubbing lacks a comprehensive automated solution. We introduce Foley Agent, an automatic movie sound design and mixing agent driven by large language models (LLMs). It processes the movie in three stages: resource collection, sound synchronization, and mixing. First, it comprehends the content of a video clip by querying a Visual LLM and searching for sound effect resources. Subsequently, it adjusts the sound signal to match the motion in the clips. Finally, it mixes the audios based on reasoning. Our approach results in structured and controllable sound with lossless quality, particularly maintaining spatial awareness in multi-channel audio. We provide insights into the capabilities of LLMs for general tasks. To the best of our knowledge, this is the first attempt to use LLMs for film dubbing and mixing.

**Keywords:** Sound · Videos · Agent · Large Language Models

## 1 Introduction

Computer-simulated animations are typically devoid of sound, and games and movies necessitate frequent attention to sound design and mixing. Nevertheless, current AIGC methods often yield subpar, unsynchronized audio quality. The outcomes are amalgamated in a way that prevents human interaction with the models or further editing of the soundtracks.

Incorporating sound effects into videos is a comprehensive task. Initially, a thorough understanding of the clip's content is essential to ensure the relevance of the sound. Secondly, it is crucial to extract the key points of the motion for precise synchronization of the added sound. Once the matching soundtracks are integrated, another challenge arises-mixing the soundtracks to impart artistic effects and maintain correct physical attributes.

Current methods for video sound synthesis primarily include feature fusion [1–3] and feature alignment [4]. Feature fusion methods enable the model to understand video and audio. However, the information in this approach is entirely hidden from the user, making it impossible to intervene dubbing process.

© The Author(s), under exclusive license to Springer Nature Singapore Pte Ltd. 2025
N. Magnenat Thalmann et al. (Eds.): CASA 2024, CCIS 2374, pp. 177–192, 2025.
https://doi.org/10.1007/978-981-96-2681-6_13

On the other hand, feature alignment methods train video and audio encoders through contrastive learning, compared to feature fusion, this method offers greater controllability due to the ease of incorporating control conditions. However, the features are hard to fully aligned, so the generated audio often deviates from the video content. Additionally, methods based on generative models tend to produce artifacts and distortions, resulting in the loss of multi-channel information and highlighting the inefficiency of current methods in utilizing data effectively.

Our work differs from other Foley models in that we consider the frequent interaction requirements with audio tracks during the sound production process. We also address audio storage and computation issues in the Foley process, rather than treating it as an end-to-end procedure. The task is demonstrated in Fig. 1.

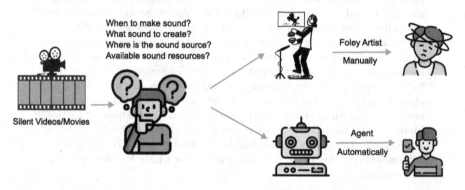

**Fig. 1.** Task of Foley Agent. The task of the Foley Agent is to ease the Foley process.

To achieve this goal, we introduce Foley Agent-an automatic agent for sound design and mixing in videos. The system operates through three key stages: resource collection, sound synchronization, and mixing. Initially, it comprehends the content of a video clip by employing basic visual question-answering models and semantic segmentation models. It then utilizes HTTP requests to search for relevant sound resources. Subsequently, it extracts motion information through a divide-and-conquer strategy, adjusting the signal to synchronize the amplitude with the motion in the clips. Finally, the system mixes the audio based on logical and physical schemes.

Our contributions primarily encompass the following aspects:

- We introduce a comprehensive pipeline for video sound design and mixing, addressing the challenges posed by current methods, including low quality, lack of synchronization, and difficulty in control.
- We delineate the segregation of distinct operations in mixing, substituting the empirical part with physical simulation to enhance the spatial sound effects.
- We design non-data-driven, fast, and efficient video content analysis algorithms combining nearest neighbor algorithms with Euler grid and two-

dimensional divide-and-conquer strategy, as well as difference calculation, enabling adjustable video content analysis.

This paper is structured as follows: The first section introduces the background and motivation of the proposed Foley Agent. Section 2 provides an overview of the related work supporting the Foley Agent. Section 3 outlines the method employed in Foley Agent, covering its working pipeline, the definition, and our novel insights into the mixing task in movie sound production, as well as the design of the Agent. Section 4 presents our results and compares them with existing state-of-the-art methods. Section 5 discusses important conclusions drawn during the development of the Foley Agent. Finally, Sect. 6 addresses the limitations and suggests future work for this endeavor.

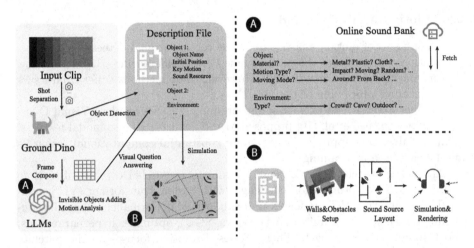

**Fig. 2.** Our framework comprises a primary module based on LLMs, complemented by image recognition and tracking models and algorithms for video analysis. Inputs and outputs of each module are organized through human-readable formatted text files in JSON. Concerning sound generation, based on the tags generated by the video analysis module, HTTP requests are sent to an online remote sound library to gather appropriate audio. Regarding sound mixing, physical mixing is achieved by laying out sound in space for spatial mixing.

## 2    Related Work

### 2.1    Sound Generation for Silent Clips

In the realm of multimedia technology, the focus on adding sound to silent videos has garnered considerable interest. This paper delves into various methodologies within this domain. GAN models [1] and diffusion models [4] have been proposed to generate soundtracks by aligning visual action sequences with audio cues. However, synthesized sounds often suffer from artifacts and homogenization. AutoFoley, developed by Ghose et al., stands as a deep-learning tool for autonomously synthesizing audio tracks for videos [2]. It proves beneficial in scenarios where original audio is absent, albeit its efficacy may vary with the complexity of video content. Su et al.'s physics-driven diffusion model achieves high-quality impact sounds for silent videos, yet its generalization remains limited [5]. Zhou et al.'s hierarchical recurrent neural network framework encodes visual information for sound generation, presenting a comprehensive system that may necessitate extensive training data [6]. Guided by insights from these studies, we posit that directly synthesizing sound with AI may struggle to achieve high quality, thus advocating for an approach leveraging intelligent editing of networked audio resources.

## 2.2 Motion Analysis in Videos

The main focus of motion analysis in videos centers around detecting collisions. Conventional methods for this task include Frame Differencing [7], Optical Flow [8], and Background Subtraction [9]. However, these methods suffer from issues such as shadow processing of the video.

Another approach to extract sound-producing events involves Visual Question Answering. Seo et al. [10] proposed MASN, it utilizes cross-modal features. While reliable, this approach may require substantial computational resources and labeled data for training.

Another approach to extract sound-producing events Is Deep Learning. Xiao et al. [11] address optimization challenges with Vision Transformer (ViT) models. They found that ViT models exhibit suboptimal performance, especially concerning the choice of optimizer (AdamW vs. SGD), optimizer hyperparameters, and training schedule length. Their proposed solution focuses on the patchify stem of ViT models, suggesting improvements to convolutional operations for enhanced performance. However, implementing these enhancements may introduce additional complexity to the model architecture and training process.

## 2.3 Audio Processing

**Automatic Audio Editing.** To make the sound synchornized with the event in videos, the main operation is to translate the signal on the time domain. Otung [12] focuses on a time domain description and analysis of signals and systems. It begins with a discussion of basic signal operations on which are built other more complex signal manipulations in the time domain, e.g. autocorrelation, convolution, etc. Keller [13] introduces the transformation from time-domain to frequency-domain and vice versa. It explains how electrical signals-periodic or nonperiodic-can be measured in the time-domain (e.g., with an oscilloscope) or in the frequency-domain (e.g., with a spectrum analyzer). Kang et al. [14] explain various time-domain analog signal processing techniques with some experimental results. O'shea [15] provides a time domain analysis of continuous time systems.

**Automatic Mixing.** Martínez-Ramírez et al. [16] explore the use of out-of-domain data such as wet or processed multitrack music recordings to train supervised deep learning models for automatic music mixing. De Man et al. [17] reflect on a decade of Automatic Mixing systems for multitrack music processing, positions the topic in the wider field of Intelligent Music Production, and highlights some promising directions for future research. Reiss and Brandtsegg [18] provide a systematic review of cross-adaptive audio effects and their applications, most notably in automatic mixing and as a new form of interaction in collaborative performance.

## 2.4 LLMs-Driven Agents

Wang et al. [19] present a comprehensive survey of studies investigating LLM-based autonomous agents. This work [20] considers a fundamental problem in multi-agent collaboration: consensus seeking. Feldt et al. [21] present a taxonomy of LLM-based testing agents based on their level of autonomy. Hu et al. [22] explore how to enable intelligent cost-effective interactions between the agent and an LLM. Huang et al. [23] propose a multi-modal AI system named AudioGPT, which complements LLMs (i.e., ChatGPT) with foundation models to process complex audio information and solve numerous understanding and generation tasks.

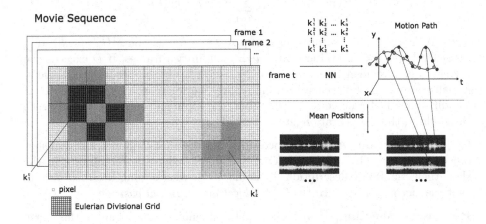

**Fig. 3.** Given the input sequence of video frames, we perform a divide-and-conquer computation of dissimilarity using the Eulerian grid, and then conduct nearest neighbor (NN) search on the dissimilarity between frames to classify them into different categories with continuous positional changes, thereby obtaining the motion path curves of the objects. Subsequently, we use the average position of each category as a visual cue to inquire about the sound corresponding to that position from a language model. During the audio shifting process, we align the peaks of the audio with the extrema of the motion path curves. In this context, $k_j^i$ are the kernels on the grid that have relatively larger difference.

# 3  Method

The pipeline is guided by a JSON description file to ensure that all outputs and inputs align with the text format. This allows them to be easily read and understood by humans, facilitating interaction and providing control, intervention, and modification capabilities.

## 3.1  Pipeline

The pipeline of this work is shown in Fig. 2.

**Preprocess.** It is necessary to check whether the clip is moving smoothly, without any abrupt camera switches, to ensure proper motion analysis. Given a video clip as input, when dealing with a silent video, we first separate different shots using Frame Differencing.

We found that the combination of Mean Absolute Difference (MAD) with a dissimilarity threshold and a minimum inter-frame difference threshold to prevent frequent segmentation of high-frequency flickering scenes can effectively achieve this goal. For each frame $F_i$ of the video, we calculate its MAD $D_i$ with the previous frame $F_{i-1}$ as

$$D(F_i, F_{i-1}) = \frac{1}{N} \sum_{k=1}^{N} |F_1(k) - F_2(k)|, \tag{1}$$

where $N$ represents the total number of pixels in a frame, and $F_i(k)$ and $F_{i-1}(k)$ respectively denote the values of the $i$ th pixel in two frames. If $D$ exceeds the threshold $\theta$, a segmentation site $S = [S_1, S_2, ..., S_n]$ is recorded. After traversing all frames, the difference in frame counts between each site is checked. If the difference in frame counts is less than the minimum inter-frame difference threshold $\gamma$, the segmentation site is deleted.

**Object Detection.** After preprocessing, the pretrained model for zero-shot object detection, Grounding DINO [24] is employed to detect objects in the shot, then the JSON description file is modified, with adding detected objects as items, accompanied with the fields *object name, initial position*.

**Resource Collecting.** Utilizing the API of online sound banks, this stage searches for sound effects on the sound banks through provided APIs. Subsequently, it adds a list field *urls* for each sound object in the JSON description file. To provide more options for the user to choose from, 5 urls are recorded by default in the filed, and user can modify this number in a config file.

**Motion Analysis.** We extract the motion information through Visual Question Answering (VQA), so that the result is human controllable. To achieve this, the video frames are skipped sampled and place on a grid on a single image, then, the grid image is sent to a LLM with a prompt *"Is the object moving in the frames?"* for each object detected. If the answer is *"yes"*, another question is asked: *"On which frames did the object collide with other objects?"*. Te questions are formatted with Langchain [25]. These results will be recorded into the JSON description file, as the fields.

To enhance the alignment accuracy of keypoints obtained from VQA, we introduce a novel disparity computation method known as Eulerian Divisional Disparity for motion detection, as shown in Fig. 3. This approach effectively distinguishes between stationary backgrounds and moving objects. The video frames are partitioned into equidistant Eulerian grids $G = G_{ij} | 1 \leq i \leq m, 1 \leq j \leq n$, where $m$ is the number of rows in the grid and $n$ is the number of columns in the grid. Each $G_{ij}$ represents a specific two-dimensional Euler grid. Similarity calculations are performed for each grid $G_{ij}$ to obtain the total difference within that grid. For example, if $p_{xy}$ represents the pixel point located in row $x$ and column $y$ of the $G_{ij}$ grid, then the total difference $T_{ij}$ of $G_{ij}$ can be calculated as follows:

$$T_{ij} = \sum_{x=1}^{|G_i|} \sum_{y=1}^{|G_j|} D(p_{xy}). \tag{2}$$

wherein, $|G_i|$ and $|G_j|$ represent the number of pixel points in the row and column of the grid $G_{ij}$, respectively, while $D(p_{xy})$ represents the difference degree of the pixel point $p_{xy}$. The accumulated disparities are then sorted, and those with lower values, which likely correspond to stationary backgrounds, are discarded. For the regions with higher disparities, extreme values are computed, and the corresponding time instances are designated as key motion points.

**Signal Shifting.** For each object, when the sound resource are loaded, user can choose to perform a signal shifting or not. In the signal shifting process, the audio is sliced in to individual patches according to the amplitudes. Then, each patch will be assigned to each *key points* with their peaks aligned with the frame number to make them synchronized with the video. If the number of the patches are insufficient, they will be repeated.

**Automatic Mixing.** At the final stage, automatic mixing is performed. This will be discussed at Sect. 3.2.

### 3.2   Automatic Mixing

**Mixing Operations.** Mixing soundtracks involves five key operations that require precision for optimal results: Equalization (EQ), Gain, Dynamic Range Compression (DRC), Panning, and Reverb. Panning and Reverb are adjusted manually based on empirical observation. These operations are pivotal in sound mixing, enhancing the quality and aesthetic appeal of the final audio output.

**Logical and Physical Insights.** To optimize the functionality of the physical components, we categorize these five operations into two parts: the Psychoacoustics part, which encompasses EQ, Gain, and DRC, and the Physical Acoustic

Part, which includes Panning and Reverb. Operations within the Psychoacoustics part will be logically executed by an LLM, while operations in the Physical Acoustic part will be simulated using computational code.

**Question Definition.** With the specification of two distinct requirements for mixing operations, we can now provide the definition of Automatic Mixing in movie sound production.

In the context of a given scenario $\mathcal{C}$, we consider multiple dry audio tracks $\{s_1, s_2, ..., s_n\}$, along with their respective temporal instances $\{t_1, t_2, ..., t_n\}$. Each dry audio track is associated with a parameter set $\mathcal{T}_i = \{g, e, d\}$, encompassing the gain, EQ parameters, and DRC parameters of the audio track, in addition to spatial coordinates $\{p_1, p_2, ..., p_n\}$. The spatial data approximates the given scene $\mathcal{S}$, enabling the positioning of each sound source in space to achieve sound rendering that aligns with the distinctive characteristics of $\mathcal{C}$.

### 3.3   Agent Design

**Components.** The components of our designed agent include LLMs, memory, planning skills, and tool-use capabilities. The language model serves as the cognitive engine, enabling the agent to comprehend and process linguistic inputs. Memory facilitates information retention and retrieval, supporting the agent's learning and adaptive capabilities. Planning skills empower the agent to strategize and execute tasks efficiently, ensuring a coherent and goal-oriented approach. Lastly, the tool-use capabilities equip the agent with the practical skills needed to interact with external tools and resources, augmenting its problem-solving capacities.

**Prompt Design.** Effective interaction with the LLMs requires a well-crafted prompt design. The design of prompts plays a crucial role in guiding the agent's responses and eliciting desired information.

As shown in Fig. 4, while delving into the technology of automatic video mixing, we have proposed a discretized method that utilizes LLMs to analyze the images composed of video frames and extract key information to guide the mixing process. The core concept of this method lies in transforming complex video content into a series of discrete and easily comprehensible queries, enabling language models to efficiently process and return the required information, including planar position, depth information, and motion patterns.

For planar position, we discretize it into three basic levels: left, center, and right. For depth information, we adopt a similar discretization strategy, dividing it into three basic levels: near, medium, and far. Regarding motion patterns, we simplify them into two basic modes: translation and moving around.

## 4   Results

Our framework comprises a client, a remote LLM server, and a remote sound database. Among them, the client operates on Blender [26] version 3.3 along with

You are a versatile agent with the ability to comprehend images, 3D space, objects, and sound. Your capabilities include analyzing and integrating this information into a descriptive file. Additionally, you can utilize APIs to perform tasks such as adding objects, adjusting their positions, inserting keyframes, incorporating sound, and executing various sound-related operations. In your task, you will be provided with:

| A high-resolution representative image of the shot, including the first frame. [Image] | A frame sequence of this shot consolidated into a single image. [Image] |
|---|---|

### Stage 1: Scene Comprehending

In this stage, interpret the representative image as specified by the user:

1. Enumerate objects in the shot, adhering to the [style-name] style, using *add_object(object_name, object_description)*.
2. Identify dynamic objects and introduce potential sounds through *add_sound(object_name, sound_name, sound_description)*.
3. Recognize background elements; if likely to contribute to an ambient sound, use *add_sound(environment, sound_name, sound_description)*.
4. Incorporate additional information from [user option prompts], adding objects and sounds based on user preferences.

### Stage 2: Scene Layout

In this phase, arrange and animate scene objects:

1. Utilize *goto_frame(frame_num)* to navigate to a specific frame.
2. Use *move(object_name, position)* to animate an object, moving it from the current position to a target position.
3. Employ *save_frame()* to preserve the current frame's state.
4. If the given frames are insufficient for analysis, invoke *track()* to acquire additional temporal information.

### Stage 3: Sound Selection

In this phase, match the sound track to the scene and motion:

1. Use *request(tags)* to obtain descriptions, durations, and URLs of sound track resources.
2. Select the most suitable resource; if none is found, utilize *edit_audio()* for deep editing.
3. Call *add_sound()* to integrate the chosen or edited sound track into the scene.

**Fig. 4.** Prompt template. Prompt is the instruction that enables LLMs to exert its planning skill, and it is also the medium for LLMs to read memory and invoke tools. In the design of prompt, we split the tasks of video understanding and object location identification apart, and instruct LLMs to generate useful data step by step, reducing the difficulty of LLMs' understanding tasks and extracting information, and preventing LLMs from generating absurd results at once. In this context, "Memory" refers to the JSON description file. As for "Tools", they refer to the Blender Python API that has a certain level of encapsulation.

the corresponding Blender Python API (bpy) and Python 3.10.6. The remote LLM server includes LLaVa [27], CogVLM [28], Qwen-VL [29] and Minigpt-4 [30]. These are all free demos of visual LLMs, and anyone can easily get started with our framework or replace them with commercial visual LLMs such as GPT-4V [31] to achieve better results. The remote sound database encompasses FreeSound and PixaBay.

**Samples.** As depicted in Fig. 5, our examples are all from open-source animations in Blender Studio, covering 3D realism and 2D cartoon types, as well as different themes such as science fiction and nature. Table 1 shows the name of each example's shots, their themes, duration, complexity, synchronization, spatial characteristics, and other evaluation results.

The participants of subjective evaluation included 7 males and 7 females with an average age of 23. The voting results for LLMs were averaged to evaluate their performance under different amounts of information. Figure 6 shows the subjective evaluation distribution of tags generated by a Shot LLMs. Figure 7 shows the subjective evaluation of spatial audio quality for 6 examples.

LLMs play a pivotal role in this task. To assess their performance, we evaluated the rationality of tag generation, the accuracy of object position identification, and the precision in recognizing object motion patterns and crucial motion judgments using four freely available visual models. The results are presented in Table 3.

**Fig. 5.** Examples. From left to right and from top to bottom, they correspond to the examples named as Machine, Going out, Spray, Dog, Mushroom, and Goat, respectively.

### 4.1   Metrics

#### 4.1.1   Objective Metrics
**Complexity:** Complexity is a metric that measures the difficulty of Foley work required for a scene, ranging from levels 1 to 5. The calculation of complexity is defined as:

$$C = \max(5, \sum_i R_i \cdot \max(1, (k-1))), \tag{3}$$

where $R_i$ is a Boolean value indicating whether the $i^{th}$ sound in the shot needs to be synchronized with motion, (e.g., collision and mechanical arm rotation are

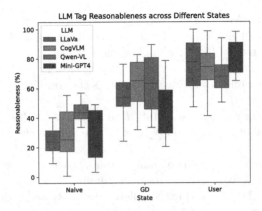

**Fig. 6.** Subjective evaluation of rationality. The corresponding shots and tags generated by LLMs can be referenced in Appendix A, Fig. 1 and Fig. 2.

different types of sound that need to be synchronized), and $k$ represents the number of times a sound is emitted.

**Synchronization:** Determined by calculating the alignment between sound peaks $P = (p_1, p_2, ..., p_n)$ and key points $Q = (q_1, q_2, ..., q_n)$, providing a measure of sound synchronization.

$$S = \|P - Q\|. \tag{4}$$

Objective assessment of **Auditory Masking**: Auditory masking is the reduction of perception of one sound by the presence of another sound, used to evaluate the quality of results for EQ, DRC, and Gain. Given a sound with center frequency $f$, the critical band (bark) of it is

$$Bark(z) = 13 \arctan(\frac{0.00076}{f})$$
$$+3.5 \arctan((\frac{f}{7500})^2). \tag{5}$$

By comparing level of masking sound and target sound on Masking Curve [32], it can be decided whether the signal is masked.

**Loss** of audio results: The discrepancy between the generated audio and the ground truth audio is measured to evaluate the audio quality of the model's output. It is computed as

$$\text{MSE Loss} = \frac{1}{N}\sum_{i=1}^{N}(X_i - Y_i)^2, \tag{6}$$

where $X_i$ and $Y_i$ are the values of the true audio signal and generated audio signal at the $i$th sample point, respectively, and $N$ is the total number of samples. The smaller the value of MSE, the closer the generated audio to the true audio, and the better the quality of the model's audio generation.

### 4.1.2  Subjective Metrics

To obtain the overall rationality of Shot A, based on the average rationality of all the tags generated by LLMs, we follow these steps:

(1). For each tag $a_i$, calculate its rationality $r_i$: $r_i = \frac{v_i}{t_i}$ where $v_i$ is the number of votes for "1" (reasonable) for tag $a_i$, and $t_i$ is the total number of votes (both "1" and "0") for tag $a_i$.

(2). Calculate the average rationality $R$ of all the tags: $R = \frac{1}{n} \sum_{i=1}^{n} r_i$, where $n$ is the total number of tags, and $\sum_{i=1}^{n} r_i$ is the sum of the rationalities of all the tags.

The final result is a single rationality value $R$, which represents the overall rationality of Shot A based on all its tags generated by LLMs. This value will range from 0 to 1, where 1 indicates complete rationality and 0 indicates complete irrationality. You can use this value to assess the overall rationality of the tags generated by LLMs for Shot A.

Similarly, we conducted a questionnaire survey on the quality of spatial hearing of sound $G$, which was divided into 5 levels according to the sense of space from bad to good. Finally, the spatial hearing of a certain example was obtained by calculating the average value.

**Table 1.** Results of our work, where the numbers 1–6 in Example correspond to the segments in the order of the demo, and each name in Movie only identifies the first word. Each example is composed of 2–4 shots. For synchronization, the smaller the value, the better the synchronization. For MSE loss, the smaller the value, the smaller the gap with the ground truth. Masking is a boolean value.

| number | movie | duration | complexity | synchronization | masking | MSE Loss |
|---|---|---|---|---|---|---|
| Machine | Charge | 11 s | 3 | 24 | No | 0.005 |
| Going Out | Charge | 7 s | 3 | 43 | No | 0.062 |
| Spray | Charge | 5 s | 2 | 23 | No | 0.003 |
| Dog | Spring | 9 s | 3 | 17 | No | 0.003 |
| Mushroom | Cosmos | 12 s | 3 | 33 | Yes | 0.001 |
| Goat | Sprite | 7 s | 2 | 12 | No | 0.013 |

**Table 2.** Shot length distribution. In terms of the distribution of shots with different durations in the example, we were surprised to find that most shots only lasted for 0 to 2 s. As for longer shots, they seemed to be able to reduce complexity through segmentation.

| Movie | 0–2 | 2–4 | 4–6 | 6–8 |
|---|---|---|---|---|
| Charge | 64% | 14% | 18% | 4% |
| Spring | 28% | 32% | 18% | 11% |
| Cosmos | 31% | 33% | 14% | 3% |
| Sprite | 43% | 29% | 17% | 0% |

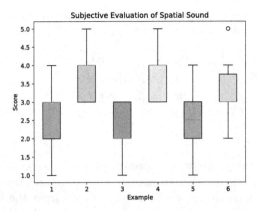

**Fig. 7.** Subjective evaluation of spatial sound.

**Table 3.** Statistics on tag rationality generated by the language model. Naive: Without additional user prompts nor object detection information provided by Ground Dino [24]; GD: With Ground Dino; User: with user prompt.

| Model | Naive | GD | User |
|---|---|---|---|
| LLaVa [27] | 44% | 63% | 78% |
| CogVLM [28] | 38% | 65% | 78% |
| Qwen-VL [29] | 63% | 76% | 78% |
| Minigpt-4 [30] | 23% | 27% | 75% |

## 4.2  Comparison

In comparison with existing methods, we conducted a qualitative assessment, as presented in Table 4, demonstrating that our approach exhibits stronger controllability, ability to handle complex scenes, high audio quality, and multi-track spatial characteristics, among other advantages, when compared to existing methods.

Comparison with Baseline. The current state of the art in visual-to-sound generation is Diff Foley [4]. We use this model as the baseline. We input our examples into the pre-trained Diff Foley model, using the CAVP checkpoint publicly available at 66 epochs and the IDM checkpoint publicly available at 240 epochs. We found that the results produced by Diff Foley exhibit significant noise, audio artifacts, and homogenization, and it lacks control over the generated style. Additionally, Diff Foley is unable to handle complex situations involving multiple sound sources, whereas our method does not encounter these issues. This indicates that our method outperforms the current state-of-the-art model in several key aspects.

**Table 4.** Comparison across existing methods. A: Synchronization, B: Complex Scene; C: Spatial Characteristic; D: Diverse Scene.

| Method | A | B | C | D |
|---|---|---|---|---|
| FoleyGAN [1] | ✓ | ✗ | ✗ | ✓ |
| Physics [5] | ✓ | ✗ | ✗ | ✗ |
| Ours | ✓ | ✓ | ✓ | ✓ |

The experimental results will be presented in the accompanied demo video. We have presented our results in a manner that compares them favorably with the professional sound design and mixing outputs from the Ground Truth – Blender Studio team. Our results demonstrate a remarkable similarity to the standards set by professional sound design and mixing, indicating a level of proficiency that rivals industry-leading standards. It is recommended to use headphones while viewing.

## 5    Conclusion

This work investigates and implements an automated pipeline for movie sound production, defining the problem of film mixing. It designs an agent driven by a LLMs to address the mixing issues in movies from both logical and physical perspectives. The proposed agent demonstrates the capability to handle sound matching and mixing challenges in complex cinematic scenes, yielding satisfactory results.

During this process, we have derived two critical conclusions: (1) The mixing operations in filmmaking can be divided into two components - psychoacoustic and acoustic - which can be addressed using logical and physical methods, respectively. (2) The description file aligns various modalities, including visual, auditory, textual, and temporal aspects, to text, serving as an effective means for collaborative problem-solving among humans, LLMs, and machine code.

Furthermore, we made several unexpected findings: (1) The majority of film shots are quite short, averaging around 2 to 3 s in duration; (2) According to our evaluation method, the complexity of most shots does not exceed 3, indicating they contain 2 or fewer sound elements requiring synchronization with motion; (3) Additionally, we were surprised to discover that in most cases, placing the sound directly at the start of the shot (frame 0) resulted in correct synchronization. (4) In the statistics of complexity, we found that the most frequent sound in the film lens is collision sound, followed by footsteps, and finally special effects sound, such as spray, mechanical arm and other special effects.

## 6    Limitations and Future Work

The limitations of this study are as follows: (1). The accuracy of the process and methods employed in video motion analysis may be subject to inaccuracies; (2).

The method of selecting audio from online audio websites by the model can be improved. The current method only searches through a single tag for each sound event, which can be changed to searching through descriptions, etc., to reduce the monotony of audio; (3). In sound matching, audio resources are obtained from online repositories. While these sound repositories are considered to have ample sound assets, they cannot guarantee full satisfaction of the requirements for film sound production.

Future work in terms of sound synchronization could focus on enhancing the accuracy of video motion analysis and improving the model's ability to handle complex scenes. Additionally, there is potential to generate synchronized sounds with matching tonal characteristics to video motion based on examples.

**Acknowledgements.** The author would like to express gratitude to the anonymous reviewers for their insightful comments. This paper was supported by National Natural Science Foundation of China under Grant no. 62072328. Special thanks are also extended to Blender Studio for their open movies, which provided invaluable visual resources and inspiration. Additionally, the author is thankful for the sound resources made available by Free Sound, which significantly enhanced the auditory aspects of this project.

# References

1. Ghose, S., Prevost, J.J.: FoleyGAN: visually guided generative adversarial network-based synchronous sound generation in silent videos. IEEE Trans. Multimedia **25**, 4508–4519 (2022)
2. Ghose, S., Prevost, J.J.: Autofoley: artificial synthesis of synchronized sound tracks for silent videos with deep learning. IEEE Trans. Multimedia **23**, 1895–1907 (2020)
3. Guo, Z., et al.: Audio generation with multiple conditional diffusion model (2023)
4. Luo, S., Yan, C., Chenxu, H., Zhao, H.: Synchronized video-to-audio synthesis with latent diffusion models, Diff-foley (2023)
5. Su, K., Qian, K., Shlizerman, E., Torralba, A., Gan, C.: Physics-driven diffusion models for impact sound synthesis from videos. In: Proceedings of the IEEE/CVF Conference on Computer Vision and Pattern Recognition, pp. 9749–9759 (2023)
6. Zhou, Y., Wang, Z., Fang, C., Bui, T., Berg, T.L.: Visual to sound: generating natural sound for videos in the wild. In: Proceedings of the IEEE Conference on Computer Vision and Pattern Recognition, pp. 3550–3558 (2018)
7. Singla, N.: Motion detection based on frame difference method. Inter. J. Inform. Comput. Technol. **4**(15), 1559–1565 (2014)
8. Beauchemin, S.S., Barron, J.L.: The computation of optical flow. ACM Comput. Surv. (CSUR) **27**(3), 433–466 (1995)
9. Piccardi, M.: Background subtraction techniques: a review. In: 2004 IEEE International Conference on Systems, Man and Cybernetics, vol. 4, pp. 3099–3104. IEEE (2004)
10. Seo, A., Kang, G.-C., Park, J., Zhang, B.-T.: Attend what you need: Motion-appearance synergistic networks for video question answering. arXiv preprint arXiv:2106.10446 (2021)

11. Xu, D., et al.: Video question answering via gradually refined attention over appearance and motion. In: Proceedings of the 25th ACM international conference on Multimedia, pp. 1645–1653 (2017)
12. Otung, I.: Time Domain Analysis of Signals and Systems, pp. 127–201. Wiley Telecom (2021)
13. Keller, R.B.: Time-Domain and Frequency-Domain, pp. 41–48. Springer International Publishing, Cham (2023)
14. Kang, J.-G., Kim, K., Yoo, C.: Time-domain analog signal processing techniques. J. Semiconductor Eng. 1(2), 64–73 (2020)
15. O'shea, R.: An improved frequency time domain stability criterion for autonomous continuous systems. IEEE Trans. Autom. Control 12(6), 725–731 (1967)
16. Martínez-Ramírez, M.A., Liao, W.-H., Fabbro, G., Uhlich, S., Nagashima, C., Mitsufuji, Y.: Automatic music mixing with deep learning and out-of-domain data. arXiv preprint arXiv:2208.11428 (2022)
17. De Man, B., Reiss, J., Stables, R.: Ten years of automatic mixing. In: The 3rd Workshop on Intelligent Music Production (WIMP) (2017)
18. Reiss, J.D., Brandtsegg, O.: Applications of cross-adaptive audio effects: automatic mixing, live performance and everything in between. Front. Digital Human. 5, 17 (2018)
19. Wang, L., et al.: A survey on large language model based autonomous agents. arXiv preprint arXiv:2308.11432 (2023)
20. Chen, H., Ji, W., Xu, L., Zhao, S.: Multi-agent consensus seeking via large language models. arXiv preprint arXiv:2310.20151 (2023)
21. Feldt, R., Kang, S., Yoon, J., Yoo, S.: Towards autonomous testing agents via conversational large language models. arXiv preprint arXiv:2306.05152 (2023)
22. Hu, B., et al.: Enabling intelligent interactions between an agent and an LLM: A reinforcement learning approach. arXiv preprint arXiv:2306.03604v2 (2023)
23. Huang, R., et al.: AudioGPT: Understanding and generating speech, music, sound, and talking head. arXiv preprint arXiv:2304.12995 (2023)
24. Liu, S., et al.: Grounding dino: Marrying dino with grounded pre-training for open-set object detection. arXiv preprint arXiv:2303.05499 (2023)
25. Topsakal, O., Akinci, T.C.: Creating large language model applications utilizing langchain: A primer on developing LLM apps fast. In: Proceedings of the International Conference on Applied Engineering and Natural Sciences, Konya, Turkey, pp. 10–12 (2023)
26. van Gumster, J.: Blender For Dummies. For Dummies, 3rd edition (2015)
27. Liu, H., Li, C., Wu, Q., Lee, Y.J.: Visual instruction tuning (2023)
28. Wang, W., et al.: Cogvlm: Visual expert for pretrained language models. arXiv preprint arXiv:2311.03079 (2023)
29. Bai, J., et al.: Qwen-vl: A frontier large vision-language model with versatile abilities. arXiv preprint arXiv:2308.12966 (2023)
30. Zhu, D., Chen, J., Shen, Z., Li, X., Elhoseiny, M.: Minigpt-4: enhancing vision-language understanding with advanced large language models. arXiv preprint arXiv:2304.10592 (2023)
31. Yang, Z., et al.: The dawn of LLMs: Preliminary explorations with GPT-4V (ision), vol. 9(1), p. 1. arXiv preprint arXiv:2309.17421 (2023)
32. Zwicker, E., Fastl, H.: Psychoacoustics: Facts and models, vol. 22. Springer Science & Business Media (2013)

# Deep Metric Learning with Feature Aggregation for Generalizable Person Re-identification

Mingfu Xiong[1], Yang Xu[1], Xiangguo Huang[2]([✉]), Yi Wen[3], Tao Peng[1], and Xinrong Hu[1]

[1] School of Computer and Artificial Intelligence, Wuhan Textile University, Wuhan, China
xmf2013@whu.edu.cn, {pt,hxr}@wtu.edu.cn
[2] Hubei Technology Exchange, Wuhan, China
huangxiangguo@51kehui.com
[3] Department of Information and Technology, Hubei Branch of PICC Property and Casualty Company Limited, Wuhan, China
wenyi06@hub.picc.com.cn

**Abstract.** Person re-identification (ReID) methods based on metric learning can adaptively learn metric matrixs with small sets to further improve the retrieval accuracy of existing models. However, inputs of metric learning are often single-scale discriminative features from deep networks via forward propagation in existing metric learning, which cannot adapt to varies poses and scales. To alleviate above issue, we proposes a metric learning method based on deep aggregate feature representation. Especially, we designs a hierarchical feature extraction module (HFE) that employs multiple large kernel convolutions to enhance the discriminative ability of features. Furthermore, an adaptive feature aggregation module (AFA) is proposed, which can utilize the complementary information of features at different layers more effectively and improve the robustness of feature representation. Experiments on four public datasets demonstrate that the proposed method can significantly improve the generalization performance of existing models.

**Keywords:** Person ReID · Hierarchical Feature · Feature Aggregation · Generalizable

## 1 Introduction

Due to the needs of surveillance video applications, generalizable person ReID for pedestrian matching across cameras has undergone significant advancement [1]. Nonetheless, due to the uncontrollability of surveillance scenes and the movement of pedestrians relative to cameras result in person images captured are varies poses and scales, which still poses a huge challenge for retrieval. Recently, most person ReID methods [1–3] have focused on enhancing feature discriminative representation by designing complex networks, which require large training samples and inevitably reduce the computational efficiency of models. Person ReID methods based on metric learning can adaptive learn a metric matrix to improve the ReID performance quickly with small sets, which has received more and more attention [4]. In this paper, we focus on learning a person ReID model to enhance cross-domain generalization capability using labeled data from the source domain.

To improve the generalization capability of models, many metric strategies are proposed to focus on enhancing the discriminative ability of feature representation [5, 6]. In [7], the pair loss is proposed to the relationship between different samples. In [8], the triple loss is proposed to constrain both the positive and negative relations in triple sample at the same time. Recently, it has been recognized that pairwise deep metric learning among small batch samples is critical [4], and they employ graph sampling to shift hard example mining by randomly choosing a class as an anchor. However, random choosing strategy is insufficient to represent a class identity for distance analysis between classes. Because the input features of this method are single-scale and cannot be adapted to the different poses and scales of captured persons.

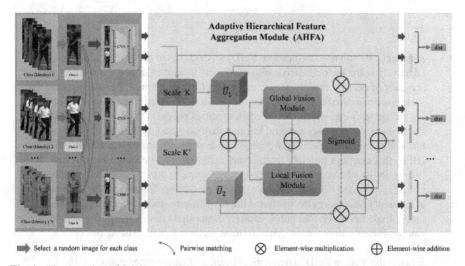

**Fig. 1.** The overview of QAConv-AHFA. We integrate our AHFA module during the paired image-matching phase of QAConv-GS. This inclusion aims to provide additional contextual information, thereby enhancing the accuracy of subsequent similarity calculations.

In order to alleviate this issue, we design a HFE module to achieve rich identity features. Motivated by [9], we introduce multiple large kernel convolutions to enhance the discriminative ability of features representation. Further-more, an AFA module that can adaptively fuse hierarchical features effectively to improve the robustness of feature representation. In details, this involves fusing features from multiple receptive fields to provide more contextual information and enhance the discriminative ability of feature representation. And we design a local and global attention fusion module to address context aggregation to improve the discriminative ability of a single data point. It ensures that the structure of graph relationship obtained through graph sampling is more accurate, which improves the discriminative and generalization ability of models.

In summary, the main contributions can be summarized as follows:

- We propose a deep metric learning method based on deep aggregate feature to improve the accuracy of the structure of graph relationship.
- This work presents a module, namely, HFE, which is used to enhance the discriminative ability of feature representation, and proposes an AFA module to improve the robustness of feature representation. Combining the two modules together, we refer to it as the Adaptive Hierarchical Feature Aggregation Module (AHFA).
- We've significantly improved the latest baseline for Person ReID. By training a single dataset on multiple datasets, the proposed method improves the Rank-1 accuracy and mAP on the three test sets of CUHK03, Market-1501 and MSMT17.

## 2   Related Work

Over the past few years, researchers in person ReID have made notable progress by incorporating key techniques such as Multi-Scale Receptive Field and Attention Mechanism. Cheng et al. innovatively proposed an approach for person ReID by introducing a convolutional neural network (CNN) based on multi-channel parts and an improved triplet loss function [10]. Fan et al. presented SphereReID, a deep spherical manifold embedding method for person ReID [11]. Fu et al. proposed a Horizontal Pyramid Matching method to enhance person ReID performance [12]. Furthermore, Zhang et al. presented an approach for learning discriminative spaces by introducing a multi-channel attention mechanism [13]. By modeling multi-scale features and key regions, these research contributions have brought valuable innovations and improvements to the person ReID task.

Recently, research in person ReID have prominently focused on achieving generalizability, leading to theemergence of effective methodologies. Song et al. presented a meta-learning-based domain-invariant mapping network [1]. Jia et al. applied instance and feature normalization to alleviate stylistic and content differences across datasets [14]. Zhou et al. introduced OSNet, a novel backbone network with notable advantages in generalizing deep models [2]. Jin et al. introducing a module for style normalization and restitution, exhibiting commendable generalization performance [3]. Yuan et al. concentrated on explicitly learning to disentangle identity-related features from challenging variations [15]. Zhuang et al. introduced a camera-based batch normalization (CBN) approach for learning domain-invariant representations [16]. Meta-learning methods have proven effective in acquiring models with generalization capabilities [17]. These methods use different metric learning techniques to design loss functions and deep feature matching schemes, which not only emphasize the importance of generalization performance but also significantly promote the development of the field of person ReID. They offer valuable insights for overcoming challenges associated with diverse feature scales, enhancing model generalization, and improving real-world application performance.

## 3   Methods

### 3.1   The Proposed Network Architecture

As shown in Fig. 1, building upon the concepts of QAConv-GS [4], at the start of each epoch, a representative image is randomly selected for each class. Pairwise computations are then performed by randomly choosing images, treating the matching similarity between images as the similarity between classes. Subsequently, a nearest-neighbor relationship graph is formed based on the similarity of images. However, using images instead of classes for similarity computation poses a challenge, as it may lead to weak representativeness, resulting in in- accuracies in the final relationship graph and a decrease in the model's generalization performance. To address the issue of insufficient representativeness when using images to compute similarity, we introduce the AHFA (Adaptive Hierarchical Feature Aggregation) module before conducting pairwise matching. This forms the basis of our designed QAConv-AHFA network framework, which more effectively leverages complementary information from various layers. This enhancement aims to improve the robustness of feature representation, leading to a more accurate relationship graph between classes. Ultimately, this contributes to an improvement in the overall generalization performance of the model. QAConv-AHFA is a repeating block in the backbone network, inspired by AFF [18] and LSKNet [9]. Each AHFA consists of two modules: the HFE sub-block and the AFA sub-block.

The HFE sub-block is introduced to enhance the discriminative ability of features by utilizing multiple large kernel convolutions. The AFA sub-block combines features from different receptive fields through the fusion of global and local feature attention mechanisms. After applying the sigmoid activation function, the output values range from 0 to 1. Weighted averaging is then applied to the initial features from the HFE submodule. This involves using 1 minus the obtained fusion weight as a mechanism for soft selection. Through training, the network determines the respective weights. Subsequently, the features pass through a fully connected layer, followed by a deep convolution, and then a residual module to obtain the final enhanced features, as illustrated in Fig. 2.

## 3.2  Hierarchical Feature Extraction

During each epoch when constructing the graph relation network, randomly sample one image from each class. Due to the limited number of pedestrian images, the information provided by the convolution operation is relatively scarce. Therefore, the information obtained from pedestrian feature extraction is particularly important. The traditional small-core fully connected layer has a limited sensing range and is difficult to capture global information, resulting in information loss and insensitivity to spatial changes. To overcome this problem, we designed the HFE module, which uses multiple large kernel convolutions to expand the receptive field of features to enhance the discriminative ability of features, bringing double advantages to pedestrian feature similarity comparisons.

Firstly, a larger receptive field enables the model to comprehensively understand the relationship between pedestrians and their surrounding environment, providing more contextual information and enhancing the global representation capability of features. Secondly, by enlarging the receptive field, the model can cover features of different scales, effectively handling details and overall structures in pedestrian images, thereby improving the diversity and richness of features. This comprehensive effect is expected to enhance the model's performance in pedestrian feature similarity comparison tasks, making it more adaptable to complex scenes and diverse pedestrian features. Therefore, we construct a larger kernel convolution by explicitly decomposing it into a sequence of convolutions with a large growing kernel and increased dilation. Specifically, the enlargement of the kernel size k dilation rate d, and the receptive field RF of the i − th depth-wise convolution in the series are defined as follows:

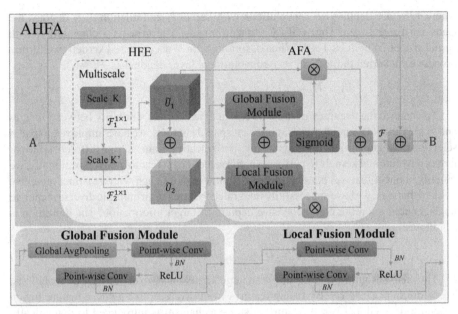

**Fig. 2.** Conceptual Explanation of the AHFA Module: The AHFA module is composed of two key components, namely the HFE module and the AFA module. The use of '⊕' denotes element-wise addition, and '⊗' signifies element-wise multiplication.

$$d_{i-1} < d_i \leq RF_{i-1}$$
$$RF_i = d_i(k_i - 1) + RF_{i-1} \tag{1}$$

where $k_{i-1} \leq k_i$, $d_1 = 1$ and $RF_1 = k_1$. By increasing the kernel size k and dilation rate d, we can rapidly expand the receptive field RF. Based on the determination of experimental parameters, the HFE module decomposes a large kernel into two depth-wise convolutions. This is elaborated solely within the specific implementation details of the experiment module. Such a design simplifies the selection of kernels because we can choose different receptive field sizes as needed without relying on a single fixed-size kernel. Simultaneously, by generating multiple features with distinct receptive fields, we enhance the model's ability to represent multiscale information. Additionally, we adopt a strategy of sequential decomposition, which is more efficient than simply applying a larger kernel.

By decomposing a large kernel into multiple smaller depth-wise convolutions, we reduce computational complexity and enhance the network's nonlinear representation capability. This decomposition method maintains the receptive field range while reducing computational costs and the number of parameters. To capture rich contextual information from different ranges for input $A \in R^{2C \times H \times W}$, a series of decomposed depth-wise convolutions with distinct receptive fields is defined as follows:

$$U_0 = \gamma(Conv_{1\times1}(A)), U_{i+1} = \mathcal{F}_i^{dw}(U_i),\tag{2}$$

where $\mathcal{F}_i^{dw}(\cdot)$ are depth-wise convolutions with kernel $k_i$ and dilation $d_i$, $\gamma$ denotes the Gaussian Error Linear Unit (GELU), and $Conv_{1\times1}(\cdot)$ represents a convolution with kernel size of $2C \times 2C \times 1 \times 1$. When designing with $N$ decomposed kernels, we further process each kernel through a $1 \times 1$ convolutional layer denoted as $\mathcal{F}^{1\times1}(\cdot)$.

$$\tilde{U}_i = \mathcal{F}_i^{1\times1}(U_i), i \in \{1, 2, \cdots, N\},\tag{3}$$

To enhance the accuracy of the network in assessing the similarity between images and to improve its focus on the most relevant spatial contexts, we have employed a spatial selection mechanism. This mechanism involves selecting features from different scales of large convolutional kernels to perform spatial selection on feature maps. Specifically, we initially connect features obtained from different kernels, each with a distinct receptive field. In this way, we have successfully integrated features from multiple diverse receptive fields, enabling a more comprehensive capture of target information. The definition is as follows:

$$\tilde{U} = \tilde{U}_1 + \tilde{U}_2 + \cdots + \tilde{U}_i.\tag{4}$$

The AHFA framework decomposes a large kernel into two depth-wise convolutions. Therefore, $\tilde{U} = \tilde{U}_1 + \tilde{U}_2$. By fusing features from two receptive fields, a feature fusion is achieved. A Global-Local Feature Fusion mechanism is introduced to dynamically select features from multiple scales, facilitating attentional feature fusion with different target-aware kernel selections.

### 3.3 Adaptive Feature Aggregation

Feature fusion is a ubiquitous operation in deep learning networks, usually implemented through simple linear summation or concatenation. However, these common operations may lead to information loss, limit the model's ability to model complex relationships, and are not suitable for specific tasks when performing multi-layer feature fusion. In order to overcome the above difficulties, we designed the AFA module to use attention feature fusion to more effectively utilize the complementary information of each layer of features and improve the robustness of feature representation. The specific implementation is as follows: from the Receptive Field Fusion, we obtain intermediate features $\tilde{U} \in R^{C\times H\times W}$, where C represents the number of channels, and the size of the feature map is H $\times$ W. The global average pooling (GAP) $g(\tilde{U})$ can be computed as follows:

$$g(\tilde{U}) = \frac{1}{H \times W}\sum_{i=1}^{H}\sum_{j=1}^{W}\tilde{U}_{[:,i,j]},\tag{5}$$

To enhance our model's effectiveness in comprehending the complex information of the Multi-Scale Receptive Field Fusion Feature and thereby improve its accuracy in distance measurement during pairwise matching, we introduce the global feature context $g(\tilde{U})$, defined as follows:

$$g(\tilde{U}) = \mathcal{B}(D_2\delta(\mathcal{B}(D_1(g(\tilde{U}))))),\tag{6}$$

where $\delta$ denotes the Rectified Linear Unit (ReLU), and $\mathcal{B}$ signifies Batch Normalization. This process is achieved through a bottleneck structure consisting of two fully connected layers. Specifically, $D_1 \in R^{\frac{C}{r} \times C}$ serves as the dimension reduction layer, while $D_2 \in R^{C \times \frac{C}{r}}$ functions as the dimension increasing layer. The variable r represents the channel reduction ratio.

We have noticed that the global feature attention compresses each feature map of size $H \times W$ into a scalar. This extremely coarse handling may lead to the loss of crucial image information, especially considering that every pixel's information is essential when dealing with individual pedestrian images. Therefore, the internal attention within the module should be more focused, integrating multi-scale feature context to flexibly adapt to scale variations and improve the accuracy of distance calculations for matching features in single pedestrian images. Hence, we introduce the local channel context $l(\tilde{U})$ defined as follows:

$$l(\tilde{U}) = B(PwC_2(\delta(B(PwC_1(\tilde{U}))))), \tag{7}$$

the kernel sizes for $PwC_1$ and $PwC_2$ are $\frac{C}{r} \times C \times 1 \times 1$ and $C \times \frac{C}{r} \times 1 \times 1$, respectively. It's worth noting that $l(\tilde{U})$ has the same shape as the input feature, preserving and highlighting subtle details in low-level features.

Based on the aforementioned the global feature context $g(\tilde{U})$ and the local feature context $l(\tilde{U})$, we fuse the two to achieve a balance between global and local feature information. This aims to enable the model to achieve optimal performance in understanding both global structure and local details. We define the balanced weights $w(\tilde{U})$ as follows:

$$w(\tilde{U}) = \sigma(g(\tilde{U}) + l(\tilde{U})), \tag{8}$$

where $\sigma$ is the Sigmoid function. With the balanced weights obtained, we perform attention feature fusion, which can be expressed as follows:

$$\tilde{U}' = w(\tilde{U}) \otimes \tilde{U}_1 + (1 - w(\tilde{U})) \otimes \tilde{U}_2, \tag{9}$$

where $\tilde{U}' \in R^{C \times H \times W}$ is the fused feature, As shown in Fig. 2, the dashed line represents $(1 - w(\tilde{U}))$. It is important to note that the fusion weights $w(\tilde{U})$ and $(1 - w(\tilde{U}))$ consist of real numbers between 0 and 1. This allows the network to perform a soft selection or weighted average between $\tilde{U}_1$ and $\tilde{U}_2$.

Then, at the end of the module, we designed a residual network to accelerate network training while mitigating the impact of gradient explosions on the final performance. This operation can be expressed as follows:

$$B = F_{1 \times 1}(Conv_{1 \times 1}(\tilde{U}')) + A, \tag{10}$$

where $B \in R^{2C \times H \times W}$ represents the final output of the AHFA module, $Conv_{1 \times 1}(\cdot)$ represents the dimension increasing operation, and $\mathcal{F}_{1 \times 1}$ involves a linear transformation through a $1 \times 1$ convolution in the channel dimension, facilitating subsequent operations on the final output.

## 3.4 The Optimization and Loss Functions

We computed similarity values between image pairs using QAConv [20] and processed them in mini-batches with the GS sampler in QAConv-GS [4]. To address the ranking learning problem, we adopted a triplet-based approach and utilized the batch OHEM triplet loss function [8]. This loss function is designed to optimize the metric learning process, thereby improving the model's performance on the task. The definition of this loss function is as follows:

$$l(\delta; X) = \sum_{i=1}^{P} \sum_{a=1}^{K} [m - \min_{p=1...K} s(f_\delta(x_i^a), f_\delta(x_i^p))$$
$$+ \max_{\substack{j=1...P \\ j \neq i \\ n=1...K}} s(f_\delta(x_i^a), f_\delta(x_j^n))]_+ \tag{11}$$

where each mini-batch, $X = \{x_i^a, i \in [1, P], a \in [1, K]\}$ contains P classes and $K$ images per class that are randomly sampled, $\delta$ represents the network parameters, $f_\delta$ denotes the feature extractor, $s(\cdot, \cdot)$ represents similarity, and $m$ indicates the margin. $[\varphi]_+$ is max($\varphi$, 0), following most methods.

**Table 1.** Comparison with the Latest Methods on the CUHK03, Market-1501, DukeMTMC-reID, and MSMT17 dataset. MSMT17 (all) indicates that all images are used for training. The gray cells represent within-dataset evaluations for reference." -" denotes data not reported or not applicable

| Method | Venue | Training | CUHK03-NP | | Market-1501 | | MSMT17 | |
|---|---|---|---|---|---|---|---|---|
| | | | Rank-1 | mAP | Rank-1 | mAP | Rank-1 | mAP |
| M³L [17] | CVPR'21 | Multi | 33.1 | 32.1 | 75.9 | 50.2 | 36.9 | 14.7 |
| MuDeep [19] | TPAMI'20 | Market-1501 | 10.3 | 9.1 | 95.3 | 84.7 | – | – |
| QAConv [20] | ECCV'20 | Market-1501 | 9.9 | 8.6 | – | – | 22.6 | 7.0 |
| OSNet-AIN [21] | TPAMI'21 | Market-1501 | – | – | 94.2 | 84.4 | 23.5 | 8.2 |
| CBN [16] | ECCV'20 | Market-1501 | – | – | 91.3 | 77.3 | 25.3 | 9.5 |
| QAConv-GS [4] | CVPR'22 | Market-1501 | 19.1 | 18.1 | 91.6 | 75.5 | 45.9 | 17.2 |
| QAConv-AHFA | Ours | Market-1501 | **21.6** | **20.7** | 92.3 | 77.4 | **46.0** | **17.7** |
| ADIN [15] | WACV'20 | MSMT17 | – | – | 59.1 | 30.3 | – | – |
| SNR [3] | CVPR'20 | MSMT17 | – | – | 70.1 | 41.4 | – | – |
| CBN [16] | ECCV'20 | MSMT17 | – | – | 73.7 | 45.0 | 72.8 | 42.9 |
| QAConv-GS [4] | CVPR'22 | MSMT17 | 20.9 | 20.6 | 79.1 | 49.5 | 79.2 | 50.9 |
| QAConv-AHFA | Ours | MSMT17 | **24.1** | **23.2** | **80.6** | **51.9** | 80.6 | 54.2 |
| OSNet-AIN [21] | TPAMI'21 | MSMT17 (all) | – | – | 70.1 | 43.3 | – | – |
| QAConv [20] | ECCV'20 | MSMT17 (all) | 25.3 | 22.6 | 72.6 | 43.1 | – | – |
| QAConv-GS [4] | CVPR'22 | MSMT17 (all) | 27.6 | 28.0 | 82.4 | 56.9 | – | – |
| QAConv-AHFA | Ours | MSMT17 (all) | **31.8** | **30.8** | **84.1** | **60.0** | – | – |
| RP Baseline [22] | ACMMM'20 | RandPerson | 13.4 | 10.8 | 55.6 | 28.8 | 20.1 | 6.3 |
| CBN [16] | ECCV'20 | RandPerson | – | – | 64.7 | 39.3 | 20.0 | 6.8 |
| QAConv-GS [4] | CVPR'22 | RandPerson | 18.4 | 16.1 | **76.7** | 46.7 | **45.1** | 15.5 |
| QAConv-AHFA | Ours | RandPerson | **18.6** | **17.2** | 76.1 | **47.1** | 44.2 | **15.5** |

# 4 Experiments

## 4.1 Implementation Details

We employ ResNet-50 [23] used as the backbone, incorporating IBN-b layers, following recent studies. The output of the third layer feature maps is utilized, and the final feature maps include a neck convolution of 128 channels. Input images are resized to $384 \times 128$ pixels. Standard data augmentation techniques are employed, including random cropping, flipping, occlusion [20], and color jittering. A batch size of 64 is used during training. We utilize the SGD optimizer, setting the learning rate to 0.0005 for the backbone and 0.005 for newly added layers. Training is conducted for a maximum of 60 epochs. After reducing the initial loss by a factor of 0.7, the learning rates decay by 0.1. Early stopping is triggered after an additional half of the already completed epochs. Gradient clipping is set at $T = 8$. PyTorch's Automatic Mixed Precision (AMP) is employed to accelerate training. The model utilizes the hard triplet loss [8], with a margin m of 16, and the number of instances per class in a batch $K$ is set to 2. The overall receptive field $RF$ for all convolution kernels is set to 23, and the expansion of the kernel size $k$ and dilation rate $d$ for these two depth-wise convolutions is configured as (5, 1) and (7, 3), and the channel reduction ratio $r = 4$.

## 4.2 Datasets

Our experiments make use of four prominent large-scale person ReID datasets: CUHK03 [24], Market-1501 [25], MSMT17 [26], and RandPerson [22], which align with the dataset selection in the original work. The CUHK03 dataset comprises 1,360 persons in its challenging "detected" subset, following the CUHK03-NP [27] protocol. Market-1501 consists of 32,668 images featuring 1,501 identities, with training and test subsets of 12,936 and 19,732 images, respectively. MSMT17 includes 4,101 identities and 126,441 images, divided into training and test sets. The RandPerson synthetic dataset holds 8,000 persons and 1,801,816 images, with a subset of 132,145 images utilized for widespread training and generalization testing. Cross-dataset evaluation involves training on one dataset and testing on another, with performance measured by Rank-1 accuracy and mean average precision (mAP) under the single-query evaluation protocol.

## 4.3 Comparison with the Latest Methods

Table 1 presents a comparison with the latest methods in generalizable person ReID. Due to privacy concerns in the DukeMTMC-reID dataset, similar to the baseline comparison approach, we utilize three other datasets in the person ReID domain for training, with the remaining three used for testing. Specifically, we employ the MSMT17 dataset for training, with one configuration involving the use of all images without considering subset segmentation, denoted as MSMT17 (all).

Several recently published generalizable person ReID methods are compared, including OSNet-AIN [21], MuDeep [19], SNR [3], QAConv [20], CBN [16], ADIN [15], M3L [17], and QAConv-GS [4]. Table 1 demonstrates that QAConv-AHFA significantly improves upon previous methods. Taking Market-1501→CUHK03 as an example, the Rank-1 accuracy and mAP are enhanced by 2.5% and 2.6%, respectively.

With MSMT17→CUHK03, the improvements are 3.2% and 2.6%, respectively. Using MSMT17(all)→CUHK03, the improvement rates for Rank-1 accuracy and mAP are 4.2% and 2.8%, respectively.

**Table 2.** Comparing the final effects of multiple convolution kernels at different scales within the AHFA framework. Here, $k$ refers to the kernel size, and $d$ refers to dilation.

| $(k,d)$ sequence | CUHK03-NP | | Market-1501 | | MSMT17 | |
|---|---|---|---|---|---|---|
| | Rank-1 | mAP | Rank-1 | mAP | Rank-1 | mAP |
| (3,1) | 19.6 | 18.7 | 91.8 | 76.6 | 45.7 | 17.4 |
| (5,1) | 19.7 | 18.4 | 91.3 | 76.6 | 45.8 | 17.6 |
| (7,1) | 20.6 | 19.3 | 91.6 | 76.6 | 44.4 | 16.8 |
| (3, 1) → (3, 2) → (3, 3) | 19.4 | 18.4 | 91.0 | 75.8 | 45.7 | 17.6 |
| (3, 1) → (5, 1) → (7, 1) | 19.2 | 18.3 | 91.4 | 77.1 | 44.9 | 17.3 |
| (3, 1) → (5, 1) → (7, 1) → (9, 1) | 19.6 | 19.1 | 91.4 | 76.6 | 44.8 | 17.6 |
| **(5,2) → (7,3)(Ours)** | **21.6** | **20.7** | **92.3** | **77.4** | **46.0** | **17.7** |

**Table 3.** Component Ablation Experiments in AHFA

| HFE | AFA | CUHK03-NP | | Market-1501 | | MSMT17 | |
|---|---|---|---|---|---|---|---|
| | | Rank-1 | mAP | Rank-1 | mAP | Rank-1 | mAP |
| ✕ | ✕ | 19.1 | 18.1 | 91.6 | 75.5 | 45.9 | 17.2 |
| ✕ | ✓ | 18.8 | 17.8 | 91.2 | 76.4 | 45.2 | 17.1 |
| ✓ | ✕ | 19.8 | 18.8 | 90.9 | 76.4 | 45.6 | 17.5 |
| ✓ | ✓ | **21.6** | **20.7** | **92.3** | **77.4** | **46.0** | **17.7** |

Despite RandPerson being a synthetic dataset with strong randomness when used as training data, our method still shows improvement across the three test sets. It is important to note that $M^3L$ [17] is trained on three datasets selected from CUHK03, Market-1501, DukeMTMC-reID, and MSMT17, with another dataset reserved for testing. This involves different evaluation protocols, making direct comparisons challenging. However, training on MSMT17 and testing on Market-1501 yields better Rank-1 accuracy and mAP compared to $M^3L$, with improvements of 4.7% and 1.7%, respectively. Additionally, training on Market-1501 and testing on MSMT17 significantly outperforms $M^3L$, with Rank-1 accuracy and mAP improvements of 9.1% and 3.0%, respectively. Despite using subsets of the training dataset employed by $M^3L$, our approach proves to be more effective in both scenarios, demonstrating the efficacy of our work.

### 4.4  Ablation Study

#### 4.4.1  Multi-scale Parameter Analysis

The HFE module we designed performs multiple convolution operations sequentially by altering the values of the kernel size k and dilation rate d to obtain features at different scales. While balancing the receptive field size and model complexity of the selected parameters, we experimented with multiple convolution kernels on the Market-1501 dataset. At different ranges, it obtains features for input A with rich contextual information. As shown in Table 2, the simple fusion of features from multiple scales does not effectively improve the model's final performance. Through parameter tuning, we discovered that the optimal performance is achieved when the values of the kernel size k and dilation rate d are set to $(5, 2) \rightarrow (7, 3)$.

#### 4.4.2  Component Performance Analysis

To validate the performance of our proposed method, we assess the effectiveness of the components within AHFA, namely the HFE sub- module and AFA submodule. Specifically, we train on Market-1501 and test on the other three datasets. We report the final results of the trained QAConv-AHFA, as shown in Table 3. We can observe that adding the AFA or HFE modules alone does not significantly differ from the baseline's final performance. However, the simultaneous use of both modules results in a substantial increase in Rank-1 accuracy and mAP. This strongly indicates the correctness of our approach, demonstrating that leveraging multiple receptive fields to gather contextual information and then fusing global and local features can make the final features more representative, thereby enhancing the model's overall performance.

#### 4.4.3  Attention Analysis of the AFA Module

To further validate the effectiveness of the attention selection in the proposed AFA module and analyze the impact of different attentions on the generalization task within the module, we conducted three tests: (1) "Global + Global", where features from two different receptive fields undergo global attention processing; (2) "Local + Local", where features from two different receptive fields undergo local attention processing; (3) Our method, using "Global + Local", where features from two different receptive fields undergo global attention processing and local attention processing, respectively. The results are shown in Table 4. Because the RandPerson dataset is large-scale, global and local features originate from information at different scales. Fusing these features may introduce more severe conflicts, affecting the model's learning and generalization capabilities. However, optimal performance can still be achieved on typical pedestrian recognition datasets. This indicates that the combined use of both global and local attention outperforms directly applying a single attention mechanism, demonstrating that global attention can capture overall contextual information of input data. In contrast, local attention can focus on details and local features. The model can more comprehensively understand and process input data by applying these two attention mechanisms. The combination of global and local attention helps the model focus on essential regions while ignoring irrelevant or minor information, thereby improving the accuracy and robustness of the model.

#### 4.4.4 Parameter Analysis

When designing our method, we considered both performance and computational efficiency to strike a balance between cost-effectiveness and efficiency. Therefore, we illustrate the performance efficiency. Therefore, we illustrate the performance of our proposed method with various channel reduction ratios r. Specifically, the training is conducted on Market-1501, and testing is performed on CHUK03. The variation in the final Rank-1 and mAP performance with different channel reduction ratios r is depicted in Fig. 3. Generally, we observe an inverted U-shaped trend in accuracy with the increase of the channel reduction ratio r. It is evident that the accuracy reaches saturation when the channel reduction ratio is "$r = 4$".

**Table 4.** Internal Ablation of the AFA Module.

| Method | Training | CUHK03-NP | | Market-1501 | | MSMT17 | |
|---|---|---|---|---|---|---|---|
| | | Rank-1 | mAP | Rank-1 | mAP | Rank-1 | mAP |
| Global + Global | Market-1501 | 21.6 | 19.7 | 91.0 | 76.1 | 44.6 | 17.0 |
| Local + Local | Market-1501 | 21.1 | 19.4 | 91.2 | 75.8 | 45.8 | **18.0** |
| Ours | Market-1501 | **21.6** | **20.7** | **92.3** | **77.4** | **46.0** | 17.7 |
| Global + Global | MSMT17 | 22.6 | 22.0 | 79.8 | 51.0 | 79.9 | 51.1 |
| Local + Local | MSMT17 | 23.6 | 23.0 | 79.9 | **52.7** | 80.2 | 52.8 |
| Ours | MSMT17 | **24.1** | **23.2** | **80.6** | 51.9 | **80.6** | **54.2** |
| Global + Global | MSMT17-all | 17.4 | 17.6 | 77.7 | 47.6 | 76.0 | 46.4 |
| Local + Local | MSMT17-all | 30.1 | 30.2 | 83.0 | 59.1 | 88.9 | **72.1** |
| Ours | MSMT17-all | **31.8** | **30.8** | **84.1** | **60.0** | **89.0** | 71.8 |
| Global + Global | RandPerson | 16.7 | 15.7 | 74.9 | 44.7 | 44.3 | 15.1 |
| Local + Local | RandPerson | 18.5 | 16.7 | **77.0** | 46.5 | **45.5** | **17.3** |
| Ours | RandPerson | **18.6** | **17.2** | 76.1 | **47.1** | 44.2 | 15.5 |

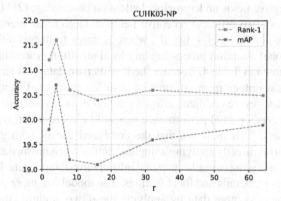

**Fig. 3.** Effect of the channel reduction ratio $r$.

# 5   Conclusion

Through this research, we demonstrate that the method of multi-scale feature fusion dynamically adjusts the spatial receptive fields of features generated from a randomly selected image for each class. Subsequently, these features from multiple receptive fields are fused, providing additional contextual information to enhance the global representational capability of features. Effective local and global attention integration further addresses context aggregation and initial feature incorporation challenges. This improves the representativeness of individual data samples and enhances the accuracy of the graph relationship structure obtained through graph sampling. Overall, these advancements significantly elevate the model's discriminative and generalization abilities.

**Acknowledgements.** This study was supported by the Science Foundation of Hubei Province (2021CFB568), the National Natural Science Foundation of China (62371350, 62202345).

# References

1. Song, J., Yang, Y., Song, Y.-Z., Xiang, T.,  Hospedales, T.M.: Generalizable person re-identification by domain-invariant mapping network. In: Proceedings of the IEEE/CVF conference on Computer Vision and Pattern Recognition, pp. 719–728 (2019)
2. Zhou, K., Yang, Y., Cavallaro, A., Xiang, T.: Omni-scale feature learning for person re-identification. In: Proceedings of the IEEE/CVF International Conference on Computer Vision, pp. 3702–3712 (2019)
3. Jin, X., Lan, C., Zeng, W., Chen, Z., Zhang, L.: Style normalization and restitution for generalizable person re-identification. In: proceedings of the IEEE/CVF conference on computer vision and pattern recognition, pp. 3143–3152 (2020)
4. Liao, S., Shao, L.: Graph sampling based deep metric learning for generalizable person re-identification. In: Proceedings of the IEEE/CVF Conference on Computer Vision and Pattern Recognition, pp. 7359–7368 (2022)
5. Wang, G., Yuan, Y., Chen, X., Li, J., Zhou, X.: Learning discriminative features with multiple granularities for person re-identification. In: Proceedings of the 26th ACM international conference on Multimedia, pp. 274–282 (2018)
6. Shen, Y., Li, H., Xiao, T., Yi, S., Chen, D., Wang, X.: Deep group-shuffling random walk for person re-identification. In: Proceedings of the IEEE Conference on Computer Vision and Pattern Recognition, pp. 2265–2274 (2018)
7. Deng, W., Zheng, L., Ye, Q., Kang, G., Yang, Y., Jiao, J.: Image-image domain adaptation with preserved self-similarity and domain-dissimilarity for person re-identification. In: Proceedings of the IEEE Conference on Computer Vision and Pattern Recognition, pp. 994–1003 (2018)
8. Hermans, A., Beyer, L., Leibe, B.: In defense of the triplet loss for person re-identification. arXiv preprint arXiv:1703.07737, (2017)
9. Li, Y., Hou, Q., Zheng, Z., Cheng, M.-M., Yang, J., Li, X.: Large selective kernel network for remote sensing object detection. arXiv preprint arXiv:2303.09030, (2023)
10. Cheng, D., Gong, Y., Zhou, S., Wang, J., Zheng, N.:Person re-identification by multi-channel parts-based cnn with improved triplet loss function. In: Proceedings of the IEEE Conference on Computer Vision and Pattern Recognition, pp. 1335–1344 (2016)
11. Fan, X., Jiang, W., Luo, H., Fei, M.: Spherereid: Deep hypersphere manifold embedding for person re-identification. J. Vis. Commun. Image Represent. **60**, 51–58 (2019)

12. Yang, F., et al.: Horizontal pyramid matching for person re-identification. In Proceedings of the AAAI Conference on Artificial Intelligence,vol. 33, pp. 8295–8302 (2019)
13. Zhang, L., Xiang, T., Gong, S.: Learning a discriminative null space for person re-identification. In: Proceedings of the IEEE Conference on Computer Vision and Pattern Recognition, pp. 1239–1248 (2016)
14. Jia, J., Ruan, Q., Hospedales, T.M.: Frustratingly easy person re-identification: generalizing person re-id in practice. arXiv preprint arXiv:1905.03422, (2019)
15. Yuan, Y., et al.: Calibrated domain-invariant learning for highly generalizable large scale re-identification. In: Proceedings of the IEEE/CVF Winter Conference on Applications of Computer Vision, pp. 3589–3598 (2020)
16. Zhuang, Z., et al.: Re-thinking the distribution gap of person re-identification with camera-based batch normalization. In: Computer Vision–ECCV 2020: 16th European Conference, Glasgow, UK, 23–28 August 2020, Proceedings, Part XII 16, pp. 140–157. Springer (2020)
17. Zhao, Y., et al.: Learning to generalize unseen domains via memory-based multi-source meta-learning for person re-identification. In: Proceedings of the IEEE/CVF conference on computer vision and pattern recognition, pp. 6277–6286 (2021)
18. Dai, Y., Gieseke, F., Oehmcke, S., Wu, Y., Barnard, K.: Attentional feature fusion. In: Proceedings of the IEEE/CVF Winter Conference on Applications of Computer Vision, pp. 3560–3569 (2021)
19. Qian, X., Fu, X., Tao, X., Jiang, Y.-G., Xue, X.: Leader-based multi-scale attention deep architec-ture for person re-identification. IEEE Trans. Pattern Analy. Mach. Intell. **42**(2), 371–385 (2019)
20. Liao, S., Shao, L.: Interpretable and generalizable person re-identification with query-adaptive convolution and temporal lifting. In: Computer Vision–ECCV 2020: 16th European Conference, Glasgow, UK, August 23–28, 2020, Proceedings, Part XI 16, pp. 456–474. Springer (2020)
21. Zhou, K., Yang, Y., Cavallaro, A., Xiang, T.: Learning generalisable omni-scale representations for person re-identification. IEEE tRans. Pattern Analy. Mach. intell. **44**(9), 5056–5069 (2021)
22. Wang, Y., Liao, S., Shao,L.: Surpassing real-world source training data: random 3d characters for generalizable person re-identification. In: Proceedings of the 28th ACM international conference on multimedia, pp. 3422–3430 (2020)
23. He, K., Zhang, X., Ren, S., Sun, J.: Deep residual learning for image recognition. In: Proceedings of the IEEE Conference on Computer Vision and Pattern Recognition, pp. 770–778 (2016)
24. Li, W., Zhao, R., Xiao, T., Wang, X.-G.: Deepreid: deep filter pairing neural network for person re-identification. In: Proceedings of the IEEE Conference on Computer Vision and Pattern Recognition, pp. 152–159 (2014)
25. Zheng, L., Shen, L., Tian, L., Wang, S., Wang, J., Tian, Q.: Scalable person re-identification: A benchmark. In: Proceedings of the IEEE International Conference on Computer Vision, pp. 1116–1124 (2015)
26. Wei, L., Zhang, S., Gao, W., Tian, Q.: Person transfer gan to bridge domain gap for person re-identification. In: Proceedings of the IEEE conference on computer vision and pattern recognition, pp. 79–88 (2018)
27. Zhong, Z., Zheng, L., Cao, D., Li, S.:Re-ranking person re-identification with k-reciprocal encoding. In: Proceedings of the IEEE Conference on Computer Vision and Pattern Recognition, pp. 1318–1327 (2017)

# Diverse 3D Human Pose Generation in Scenes Based on Decoupled Structure

Bowen Dang and Xi Zhao$^{(\boxtimes)}$

Xi'an Jiaotong University, Xi'an, China
`xi.zhao@mail.xjtu.edu.cn`

**Abstract.** This paper presents a novel method for generating diverse 3D human poses in scenes with semantic control. Existing methods heavily rely on the human-scene interaction dataset, resulting in a limited diversity of the generated human poses. To overcome this challenge, we propose to decouple the pose and interaction generation process. Our approach consists of three stages: pose generation, contact generation, and putting human into the scene. We train a pose generator on the human dataset to learn rich pose prior, and a contact generator on the human-scene interaction dataset to learn human-scene contact prior. Finally, the placing module puts the human body into the scene in a suitable and natural manner. The experimental results on the PROX dataset demonstrate that our method produces more physically plausible interactions and exhibits more diverse human poses. Furthermore, experiments on the MP3D-R dataset further validates the generalization ability of our method.

**Keywords:** Human Pose Generation in Scenes · Human-Scene Interaction · Virtual Humans

## 1 Introduction

Generating natural and diverse human poses is a challenging research problem with wide-ranging applications, such as AR/VR, computer games, and generating training data for vision and graphics tasks. Most methods focus on generating human poses without considering scene constraints [1,2]. With the development of the human-scene interaction dataset [3,4], many recent methods [5–10] have been dedicated to generating human poses in scenes. In this case, the generated human body must be coherent with the scene's semantic and geometric features to form reasonable spatial relationships with the scene. Our work belongs to this category as well. We focus on generating diverse 3D human poses in scenes with semantic control.

Existing methods [5,6] can generate human poses given the surrounding 2D or 3D scene information. However, these methods lack controllability and require manual labor to search for desired interaction types. Recently, some methods have incorporated semantic control into pose generation [8–10]. Despite their

© The Author(s), under exclusive license to Springer Nature Singapore Pte Ltd. 2025
N. Magnenat Thalmann et al. (Eds.): CASA 2024, CCIS 2374, pp. 207–223, 2025.
https://doi.org/10.1007/978-981-96-2681-6_15

capability to generate semantically plausible human poses, these methods heavily rely on the specific human-scene interaction dataset, and it is challenging for these methods to create diverse human poses that never appear in the interaction dataset. In summary, current works have difficulty generating controllable and diverse human poses while maintaining natural interactions.

We propose a new system based on the decoupled structure to deal with the above problems. Our main idea is to decouple the pose and interaction process. This design enables us to learn a rich pose prior on the large human dataset such as AMASS [11], so as to minimize the reliance on the human-scene interaction dataset. We generate specified interactions based on the given word instruction that provides the action and object type. The action type controls the generated pose, while the object type controls the interaction mode. By separating the pose and interaction generation modules, our system can produce more diverse human body poses and ensure reasonable interactions.

Our method includes three stages. The first stage is to generate the desired human body pose. We train the pose generator on the human dataset, which is easy to get and has rich annotations. So we can generate various poses to enrich the results. The second stage involves the generation of a contact feature map for the previously generated human body. We train the contact generator on the human-scene interaction dataset to capture the human-scene contact prior. The final stage is to place the human body in the scene. In this stage, we first select initial positions to put the human body. Then, we propose an effective physical feasibility test to remove unsuitable initial results. Finally, we optimize the human body pose to make the result look more natural.

In summary, our contributions are as follows:

1. A multi-stage generation framework that decouples the pose and interaction generation process;
2. A simple yet effective physical feasibility test module to ensure the physical feasibility of the generated results;
3. We demonstrate that our method can generate more physically plausible interactions with more diverse human poses in scenes compared to other methods.

## 2   Related Work

**3D Human Pose Generation in Scenes**: Generating 3D human poses in scenes has been a challenging research problem, and various methods based on different settings have been proposed. Some methods generate the human poses conditioned solely on the scene feature [5–7,12]. Zhang et al. [5] propose to extract the scene feature from the scene semantic segmentation and depth map, and use the feature to generate semantically plausible human poses. Zhang et al. [6] model the proximal relationship between the human body and the scene using BPS [13] feature. Hassan et al. [7] propose a body-centric representation that encodes geometric and semantic information of the given human body, and use it to guide the search for the most likely position in the scene. Kim et al. [12] introduce a geometric alignment term in the optimization stage to ensure more natural contact with the scene. Recently, some methods introduce semantic control to make the generation process controllable [8,9]. Zhao et al. [8] first generate a plausible human pelvis location and then generate the human body. The proposed method can support atomic and compositional interactions. Xuan et al. [9] propose to reason the relationship of the scene structure and use it to generate the desired human poses according to textual descriptions. Our method tackles the same task with COINS [8] and we focus on improving the diversity of the human poses by decoupling the pose and interaction generation process.

**Human-Scene Interaction Representation**: Human-scene interaction has also been widely studied in other tasks such as human or/and scene reconstruction [14,15] and scene generation [16,17]. Dang et al. [14] propose to estimate the possible region the human body can be positioned from the scene information, and use it to constrain the human pose for human pose reconstruction under severe occlusions. Yi et al. [15] propose a framework to reconstruct the plausible scene layout from the video and human movement. Savva et al. [16] propose to learn a joint distribution of human poses and object arrangements and generate a plausible interaction by sampling from the distribution. Ye et al. [17] propose to generate the scene layout from the human motions. We focus on generating diverse human poses in scenes. Our method incorporates semantic information while generating the body pose and contact feature.

## 3   Method

Our goal is to generate 3D human poses in scenes. Our main idea is to decouple the pose and interaction generation process to minimize the reliance on the human-scene interaction dataset. In this section, we present details of our method.

### 3.1   Overview

Our method takes an action-object pair and the scene mesh as input and generates the human body mesh placed in the scene as output. As shown in Fig. 1, our method comprises three stages. In the first stage, we use a pose generator to produce a desired human body model. In the second stage, we employ a contact generator to create a contact feature map for the human body mesh. Finally, we place the human body in the scene, which involves three sub-stages: initial position selection, physical feasibility test, and optimization.

We adopt the SMPL-X human body model [18] to represent the human, which is a differentiable function that takes shape parameters $\beta$, pose parameters $\theta$, facial expression parameters $\psi$, and global translation $t$ as input. The output is a human body mesh $M_b = (V_b, F_b)$, comprising vertices $V_b$ and faces $F_b$. Throughout our method, we focus on the human body pose $\theta_b$ while keeping

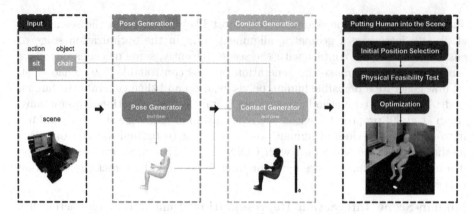

**Fig. 1.** The overview of our method. The input are an action-object pair and the scene mesh. The output is the human body mesh placed in the scene. In the first stage, we generate a desired human body model using the pose generator. In the second stage, we generate the contact feature map for the human body mesh using the contact generator. Finally, we put the human body into the scene. The last stage can be further divided into three sub-stages, including initial position selection, physical feasibility test, and optimization.

the other parameters constant. We assume the scene has semantic and instance segmentation, allowing us to search for plausible positions around the object to place the human body.

### 3.2   Pose Generator

Existing methods typically employ a generator trained on the human-scene interaction dataset to directly generate human poses in scenes [5,6,9]. However, the limited availability of interaction dataset [3,4] and the restricted range of human poses they contain hinder the diversity of the generated results. To alleviate this dependence on the interaction dataset, we propose an action-conditioned pose generator that is independent of other stages. By training the pose generator on the readily available human dataset with rich annotations, it can learn a rich pose prior, ultimately enhancing the diversity of the generated human poses.

As illustrated in Fig. 2, our approach employs a VAE-based [18,19] network architecture to generate body poses from given action types. The input body pose $\hat{\theta}_b \in R^{63}$ is encoded using a multi-layer perceptron (MLP) encoder, which outputs the mean $\mu \in R^{64}$ and variance $\sigma \in R^{64}$ of the Gaussian distribution that $\hat{\theta}_b$ belongs to. Subsequently, we obtain the reconstructed body pose $\theta_b \in R^{63}$ by feeding the sampled latent code $z \in R^{64}$ into an MLP decoder. The action code $c_a \in R^3$ is defined as the one-hot code representing the action type. It serves as a conditional input to control the generated body pose and is concatenated with the hidden features of both the encoder and decoder. During the testing stage, we only use the decoder part to generate the body pose.

The training loss for the pose generator can be formulated as follows:

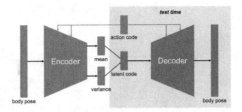

**Fig. 2.** The network structure of the pose generator. The input and output are both the body pose. The action code serves as the conditional input to control the generated body pose.

$$L_{\text{Pose}} = \lambda_m L_m + \lambda_v L_v + \lambda_j L_j + \lambda_{\text{kl}} L_{\text{kl}} \tag{1}$$

$$L_m = \text{Geodesic}(M(\theta_b), M(\hat{\theta}_b)) \tag{2}$$

$$L_v = \|V(\theta_b) - V(\hat{\theta}_b)\|_1 \tag{3}$$

$$L_j = \|J(\theta_b) - J(\hat{\theta}_b)\|_1 \tag{4}$$

$$L_{\text{kl}} = \text{KL}(q(Z|\hat{\theta}_b)\|N(0, I)) \tag{5}$$

$L_m$ denotes the pose reconstruction loss and is calculated as the Geodesic distance of rotation matrixs representing the input and reconstructed body pose [20]. $M(\cdot)$ denotes the function to transform the body pose from axis angle format to rotation matrix format. $L_v/L_j$ denotes the vertices/joints reconstruction loss and is calculated as the mean L1 distance between the input and reconstructed body vertices/joints. $V(\cdot)/J(\cdot)$ denotes the function to get the human body vertices/joints. $L_{\text{kl}}$ denotes the KL divergence and is used to encourage the latent space distribution to be close to a prior distribution such as the standard normal distribution. $\lambda_*$ denotes the weight for each loss term.

### 3.3  Contact Generator

After obtaining the desired human body model, we need to place it in the scene and ensure that it interacts naturally with the environment. Since most interactions involve contact, the key challenge is to ensure that the human body makes reasonable contact with the scene. To achieve this, we propose learning the human-scene contact prior from the human-scene interaction dataset and using the prior information to guide the human body to contact the surrounding environment naturally. We introduce an object-conditioned contact generator to produce a contact feature for the human body model, which represents the contact probability for each vertex on the human body mesh. The original SMPL-X human body model has a dense (10475 vertices) and uneven vertex distribution. To address this, we adopt the mesh simplification method from POSA [7] to downsample the vertices to 655, resulting in a more uniform distribution and reducing the number of parameters in the contact generator.

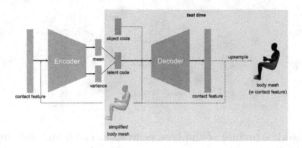

**Fig. 3.** The network structure of the contact generator. The input and output are both the contact feature. The simplified body mesh and object code serve as the conditional input to control the generated contact feature.

As shown in Fig. 3, we utilize a VAE-based architecture to generate the body contact feature [7,19]. The input contact feature $\hat{f} \in R^{655}$ and the corresponding simplified body mesh vertices $V_s \in R^{655 \times 3}$ are concatenated and fed into an encoder composed of spiral convolutions [21,22], which outputs the mean $\mu \in R^{256}$ and variance $\sigma \in R^{256}$ of the Gaussian distribution. The simplified body mesh vertices $V_s$, sampled latent code $z \in R^{256}$, and the object code $c_o \in R^{42}$ are then fed into the decoder composed of spiral convolutions to obtain the reconstructed contact feature $f \in R^{655}$. The object code is defined as a one-hot code representing the object type and used to control the generator to produce different contact features when interacting with different objects at the same pose. During testing, we only use the decoder to generate the contact feature for a given simplified human body mesh, and then upsample the contact feature to obtain the complete contact feature.

The training loss for the contact generator can be formulated as follows:

$$L_{\text{Contact}} = \lambda_{\text{rec}} L_{\text{rec}} + \lambda_{\text{kl}} L_{\text{kl}} \tag{6}$$

$$L_{\text{rec}} = \|f - \hat{f}\|_2^2 \tag{7}$$

$$L_{\text{kl}} = \text{KL}(q(Z|V_s, \hat{f}) \| N(0, I)) \tag{8}$$

$L_{\text{rec}}$ denotes reconstruction loss and is calculated as the mean squared error between the input and reconstructed contact feature. $L_{\text{kl}}$ denotes the KL divergence and is used to encourage the latent space distribution to be close to a prior distribution such as the standard normal distribution. $\lambda_*$ denotes the weight for each loss term.

### 3.4  Putting Human into the Scene

#### 3.4.1  Initial Position Selection

After obtaining the human body model and its corresponding contact feature, the subsequent step involves placing the human body in the scene based on the

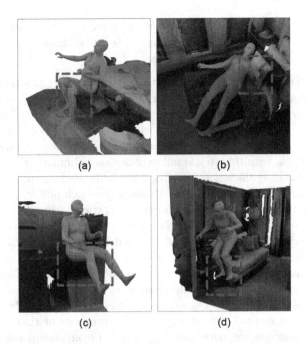

**Fig. 4.** Examples of bad positions. (a) and (b) show the situations with severe penetrations. (c) and (d) show the situations without reasonable contact.

contact feature. It is crucial to select appropriate initial positions and orientations to ensure interaction between the human body and the target object. Some methods utilize generative models to generate potential positions and orientations around the target object [8]. The diversity of the generated results heavily depends on the human-scene interaction dataset. For instance, when dealing with interactions like sitting on a chair, it becomes challenging to generate humans sitting sideways at a table if the interaction dataset only includes humans sitting facing a table.

To enhance the diversity of the generated results, we employ a simple yet effective method for obtaining initial positions and orientations. Given that the scene's semantic and instance segmentation are already known, we can directly query the target objects and calculate their bounding boxes. We then uniformly sample grid points within the bounding box as initial positions above the target object. For each position, we assign four directions: front, back, left, and right. This approach enables us to obtain a diverse collection of initial positions and orientations.

### 3.4.2  Physical Feasibility Test

While the above-mentioned initial positions and orientations guarantee contact between the human and the target object, they may not always yield reasonable results. Placing the human body directly at these positions may lead to issues illustrated in Fig. 4. To address this concern, we introduce two physical feasibility tests including a penetration test and a contact test to eliminate unsuitable initial results.

**Penetration Test**: The penetration test is used to identify positions where the human body exhibits severe penetrations that are challenging to resolve through optimization. We refer to this type of penetration as "thorough penetration". Figure 4 (a) and (b) illustrate scenarios where the human body is divided into multiple parts due to thorough penetration. In (a), the left leg penetrates through the thin chair back, resulting in a small penetration volume that makes the penetration term too insignificant to be effectively addressed through optimization. In (b), the left hand penetrates deeply through the thick pillow, posing a significant challenge to resolve despite the large penetration term.

To detect such situations, we design a geometry-based algorithm. Specifically, we compute the scene's signed distance field (SDF) value for each vertex of the human body. We then remove faces that connect vertices with different SDF signs, which indicates the presence of penetration edges. Next, we treat the human body mesh as a graph and analyze its connected components, distinguishing between positive and negative components. If we identify two or more positive connected components, it suggests the presence of thorough penetrations, and we eliminate the corresponding position from consideration.

**Contact Test**: The contact test is employed to identify situations where the human body lacks "reasonable contact" with the scene. It is important for the human body to have support from the scene in order to ensure physically plausible interactions. In Fig. 4 (c) and (d), even though certain body parts, such as the left arm and left leg in (c), or the right leg in (d), are close to the scene, the body parts that should be in contact with the scene are not actually making contact. For example, in a standing pose, the soles of the feet should be in contact; in a sitting pose, the thighs; and in a lying pose, the back, thighs, and legs.

To detect these situations, we propose using the contact feature generated in the last stage. We define the real contact vertices as those vertices that not only have a high contact probability but are also close to the target object. For each position, we calculate the number of real contact body vertices and remove positions where this number falls below a certain threshold. This ensures that only positions with a sufficient number of body vertices in genuine contact with the target object are retained.

### 3.4.3    Optimization

Although the penetration test and the contact test eliminate most unreasonable results, some slight penetrations or lack of necessary contact may still exist in the initial results. To further enhance the realism of the results, we additionally optimize the human pose. The objective function is defined as follows:

$$E = \lambda_{wc} E_{wc} + \lambda_{vp} E_{vp} + \lambda_r E_r \tag{9}$$

$E_{\mathrm{wc}}$ denotes the weighted contact term and is used to enforce necessary contact between the human body and the target object. $E_{\mathrm{vp}}$ denotes the volume penetration term and is used to reduce the penetrations between the human body and the scene. $E_r$ is the regularization term to minimize the mean squared error between the current body pose and the initial body pose. $\lambda_*$ denotes the weight for each term.

**Weighted Contact Term**: We consider body vertices with contact probability above a certain threshold as contact vertices $V_c$. We sample points on the target object to get object points $P_o$. Then, we minimize the weighted distances from $V_c$ to $P_o$ to match the human body with the target object:

$$E_{\mathrm{wc}} = \sum_{v_i \in V_c} f_i \rho(\min_{p_j \in P_o} \|v_i - p_j\|_2) \tag{10}$$

$\rho(\cdot)$ denotes a robust Geman-McClure error function [23] for down weighting the vertices in $V_c$ that are far from $P_o$. $f_i$ denotes the contact probability of contact vertex $v_i$.

**Volume Penetration Term**: We extract the human body internal points $P_{\mathrm{int}}$ by treating the human body as a volume [14]. Then we minimize the sum of the absolute values of the scene SDF for internal points with a negative scene SDF $P_{\mathrm{int}}^-$ to reduce penetrations between the human body and the scene:

$$E_{\mathrm{vp}} = \sum_{p_i \in P_{\mathrm{int}}^-} |\mathrm{SDF}(p_i)| \tag{11}$$

$\mathrm{SDF}(\cdot)$ denotes the function to search for the scene SDF for a given point.

## 4 Experiments

### 4.1 Datasets

The dataset we used consists of three parts: the human dataset (e.g. AMASS [11]), the human-scene interaction dataset (e.g. PROX [3]), and the scene dataset (e.g. MP3D-R [5,24]).

**AMASS**: We utilize the AMASS dataset to train the pose generator. BABEL dataset [25] provides sequence-based and frame-based annotations, enabling us to train the pose generator with action conditioning. Specifically, we use 4 subsets including ACCAD, HDM05, CMU, and BMLrub.

**PROX**: We leverage the PROX dataset [3] to train both the pose generator and the contact generator. Following the split of PSI [5], we use 8 scenes as the training set and 4 scenes as the testing set.

**MP3D-R**: To further evaluate the generalization ability of our method, we also test our approach on scenes from the MP3D-R dataset [5,24].

## 4.2 Experiment Details

**Pose Generator**: We train the pose generator using the Adam optimizer [26] with a learning rate of 1e-3. The weights for each loss term are set as follows: $\lambda_m = 2$, $\lambda_v = 4$, $\lambda_j = 2$, and $\lambda_{kl} = 0.005$.

**Contact Generator**: We create the training data for the contact generator using LEMO [27] fitting. For each body vertex, we calculate the ground truth contact probability as $\text{Clamp}(1 - \frac{d}{\delta})$, where $d$ denotes the minimum distance from the body vertex to the scene, and $\delta$ is the distance threshold set to 0.05. The $\text{Clamp}(\cdot)$ function clamps the value to $0 \sim 1$. We train the contact generator using the Adam optimizer with a learning rate of 1e-3. The weights for each loss term are set as follows: $\lambda_{rec} = 1$, and $\lambda_{kl} = 0.001$.

**Optimization**: We employ the same optimizer as SMPLify-X [18]. The weights for each term are set as follows: $\lambda_{wc} = 1$, $\lambda_{vp} = 10$, and $\lambda_r = 50$.

## 4.3 Results

Figure 5 presents a gallery of our results. We test our method on some common interactions that appear frequently in the dataset, such as standing on the floor, sitting on the chair, sitting on the sofa, or lying on the bed. The first and second rows show results on the PROX and MP3D-R dataset respectively. We can see that our method can generate physically plausible interactions for different action-object pairs. By decoupling the pose and interaction process, our method can generate some uncommon body poses, such as bending the knees (row 1, column 1) or crossing the legs (row 1, column 4). The contact generator can ensure necessary contact so the human body looks more natural without feeling isolated from the scene (row 2, column 1–3). It should be noted that the strip-shaped mesh above the human body is part of the original scene mesh (row 2, column 4).

In the third row of Fig. 5, we test our method on some uncommon interactions that never appear or seldom appear in the dataset, such as standing on the sofa, sitting on the table, or lying on the chair, to further validate the generalization ability of our method. We can see that our method can still generate reasonable interactions.

## 4.4 Comparison and Evaluation

In this section, we present the comparison results of our method with other methods on the PROX dataset.

### 4.4.1 Evaluation Metrics
We evaluate the performance using a set of metrics, which can be categorized into physical plausibility and pose diversity metrics.

**Physical Plausibility**: To evaluate the physical plausibility, we employ the Non-Collision (NC) and Contact metric introduced in PSI [5]. NC is used to

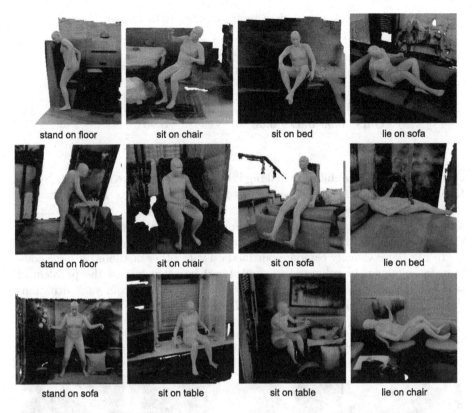

**Fig. 5.** Gallery of our results. The first and second row denotes results on the PROX and MP3D-R dataset respectively. The last row denotes results under uncommon interactions.

measure the penetration and is calculated as the ratio of body vertices with a positive scene SDF value. Contact is 1 if any body vertex has a negative scene SDF value, otherwise, it will be 0. We additionally use the Volume Non-Collision (VNC) to compensate for the defect of NC [14].

**Pose Diversity**: Following PSI, we cluster the body poses into 50 clusters using K-Means [28]. Then we calculate two metrics to evaluate the diversity. The first is the entropy of the cluster-ID histogram. It measures the average degree of all clusters. The second is the cluster size which is calculated as the average distance between the cluster center and the samples belonging to it. It measures the diversity degree of each cluster.

### 4.4.2   Comparison Results

We compare our method with POSA [7] and COINS [8]. To enable POSA to support the same input, we randomly select corresponding poses from the PROX dataset and sample initial positions around the object. The comparison results are listed in Table 1. For the physical plausibility metrics, the penetration and

**Table 1.** Comparison results on the PROX dataset.

| | Physical Plausibility | | | Diversity | |
|---|---|---|---|---|---|
| | NC ↑ | VNC ↑ | Contact ↑ | Entropy ↑ | Cluster Size ↑ |
| POSA | 0.96 | 0.94 | 0.95 | 3.60 | 0.68 |
| COINS | **0.99** | 0.98 | 0.89 | **3.77** | 0.61 |
| **Ours** | **0.99** | **0.99** | **0.96** | 3.69 | **0.90** |

contact metrics are conflicting, making it challenging to strike a balance. Nevertheless, our method achieves the highest value for all metrics. In terms of pose diversity metrics, the Entropy metric shows no significant differences among all methods. However, our method demonstrates a notable improvement on the Cluster Size metric, indicating that our pose generator learns richer pose prior.

In Fig. 6, we visually compare our method with other methods on some common interactions. In column 1, 2, and 4, other methods face the problem of severe penetrations or no contact, while our method can avoid such situations due to the physical feasibility test module. In scenes with constrained space, it

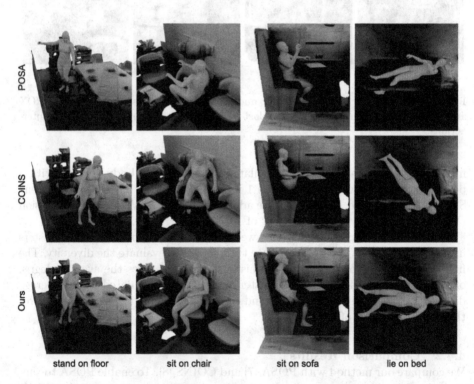

**Fig. 6.** Comparison of the generated results by our method with those of POSA and COINS.

is hard to put the human body at a suitable place with no penetrations at one time, such as the sofa in column 3. Our method can adjust the human pose to reduce the penetrations using the optimization module.

**Table 2.** Evaluation based on different actions.

| | Stand | | | Sit | | | Lie | | |
|---|---|---|---|---|---|---|---|---|---|
| | NC ↑ | VNC ↑ | Contact ↑ | NC ↑ | VNC ↑ | Contact ↑ | NC ↑ | VNC ↑ | Contact ↑ |
| POSA | 0.97 | 0.98 | 0.87 | 0.96 | 0.93 | 0.99 | 0.96 | 0.93 | 0.97 |
| COINS | 0.98 | 0.99 | 0.80 | **0.99** | 0.97 | **1.00** | **0.99** | **0.99** | 0.65 |
| **Ours** | **0.99** | **1.00** | **0.90** | **0.99** | **0.99** | 0.98 | **0.99** | **0.99** | **1.00** |

We further analyze the results by actions in Table 2. Our method outperforms others in all metrics, except for the Contact metric of the sitting pose. For the standing pose, since the human body only contacts the scene with the soles of the feet, it is easy to encounter floating issues. In contrast, sitting or lying poses involve more contact with the scene, which can lead to penetrations. Achieving a balance between less penetration and more contact is a challenging task. However, our method successfully strikes a balance for different actions.

## 4.5 Ablation Study

We conduct the ablation study on the PROX dataset. We consider the following ablation versions:

- Ours (w/o PFT): we test how our method performs when the Physical Feasibility Test module is removed.
- Ours (w/o OPT): we test how our method performs when the OPTimization module is removed.

As shown in Table 3, the final version which includes all the proposed components achieves the best overall performance.

**Table 3.** Ablation study on the PROX dataset.

| | PFT | OPT | NC ↑ | VNC ↑ | Contact ↑ |
|---|---|---|---|---|---|
| Ours (w/o PFT) | | ✓ | 0.97 | 0.96 | 0.95 |
| Ours (w/o OPT) | ✓ | | **0.99** | 0.98 | 0.87 |
| **Ours** | ✓ | ✓ | **0.99** | **0.99** | **0.96** |

Without the physical feasibility test module, severe penetrations may occur in the initial results, leading to a decline in the NC and VNC metrics. As shown

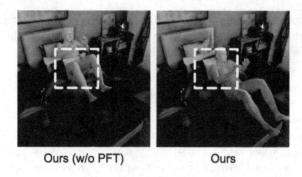

Ours (w/o PFT)    Ours

**Fig. 7.** Ablation study: compare our method with the version without physical feasibility test.

in Fig. 7, the physical feasibility test module enables us to avoid undesirable results, such as the human body penetrating through a pillow, thereby ensuring more realistic and physically plausible interactions.

When the optimization module is removed, the direct placing result may exhibit penetrations or fail to establish required contact with the scene, resulting in a significant decline in the Contact metric. As illustrated in Fig. 8, even with a suboptimal initial result, the optimization module can effectively guide the human to sit in a comfortable and natural manner.

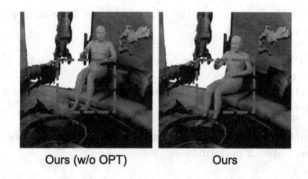

Ours (w/o OPT)    Ours

**Fig. 8.** Ablation study: compare our method with the version without optimization.

## 5    Conclusion

We present a novel method for generating diverse 3D human poses in scenes with semantic control. Our main idea is to decouple the pose and interaction generation process so that we can minimize the reliance on the human-scene interaction dataset. This decoupled structure enables us to learn a richer pose prior, resulting in more diverse human poses. We introduce a physical feasibility test module to eliminate undesirable positions, avoiding severe penetrations or lack of reasonable contact. An optimization module is also proposed to fine-tune the human pose, making the result appear more natural. Extensive experiments demonstrate that our method can generate more physically plausible interactions with more diverse human poses compared to other methods.

**Limitations and Future Work**: Our method can only handle fixed text descriptions in the form of "action + object", which restricts its usability. A potential direction for future work is to integrate language models that can extract key control information from complex descriptions. This will provide more precise control over the generated results. Furthermore, our experiments are confined to indoor scene datasets, whereas outdoor scenes present distinct object categories and structures with different human-scene interactions. Future work can extend 3D human generation to outdoor scenes to enhance the generality.

**Acknowledgements.** This work was supported by the National Natural Science Foundation of China (62072366, U23A20312) and National Key R&D Program of China (2022YFB3303200).

# References

1. Petrovich, M., Black, M.J., Varol, G.: Action-conditioned 3d human motion synthesis with transformer vae. In: Proceedings of the IEEE/CVF International Conference on Computer Vision, pp. 10985–10995 (2021)
2. Petrovich, M., Black, M.J., Varol, G.: Temos: generating diverse human motions from textual descriptions. In: European Conference on Computer Vision, pp. 480–497. Springer (2022). https://doi.org/10.1007/978-3-031-20047-2_28
3. Hassan, M., Choutas, V., Tzionas, D., Black, M.J.: Resolving 3d human pose ambiguities with 3d scene constraints. In: Proceedings of the IEEE/CVF International Conference on Computer Vision, pp. 2282–2292(2019)
4. Zhang, S., et al.: Egobody: human body shape and motion of interacting people from head-mounted devices. In European Conference on Computer Vision, pp. 180–200. Springer (2022). https://doi.org/10.1007/978-3-031-20068-7_11
5. Zhang, Y., Hassan, M., Neumann, H., Black, M.J., Tang, S.: Generating 3d people in scenes without people. In: Proceedings of the IEEE/CVF Conference on Computer Vision and Pattern Recognition, pp. 6194–6204 (2020)
6. Zhang, S., Zhang, Y., Ma, Q., Black, M.J., Tang, S.: Place: proximity learning of articulation and contact in 3d environments. In 2020 International Conference on 3D Vision (3DV), pp. 642–651. IEEE (2020)
7. Hassan, M., Ghosh, P., Tesch, J., Tzionas, D., Black, M.J.: Populating 3d scenes by learning human-scene interaction. In: Proceedings of the IEEE/CVF Conference on Computer Vision and Pattern Recognition, pp. 14708–14718 (2021)

8. Zhao, K., Wang, S., Zhang, Y., Beeler, T., Tang, S.: Compositional human-scene interaction synthesis with semantic control. In European Conference on Computer Vision, pages 311– 327. Springer (2022). https://doi.org/10.1007/978-3-031-20068-7_18

9. Xuan, H., Li, X., Zhang, J., Zhang, H., Liu, Y., Li, K.: Narrator: towards natural control of human-scene interaction generation via relationship reasoning. arXiv preprint arXiv:2303.09410 (2023)

10. Li, L., Dai, A.: Genzi: zeroshot 3d human-scene interaction generation. arXiv preprint arXiv:2311.17737 (2023)

11. Mahmood, N., Ghorbani, N., Troje, N.F., Pons-Moll, G., Black, M.J.: Amass: archive of motion capture as surface shapes. In: Proceedings of the IEEE/CVF International Conference on Computer Vision, pp. 5442–5451 (2019)

12. Kim, M., Kang, C., Park, J., Joo, K.: Pose-guided 3d human generation in indoor scene. In: Proceedings of the AAAI Conference on Artificial Intelligence, vol. 37, pp. 1133–1141 (2023)

13. Prokudin, S., Lassner, C., Romero, J.: Efficient learning on point clouds with basis point sets. In: Proceedings of the IEEE/CVF International Conference on Computer Vision, pp. 4332– 4341 (2019)

14. Dang, B., Zhao, X.,Bowen Zhang, and He Wang. Reconstructing 3d human pose from rgb-d data with occlusions. Comput. Graph. Forum **42**, e14982 (2023)

15. Yi, H., et al.: Human-aware object placement for visual environment reconstruction. In: Proceedings of the IEEE/CVF Conference on Computer Vision and Pattern Recognition, pp. 3959–3970 (2022)

16. Savva, M., Chang, A.X., Hanrahan, P., Fisher, M., Nießner, M.: Pigraphs: learning interaction snapshots from observations. ACM Trans. Graph. (TOG) **35**(4), 1–12 (2016)

17. Ye, S., et al.: Scene synthesis from human motion. In: SIGGRAPH Asia 2022 Conference Papers, pp. 1–9 (2022)

18. Pavlakos, G., et al.: Expressive body capture: 3d hands, face, and body from a single image. In: Proceedings of the IEEE/CVF conference on computer vision and pattern recognition, pp. 10975–10985 (2019)

19. Kingma, D.P., Welling, M.: Auto-encoding variational bayes. arXiv preprint arXiv:1312.6114 (2013)

20. Salehi, S.S.M., Khan, S., Erdogmus, D., Gholipour, A.: Real-time deep registration with geodesic loss. arXiv preprint arXiv:1803.05982 (2018)

21. Bouritsas, G., Bokhnyak, S., Ploumpis, S., Bronstein, M., Zafeiriou, S.: Neural 3d morphable models: Spiral convolutional networks for 3d shape representation learning and generation. In: Proceedings of the IEEE/CVF International Conference on Computer Vision, pp. 7213–7222 (2019)

22. Gong, S., Chen, L., Bronstein, M., Zafeiriou, S.: Spiralnet++: a fast and highly efficient mesh convolution operator. In Proceedings of the IEEE/CVF International Conference on Computer Vision Workshops (2019)

23. Geman, S.: Statistical methods for tomographic image restoration. Bull. Internat. Statist. Inst. **52**, 5–21 (1987)

24. Chang, A., et al.: Matterport3d: Learning from rgb-d data in indoor environments. arXiv preprint arXiv:1709.06158 (2017)

25. Punnakkal, A.R., Chandrasekaran, A., Athanasiou, N., Quiros-Ramirez, A., Black, M.J.: Babel: bodies, action and behavior with english labels. In: Proceedings of the IEEE/CVF Conference on Computer Vision and Pattern Recognition, pp. 722– 731 (2021)

26. Kingma, D.P., Ba, J.: Adam: A method for stochastic optimization. arXiv preprint arXiv:1412.6980 (2014)
27. Zhang, S., Zhang, Y., Bogo, F., Pollefeys, M., Tang, S.: Learning motion priors for 4d human body capture in 3d scenes. In: Proceedings of the IEEE/CVF International Conference on Computer Vision, pp. 11343–11353 (2021)
28. MacQueen, J., et al.: Some methods for classification and analysis of multivariate observations. In: Proceedings of the fifth Berkeley symposium on mathematical statistics and probability, Oakland, CA, USA, vol. 1, pp. 281–297 (1967)

# A Combination Simulation Method for Low Orbit Large Scale Satellites via STK and NS2

Maolin Xiong[1,2] (iD), Haowen Wu[1] (iD), Yong Wang[2,3], Yan Zhang[2,3], and Wei Ren[1,2](✉) (iD)

[1] School of Computer Science, China University of Geosciences, Wuhan, China
weirencs@cug.edu.cn
[2] Anhui Province Key Laboratory of Electronic Restriction, Hefei 230037, China
[3] College of Electronic Engineering, National University of Defense Technology, Hefei 230037, China

**Abstract.** Satellite communication is envisioned as a next generation communications due to its global coverage without relying on pre-deployed base station. There are many network simulators nowadays e.g., OPNET, Mininet and NS2. However, few simulators can simulate the exact trace of constellation while testing network performance. Satellite Tool Kit (STK) is an analysis software which is capable of generating orbit/ballistic ephemeris. In this paper, we present a co-simulation framework that integrates STK with NS2. We discuss the key components of the framework, including data exchanging and the synchronization of simulation time. We describe the process of modeling satellite constellations and configuring network nodes in NS2 using the data imported from STK. Additionally, we demonstrate the utility of the framework through a case study on the performance evaluation of a satellite communication system. The results of our experiments show that the co-simulation provides a more comprehensive understanding of satellite communication systems. It allows researchers to analyze the impact of various factors, such as satellite orbit parameters, network topologies, and communication protocols on the overall communication performance.

**Keywords:** Simulation · Satellite · STK · NS2

## 1 Introduction

Satellite communication is envisioned as a next generation and enhanced communications for 5G, as the signal can reach anywhere without the deployment of base stations in advance. The performance of satellite communication usually relies on the simulation tools, e.g., NS2/3 [1], OPNET [2].

However, with a high frequency of transforming based on position and topological structure brought by a large LEO constellation, simulation imposes more difficulties compared with the normal 5G simulations [3]. For example, the orbit trace data is generated by STK [4], the networking simulation is conducted by NS2/3. Then, the trace data should be imported into NS2, which is a complex task, e.g., the number of orbits, satellites per plane, and so on.

© The Author(s), under exclusive license to Springer Nature Singapore Pte Ltd. 2025
N. Magnenat Thalmann et al. (Eds.): CASA 2024, CCIS 2374, pp. 224–240, 2025.
https://doi.org/10.1007/978-981-96-2681-6_16

Thus, the problem falls to three points: how to generate and import the trace data intoNS2, and how to utilize those data for networking simulations.

The main contribution of the paper is as follows:

1. We propose a method for the interaction between STK and NS2.
2. We also give a concrete illustration on the network simulation performance under large scale satellites.

The paper is organized as follows: Related work is reviewed in Sect. 2. Section 3 presents proposed method. Section 4 presents experiment result and we conclude the paper in Sect. 5.

## 2  Related Work

There are many aspects in satellite communication simulations such as the performance of simulators, optimization strategy and data transmission etc. In the following paragraphs, We discuss other scholars' effort on satellite network simulation.

### 2.1  Performance of Simulators

There are many network simulation tools available. Mininet is an extendable simulator with fast start speed and large bandwidth [5], Mininet has no dedicated OpenFlow controller. If routing or switching behavior needs to be customized, you need to find or develop a controller with the desired functionality. OPNET is a powerful simulator which uses a discrete event-driven simulation mechanism that only when the network state changes [6], the simulator works. No analog calculation is performed during the period when the network status does not change [7–10], but it's an expensive commercial software which limits its adoption. Mini-Savi is a relatively new tool for mega constellation simulations which combines both Mininet and orbit simulation tool Savi, but there are a few tutorials so the learning difficulty is slightly higher than other simulators. Based on the combination of the network simulation tool Mininet and the orbit simulation tool Savi, Zhu Tang et al. proposed the satellite network-orbit integrated simulation platform (Mini-Savi) for large satellite constellations [11]. NS2 is an open source simulator and the tutorial are extensive and detailed. NS2 adopts discrete event driving mechanism for simulation. Its architecture strictly follows the OSI seven-layer network model. So we choose to use NS2 to simulate.

But the satellite module of NS2 does not support LEO satellites, the satellite node in NS2 is immobile. So in order to run the simulation with authentic movement of satellites, we choose to combine NS2 with another simulator which is capable of simulating the orbit of the whole constellation. STK (Satellite Tool Kit) is a powerful satellite constellation modeling, simulation and analysis software. The satellite constellation was designed based on STK and OPNET simulation software. Shiying Xu et al. modeled the three-layer network domain, node domain and process domain, and adopted static routing [12].

Few studies has explored the integration of Satellite Tool Kit (STK) and Network Simulator 2 (NS2) to analyze and evaluate routing algorithms in satellite communication systems. This unique approach allows for the combined benefits of STK's accurate and detailed satellite orbit modeling and NS2's network simulation capabilities. By leveraging this integration, researchers can gain insights into the performance of routing algorithms that consider both the physical characteristics of satellite orbits and the network protocols.

## 2.2  Network Optimization Strategy

Optimization of satellite communications includes a range of strategies at different levels aiming at improving the efficiency, reliability and performance of communications [13–16]. We provide an unparalleled level of detail in trajectory analysis by jointly simulating the orbital characteristics and network behavior of satellites. By closely coordinating STK's robust orbital mechanics with NS2's comprehensive network simulation capabilities, we achieve a granular level of insight into the timing, duration, and quality of network connections. This includes analyzing handover events, signal attenuation, and bandwidth allocation during various operational phases of the satellites.

## 2.3  Data Transmission

In order to realize real-time data transmission, we use STK API and NS2 programming interface. STK can provide real-time track and signal data, which can be transferred to NS2 for real-time network simulation. In NS2, we parse and use this data to configure specific network topology and performance parameters. In the event-driven interface, we define how to trigger the corresponding action or event of NS2 when a particular event occurs in STK. For example, when the position of a satellite changes, we transmit the new location information to NS2 through an event notification mechanism, then updating the network topology and routing information. Once the data is transferred between STK and NS2, we transmit the routing and network performance data generated by NS2 back to STK for further analysis and visualization after the simulation. The current landscape of research in satellite routing algorithms reflects a multiplicity of approaches aiming at optimizing data transmission across a complex and dynamic network of satellites. This body of work encompasses various strategies designed to manage the unique challenges presented by satellite communication, including high-latency links, limited bandwidth, dynamic topology, and the need for robust fault tolerance [17–19]. In summary, while existing research addresses the importance of considering delay and bandwidth factors in satellite routing algorithms, this work builds upon those efforts by leveraging the distinctive strength of STK in conjunction with NS2. Our innovative approach aims to advance the field by providing a comprehensive and accurate evaluation of routing algorithms that consider both physical and network-level characteristics in satellite communication systems.

# 3 Proposed Method

## 3.1 STK Simulation Method

The position and orbit of satellite affect the topology of communication network, so it is vital to use simulation software to calculate the position of all satellites.

### 3.1.1 Build the Constellation

1. By walker component. To begin with, inserting several root satellites to the scenario, each root satellite should be different from each other in both orbital inclination and altitude. For calculating the signal coverage, inserting one sensor to all root satellites is required. Then find the 'Walker' feature in the right-click menu and create constellation you need. The 'Walker' feature will automatically insert satellites that share the same height and inclination as the root satellite, while RAAN is evenly distributed over the Earth (Fig. 1).

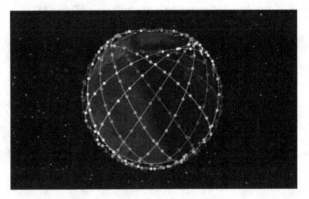

**Fig. 1.** Satellite constellation established by STK

2. By importing Two-Line Orbital Element (TLE) file. Click Insert -> Satellite -> From TLE file to import satellites (5000 objects maximum each time). Satellites imported by this way have no component, so in order to run the coverage analysis, we need to use MATLAB to insert sensors to all satellites.

Establish MATLAB with STK. The pseudo code is shown as follows:

```
stkInit;
remMachine = stkDefaultHost;
objNames = stkObjNames;
%get object name
```

Connects to the STK by port 5001. The pseudo code is shown as follows:

```
ui app   =   act x Get Running Server . . .
( ' STK11 . appli c a t i o n ' ) ;
r o o t = ui app . P e r s o n ality 2 ;
```

Loop, Get all objects' names from 6th to the last one, then split the name by "/", add a sensor to current satellite, set the sensor's coverage as a simple cone with a top Angle of 10 degrees. The pseudo code is shown as follows:

```
for   i   = 1 : l e ngth ( stk Obj Names )
name= s t r s p li t ( objNames { i , 1 } , '/ ' ) ;
command= s prin t f ( ' New  /  */ S a t e lli t e
/% s / Sen sor  sen ' , ch ar ( name ( 5 ) ) ) ;
r o o t . ExecuteCommand ( command ) ;
command2  =  s prin t f ( . . .
' Define  */ S a t e lli t e /% s
/ Sen sor / sen  Simple Cone  10 '
, ch ar ( name ( 5 ) ) ) ;
r o o t . ExecuteCommand ( command2 ) ;
end
```

After the constellation is built, click Analysis -> Report & Graph Manager -> CR to output time-based location information table as below (Table 1).

**Table 1.**  time-based location of satellite

| Satellite-Satellite1 | | | |
|---|---|---|---|
| Time (UTCG) | x (km) | y (km) | z (km) |
| 30 Jan 2024 04:00:00 30 Jan 2024 04:01:00 | −6603.16 −6644.91 | 997.711 621.842 | 15.570 236.553 |

Here is an example for STK to generate the.TLE file of the constellation by MATLAB, the pseudo code is shown as follows:

```
ui app  =  act x Get Running Server . . .
  ( 'STK11 . application ' ) ;
r o o t  =  ui app . P e r s o n a lity 2 ;
sc  =  r o o t . Curr e nt S c e n ari o ;
j = l e ngth ( s t k ObjNames ) ;
s s c  =  60000;
fid  =  fopen ( 'TLEData . tl e ' , ' wt ' ) ;
%Get  p ath s  of  the  s a t e llit e s
s a t p a t h c o ll e c ti o n = r o o t . ExecuteCommand . . .
( 'ShowNames * Cl a s s  S a t e llit e ') ;
s a t p a t h c o ll e c ti o n . Item ( 0 ) ;
s a t P a t h s = regexp . . .
( s a t p a t h c o ll e c ti o n . Item ( 0 ) , ' ' , ' s plit ' ) ;
s a t P a t h s ( c e ll f u n ( @isempty , s a t P a t h s ) ) = [ ] ;
%G e n e r ating
for  i  =  1 : l e ngth ( s a t P a t h s )
s a t t emp = r o o t . Get Object From Path . . .
  ( s a t P a t h s {i } ) ;
s t a r t  =  sc . St art Tim e ;
  cmd1  =  [ ' GenerateTLE ' , s a t P a t h s {i } , . . .
    ' Point  " ' , s t a r t , '" ' , . . .
    s prin t f ( '%05 . 0 f ' , ssc ) , . . .
    ' 20  0 . 01  SGP4  ' , . . .
    ' ' , s a t temp . In s tance Name ] ;
r o o t . ExecuteCommand ( cmd1 ) ;
sat DP = s a t temp . D a t a Pr o v id e r s . Item . . .
  ( 'TLE  Summary  Data ' ) . Exec ( ) ;
TLEData  =  s at DP . D a t a S e t s . . .
  GetData SetByName ( 'TLE ' ) . Get Value s ;
fprin t f ( fid ,  '%s \ n%s \ n ' , . . .
  TLEData { 1 , 1 } , TLEData { 2 , 1 } ) ;
s s c  =  s s c  +1  ;
end
f c l o s e ( fid ) ;
```

### 3.1.2   Coverage Analysis

Constellation needs to connect with earth's surface, so signal coverage rate is required to calculate. Insert a coverage definition, add the con- stellation to the asset of the CoverageDefination, then click CoverrageDefination -> Compute access to generate the report.

## 3.2   Trace Data Import Method

### 3.2.1   Trace in the Form of a Rectangular Coordinate System

This form contains the coordinate position of the satellite at every moment, and in order to simulate the movement of the satellite, the file needs to be read over time, thus it is not applicable to mega constellation. Use the loop to modify the satellite position at different points in time. The pseudo code is shown as follows:

```
s e t  topo  [ new  Topography ]
$ topo  l o a d_fl a t grid \
$ opt ( x )  $ opt ( y )  $ opt ( z )
$ ns_  at  $ t  " $ ns_node \
s e t d e s t  $x  $y  $z  "
```

### 3.2.2 Trace in TLE File

Before importing into NS2,.TLE file requires additional processing by Python or STK to convert data to trace. Using Python to calculate the inclination and altitude. The pseudo code is shown as follows:

```
import ephem
me = ephem. Ob server ()
(me . lon , me . lat , me . elevation )=(
    '108.5000','34.5000',800.0)
me . date = '2024/2/1 '# ephem . now ()
f = open ( r ' fle path ' , ' r ')
lines = f . readlines ()
i =0
while i <= 15630:
    satellite = ephem . readtle (
        lines [ i ] ,
        lines [ i + 1] ,
        lines [ i + 2])
    satellite . compute (me)
    print ( satellite . alt )
    print ( satellite . inc )
    i +=3
```

Then in NS2 use code below to set the position. The pseudo code is shown as follows:

```
set n0 [ $ns node ] ;
$n0 set −position \
$ alt $ inc 0 0 $ plane
```

## 3.3  NS2 Simulation Method

### 3.3.1  Overview

NS2 runs discrete event simulation which specifies changes in the system state that occur only when events happen. Typical events include packet arrivals and clock timeouts in network simulators. The advancement of the simulation clock is determined by the time at which events occur, so the rate at which the simulation process progresses does not directly correspond to real-time. Processing one event may trigger subsequent events and the simulator will continuously process events until all events have been processed or a specific event occurs.

STK is capable of generating orbit/ballistic ephemeris, remote sensor analysis, attitude analysis and visual calculations. The position and orbit of satellite affect the topology of the communication network, so it is vital to use simulation software to calculate the position of all satellites.

Awk is a programming language that possesses powerful data processing capabilities, allowing for easy manipulation, analysis, extraction and comparison of text files using concise code. If one were to implement these functionalities using languages like C or Pascal, it would require more time and longer code. The primary functionality of gawk is to search for specified patterns in each line of a file. When a line matches the specified patterns, gawk executes the corresponding actions. Gawk sequentially processes the input file, line by line, until the end of the file is reached. Gawk can read input from either standard input or specified files.

Before conducting a simulation, it is necessary to analyze the level at which the simulation is performed. NS2 simulation is divided into two levels: One is based on Otcl programming, utilizing existing network elements in NS2 for simulation without modifying NS2 itself, requiring only the creation of Otcl scripts; The other level involves programming in C++ and Otcl. If the desired network elements are not available inNS2, NS2 needs to be extended by adding the required network elements using the split-object model mentioned earlier. This involves adding new C++ and Otcl classes, followed by scripting in Otcl. The premise is that we have completed the extension of NS2, or the components contained inNS2 have met the requirements, the general steps for a simulation are as follows:

1) Start scripting in Otcl. Configure the simulated network topology, determining the basic characteristics of links such as delay, bandwidth, and loss strategies.
2) Establish protocol agents. It includes protocol bindings for end devices and the establishment of communication traffic models.
3) Configure parameters of the traffic model to determine the distribution of traffic on the network.
4) Import trace objects. Trace objects record specific types of events occurring during the simulation process in a trace file. NS2 uses the trace file to capture the entire simulation process. After the simulation, users can analyze and study the trace file.
5) Write other auxiliary procedures, set the simulation end time, and complete the scripting in Otcl.
6) Execute the Otcl script using NS2 for interpretation and execution.
7) Analyze the trace file to extract useful data. Tools like Nam can be used to observe the simulation process
8) Adjust the configuration of the topology and traffic models, and repeat the simulation process described above.

### 3.3.2  Main Flow of Simulation

NS2 is an event-driven simulator that currently supports two types of event schedulers: non- real-time and real-time. The non-real-time schedulers are further divided into three forms: linked list, heap, and calendar, with the latter being the default option. Although these three schedulers are logically identical, they utilize different underlying data structures. The primary reason for retaining these three schedulers is to ensure NS2's backward compatibility. Therefore, when using a non-real-time scheduler, it is typically sufficient to use the default calendar scheduler.

The main function of a scheduler is to manage packet delays and act as a timer. The workflow of a scheduler is as follows: it selects the earliest occurring event from all pending events, calls its handler function, completes that event, and then selects the next earliest occurring event from the remaining events for processing, repeating this cycle. NS2 only supports single-threaded operation, meaning that at any given moment, only one event can be executed. If multiple events are scheduled at the same time, they will be executed in the order in which their event codes were inserted into the system. This section describes the main simulation process and some key codes.

1) Nodes

Setting up a node refers to determining its various characteristics before the actual creation of the node. These characteristics include the category of the node's address, the types of network components for mobile nodes, the type of routing protocol used by mobile nodes in ad hoc networks, as well as whether to activate tracking functions at different levels such as the Agent layer, Router layer, and Media Access Control (MAC) layer, among others.

A node represents a satellite in a satellite network. This section shows how to establish the satellite node and the specific location of the satellite node, including longitude, latitude, altitude, satellite inclination and orbital plane. When you need to create a large number of nodes, you can use loops. Implemented by the following code. The pseudo code is shown as follow:

```
set node($i) [$ns node]
$n($i) set-position $alt $inc \
$lon $alpha $plane
```

Switching efficiency will be optimized by setting the next satellite node of the satellite. The pseudo code is shown as follow:

```
$n($k) set_next $n($m)
```

Next set up terrestrial nodes. Ground nodes only need to set longitude and latitude. We used two ground nodes Berkeley and Boston. The pseudo code is shown as follow:

```
$ns node-config -satNodeType \
terminal
set n(100) [$ns node]
$n(100) set-position 37.9\
-122.3; # Berkeley
set n(101) [$ns node]
$n(101) set-position 42.3\
-71.1; # Boston
```

2) Agent

In NS2, there are two types of TCP proxies: one-way agents and two-way agents. One-way agents consist of a variety of TCP senders, which operate based on different congestion control and error control algorithms, as well as corresponding TCP receivers (known as TCPSink). On the other hand, two-way agents can act both as senders and receivers. Currently, the predominant types of two-way TCP proxies include BayFullTcp and FullTcp. The following contains the code to set up the TCP agent, and showed how to add a TCP agent to a satellite node:

```
set src($i)  [new Agent\
/TCP/FullTcp]
set sink($i)  [new Agent\
/TCP/FullTcp]
$ns attach -agent $node($i)\
$src($i)
$ns attach -agent $node($i)\
$sink($i)
```

3) Application layer

In NS2, applications at the application layer are built upon transport layer agents, and they are divided into two main categories: traffic generators, which are responsible for generating network traffic, and simulated applications, which are used to emulate behaviors of real-world applications. The following code shows how to set up a CBR traffic generator to simulate the sending of traffic, and the traffic generator is added to the tcp proxy:

```
set cbr($i)  [new \
Application/Traffic/CBR]
$cbr($i)  attach -agent \
$src($i)
```

The next step is to set some parameters of the traffic generator, including the size of the packet sent each time, the sending rate, the duration of sending, the stop sending time, the start of listening to the sender, the receiver's window size, the start of sending packets at 1 second and the stop of sending packets at 2000 seconds. The pseudo code is shown as follow:

```
$cbr($i)  set packetSize 480
$cbr($i)  set rate 64k
$cbr($i)  set burst_time 500ms
$cbr($i)  set idle_time 500ms
$sink($i)  listen
$src($i)  set window_ 100
$ns at 1.0  "$cbr($i) start"
$ns at 2000.0  "$cbr($i) stop"
```

4) Links between nodes

The SimpleLink class implements a simple point-to-point link with queue and delay. It is a subclass of the link class in Otcl, and the functionality for simulating packet delivery delay is implemented by the LinkDelay class in C++. This section describes how to establish a link between satellite nodes, as well as the parameters of the link: bandwidth, latency, queue type, and establish the link at the transport layer. The pseudo code is shown as follow:

```
$ns  simplex - link  $node ( $i )\
$node ( $j )  5Mb  2ms  Drop Tail
$ns  connect  $ src ( $ i )  $ sink ( $j )
```

This is used to add inter-satellite links within orbital planes and inter-satellite links between orbital planes. The pseudo code is shown as follow:

```
$ns  add - i s l  intr apl ane  $n ( $k )\
$n ( $m )  $ opt ( bw_isl )\
$ opt ( ifq )  $ opt ( q lim )
$ns  add - i s l  interpl ane  $n ( $i )\
$n ( $j )  $ opt ( bw_isl )
$ opt ( ifq )  $ opt ( q lim )
```

Next, add a satellite-ground link for the ground base station and satellite node 100. The parameters here are taken from the global parameter list. The pseudo code is shown as follow:

```
$n ( 1 0 0 )  add - g s l  p o l ar  $ opt ( ll )\
$ opt ( ifq )  $ opt ( q lim )\
$ opt ( mac )  $ opt ( bw_up )  \
$ opt ( phy )  [ $n ( 0 )  s e t  down link_ ]\
[ $n ( 0 )  s e t  up link_ ]
```

5) Global configuration parameters

Next set the global parameters. Due to the large number of parameters, the code is put into our github repository: repository link

We're using a centralized routing genie. Create and start ithere. The pseudo code is shown as follow:

```
set  s at route obj e c t_  [ new\
S at R oute Object ]
$ s a t r o u te obj e c t_  compute_route s
```

## 4  Experimental Results and Analysis

### 4.1  Simulation Setup

In order to build a simulation environment, this paper installs Linux operating system ubuntu (version 16.04) on the VMware Workstation virtual machine, and installs NS-2.35, as a simulation tool under ubuntu. The number of satellite nodes was set as 600 (Tables 3 and 4).

**Table 2.** Trace data file format

| event | time | | from node | to node | pkt type |
|---|---|---|---|---|---|
| pkt size | flage | | fid | src addr | dst addr |
| seq num | pktid | | | | |

**Table 3.** The first five lines of the Sat.tr file

| + | 1 | 0 | 19 | tcp | 40 | – | 0 | 0.0 | 19.1 | 0 | 0 |
|---|---|---|---|---|---|---|---|---|---|---|---|
| – | 1 | 0 | 19 | tcp | 40 | – | 0 | 0.0 | 19.1 | 0 | 0 |
| + | 1 | 1 | 19 | tcp | 40 | – | 0 | 1.0 | 19.1 | 0 | 1 |
| – | 1 | 1 | 19 | tcp | 40 | – | 0 | 1.0 | 19.1 | 0 | 1 |
| + | 1 | 2 | 19 | tcp | 40 | – | 0 | 2.0 | 19.1 | 0 | 2 |

**Table 4.** The first five lines of the delay.tr file

| time | delay |
|---|---|
| 1.015000 | 0.002922 |
| 1.017922 | 0.002064 |
| 1.019986 | 0.002550 |
| 1.030000 | 0.002922 |
| 1.034986 | 0.002550 |

## 4.2 Trace Analysis

The function of trace is to meticulously record the simulation process, allowing for the capture of any detail as required by the user. After the completion of a simulation, the sole document left is the trace file, which all subsequent analysis of the simulation is based upon, highlighting the critical importance of trace. To support trace recording, each packet incorporates a unique common packet header. This header contains vital information such as the packet's sequence number, the type of packet (set by the Agent that generated it), the size of the packet (in bytes, which determines the transmission time), and port identifiers, among other details. The trace feature is realized within the C++ environment, with NS2 providing a number of sample scripts in Tcl that function as interfaces to the trace object in C++. The trace object contains the source address, destination address, type field, current time, and individual packet header fields (including packet type, size, flag bit, stream label, source and destination packet header fields, serial number, and unique identifier of the packet).

Now we analyze the resulting trace file. The parameters of the trace file are shown in Table 2. In the following analysis of the trace file, the first column indicates that the first packet is an entry event, and correspondingly, the second packet is an exit event. The packet is sent from node 0 to node 19 and is a tcp data packet with the source address being port 0 of node 0. The destination address is port 1 of node 19, and the packet size is obviously 40 bytes.

Calculate the number of packets sent by node 0 by searching the entire trace file and ACK confirmation, calculate the number of packets sent by node 0, port 0 of node 0 is used to send packets, where the trace file is named SatRouting, the pseudo code is shown as follow:

```
gawk   '$9 == "0.0"  {sum++}\
END  {print  sum} ' SatRouting.tr
```

Calculate the number of ACK acknowledgements sent by node 0. Port 1 of node 0 is used to send ACK acknowledgements. The pseudo code is shown as follow:

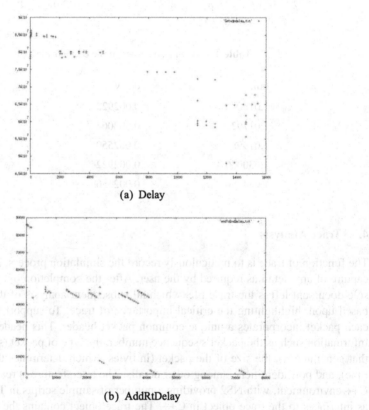

(a) Delay

(b) AddRtDelay

**Fig. 2.** Performance comparison between the two cases

```
gawk   '$9 == "0.1"  {sum++}\
END  {print  sum} ' SatRouting.tr
```

We use the gawk tool to analyze the trace data, using the following awk code edited, where SatRouting is the original trace data, delay is the processed trace data. The pseudo code is shown as follow:

```
gawk  − f  del ay . awk \
S at R outing . tr > del ay . tr
```

The processed trace data we get is shown in Table 2, where the first column represents the point in time and the second column represents the delay.

In Fig. 2, by comparing the results, we find that before adding the satellite node to the routing table, the transmission delay is unstable. The transmission delay is reduced by about 50% and stabilizes, and the transmission performance is greatly improved. Figure 3 shows jitter and throughput, which are both slow and smooth. After using both NS2 and STK instead of only using NS2, the proposed combination simulator runs with position of satellites updating all the time, and the movement of satellites is more precise than before.

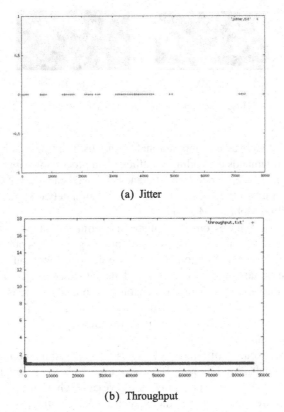

(a) Jitter

(b) Throughput

**Fig. 3.** Performance comparison between the two cases

### 4.3 Advanced Discussion

The co-simulation of STK and NS2 provides an advanced platform for studying and analyzing various aspects of satellite communication systems. Three specific cases highlight the capabilities and insights offered by this co-simulation framework:

Case I: Routing Protocols

The STK simulation reveals that low-earth orbit satellites operate at high speed, providing only a brief window of approximately 180 seconds for establishing links between neighboring satellites and ground stations. As a result, routing protocols like AODV require flooding to maintain routing tables, which incurs significant additional overhead. However, since the relative positions of satellites within the same plane remain constant, we can implement a layered routing strategy among satellites to reduce communication costs and improve data transmission efficiency. Instead of flooding, we can select a few leading satellites in each plane to establish connections, and only the leading satellites are responsible for forwarding packets to their destinations and maintaining fixed routes (Fig. 4).

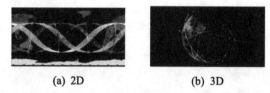

(a) 2D                    (b) 3D

**Fig. 4.** Connection between leader satellites

While this protocol saves computational resources, it introduces increased latency and places higher demands on leading satellites' data processing capabilities. With this approach, we strike a balance between efficiency and overhead, paving the way for more optimized and resource-efficient satellite communication networks [20].

Case II: Satellite Mobility Modeling

The second case focuses on the realistic modeling of satellite mobility patterns within the co-simulation framework. By incorporating STK's accurate satellite orbit data and NS2's network simulation, we can mimic the movement of satellites with different orbits and study the effects on network performance, such as handover latency and signal strength variations. This case enables us to analyze the trade-offs between satellite mobility, network coverage, and connectivity, leading to optimized satellite constellation designs and resource allocation strategies.

Case III: Communication Establishment Methods

The third case explores different techniques for establishing communication links between satellites and ground stations. By leveraging STK's precise modeling of satellite antenna patterns and NS2's network simulations, we can evaluate the performance of various communication establishment methods, such as beamforming, frequency allocation, and handover protocols. This case provides insights into optimizing the communication establishment process, reducing latency, and improving the overall quality of service in satellite communication systems.

These three cases exemplify the versatility and in-depth analysis made possible by the co-simulation of STK and NS2. This unified approach allows researchers and engineers to understand and optimize routing protocols, satellite mobility models, and communication establishment methods within satellite communication systems.

## 5 Conclusion

The co-simulation of STK and NS2 offers an effective approach for studying and analyzing the performance of communication systems involving satellites. Through the proposed co-simulation framework, we have discovered and proved the successful integration of STK and NS2, and realized the data exchange and simulation time synchronization between the two simulators. Our transmission latency is stable over time and after adding the appropriate routing table, the latency is even lower. The framework allows for the modeling of satellite constellations and network nodes in NS2 using information from STK, facilitating comprehensive performance evaluations of satellite communication systems. The ability to analyze satellite orbit parameters, network topologies, and communication protocols in a combined simulation environment is critical for designing and optimizing satellite communication systems.

**Acknowledgement.** The research was financially supported by the Open Project of Anhui Province Key Laboratory of Electronic Restriction (No. ERKL2023KF05).

## References

1. Zhang, D.-y., Liu, S., Yin, M.-l.: A satellite routing algorithm based on optimization of both delay and band- width. In: 2011 7th International Conference on Wireless Communications, Networking and Mobile Computing, pp. 1–4 (2011)
2. Firouzja, S.A.N., Yousefnezhad, M., Othman, M.F., Samadi, M.: A wised routing protocols for leo satellite networks. In: 2015 10th Asian Control Conference (ASCC), pp. 1–6 (2015)
3. Tang, F., Zhang, H., Yang, L.T.: Multi- path cooperative routing with efficient ac- knowledgement for leo satellite networks. IEEE Trans. Mob. Comput. **18**(1), 179–192 (2019)
4. Bai, X., Wu, X.: A simulation and visualization platform for fractionated space- craft attitude control system. In: 2011 IEEE International Conference on Mechatronics and Automation, pp. 2033–2038 (2011)
5. Software defined networks using mininet. Inter. J. Recent Technol. Eng. **9**, 843–849 (2020)
6. Yang, Y.. Guo, X., Xu, Z., Zhu, Y., Yi, X.: Design and implementation of leo micro-satellite network routing protocol based on virtual topology. In: 2021 IEEE 5th Information Technology, Networking, Electronic and Automation Control Conference (IT- NEC), vol. 5, pp. 1490–1496 (2021)
7. Li, L.-m., Zhu, L.-d., Wu, S.-q.: Design on the simulation platform for mobility management in leo satellite network based on opnet. In: Future Generation Communication and Networking (FGCN 2007), vol. 2, pp. 198–202 (2007)
8. Nie, L., Hu, S.: Simulation and analysis of campus network based on opnet. J. Computational Methods Sci. Eng. **19**(3–12) (2018)
9. Wang, P., Zhang, J., Zhang, X., Liu, L., Wang, Y., Ouyang, L.: Performance evaluation of double-edge satellite terrestrial networks on opnet platform. In:2018 IEEE/CIC International Conference on Communications in China (ICCC Workshops), pp. 37–42 (2018)

10. Jiang, W., Zong, P.: Analysis and validation of a new path loss model for leo satellite communication systems. In: 2010 2nd International Conference on Computer Engineering and Technology, vol. 2, pp. V2–523–V2–527 (2010)

11. Tang, Z., et al.: Mini-savi: realistic satellite network simulation platform based on open-source tools. In: 2023 Fourth International Conference on Frontiers of Computers and Communication Engineering (FCCE), 27–30 (2023)

12. Xu, S., Chen, Z., Zhang, X., Bian, J., Zhai, R.: Static routing-based delay analysis for low-orbiting satellite networks. In: 2021 IEEE 21st International Conference on Software Quality, Reliability and Security Companion (QRS-C), pp. 596– 601 (2021)

13. Duan, C., Feng, J., Chang, H., Song, B., Xu, Z.: A novel handover control strategy combined with multi-hop routing in leo satellite networks. In: 2018 IEEE International Parallel and Distributed Processing Symposium Workshops (IPDPSW), pp. 845–851 (2018)

14. Li, C., Liu, C., Jiang, Z., Liu, X., Yang, Y.: A novel routing strategy based on fuzzy theory for ngeo satellite networks. In: 2015 IEEE 82nd Vehicular Technology Conference (VTC2015-Fall), pp. 1–5 (2015)

15. Obata, H., Nishimoto, S., Ishida, K.: Tcp congestion control method of im- proving friendliness over satellite inter- net. In: 2009 7th International Conference on Information, Communications and Signal Processing (ICICS), pp. 1–4 (2009)

16. Hui, C., Jun, W., Xiaolin, F.: New strategy of improving stream control transmission protocol performance over satellite link. In: 2008 27th Chinese Control Conference, pp. 307–310 (2008)

17. Li, H.:Queue state based dynamical routing for non-geostationary satellite networks. In: 2018 IEEE 32nd International Conference on Advanced Information Networking and Applications (AINA), pp. 1–8 (2018)

18. Li, X., Tang, F., Chen, L., Li, J.: A state- aware and load-balanced routing model for leo satellite networks. In: GLOBECOM 2017 - 2017 IEEE Global Communications Conference, pp. 1–6 (2017)

19. Chen, Q., Zheng, K., Ouyang, F., Gan, X., Xu, Y., Tian, X.: A shortest path routing algorithm based on virtual coordinate in nels. In: 2016 8th International Conference on Wireless Communications Signal Processing (WCSP), pp. 1–5 (2016)

20. Liu, X., Yan, X., Jiang, Z, Li, C., Yang, Y.: A low-complexity routing algorithm based on load balancing for leo satellite networks. In: 2015 IEEE 82nd Vehicular Technology Conference (VTC2015- Fall), pp. 1–5 (2015)

# Semantic-Guided Prompt Learning Network for Generalized Zero-Shot Learning

Yongli Hu, Lincong Feng, Huajie Jiang[✉], Mengting Liu, and Baocai Yin

Beijing University of Technology, Chaoyang, China
{huyongli,jianghj,ybc}@bjut.edu.cn,
{fenglincong,Foreward}@emails.bjut.edu.cn

**Abstract.** Generalized zero-shot learning (GZSL) addresses the challenge of recognizing both seen and unseen classes with only training data from the seen classes. While the large-scale model CLIP holds promise for GZSL, a significant obstacle remains: the scarcity of high-quality prompts. To overcome this, we present a novel prompt learning approach for GZSL that leverages semantic information to guide the construction of a generic prompt template applicable to both seen and unseen classes. Specifically, we propose a semantic-guided prompt tuning network, which effectively learns the prompt template using semantic knowledge, enabling its utilization across seen and unseen classes. We extensively evaluate our approach on three GZSL datasets, where our network consistently achieves competitive performance across all three datasets. By addressing the challenge of prompt quality, our method demonstrates the potential of CLIP in GZSL tasks and highlights the importance of semantic guidance in learning effective prompt templates.

**Keywords:** Generalized Zero-Shot Learning · Prompt Learning · Image recognition

## 1 Introduction

Computer vision tasks like image classification and object recognition have made significant progress in recent years. However, these advanced technologies heavily rely on large-scale labeled data for training. Additionally, traditional recognition models can recognize trained categories, but fail to recognize the new classes. Therefore, zero-shot learning has drawn increasing attention as it can recognize novel classes without requiring a large number of labeled training data.

Zero-shot learning (ZSL) [1,2] aims to recognize the unseen samples by transferring knowledge from seen classes. A more challenging task is generalized zero-shot learning(GZSL), which requires identifying both seen and unseen classes.

The early GZSL methods are embedding-based [3,4], aiming to align visual features and semantics in latent space. Recent works focus on learning discriminative features: [5] tries to enhance feature distinctiveness distinguished by attributes matching; [6] improves the discriminability of features by optimizing the similarity between samples and their respective prototypes, while minimizing the similarity between non-corresponding prototypes. However, due to bias problems [7], unseen samples are easily misclassified as seen classes.

N. Magnenat Thalmann et al. (Eds.): CASA 2024, CCIS 2374, pp. 241–253, 2025.
https://doi.org/10.1007/978-981-96-2681-6_17

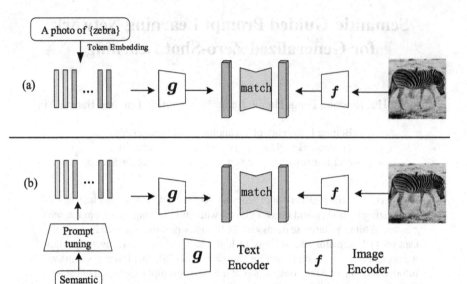

**Fig. 1.** Comparisons between CLIP (a) and Semantic-Guided Prompt Learning Network (SGPLN) (b) in GZSL, where CLIP uses fixed prompts while SGPLN learns adaptive prompts guided by semantic information.

To alleviate the identification bias problem, generative methods [2] have been proposed, which generate synthetic features for unseen classes using generative models such as GAN [8] or VAE [9]. Although these generative methods improve GZSL performance, they still face the feature confusion problem [10]. To solve this problem, [11,12] splits GZSL task into a supervised learning task and ZSL task by gating mechanism. However, these methods are trained from the blank and do not effectively utilize the preparatory knowledge of existing models.

Recently, there has been a significant advancement in zero-shot recognition with the CLIP [13] model. This model undergoes pre-training on an extensive dataset of image-text pairs through contrastive learning, effectively aligning image and text features within a latent space. During the inference process, zero-shot recognition is achieved by supplying a manually designed prompt, such as 'a photo of class name,' as illustrated in Fig. 1(a). Although this approach has demonstrated promising outcomes in zero-shot learning tasks, its dependency on manually crafted prompts introduces limitations to the current zero-shot recognition framework. Such prompts often necessitate human intervention and may fall short of encapsulating the complete essence of the target class. As a result, there arises a necessity to explore alternative methods that can automatically generate prompts, aiming to enhance the overall performance of the CLIP model in zero-shot recognition scenarios.

Motivated by the concept of prompt tuning in Visual-language interaction work (Coop) [14], our contribution introduces the Semantic-Guided Prompt Learning Network (SGPLN). In contrast to relying on manually designed prompts for Generalized Zero-Shot Learning (GZSL), as depicted in Fig. 1(b), our approach leverages semantic information to dynamically generate prompts. We harness two distinct types of semantic information for this purpose: attribute names, which contribute to the acquisition of generalized prompts, and attribute annotations, strategically employed to generate prompts that adapt effectively to the nuances of specific tasks.

To assess the effectiveness of our proposed framework, we conducted comprehensive experiments on three well-established Generalized Zero-Shot Learning (GZSL) benchmarks, namely AWA2, CUB, and SUN. Our method, Semantic-Guided Prompt Learning Network (SGPLN), consistently demonstrates outstanding performance across these diverse datasets. The noteworthy contributions of our work can be succinctly summarized as follows:

- We propose a semantic-guided prompt learning framework for GZSL, which utilizes semantic information to learn more effective prompts.
- We utilize two types of semantic information to learn semantic-related prompts: the attribute names for general prompts and the attribute annotation for task-specific prompts.
- Compared with the baseline(Manual prompts), the proposed method achieves remarkable performance on three ZSL benchmarks, improving the harmonic mean on the popular benchmark by about 10% on average.

## 2  Related Work and Preliminary

### 2.1  Generalized Zero-Shot Learning

Generalized zero-shot learning can be divided into two main categories: embedding-based and generative-based methods. The key challenge in GZSL is to establish the relationship between visual features and semantics. Embedding-based GZSL methods learn a space in which visual features and class semantics are related and can be further categorized into semantic embedding [15], visual embedding [16,17], and common space embedding [4,18] approaches. Semantic embedding methods learn transformations from the visual space to the semantic space and perform zero-shot recognition in the semantic space, while visual embedding methods do the opposite LDR [18] aligns visual and semantic information directly in latent spaces. AREN [19] learns more discriminative features by learning local features with attention. Common space embedding approaches [3,20] learn a common latent space to align visual features and class semantics for effective knowledge transfer. However, previous embedding methods have been troubled by the bias problem, where unseen classes are misclassified into seen classes. To alleviate this issue, co-representation network (CoNet) was proposed in [7], which uses a single-layer cooperation module with a parallel structure to learn a more uniform embedding space with better representation.

Generative-based GZSL methods [2,21–25] aim to generate visual features for unseen classes conditioned on class semantics, effectively transforming GZSL into a traditional supervised classification(CZSL) problem. Popular generative approaches include generative adversarial networks (GAN) [26] and variational autoencoder (VAE) [9]. GAN is used in [2] to generate visual features conditioned on class semantics, where a discriminator is used as supervision to learn robust generative models. VAE is used in

[21] to align the visual space and semantic space in a common latent space. Although generative methods significantly improve GZSL performance, they suffer from the feature confusion problem, as noted in [10]. The recently proposed dual-aligned framework in [27] aims to mitigate this problem but it is not completely solved. Although generative-based methods can alleviate the identification bias problem, they introduce a new problem where the generated features lack discrimination and may be confused with each other.

## 2.2 Vision-Language Pre-training

The pre-trained vision-language model, CLIP [13], consists of both an image encoder and a text encoder. The image encoder facilitates the transformation of images into a lower-dimensional embedding space, while the text encoder generates corresponding text representations. CLIP aligns these image and text embedding spaces using a contrastive loss during its training phase. The model is trained on an extensive dataset of image-text pairs, enabling it to capture diverse visual concepts. Notably, there has been a significant breakthrough in zero-shot recognition leveraging the capabilities of the CLIP model. During the inference process, zero-shot recognition is executed by providing a manually designed prompt, such as 'a photo of class name,' as illustrated in Fig. 1(a).

## 2.3 Prompt Learning

Prompting [28] is a technique that adapts a pre-trained upstream task to a downstream task. This topic originates from the NLP domain. The motivation was to view pre-trained language models, such as BERT [29] or GPT [30], as knowledge bases from which information useful to downstream tasks is elicited [31]. Concretely, given a pre-trained language model, the task is often formulated as a "fill-in-the-blank" cloze test, such as asking the model to predict the masked token in "No reason to watch. It was [MASK]" as either "positive" or "negative" for sentiment classification. The key lies in how to design the underlined part, known as prompt (template), in such a format familiar to the model.

Recently, prompt learning has made significant progress in Computer vision and multimodal tasks. Typical work, such as Clip [13] model, which usds the manually designed prompt 'a photo of ......' to image recognition. With the rapid development of prompt engineering, manually designed prompts cannot fully meet our needs. As a result, people are exploring prompt learning to replace traditional manually designed prompts, and achieving satisfactory results. Typical work, such as VPT [32], involves adding learnable tokens to a pre-trained ViT model for fine-tuning, thereby adapting it to various downstream tasks. Prompt learning is also extensively applied in multimodal tasks, for instance, COOP [14] and CoCoOp [33], which embed learnable tokens in the vision encoder of CLIP to learn prompt templates. This replaces the original manually designed prompt 'a photo of', thus enabling zero-shot recognition and inference.

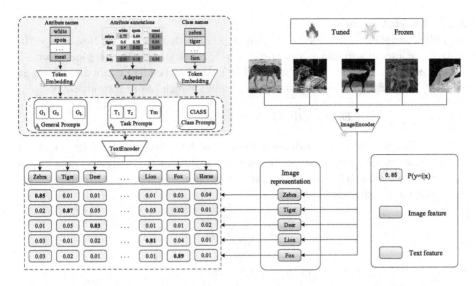

**Fig. 2.** The framework of the Semantic-Guided Prompt Learning Network, which contains three kinds of prompts: general prompts, task prompts and class prompts. The general prompts and task prompts are guided by attribute names and attribute annotations, respectively, and the class prompts are guided by class names. The image encoder and text encoder are fixed CLIP [13] encoders.

## 3 Methodology

### 3.1 Problem Formulation

In generalized zero-shot learning, assume that we have training data $\mathcal{D}^s = \{(x_i^s, y_i^s)\}$ with $C^s$ seen classes, where $x_i^s \in \mathcal{X}$ denotes image i of seen classes, and $y_i^s \in \mathcal{Y}^s$ is the corresponding class label. Another set of unseen classes $C^u$ has unlabeled sample $\mathcal{D}^u = \{(x_i^u, y_i^u)\}$, where $x_i^u \in \mathcal{X}$ is the unknown image i, and $y_i^u \in \mathcal{Y}^u$ is the corresponding label. Note that the seen and unseen classes are disjoint, *i.e.* $\mathcal{Y}^s \cap \mathcal{Y}^u = \emptyset$. A set of class attributes for all classes $\mathcal{A} = \{a_i\}$ are given to make knowledge transfer from seen to unseen classes. The goal of GZSL is to learn more general visual classifiers to recognize samples of all classes $f_{gzsl} : \mathcal{X} \to \mathcal{Y}^s \cup \mathcal{Y}^u$.

### 3.2 Semantic-Guided Prompt Learning Framework

In the subsequent section, we present our Semantic-Guided Prompt Learning framework, as depicted in Fig. 2. The architecture of our model integrates two distinct forms of semantic guidance aimed at acquiring proficient prompts: general prompts acquired from attribute names and task-specific prompts guided by attribute annotations. Elaboration on these components will be provided in the ensuing sections for a comprehensive understanding.

### 3.2.1 General Prompts

We utilize attribute names to learn the general prompts that apply to all classes. Specifically, given a set of attribute names $\{na_i\}$, $i = 1, 2...m$, such as "black, blue, green...", we embed the $m$ attribute names using CLIP's word embedding method to obtain an $\mathbf{E} \in \mathbb{R}^{m \times L \times d}$ representation of the attribute names, which can be formulated as:

$$\mathbf{E}_i = \text{CLIP}_{\text{embed}}(na_i), \quad i = 1, 2, \ldots, m \tag{1}$$

where $m$ is the number of attribute names, $L$ is the maximum word length of the attribute names, and $d$ represents the embedding dimension. To create a representation of the semantic background, an average pooling operation is performed on the embedding of the attributes names $\mathbf{E}$:

$$\mathbf{G} = \frac{1}{m} \sum_{i=1}^{m} \mathbf{E}_i \tag{2}$$

where $\mathbf{G} \in \mathbb{R}^{L \times d}$ represents the obtained general prompts.

### 3.2.2 Task-Specific Prompts

We utilize the attribute annotations to learn prompts for a specific task.

The attributes attribute annotations of all classes are represented by a matrix $\mathbf{A} \in \mathbb{R}^{N \times m}$, where $N$ denotes the number of classes and $m$ represents the number of attributes. First, we use two fully connected layers to learn a mapping from attribute representation space to the token embedding space (512 for CLIP), which can be formulated as:

$$\mathbf{A}' = \sigma(\sigma(\mathbf{A}\mathbf{W}_1)\mathbf{W}_2) \tag{3}$$

where $\mathbf{W}_1 \in \mathbb{R}^{m \times m}$ and $\mathbf{W}_2 \in \mathbb{R}^{m \times d}$ are the parameters, and $\sigma$ denotes the activation function. Then, we combine the token embeddings to learn the task-specific prompts:

$$\mathbf{T} = (\mathbf{A}')^{\mathrm{T}}\mathbf{W}_3 \tag{4}$$

where $\mathbf{W}_3 \in \mathbb{R}^{N \times n}$ is a learnable weight matrix and $n$ represents the desired number of task-specific prompts.

### 3.2.3 Class Prompts

Finally, category-related information is introduced through class name information. Specifically, given class names of $i$-th class, we embed it as a class-specific prompt using CLIP's word embedding method to obtain an $\mathbf{C}_i \in \mathbb{R}^{L_i \times d}$, where $L_i$ represents the length of $i$-th class name.

Finally, the general prompts, the task-specific prompts as well as the class-specific prompts are concatenated together as the ultimate prompts:

$$\mathbf{t}_i = [\mathbf{G}]_1[\mathbf{G}]_2...[\mathbf{G}]_L||[\mathbf{T}]_1[\mathbf{T}]_2...[\mathbf{T}]_n||[\mathbf{C_i}] \tag{5}$$

where $i$ represents the label of $i$-th class.

### 3.3 Training

Given an image $x$, a set of attribute names $\{na_i\}, i = 1, 2...m$, attribute values $\mathbf{A} \in \mathbb{R}^{N \times m}$, and a set of category names $\{\mathbf{C_i}\}, i = 1, 2...N$, we use CLIP image encoder $f(.)$ to extract 512-dimensional image features $f(x) \in \mathbb{R}^{512}$. The attribute names, attribute values, and category names are fed into our prompts-generating network, and then we get the prompt of each class $t_i \in \mathbb{R}^{(L+n+l_i) \times 512}$, where $l_i$ is the length of the class name. We use CLIP text encoder $g(.)$ to extract 512-dimensional text features. Then, we compute the probability of image $x$ belonging to class $i$ by:

$$p(y = i \mid x) = \frac{\exp\left(\cos\left(g(t_i), f(x)\right)\right)}{\sum_{j=1}^{N} \exp\left(\cos\left(g(t_j), f(x)\right)\right)} \tag{6}$$

In the end, we use cross-entropy loss to optimize our prompt and prompt learning network:

$$L_{CE} = -\sum_{i=1}^{N} y_i \log(p(y = i \mid x)), \tag{7}$$

where $N$ is the number of categories and $y_i$ is one-hot embedding of the ground truth label for category $i$.

### 3.4 Generlized Zero-Shot Inference

Given a test image $x_t$, we can infer the category of the sample by:

$$\hat{y} = \arg\max_i p(y = i \mid x_t)$$
$$p(y = i \mid x_t) = \Psi(x_t) \cdot \Phi(t_i) \tag{8}$$

where $\Psi(.)$ and $\Phi(.)$ is image encoder and text encoder of Clip model, respectively.

## 4 Experiments

### 4.1 Datasets

We evaluate the effectiveness of our framework on three widely-used GZSL datasets: AWA2 (coarse-grained), CUB, and SUN Attribute (both fine-grained). The AWA2 dataset comprises 37,322 images of 50 animal classes with 85 attributes. It is split into 40 seen classes and 10 unseen classes. The CUB dataset consists of 11,788 images of 200 bird species with 312 attributes, with 150 classes considered as seen and 50 classes as unseen. The SUN dataset contains 14,340 images from 717 scene classes and is accompanied by 102 attributes. Each attribute is represented by a word or phrase combination, such as "crooked mouth." Our evaluation follows the settings proposed in [44], ensuring that the pre-trained models have no prior knowledge of the unseen classes.

## 4.2   Evaluation Protocols

During testing, we follow the evaluation protocol proposed in [45]. The average per-class top-1 accuracy of seen classes (S) and unseen classes (U), as well as the harmonic mean ($H = 2 \times s \times u/(s+u)$), are used to evaluate the comprehensive performance in the GZSL setting. $H$ is the general metric used to measure the performance of GZSL.

## 4.3   Comparison with State-of-the-Art Methods

In this section, we compare our semantic-guided prompt learning method with state-of-the-art embedding-based and generative-based zero-shot learning methods to evaluate their performance. As is shown in Table 1, our proposed method demonstrates strong performance on AWA2 and SUN, highlighting the effectiveness of leveraging semantic-guided prompt learning. However, we do observe relatively lower performance on fine-grained CUB dataset. We attribute this limitation to the less effective visual representation provided by the general CLIP model. Since CUB is a specific the fine-grained bird dataset, it may require more specialized visual features that are not adequately addressed by the general CLIP model. Furthermore, we conduct a comparative analysis involving popular prompt-based learning methods, such as CoOp [14], CoCoOp [33], and kgCoOp [43]. Our approach consistently outperforms these methods across all evaluation metrics, which demonstrates the effectiveness of using semantics as guidance in our method, since semantic information can improve the generalization of the generated prompts.

**Table 1.** Generalized Zero-Shot Learning Results on AWA2, CUB, and SUN Datasets. U, S, and H represent Top-1 accuracy of unseen classes, seen classes, and harmonic mean, respectively. FT indicates fine-tuning the backbone network.

| Method | | FT | Source | CUB | | | AWA2 | | | SUN | | |
|---|---|---|---|---|---|---|---|---|---|---|---|---|
| | | | | U | S | H | U | S | H | U | S | H |
| Generative | f-CLSWGAN [2] | × | CVPR'2018 | 43.7 | 57.7 | 49.7 | 57.9 | 61.4 | 59.6 | 42.6 | 36.6 | 39.4 |
| | SABR-I [34] | × | CVPR'2019 | 55.0 | 58.7 | 56.8 | 30.3 | 93.9 | 46.9 | 50.7 | 35.1 | 41.5 |
| | f-VAEGAN-D2 [35] | × | CVPR'2019 | 48.4 | 60.1 | 53.6 | 57.6 | 70.6 | 63.5 | 45.1 | 38.0 | 43.1 |
| | FREE [24] | × | ICCV'2021 | 55.7 | 59.9 | 57.7 | 60.4 | 75.4 | 67.1 | 47.4 | 37.2 | 41.7 |
| | MCGM-VAE [36] | × | SPL'2020 | 51.1 | 58.0 | 54.3 | 60.9 | 69.3 | 64.8 | 38.7 | 43.8 | 41.1 |
| Embedding | TripletLoss [37] | √ | ICCV'2019 | 55.8 | 52.3 | 53.0 | 48.5 | 83.2 | 61.3 | 47.9 | 30.4 | 36.8 |
| | APN [38] | √ | NIPS'2020 | 65.3 | 69.3 | 67.2 | 56.5 | 78.0 | 65.5 | 41.9 | 34.0 | 37.6 |
| | HSVA [25] | √ | NIPS'2021 | 52.7 | 58.3 | 55.3 | 59.3 | 76.6 | 66.8 | 48.6 | 39.0 | 43.3 |
| | Transzero [39] | √ | AAAI'2022 | 69.3 | 68.3 | **68.8** | 61.3 | 82.3 | 70.2 | 52.6 | 33.4 | 40.8 |
| | MSDN [40] | √ | CVPR'2022 | 68.7 | 67.5 | 68.1 | 62.0 | 74.5 | 67.7 | 52.2 | 34.2 | 41.3 |
| | TDCSSF [41] | √ | CVPR'2022 | 42.2 | 62.8 | 51.9 | 59.2 | 74.9 | 66.1 | – | – | – |
| | BGSNet [42] | √ | TMM'2023 | 60.9 | 63.6 | 66.7 | 61.0 | 81.8 | 69.9 | 45.2 | 34.3 | 39.0 |
| Prompt-based | CLIP [13] | × | ICML'2021 | 48.9 | 50.1 | 47.6 | 83.2 | 88.3 | 85.7 | 48.1 | 47.1 | 47.6 |
| | CoOp [14] | × | IJCV'2022 | 48.1 | 52.3 | 50.1 | 86.7 | 85.0 | 85.8 | 46.8 | 48.1 | 47.4 |
| | CoCoOp [33] | × | CVPR'2022 | 50.3 | 49.1 | 49.7 | 79.7 | 90.6 | 84.8 | 50.1 | 48.7 | 49.4 |
| | KgCoOp [43] | × | CVPR'2023 | 50.0 | 51.2 | 50.6 | 85.9 | 86.9 | 86.4 | 51.8 | 53.2 | 52.5 |
| | SGPLN | × | OURS | 54.5 | 62.4 | 58.2 | 88.4 | 93.2 | **90.7** | 60.2 | 62.7 | **61.4** |

**Fig. 3.** Similarity representations of unseen class samples on AWA2. Top five similar classes are shown

## 4.4  Similarity Score

Similarity scores between images and categories serve as indicators of the model's recognition capabilities. We randomly selected several examples and displayed their top 5 highest similarity scores. From Fig. 3 , it is evident that SGPLN can effectively distinguish highly similar categories. For instance, the resemblance between a leopard and a tiger is striking, yet the model accurately distinguishes between them. However, there are instances of misclassification, such as Deer and Squirrel. Examining the model's scores, these misclassifications appear reasonable. Given the similarity in external appearance between Deer and Antelope, as well as between Mouse and Squirrel, recognizing Antelope as Deer and Squirrel as Mouse is justifiable. Addressing such "challenging samples" requires further learning of fine-grained features, which is a focal point for our upcoming efforts.

## 4.5  Ablation Study

We performed ablation experiments to assess the effectiveness of our proposed method on CUB, AWA2, and SUN datasets. We compared our method with three alternatives: 1:learning prompts from randomly initializing vectors(without semantic); 2:only use attribute names to learn general prompts; 3:only use attribute annotation to learn task-specific prompts. Through comprehensive experiments, we present the results in the Table 2. Compared with randomly initializing, the improvement rates for the three datasets are 8.1%, 4.9%, and 14.0%, respectively. Overall, our model exhibits the most significant improvement on fine-grained datasets, CUB and SUN, indicating its ability to learn more nuanced and discriminative features. When examining each component

**Table 2.** Ablation study of different components for the proposed framework. The best results are marked in bold.

| component | | CUB | | | AWA2 | | | SUN | | |
|---|---|---|---|---|---|---|---|---|---|---|
| attribute names | attribute annotations | U | S | H | U | S | H | U | S | H |
| × | × | 48.1 | 52.3 | 50.1 | 86.7 | 85.0 | 85.8 | 46.8 | 48.1 | 47.4 |
| √ | × | 52.2 | 55.5 | 53.8 | 86.7 | 88.0 | 87.3 | 50.8 | 49.1 | 49.9 |
| × | √ | 54.0 | 57.3 | 55.6 | 87.1 | 92.4 | 89.7 | 53.5 | 53.7 | 53.6 |
| √ | √ | 54.5 | 62.4 | **58.2** | 88.4 | 93.2 | **90.7** | 60.2 | 62.7 | **61.4** |

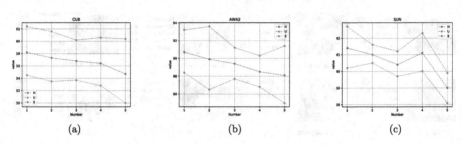

(a)                                    (b)                                    (c)

**Fig. 4.** The influence(H) of gereral prompt number in generalized zero-shot learning on CUB, AWA2, SUN

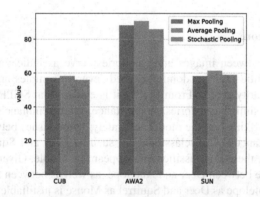

**Fig. 5.** Influence of different pooling methods on generalized zero-shot learning.

individually, attribute annotations have the most substantial impact on the model's gain, contributing increases of 5.5%, 3.9%, and 6.2% for each dataset, respectively. This is because attribute annotations are the sole source of semantic information capable of representing the characteristics of each category. To sum up, our method consistently outperforms the alternatives, showcasing the effectiveness of our approach.

### 4.6   Influence of General-Prompt Number

General-prompt plays a important role in our network. In this section, we investigate the impact of the number of general prompts on generalized zero-shot learning. Therefore, we conduct experiments for different numbers of general-prompts on three datasets

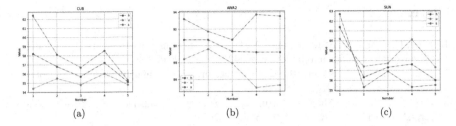

**Fig. 6.** The influence(H) of task prompt number in generalized zero-shot learning on CUB, AWA2, SUN

and the results are shown in Fig. 4. To obtain different numbers of universal prompts, we configure the model with various average pooling kernel sizes. We can see that the model performs best with a single prompt and the performance declines with an increasing number of prompts. In addition, we compared the effects of three different pooling methods on the generalization of zero-shot recognition, namely Max Pooling, Average Pooling, and Stochastic Pooling. In Fig. 5, we find that using Max Pooling achieved the best performance across all three datasets.

### 4.7   Influence of Task-Prompt Number

The essence of our framework lies in leveraging semantic information to acquire adaptive prompts for Generalized Zero-Shot Learning (GZSL), where the number of prompts significantly impacts our model. Consequently, we conducted experiments varying the number of prompts on three datasets, and the outcomes are visually depicted in Fig. 6. It is evident from the results that the model attains its optimal performance with a single prompt, and the performance gradually diminishes as the number of prompts increases. This observation implies that an excessive number of prompts can potentially lead to overfitting, undermining the model's generalization ability. Therefore, striking a balance in the number of prompts becomes crucial for achieving optimal performance.

## 5   Conclusion

In this paper, we present an innovative semantic-guided prompt learning network tailored for generalized zero-shot learning. This network strategically generates multi-level prompts to enhance the robustness of recognition. The general prompts, influenced by attribute names, are designed to augment the model's capacity for generalization. Concurrently, task prompts, derived from attribute annotations, focus on capturing class relationships specific to the task at hand. Additionally, class prompts, originating from class names, aim to facilitate the effective recognition of diverse classes. The empirical validation of our proposed approach is demonstrated through experiments conducted on three distinct datasets, showcasing its effectiveness and promising results.

# References

1. Jiang, H., Wang, R., Shan, S., Yang, Y., Chen, X.: Learning discriminative latent attributes for zero-shot classification. In: ICCV, pp. 4223–4232 (2017)
2. Xian, Y., Lorenz, T., Schiele, B., Akata, Z.: Feature generating networks for zero-shot learning. In: CVPR, pp. 5542–5551 (2018)
3. Jiang, H., Wang, R., Shan, S., Chen, X.: Transferable contrastive network for generalized zero-shot learning. In: ICCV, pp. 9765–9774 (2019)
4. Jiang, H., Wang, R., Shan, S., Chen, X.: Learning class prototypes via structure alignment for zero-shot recognition. In: ECCV, pp. 118–134 (2018)
5. Yang, S., Wang, K., Herranz, L., van de Weijer, J.: On implicit attribute localization for generalized zero-shot learning. IEEE Signal Process. Lett. **28**, 872–876 (2021)
6. Huang, S., Lin, J., Huangfu, L.: Class-prototype discriminative network for generalized zero-shot learning. IEEE Signal Process. Lett. **27**, 301–305 (2020)
7. Zhang, F., Shi, G.: Co-representation network for generalized zero-shot learning. In: ICML, pp. 7434–7443. PMLR (2019)
8. Goodfellow, I., et al.: Generative adversarial networks. Commun. ACM **63**(11), 139–144 (2020)
9. Kingma, D.P., Welling. M.: Auto-encoding variational bayes. arXiv (2013)
10. Li, J., Jing, M., Lu, K., Zhu, L., Yang, Y., Huang, Z.: Alleviating feature confusion for generative zero-shot learning. In: Multimedia, pp. 1587–1595 (2019)
11. Ding, J., Xiao, H., Zhong, X.: A semantic encoding out-of-distribution classifier for generalized zero-shot learning. IEEE Signal Process. Lett. **28**, 1395–1399 (2021)
12. Hu, Y., Feng, L., Jiang, H., Liu, M., Yin, B.: Domain-aware prototype network for generalized zero-shot learning. IEEE Trans. Circuits Syst. Video Technol. **34**(5), 3180–3191 (2023)
13. Radford, A., et al.: Learning transferable visual models from natural language supervision. In: International Conference on Machine Learning, pp. 8748–8763. PMLR (2021)
14. Zhou, K., Yang, J., Loy, C.C., Liu, Z.: Learning to prompt for vision-language models. Int. J. Comput. Vis. **130**(9), 2337–2348 (2022)
15. Lampert, C.H., Nickisch, H., Harmeling, S.: Learning to detect unseen object classes by between-class attribute transfer. In: CVPR, pp. 951–958 (2009)
16. Changpinyo, S., Chao, W.L., Sha, F.: Predicting visual exemplars of unseen classes for zero-shot learning. In: ICCV, pp. 3496–3505 (2017)
17. Wang, X., Ye, Y., Gupta, A.: Zero-shot recognition via semantic embeddings and knowledge graphs. In: CVPR, pp. 6857–6866 (2018)
18. Reed, S., Akata, Z., Lee, H., Schiele, B.: Learning deep representations of fine-grained visual descriptions. In: CVPR, pp. 49–58 (2016)
19. Xie, G.-S., Zhang, Z., Xiong, H., Shao, L., Li, X.: Towards zero-shot learning: a brief review and an attention-based embedding network. IEEE Trans. Circuits Syst. Video Technol. **33**(3), 1181–1197 (2022)
20. Sung, F., Yang, Y., Zhang, L., Xiang, T., Torr, P.H., Hospedales, T.M.: Learning to compare: relation network for few-shot learning. In: CVPR, pp. 1199–1208 (2018)
21. Schonfeld, E., Ebrahimi, S., Sinha, S., Darrell, T., Akata, Z.: Generalized zero-and few-shot learning via aligned variational autoencoders. In: CVPR, pp. 8247–8255 (2019)
22. Huang, H., Wang, C., Yu, P.S., Wang, C.D.: Generative dual adversarial network for generalized zero-shot learning. In: CVPR, pp. 801–810 (2019)
23. Wu, J., Zhang, T., Zha, Z.J., Luo, J., Zhang, Y., Wu, F.: Self-supervised domain-aware generative network for generalized zero-shot learning. In: CVPR, pp. 12767–12776 (2020)
24. Wu, J., Zhang, T., Zha, Z.J., Luo, J., Zhang, Y., Wu, F.: Free: feature refinement for generalized zero-shot learning. In: ICCV, pp. 122–131 (2021)

25. Chen, S., et al: HSVA: hierarchical semantic-visual adaptation for zero-shot learning. Adv. Neural Info. Process. Syst. **4** (2021)
26. Goodfellow, I., et al.: Generative adversarial nets. Adv. Neural Info. Process. Syst. **27** (2014)
27. Su, H., Li, J., Lu, K., Zhu, L., Shen, H.T.: Dual-aligned feature confusion alleviation for generalized zero-shot learning. IEEE Trans. Circuits Syst. Video Technol. **33**(8), 3774–3785 (2023)
28. Liu, P., Yuan, W., Jinlan, F., Jiang, Z., Hayashi, H., Neubig, G.: Pre-train, prompt, and predict: a systematic survey of prompting methods in natural language processing. ACM Comput. Surv. **55**(9), 1–35 (2023)
29. Devlin, J., Chang, W.C., Lee, K., Toutanova. K.: BERT: pre-training of deep bidirectional transformers for language understanding. arXiv preprint arXiv:1810.04805 (2018)
30. Radford, A., Jeffrey, W., Child, R., Luan, D., Amodei, D., Sutskever, I., et al.: Language models are unsupervised multitask learners. OpenAI blog **1**(8), 9 (2019)
31. Petroni, F., et al.: Language models as knowledge bases? arXiv preprint arXiv:1909.01066 (2019)
32. Jia, M., et al.: Visual prompt tuning. In: European Conference on Computer Vision, pp. 709–727. Springer (2022)
33. Zhou, K., Yang, J., Loy, C.C., Liu, Z.: Conditional prompt learning for vision-language models. In: Proceedings of the IEEE/CVF Conference on Computer Vision and Pattern Recognition, pp. 16816–16825 (2022)
34. Paul, A., Krishnan, N.C., Munjal, P.: Semantically aligned bias reducing zero shot learning. In: CVPR, pp. 7056–7065 (2019)
35. Xian, Y., Sharma, S., Schiele, B., Akata, Z.: F-VAEGAN-D2: a feature generating framework for any-shot learning. In: CVPR, pp. 10275–10284 (2019)
36. Shao, J., Li, X.: Generalized zero-shot learning with multi-channel gaussian mixture VAE. IEEE Signal Process. Lett. **27**, 456–460 (2020)
37. Cacheux, Y.L., Borgne, H.L., Crucianu, M.: Modeling inter and intra-class relations in the triplet loss for zero-shot learning. In: ICCV, pp. 10333–10342 (2019)
38. Wenjia, X., Xian, Y., Wang, J., Schiele, B., Akata, Z.: Attribute prototype network for zero-shot learning. NIPS **33**, 21969–21980 (2020)
39. Chen, S., et al.: TransZero: attribute-guided transformer for zero-shot learning. In: AAAI, vol. 2, p. 3 (2022)
40. Chen, S., et al.: MSDN: mutually semantic distillation network for zero-shot learning. In: CVPR, pp. 7612–7621 (2022)
41. Feng, Y., Huang, X., Yang, P., Yu, J., Sang, J.: Non-generative generalized zero-shot learning via task-correlated disentanglement and controllable samples synthesis. In: CVPR, pp. 9346–9355 (2022)
42. Li, Y., Liu, Z., Chang, X., McAuley, J., Yao, L.: Diversity-boosted generalization-specialization balancing for zero-shot learning. IEEE Trans. Multimedia **25**, 8372–8382 (2023)
43. Yao, H., Zhang, R., Xu, C.: Visual-language prompt tuning with knowledge-guided context optimization. In: Proceedings of the IEEE/CVF Conference on Computer Vision and Pattern Recognition, pp. 6757–6767 (2023)
44. Xian, Y., Lampert, C.H., Schiele, B., Akata, Z.: Zero-shot learning-a comprehensive evaluation of the good, the bad and the ugly. PAM **41**(9), 2251–2265 (2018)
45. Xian, Y., Lorenz, T., Schiele, B., Akata, Z.: Feature generating networks for zero-shot learning. In: CVPR, pp. 5542–5551 (2018)

# MiT-Unet: Mixed Transformer Unet for Transmission Line Segmentation in UAV Images

Jianwei Chen[1], Yuan Liu[2], Lifang Li[2], Shuifa Sun[1], and Ning Wei[1(✉)]

[1] Hubei Key Laboratory of Intelligent Vision-Based Monitoring for Hydroelectric Engineering, College of Computer and Information Technology, China Three Gorges University, Hubei 443002, Yichang, China
**weininglz@163.com**
[2] State Grid Yichang Electric Power Supply Company, Hubei 443002, Yichang, China

**Abstract.** The segmentation of power lines in drone images is one of the challenging tasks in the field of computer vision. Although power lines share the same difficulties with tiny object segmentation, occupying only a very small proportion of pixel areas in the images, the greater challenge is that they also have a very large visual perspective field. Therefore, the results obtained by traditional convolutional neural network-based segmentation methods are still unsatisfactory. To tackle these problems, we propose MiT-Unet(Mixed Transformer Unet), which has an analogous multi-level convolutional neural network structure similar to Unet for encoding and decoding transmission line detailed features. However, when dealing with excessive scales, we employ Efficient Self-Attention based module to enhance and fusion the global features of straight lines. Experimental results demonstrate that our proposed method achieves state-of-the-art performance in transmission line segmentation on the public TTPLA dataset. Moreover, the computational efficiency of the proposed model makes it potentially deployable on mobile platforms.

## 1 Introduction

Transmission line detection is an important process to ensure the safe and reliable operation of transmission lines. Regular inspections using UAV equipped with high-resolution cameras are commonly employed to identify potential safety hazards and implement preventive maintenance and repair measures for the normal functioning of transmission lines.

Various methods based on traditional local line features have been developed for the detection of transmission lines in UAV aerial images. Li et al. [1] utilized a PCNN filter to remove background noise in aerial images and detected lines using the Hough transform. Damodaran et al. [2] combined various image segmentation methods, including adaptive edge detection, OTSU thresholding, morphological reconstruction, and conditional random field post-processing, to detect transmission lines in aerial images. Shuai et al. [3] proposed a method

N. Magnenat Thalmann et al. (Eds.): CASA 2024, CCIS 2374, pp. 254–267, 2025.
https://doi.org/10.1007/978-981-96-2681-6_18

based on the Ratio operator and fast Hough transform for extracting transmission lines and measuring their distances from aerial images. These methods require predefined rules and thresholds for line clustering, making them unsuitable for complex scenes and conditions.

In recent years, deep learning has rapidly developed and been widely applied to transmission line detection, overcoming the limitations of traditional image processing algorithms. Lu et al. [4] proposed a transmission line detection method based on the YOLOv5s model. The method designed a dynamic adaptive weight allocation module and a cross-scale connection module to enhance the feature fusion effect. Zhu et al. [5] proposed a novel lightweight transmission line detection model Fast-PLDN that utilizes low-high pass block and edge attention fusion modules to construct a semantic segmentation model. This model effectively extracts spatial and semantic information to improve the accuracy of power line detection at boundaries. Rao et al. [6] introduced a multi-level Transformer model called Quadformer, which incorporated a pseudo-label correction scheme to denoise pseudo-labels for unsupervised transmission line segmentation research.

Compared to traditional methods, deep learning models have enabled automation and improved efficiency in transmission line detection, greatly enhancing the detection and segmentation process. However, there are still limitations in using deep learning models for transmission line detection, including: Interference from external factors such as lighting, environment, and occlusion may lead to false detections or low integrity of detected power lines; Power lines have a small pixel proportion but a large spatial span, requiring the model to focus on local features while taking into account the global attention of lines; When utilizing traditional sampling method, such as bilinear interpolation patch merging for downsampling or upsampling multi-level features, vulnerable transmission line feature is more likely to be lost, leading to fragmented and incomplete segmentation results for lines.

To address these issues, we propose a transmission line segmentation method that combines Transformer and CNN. Our main contributions include:

- We propose a novel MiT-Unet(Mixed Transformer Unet) for transmission line segmentation, which leverages both the advantage of the global encoding capability of Transformer and the multi-level local feature fusion and extraction Unet structure.
- Transfomer-based MiT-Down and MiT-Up modules for feature maps downsampling and upsampling are proposed. We deploy Efficient Self-Attention for global line feature enhancement and propose TLFM and PLFE modules for feature fusion and sampling to separate the vulnerable line feature from complex backgrounds.
- Experiments on challenging public dataset TTPLA that the MiT-Unet framework outperforms state-of-the-art segmentation models in terms of the main evaluation metrices.

## 2    Related Work

### 2.1    Image Segmentation Model Based on CNN

In recent years, CNN-based image segmentation methods have achieved significant success in various fields. A lightweight end-to-end image segmentation model called Unet was proposed in [7], which consists of a U-shape encoder-decoder structure and incorporates Skip Connection to fuse multi-level features from the encoder and decoder. Due to its simplicity and high efficiency, many improved models base on Unet have emerged. DoubleUnet [8] utilizes a dual Unet construction and adds Skip Connection between one Unet to the other one, which enhances feature representation. Unet++ [9] introduces dense connections and deep supervision, improving the Skip Connection to better integrate features of different scales. Unet 3+ [10] further extends Unet++ by proposing full-scale connections, enabling every layer of the encoder and decoder to be connected, thereby fully exploiting multi-level information.

### 2.2    Transformer Model

Transformer is a deep learning model architecture for processing sequential data, initially proposed in [11]. The basic idea is to capture the dependencies between different positions in the input sequence through self-attention mechanism. ViT [12] first apply Transformer to the field of computer vision by dividing the input image into $16 \times 16$ patches and transforming it into a one-dimensional sequence. Then, the Transformer's self-attention mechanism is used to encode the sequence. The Transformer model has strong global encoding capability, enabling it to capture wide-range dependencies in images and detect large objects effectively. However, it has limitations such as high computational complexity, single feature scale, the need for position encoding, and unfriendliness to tiny object detection.

In image processing, high-resolution images are often provided as inputs, which impose a significant computational burden on the transformer encoding. Swin Transformer [13] introduces the sliding window mechanism, which allows the model to perform self-attention computation within local windows, reducing the computational complexity. Additionally, it enables information interaction across windows through window shifting and merging. [14] proposes a lightweight multi-level image segmentation model called SegFormer, which designs an Efficient Self-Attention mechanism to reduce the computational complexity by reducing the length of the sequence.

### 2.3    Models Combining Transformer and CNN

To complement the shortcomings of Transformer and CNN, many models combining the two have emerged. [15] stacks convolutional layers and self-attention layers alternately, utilizing convolutional layers to extract local features and self-attention layers to capture global features. [16] embed the self-attention mechanism of Transformer into convolutional layers. [17] uses ViT as the encoder and adds convolutional blocks and upsampling in the decoder. [18] proposes a novel dual-branch architecture called TransFuse, which combines Transformers and CNN in a parallel manner to effectively capture global information and local features. [19] [20] combines Transformer and Unet, utilizing Transformer's global self-attention mechanism and Unet's multi-level feature fusion to extract image features and achieve precise feature localization.

Although these methods effectively improve the precision of small object segmentation, there is still room for improvement in the segmentation of power lines having large spatial extents but occupying a tiny portion of images. Some of the difficulties are attributed to mult-level transition where improper sampling layers would lead to vulnerable line feature losing and result in poor segmentation performance.

# 3 Method

## 3.1 Architecture Overview

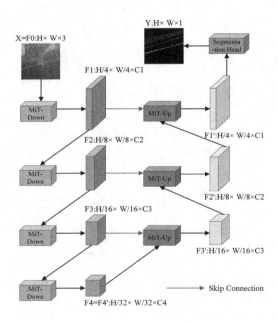

**Fig. 1.** Overall architecture of MiT-Unet.$X$ i.e. $F_0$ represents the input color image, $Y$ represents the final segmentation result.

The overall architecture of the proposed method is represented in Fig. 1, which has a similar structure to Unet. It encodes features from low to high levels in the encoding stage(from $F_1$ to $F_4$) and decodes them in the decoding stage in the reverse order of the corresponding resolution(from $F_4'$ to $F_1'$). Although, the fine detail feature is encoded in the high-resolution feature maps and the global semantic feature is encoded in low-resolution feature maps, the down and up-sampling process is crucial for extracting vulnerable transmission line features. Therefore, unlike traditional Unet, we propose the MiT-Down module at the encoding stage and the MiT-Up module at the decoding stage, which introduce an Efficient Self-Attention mechanism to enhance global semantic features during upsampling and improve the anti-interference capability of transmission line features.

As shown in Fig. 2, these two modules are deployed by Efficient Self-Attention to enhance the global semantic transmission line features and with TLFM(Transmission Line Feature Merging module) and TLFE(Transmission Line Feature Expanding module) to sample and fuse transmission line features.

## 3.2  MiT-Down Module

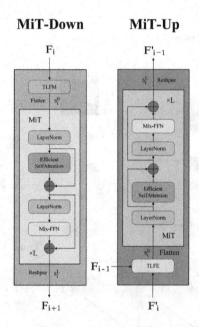

**Fig. 2.** The left is the MiT-Down module, and the right is the MiT-Up module. $\times L$ indicates that the MiT module is repeated for $L$ times.

MiT-Down module is composed of TLFM and MiT module, as shown in Fig. 2. The TLFM module is responsible for downsampling and fusing the feature maps, while the MiT module extracts the global transmission line feature. The formula for the MiT-Down module is as follows:

$$
\begin{aligned}
S_i^0 &= Flatten(TLFM(F_i)), \\
S_i^{j+1} &= MiT(S_i^j), j = (0,1,2,...,L-1), \\
F_{i+1} &= Reshape(S_i^L), i = (0,1,2,3),
\end{aligned}
\tag{1}
$$

where $F_i$ represents the output of the feature maps from the high-resolution with a shape of $\frac{H}{2^{i+1}} \times \frac{W}{2^{i+1}} \times C_i(F_0$ is $H \times W \times 3)$ for initialization. After TLFM and flatten operation, the output sequence feature $S_i^0$ is with a shape of $(\frac{H}{2^{i+2}} \times \frac{W}{2^{i+2}}) \times C_{i+1}$. The $MiT(\cdot)$ is a recursive operator, as shown in Fig. 2, which repeats $L$ times. Then, the features are reshaped back to two-dimensional feature maps, and output as $F_{i+1}$ with a shape of $\frac{H}{2^{i+2}} \times \frac{W}{2^{i+2}} \times C_{i+1}$. $L$ and $C$ are hyper-parameters, we defined models(from b0 to b5) of different scales based on various hyper-parameters, as shown in Table 2.

**TLFM:** Currently, there are various downsampling methods, such as traditional bilinear interpolation, max pooling used in Unet [7] and patch merging proposed in ViT [12]. Although these methods partially retain the semantic information and spatial coherence of the original feature map, they perform poorly in retaining vulnerable line features, as shown in Table 3. To address it, we propose a convolutional layer to generate and fuse low-resolution feature maps, aiming to capture the information of local small targets on power transmission lines, preserve spatial position information, and facilitate feature extraction learning. This approach reduces the noise and loss introduced by continuous sampling of power transmission line images. We formulate the TLFM as:

$$TLFM(F_i) = \begin{cases} Conv_{7 \times 7}^{d=4}(F_i), & i = 0, \\ Conv_{3 \times 3}^{d=2}(F_i), & i = (1, 2, 3), \end{cases} \tag{2}$$

where $d$ represents the stride of the convolution. When $i = 0$, $F_i$ is downsampled using a convolution with kernel of size $7 \times 7$, stride of 4, and padding of 3. When $i = (1, 2, 3)$, $F_i$ are downsampled using a convolution with kernel of size $3 \times 3$, stride of 2, and padding of 1. Both of the convolutions have an input channel of $C_i$ and an output channel of $C_{i+1}$.

### 3.3   MiT-Up Module

MiT-Up is an inverse of MiT-down, which consists of TLFE and MiTmodule, as shown in Fig. 2. TLFE module first performs upsampling on the image, then concatenates it with the corresponding resolution feature from the encoder, and finally passes it to the MiT module for global feature restoration. The formula for the MiT-Up module is as follows:

$$S_i^0 = Flatten(TLFE(F_i', F_{i-1})),$$
$$S_i^{j+1} = MiT(S_i^j), j = (0, 1, 2, .., L - 1) \tag{3}$$
$$F_{i-1}' = Reshape(S_i^L), i = (4, 3, 2),$$

similar to the MiT-Down module, the shape of $F_i'$ is $\frac{H}{2^{i+1}} \times \frac{W}{2^{i+1}} \times C_i$. Specifically, We set $F_4 = F_4'$ for the initialization of the decoding. After $L$ times repeating of the MiT module, we reshape $S_i^L$ back to two-dimensional feature maps, and output it as $F_{i-1}'$ with the shape of $\frac{H}{2^i} \times \frac{W}{2^i} \times C_{i-1}$ to the next level.

**TLFE:** We employ transposed convolution for upsampling, which allows for learning more complex image transformation patterns compared to traditional Bilinear Interpolation method. The proposed approach can better preserve fine details and recover missing information when enlarging feature maps. The formula for TLFE is as follows:

$$\begin{aligned}
F_{i-1} &= Linear(C_{i-1}, C_i/2)(F_{i-1}), \\
F_i' &= Cat(UpConv_{3 \times 3}(F_i'), F_{i-1}), \\
i &= (4, 3, 2),
\end{aligned} \tag{4}$$

where UpConv represents transposed convolution. In order to maintain the same number of channels after concatenation, $F_{i-1}$ reduces the number of channels from $C_{i-1}$ to $C_i/2$ using a linear layer. Then, $F_i'$ performs upsampling with transposed convolution and concatenates with $F_{i-1}$. The convolution kernel of Transposed Convolution is $3 \times 3$, the number of input channel is $C_i$ and the number of output channel is $C_i/2$, ensuring that the number of channels after concatenation remains as $C_i$.

### 3.4  MiT Module

The MiT module, as illustrated in the light-colored region of Fig. 2. It combines Transformer and convolutional methods and primarily consists of two major modules: Efficient Self-Attention and Mix-FFN.

**Efficient Self-attention:** Typically, the features of power lines in images are very subtle, but UAV images typically have relatively high resolution. Therefore, simply reducing the resolution of the image to speed up self-attention computation can easily result in the loss of local details of the power lines, leading to poor segmentation results. Consequently, we introduce Efficient Self-Attention to reduce the computational complexity of self-attention. The formula for Efficient Self-Attention is as follows:

$$\begin{aligned}
\hat{K} &= Reshape(\frac{N}{R^2}, C \cdot R^2)(K), \\
K &= Linear(C \cdot R^2, C)(\hat{K}), \\
\hat{V} &= Reshape(\frac{N}{R^2}, C \cdot R^2)(V), \\
V &= Linear(C \cdot R^2, C)(\hat{V}),
\end{aligned} \tag{5}$$

where $K, V$ is the input sequence of query and value and $\hat{K}$ and $\hat{V}$ is the sequence after length reduction, $R$ is the reduction ratio, and $C$ is the number of channels. The following formula reshapes the input sequence $K$ and $V$, which has dimension $N \times C$, into $\frac{N}{R^2} \times (C \cdot R^2)$ to obtain $\hat{K}$ and $\hat{V}$. Then they passed through a linear layer with an input channel size of $C \cdot R^2$ and an output channel size of $C$, resulting in a new sequence, denoted by $K$ and $V$.

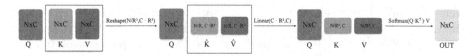

**Fig. 3.** Efficient Self-Attention. The orange, green, and blue blocks represent the sequence $Q$, $K$, and $V$, and their corresponding reshaped sequence $\hat{K}, \hat{V}$, respectively. The Linear($\cdot$) operator only exerts on the sequence, packed in black rectangle. The beige blocks represent the out sequence. (Color figure online)

As shown in Fig. 3, the calculation process of Efficient Self-Attention is depicted. In this process, $Q$ remains unchanged, while $K$ and $V$ undergo sequence reduction and linear layer transformations to attain a size of $\frac{N}{R^2} \times C$. The transpose multiplication between $Q$ and $K$ is then passed through a softmax layer to obtain the self-attention weights, which are ultimately multiplied with the sequence $V$ to yield the output of Efficient Self-Attention. By employing these operations, the computational complexity of self-attention is reduced from $O(N^2)$ to $O(\frac{N^2}{R^2})$. Finally, the efficient attention mechanism sets different numbers of attention heads $M$ at each stage. $R$ and $M$ are hyper-parameters, we defined models(from b0 to b5) of different scales based on various hyper-parameters, as shown in Table 2.

**Mix-FFN:** We use convolution instead of positional encoding to introduce positional information and increase the robustness of the model. However, regular convolutions result in excessive computational complexity due to multiple iterations of the module. Inspired by [21], we utilizes a depthwise separable convolution(DW convolution) and MLP to construct the Mix-FFN module, which can be represented as follows:

$$X_{out} = Mlp(GELU(Conv(Mlp(X_{in})))) + X_{in}, \tag{6}$$

where $X_{in}$ represents the input of the Mix-FFN module, while $X_{out}$ represents the output. $X_{in}$ first goes through an MLP layer for dimensionality expansion, followed by a $3 \times 3$ DW convolution to introduce positional information. After activation with the GELU function, the MLP layer reduces the dimensionality back to the input dimension, and finally, it is connected with the input residual to generate the output $X_{out}$. Through this non-linear transformation, the expressive power of the features is enhanced.

### 3.5 Segmentation Head

The Segmentation Head consists of a deconvolutional layer followed by two linear layers. The formula is as follows:

$$\begin{aligned} Y &= UpConv_{7\times7}(F_1'), \\ \hat{Y} &= Linear(C_1, 4C_1)(Y), \\ Y &= Linear(4C_1, 1)(\hat{Y}), \end{aligned} \tag{7}$$

where $F_1'$ and $C_1$ represent the output features and channel number of the 7th stage, respectively, and $Y$ represents the final segmentation result. The $F_1'$ with a shape of $\frac{H}{4} \times \frac{W}{4} \times C_1$ is upsampled through $7 \times 7$ transpose convolution to restore its shape to $H \times W \times C_1$, followed by two linear layers for dimensionality expansion and reduction, resulting in an output with a shape of $H \times W \times 1$ for the transmission line segmentation map. This approach of dimensionality expansion and reduction allows for the combination of various types of features while eliminating low discriminatory combination features, thereby improving the segmentation performance of the model.

### 3.6   Loss Function

As the task at hand involves distinguishing transmission lines from the background, which is a binary classification problem, we utilizes Binary CrossEntropy Loss(BCE Loss) to compute the loss. The formula for calculating BCE Loss is as follows:

$$Loss = -\frac{1}{n} \sum_{i=1}^{n} [y_i^{gt} log(y_i) + (1 - y_i^{gt}) log(1 - y_i)], \tag{8}$$

where $y_i$ represents the pixel point in the segmentation result $Y$, $y_i^{gt}$ represents the pixel point in the ground truth, and $n$ represents the number of pixel points.

## 4   Experiments

### 4.1   Experimental Settings

**Dataset:** We utilized the aerial image dataset TTPLA [22] for transmission line detection in our study. This dataset comprises 1,234 drone aerial images with a resolution of $3,840 \times 2,160$ pixels. To facilitate model training, we resized the images to a dimension of $512 \times 512$. Among these, 1,125 images were allocated for training, while 109 images were set aside for validation, serving as a substitute for the test set.

**Training:** The encoder of the model is initialized using the weights of SegFormer [14] delete this and add information about the traning platform. The training was conducted for 50 epochs with a batch size of 8. The Adam optimizer was employed to adjust the model parameters, with an initial learning rate of 1e-4. To ensure fairness and reproducibility in the comparative experiments, all trials were performed with the same random seed.

**Evaluation Metrics:** We use four metrics: precision, recall, F1-score, and IoU, for evaluating the segmentation results.

### 4.2   Comparative Experiments

Table 1 demonstrates the quantitative comparison of our method and the other state-of-the-art benchmarks. On the highly challenging TTPLA dataset, it shows that the proposed MiT-Unet(b1, b2) achieves significantly better performance

**Table 1.** The comparative results of various models on the TTPLA dataset.

| Method | Params(M) | FLOPs(G) | Precision(%) | Recall(%) | F1score(%) | IoU(%) |
|---|---|---|---|---|---|---|
| Unet | 31.04 | 218.95 | 79.39 | 76.77 | 78.06 | 60.58 |
| SegFormer(b1) | **13.24** | **13.68** | 72.82 | 63.17 | 67.66 | 46.71 |
| SegFormer(b2) | 27.35 | **56.70** | 77.06 | 68.18 | 72.35 | 51.10 |
| Swin-Unet | 231.96 | 180.32 | 80.10 | 74.79 | 77.35 | 60.26 |
| MiT-Unet(b1) | **19.27** | 73.25 | **81.34** | **81.31** | **81.32** | **65.24** |

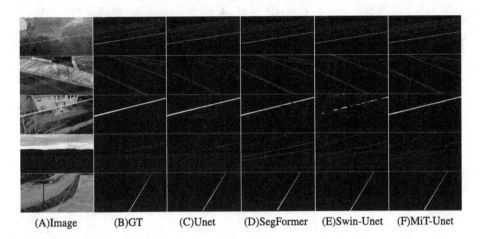

(A)Image    (B)GT    (C)Unet    (D)SegFormer    (E)Swin-Unet    (F)MiT-Unet

**Fig. 4.** Visualization of segmented results on the TTPLA dataset.

over other benchmarks in all four evaluation metrics. Specifically, compared to the third-best Unet, our model(MiT-Unet(b2)) achieves 2.83%, 6.28%, 4.57% and 7.88% improvement in Precision, Recall, F1-score, and IoU respectively. Moreover, our model exhibits excellent computational efficiency in parameter numbers and FLOPs compared with other models.

Figure 4 demonstrates a qualitative evaluation of the segmentation results obtained by various methods. It is evident that power line features face significant interference from the background, including elements like zebra crossings and lane markings. Additionally, due to the delicate nature of power lines, their wire features exhibit weaker contrast compared to other linear objects. Compared with other benchmarks, the proposed model delivers more robust results, preserving the continuity of power lines while producing fewer instances of false segmentation, leading to relatively clear segmentation results.

## 4.3 Ablation Experiments

*A. MiT-Unet with different scale hyper-parameters*
We propose six versions of MiT-Unet(from b0 to b5), which have different hyper-parameter scales, as shown in Table 2, where $R$ represents the reduction ratios

**Table 2.** MiT-Unet defines six models(from b0 to b5) with different hyper-parameter scales.

| | R | M | L | C |
|---|---|---|---|---|
| b0 | [8, 4, 2, 1, 2, 4, 8] | [1, 2, 5, 8, 5, 2, 1] | [2, 2, 2, 2, 2, 2, 2] | [32, 64, 160, 256, 160, 64, 32] |
| b1 | [8, 4, 2, 1, 2, 4, 8] | [1, 2, 5, 8, 5, 2, 1] | [2, 2, 2, 2, 2, 2, 2] | [64, 128, 320, 512, 320, 128, 64] |
| b2 | [8, 4, 2, 1, 2, 4, 8] | [1, 2, 5, 8, 5, 2, 1] | [3, 3, 6, 3, 6, 3, 3] | [64, 128, 320, 512, 320, 128, 64] |
| b3 | [8, 4, 2, 1, 2, 4, 8] | [1, 2, 5, 8, 5, 2, 1] | [3, 3, 18, 3, 18, 3, 3] | [64, 128, 320, 512, 320, 128, 64] |
| b4 | [8, 4, 2, 1, 2, 4, 8] | [1, 2, 5, 8, 5, 2, 1] | [3, 8, 27, 3, 27, 8, 3] | [64, 128, 320, 512, 320, 128, 64] |
| b5 | [8, 4, 2, 1, 2, 4, 8] | [1, 2, 5, 8, 5, 2, 1] | [3, 6, 40, 3, 40, 6, 3] | [64, 128, 320, 512, 320, 128, 64] |

**Table 3.** Performance comparison of different scale versions of MiT-Unet on TTPLA dataset.

| Method | Params(M) | FLOPs(G) | Precision(%) | Recall(%) | F1score(%) | IoU(%) |
|---|---|---|---|---|---|---|
| MiT-Unet(b0) | **4.87** | **18.48** | 80.46 | 78.57 | 79.51 | 62.25 |
| MiT-Unet(b1) | 19.27 | 73.25 | 81.34 | 81.31 | 81.32 | 65.24 |
| MiT-Unet(b2) | 38.18 | 88.48 | 82.22 | 83.05 | 82.63 | 68.46 |
| MiT-Unet(b3) | 77.93 | 117.78 | **85.53** | 80.46 | 82.92 | 68.45 |
| MiT-Unet(b4) | 111.48 | 145.90 | 85.21 | 80.99 | 83.05 | 68.29 |
| MiT-Unet(b5) | 152.68 | 174.56 | 82.96 | **83.66** | **83.30** | **69.36** |

of the Efficient Self-Attention (Eq. 5); $M$ represents the head numbers of the Efficient Self-Attention; $L$ represents the numbers of encoder layers, as shown in Fig. 2; $C$ represents the output channel numbers in MiT-down and MiT-up modules. For each model, there are seven elements in each bracket, which correspond to seven level transitions, including MiT-Down and MiT-Up, from $F_1$ to $F_1'$ at the encoding and decoding procedures.

From b0 to b5, the complexity of the model gradually increases, as shown in the Params(M) and FLOPs(G) columns of Table 3. It also shows that when the model scale reaches b2, the gain from further increasing the parameter scale is plateaus, as shown in F1-score and IoU. Therefore, we only focus on the performance of MiT-Unet (b0,b1,b2) in experiments.

### B.  Comparison of Sampling Methods

Since the proposed model integrates transformer encoder features and convolutional neural network features, the upsampling module TLFM and the downsampling module TLFE in MiT-Down and MiT-Up modules play a very important role. Table 4 illustrates the impact of the proposed TLFM and TLFE and their potential alternative scheme on segmentation results. It shows that the Bilinear Interpolation and the Patch Merging and Patch Expanding [12, 20] exhibit inferior performance for transmission line segmentation. This may be attributed to the limitations of bilinear interpolation, which solely relies on the local features for interpolation and fails to leverage high-level contextual information of

**Table 4.** Performance comparison of TLFM and TLFE modules with other sampling methods on TTPLA dataset.

| Sampling Method | F1score(%) | IoU(%) |
|---|---|---|
| TLFM and TLFE | **79.51** | **62.25** |
| Bilinear Interpolation | 63.24 | 49.09 |
| Patch Merging andPatch Expanding | 66.01 | 54.26 |

**Table 5.** Ablation experiment results for ESA (Efficient Self-attention) and MixFFN modules on TTPLA dataset.

| +ESA | +MixFFN | F1score(%) | IoU(%) |
|---|---|---|---|
| ✗ | ✗ | 60.92 | 41.88 |
| ✓ | ✗ | 64.88 | 46.41 |
| ✗ | ✓ | 73.79 | 55.88 |
| ✓ | ✓ | **79.51** | **62.25** |

power lines. On the other side, patch-based sampling methods, depending on the selection and merging techniques employed for the patches, could lead to lost vulnerable line features in complex backgrounds.

*C.   Ablation of various modules*

We conduct our ablation experiment based on MiT-Unet(b0) model to verify the effectiveness of Efficient Self-Attention module and MixFFN module. In the baseline module, we directly shield Efficient Self-Attention and MixFFN in MiT module. It is shown in Table 5 that compared to the baseline, Efficient Self-Attention and MixFFN individually achieve 3.96% and 12.87% improvements on F1-score and 4.53% and 14% on IoU. When the two modules are combined, it can obtain an additional improvement of 5.72% on F1-score, and 6.37% on IoU.

## 4.4   Self-attention Visualization

To validate the effectiveness of this module, we conduct an experiment to analysis of the self-attention matrices in each MiT module. Figure 5 demonstrates the rendered self-attention matrix in each level, which is based on Mit-Unet(b0) model. It shows that for a specific pixel located on the power line, red point, its self-attention matrix effectively focuses on similar pixels located on power lines, especially at the decoder stage at high-resolution levels ($F_3'toF_2'andF_2'toF_1'$), which enhances power line features from the background, thus, improving the completeness and accuracy of power line segmentation.

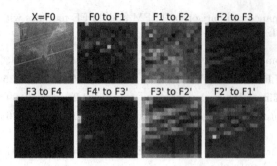

**Fig. 5.** For a specific pixel (red point in the original image) located on the transmission line, its self-attention matrix in each level transition MiT module is rendered. (Color figure online)

## 5   Conclusion

In this paper, we propose MiT-Unet, which incorporates the lightweight transformer encoding and CNN-based Unet structures, allowing for the extraction and segmentation of features from local small targets while maintaining a large receptive field. Experimental results demonstrate that our model achieves superior performance on multiple metrics compared to state-of-the-art image segmentation methods, even on our smaller-scale version. In the future, we may embed the small scale model into UAV for applications related to transmission line detection.

## References

1. Li, Z., Liu, Y., Hayward, R., Zhang, J., Cai, J.: Knowledge-based power line detection for UAV surveillance and inspection systems. In: 2008 23rd International Conference Image and Vision Computing New Zealand, pp. 1–6. IEEE (2008)
2. Damodaran, S., Shanmugam, L., Jothi Swaroopan, N.M.: Overhead power line detection from aerial images using segmentation approaches. Automatika **65**(1), 261–288 (2024)
3. Shuai, C., Wang, H., Zhang, G., Kou, Z., Zhang, W.: Power lines extraction and distance measurement from binocular aerial images for power lines inspection using UAV. In: 2017 9th International Conference on Intelligent Human-Machine Systems and Cybernetics (IHMSC), vol. 2, pp. 69–74. IEEE (2017)
4. Lihui, L., Chen, Z., Wang, R., Liu, L., Chi, H.: Yolo-inspection: defect detection method for power transmission lines based on enhanced yolov5s. J. Real-Time Image Proc. **20**(5), 104 (2023)
5. Zhu, K., Xu, C., Wei, Y., Cai, G.: Fast-PLDN: fast power line detection network. J Real-Time Image Process. **19**(1), 1–11 (2022)
6. Rao, P.P., et al.: QuadFormer: quadruple transformer for unsupervised domain adaptation in power line segmentation of aerial images. arXiv preprint arXiv:2211.16988 (2022)

7. Ronneberger, O., Fischer, P., Brox, T.: U-net: convolutional networks for biomedical image segmentation. In: Medical Image Computing and Computer-Assisted Intervention–MICCAI 2015: 18th International Conference, Munich, Germany, October 5-9, 2015, Proceedings, Part III 18, pp. 234–241. Springer (2015)

8. Jha, D., Riegler, M.A., Johansen, D., Halvorsen, P., Johansen, H.D.: DoubleU-Net: a deep convolutional neural network for medical image segmentation. In: 2020 IEEE 33rd International Symposium on Computer-Based Medical Systems (CBMS), pp. 558–564. IEEE (2020)

9. Zhou, Z., Rahman Siddiquee, M.M., Tajbakhsh, N., Liang, J.: UNet++: a nested U-Net architecture for medical image segmentation. In: Deep Learning in Medical Image Analysis and Multimodal Learning for Clinical Decision Support: 4th International Workshop, DLMIA 2018, and 8th International Workshop, ML-CDS 2018, Held in Conjunction with MICCAI 2018, Granada, Spain, September 20, 2018, Proceedings 4, pp. 3–11. Springer (2018)

10. Huang, H., et al.: UNet 3+: a full-scale connected UNet for medical image segmentation. In: ICASSP 2020-2020 IEEE International Conference on Acoustics, Speech and Signal Processing (ICASSP), pp. 1055–1059. IEEE (2020)

11. Vaswani, A., et al.: Attention is all you need. Adv. Neural Info. Process. Syst. **30** (2017)

12. Dosovitskiy, A., et al.: An image is worth $16 \times 16$ words: transformers for image recognition at scale. arXiv preprint arXiv:2010.11929 (2020)

13. Liu, Z., et al.: Swin Transformer: hierarchical vision transformer using shifted windows. In: Proceedings of the IEEE/CVF International Conference on Computer Vision, pp. 10012–10022 (2021)

14. Xie, E., Wang, W., Yu, Z., Anandkumar, A., Alvarez, J.M., Luo, P.: SegFormer: simple and efficient design for semantic segmentation with transformers. Adv. Neural Info. Process. Syst. **34**, 12077–12090 (2021)

15. Liu, Z., et al.: ConvTransformer: a convolutional transformer network for video frame synthesis. arXiv preprint arXiv:2011.10185 (2020)

16. Guo, J., et al.: CMT: convolutional neural networks meet vision transformers. In: Proceedings of the IEEE/CVF Conference on Computer Vision and Pattern Recognition, pp. 12175–12185 (2022)

17. Zheng, S., et al.: Rethinking semantic segmentation from a sequence-to-sequence perspective with transformers. In: Proceedings of the IEEE/CVF Conference on Computer Vision and Pattern Recognition, pp. 6881–6890 (2021)

18. Zhang, Y., Liu, H., Hu, Q.: TransFuse: fusing transformers and CNNs for medical image segmentation. In: de Bruijne, M., et al. (eds.) MICCAI 2021. LNCS, vol. 12901, pp. 14–24. Springer, Cham (2021). https://doi.org/10.1007/978-3-030-87193-2_2

19. Chen, J., et al.: TransUNet: transformers make strong encoders for medical image segmentation. arXiv preprint arXiv:2102.04306 (2021)

20. Cao, H., et al.: Swin-UNet: UNet-like pure transformer for medical image segmentation. In: European conference on computer vision, pp. 205–218. Springer (2022)

21. Howard, A.G., et al.: MobileNets: efficient convolutional neural networks for mobile vision applications. arXiv preprintarXiv:1704.04861 (2017)

22. Abdelfattah, R., Wang, X., Wang, S.: TTPLA: an aerial-image dataset for detection and segmentation of transmission towers and power lines. In: Proceedings of the Asian Conference on Computer Vision (2020)

# Semantic-Driven Multi-character Multi-motion 3D Animation Generation

Hui Liang[1(✉)], Fan Xu[1], Junjun Pan[2], and Zhaolin Zhang[1]

[1] Zhengzhou University of Light Industry, Zhengzhou 450002, China
hliang@zzuli.edu.cn
[2] Beihang University, Beijing 100191, China

**Abstract.** Semantic-driven animation generation significantly eases the workload of animators, but it still confronts a variety of challenges (e.g., natural language input, temporal reasoning under visualization, linking natural language with graphical systems, etc.). This paper tackles the issue of synchronized motion juxtaposition in terms of temporal visualization. We utilize semantic dependency analysis, prior probabilities and the Semantic Action Graph to extract and fuse synchronous motions, thus creating an advanced system for generating Semantic-driven 3D animations. The results demonstrate that our system proficiently generates natural and coherent 3D animations from text descriptions involving multiple characters and actions. This effectively overcomes the synchronized motion juxtaposition challenge and advances the field of Semantic-driven animation creation.

**Keywords:** synchronized motion · synchronized motion juxtaposition challenge · semantics · animation generation

## 1 Introduction

3D animation is extensively employed in various sectors including advertisement, games, and education [1]. The concept of generating 3D animations driven by semantics has gained popularity in recent times [2], despite facing hurdles such as interpreting natural language inputs, handling temporal reasoning, and connecting natural language with graphic interfaces [3]. Key among these is the challenge of motion timeliness, which includes the alignment of one motion with a preceding one and synchronized motion juxtaposition. Our focus in this paper is on the latter challenge. The term 'synchronized motion juxtaposability' pertains to the concurrent alignment of multiple actions in a timeline [3]. Synchronized motion consists of two scenarios: between different characters, and in the varied actions of a single character. For instance, in the sentence "Zhang Hua is running and Li Ming is walking his dog," both characters are engaged in distinct actions that occur concurrently. In another example, "Zhang Hua is running and waving at the same time," a single character is performing two actions at the same time.

In systems designed for generating 3D animations based on semantic inputs, the issue of synchronized motion juxtaposition poses a significant challenge, particularly when

N. Magnenat Thalmann et al. (Eds.): CASA 2024, CCIS 2374, pp. 268–280, 2025.
https://doi.org/10.1007/978-981-96-2681-6_19

dealing with complex input sentences. If the system is limited to processing sentences that describe a single motion, the challenge of synchronized motion juxtaposition does not arise. However, when the system is equipped to handle sentences that describe multiple motions for a single character, the potential for these motions to occur in synchrony becomes a pertinent issue. The complexity further increases if the system also accommodates sentences involving multiple characters, elevating the likelihood of needing to coordinate motions among different characters. Therefore, it is evident that animation generation systems capable of interpreting complex sentences with multiple characters and a variety of motions must tackle the issue of synchronized motion juxtaposition effectively. At this juncture, the critical challenge lies in how to analyze and interpret the relationships of juxtaposition or succession among the various motions described in a sentence.

Semantic-driven 3D animation generation systems face another critical challenge when it comes to creating synchronized motion juxtapositions. This involves synthesizing animations where motions are perfectly timed either in a single character or among multiple characters. These two scenarios are fundamentally different and require varied approaches. When synchronizing motion among multiple characters, the primary task is to create individual animations for each character that coincide in time. In this scenario, the animations for all characters are designed to align in the same timeframe, resulting in a cohesive overlap on the timeline. Conversely, synchronizing different movements in a single character presents a different set of challenges. Here, the focus shifts to merging various motion animations into one for the same character. These animations overlap in the timeline, and for synchronized motion between different movements of a single character, this method is not applicable. The integration of diverse movements in a single character's animation is a crucial aspect that needs resolution.

This paper develops a system for generating 3D animations that can handle multiple characters and multiple motions simultaneously, driven by semantic analysis. This system addresses the complex task of aligning motions in sync by leveraging semantic dependency analysis, prior probabilities, and the Semantic Action Graph. As a result, it can produce 3D animations that accurately reflect complex sentences involving numerous characters and varied movements. The system is user-friendly, allowing even beginners to craft detailed animations by utilizing pre-existing motion templates.

In summary, our contribution is as follows:

- Semantic dependency analysis, prior probability and Semantic Action Graph are introduced to address the challenge of synchronized motion juxtaposition in semantically driven animation generation.
- A semantically-driven multi-character, multi-motion 3D animation generation system is constructed to create complex 3D animations containing multiple characters and multiple motions.

The structure of this paper is as follows: Sect. 2 provides a concise review of relevant research. Section 3 elaborates on the methodology employed to overcome the challenges in synchronized motion juxtaposition. Section 4 outlines the design and implementation of our semantically driven animation system, which can handle multiple characters and motions. Section 5 delves into the experimental results and their assessment. Finally, Sect. 6 offers a comprehensive summary of the paper.

## 2 Related Work

In the periods of the mid-2000s and mid-late 2010s, there was a significant increase in the development of semantic-driven animation systems [3]. Presently, research in this field is primarily divided into two streams. The first stream focuses on the motion semantics of natural language, exploring ways to manipulate a character model's skeleton in real time to generate realistic bodily movements [4], such as running, jumping, and bending legs. The second stream assesses the integration of character motion animations into action animations, aiming to visually represent events in a graphics system based on descriptions of events in natural language [5]. Our paper concentrates on the latest advancements in synchronized motion juxtaposition, specifically in the second research category.

Zhang's approach [6] builds upon Cardinal's work [7] by incorporating a module for simplifying sentences based on rules, which allows their system to process complex sentences found in movie scripts. The complexity addressed here involves scenarios with a character performing multiple actions, exemplified by sentences such as "Felix crawls out of the tent, and walks over to Tina. He trips and falls, landing on the rock." In such instances, despite the presence of two characters, only one engages in various movements. A limitation of Zhang's system is its inability to manage simultaneous actions performed by different characters.

Mashad's system [8] employs Named Entity Recognition (NER) and co-reference resolution in aiding the generation of animations that involve various characters executing multiple actions. The primary focus of this system is on analyzing the subject-action-object (SAO) dynamics in the text. However, it does not account for temporal aspects, rendering it ineffective for texts that describe concurrent actions.

Currently, few research systems tackle the challenge of synchronized motion juxtaposition. One such system is Oshita's [9], which analyzes the grammatical structure using a rule-based module that identifies temporal relationships between different actions. This enables it to determine which actions occur concurrently. However, such as Zhang's system, Oshita's does not address the synchronization of varied movements performed by a single character. Moreover, Oshita's method, primarily tailored for English text analysis, becomes more complex when applied to Chinese texts.

## 3 Methodology

### 3.1 Determining Synchronized Motion Using Semantic Dependency Analysis

The contemporary advancements in natural language processing (NLP) are opening up new possibilities. The architecture of HanLP draws inspiration from the CoreNLP [10] tool developed by Stanford University's NLP group. As a toolkit based on deep learning for NLP, HanLP offers an extensive array of functionalities and models. These include Chinese text segmentation, lexical annotation, named entity recognition, dependency syntactic analysis, semantic role labeling, and other tasks applicable across various domains [11]. HanLP is renowned for its user-friendliness and high-performance capabilities, making it a preferred tool in Chinese [12].

In HanLP, semantic dependency analysis is a specific task that evaluates the semantic relationships among words in a sentence, presenting them in the form of graph structures [13]. This method stands out from the dependency syntactic analysis typically employed in other research. It can more adeptly extract complex semantic relations. For instance, HanLP's semantic dependency analysis is adept at discerning relationships among multiple actions in Chinese texts. This feature simplifies the task of handling synchronized motion juxtaposition. To illustrate, consider the sentence "张华在遛狗时，李明在跑步，突然，他摔倒了。(Zhang Hua is walking the dog while Li Ming is running, but suddenly, he falls down.)". Here, conventional dependent syntactic analysis may not effectively identify that "遛(walking)" and "跑步(running)" are juxtaposed, and that "跑步(running)" and "摔倒(fell down)" follow each other (as shown in Fig. 1). Semantic dependency analysis, however, can accurately reflect these dynamics, indicating the parallelism of "遛(walking)" and "跑步(running)" and the sequential nature of "跑步(running)" and "摔倒(fell down)" (as shown in Fig. 2). Similarly, this analysis can be employed to extract the synchronization of different actions performed by a single character, as well as to gather insights into subject, object, and manner, etc.

**Fig. 1.** Dependency syntactic analysis results. The relation between the verbs "遛(walking)", "跑步(running)" and "摔倒(fell down)" is conj, conj = conjunct.

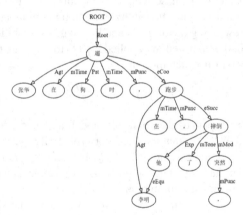

**Fig. 2.** Semantic dependency analysis results. eCoo = event Coordinating relationship, eSucc = event Successive relationship.

## 3.2 Fusing Animations Using Animation Controllers and a Priori Probabilities

In Unity, the animation controller [14] plays a crucial role in managing animation states and implementing animation logic. It enables the developer to craft and manipulate a character's motion animations, toggling between various animations based on the underlying animation logic. A key feature of the animation controller is its layers, which allow the developer to simultaneously handle multiple sets of motion animations for a character. Each layer possesses its unique states and transitions, operating independently from others. This feature is particularly beneficial for managing complex characters with multi-layer animations (e.g. facial expressions, gestures, etc.). Utilizing these capabilities, our system employs animation controller layers to merge synchronized motion animations of a character's different movements. This is achieved by superimposing the motion animation from one layer onto another at the appropriate moment.

Every motion animation governs the character's entire body. Overlaying one motion animation directly onto another would lead to the latter being entirely obscured. To address this, it is essential to designate specific parts of the character for coverage in the overlay layer. The remaining parts will then display according to the motion animation of the overlay layer.

The selection of the character parts for overlay coverage is guided by the a priori probability. This probability is derived from the statistical analysis of the motion dataset.

Our dataset of motions is sourced from Mixamo [15], featuring 2484 character template animations. First and foremost, we consolidated the bones frequently manipulated by the character models in these template animations into six comprehensive body sections, yielding the following parts: head, upper body, left arm, right arm, left leg, and right leg. Thereafter, we undertook a detailed annotation process on the dataset. This involved labeling each template animation with the names of the motions it includes and the specific body parts engaged in these motions. For every template animation, we divided it during the annotation phase. This division aimed to separate fused animations comprising multiple motions into their individual motion components. Figure 3 illustrates this process, showcasing the division and labeling of a specific Hip Hop Dancing template animation. In the final step, we applied Eq. (1) to calculate the prior probability of needing each body part for each motion.

$$P(B_i|M) = \frac{C(B_i, M)}{C(M)} \tag{1}$$

where $B_i$ denotes a body part of the character model, and $1 \leq i \leq 6$; $M$ denotes the character motion; and $P(B_i|M)$ denotes the prior probability that the body part $B_i$ will be utilized under the character motion M; $C(B_i, M)$ denotes the number of the body part $B_i$ is utilized under the character motion $M$; $C(M)$ denotes the number of template animations that contain character motion $M$.

The concept of prior probability here serves to evaluate the significance of each character part in a chosen motion. The subsequent phase involves determining the most suitable animation for each character part in the fused animation. To make this selection, we employ Eq. (2), which aids in identifying the most fitting animations, among those available for fusion, that include the required motion.

$$O(B_i, A_j, A_{j+1}) = \begin{cases} (B_i, A_j), P(B_i|A_j) \geq P(B_i|A_{j+1}) \\ (B_i, A_{j+1}), P(B_i|A_j) < P(B_i|A_{j+1}) \end{cases} \tag{2}$$

where $A_j$ denotes the animation which contain character motion $M_j$, and $1 \leq j <$ The number of animations to be fused; $(B_i, A_j)$ denotes the movement of body part $B_i$ follows the animation $A_j$; $P(B_i|A_j)$ indicates the prior probability that the body part $B_i$ will be utilized under the character motion $A_j$; $O(B_i, A_j, A_{j+1})$ denotes which animation, $A_j$ or $A_{j+1}$, should be referenced for the motion of body part $B_i$.

**Fig. 3.** Split results and labeling for a particular Hip Hop Dancing template animation

We integrate various motion animation clips of a single character in the initial layer and a newly established layer. This involves setting the weight parameter of the new layer to match that of the initial layer, switching the new layer to override mode, and assigning a fresh Avatar to this layer. The purpose of the weight parameter is to manage the extent to which the animation in one layer blends with animations in other layers. The avatar's role is to define which body part should be blended or animated in the motion animation clips. As it is not feasible to introduce a parameter directly to the transition between the ENTRY state and the animation clip in each layer, we circumvent this limitation by inserting an empty state between them. We then add a parameter to the transition from this empty state to the animation clip. This parameter outlines the specific conditions that trigger the transition.

Take, for instance, the fusion process of motion animations "走(Walk)" and "挥手(Wave)", as illustrated in Fig. 4.

## 4  Semantic-Driven Multi-character Multi-motion 3D Animation Generation System

### 4.1  System Overview

In this section, we will explain the flow of the system as depicted in Fig. 5. The process begins with the system analyzing the input text to identify multiple motion tuples. This is achieved via semantic dependency analysis, which allows us to extract the subject, object, and manner, among other things. These motion tuples are then organized into Semantic Action Graph. Thereafter, the system searches the motion database to find suitable motion animations for each identified motion. These selected animations are then arranged based on the binary tree structure of the Semantic Action Graph. This arrangement is utilized to

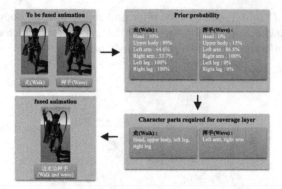

**Fig. 4.** Motion animation fusion process of "走(Walk)" and "挥手(wave)".

animate the previously chosen virtual object model. Throughout this phase, the system merges the motion animations as needed.

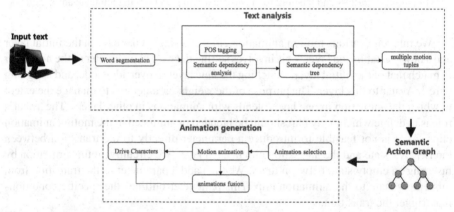

**Fig. 5.** System flow

## 4.2 Chinese Text Analysis

Firstly, we segment the input text using HanLP. Following this segmentation, we perform lexical annotation and semantic dependency analysis. The final step involves identifying individual motion tuples based on the semantic dependency analysis's dependency tree.

Lexical annotation aims to identify verbs in the text, which are then stored in a collection. This collection serves as a reference point to initiate the analysis for extracting motor tuples from the semantic dependency analysis results.

The purpose of semantic dependency analysis is to create a dependency tree. This tree represents the semantic interconnections among words in the text. In this structure, the verb functions as the primary node, with related words as subordinate nodes.

Additionally, this tree labels the semantic interrelations between each pair of connected words. Our system pays special attention to the semantic relations among different verbs.

We analyze the dependency tree using specific rules. This analysis is aimed at determining all motion tuples, anchored in the semantic relations depicted in the tree (subject, object, manner, tendency, final location, quantity, subsequent motion tuple, and concurrent motion tuple, etc.). A sample of these frequently employed semantic relations is presented in Table 1.

1) Create each motion tuples. Treat every verb in the set independently as a name for a motion tuple. The motion contained in this motion tuple is identical to the verb itself. In instances where the same verb appears multiple times in the set, assign ordinal numbers to differentiate between them, e.g., 'hit 1', 'hit 2'.

2) Enrich the details for each motion tuples. Go through the verbs in the set and determine the subject, object, and manner, etc., based on the semantic relationships correlated to the verb in the dependency tree. Incorporate these details into the respective motion tuple. Note that some actions may not require an object, or there might be an absence of a concurrent motion category, etc. In such scenarios, the symbol "^" is utilized to indicate the absence of that component in the motion tuple.

**Table 1.** Several commonly utilized semantic relations

| Marker word | Meaning |
| --- | --- |
| eCoo | event Coordination |
| eSucc | event Successor |
| Agt | Agent |
| Pat | Patient |
| Mann | Manner |
| Lfin | Location-final |
| Nmod | Name-modifier |
| mAux | Auxiliary Marker |
| mPrep | Preposition Marker |
| Desc | Description |
| Quan | Quantity |

## 4.3  Semantic Action Graph

The system then proceeds to identify all motion tuples in the text, and generating the Semantic Action Graph. This graph arranges all motion tuples chronologically. It is stored as a binary tree structure. Due to the limitations of semantic dependency analysis, which can only process one sentence at a time, our system assumes that the motion relationships between different sentences have a sequential dependency.

For instance, the sentence "李明一边架起手臂，一边持续左转地走回张华的旁边。而后李明以弓步姿态亮相，张华同时以单腿站立姿态亮相。(Li Ming raises his arms and continues to turn left as he walks back to Zhang Hua's side. Thereafter, Li Ming poses in a horse stance position, paralleled by Zhang Hua making a pose in a one-legged standing posture.)" illustrates the sequential timing of the movements. The Semantic Action Graph of this sentence evidently exhibits the temporal sequence of the movements, as presented in Fig. 6.

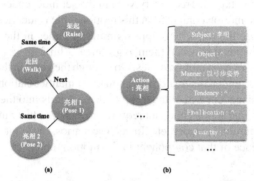

**Fig. 6.** Semantic Action Graph. (a) displays a binary tree structure, wherein the left child node represents the side-by-side movement, and the right child denotes the subsequent motion. (b) details the node information of the binary tree, where each node corresponds to a motion tuple. "∧" represents missing information.

### 4.4   Semantic Label Definition for Motion Animation and 3D Models

To ensure semantic matching between the semantic processing results of text and animations, it is crucial to assign relevant semantic labels to each motion animation in our database. These labels include motion, subject, object, manner, and tendency, etc. While annotating each animation, we deconstruct it, ensuring that animations composed of multiple motions are segmented into individual motions. Figure 7 shows an example of semantic annotation.

In animation, changes often occur in the spatial positioning of a model. To address this, we assign semantic labels to describe the model's spatial position. These include: '上' (up), '下' (down), '左' (left), '右' (right), '前' (front), '后' (back), '周围' (around), '远' (far), and '近' (near). The term 'surrounding' refers to the nearness of each direction.

To differentiate between "far" and "near", our system calculates the average of the sum of the model's dimensions along the X, Y, and Z axes. The definition of the coordinate system is the same as in Unity 3D. A measurement equal to or less than this average is categorized as "near", while anything exceeding it is classified as "far".

### 4.5   Animation Generation

The process of creating animations from motion tuples in Unity involves an first step of selecting the most appropriate motion animation from a database, matching it to the

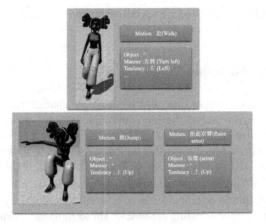

**Fig. 7.** Semantic annotation of a particular Hip Hop Dancing template animation.

given motion tuple. This selection is guided by the semantic tags associated with the motion animations. The diversity in textual expressions, however, adds complexity to the task of retrieving motion animations from the database. In this context, we employ the Word2Vec model to facilitate a more effective search for the motion animation that aligns closely with the motion tuple in the database. This search is carried out in two steps.

In the first step, we select a motion animation from the database, which includes the specific movements described in the motion tuple, as a potential option.

In the second step, we assess all potential motion animations. This evaluation employs Word2Vec to analyze the semantic labels and modality tendencies associated with each candidate motion animation. Through this process, we identify the motion animation that most closely aligns with our criteria, indicated by the highest degree of similarity.

Word2Vec, an unsupervised learning model in a neural network, is critical here. It transforms words into vector representations in a 300-dimensional space. This conversion facilitates the comparison of word similarities [16]. For accurate similarity measurement, we employ the cosine similarity formula [17]. This formula calculates the similarity based on the angle between two word vectors: a smaller angle indicates greater similarity. The specific details of this formula are provided in (3).

$$Similarity(A, B) = \frac{A \cdot B}{||A|| ||B||} \tag{3}$$

Of these, the $A$ and $B$ are two vectors, and $A \cdot B$ is the inner product, and $||A||$ denotes the vector $A$ modulo.

Following this, our system activates the chosen animation, guiding the character model to replicate the motion as outlined in the semantic motion graph. At this stage, it is crucial to determine whether there appears to be a necessity to synthesize animation. This decision depends on the subject of the motion and the relationship between different motions. The character models and scenes utilized in our system are pre-established and selected by the user before text input.

## 5  Results and Discussion

In Chinese opera, performances often involve multiple characters and complex movements. Therefore, we demonstrate the animation capabilities of our system in the context of Chinese opera performances.

Figures 8 and Fig. 9 depict the scene where "李明一边架起手臂，一边持续左转地走回张华的旁边。而后李明以弓步姿态亮相，张华同时以单腿站立姿态亮相。(Li Ming raises his arms and continues to turn left as he walks back to Zhang Hua's side. Thereafter, Li Ming poses in a horse stance position, paralleled by Zhang Hua making a pose in a one-legged standing posture.)" These movements are typical of opera performances.

**Fig. 8.** Animation generated from the previous sentence. The character on the right is Li Ming, whose movement is a combination of "walk left turn" and "raise arms".

**Fig. 9.** Animation generated by the text of the latter sentence. The character on the left is Zhuang hua, and he and Li ming make their respective movements at the same time.

We invited 30 participants (15 females), aged between 10 to 60 years. We created five animations based on the described motions and requested the participants to evaluate them. They rated each animation on a scale from 1 (least favorite) to 5 (most favorite) according to three specific criteria. Figure 10 represents these comprehensive findings. Naturalness reflects the coordination of a character's motion, especially in fused animations. Acceptability indicates whether the animations, as derived from the text, are considered suitable or appropriate, while plausibility represents if the timing of characters' movements in the animations aligns with the motion description in the text.

In the evaluation, participants were considered to have given positive feedback on our work when their scores exceeded 3. Out of 450 responses, we received 363 instances of positive feedback. Applying the Wilson score confidence interval for Bernoulli trials [18], our analysis indicated a 95% probability that users will appreciate the animations produced by our method at least 78.3% of the time.

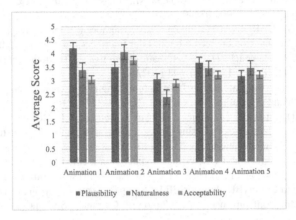

**Fig. 10.** Detailed findings

## 6  Conclusion

This paper introduces a novel method for generating 3D animations. It integrates semantic dependency analysis, a priori probability, and a Semantic Action Graph, including a range of motions for various characters. A key feature of this method is the animation fusion, which allows a single character to execute multiple motions simultaneously in different body parts. The resulting animations closely mirror the provided textual descriptions, showcasing our method's adeptness in overcoming the challenges of synchronized motion juxtaposition in Semantic-driven 3D animation creation.

However, the complexity of Chinese expressions sometimes hinders the identification of exact corresponding motion animations, impacting the effectiveness of our animation fusion approach. Additionally, our current method faces challenges in analyzing texts with multiple sentences, as the motion across different sentences is managed based solely on their interrelation. Future work will focus on enhancing our method to resolve these issues.

## References

1. Ma, M., Kevitt, P.M.: Virtual human animation in natural language visualisation. In: Special Issue on the 16th Artificial Intelligence and Cognitive Science Conference (AICS-05), Artificial Intelligence Review, vol. 25 (1–2), pp. 37–53 (2006)

2. Ma, M.: Automatic conversion of natural language to 3D animation. Ph.D. dissertation, Dept. Eng., Univ. Ulster, Coleraine, U.K. (2006)
3. Bouali, N., Cavalli-Sforza, V.: A review of text-to-animation systems. IEEE Access 11, 86071–86087 (2023)
4. Sarma, H., Porzel, R., Smeddinck, J.D., Malaka, R., Samaddar, A.B.: A text to animation system for physical exercises. Comput. J. 61(11), 1589–1604 (2018)
5. Zhang, J.Q., et al.: Write-an-animation: high-level text-based animation editing with character-scene interaction. Comput. Graph. Forum 40(7), 217–228 (2021)
6. Zhang, Y., Tsipidi, E., Schriber, S., Kapadia, M., Gross, M., Modi, A.: Generating animations from screenplays. arXiv:1904.05440 (2019)
7. Marti, M., et al.: CARDINAL: Computer assisted authoring of movie scripts. In: Proceedings of 23rd International Conference on Intell, User Interfaces, pp. 509–519 (2018)
8. El-Mashad, S.Y., Hamed, E.-H.-S.: Automatic creation of a 3D cartoon from natural language story. Ain. Shams Eng. J. 13(3), 101641 (2022)
9. Oshita, M.: Generating animation from natural language texts and semantic analysis for motion search and scheduling. Vis. Comput. 26, 339–352 (2010)
10. Manning, C.D., Surdeanu, M., Bauer, J., Finkel, J., Bethard, S.J., Mcclosky, D.: The Stanford CoreNLP natural language processing toolkit. In: Association for Computational Linguistics (ACL) System Demonstrations, pp. 55–60 (2014)
11. Wu, Q., et al.: A film and TV news digest generation method based on HanLP. 18th IEEE Int Symp on Parallel and Distributed Proc with Applicat (ISPA)/10th IEEE Int Conf on Big Data and Cloud Comp (BDCloud)/IEEE Int Symp on Social Comp and Networking (Social-Com)/IEEE Int Conf on Sustainable Comp and Commun (SustainCom), Electr Network (2021)
12. Yang, Y., Ren, G.: HanLP-based technology function matrix construction on Chinese process patents. Int. J. Mob. Comput. Multimedia Commun. 11(3), 48–64 (2020)
13. He, H., Choi, J.D.: The stem cell hypothesis: Dilemma behind multi-task learning with transformer encoders. arXiv preprint arXiv:2109.06939 (2021)
14. Kitsikidis, A., et al.: A game-like application for dance learning using a natural human computer interface. In: International Conference on Universal Access in Human-Computer Interaction, Springer, Cham (2015)
15. INC A. S.: Mixamo (2023). https://www.mixamo.com
16. Asr, F.T., Zinkov, R., Jones, M.: Querying word embeddings for similarity and relatedness. In: Proceedings of the 2018 Conference of the North American Chapter of the Association for Computational Linguistics: Human Language Technologies, vol. 1 (Long Papers) (2018)
17. El-Mashad, S.Y., Shoukry, A.: A more robust feature correspondence for more accurate image recognition. In: 2014 Canadian Conference on Computer and Robot Vision. IEEE (2014)
18. Agresti, A., Coull, B.A.: Approximate is better than "exact" for interval estimation of binomial proportions. Am. Stat. 2, 119–126 (1998)

# MSAR: A Mask Branch Module Integrating Multi-scale Attention and RefineNet

Ping Han[1], Zhicheng Liu[1], and Huahong Zuo[2(✉)]

[1] School of Information Engineering, Wuhan University of Technology, Wuhan, China
{hanping,285393}@whut.edu.cn
[2] Wuhan Chuyan Information Technology Co., Ltd., Wuhan, China
q3163068148@gmail.com

**Abstract.** Aiming to address the issue of inadequate and singular feature extraction in instance segmentation and drawing inspiration from the design concept of RefineNet and relative multi-scale attention, we propose a novel mask branch module known as MSAR (Multi-Scale Attention Refinenet). Initially, features extracted by the backbone network or FPN at different scales are utilized as input. Subsequently, high-level and low-level feature maps are generated through relative multi-scale attention. These generated feature maps are then fused using the RefineNet module to produce the final mask. Testing on the COCO dataset reveals that when MSAR is incorporated into BlendMask, the mask AP can reach 35.55%, indicating that MSAR can enhance the accuracy of masks generated by instance segmentation networks.

**Keywords:** instance segmentation · RefineNet · multi-scale attention

## 1 Introduction

The current trend in computer animation necessitates the utilization of computer vision technology for post-processing, which is widely recognized for its efficiency. Instance segmentation in computer vision presents significant challenges, with current methods broadly categorized into two types: two-stage and one-stage. The former is further divided into top-down and bottom-up approaches. Due to the complexity of parameters and post-processing involved in two-stage instance segmentation methods, there is a growing preference for one-stage methods.

One-stage instance segmentation methods are influenced by one-stage object detection methods, sharing some similarities in their approaches. In 2019, Daniel Bolya et al. proposed Yolact [1], which initially generates a set of prototype masks, linear combination coefficients, and bounding boxes for each instance. Subsequently, the predicted coefficients are linearly combined with the prototype masks, and the resulting masks are clipped using the bounding boxes to obtain the final instance masks. In the same year, they introduced Yolact++ [2], building upon the original model by incorporating deformable convolution, a fast rescoring network, and increased scales and sizes of anchor boxes to improve accuracy at a slight compromise to speed significantly. In 2020, Xie Enze et al. presented PolarMask [3], based on FCOS [4] but utilizing polar coordinates for mask prediction and proposing Polar IoU Loss for polar coordinate predictions. During this period, Wang Xinlong et al. introduced SOLO [5], focusing on separating object instances based on location and size before subsequently proposing SOLOv2 [6]. The improvements include decomposing SOLO's mask branch into separate branches for mask features and mask convolution kernels whose outputs are combined into the mask output to reduce model parameters and implementing Matrix NMS for post-processing to reduce processing time. In 2020, Chen Hao et al. developed BlendMask [7], where a blending module effectively combines top-down and bottom-up methods to achieve improved mask predictions.

Limited research has been conducted on the feature extraction of the backbone network in the aforementioned one-stage instance segmentation methods, and deficiencies persist in feature fusion.

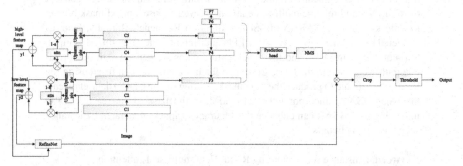

**Fig. 1.** Improved network architecture utilizing YOLACT as a foundation.

The convolutional network extracts image features through the convolutional layers, where high-level and low-level features are limited in neural networks. Semantic and geometric information features become prominent after the fusion of image features at different scales. Therefore, it is essential to utilize features of different scales in instance segmentation fully. In 2016, Lin Guosheng et al. proposed RefineNet [8], which utilizes all downsampling information through multi-paths to maintain high-resolution semantic segmentation predictions. In the same year, Tsung-Yi Lin et al. proposed FPN [9], which fuses feature maps from multiple stages, providing high-level semantic and low-level contour information. In 2017, Zhao Hengshuang et al. proposed PSPNet [10], where the SPP module within the model performs spatial pooling at various grid scales and demonstrates excellent performance on several semantic segmentation benchmarks. In the same year, Liang-Chieh Chen et al. improved Deeplabv3 [11]. The ASPP module inside is similar to the SPP module in PSPNet but uses atrous convolution instead. In 2020, Andrew Tao et al. proposed multi-scale attention [12], which predicts attention between adjacent scales and uses it as a weight to combine image features obtained from different scales, ultimately producing the final mask.

In response to the issue of inadequate and limited feature extraction in the aforementioned instance segmentation network, this paper introduces the MSAR (Multi-Scale Attention Refinenet) module. This module integrates the RefineNet with the backbone of a one-stage instance segmentation network to establish a novel feature extraction network. Additionally, it incorporates a relative multi-scale attention module for improved mask prediction. Integrating this module into the one-stage instance segmentation network allows for consideration of disparities between high-level and low-level features during feature fusion, resulting in more comprehensive features encompassing both advantages.

The paper is organized as follows: Sect. 1 outlines the current research status and existing shortcomings of the instance segmentation task, along with a brief explanation of the new module MSAR proposed in this paper. Section 2 provides a detailed explanation of the working principle and two main modules of the MSAR. In Sect. 3, we discuss the results of both the ablation experiment and the horizontal comparison experiment. Finally, in Sect. 4, we briefly describe the arrangements for follow-up work.

## 2   MSAR Module Introduction

This section proposes a new module, the MSAR (Multi-Scale Attention Refinenet) module.

### 2.1   Overall Structure

The MSAR module constructed in this paper is shown in Fig. 1.

As shown in Fig. 1, The input image undergoes processing by the backbone extraction network, resulting in four output feature maps. These can be obtained through either the backbone network or FPN. Initially, the MRF module [8] in RefineNet processes these output feature maps (via 3 × 3 convolution and upsampling) to maintain consistent feature map sizes and facilitate subsequent processing. Subsequently, the third and fourth-layer output feature maps are combined linearly using weights predicted by the relative multi-scale attention module to produce the high-level feature map y1. Similarly, the first and second-layer output feature maps are combined into the low-level feature map y2 using this same relative multi-scale attention approach. Furthermore, y1 then undergoes complete RefineNet [8] processing before fusing with y2 in the MRF module to generate masks.

Organizing the mask branch extracts more valuable high-level and low-level information through relative multi-scale attention [12], enhancing its focus on the object. This paper aims to integrate high-level and low-level information using this module, improving mask predictions and performance in instance segmentation tasks. The RefineNet module not only leverages multiple levels of features but also incorporates numerous residual structures, resulting in easier and more efficient training.

Compared to the previous architecture, we have modified the input mode in the relatively multi-scale attention module by replacing the parallel processing of three inputs with one-way processing, significantly reducing the number of parameters. Additionally, we have positioned RefineNet's MRF module for size processing after the convolutional layer output, pre-processing the feature map size to ensure consistency before fine-tuning.

## 2.2  Backbone Relative Multi-scale Attention

In the context of relative multi-scale attention [12], the backbone network is required to process input images at various scales for feature extraction. This leads to a complex network structure and excessive parameters, resulting in redundant architecture.

However, in this paper, the convolution process in the backbone network can be interpreted as a gradual downscaling of the image. Consequently, the feature maps obtained at different layers within the backbone network can be viewed as images at varying scales. These feature maps are then combined linearly using weights derived from relative multi-scale attention to produce the final result. The enhanced network framework is illustrated in Fig. 2.

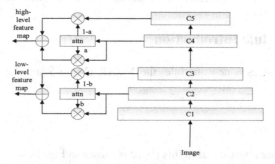

**Fig. 2.**  Enhanced multi-scale attention framework

As depicted in Fig. 2, the input image undergoes the ResNet backbone network (or FPN) processing, resulting in output feature maps from each intermediate layer. These output feature maps are treated as input images at varying scales. In this study, we utilize relative multi-scale attention weights to predict the output feature maps of the last two and first two layers, capturing more suitable high-level and low-level information. These are then concatenated to produce the final output result. The output results of high-level feature maps and low-level feature maps can be represented as:

$$L_{(low-out)} = (1 - b) * L_{c3} + b * L_{c2} \tag{1}$$

$$L_{(high-out)} = (1 - a) * L_{c5} + a * L_{c4} \tag{2}$$

where L denotes the output feature of the current layer in the neural network.

## 2.3  Feature Fusion Based on Single-RefineNet

After careful consideration, this paper introduces the Single-RefineNet into the new feature extraction module to ensure high-resolution predictions for the masks by leveraging all the information obtained during the downsampling process through residual connections. This is unlike current instance segmentation network architectures, which have relatively simple and single feature extraction methods.

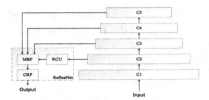

**Fig. 3.** Single-RefineNet

The Single-RefineNet module is depicted in Fig. 3.

Compared to the original architecture, the Single-RefineNet incorporates a single complete RefineNet module positioned after the initial layer output of the backbone network. Following a $3 \times 3$ convolution and upsampling, the feature outputs from subsequent layers are adjusted to match the size of the first layer, facilitating feature fusion within the MRF module [8]. After passing through the RCU module [8], the feature map output from the initial layer is combined with processed feature maps from other layers in the MRF module. Then it undergoes further processing in the CRP module [8], The resulting fused feature map represents our desired output.

The Single-RefineNet preserves RefineNet's essential characteristics, effectively leveraging features from all levels of the backbone network to ensure high-resolution mask predictions while also optimizing the network framework and reducing parameter count.

## 3    Experiment

### 3.1    Experimental Datasets and Experimental Details

During the experiment, both the SBD dataset [13] and the COCO2017 dataset [14] were utilized. The SBD dataset is an improved version of the VOC2011 dataset, sharing the same 20 categories. It consists of 8498 training images and 2857 validation images. The COCO2017 dataset is a widely used large-scale instance segmentation dataset, encompassing 80 object categories and including 118,287 training and 5,000 validation images.

The experimental setup employed an Intel Core i9-10900K CPU@3.70GHz and a GeForce RTX 3090 GPU, with a total memory size of 64GB. The entire network training was conducted using Stochastic Gradient Descent (SGD) with a momentum of 0.9 and weight decay of 0.0005. The batch size was configured to 1, totaling 960,000 iterations. The initial learning rate was set at 0.001, decreasing to one-tenth of its original value at the 48,000th and 800,000th iterations.

### 3.2    Ablation Experiment

This experiment aims to demonstrate the efficacy of the two network modules introduced in Sect. 2. The SBD dataset is used for experimentation, with Yolact as the baseline model and evaluation metrics encompassing AP, AP50, and AP75. Specifically, AP denotes the average precision computed at intervals of 0.05 within the threshold range from 0.5 to

0.95. AP50 represents the mAP value at a threshold of 0.5, while AP75 represents the mAP value at 0.75. All backbone networks are based on ResNet50 architecture. Table 1 presents the experimental findings, where 'a' signifies the RefineNet module and 'b' signifies the multi-scale attention module.

**Table 1.** Comparative Experiment Results

| Model | | AP | $AP_{50}$ | $AP_{75}$ |
|---|---|---|---|---|
| YOLACT | Box | 45.81 | 71.31 | 49.82 |
| | Mask | 44.96 | 68.58 | 47.47 |
| YOLACT + a | Box | 45.94 | 70.98 | 49.58 |
| | Mask | 46.31 | 69.06 | 49.12 |
| YOLACT + a + b | Box | 45.84 | 70.77 | 49.86 |
| | Mask | 46.63 | 68.73 | 49.99 |

The results presented in Table 1 demonstrate that adding YOLACT + a leads to improvements in mask AP by 1.35%, AP50 by 0.48%, and AP75 by 1.65% compared to YOLACT alone. The box AP for both models remains within a similar range, indicating that the RefineNet module, denoted as module a, enhances mask accuracy in instance segmentation when integrated into the backbone network. Furthermore, compared with YOLACT + a, there is an increase of 0.32% in mask AP and 0.87% in AP75, although there is a slight decrease of 0.33% in AP50. Including the RefineNet and multi-scale attention modules improve mask accuracy without significantly impacting box AP.

### 3.3  Comparative Experiment

Subsequently, a comparison will be made with other instance segmentation methods by replacing the mask branch of BlendMask with the mask branch proposed in this paper and observing its impact. The experimental dataset used is the coco2017 dataset, and the evaluation metrics employed are consistent with those used in the ablation experiment. All backbone networks utilized are ResNet50. Throughout this phase, the entire network training uses SGD with a momentum of 0.9 and weight decay of 0.0005. The batch size is set at 4, with 360,000 iterations. The initial learning rate is 0.01 and decays to one-tenth of its original value at 24,000 and 320,000 iterations. Table 2 presents a horizontal comparison of experimental results.

The results in Table 2 indicate a significant enhancement in BlendMask's performance following the replacement of the mask branch. Specifically, there was an increase of 0.21% in mask AP and 0.38% in AP50, with a more modest increase of 0.04% in AP75. These findings underscore the substantial improvement brought about by the newly proposed mask branch, which effectively enhances feature fusion and elevates the accuracy of mask and instance segmentation.

Surprisingly, there is an unexpected enhancement in the box AP solely by modifying the mask branch, contrary to the findings of the ablation experiments. It is evident that

**Table 2.** Ablation Experiment Results

| model | | AP | AP$_{50}$ | AP$_{75}$ |
|---|---|---|---|---|
| YOLACT | Box | 28.26 | 46.07 | 29.96 |
| | Mask | 26.58 | 43.03 | 27.69 |
| SOLOv2 | Box | – | – | – |
| | Mask | 32.73 | 51.42 | 34.93 |
| BlendMask | Box | 39.58 | 57.44 | 42.76 |
| | Mask | 35.34 | 54.99 | 37.82 |
| BlendMask + MSAR | Box | 39.70 | 57.91 | 43.13 |
| | Mask | 35.55 | 55.37 | 37.86 |

replacing the mask branch results in a 0.12% increase in box AP, a 0.47% increase in AP50, and a 0.36% increase in AP75. This suggests that the mask branch impacts both mask accuracy and bounding boxes. Despite being processed separately within the network architecture, alterations to the mask branch can influence the prediction branch through the shared backbone network, thereby affecting bounding box accuracy.

### 3.4 More Qualitative Results

The qualitative comparison between BlendMask + MSAR and SOLOv2 is presented in Fig. 4.

(a)input          (b)solov2          (c)ours

**Fig. 4.** Qualitative results with different networks

As depicted in Fig. 4, SOLOv2 consistently exhibits misjudgments during the instance segmentation process, particularly in architectural contexts where attention may not be necessary, resulting in decreased accuracy. In contrast, our model demonstrates superior performance and excels in accurate instance segmentation. This indicates that the MSAR module's feature extraction effect is more pronounced, and the backbone network with relative multi-scale attention enables the network to prioritize image information while disregarding background and blurred details. Whether handling overlapping categories or scenarios with numerous instances of the same category, BlendMask + MSAR can precisely identify and segment masks, showcasing its high precision in instance segmentation. By generating precise masks and bounding boxes, it further underscores the exceptional performance of BlendMask + MSAR.

## 4 Conclusion

This paper presents a feature fusion module method named MSAR. Specifically, the RefineNet and multi-scale attention modules are integrated into the backbone network to enhance feature fusion capabilities. This addresses the need for more robust feature fusion in one-stage instance segmentation methods. Experimental results demonstrate that incorporating these two modules significantly enhances instance segmentation.

In our future research, we will investigate the modification of only the prediction branch to evaluate its impact on mask accuracy and to demonstrate the interaction between these two components. The MSAR module will also be tested on additional data sets to demonstrate its generalizability through experiments.

**Acknowledgements.** We gratefully acknowledge the valuable discussions we had with our teacher and classmates. This research was supported by the National Natural Science Foundation of China (grant number 51405360) and the Central University Basic Research Fund (grant number 2018III069GX). Thank you for your support.

## References

1. Bolya, D., Zhou, C., Xiao, F., Lee, Y.J.: YOLACT: real-time instance segmentation. In: 2019 IEEE/CVF International Conference on Computer Vision (ICCV), pp. 9156–9165 (2019)
2. Bolya, D., Zhou, C., Xiao, F., Lee, Y.J.: YOLACT++ better real-time instance segmentation. In: IEEE Transactions on Pattern Analysis and Machine Intelligence, pp. 1108–1121 (2022)
3. Xie, E., et al.: PolarMask: single shot instance segmentation with polar representation. In: 2020 IEEE/CVF Conference on Computer Vision and Pattern Recognition (CVPR), pp. 12190–12199 (2020)
4. Tian, Z., Shen, C., Chen, H., He, T.: FCOS: a simple and strong anchor-free object detector. In: IEEE Transactions on Pattern Analysis and Machine Intelligence, pp. 1922–1933 (2022)
5. Wang, X., Zhang, R., Shen, C., Kong, T., Li, L.: SOLO: a simple framework for instance segmentation. In: IEEE Transactions on Pattern Analysis and Machine Intelligence, pp. 8587–8601 (2022)
6. Wang, X., Zhang, R., Kong, T., Li, L., Shen, C.: SOLOv2: dynamic and fast instance segmentation. In: Advances in Neural Information Processing Systems, pp. 17721–17732 (2020)
7. Chen, H., Sun, K., Tian, Z., Shen, C., Huang, Y., Yan, Y.: BlendMask: top-down meets bottom-up for instance segmentation. In: 2020 IEEE/CVF Conference on Computer Vision and Pattern Recognition (CVPR), pp. 8570–8578 (2020)
8. Lin, G., Milan, A., Shen, C., Reid, I.: RefineNet: multi-path refinement networks for high-resolution semantic segmentation. In: 2017 IEEE Conference on Computer Vision and Pattern Recognition (CVPR), pp. 5168–5177 (2017)

9. Lin, T.-Y., Dollár, P., Girshick, R., He, K., Hariharan, B., Belongie, S.: Feature pyramid networks for object detection. In: 2017 IEEE Conference on Computer Vision and Pattern Recognition (CVPR), pp. 936–944 (2017)
10. Zhao, H., Shi, J., Qi, X., Wang, X., Jia, J.: Pyramid scene parsing network. In: 2017 IEEE Conference on Computer Vision and Pattern Recognition (CVPR), pp. 6230–6239 (2017)
11. Chen, L.C., Papandreou, G., Schroff, F.: Rethinking atrous convolution for semantic image segmentation. ArXiv preprint arXiv:1706.05587 (2017)
12. Tao, A., Sapra, K., Catanzaro, B.: Hierarchical multi-scale attention for semantic segmentation. ArXiv preprint arXiv:2005.10821 (2020)
13. Hariharan, B., Arbeláez, P., Bourdev, L., Maji, S., Malik, J.: Semantic contours from inverse detectors. In: 2011 International Conference on Computer Vision, pp. 991–998 (2011)
14. Lin, T.Y., Maire, M., Belongie, S., Hays, J., Zitnick, C.L.: Microsoft COCO: common objects in context. In: Springer International Publishing, pp. 740–755 (2014)

# Multi-level Knowledge Distillation
# for Class Incremental Learning

Yongli Hu, Mengting Liu, Huajie Jiang$^{(\boxtimes)}$, Lincong Feng, and Baocai Yin

Beijing University of Technology, Beijing, China
{huyongli,jianghj,ybc}@bjut.edu.cn, Foreward@emails.bjut.edu.cn,
fenglincong@emails.bjut.edu.cn

**Abstract.** Incremental learning aims to train a model on a sequence of tasks while preserving previously learned knowledge, whereas catastrophic forgetting is a widely-studied problem. To tackle this concern, we design a multi-level knowledge distillation framework (MLKD), which combines coarse-grained and fine-grained distillations to effectively memorize past knowledge. For the coarse-grained distillation, we enforce the model to memorize the neighborhood relationships among samples. For the fine-grained distillation, we aim to memorize the activation logits within each sample. Through the multi-level knowledge distillation, we can learn more robust incremental learning models. In order to assess the efficacy of the MLKD, we perform experiments on two popular incremental learning benchmarks(CIFAR100 and Mini-ImageNet), and our approach achieves good performance.

**Keywords:** Catastrophic forgetting · Knowledge distillation · Incremental learning

## 1 Introduction

Machine learning models have demonstrated remarkable achievements across diverse domains such as computer vision and natural language processing in recent years. In some cases, they have demonstrated exceptional performance, surpassing human capabilities in specific tasks, such as mastering Atari games [1] and achieving remarkable object recognition accuracy [2]. However, these models often encounter a common problem known as catastrophic forgetting [3], which means that the model tends to forget previously learned knowledge when presented with new data, leading to a considerable performance drop in previously mastered tasks. In order to mitigate this problem, incremental learning is receiving increasing attention, and the concepts and techniques of incremental learning are increasingly being employed across various domains [4].

In incremental learning, the model is trained on a sequence of tasks, with the objective of minimizing forgetting of the previously learned tasks while maximizing performance on the current task. To lessen the impact of this issue, researchers have proposed different approaches. These can be categorized into

N. Magnenat Thalmann et al. (Eds.): CASA 2024, CCIS 2374, pp. 290–305, 2025.
https://doi.org/10.1007/978-981-96-2681-6_21

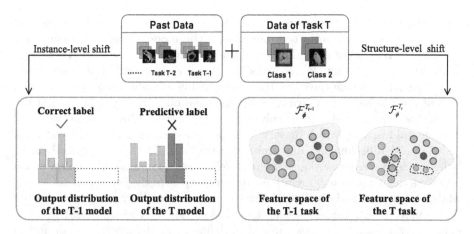

**Fig. 1.** Two types of shift issues: instance-level shift and structural shift. Orange circles represent samples from past tasks and purple circles represent samples from current tasks. (Color figure online)

three primary groups: approaches that depend on regularization [5], network expansion [6], and rehearsal [7]. Regularization-based methods penalize changes in the network parameters to preserve previously learned knowledge. Network expansion-based methods assign different network branches to different tasks to prevent interference. Rehearsal-based methods involve the maintenance of a memory buffer, which stores samples from previous tasks. These stored samples are then replayed during the training process to reinforce and consolidate knowledge. Among these approaches, rehearsal-based methods have demonstrated more effective in dealing with challenging incremental learning tasks [8].

As illustrated in Fig. 1, contemporary rehearsal-based methods in machine learning encounter two primary forms of knowledge shifts: structure-level shift and instance-level shift. Structure-level shift occurs when samples that were neighbors in the feature space of previous tasks undergo drastic transformations in the feature space of subsequent tasks. This shift can cause significant disruptions in the model's understanding of data relationships and patterns, leading to a degradation in its ability to generalize from past learnings to new scenarios.

In contrast, the instance-level shift highlights a notable issue where models exhibit a bias towards the most recent task. This bias stems from an insufficient representation of historical data in the training process. Consequently, this leads to an increased likelihood of misclassifying samples that belong to previously learned categories. Such a tendency not only undermines the model's overall accuracy but also signals a failure in retaining past learning effectively.

Current methodologies in the field of machine learning primarily focus on addressing either structure-level transfer or instance-level problems. Focusing solely on structure-level problems means ensuring that the model preserves the overall data structure and relationships between data points across tasks. However, this approach may not pay enough attention to the finer details and specific characteristics of individual instances. On the other hand, the instance-level transfer approach primarily concentrates on the model's ability to accurately classify and remember individual data points or instances from previous tasks. While this is important, it overlooks the broader structural relationships and patterns that underpin the data. By concentrating on only one of these aspects, current approaches fail to provide a holistic solution to catastrophic forgetting.

In this paper, we design a multi-level knowledge distillation framework for incremental learning, which preserves the previous knowledge by coarse-grained knowledge distillation and fine-grained distillation. The coarse-grained distillation aims to memorize the structure-level information among samples, which preserves the neighborhood relationships for samples in the feature space. Meanwhile, the fine-grained distillation aims to memorize the logit activations within the sample, which preserves the class information in the continued learning phases. By combining coarse-grained and fine-grained knowledge, our model achieves to achieve better performance and effectively mitigates catastrophic forgetting in incremental learning tasks. Our work contributes in the following ways:

- We propose a multi-level distillation framework for incremental learning, which combines coarse-grained distillation and fine-grained distillation to deal with catastrophic forgetting problems.
- We combine structure-level information (coarse-grained) and instance-level information (fine-grained) for more effective memory, which can effectively preserve the previous knowledge.
- We conduct experiments on two widely recognized benchmark datasets for CIL, and our model achieves excellent performance.

## 2    Related Work and Preliminary

### 2.1    Incremental Learning Settings

The initial research in incremental learning (IL), particularly in the domain of task-incremental learning (Task-IL) [9], laid the groundwork for understanding how models can sequentially acquire new knowledge across distinct tasks. Early key studies in this area emphasized models trained on a series of discrete tasks, each distinct from the other with no overlapping content. In these models, the task identity was typically known both during the training and testing phases, which simplified the learning process.

However, recent developments in the field have pivoted towards scenarios that better reflect real-world conditions, where the demarcation between different tasks is not always clear and may evolve over time. This paradigm shift has given rise to the concept of class incremental learning (Class-IL) [10], a more nuanced and realistic approach to IL. Unlike Task-IL, Class-IL does not provide explicit task identifiers during testing. This scenario is inherently more complex as it closely mimics how humans encounter and process new information over time without clear categorization.

Class-IL poses unique challenges that demand advanced and sophisticated methods to address effectively. These challenges include but are not limited to managing maintaining knowledge from previous classes while acquiring new ones, and accurately classifying data in the absence of task labels. Therefore, given its relevance to practical applications and its inherent complexity, our research is dedicated to exploring and advancing Class-IL. We aim to develop innovative solutions that can effectively learn from a continuous stream of data, akin to how learning occurs in natural settings.

## 2.2   Incremental Learning Approaches

According to current research, there are several mainstream approaches to solving tasks in incremental learning, including structure-based approaches, regularity-based approaches, and replay-based approaches.

Structure-based approaches generally involve making modifications to the model's architecture, often by introducing task-specific parameters that increase the model's capacity dynamically. One popular approach [11] is a novel method for Class-IL that introduces a dynamically expandable representation to mitigate catastrophic forgetting. The method expands the representation of each class by incrementally adding new subspaces to the original feature space. Another approach [12] utilizes a mask to protect the parameters of previous tasks during backward passing and chooses which parameters to use during forward passing, allowing a single network to adapt to multiple tasks without catastrophic forgetting.

Regularity-based approaches aim to encourage the stability of previous tasks and prevent catastrophic forgetting by incorporating regularization terms in the loss function. By estimating the importance of parameters from previous tasks, EWC [9] constrains the change of important parameters during training on new tasks, thus preventing them from being forgotten. Synaptic Intelligence [13] is a regularization-based method that uses historical gradient and parameter adjustment information to measure the importance of each weight in the network. The Learning without Forgetting (LWF) [14] algorithm introduced knowledge distillation in incremental learning, where the knowledge from a previously trained model is transferred to a new model trained on a new task. Knowledge distillation has been shown to be effective in preserving the knowledge of previously learned tasks and improving the performance of the model on new tasks. It has been extended in various ways, such as dark knowledge [15] distillation.

The replay-based approach maintains a memory buffer that stores past task samples to be used during the training of new tasks. Chaudhry et al. introduced the empirical replay (ER) [16] approach, which combines data from new tasks with memories from the past. Rainbow Memory [17] is a improved method of memory management that uses predictive uncertainty estimation to better manage the memory buffer. The method also employs a data enhancement strategy to further improve the diversity of the samples. However, the security and privacy of data can be a concern when using such methods. To address this, some methods use Generative Adversarial Network (GAN) [18] or a Variational AutoEncoder

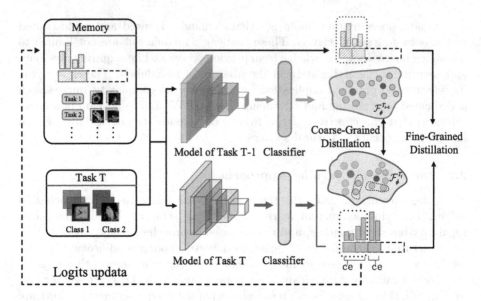

**Fig. 2.** MLKD combines coarse-grained and fine-grained distillations, which are responsible for the memory of the sample's neighbor information and activation logits, respectively.

[19] to generate replay samples, ensuring the security and privacy of the original data. Overall, these replay-based approaches have proven to be effective in improving the learning process of machine learning models.

## 3   Proposed Model

We describe the multi-level knowledge distillation framework in this section. As is shown in Fig. 2. The details will be introduced in the following part.

### 3.1   Problem Formulation

We focus on Class Incremental Learning (CIL) and considers a sequential arrangement of tasks denoted as $\mathcal{T}_1, \mathcal{T}_2, ..., \mathcal{T}_n$. Each task is associated with a training set $D_t$, which comprises samples from a specific set of classes denoted as $\mathcal{C}_t$. Notably, each incremental step introduces new classes, ensuring that the intersection of classes across all tasks is an empty set, denoted as $\bigcap_{t=0}^{T} \mathcal{C}_t = \varnothing$. The key to incremental learning is effectively learning new knowledge from the current task $\mathcal{T}_t$ while keeping the information from previous tasks $\mathcal{T}_1, \mathcal{T}_2, ..., \mathcal{T}_{t-1}$, where catastrophic forgetting has a bad influence. To deal with this problem, we propose to memorize the structure-level information and instance-level information by coarse-grained knowledge distillation and fine-grained distillation respectively.

## 3.2    Coarse-Grained Knowledge Distillation

Coarse-grained knowledge distillation aims to preserve the neighborhood relationships among samples during the learning process. It begins with the extraction of features from a sample $x$ using a previously trained model $f_{t-1}$. Once these features are extracted, the $k$ nearest neighbors $N_k(x)$ of the sample in the feature space are identified, with cosine similarity serving as the metric for measuring distance. These neighbors, along with the original sample, are then fed into the new model $f_t$. The output of this process is the calculation of the average logits $p_c(x)$, represented mathematically as:

$$p_c(x) = \frac{1}{k+1}( \sum_{x_i \in N_k(x)} f_t(x_i) + f_t(x)) \tag{1}$$

We retain the sample structure of the previous task by enforcing the combined logits to be close to the true value of sample x, which is expressed as

$$\mathcal{L}_{CGD}(x) = ||p_c(x) - y(x)||^2 \tag{2}$$

where $y(x)$ is the one-hot encoding label for sample $x$. As the quantity of tasks rises, we anticipate the model will gradually improve its ability to retain previously learned knowledge during training. To prevent the model from overly focusing on maintaining the performance of old tasks, which could hinder its ability to learn new information, we propose an adaptive weight to the current task: $\beta = \beta_{base}/t$, where $\beta_{base}$ is the base weight value and $t$ represents the cumulative number of tasks learned by the model. Then an adaptive coarse-grained distillation loss can be denoted as:

$$\mathcal{L}_A(x) = \begin{cases} \alpha||p_c(x) - y(x)||^2 & y \in \mathcal{C}_{1:t-1} \\ \beta||p_c(x) - y(x)||^2 & y \in \mathcal{C}_t \end{cases} \tag{3}$$

In this equation, $\alpha$ acts as a hyperparameter. This adaptive loss function effectively balances the need to remember previous tasks $\mathcal{C}_{1:t-1}$ and the requirement to learn new tasks $\mathcal{C}_t$. The division of the loss function into two cases allows the model to apply different levels of emphasis based on whether the current task is new or previously encountered.

## 3.3    Fine-Grained Knowledge Distillation

Fine-grained knowledge distillation preserves the class information from the local instance level. To facilitate the preservation of past knowledge, we employ a compact replay buffer denoted as $\mathcal{M}$. This buffer is designed to store a limited number of previous examples $x$, accompanied by the corresponding model outputs $\ell_x$. These outputs represent the model's learned response or prediction for each example.

Once these examples and their associated outputs are stored in $\mathcal{M}$, they are periodically reintroduced into the model $f_t$, which is currently being trained for a new task. This reintroduction allows the model to 're-experience' past data, thereby aiding in the retention of previously learned information. When the data from the buffer is fed into $f_t$ , it produces new outputs $z_t(x)$, which reflect the model's current understanding and interpretation of the data. The critical aspect of this process is captured in the fine-grained distillation loss. This loss is formulated to quantify and minimize the divergence between the model's current outputs on the replayed examples $z_t(x)$ and the outputs stored in the replay buffer $\ell_x$. By doing so, it helps to ensure that the model does not 'forget' or significantly alter its responses to these previously learned instances. The fine-grained distillation loss is mathematically expressed as:

$$\mathcal{L}_F = \frac{1}{|\mathcal{B}|} \sum_{i=1}^{N_o} \sum_{x \in C_i} \mathcal{H}\left(z_t(x), \ell_x\right) \tag{4}$$

where $\mathcal{B}$ is the size of batchsize, $C_i$ denotes the i-th category and $\mathcal{N}_o$ represents the number of categories associated with the old tasks, and the loss function $\mathcal{H}$ measures the similarity between the predicted and actual distributions. In this paper, $\mathcal{H}$ is the mean square error function. By minimizing this loss, the current model can mitigate catastrophic forgetting by remembering the activation response of a single sample. Overall, our distillation loss can ultimately be defined as:

$$\mathcal{L}_{GD} = \mathcal{L}_A + \gamma \mathcal{L}_F \tag{5}$$

### 3.3.1  Logits Update

In incremental learning, the model may need to handle a growing number of classes as time goes on. We represent the number of categories in the new task as $\mathcal{N}_e$. This requires updating the dimensions of the stored logits $\ell^\mathcal{M} : \mathbb{R}^{N_o}$. One straightforward method is to take samples from the memory buffer and input them into the current model. This allows us to obtain the output specific to the current task $\ell^{cur} : \mathbb{R}^{N_e}$. Then, we can concatenate this output with the logits stored in the memory buffer to form $\ell^\mathcal{M}_{update} : \mathbb{R}^{N_o+N_e}$. Since the samples corresponding to the current task are far more than those stored in memory, the network may be biased against the current class, and directly concating the output logits will exacerbate the problem. To address this problem, we use the following equation to scale the logits corresponding to the current task $\ell^{cur}$:

$$\ell^{cur} \longleftarrow \ell^{cur} \cdot \min(\eta \frac{\ell^\mathcal{M}_{gd}}{\ell^{cur}_{max}}, 1) \tag{6}$$

$\ell^\mathcal{M}_{gd}$ is the logit value corresponding to groudtruth. $\ell^{cur}_{max}$ is the maximum logit in $\ell^{cur}$. We denote $\eta \in [0, 1]$ as a hyperparameter and we set it to 0.75 in our experiments.

### 3.4  Classifier

Previous research [20] has shown a crucial challenge in the realm of incremental learning: the risk of imbalanced predictions when integrating logits from both old and new tasks into a single softmax function. This imbalance can significantly skew the model's performance, favoring either the new or old tasks, thereby compromising the overall effectiveness of the learning process. To avoid this, we adopt separate softmax functions for the old and new tasks. For the incremental task t, which can be formulated as:

$$\mathcal{L}_{\text{CE-SS},t}((\boldsymbol{x},y),\boldsymbol{\theta}) =$$
$$\lambda\mathcal{L}_{\text{CE},t-1}(y_{t-1}, f_t^{1:t-1}(x)) \cdot \mathbb{I}\{y \in \mathcal{C}_{1:t-1}\} \tag{7}$$
$$+ \mathcal{L}_{\text{CE},t}(y_t, f_t^{t-1:t}(x)) \cdot \mathbb{I}\{y \in \mathcal{C}_t\}$$

$\mathcal{C}_t$, $\mathcal{C}_{1:t-1}$ represent the categories of new and old tasks respectively. In which $y_{t-1}$, $y_t$ respectively represent the one-hot vector of the corresponding label in $\mathbb{R}^{\mathcal{N}_o}$, $\mathbb{R}^{\mathcal{N}_e}$. $f_t^{m:n}(x)$ stands for the corresponding classifier head output from the m task to n tasks.

### 3.5   Overall

Finally, the overarching loss function for our model can be defined as follows:

$$\mathcal{L} = \mathcal{L}_{\text{GD}} + \mathcal{L}_{\text{CE-SS},t} \tag{8}$$

This equation consists of three hyperparameters $\alpha$, $\beta$, $\gamma$, $\lambda$ which respectively represent the weight of the corresponding part. In Sect. 4.5, we will analyze the sensitivity of the parameters.

## 4   Experiments

### 4.1   Datasets

In order to thoroughly evaluate the efficacy of our proposed approach, we have chosen to conduct experiments using two extensively recognized and widely used datasets in the field of machine learning: CIFAR-100 [21] and Mini-ImageNet [22]. These datasets have been selected due to their complexity and diversity, making them ideal for testing the robustness and adaptability of our approach in a variety of scenarios. The CIFAR-100 dataset comprises a training set, which encompasses a collection of 50,000 images, and a corresponding test set consisting of 10,000 images, each belonging to one of 100 fine-grained classes. To establish a sequential learning framework, we partition CIFAR-100 into 10 tasks, with each task encompassing 10 classes. On the other hand, Mini-ImageNet is a subset of the larger ImageNet dataset, comprising 60,000 images that are categorized into 100 classes. We divide Mini-ImageNet into 20 tasks, each of which includes 5 classes. To assess the performance of our method, we evaluate both datasets using different buffer sizes. An important aspect of our evaluation strategy involves testing the performance of our model across different buffer sizes. For the CIFAR-100 dataset, we conduct experiments using buffer sizes of 500 and 2000, which allows us to observe how our model performs with varying degrees of memory capacity. Similarly, for Mini-ImageNet, we examine the model's performance with buffer sizes of 2000 and 5000.

## 4.2  Implementation Details

For our experiments, we use ResNet18 [23] as the backbone network for the CIFAR-100 dataset. For Mini-ImageNet, we use the EfficientNetV2 [24] architecture as the backbone network. We implement our models using the PyTorch deep learning framework. We utilize a batch size of 32 for both CIFAR-100 and Mini-ImageNet. To optimize the training process, we employed the widely-used Stochastic Gradient Descent (SGD) optimizer. For the CIFAR-100 dataset, we set the learning rate to 0.03, whereas for the Mini-ImageNet dataset, we utilized a learning rate of 0.1. We will use the final average accuracy to evaluate our model. The final average accuracy is calculated as the average accuracy over all tasks. We introduce the notation $a_i^t$ to represent the model's accuracy on the $i^{th}$ task after undergoing training on task $T_t$. Then, the final average accuracy ($FAA$) can be calculated as:

$$\text{FAA} = \frac{1}{T} \sum_{i=0}^{T-1} a_i^{T-1} \tag{9}$$

Nonetheless, this approach offers only a glimpse into the model's state following the completion of the last task. To gain a comprehensive understanding of the model's performance throughout the entire sequence of tasks, we adopt a strategy used in other studies [25] and utilize the Final Forgetting (FF) metric. This metric provides a more holistic view of how well the model retains information over the course of sequential learning tasks.

The Final Forgetting metric is defined as follows:

$$\text{FF} \triangleq \frac{1}{T-1} \sum_{j=0}^{T-2} f_j, \tag{10}$$

$$\text{s.t. } f_j = \max_{l \in \{0,\dots,T-2\}} a_j^l - a_j^{T-1}$$

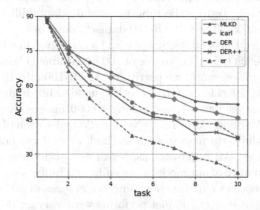

**Fig. 3.** The final average accuracy trend of different methods at the end of each task with a buffer set of 500 on the cifar100 dataset.

T represents the number of tasks, and $f_j$ is calculated as the maximum discrepancy between $a_j^l$ and $a_j^{T-1}$ over all tasks.

## 4.3   Result of Multi-level Knowledge Distillation

To provide a clear understanding of the performance of our proposed method, we compare it to two other approaches. The first method is a lower bound known as Finetuning (FT). This approach continually finetunes the most recent task without any remedy for catastrophic forgetting. The second method acts as an upper bound known as Joint-Training (JT). This approach trains a model jointly on all data, allowing optimal performance without considering the incremental learning scenario. In addition, we also compared it with several other incremental learning methods, all with varying degrees of improvement.

The results in Table 1 show that our proposed method is superior to other methods such as XDER and the latest R-STAR method on both CIFAR-100 and Mini-ImageNet datasets. Notably, the performance improvement is significant for different buffer sizes. Specifically, for the CIFAR-100 dataset, our method improves the buffer500 setting by 3.75% and the buffer2000 setting by 1.9% compared to R-STAR. We attribute this to the fact that XDER solves the catastrophic forgetting problem primarily through memorizing the instance-level knowledge and ignores the relationships among samples. In the same way, although R-STAR made the model aware of score bias, it gained only a slight advantage over XDER because it did not recognize the importance of structure-level knowledge. In contrast, our method considers not only the fine-

**Table 1.** Comparisons with different class incremental learning approaches, where the performance is measured by Final Average Accuracy (FAA).

| $FAA[\uparrow]$ | CIFAR-100 | | Mini-ImageNet | |
|---|---|---|---|---|
| JT(upper bound) | 70.44 | | 53.35 | |
| FT(lower bound) | 9.43 | | 4.51 | |
| $\mathcal{M}_{size}$ | 500 | 2000 | 2000 | 5000 |
| ER [26] | 22.10 | 38.58 | 14.57 | 21.42 |
| GDumb [27] | 9.98 | 20.66 | 15.22 | 27.79 |
| ER-ACE [28] | 38.75 | 49.72 | 22.60 | 27.92 |
| RPC [29] | 22.34 | 38.33 | 15.60 | 24.69 |
| BiC [30] | 36.02 | 46.39 | 12.96 | 14.45 |
| iCaRL [25] | 46.52 | 49.82 | 22.58 | 22.78 |
| LuCIR [31] | 40.59 | 41.73 | 14.97 | 17.61 |
| DER [15] | 36.60 | 51.89 | 22.96 | 29.83 |
| DER++ [15] | 38.25 | 53.63 | 23.44 | 30.43 |
| X-DER [32] | 48.08 | 57.58 | 28.19 | 32.32 |
| R-STAR [33] | 48.47 | 57.60 | 28.87 | 32.99 |
| our method | **52.22** | **59.50** | **32.43** | **37.54** |

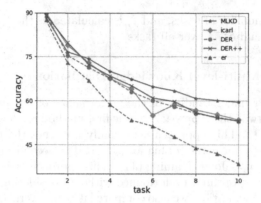

**Fig. 4.** The final average accuracy trend of different methods at the end of each task with a buffer set of 2000 on the cifar100 dataset.

grained instance-level knowlege but also the coarse-graind structure-level knowlege, which is more benificial to prevent the catastrophic forgetting. For the Mini-ImageNet dataset, our method yields even more extensive improvements, with 3.56% and 4.55% increases for the buffer2000 and buffer5000 settings, respectively.

In Table 2, we present a detailed comparison of the forgetting rates between our method and the current leading approaches in the field. This table provides a clear and quantifiable insight into the effectiveness of our method. Notably, under the configurations with memory buffer sizes of 2000 and 5000, the forgetting

**Table 2.** Result on Split Mini-ImageNet for CIL. Comparisons with different class incremental learning approaches, where the performance is measured by the Final Forgetting(FF).

| $FF[\downarrow]$ | Mini-ImageNet | |
|---|---|---|
| **FT(lower bound)** | 77.38 | |
| $\mathcal{M}_{size}$ | 2000 | 5000 |
| **ER** [26] | 64.49 | 50.36 |
| **ER-ACE** [28] | 23.74 | 19.72 |
| **RPC** [29] | 61.00 | 46.34 |
| **BiC** [30] | 57.19 | 56.55 |
| **iCaRL** [25] | 16.46 | 16.37 |
| **LuCIR** [31] | 43.83 | 39.01 |
| **DER** [15] | 48.78 | 36.38 |
| **DER++** [15] | 46.69 | 37.11 |
| **X-DER** [32] | 44.20 | 26.02 |
| **R-STAR** [33] | 42.47 | 24.52 |
| **our method** | **15.53** | **13.60** |

rates of our methods were 15.53% and 13.60%, respectively, which are 26.94% and 10.92% lower than those of the most advanced methods currently available. This indicates a significant improvement in retaining learned information when compared to the benchmarks.

These results indicate the superiority of our approach in handling catastrophic forgetting and adapting to different memory buffer sizes, making it a promising solution for incremental learning tasks. Moreover, our approach demonstrates superior performance over the comparison approachs on every task, as depicted in Fig. 3. This indicates that our method consistently impacts the model's performance, regardless of the task. These findings suggest that our method is effective and can serve as a promising solution for incremental learning tasks.

In our research, we analyzed the impact that varying buffer sizes have on the accuracy of our data processing algorithms. This was a crucial part of our study because buffer size directly influences how much data can be temporarily stored and processed at any given time. As illustrated in Fig. 5, we observed a clear trend: as the number of samples stored in the buffer increases, there is a corresponding rise in the final average accuracy of the data processing. This finding suggests that larger buffers allow for more comprehensive data analysis, likely because they can accommodate more samples for processing, leading to a more robust and accurate outcome.

### 4.4   Ablation Studies

In the subsequent section of our analysis, we delve deeper into the individual impacts of the various components that constitute our method. Specifically, we aim to understand how each component contributes to the overall efficacy of our model. To this end, we have conducted a series of experiments where we isolate and remove key elements from our method, namely the Fine-grained and Coarse-grained knowledge distillation processes, and observe the resulting changes in performance. These findings are meticulously compiled and presented in Table 3. Upon examining the results in Table 3, it becomes evident that both Fine-grained and Coarse-grained knowledge distillation play significant roles in enhancing the performance of our model. When we evaluated the model in the absence of Fine-grained knowledge distillation, We noticed a drop in performance. Similarly, the removal of Coarse-grained knowledge distillation leads to a noticeable impact on the model's performance. This component is primarily responsible for preserving the broader, more general features and relationships among the data samples. Its absence underscores its importance in maintaining the overall structural integrity and general knowledge base of the model across different learning stages.

### 4.5   Parameter Sensitivity

The hyperparameter sensitivity experiment focused on investigating the impact of four hyperparameters in the loss function. These hyperparameters determine the importance of coarse-grain distillation $\alpha$, $\beta$, fine-grained distillation $\gamma$, and

**Table 3.** Ablation studies of coarse-grained distillation and fine-grained distillation on cifar100 with buffer500.

| Fine-grained | Coarse-grained | Acc |
|:---:|:---:|:---|
| | | 44.95 |
| | ✓ | 46.55 |
| ✓ | | 49.38 |
| ✓ | ✓ | 52.22 |

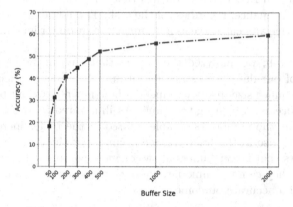

**Fig. 5.** The performance on CIFAR 100 for different buffer sizes.

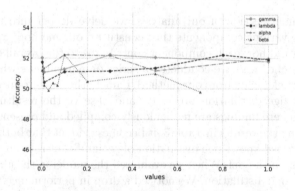

**Fig. 6.** The influence of different parameter values, where the performance is reported by the final average accuracy at the end of each task with a buffer set of 500 on the cifar100 dataset.

Cross entropy loss corresponding to the current task $\lambda$. As depicted in Fig. 6, we conducted experiments using a range of values from 0.001 to 1. We conducted hyperparameter sensitivity experiments with initial settings of $\alpha = 1$, $\beta = 0.1$, $\lambda = 0.5$, and $\gamma = 0.3$. When investigating the effect of varying one hyperparameter within a specific range, the other hyperparameters were kept constant at their baseline values. Ultimately, the optimal hyperparameter combination we determined is $\alpha = 0.1$, $\beta = 0.1$, $\lambda = 0.5$, and $\gamma = 0.3$. The experiment results also revealed that the accuracy remained consistent for different hyperparameter values, which shows that our suggested strategy is not very sensitive to these particular hyperparameters.

## Conclusion

This paper delves into the issue of catastrophic forgetting within the realm of incremental learning. To tackle this intricate issue, we design a multi-level knowledge distillation framework, which combines coarse-grained and fine-grained distillation techniques. Coarse-grained distillation maintains the adjacent relations in the new feature space, which preserves the global structure information for the samples. Meanwhile, the fine-grained distillation retains the logits of old samples in memory storage to avoid the gradual deviation of teachers, which preserves the class information within each sample from the local instance-level. We demonstrate that our approach achieves better performance and mitigates catastrophic forgetting in incremental learning tasks by evaluating on two popular incremental learning benchmarks. We emphasize the importance of maintaining both instance-level and structure-level knowledge to achieve better performance in incremental learning tasks, and we believe that our proposed approach is a step towards developing more sophisticated and comprehensive replay-based methods.

## References

1. Silver, D., et al.: A general reinforcement learning algorithm that masters chess, shogi, and go through self-play. Science **362**(6419), 1140–1144 (2018)
2. Russakovsk, O., et al.: ImageNet large scale visual recognition challenge. Int. J. Comput. Vision **115**, 211–252 (2015)
3. McCloskey, M., Cohen, N.J.: Catastrophic interference in connectionist networks: the sequential learning problem. In: Psychology of Learning and Motivation, vol. 24, pp. 109–165. Elsevier (1989)
4. Wang, Z., et al.: Learning representations for new sound classes with continual self-supervised learning. IEEE Signal Process. Lett. **29**, 2607–2611 (2022)
5. Ritter, H., Botev, A., Barber. D.: Online structured Laplace approximations for overcoming catastrophic forgetting. Adv. Neural Info. Process. Syst. **31** (2018)
6. Yoon, J., Yang, E., Lee, J., Hwang, S.J.: Lifelong learning with dynamically expandable networks. arXiv preprint arXiv:1708.01547 (2017)
7. Chaudhry, A., Ranzato, M.A., Rohrbach, M., Elhoseiny, M.: Efficient lifelong learning with a-gem. arXiv preprint arXiv:1812.00420 (2018)
8. Farquhar, S., Gal, Y.: Towards robust evaluations of continual learning. arXiv preprint arXiv:1805.09733 (2018)
9. Kirkpatrick, J., et al.: Overcoming catastrophic forgetting in neural networks. Proc. Nat. Acad. Sci. **114**(13), 3521–3526 (2017)
10. Hou, S., Pan, X., Loy, C.C., Wang, Z., Lin, D.: Learning a unified classifier incrementally via rebalancing. In: 2019 IEEE/CVF Conference on Computer Vision and Pattern Recognition (CVPR) (2020)

11. Yan, S., Xie, J., He, X.: DER: dynamically expandable representation for class incremental learning. In: 2021 IEEE/CVF Conference on Computer Vision and Pattern Recognition (CVPR) (2021)
12. Mallya, A., Davis, D., Lazebnik, S.: Piggyback: adapting a single network to multiple tasks by learning to mask weights. In: Proceedings of the European Conference on Computer Vision (ECCV), pp. 67–82 (2018)
13. Zenke, F., Poole, B., Ganguli, S.: Continual learning through synaptic intelligence. In: International Conference on Machine Learning, pp. 3987–3995. PMLR (2017)
14. Li, Z., Hoiem, D.: Learning without forgetting. IEEE Trans. Pattern Anal. Mach. Intell. **40**(12), 2935–2947 (2017)
15. Buzzega, P., Boschini, M., Porrello, A., Abati, D., Calderara, S.: Dark experience for general continual learning: a strong, simple baseline (2020)
16. Chaudhry, A., et al.: Continual learning with tiny episodic memories (2019)
17. Bang, J., Kim, H., Yoo, Y., Ha, J.-W., Choi, J.: Rainbow memory: Continual learning with a memory of diverse samples. In: 2021 IEEE/CVF Conference on Computer Vision and Pattern Recognition (CVPR) (2021)
18. Goodfellow, I., et al.: Generative adversarial networks. Commun. ACM **63**(11), 139–144 (2020)
19. Kingma, D.P., Welling, M.: Auto-encoding variational bayes (2013)
20. Ahn, H., Kwak, J., Lim, S., Bang, H., Kim, H., Moon, T.: SS-IL: separated softmax for incremental learning. In: 2021 IEEE/CVF International Conference on Computer Vision (ICCV) (2022)
21. Krizhevsky, A., Hinton, G.: Learning multiple layers of features from tiny images. Handbook of Systemic Autoimmune Diseases **1**(4) (2009)
22. Vinyals, O., Blundell, C., Lillicrap, T., Wierstra, D., et al.: Matching networks for one shot learning. Adv. Neural Inf. Process. Syst. **29** (2016)
23. He, K., Zhang, X., Ren, S., Sun, J.: Deep residual learning for image recognition. In: Proceedings of the IEEE Conference on Computer Vision and Pattern Recognition, pp. 770–778 (2016)
24. Tan, M., Le, Q.: EfficientNet: rethinking model scaling for convolutional neural networks. In: International Conference on Machine Learning, pp. 6105–6114. PMLR (2019)
25. Rebuffi, S.-A., Kolesnikov, A., Sperl, G., Lampert, C.H.: iCaRL: incremental classifier and representation learning. In: 2017 IEEE Conference on Computer Vision and Pattern Recognition (CVPR) (2017)
26. Riemer, M., et al.: Learning to learn without forgetting by maximizing transfer and minimizing interference. arXiv preprint arXiv:1810.11910 (2018)
27. Prabhu, A., Torr, P.H.S., Dokania, P.K.: GDumb: a simple approach that questions our progress in continual learning. In: Vedaldi, A., Bischof, H., Brox, T., Frahm, J.-M. (eds.) ECCV 2020. LNCS, vol. 12347, pp. 524–540. Springer, Cham (2020). https://doi.org/10.1007/978-3-030-58536-5_31
28. Caccia, L., Aljundi, R., Asadi, N., Tuytelaars, T., Pineau, J., Belilovsky, E.: New insights on reducing abrupt representation change in online continual learning. arXiv preprint arXiv:2203.03798 (2022)
29. Pernici, F., Bruni, M., Baecchi, C., Turchini, F., Del Bimbo, A.: Class-incremental learning with pre-allocated fixed classifiers. In: 2020 25th International Conference on Pattern Recognition (ICPR), pp. 6259–6266. IEEE (2021)
30. Wu, Y., et al.: Large scale incremental learning. In: Proceedings of the IEEE/CVF Conference on Computer Vision and Pattern Recognition, pp. 374–382 (2019)

31. Hou, S., Pan, X., Loy, C.C., Wang, Z., Lin, D.: Learning a unified classifier incre-
    mentally via rebalancing. In: Proceedings of the IEEE/CVF Conference on Com-
    puter Vision and Pattern Recognition, pp. 831–839 (2019)
32. Boschini, M., Bonicelli, L., Buzzega, P., Porrello, A., Calderara, S.: Class-
    incremental continual learning into the extended der-verse. IEEE Transactions on
    Pattern Analysis and Machine Intelligence (2022)
33. Luoa, Y., Gaoa, Y., Wub, H., Mab, R., Lua, Z.: R-star: robust self-taught task-wise
    reweighting for rehearsal-based class incremental learning (2023)

# Research on the Algorithm of Helmet-Wearing Detection Based on the Optimized Mobilevit and Centernet

Min Li, Chun Wang$^{(\boxtimes)}$, Peng Luo, and Menghan Ai

Wuhan Textile University, Wuhan, China

`2008031@wtu.edu.cn, 993583291@qq.com, thornluo@whu.edu.cn`

**Abstract.** On construction sites, wearing a safety helmet is a crucial and effective measure to protect workers from unforeseen injuries. In order to ensure timely reminders for workers to wear safety helmets, it is necessary to automate the detection process of safety helmet-wearing. However, Limited to the camera distance and environment, detecting relatively small targets can be challenging, this study constructs a safety helmet-wearing detection algorithm based on MobileViT and Centernet. Firstly, in the feature extraction stage, a more lightweight MobileViT algorithm is employed to replace the original Resnet50 algorithm. Additionally, the efficient channel attention (ECA-Net) module is introduced in the first two layers to weight feature information, thereby reducing the degree of target information loss. Secondly, the introduction of the ASFF-FPN structure strengthens the network's cross-scale feature fusion capability, enabling it to effectively detect small targets. Lastly, a lightweight CARAFE upsampling operator is employed for upsampling operations to reduce the model's parameters. The final model achieves an average precision of 86.37% in the task of safety helmet detection, with an increase of 6.24% compared with that of the original Centernet. On the GeForce RTX 3060 Ti graphics card, there is a 17.8 FPS improvement.

**Keywords:** Safety helmet detection · Centernet · MobileVit · ECA-Net · Carafe upsampling operator

## 1 Introduction

There are various safety hazards on construction sites, among which head injuries are the most fatal. In this context, the wearing of safety helmets has become a fundamental protective measure. Currently, the majority of construction projects typically rely on manual on-site inspections. However, depending solely on human supervision can incur significant time and labor costs. Therefore, with the development of computer vision, the detection of safety helmet wear has become a significant research project in the field of construction site safety protection.

Many researchers have proposed using object detection methods as a substitute for manual detection. Currently, there are two main types of object detection algorithms: anchor-based and anchor-free. In the research on anchor- based algorithms, the earliest

© The Author(s), under exclusive license to Springer Nature Singapore Pte Ltd. 2025
N. Magnenat Thalmann et al. (Eds.): CASA 2024, CCIS 2374, pp. 306–318, 2025.
https://doi.org/10.1007/978-981-96-2681-6_22

studies originate from the R-CNN series, including R-CNN [1], Fast R-CNN [2], and Faster R-CNN [3]. Sun et al. [4] improved the ability of Faster R-CNN to detect small objects by employing attention mechanisms and an anchor box supplementation method. The enhanced algorithm ultimately demonstrated a 6.4% increase in mAP compared to the original algorithm in the task of detecting the wearing of safety helmets. However, because the R-CNN series of networks requires the pregeneration of candidate boxes, the detection speed is slow. Unlike the R-CNN series, the yolo [5–8] series algorithm and the SSD [9] algorithm, don't need to generate candidate boxes, resulting in faster detection speeds. Wu et al. [10] improved the accuracy of safety helmet detection by replacing the original feature extraction network of YOLOv3 with the DenseNet network. However, the model exhibited poor performance in detecting blurred and small targets. Zeng et al. [11] enhance the capabilities of YOLOv4 for detecting small targets through changing the yolov4 feature layer output and linear transformation of anchors. However, there is still room for improvement in terms of detection speed. Liang et al. [12] replaced the original backbone network with MobileNet, significantly reducing the network parameters and improving the detection speed of the model. But their experiments also indicate a marginal reduction in the model's detection accuracy.

The aforementioned studies are all based on anchor-based detection frameworks, while in recent years, many new studies have shifted towards anchor-free detection frameworks. In contrast to anchor-based detection frameworks, anchor-free detection frameworks offer the following advantages: (1) Anchor-free frameworks don't rely on predetermined anchor boxes with fixed parameters, making the training process more flexible. (2) Anchor-free frameworks overcome a constraint in anchor-based frameworks where the fixed anchor boxes might encounter difficulty in precisely aligning with the sizes of target objects. CenterNet, as a typical anchor- free algorithm, directly utilizes the feature information of the target object's center point for target classification and bounding box regression. Zhou et al. [13] introduce of the Feature Pyramid Module, Global Guidance Module, and Feature Integration Module enlarges the receptive field of the CenterNet, enhancing the accuracy of detecting small targets in the task of safety helmet detection. However, the feature fusion method increases the model's complexity, impacting the detection speed. Zhao et al. [14] improved CenterNet by introducing the ACNet module and optimizing the loss function. The modified CenterNet exhibits enhanced detection accuracy without a significant change in speed. However, due to insufficient feature extraction, it may lead to false positives for the surrounding environment.

The majority of the improvements mentioned above failed to comprehensively consider issues related to speed and small target detection. Therefore, this study constructs a safety helmet detection algorithm based on MobileViT and Centernet. Firstly, we use the MobileViT model as the backbone network for feature extraction, improving the model's detection speed and achieving model lightweighting. Simultaneously, the ECA attention mechanism is introduced in the first two layers to reduce information diffusion and strengthen the network's anti-interference capability in complex environments. Secondly, we combine the adaptive feature fusion module with the feature pyramid structure to reuse features extracted by the back- bone network, thereby enhancing the model's ability to detect small targets. Finally, we use Carafe to replace the first two deconvolution layers for upsampling operations, further reducing the computational load of the network.

## 2   Proposed Method

To address the aforementioned issues, this paper proposes an improved safety helmet-wearing detection algorithm based on MobileViT and Centernet. First, for the feature extraction stage, we use a more lightweight MobileViT (Mobile Vision Transformer) as the backbone, along with the introduction of the Efficient Channel Attention (ECA) mechanism, reducing false alarms caused by complex environmental factors. Second, in decoding stage, we combine the Feature Pyramid Networks (FPN) structure with the Adaptively Spatial Feature Fusion (ASFF) module, achieving multi-scale adaptive fusion of features. This fusion integrates high-level semantic information with low-level semantic information, allowing the network to retain more information about small targets. Last but not least, the introduction of the Context-Aware Refinement (Carafe) for upsampling operations, significantly reduces the model's parameters. The improved structure is illustrated in Fig. 1.

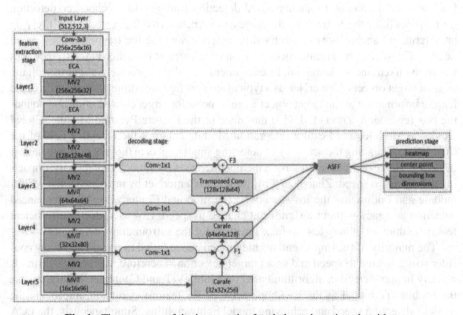

**Fig. 1.** The structure of the improved safety helmet detection algorithm

### 2.1   Centernet Model

The CenterNet model [15] is anchor-free object detection network structure, which can be divided into three stages: feature extraction stage, decoding stage and prediction stage. The feature extraction stage typically employs architectures such as ResNet-50 [16], Hourglass [17], to extract features from input images and obtain rich semantic information. During the decoding stage, upsampling operations are performed through three deconvolutional layers to obtain an output feature map of $128 \times 128 \times 64$. In the prediction phase, three convolutional operations are applied to the output feature map, yielding predictions for heatmap, center point, and bounding box dimensions. The heatmap prediction determines the category of the hot point. The center point prediction provides the offset of the hot point from the object center, and the width and height predictions yield the dimensions of the object. Finally, a bounding box is drawn based on the prediction results. This algorithm focuses on detecting the central point of each target and performs well in terms of both speed and precision. Therefore, it is well-suited for scenarios with high real-time requirements, such as safety helmet detection.

## 2.2 Backbone

In order to reduce the model's parameter quantity and better meet the requirements of realtime monitoring, this study replaced the original ResNet50 with MobileViT as the feature extraction network. MobileViT [18] is a lightweight model that combines both CNN and Transformer architectures. The CNN architecture helps address the training difficulties and lack of spatial inductive biases in the Transformer architecture, enhancing training stability and accelerates network convergence. The self-attention mechanism and global perspective inherent in the Transformer facilitate better learning of both local features and global representations. Therefore, it outperforms typical lightweight CNN architectures in terms of performance, ensuring both improved detection speed and accuracy. As shown in Fig. 1, "MViT" represents the MobileViT module, while "MV2" denotes the linear bottleneck inverted residual module in MobileNetV2 [19].

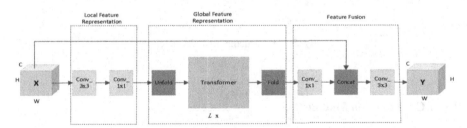

**Fig. 2.** The structure of MobileViT block

The MobileViT module, as illustrated in Fig. 2, consists of three parts: local feature representation, global feature representation, and feature fusion. First, using a 3x3 convolution operation to extract local feature information from the input feature map. Next, In the global feature representation, the image is divided into patches, as illustrated in Fig. 3, self-attention operations are performed only on the pixels at corresponding positions to reduce computational complexity. Finally, feature fusion is performed using a $3 \times 3$ convolutional operation to obtain the output result.

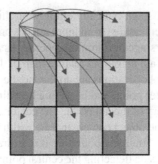

**Fig. 3.** Obtaining global features from pixels at corresponding positions

The MobileNetV2 module, as depicted in Fig. 4, employs an inverted residual structure. Expand the dimensions first, and then reduce them. This structure extracts features more comprehensively than the residual structure, achieving higher accuracy while maintaining speed.

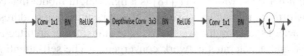

**Fig. 4.** The structure of MV2 block

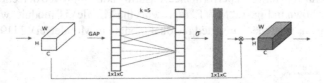

**Fig. 5.** The structure of ECA block

### 2.3 ECA Attention Module

The ECA (Efficient Channel Attention) module [20] is a type of channel attention module that enhances model performance with only a minimal increase in parameters. As an improved version of the SE (Squeeze- and-Excitation) module, the ECA module introduces two improvements compared to SE: (1) ECA (Efficient Channel Attention) mitigates the feature dimension reduction between two fully connected (FC) layers. (2) Using one-dimensional convolution accomplishes local interactions between channels. This enables a more comprehensive enhancement of detailed features in the lower-level feature maps, strengthening the focus on the target, and reducing false detections of surrounding environmental objects. The ECA structure, as shown in Fig. 5, starts by applying global pooling to the input feature map. Subsequently, an one-dimensional convolution and an activation function are utilized for adjustments, resulting in channel weight parameters. These parameters are then multiplied with the input feature map, yielding the final feature map enhanced through channel attention.

ECA utilizes a one-dimensional convolution kernel with a channel size of k to adaptively adjust the interaction rate, allowing layers with a greater number of channels to perform more interactions. The calculation of kin relation to the channel number C is described by Eq. (1).

$$k = \psi(C) = \left| \frac{\log_2(C)}{r} + \frac{b}{r} \right|_{obb} \tag{1}$$

## 2.4 ASFF-FPN

After four rounds of downsampling, the feature extraction network produces a $16 \times 16 \times 96$ feature map. The pixel information is heavily compressed at this stage. Due to the limited amount of pixel information contained in the $16 \times 16 \times 96$ feature map, leading to missed detections of small objects. Introducing the FPN structure allows for the fusion of high-level semantic information with low-level semantic information, preserving more spatial details. This is conducive to more accurate detection of small targets. We introduce ASFF [21] on the basis of FPN, conducting adaptive fusion processing yields rich cross-scale semantic information, further enhancing the precision of small target detection.

As illustrated in Fig. 6, ASFF first performs upsampling on F1 and F2 to match their sizes with the feature map F3, resulting in S1, S2, and S3. These three feature maps are then multiplied by α, β and γ, followed by dimension-wise summation. The final result is obtained through a $3 \times 3$ convolution operation. The principles can be represented by Eq. (2).

$$F_{out} = \alpha \times S_3 + \beta \times S_2 + \gamma \times S_3 \tag{2}$$

After training, α, β and γ represent the important relationships among feature maps at three different scales. If certain regions exhibit conflicting information between shallow and deep features, those features will be discarded. If the features in the corresponding regions contain more discriminative information beneficial for image recognition, these features will receive a larger proportion of weights during the reassignment, making the network more adept at distinguishing the category to which an object belongs.

## 2.5 Carafe Upsample Operator

The original network used deconvolution for upsampling operations. The main drawback of deconvolution is its high computational cost. Employing the Carafe [22] for upsampling operations can effectively address this issue. As illustrated in Fig. 7, this paper replaces the first two deconvolution layers with Carafe, and the final layer is not replaced. This approach achieves a reduction in the number of parameters while nearly maintaining the detection performance. The specific steps are as follows:

(1) First, use a $1 \times 1$ convolutional kernel as a channel compressor to reduce the number of channels.

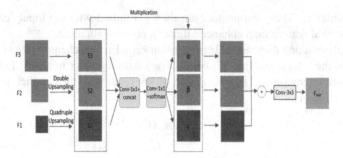

**Fig. 6.** The structure of ASFF

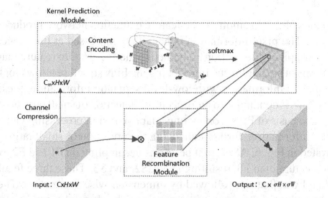

**Fig. 7.** The structure of Carafe

(2) A kup ×kup convolution was used to perform content encoding as an encoder, resulting in a $\alpha^2$ ($\alpha$ is the upsampling factor)$\times$kup$^2\times$H$\times$W output feature map. Subsequently, apply sub-pixel convolution (PixelShuffle) to the output feature map, extracting and unfolding pixels on the same channel, resulting in a kup$^2\times\alpha$H$\times\alpha$W.

(3) Perform softmax normalization to the feature map, and then adjust the shape of the feature map to obtain the final predicted feature kernel, preparing for the fusion operation.

(4) Conduct a convolution operation on the input feature map using the predicted feature kernel to obtain the final output result.

## 3   Experiments and Results

### 3.1   Source of Experimental Data Set

The data set we used was derived from a self-annotated dataset of electrical power scenes. A total of 9081 images were used in the experiment, including 10444 instances with wearing safety helmets and 11519 instances without safety helmets. The dataset is divided into training, validation, and test sets with a ratio of 8:1:1. However, Some images in the dataset present challenges for the model detection, such as small targets and blurry faces. The statistics of target sizes are shown in Fig. 8, small targets have fewer than 32×32 pixels, medium targets have pixels ranging from 32×32 to 96×96, large targets have more than 96×96 pixels.

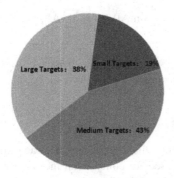

**Fig. 8.** Proportion of targets for each size

## 3.2 Experimental Environment and Experimental Parameters

The experiment used the Ubuntu 20.04 operating system, training framework python3.8.16 and pytorch 1.12.1. During the model training, the images are uniformly resized to 512×512, with batch size set to 5, initial learning rate set to 0.0005, the minimum learning rate set to 0.000005, the optimization function used is Adam, the learning rate decay is cosine decay and a total of 200 epoch.

## 3.3 Evaluation Metrics

The assessment criteria used in the experiment include Mean Average Precision (mAP), F1 Score (F1), Frames Per Second (FPS) and parameter quantity, among which F1 combines both precision and recall into a single metric, formula is shown in Eq. (3), FPS represents detection speed. The following are the calculation Equation for F1, precision and recall.

$$F1 = \frac{2 \times P \times R}{P + R} \tag{3}$$

$$P = \frac{TP}{TP + FP} \tag{4}$$

$$R = \frac{TP}{TP + FN} \tag{5}$$

Equation (4) shows the formula of the precision while Eq. (5) indicates the formula of the recall, in which TP signifies the count of positive samples that are predicted as positive; FP denotes the count of negative samples that are falsely predicted as positive; FN indicates the count of positive samples that are falsely predicted as negative.

The formula for calculating mAP is as shown in Eq. (6), among which N is the total number of all classes in safety helmet detection, while APi is the Average Precision of the i-th class. The expression for Average Precision (AP) is shown as Eq. (7).

$$mAP = \frac{1}{N} \sum_{i=1}^{N} AP_i \tag{6}$$

$$AP = \int_0^1 P\,dR \tag{7}$$

## 3.4  Ablation Experiment

Through ablation experiments, the effectiveness of each improvement was validated, and the evaluation metrics used for comparison include F1, mAP0.5 and the model's parameter quantity. The results of the ablation experiments are presented in Table 1.

Experiment 2 replaced the feature extraction network based on the original model, after replacing ResNet50 with MobileViT-XS, the model's parameters decreased by approximately ten times compared to the original model, with little impact on mAP.

**Table 1.**  Ablation experiment

| | MobileViT-XS | ASFF-FPN | ECA | Carafe(first two layers) | Carafe (all layers) | Hat F1 | Person F1 | Map (0.5)/% | Parameter quantity/M |
|---|---|---|---|---|---|---|---|---|---|
| 1 | | | | | | 0.84 | 0.77 | 80.13 | 32.67 |
| 2 | ✓ | | | | | 0.84 | 0.75 | 79.40 | 3.06 |
| 3 | ✓ | ✓ | | | | 0.84 | 0.81 | 85.98 | 3.12 |
| 4 | ✓ | ✓ | ✓ | | | 0.85 | 0.82 | 86.44 | 3.13 |
| 5 | ✓ | ✓ | ✓ | ✓ | | 0.85 | 0.82 | 86.37 | 2.57 |
| 6 | ✓ | ✓ | ✓ | | ✓ | 0.84 | 0.81 | 84.96 | 2.47 |

Experiment 3 introduced the ASFF-FPN structure based on Experiment 2, enhancing the model's capability to extract feature information from small targets, and significantly improving accuracy. However, ASFF-FPN would complicate the model's architecture. Resulting in an increase in the number of parameters.

Experiment 4 incorporated the ECA module after the first convolutional layer and lay1 based on Experiment 3. This improvement increased the model's focus on targets in complex backgrounds, reducing false detections of surrounding similar objects. With a mere 0.01M increase in parameters, the mAP improved by 0.46%.

Experiment 5 improved the model's upsampling stage based on Experiment 4. It replaced the deconvolutions in the first two layers of the original model with the Carafe, while retaining deconvolution in the final layer. According to the experimental data, the parameter quantity decreased by 0.56M, with only a slight decrease of 0.07% in mAP.

Experiment 6 replaced all the deconvolutions with the Carafe. Despite a reduction in parameter count by only 0.1M compared to Experiment 5, there was a notable decrease of 1.41% in mAP. F1 scores also experienced a decrease of 0.01 for each category. Due to the fewer channels of the final deconvolution, would not incur a substantial increase in computational load. Therefore, the improvement method from Experiment 5 was ultimately adopted.

**Fig. 9.** The left shows the detection results of the original network, and the right shows the detection results of the improved network.

### 3.5  The Actual Detection Effect of the Optimized Network

The detection results of the original network are displayed on the left, while the enhanced network detection results are presented on the right. As shown in Fig. 9, the predicted instances without safety helmets are denoted by the blue boxes, while those with safety helmets are represented by the red boxes. It can be observed that the original Centernet model has issues with missing small targets and may incorrectly detect objects in the surrounding area with colors and shapes similar to a safety helmet as instances of heads wearing safety helmets. However, The proposed model in this paper has improved abilities to detect small targets and resist interference, better meeting the detection requirements in practical operational environments.

### 3.6  Comparative Experiment

This experiment compares the original Centernet, EfficientDet, RefineDet, Faster-RCNN, Deformable DETR, and the improved Centernet in terms of parameters, mAP and FPS. The specific data is presented in Table 2. Compared to the original model, the improved Centernet showed a 6.24% increase in mAP and a 17.8 FPS improvement. EfficientDet [23] also utilizes a lightweight model as the feature extraction network, making it the fastest among these networks. However, its precision is lower compared to our proposed model. RefineDet [24] and Faster R-CNN lag behind our proposed model in both detection speed and accuracy. Deformable DETR [25] performs well in accuracy, but it significantly lags behind our proposed model in terms of speed.

**Table 2.** Performance comparison between the improved model and different models

| Model | Parameter quantity/M | Map (0.5)/% | FPS |
|---|---|---|---|
| Centernet | 32.67 | 80.13 | 87.9 |
| Ours | 2.28 | 86.37 | 105.7 |
| Efficientdet-D0 | 3.93 | 76.2 | 109.1 |
| RefineDet | 28.46 | 73.32 | 64.6 |
| Faster-RCNN | 137.10 | 70.42 | 13.1 |
| Deformable DETR | 39.82 | 86.2 | 9.53 |

## 4  Conclusions

To address the issues of missed detection for small objects and false detection of surrounding similar objects, improvements were made to the Centernet model. To address the loss of pixel information during the downsampling process, the AFSS-FPN was employed for multi- scale adaptive feature fusion. This approach facilitates the reuse of low-level pixel information and cross-scale information integration. Additionally, the ECA attention mechanism was introduced into the backbone network to enhance the model's focus on the targets, thereby reducing instances of false detection and missed detection. By replacing the original backbone network ResNet50 with the MobileViT network and substituting the CARAFE for the original deconvolution, model parameters were reduced, leading to an improvement in detection speed.

The experimental results indicate that the improved Centernet model achieves higher precision on the basis of faster detection speed compared to the original model. The improved mAP has increased by 6.24% and the FPS has been boosted by 17.8. This enhancement demonstrates better accuracy and speed in the task of detecting whether safety helmets are worn.

**Acknowledgements.** We thank reviewers for their valuable comments and help. This project is supported by the Education Commission of Hubei Province (No. D2021701).

# References

1. Girshick, R., Donahue, J., Darrell, T.: Rich feature hierarchies for accurate object detection and semantic segmentation. In: Proceedings of the IEEE Conference on Computer Vision and Pattern Recognition (CVPR), pp. 580–587. IEEE (2014)
2. Girshick, R.: Fast R-CNN. In: Proceedings of the IEEE Conference on Computer Vision and Pattern Recognition (CVPR), pp. 1440–1448. IEEE (2015)
3. Ren, S., He, K., Girshick, R.: Fasterr- CNN: towards real-time object detection with region proposal networks. In: IEEE Trans. Pattern Anal. Mach. Intell, pp. 1137–1149. IEEE (2016)
4. Sun, D., LI, C., Zhang, H.: Safety helmet wearing detection method fused with self-attention mechanism. Comput. Eng. Appl. **58**(20), 300–304 (2022)
5. Redmon, J., Divvala, S., Girshick, R.: You only look once: unified, real-time object detection. In: Proceedings of the IEEE Conference on Computer Vision and Pattern Recognition, pp. 779–788. IEEE (2016)
6. Redmon, J., Farhadi, A.: YOLO9000: better, faster, stronger. In: Proceedings of the IEEE Conference on Computer Vision and Pattern Recognition, pp. 7263–7271. IEEE (2017)
7. Redmon, J., Farhadi, A.: YOLOv3: an incremental improvement. In: arXiv preprint arXiv: 1804.02767. IEEE (2018)
8. Bochkovskiy, A., Sang, W., Markovtsev, V.: YOLOv4: Optimal speed and accuracy of object detection. arXiv preprint arXiv:2004.10934 (2020)
9. Liu, W., Anguelov, D., Erhan, D.: SSD: single shot multibox detector. European Conference on Computer Vision, pp. 21–37 (2016)
10. Wu, F., Jin, G., Gao, M.: Helmet detection based on improved YOLO v3 deep model. In: IEEE 16th International Conference on Networking Sensing and Control (ICNSC), pp. 363–368 (2019)
11. Zeng, L., Duan, X., Pan, Y.: Research on the algorithm of helmet-wearing detection based on the optimized yolov4. Vis. Comput. **39**, 2165–2175 (2023)
12. Liang, W., Jing, C., Zhou, Z.: Research on detection algorithm of helmet wearing state in electric construction. In: 14th National Conference on Signal and Intelligent Information Processing and Application, pp. 508–512 (2021)
13. Zhou, M., Zhang, Z., Gong, R.: Detection of nonhardhat-use based on new feature fusion. Comput. Eng. Des. **4211**, 3181–3187 (2021)

14. Zhao, J., Wang, H., Wu, L.: FPN centernet helmet wearing detection algorithm. Comput. Eng. Appl. **58**(14), 114–120 (2022)
15. Zhou, X., Wang, D., Krhenb¨uhl, P.: Objects as points. arXiv preprint arXiv:1904.07850 (2019)
16. He, K., Zhang, X., Ren, S., Sun, J.: Deep residual learning for image recognition. In: Proceedings of the IEEE Conference on Computer Vision and Pattern Recognition (CVPR), pp. 770–778. IEEE (2016)
17. Newell, A., Yang, K., Jia, D.: Stacked hourglass networks for human pose estimation. In: Proceedings of the 2016 European Conference on Computer Vision (ECCV), pp. 981–990. Springer (2016)
18. Mehta, S., Rastegari, M.: Light- weight, general-purpose, and mobile- friendly vision transformer. arXiv preprint arXiv:2110.02178 (2021)
19. Sandler, M., Howard, A., Zhu, M.: Inverted residuals and linear bottlenecks: Mobile networks for classification, detection and segmentation. In: Proceedings of the IEEE Conference on Computer Vision and Pattern Recognition (CVPR), pp. 4510–4520. IEEE (2018)
20. Wang, Q., Wu, B., Zhu, P.: ECA-Net: efficient channel attention for deep convolutional neural networks. In: Conference on Computer Vision and Pattern Recognition (CVPR), pp. 1131–1139. IEEE (2020)
21. Zhao, X., Deng, Z., Xia, Z.: Light- weight, general-purpose, and mobile-friendly vision transformer. arXiv preprint arXiv:1911.09516 (2019)
22. Wang, J., Chen, K., Xu, R.: CARAFE: content-aware reassembly of features. In: International Conference on Computer Vision (ICCV), pp. 3007–3016. IEEE (2019)
23. Tan, M., Pang, R., Le, Q.: EfficientDet: scalable and efficient object detection. In: Conference on Computer Vision and Pattern Recognition (CVPR), pp. 10778–10787. IEEE (2020)
24. Zhang, S., Wen, L., Bian, X.: Single-shot refinement neural network for object detection. In: IEEE Conference on Computer Vision and Pattern Recognition. IEEE, pp. 4203–4212 (2018)
25. Wang, J., Chen, K., Xu, R.: Deformable DETR: Deformable transformers for end-to-end object detection. arXiv preprint arXiv:2005.12872 (2020)

# Better Sampling, Towards Better
# End-to-End Small Object Detection

Zile Huang, Chong Zhang, Mingyu Jin, Fangyu Wu, Chengzhi Liu,
and Xiaobo Jin$^{(\boxtimes)}$

Xi'an Jiaotong-Liverpool University, Suzhou, China
{Zile.Huang21,Chong.zhang19,mingyu.jin19}@student.xjtlu.edu.cn,
{Fangyu.Wu02,Xiaobo.Jin}@xjtlu.edu.cn

**Abstract.** While deep learning-based general object detection has made significant strides in recent years, the effectiveness and efficiency of small object detection remain unsatisfactory. This is primarily attributed not only to the limited characteristics of such small targets but also to the high density and mutual overlap among these targets. The existing transformer-based small object detectors do not leverage the gap between accuracy and inference speed. To address challenges, we propose methods enhancing sampling within an end-to-end framework. Sample Points Refinement (SPR) constrains localization and attention, preserving meaningful interactions in the region of interest and filtering out misleading information. Scale-aligned Target (ST) integrates scale information into target confidence, improving classification for small object detection. A task-decoupled Sample Reweighting (SR) mechanism guides attention toward challenging positive examples, utilizing a weight generator module to assess the difficulty and adjust classification loss based on decoder layer outcomes. Comprehensive experiments across various benchmarks reveal that our proposed detector excels in detecting small objects. Our model demonstrates a significant enhancement, achieving a 2.9% increase in average precision (AP) over the state-of-the-art (SOTA) on the VisDrone dataset and a 1.7% improvement on the SODA-D dataset.

**Keywords:** small object detection · label assignment · deformable attention

## 1   Introduction

Since the emergence of deep convolutional neural networks (CNN), the performance of object detection methods has improved rapidly. There are two main approaches: two-stage proposal-based models with accuracy advantages [1] and single-stage proposal-free models with speed advantages [2]. However, despite recent tremendous advances in object detection, detecting objects under certain conditions is still difficult, such as being small, occluded, or truncated (Fig. 1).

This work was partially supported by the "Qing Lan Project" in Jiangsu universities, Research Development Fund with No. RDF-22-01-020 and Suzhou Science and Technology Development Planning Programme (Grant No. ZXL2023176).

N. Magnenat Thalmann et al. (Eds.): CASA 2024, CCIS 2374, pp. 319–335, 2025.
https://doi.org/10.1007/978-981-96-2681-6_23

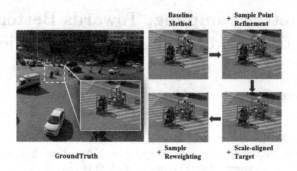

**Fig. 1.** Visualization of our methods within challenging scenes featuring crowds and overlapping objects. Our visual illustration emphasizes the effectiveness of scale-aligned target, sample reweighting, and sample point refinement within intricate scenes, allowing for a comparative analysis with a standard or baseline method.

Small target detection problems are mainly divided into four categories: multi-scale representation, contextual information, super-resolution and region proposal. Due to the tiny size and low resolution of small objects, location details are gradually lost in high-level feature maps. Multi-scale representation [3] combines the location information of low-level features and the semantic information of high-level features. Contextual information, which exploits the relationship between an object in an image and its surrounding environment, is another novel way to improve small object detection accuracy. It is very necessary to extract more additional contextual information [4] as a supplement to the original ROI (Region of Interest) features because there are too few ROI features extracted from small objects. As mentioned above, fine details are crucial for object instance localization, which means that more details for small objects should be obtained. Super-resolution technology [5] attempts to restore or reconstruct the original low-resolution image to a higher resolution, which means more details of small objects can be obtained. Region-proposal [6] is a strategy aimed at designing more suitable anchor points for small objects. The anchors of the current leading detectors mainly focus on generic objects, and the size, shape and number of anchors used in general detectors do not match small objects well.

Through the Transformer architecture, DETR [7] achieves competitive end-to-end detection performance in a one-to-one scheme, abandoning the manual components of NMS and eliminating the need for post-processing. However, the limited number and low quality of positive samples may lead to poor performance on objects of extremely limited size. Deformable DETR [8] uses deformable sampling points to enhance its feature decoding capabilities, but its performance in densely populated and overlapping scenes is unsatisfactory, and the ongoing challenge of effectively distinguishing positive and negative samples remains solve.

To address the inherent challenges associated with small object detection and the limitations observed in current end-to-end object detectors, we introduce three different strategies aimed at mitigating these issues from different perspectives. In this work, we focus on improving the DETR method [7] for detecting small target objects. First, to mitigate potential clutter caused by background noise and surrounding elements, our approach follows an iterative refinement paradigm similar to [8], which focuses on refining the attention mechanism by merging updated box predictions from the previous layer, and effectively reduce confusion with background elements and noise. Second, sample point refinement (SPR) constrains the distribution and attention of sample points by setting learning goals for the deformable attention module in the decoder, instead of directly discarding reference points located outside the bounding box. This intentional inhibition can serve as a strategic stimulus for the model, resulting in a more object-centered deformable attentional sampling capability without losing surrounding information. Finally, a decoupled sample reweighting (SR) mechanism integrates a scaling factor into the target confidence, making the model inherently scale-aligned. The decoupled reweighting technique helps the model refocus its focus to learning from challenging positive examples at the feature level instead of the object level.

In summary, the main contributions of this article are as follows:

- We proposed Sample Points Refinement (SPR), which imposes constraints on the localization and attention of sample points within deformable attention. This ensures the preservation of meaningful interactions within the region of interest while filtering out potentially misleading information.
- We incorporate scale information from samples into the target confidence, namely Scale-aligned Target (ST), thereby establishing a more appropriate learning objective for classification. This adjustment proves highly advantageous, particularly in the realm of small object detection.
- We present a task-decoupled Sample Reweighting (SR) mechanism aimed at guiding the model to redirect its attention toward learning from challenging positive examples. Our approach includes a weight generator module that gauges difficulty from decoder layer outcomes, facilitating the adjustment of the classification loss accordingly.
- We conduct comprehensive experiments and ablations on VisDrone [9] and SODA-D [10] to verify the effectiveness of the proposed method and the importance of correct sampling in small object detection.

## 2    Related Work

**Multi-scale Feature Learning.** The basic idea of the multi-scale feature learning method is to learn targets at different scales separately, mainly to solve the problem that small targets themselves have few discriminative features, including based on feature pyramids and based on receptive fields. The main idea of the feature pyramid-based method [11] is to integrate low-level spatial information and high-level semantic information to enhance target features. Receptive field-based methods, such as the Trident network [12], use dilated convolutions with different expansion rates to form three branches with different receptive fields, responsible for detecting objects of different scales.

**GAN-Based Methods.** Different from multi-scale feature learning methods, GAN methods solve the problem of small targets with few discriminative features by generating high-resolution images or high-resolution features. SOD-MTGAN [13] uses a trained detector (such as Faster R-CNN) to obtain a subgraph containing objects, and then uses a generator to generate corresponding high-definition images, where the detector also acts as a discriminator. After generating high-resolution features, GaN network [14] reduce the input image by 2 times, then extracts the features as low-resolution features, and the features extracted from the original image as the corresponding high-resolution features. The generator generates "fake" high-resolution features based on low-resolution features, and the discriminator is responsible for distinguishing "fake" high-resolution features from "real" high-resolution features.

**Context-Based Methods.** Context-based methods assist the detection of small objects based on the environmental information where the small objects are located or their relationship with other easily detected objects. Inside-Outside Net [15] extracts the global context information of each object in the four directions of up, down, left, and right through RNN. RelationNetwork [16] uses the relationship between objects to assist in the detection of small objects. The relationship between two objects is implicitly modeled by a Transformer, and this relationship is used to enhance the characteristics of each object.

**Loss Reweighting Methods.** This type of method makes the network pay more attention to the training of small objects by increasing the weight in the small object loss. The feedback-driven loss method [17] increases the weight of small object loss when the proportion of small object loss is low, allowing the network to treat objects of different scales more equally.

**Special Design for Small Object.** This type of method designs target detection algorithms based on the characteristics of small targets. S3FD [18] directly reduces the IoU threshold of small object positive samples, thereby increasing the number of anchors for small object matching. If there are still few anchors matching small objects, the top $N$ anchors are selected from all anchors that meet the threshold as matching anchors. Xu et al. [19] proposed a new metric to alleviate the situation where a slight shift in the prediction box of a small object causes a huge change in the IoU index. Wang et al. [20] introduced the normalized Wasserstein distance to optimize the position metric for small object detectors. However, this method is not sensitive to box offset, and a small amount of offset will not cause a sharp drop in the indicator.

## 3   Background on Deformable DETR-Based Detection

### 3.1   Deformable DETR-Based Models

Following the Deformable DETR-based models [8], our model consists of three main components: a CNN-backbone, an encoder-decoder transformer, and a prediction head.

The backbone network flattens the raw features of the input image into a sequence of tokens $X = \{x_1, x_2, \cdots, x_l\}$. The transformer then extracts information from $X$ using a set of learnable queries $Z = \{z_1, z_2, \cdots, z_n\}$.

We can compute the attention representation for the $i^{th}$ query point

$$\text{Attn}(z_i, p_i, X)$$
$$= \sum_m W_m [\sum_{l,k} A_{milk} W'_m x_l (\phi_l(p_i) + \Delta p_{milk})], \tag{1}$$

where the set of subscripts $\{m, i, l, k\}$ represents the $k$-th sampling point of the $l$-th sampling layer of the $m$-th attention head corresponding to the $i$-th query and the reference point of the $i$-th query is $p_i$. The matrices $W$ and $W'$ correspond to two linear transformations respectively. Here, $\Delta p$ and $A$ denote the tensor matrices of sampling offsets and attention weights, respectively, where the weight matrix $A$ satisfies the constraints $\sum_{l,k} A_{milk} = 1$. It is worth noting that $p_i$ is a normalized two-dimensional coordinate located at $[0,1]^2$, and the function $\phi$ will convert it to the coordinates in the original image.

Subsequently, for each query $z_i$, the decoder will output two heads: the head $H^{reg}(z_i)$ predicts the location of the object box in the image, and another head $H^{cls}(z_i)$ predicts the category of the object

$$s_i = H^{cls}(z_i), \quad b_i = H^{reg}(z_i) \tag{2}$$

where $s_i$ represents the object category corresponding to the $i$-th query, and $b_i$ is the box predicted by multiple decoders, including the upper left corner position and the length and width of the box.

## 3.2 Varifocal Loss

We adopt Varifocal Loss (VFL) [21] as our baseline method for classification loss. Varifocal Loss is an extension of Focal Loss [22], incorporating a trade-off parameter $\alpha$ that adjusts the loss based on the difficulty of each sample:

$$\hat{\mathcal{L}}_{cls} = -\sum_{i=1}^{N^+} q_i \text{BCE}(p_i, q_i) - \alpha \sum_{i=1}^{N^-} p_i^\gamma \text{BCE}(p_i, 0), \tag{3}$$

where $p_i$ is the predicted IoU-aware classification score (IACS) and $q_i$ is the target score. For a foreground point, $q_i$ is set to the IoU between the generated bounding box and its ground-truth value, otherwise it is 0. For background points, the target $q_i$ is 0 for all classes. The variables $N^+$ and $N^-$ respectively represent the number of bounding boxes containing the object.

We perform bounding box regression using a combination of norm loss $\mathcal{L}_1$ and Intersection over Union (IoU) loss $\mathcal{L}^{IoU}$, where $L1$ loss measures the absolute difference in width, height, center $x$, and center $y$ between the predicted bounding box and the ground truth, a measure of localization accuracy, while IoU computes the intersection area between the predicted and ground-truth bounding boxes divided by their union as a similarity measure and penalizes differences in spatial overlap

$$\hat{\mathcal{L}}^{\mathrm{reg}} = \sum_{i=1}^{N^+} [\mathcal{L}_1(b_i, \hat{b}_i) + \mathcal{L}^{\mathrm{IoU}}(b_i, \hat{b}_i)], \tag{4}$$

where $b_i$ and $\hat{b}_i$ represent the predicted bounding boxes and the ground truth bounding box respectively. The total loss will be presented in the following section.

# 4    Our Method

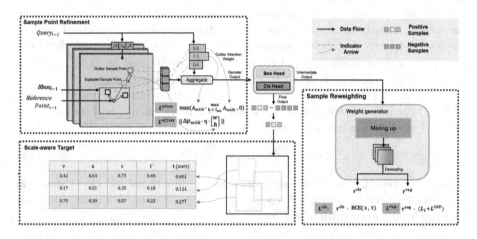

**Fig. 2.** Framework overall. We proposed a series of transferable methods to support end-to-end models to perform better in small object detection. The final loss could be represented as $\mathcal{L} = \mathcal{L}^{\mathrm{cls}} + \mathcal{L}^{\mathrm{reg}} + \mathcal{L}^{\mathrm{offset}} + \mathcal{L}^{\mathrm{atten}}$.

Our methodology involves multi-step training supervision aimed at refining sampling strategies, addressing challenges posed by box edge regression and ambiguous classification in small object detection, often caused by limited information availability. Notably, our approach maintains the original inference speed as we solely modify the training objective of the model.

## 4.1    Refinement of Sample Points Outside Box

We employ learnable offsets in deformable attention to make the convolution kernel more flexible to focus on objects with significant differences in size and shape. In Deformable DETR [8], attention is focused on the x-coordinate and width of the left or right border of the object and the y-coordinate and height of the top or bottom border. However, when the model is not constrained in learning deformation offsets, the perceptual field has a tendency to extend beyond the target, especially in the context of small objects. As in Fig. 2, the red square within the deformable attention region signifies a sample point necessitating refinement due to its substantial distance from the object, resulting in diminished informativeness.

Suppose that when we use the $i$-th query to sample in the $l$-th layer of the $m$-th attention head, the set of sampling points contained within the bounding box is $\mathcal{I}_{ilm}$, and the set of sampling points located outside the bounding box is $\mathcal{O}_{ilm}$, then in order to make the points outside the bounding box as close as possible to the bounding box, we define the following loss for sampling points outside the bounding box

$$\mathcal{L}^{\text{offset}} = \sum_{i=1}^{N^+} \left[ \sum_{m,l,k \in \mathcal{O}_{ilm}} \left\| \Delta p_{milk} - \eta \begin{bmatrix} w_i \\ h_i \end{bmatrix} \right\|_1^2 \right], \tag{5}$$

where $w_i$ and $h_i$ represent the width and height of the previous layer on the query $z_i$ in the decoder, and $\eta > 1$ is an expansion parameter indicating the expansion degree of the bounding box of the previous layer. Note that since $\eta > 1$, the sample point is still outside the bounding box. The orange dotted line box in Fig. 2 functions as an expanded buffer, preserving both local and global attention cues.

At the same time, we hope that the weight $A$ of the sampling points outside the box should be smaller than the weight of all sampling points within the box, so we define the attention loss for sampling points outside the bounding box as follows

$$\mathcal{L}^{\text{atten}} = \sum_{i=1}^{N^+} \sum_{m,l,k \in \mathcal{O}_{ilm}} \max(A_{milk} - \max_{k \in \mathcal{I}_{mil}} A_{milk}, 0). \tag{6}$$

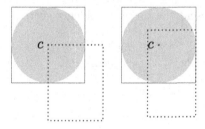

**Fig. 3.** The IoU values on the two target detection tasks are equal, but the right side has a larger area ratio (predicted box area and true box area).

## 4.2 Estimation of Target Confidence

As shown in Eq. (3), although Varifocal loss increases the penalty for negative class samples, it does not consider the interaction between target detection and target classification. To this end, we introduce the results of small target detection and redefine the target confidence $s$. For small target detection, detection performance is not only related to the intersection area between the predicted box and the grounding-truth box, but also related to the size of the predicted box (Fig. 3).

Assume that the annotations of the predicted box and the grounding-box box are $B = (x, y, w, h)$ and $\hat{B} = (\hat{x}, \hat{y}, \hat{w}, \hat{h})$, respectively, then we introduce two variables to measure the performance of the detection algorithm

$$u = \frac{\mathcal{A}(B \cap \hat{B})}{\mathcal{A}(B \cup \hat{B})} = \text{IoU}(B, \hat{B}), \tag{7}$$

$$\rho = \frac{\mathcal{A}(B)}{\mathcal{A}(\hat{B})}, \tag{8}$$

where $\mathcal{A}(\cdot)$ represents the area of the bounding box. If we define $x = \mathcal{A}(B)$, $y = \mathcal{A}(\hat{B})$ and $z = \mathcal{A}(B \cap \hat{B})$, then we have

$$u = \frac{z}{x + y - z}, \tag{9}$$

$$\rho = \frac{x}{y}. \tag{10}$$

Furthermore, we get the relationship between $u$ and $\rho$

$$\frac{z/y}{\rho + 1} = \frac{u}{1 + u}. \tag{11}$$

When IoU ($u$) is constant, $z/y \propto (\rho + 1)$. But obviously, we prefer larger $\rho$ or $z/y$, which indicates better detection results, since the area of the predicted box is closer to the area of the grounding-truth box.

Based on the above analysis, we define a function with respect to IoU $u$ and area ratio $\rho$ to re-represent the target confidence score

$$r = \sqrt{\rho}, \tag{12}$$

$$v = e^{-\theta(r-1)^2}, \tag{13}$$

$$c = u^\beta \cdot v^{1-\beta}, \tag{14}$$

$$t = c \cdot s, \tag{15}$$

where $\beta$ and $\theta$ are the hyper-parameters. Note that our goal is that the area of the predicted box is as close as possible to the area of the true box, that is, $\rho \to 1$. Therefore, we interpret the meaning of the above formula as follows: the square root operation in Eq. (12) is to make the values near 1 more concentrated; the exponential operation in Eq. (13) is to convert the distance loss into a bounded interval $[0, 1]$; Eq. (14) combines the indicators IoU ($u$) and $\rho$ through geometric mean as the proportional coefficient of $s$, where the geometric mean rather than the algorithmic mean is used to measure measurements on two different scales.

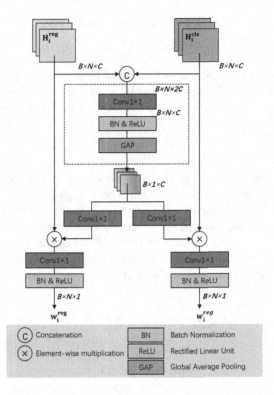

**Fig. 4.** Illustration for the weight generator in the reweighting module. The kernel size of $\text{Conv}_1$, $\text{Conv}_2$, and $\text{Conv}_3$ are $C \times 2C \times 1 \times 1$, $C \times C \times 1 \times 1$, and $1 \times C \times 1 \times 1$, respectively.

### 4.3 Reweighting of Positive Samples

Below we describe in detail our reweighting module for positive samples (boxes containing targets).

First, we generate a shared attention feature between the classification and the regression tasks through the hidden layer representation of the two tasks: the inputs $H_i^{\text{cls}}$ and $H_i^{\text{reg}}$ respectively come from the hidden layer features decoded by the classification head and the regression head that decode the query $z_i$. Then, we directly concatenate the two inputs and go through the following operations, as shown in the dotted box in Fig. 4.

$$A_i = \sigma(\mathcal{B}(\text{cov}(\text{cat}(H_i^{\text{reg}}, H_i^{\text{cls}})))), \tag{16}$$

where $\mathcal{B}$ represents ReLU and batch normalization operations and $\sigma$ is the sigmoid function.

Based on the shared attention weight $A_i$, We implement channel compression through convolution operation and BN/ReLU operation to obtain the weights $w_i^{\text{cls}}$ and $w_i^{\text{reg}}$ corresponding to query $z_i$

$$w_i^{\text{cls}} = \sigma(\mathcal{B}(\text{cov}(H_i^{\text{cls}} \otimes \text{cov}(A_i)))), \tag{17}$$

$$w_i^{\text{reg}} = \sigma(\mathcal{B}(\text{cov}(H_i^{\text{reg}} \otimes \text{cov}(A_i)))), \tag{18}$$

where $\otimes$ is the element-wise multiplication of matrices.

However, in the initial stage of training, when the model has not fully learned accurate feature representations, we discount the weights, where the weights are a decreasing function of the difference between target confidence and prediction confidence

$$r = w^{1-|t-s|}, \tag{19}$$

where $w$ can be $w_i^{\text{cls}}$ or $w_i^{\text{reg}}$ related to query $z_i$, $t$ and $s$ are respectively the target confidence and prediction confidence corresponding to $z_i$. Note that when our algorithm converges, then $t = s$ and $r = w$. Finally, we get the classification weight $r_i^{\text{cls}}$ and regression weight $r_i^{\text{reg}}$ of each bounding box containing the object.

Based on the above discussion, the reweighted loss for both classification (3) and regression (4) is derived by substituting the suppression factor on positive samples with $r_i^{\text{cls}}$, while retaining the suppression on negative samples.

$$\mathcal{L}^{\text{cls}} = \sum_{i=1}^{N^+} r_i^{\text{cls}} \text{BCE}(s_i, t_i)$$

$$+ \alpha \sum_{i=1}^{N^-} p_i^{\gamma} \text{BCE}(s_i, 0), \tag{20}$$

$$\mathcal{L}^{\text{reg}} = \sum_{i=1}^{N^+} r_i^{\text{reg}}[\mathcal{L}_1(b_i, \hat{b}_i) + \mathcal{L}^{\text{IoU}}(b_i, \hat{b}_i)]. \tag{21}$$

Finally, we train our object detection architecture using the following loss function

$$\mathcal{L} = \mathcal{L}^{\text{cls}} + \mathcal{L}^{\text{reg}} + \mathcal{L}^{\text{offset}} + \mathcal{L}^{\text{atten}}. \tag{22}$$

## 5   Experiment

### 5.1   Dataset and Metrics

We perform quantitative analysis on small object datasets in driving scenes and aerial photography scenes. SODA-D [10] and VisDrone [9]. SODA-D contains 24,828 carefully selected high-quality images associated with 278,433 instances in nine categories and annotated with horizontal bounding boxes. These images exhibit significant diversity in time periods, geographical locations, weather conditions, camera perspectives, etc., making them a significant strength of this dataset. VisDrone is a data set dedicated to the detection of drone-captured images, mainly targeting small-sized objects. It contains various environmental settings (urban and rural), scenes with different population densities, and a variety of objects, including pedestrians, vehicles, and bicycles. The dataset contains

**Table 1.** Comparison with state-of-the-art end-to-end detectors on the Visdrone2019 test-set: The subscripts S, M, and L respectively indicate the size of the object as small, medium, and large.

| Model | Publication | #epochs | AP | $AP_{50}$ | $AP_{75}$ | $AP_S$ | $AP_M$ | $AP_L$ | Params |
|---|---|---|---|---|---|---|---|---|---|
| **Non-Deformable-DETR-based** | | | | | | | | | |
| YOLOX-R50 [23] | CVPR'21 | 70 | 24.1 | 52.6 | 25.1 | 13.7 | 39.5 | 53.4 | 43M |
| Anchor-DETR-R50 [24] | AAAI'21 | 70 | 27.7 | 54.7 | 26.3 | 14.1 | 40.8 | 56.7 | 39M |
| Sparse RCNN-R50 [25] | CVPR'21 | 12 | 27.2 | 56.9 | 25.7 | 17.4 | 46.2 | 57.1 | 40M |
| ViTDet-ViT-B [26] | ECCV'22 | 50 | 28.9 | 57.1 | 25.3 | 16.5 | 47.3 | 55.4 | 47M |
| **Deformable-DETR-based** | | | | | | | | | |
| Deformable-DETR-R50 [8] | ICLR'21 | 50 | 21.7 | 48.4 | 23.5 | 11.7 | 34.8 | 49.2 | 43M |
| Conditional-DETR-R50 [27] | ICCV'21 | 50 | 26.4 | 53.7 | 27.4 | 16.2 | 46.2 | 53.6 | 44M |
| DAB-DETR-R50 [28] | ICLR'22 | 50 | 27.8 | 56.8 | 26.9 | 16.4 | 45.5 | 54.8 | 47M |
| DINO-R50 [29] | ICLR'23 | 36 | 26.8 | 58.2 | 28.9 | 17.5 | 47.3 | 58.3 | 47M |
| Co-DINO-R50 [30] | ICCV'23 | 36 | 29.4 | 58.7 | 29.5 | 18.9 | 46.8 | 61.3 | 55M |
| Baseline-R50 [31] | – | 72 | 28.9 | 57.3 | 31.1 | 19.3 | 46.0 | 57.3 | 42M |
| Ours-R50 | – | 72 | **32.3** | **66.4** | **36.7** | **23.7** | **50.0** | **60.2** | 43M |

**Table 2.** Comparison with state-of-the-art end-to-end detection approaches on the SODA-D test-set, where the subscripts ES, RS and GS represent extremely small, relatively small, generally small and normal respectively.

| Model | Publication | #epochs | AP | $AP_{50}$ | $AP_{75}$ | $AP_{ES}$ | $AP_{RS}$ | $AP_{GS}$ | $AP_N$ | Params |
|---|---|---|---|---|---|---|---|---|---|---|
| **Non-Deformable-DETR-based** | | | | | | | | | | |
| YOLOX-R50 [23] | CVPR'21 | 70 | 26.7 | 53.4 | 23.0 | 13.6 | 25.1 | 30.9 | 30.4 | 43M |
| Anchor-DETR-R50 [24] | AAAI'21 | 70 | 27.3 | 55.9 | 22.7 | 12.2 | 24.2 | 32.8 | 41.7 | 39M |
| Sparse RCNN-R50 [25] | CVPR'21 | 12 | 24.2 | 50.3 | 20.3 | 8.8 | 20.4 | 30.2 | 39.4 | 40M |
| ViTDet-ViT-B [26] | ECCV'22 | 50 | 28.1 | 55.7 | 24.8 | 10.2 | 23.9 | 35.2 | 45.4 | 47M |
| Deformable-DETR-based | | | | | | | | | | |
| Deformable-DETR-R50 [8] | ICLR'21 | 50 | 19.2 | 44.8 | 13.7 | 6.3 | 15.4 | 24.9 | 34.2 | 42M |
| Conditional-DETR-R50 [27] | ICCV'21 | 50 | 25.7 | 52.8 | 15.0 | 7.9 | 20.3 | 28.0 | 36.5 | 44M |
| DAB-DETR-R50 [28] | ICLR'22 | 50 | 27.2 | 55.1 | 20.6 | 10.3 | 22.5 | 31.9 | 37.2 | 47M |
| DINO-R50 [29] | ICLR'23 | 36 | 28.9 | 59.4 | 22.4 | 12.5 | 22.7 | 34.7 | 42.8 | 47M |
| Co-DINO-R50 [30] | ICCV'23 | 36 | 29.7 | 61.3 | 23.9 | 13.6 | 25.3 | 36.1 | 45.1 | 55M |
| Baseline-R50 [31] | – | 72 | 29.3 | 60.2 | 25.2 | 13.2 | 26.9 | 35.4 | 44.6 | 42M |
| Ours-R50 | – | 72 | **31.4** | **63.7** | **28.1** | **15.6** | **29.7** | **38.4** | **46.4** | 43M |

over 2.6 million manually annotated bounding boxes for common target objects (Tables 1 and 2).

The average precision (AP) is used to verify the performance in our experiments. The average AP across multiple IoU thresholds is between 0.5 and 0.95 with an interval of 0.05. Furthermore, $AP_{50}$ and $AP_{75}$ are calculated under a single IoU threshold of 0.5 and 0.75, respectively. The definition of AP across scales differs in Visdrone and SODA-D. In Visdrone, the scale is divided into small (S), medium (M) and large (L), including objects in the range of $(0, 32^2]$, $(32^2, 96^2]$, respectively. is $(96^2, \infty]$. In SODA-D, the scales are divided into extremely small

(ES), relatively small (RS), generally small (GS) and normal (N), including those located at $(0, 144]$, $(144, 400]$, $(400, 1024]$ and $(1024, 2000]$.

## 5.2   Setup

We adopt RT-DETR [31] as our baseline method and leverage its codebase. RT-DETR exhibits superior accuracy and speed compared to traditional CNN-based methods. During training, we use the AdamW optimizer with a base learning rate of 0.0002, weight decay configured to 0.0001, and a linear warm-up step lasting 2000 iterations. The learning rate of the backbone network will be adjusted accordingly. Additionally, we also used an exponential moving average (EMA) with an EMA decay rate of 0.9999 for stability. Our basic data augmentation strategy includes stochastic operations such as color distortion, flipping, resizing, expansion, and cropping.

## 5.3   Main Results

In this study, we conduct a thorough comparison of state-of-the-art end-to-end object detection methods. To ensure a fair comparison, we equip all baseline models with ResNet-50 as the underlying backbone architecture.

Our evaluation results clearly position our proposed method as a superior performer on both datasets considered. Notably, our method shows superior performance on the VisDrone dataset, achieving a significant overall average precision (AP) score of 32.3%. Impressively, this performance outperforms the baseline model by a significant 2.9%.

Similarly, on the SODA-D dataset, our method once again demonstrates its strength, achieving state-of-the-art performance with an overall AP of 31.3%. Compared with the baseline model, our method shows significant superiority, significantly outperforming the baseline model by 1.7%.

These results highlight the effectiveness and dominance of our proposed method in advancing object detection, especially in scenarios involving small objects. The state-of-the-art performance achieved on two datasets validates the superiority of our approach.

## 5.4   Ablation Study

**Individual Component Contribution.** We perform a series of ablations on key components, namely task-decoupled reweighting and object-oriented losses. The experimental results are listed in Table 3. All components significantly contribute to the overall performance, improving objects of different sizes, with the most significant impact observed in the case of small objects.

**Hyperparameters.** The parameter $\beta$ plays a crucial role in balancing the contribution of IoU score and scale score in the confidence objective. In a series of experiments detailed in Table 4, we observe that when $\beta$ varies from 0.3 to

**Table 3.** Ablation study on three strategies including scale-aligned target (ST), sample reweighting (SR), and sample point refinement (SPR)

| ST | SR | SPR | AP | AP$_{50}$ | AP$_S$ | AP$_M$ | AP$_L$ |
|---|---|---|---|---|---|---|---|
| ✓ | | | 29.9 | 58.1 | 20.5 | 46.9 | 58.2 |
| | ✓ | | 30.5 | 58.7 | 21.1 | 48.2 | 58.6 |
| | | ✓ | 31.2 | 61.0 | 21.5 | 48.3 | 58.5 |
| ✓ | ✓ | | 31.8 | 62.1 | 22.8 | 49.5 | 59.8 |
| ✓ | ✓ | ✓ | **32.3** | **66.4** | **23.7** | **50.0** | **60.2** |

**Table 4.** Ablation study on the effectiveness of different choices of $\beta$

| $\beta$ | 0.3 | 0.5 | 0.73 | 0.9 |
|---|---|---|---|---|
| AP | 30.4 | 31.4 | **32.3** | 31.9 |

**Table 5.** Ablation study on the effectiveness of different choices of $\theta$

| $\theta$ | 1.5 | 3 | 6 | 9 |
|---|---|---|---|---|
| AP | 30.6 | 30.9 | **32.3** | 31.7 |

**Table 6.** Ablation study on scaling factor $\alpha$ and suppression degree $\gamma$

| $\gamma$ | 1.5 | | | 1.75 | | |
|---|---|---|---|---|---|---|
| $\alpha$ | 0.25 | 0.5 | 0.75 | 0.25 | 0.5 | 0.75 |
| AP | 32.1 | **32.3** | 31.5 | 30.8 | 30.6 | 30.2 |

**Table 7.** Ablation study on the effectiveness of different choices of expansion rate $\eta$

| $\eta$ | AP | AP$_{50}$ | AP$_S$ | AP$_M$ | AP$_L$ |
|---|---|---|---|---|---|
| (1.5, 1.4, 1.3, 1.2, 1.1, 1.0) | 32.2 | 64.8 | 23.4 | 50.6 | 60.1 |
| (1.5, 1.3, 1.2, 1.1, 1.05, 1.0) | **32.3** | **66.4** | **23.7** | 50.4 | **60.2** |
| (2.0, 1.8, 1.6, 1.4, 1.2, 1.0) | 31.9 | 65.1 | 21.6 | 50.9 | 60.9 |
| (2.0, 1.6, 1.4, 1.2, 1.1, 1.0) | 32.0 | 66.0 | 22.3 | 49.7 | 59.6 |

0.9, the overall performance initially increases to 32.3% and then drops to 31.9%. Therefore, we choose $\beta = 0.73$ as the best choice for our method. This suggests that scale information plays a crucial role in small object detection.

Similarly, $\theta$ acts as a scalar controlling factor, from area ratio to scale fraction, affecting the shape of the projection. In the experiments summarized in Table 5, we found that when $\theta$ is between 1.5 and 9, the overall performance shows a trend of first increasing and then decreasing. Therefore, we choose $\theta = 6$ as the best choice for our method.

**Table 8.** Generalizability of proposed scale-aligned target (ST) and sample reweighting (SR) across different state-of-the-art label assignment methods.

| Method | AP | $AP_{50}$ | $AP_S$ | $AP_M$ | $AP_L$ |
|--------|-----|-----------|--------|--------|--------|
| GFL [32] | 29.7 | 60.7 | 23.7 | 47.7 | 52.8 |
| +ST | 30.8 | 62.1 | 24.1 | 48.6 | 53.2 |
| +SR | 31.6 | 64.5 | 23.7 | 49.8 | 60.2 |
| TOOD [33] | 29.5 | 59.4 | 21.7 | 46.6 | 55.9 |
| +ST | 30.3 | 61.1 | 22.5 | 46.8 | 55.2 |
| +SR | 31.5 | 64.2 | 23.1 | 48.0 | 57.4 |

We also conduct experiments on suppression factors $\gamma$ and $\alpha$ to determine the optimal balance between positive and negative samples shown in Table 6. The results indicate substantial variations with $\gamma$, and the combination of $\gamma = 1.5$ and $\alpha = 0.5$ yields the best performance.

In our final experiment, we investigated the impact of various settings on the expansion rate $\eta$ in the six layers of the deformable attention module, as detailed in Table 7. The settings involved six elements, each controlling the expansion rate. The first row represents a uniform reduction approach, while the second row represents an accelerated reduction method. The third and fourth rows involve a straightforward doubling of the expansion rate $\eta$. The setting of $(1.5, 1.3, 1.2, 1.1, 1.05, 1.0)$ shows the best performance of 32.3%. One potential explanation for this behavior is that deformable attention may initially explore and identify the object in the early layers and subsequently refine the bounding box in the later layers.

**Generalization.** To further verify the generalizability of our target design and target reweighting method, we apply our method to two other state-of-the-art label assignment methods GFL [32] and TOOD [33]. The experiments are based on our framework, as shown in Table 8. The results demonstrate that our Scale-aligned Target proves to be a superior choice for small object detection, and the reweighting method facilitates the model in adaptively learning from data with class and size biases.

## 5.5 Visualization

Figure 5 shows the visualization results obtained by various methods applied to images in the VisDrone dataset. It is worth noting that our method shows quite superior performance compared with other methods. Initial numbers indicate that the baseline approach shows insufficient emphasis on extremely small targets. In contrast, our sampling method significantly enhances attention distribution, demonstrating enhanced accuracy and the ability to detect very small and faint targets effectively.

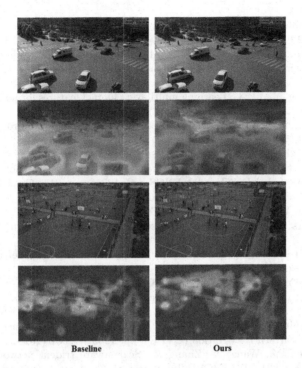

**Fig. 5.** Comparison of heatmap visualizations between the baseline and our method.

## 6    Conclusion

This paper presents sample point refinement, a novel approach to confine the localization and attention of sample points within deformable attention. This constraint ensures meaningful interactions within the region of interest while filtering out misleading information. Additionally, we introduce Scale-aligned Targets, incorporating scale information into target confidence, proving beneficial for small object detection. Furthermore, a task-decoupled sample reweighting mechanism guides the model to focus on challenging positive examples, adjusting classification loss based on difficulty assessed by a weight generator module. Extensive experiments on public datasets consistently demonstrate our approach outperforming state-of-the-art methods.

## References

1. Dai, J., Li, Y., He, K., Sun, J.: R-FCN: object detection via region-based fully convolutional networks. In: Proceedings of the 30th International Conference on Neural Information Processing Systems, NIPS'16, pp. 379–387 (2016)
2. Fu, C.Y., Liu, W., Ranga, A., Tyagi, A., Berg, A.C.: DSSD: deconvolutional single shot detector. In: CoRR abs/1701.06659 (2017)

3. Cui, L., et al.: Multi-scale deconvolutional single shot detector for small objects, Mdssd (2020)
4. Liu, Y., Cao, S., Lasang, P., Shen, S.: Modular lightweight network for road object detection using a feature fusion approach. IEEE Trans. Syst. Man Cybern. Syst. **51**(8), 4716–4728 (2021)
5. Cao, J., Pang, Y., Li, X.: Learning multilayer channel features for pedestrian detection. IEEE Trans. Image Process. **26**(7), 3210–3220 (2017)
6. Chen, Z., Kehe, W., Li, Y., Wang, M., Li, W.: SSD-MSN: an improved multi-scale object detection network based on SSD. IEEE Access **7**, 80622–80632 (2019)
7. Carion, N., Massa, F., Synnaeve, G., Usunier, N., Kirillov, A., Zagoruyko, S.: End-to-end object detection with transformers. In: Vedaldi, A., Bischof, H., Brox, T., Frahm, J.-M. (eds.) ECCV 2020. LNCS, vol. 12346, pp. 213–229. Springer, Cham (2020). https://doi.org/10.1007/978-3-030-58452-8_13
8. Zhu, X., Su, W., Lu, L., Li, B., Wang, X., Dai, J.: Deformable DETR: deformable transformers for end-to-end object detection. arXiv preprint arXiv:2010.04159 (2020)
9. Du, D., et al.: VisDrone-DET2019: the vision meets drone object detection in image challenge results. In: CVPRW (2019)
10. Cheng, G., Yuan, X., Yao, X., Yan, K., Zeng, Q., Han, J.: Towards large-scale small object detection: survey and benchmarks. TPAMI **45**, 13467–13488 (2022)
11. Guo, C., Fan, B., Zhang, Q., Xiang, S., Pan, C.: AugFPN: improving multi-scale feature learning for object detection. In: 2020 IEEE/CVF Conference on Computer Vision and Pattern Recognition (CVPR), pp. 12592–12601 (2020)
12. Li, Y., Chen, Y., Wang, N., Zhang, Z.: Scale-aware trident networks for object detection. In: 2019 IEEE/CVF International Conference on Computer Vision (ICCV), pp. 6053–6062 (2019)
13. Bai, Y., Zhang, Y., Ding, M., Ghanem, B.: SOD-MTGAN: small object detection via multi-task generative adversarial network. In: Proceedings of the European Conference on Computer Vision (ECCV) (2018)
14. Noh, J., Bae, W., Lee, W., Seo, J., Kim, G.: Better to follow, follow to be better: towards precise supervision of feature super-resolution for small object detection. In: 2019 IEEE/CVF International Conference on Computer Vision (ICCV), pp. 9724–9733 (2019)
15. Bell, S., Zitnick, C.L., Bala, K., Girshick, R.: Inside-Outside Net: detecting objects in context with skip pooling and recurrent neural networks. In: CVPR 2016, pp. 2874–2883 (2016)
16. Hu, H., Gu, J., Zhang, Z., Dai, J., Wei, Y.: Relation networks for object detection. In: 2018 IEEE/CVF Conference on Computer Vision and Pattern Recognition, pp. 3588–3597 (2018)
17. Liu, G., Han, J., Rong, W.: Feedback-driven loss function for small object detection. Image Vis. Comput. **111**, 104197 (2021)
18. Zhang, S., Zhu, X., Lei, Z., Shi, H., Wang, X., Li, S.Z.: S3FD: single shot scale-invariant face detector. In: Proceedings of the IEEE International Conference on Computer Vision, pp. 192–201 (2017)
19. Xu, C., Wang, J., Yang, W., Yu, L.: Dot distance for tiny object detection in aerial images. In: 2021 CVPRW, pp. 1192–1201 (2021)
20. Wang, J., Xu, C., Yang, W., Yu, L.: A normalized Gaussian Wasserstein distance for tiny object detection (2022)
21. Zhang, H., Wang, Y., Dayoub, F., Sunderhauf, N.: VarifocalNet: an IoU-aware dense object detector. In: Proceedings of the IEEE/CVF Conference on Computer Vision and Pattern Recognition, pp. 8514–8523 (2021)

22. Lin, T.-Y., Goyal, P., Girshick, R., He, K., Dollár, P.: Focal loss for dense object detection. In: Proceedings of the IEEE International Conference on Computer Vision, pp. 2980–2988 (2017)
23. Ge, Z., Liu, S., Wang, F., Li, Z., Sun, J.: YOLOX: exceeding YOLO series in 2021. arXiv preprint arXiv:2107.08430 (2021)
24. Wang, Y., Zhang, X., Yang, T., Sun, J.: Anchor DETR: Query design for transformer-based object detection. arXiv preprint arXiv:2109.07107, vol. 3, no. 6 (2021)
25. Sun, P., et al.: Sparse R-CNN: end-to-end object detection with learnable proposals. In: Proceedings of the IEEE/CVF Conference on Computer Vision and Pattern Recognition, pp. 14454–14463 (2021)
26. Li, Y., Mao, H., Girshick, R., He, K.: Exploring plain vision transformer backbones for object detection. In: European Conference on Computer Vision, pp. 280–296. Springer (2022)
27. Meng, D., et al.: Conditional DETR for fast training convergence. In: Proceedings of the IEEE International Conference on Computer Vision (ICCV) (2021)
28. Liu, S., et al.: DAB-DETR: dynamic anchor boxes are better queries for DETR. In: International Conference on Learning Representations (2022)
29. Zhang, H., et al.: DINO: DETR with improved denoising anchor boxes for end-to-end object detection. In: The Eleventh International Conference on Learning Representations (2022)
30. Zong, Z., Song, G., Liu, Y.: DETRs with collaborative hybrid assignments training (2022)
31. Lv, W., et al.: DETRs beat YOLOs on real-time object detection. ArXiv, abs/2304.08069 (2023)
32. Li, X., et al.: Generalized focal loss: learning qualified and distributed bounding boxes for dense object detection. Adv. Neural. Inf. Process. Syst. **33**, 21002–21012 (2020)
33. Feng, C., Zhong, Y., Gao, Y., Scott, M.R., Huang, W.: TOOD: task-aligned one-stage object detection. In: 2021 IEEE/CVF International Conference on Computer Vision (ICCV), pp. 3490–3499. IEEE Computer Society (2021)

# Stealthily Launch Backdoor Attacks Against Deep Neural Network Models via Steganography

Aolin Che[1], Miaoxia Chen[2,3], Abdul Samad Shibghatullah[2], Cai Guo[3(✉)], and Ping Li[4]

[1] Guangdong Industry Polytechnic University, Guangdong, China
[2] University College Sedaya International, Kuala Lumpur, Malaysia
abdulsamad@ucsiuniversity.edu.my
[3] Hanshan Normal University, Chaozhou, China
c.guo@hstc.edu.cn
[4] The Hong Kong Polytechnic University, Hong Kong, China
p.li@polyu.edu.hk

**Abstract.** The widespread deployment of deep neural network (DNNs) model based on image classification in the real world provides new attack scenarios for attackers. Backdoor attack is one of the most frequently used attack methods against DNNs models due to their simplicity and effectiveness. In this paper, we attempt to launch a backdoor attack by **H**ide **T**ext **T**rigger via **S**teganography (HTTS). Specifically, we propose a regular text trigger and use backdoor steganography we designed to embed the trigger in a small number of training images. When launching a backdoor attack, our triggers will be mistaken by DNNs models as hidden features of the training images. DNNs models can easily capture and learn these hidden features. In the testing phase, only the same trigger embedded in the training image can activate the backdoor of the DNNs model, causing the DNNs model to output incorrect classification results. Our experiments on the CIFAR-10 data set show that https can not only achieve an attack success rate of up to 100% but also effectively alleviate the contradiction between visual invisibility and attack performance.

**Keywords:** backdoor attack · steganography · DNNs model

## 1 Introduction

From face recognition to autopilot, models based on deep neural networks (DNNs) have been successfully deployed in numerous critical domains [1–3]. However, seemingly robust DNN models have been demonstrated to be highly vulnerable to backdoor attacks [4,5]. For instance, attackers could launch backdoor attacks on autopilot models, causing them to fail to fail to recognize "STOP" traffic signs on the sides of the road [6]. Furthermore, backdoor attacks

N. Magnenat Thalmann et al. (Eds.): CASA 2024, CCIS 2374, pp. 336–349, 2025.
https://doi.org/10.1007/978-981-96-2681-6_24

on face recognition can induce the system to incorrectly match wrong identity information to the face image to be recognized [7].

In this paper, we mainly investigate the repercussions of backdoor attacks on image classification models based on DNNs. Generally speaking, backdoor attacks are usually carried out in three steps. First of all, the attacker embeds specific triggers on randomly selected images in the clean training set, while replacing the original label of the poisoned image with a target label. Subsequently, these modified images are integrated into the clean training dataset to construct a poisoned training set. In the second step, the victim inputs the poisoned training set into the DNNs model for training. After completing training, the DNNs model outputs a poisoned classifier. In the third step, during the testing stage, the poisoned classifier will classify the test image embedded with the same trigger as the target label. But for clean test images, the classification results of the poisoned classifier are the same as their original labels.

Unfortunately, the current backdoor attacks face three critical issues that need to be solved: (1) **Limited Attack Performance.** Predominantly, existing methods consider white-box attack scenarios. Nonetheless, in the majority of real-world attack scenarios, attackers lack knowledge about the DNNs model and dataset held by the victim. (2) **Poor Visual Stealthiness.** Triggers proposed by most existing attack methods are difficult to avoid human visual inspection by the victim. Because in the context of real-world attack scenarios, if the trigger cannot be hidden in the image, it will be immediately detected and deleted by the vigilant victim. (3) **Trade-off Between Visual Stealthiness and Attack Performance.** One of the most formidable challenges in the backdoor attack is the balance between visual stealthiness and attack performance. In most scenarios, attackers can increase the attack success rate by embedding a visually visible trigger in clean images because the visually visible trigger can effectively reduce the difficulty of activating the neural network backdoor. On the contrary, if we embed an "invisible" trigger in the training image, it will make the activation of the neural network backdoor more difficult. Therefore, designing a backdoor attack method that can simultaneously fool DNN models and human visual scrutiny is quite difficult.

To tackle the problems above, we propose a backdoor attack method in this paper called **H**ide **T**ext **T**rigger via **S**teganography (HTTS). Specifically, in our approach, we first design a new text-based trigger. Our trigger is a string generated by repeating a specific word multiple times because the regular triggers are more easily captured and learned by DNNs models [8,9]. Secondly, we observed that the DNN model can sensitively capture subtle changes in the image pixels, but it is difficult for human vision to perceive small color changes. Based on this, we propose new backdoor steganography method. We embed our triggers into the image by slightly modifying the pixel values according to predefined steganography rules. We argue that the proposed attack method can efficiently induce classification errors in DNNs models and make it difficult for victims to visually inspect poisoned images in the dataset. Our contributions can be summarized as follows:

- We propose a general backdoor attack method–HTTS. Our attack method can substantially reduce the activation difficulty of the neural network backdoor under a black-box scenario and effectively evade the victim's human visual inspection. Consequently, our approach attains an optimal balance between visual stealthiness and attack performance.
- We design a novel text-based trigger that can more easily activate the backdoor of the DNNs model and improve the attack performance of our method in black-box scenarios. In particular, our trigger is generated by repeating a set of given words 100 times. During the training phase, the DNNs model readily identifies such regular trigger as a hidden feature and allocate a higher weight.
- To maintain the stealthiness of our trigger from the visual perspective, we propose a novel backdoor steganography. We first convert our trigger into a set of secret messages consisting only of the numbers 0 and 1. Then, we use the secret messages to slightly modify the RGB value of each pixel in the image according to the predefined steganography rules. Since it is difficult for humans to visually detect subtle changes in pixel values, our trigger can visually completely hidden in the image.

## 2  Related Works

### 2.1  Backdoor Attacks

Existing works have conducted a lot of researchs on backdoor attacks [10,11]. In 2017, Liu *et al.* [12] first attempted to induce neural network classification errors by embedding a visually conspicuous square trigger on the original image. They emphasized that their method achieved nearly 100% attack success rate on the LFW dataset. Nevertheless, it is important to emphasize that this high attack success rate requires the trigger to visually cover a large area of the original image.

In addition, some researchers are effort to design "invisible" triggers to enhance the stealthiness of the attack [13,14]. Dezfooli *et al.* [15] proposed an "invisible" attack method based on iterative linearization of the classifier. Their attack method can generate minimal perturbations sufficient to change the classification results output by DNNs models. Although the trigger generated by this method can be well hidden in the original image, the attack performance is not ideal. Recently, the authors in [16] attempted to generate a separate trigger for each image by training an encoder-decoder network. This will take a lot of time to generate unique triggers for each image. Furthermore, triggers generated through this method still cannot escape the meticulous inspection of human visual inspection.

To sum up, existing methods of backdoor attacks are difficult to fool both DNNs models and human checks. Striking the balance between visual stealthiness and attack performance is still a question worth discussing in the field of backdoor attacks.

## 2.2 Steganography

Steganography is a covert communication technology [17]. An attacker can embed secret message into a specific digital medium without damaging the quality of the medium. Generally speaking, these digital media can be images, audio or text. Currently, researchers have explored embedding triggers into digital media through steganography. For instance, the authors in [18] introduced a text-based backdoor attack framework called BadNL. They use steganography to insert, remove, or replace specific characters in the words of the source text to construct character-level triggers. Furthermore, in order to avoid affecting the original text content, they used syntax transfer to modify the underlying syntax rules.

Inspired by this, in this paper we try to apply steganography to the field of backdoor attacks. We propose a new backdoor steganography for embedding text-based trigger into original images. Compared with previous work, our trigger can more easily evade human visual inspection.

# 3 Backdoor Attack Process

Before describing the backdoor attack process, it is imperative to underscore the background of our attack. We consider that the victim holds a DNNs model and a image dataset $(x, l) \in D$. We assume that the attacker possesses no prior knowledge regarding the DNNs model. However, the attacker can obtain a small amount of training data held by the victim. In practical terms, it is not a arduous task for an attacker. For example, if the victim is a corporation, the attacker could obtain part of the data through bribed employees.

Now, we try to describe the backdoor attack process concretely. The complete attack process is depicted in Fig. 1. First, we divide the data in the clean data set $D$ into two parts: the training set $D_{train}$ and the test set $D_{test}$. Then, we further divide $D_{train}$ into two subsets: the clean training set $D_{train}^C$ and the training set to be attacked $D_{train}^A$. $D_{train}^A$ is a small number of clean images with original label $l_o$ obtained by the attacker from the victim. They are targets for attackers. Conversely, $D_{train}^C$ will not be attacked. They participate in the training of the model normally. Here, we present the expression of $D_{train}^A$:

$$D_{train}^A = \{(x_k, l_o), k = 0, ..., n\}, \tag{1}$$

where we use $x_k$ to represent the clean image to be attacked, and $l_o$ to represent the original label. Additionally, $n$ represents the number of images in $D_{train}^A$, and $k$ denotes the sequence number of each image to be attacked. After completing the above steps, the attacker can launch a backdoor attack. The attacker first embeds a trigger $T$ into the image of $D_{train}^A$ and then replaces the original label $l_o$ of the image in $D_{train}^A$ with the target label $l_t$. We call the poisoned $D_{train}^A$ the poisoned training dataset $D_{train}^P$. Here, we give the expression of $D_{train}^P$:

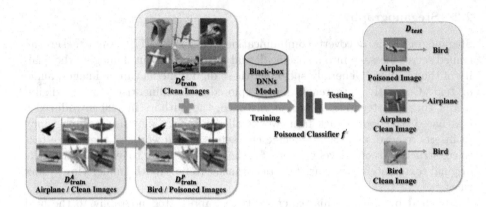

**Fig. 1.** The process of backdoor attack. We can build the poisoned training set by selecting any training image, regardless of their original labels. Then, in the training phase, the DNNs model will consider our triggers to be the most important features of the target label. Finally, in the test phase, the poisoned classifier classifies the test images with the same trigger added as the target label. In contrast, clean test images are still classified as their original labels.

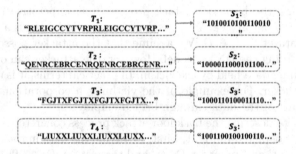

**Fig. 2.** The secret information generation process.

$$D_{train}^{P} = \left\{ (x_k^T, l_t), k = 0, ..., n \right\}, \tag{2}$$

where $x_k^T$ represents a poisoned training image and $(x_k^T, l_t)$ represents a poisoned image sample. In addition, $n$ represents the number of poisoned images, and $k$ denotes the sequence number of each poisoned image.

Finally, the attacker replaces the clean training set $D_{train}^{A}$ with $D_{train}^{P}$ before the victim updates or trains the DNNs model. As a result, the input to the DNNs model becomes $D_{train}^{C} \cup D_{train}^{P}$. When the DNNs model completes training, it will output a poisoned classifier $f'$. In the test stage, the attacker will randomly selects an image with the original label $l_o$ in $D_{test}$ and uses the same attack method to generate a poisoned image. The attacker expects $f'$ to classify the poisoned test image with the label $l_o$ as the target label $l_t$.

**Table 1.** DNN Model Structure

| Layer | Configuration |
|---|---|
| 1st Convolutional | filters = 32, kernal size = 3 × 3, stride = 1, activation = *ReLu* |
| 1st Max Pooling | kernal size = 2 × 2, stride = 1 |
| 2st Convolutional | filters = 64, kernal size = 3 × 3, stride = 1, activation = *ReLu* |
| 2st Max Pooling | kernal size = 2 × 2, stride = 1 |
| 3st Convolutional | filters = 64, kernal size = 3 × 3, stride = 1, activation = *ReLu* |
| Fully Connected | activation = *ReLu* |
| Fully Connected | activation = *Softmax* |

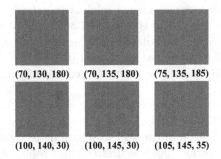

**Fig. 3.** Three different colours of blue and green. (Color figure online)

# 4   Hide Text Trigger via Steganography

We propose a backdoor attack method called HTTS. Our attack method can be divided into three parts: generate poisoned images, poisoned training, and backdoor testing.

## 4.1   Generate Poisoned Images

**Generate Text Triggers:** We discover that embedding a regular text trigger into clean images results in a regular hidden feature. Compared with other features, such regular features can be learned more easily by DNNs models and assigned a higher weight. In addition, we also find that text triggers can be better hidden in images than image triggers. Inspired by this, the trigger $T$ we designed is a string generated by repeating a given word multiple times. For example, assuming that the given word is "APPLE", the text trigger generated after repeating it m times is "APPLEAPPLEAPP...".

In our method, we generate four different text triggers, namely $T_1, T_2, T_3$ and $T_4$. They are generated by repeating four strings "RLEIGCCYTVRP", "QENRCEBRCENR", "FGJTXFGJTX" and "LIUXXLIUXX" 100 times respectively.

**Generate Secret Messages:** After generating the text triggers, we convert each letter in $T_1$, $T_2$, $T_3$ and $T_4$ into a seven-digit binary string according to the ASCII Table. These strings consisting of 0 and 1 are the secret messages we generate. We use $S_1$, $S_2$, $S_3$ and $S_4$ to represent the corresponding secret messages. Figure 2 shows the secret information generation process.

**Embedding via Steganography:** It is a well-established fact that DNNs models can sensitively capture some subtle changes in images [19,20]. However, these small changes can be difficult for human vision to perceive. As shown in Fig. 3, human vision can hardly perceive the difference between the two blue colours with RGB values (70, 130, 180) and (75, 135, 185).

Inspired by this, we designed a new backdoor steganography. We first assume that the image held by the victim is composed of $W \times H$ pixels, where the width is $W$ and the height is $H$. For colored images, the pixel value of each pixel is composed of three color values: red (R), green (G), and blue (B). Consequently, we can write the RGB values of each image sequentially into a list $L$ of length $W \times H \times 3$.

Following this, we align the secret messages $S_1$, $S_2$, $S_3$ and $S_4$ with $L$ and retain only the $W \times H \times 3$ length of each secret information. Then, we steganograph the secret information in two steps. According to the steganography rules we formulated, when performing the first steganography step, if $S_1^i = S_2^i = 1$ at the same position $i$ ($0 \leq i < W \times H \times 3$), then we add 2 to the value of the position $L_i$; if $S_1^i = 1, S_2^i = 0$, we execute the operation of $L_i = L_i - 2$. In the second steganography step, if $S_3^i = S_4^i = 1$ at the same position i, we add 1 to the value of the corresponding position in $L$; if $S_1^i = 1, S_2^i = 0$, we execute $L_i = L_i - 1$ operation. Finally, we convert the numerical values in $L$ into an RGB image with dimensions $W \times H$.

## 4.2 Poisoned Training

The essence of deep learning training is actually the process of finding an optimal weight for each feature [21]. Compared with other image features, this static and regular backdoor feature we designed is very toilless to be captured by the DNNs model. During model training, the model treats the trigger in the poisoned image as a normal image feature. In addition, since we embed the same trigger in multiple images, the DNNs model will also assign relatively higher weights to our triggers.

## 4.3 Backdoor Testing

In the backdoor testing phase of HTTS, we use the same backdoor steganography to embed the trigger $T$ into the image with the original label $l_o$ in the test set. When the poisoned classifier $f'$ captures the existence of a backdoor in the image, it will classify the poisoned test image with the original label $l_o$ as the target label $l_t$. Nevertheless, the classification results of $f'$ on clean test images are the same as clean classifier $f$.

# 5  Experimental Analysis

## 5.1  Experiment Setup

### 5.1.1  Dataset

We tested on the CIFAR-10 dataset. It comprises ten different classes (Airplane, Car, Bird, Cat, Deer, Dog, Frog, Horse, Ship and Truck), with 6000 images in each class. Throughout our experiments, we randomly select 5000 images in each category as the training set. Then, we take the remaining 1000 images in each category as the test set. It is worth mentioning that in CIFAR-10, each image is unique, which means that there will be no duplicate images.

### 5.1.2  Measurements

We conduct a comprehensive evaluation of backdoor attack methods from three aspects: attack success rate, test accuracy loss and visual stealthiness. Here, we provide a detailed explanation.

**Attack Success Rate:** We evaluate the attack performance by counting the attack success rate of the attack method on the test set. Specifically, we first embed the trigger into the 1000 test images with original label $l_o$. Subsequently, we utilize the poisoned classifier $f'$ to predict the labels of the poisoned test images. If the prediction result is that the percentage of target label $l_t$ is close to 100%, it proves that the attack performance of this attack method is better.

**Test Accuracy Loss:** In our experiments, we evaluate attack stealthiness by comparing the performance of the clean classifier $f$ and the poisoned classifier $f'$ on the clean test dataset (test accuracy loss). For the attacker, the smaller the test accuracy loss, the lower the probability of being discovered by the victim.

**Visual Stealthiness:** We evaluate the visual stealthiness of each attack method by comparing the similarity between the poisoned images and the corresponding clean images. In our experiments, we used pHash. A higher pHash score indicates a higher degree of similarity between the two images. Conversely, a lower pHash similarity score means there is a significant visual difference between the two images.

### 5.1.3  DNNs Model

In real-world attacks, attackers often lack knowledge of the model held by the victim. Based on this, we randomly selected a DNN-based image classification model. Table 1 provides the various parameters of the model in detail.

### 5.1.4  Comparison Methods

In our experiments, we conducted a comparative analysis between HTTS and two advanced backdoor attack methods: PSPM [21] and LSB [19].

## 5.2    Results of Attack Success Rate

In Fig. 4, we use a gradient of colors to illustrate the attack performance of three different backdoor methods across ninety original-target label pairs when the attacker can obtain 2500 original images. We represent lower attack success rates with deep blue and higher attack success rates with light blue.

By comparing the colour distribution of the three attack methods in Fig. 4, we can observe that our method achieves the best attack performance on the CIFAR-10 dataset. Specifically, when the original label = Bird and target label = Cat, HTTS achieves the lowest attack success rate of 96.2%, while the lowest attack success rates of PSPM and LSB are 92.6% and 81.7%, respectively.

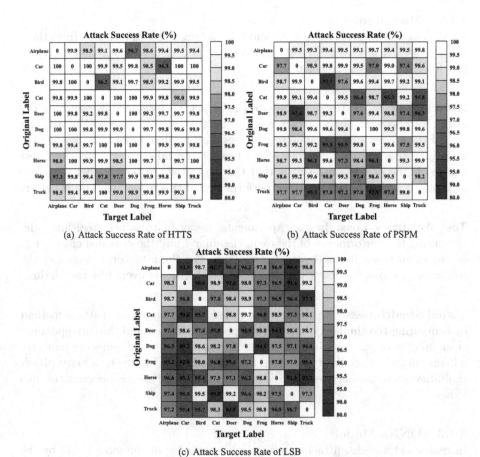

(a) Attack Success Rate of HTTS          (b) Attack Success Rate of PSPM

(c) Attack Success Rate of LSB

**Fig. 4.** We provide complete statistics of attack success rates on original-target label pairs in the CIFAR-10 dataset. We use a set of gradient blue to represent the success rate of the attack. The lighter colour indicates that the attack success rate is closer to 100%. On the contrary, the darker the colour indicates that the attack success rate is lower. (Color figure online)

Furthermore, we find that HTTS achieves a total of nineteen instances of 100% attack success rate, while the highest attack success rates of PSPM and LSB are only 99.9% and 99.7%.

## 5.3  Results of Test Accuracy Loss

We give detailed experimental results of attack stealthiness in Fig. 5. As shown in Fig. 5, when the original label = Dog and target label = Deer, the test accuracy loss of HTTS is 1.77%. At this point, our method shows a relatively higher accuracy loss on the test set. We observe that the highest test accuracy loss for PSPM is 1.72%, which is 0.05% lower than HTTS's maximum test accuracy loss. However, on the whole, HTTS has only five original-target label pairs with

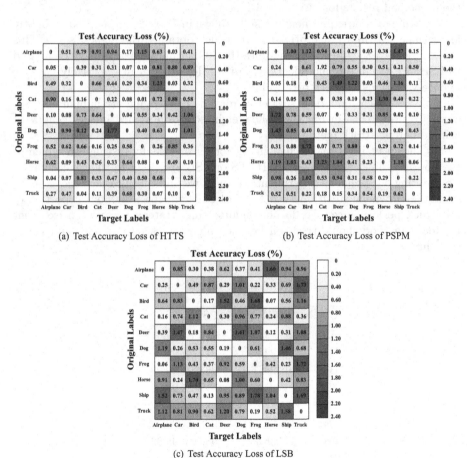

(a) Test Accuracy Loss of HTTS          (b) Test Accuracy Loss of PSPM

(c) Test Accuracy Loss of LSB

**Fig. 5.** We calculate the test accuracy loss on ninety original-target label pairs in the CIFAR-10 dataset. We use a set of gradient blue to represent the test accuracy loss of the method. The lighter the colour indicates that the test accuracy loss is closer to 0%, and the darker the colour means the test accuracy loss is higher. (Color figure online)

test accuracy loss higher than 1.00%, significantly less than PSPM's sixteen pairs. Furthermore, HTTS has 18 original-target label pairs with test accuracy loss lower than 0.1%. In the testing phase, accuracy loss within 0.1% is almost impossible to attract the attention by victim. Therefore, our attack method is proven to have a strong attack stealthiness.

## 5.4   Results of Visual Stealthiness

To precisely measure the visual stealthiness of each attack method, we calculate the pHash similarity scores between the clean image and its corresponding poisoned image (a total of 60,000 image pairs). We evaluate the visual stealthiness of each attack method by comparing the average pHash scores. Table 2 reports the numerical results for visual stealthiness.

According to the experimental results shown in Table 2, our method is slightly lower than LSB in average pHash score, which obtained the highest score. This is because HTTS significantly modifies the RGB values of each image compared to LSB. Although our modifications are subtle, pHash can sensitively capture minute variations in every pixel value.

However, such numerical subtleties may be challenging for humans to perceive. To prove this, in Fig. 6 we show eight sets of poisoned images generated using different attack methods.

As shown in Fig. 6, it is challenging for us to visually distinguish which of the poisoned images generated by HTTS or LSB are closer to the clean images. Considering our previous experimental results, we find that LSB achieves a slight advantage in visual stealthiness at the cost of sacrificing a significant portion of its attack performance. We do not endorse this strategy because an excellent backdoor method should trade-off between high attack performance and visual stealthiness.

**Table 2.** Average pHash Scores

| Classes | HTTS (Ours) | PSPM | LSB |
|---------|-------------|--------|--------|
| Airplane | 98.79% | 97.71% | 99.61% |
| Car | 98.24% | 97.16% | 99.47% |
| Bird | 98.28% | 98.41% | 99.29% |
| Cat | 98.24% | 97.91% | 98.98% |
| Deer | 97.87% | 98.70% | 99.87% |
| Dog | 98.05% | 97.70% | 99.35% |
| Frog | 97.86% | 98.53% | 98.92% |
| Horse | 98.47% | 97.48% | 99.01% |
| Ship | 98.66% | 98.00% | 99.63% |
| Truck | 98.63% | 96.22% | 99.40% |
| Average | **98.63%** | 97.78% | 99.35% |

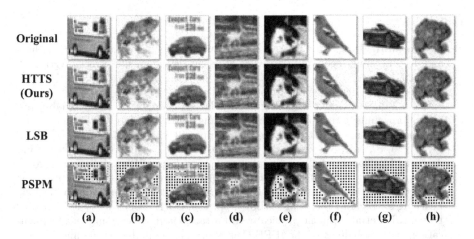

**Fig. 6.** Examples of poisoned images.

On the whole, our method achieves the optimal balance between attack performance and visual stealthiness.

## 6 Conclusion

In this paper, we propose a backdoor attack method HTTS that can be applied in the real world. Specifically, we design a text-based backdoor trigger. Our trigger is a set of regular strings generated by four specific words iterate 100 times. This type of trigger can more easily activate the backdoor of the DNNs model, significantly improving the success rate of backdoor attacks. Additionally, we propose a new backdoor steganography to hide our triggers in the image. We convert our triggers into a set of secret information consisting of the digits 0 and 1 according to the ASCII table. And then, based on these secret messages, we make minor adjustments to the RGB values of each pixel in the image. Our experiments demonstrate that our method not only achieves a 100% attack success rate but also exhibits excellent visual stealthiness. In the future, we will continue to explore the backdoor attacks and we attempt to provide a deeper explanation from the structure of the neural network.

**Acknowledgements.** This work was supported in part by Natural Science Foundation of Guangdong Province (2021A1515011091), by Educational Commission of Guangdong Province (2020ZDZX3056), by Doctor Starting Fund of Hanshan Normal University, China (QD202324), by Teaching Reform Project of Hanshan Normal University, China (E23068), and by APT Image Processing Project of Hanshan Normal University, China.

# References

1. Saleem, M.H., Potgieter, J., Arif, K.M.: Automation in agriculture by machine and deep learning techniques: a review of recent developments. Precis. Agric. **22**, 2053–2091 (2021)
2. Mystakidis, S.: Metaverse. Encyclopedia **2**(1), 486–497 (2022)
3. Xie, C., Tan, M., Gong, B., Wang, J., Yuille, A.L., Le, Q.V.: Adversarial examples improve image recognition. In: Proceedings of the IEEE/CVF Conference on Computer Vision and Pattern Recognition, pp. 819–828 (2020)
4. Li, S., Ma, S., Xue, M., Zhao, B.Z.H.: Deep learning backdoors. In: Security and Artificial Intelligence: A Crossdisciplinary Approach, pp. 313–334. Springer (2022)
5. Miller, D.J., Hu, X., Qiu, Z., Kesidis, G.: Adversarial learning: a critical review and active learning study. In: 2017 IEEE 27th International Workshop on Machine Learning for Signal Processing (MLSP), pp. 1–6. IEEE (2017)
6. Eykholt, K., et al.: Robust physical-world attacks on deep learning visual classification. In: Proceedings of the IEEE Conference on Computer Vision and Pattern Recognition, pp. 1625–1634 (2018)
7. He, C., Xue, M., Wang, J., Liu, W.: Embedding backdoors as the facial features: invisible backdoor attacks against face recognition systems. In: Proceedings of the ACM Turing Celebration Conference-China, pp. 231–235 (2020)
8. Pak, M., Kim, S.: A review of deep learning in image recognition. In: 2017 4th International Conference on Computer Applications and Information Processing Technology (CAIPT), pp. 1–3. IEEE (2017)
9. Rawat, W., Wang, Z.: Deep convolutional neural networks for image classification: a comprehensive review. Neural Comput. **29**(9), 2352–2449 (2017)
10. Dong, Y., et al.: Boosting adversarial attacks with momentum. In: Proceedings of the IEEE Conference on Computer Vision and Pattern Recognition, pp. 9185–9193 (2018)
11. Liu, Y., Ma, X., Bailey, J., Lu, F.: Reflection backdoor: a natural backdoor attack on deep neural networks. In: Vedaldi, A., Bischof, H., Brox, T., Frahm, J.-M. (eds.) ECCV 2020. LNCS, vol. 12355, pp. 182–199. Springer, Cham (2020). https://doi.org/10.1007/978-3-030-58607-2_11
12. Liu, Y., et al.: Trojaning attack on neural networks. In: 25th Annual Network And Distributed System Security Symposium (NDSS 2018). Internet Soc (2018)
13. Narodytska, N., Kasiviswanathan, S.P.: Simple black-box adversarial attacks on deep neural networks. In: CVPR Workshops, vol. 2, pp. 2 (2017)
14. Sharma, Y., Ding, G.W., Brubaker, M.: On the effectiveness of low frequency perturbations. arXiv preprint arXiv:1903.00073 (2019)
15. Moosavi-Dezfooli, S.-M., Fawzi, A., Frossard, P.: DeepFool: a simple and accurate method to fool deep neural networks. In: Proceedings of the IEEE Conference on Computer Vision and Pattern Recognition, pp. 2574–2582 (2016)
16. Li, Y., Li, Y., Wu, B., Li, L., He, R., Lyu, S.: Invisible backdoor attack with sample-specific triggers. In: Proceedings of the IEEE/CVF International Conference on Computer Vision, pp. 16463–16472 (2021)
17. Geleta, M., Punti, C., McGuinness, K., Pons, J., Canton, C., Giro-i Nieto, X.: PixInWav: residual steganography for hiding pixels in audio. In: ICASSP 2022-2022 IEEE International Conference on Acoustics, Speech and Signal Processing (ICASSP), pp. 2485–2489. IEEE (2022)
18. Chen, X., et al.: BadNL: backdoor attacks against NLP models with semantic-preserving improvements. In: Annual Computer Security Applications Conference, pp. 554–569 (2021)

19. Li, S., Xue, M., Zhao, B.Z.H., Zhu, H., Zhang, X.: Invisible backdoor attacks on deep neural networks via steganography and regularization. IEEE Trans. Dependable Secure Comput. **18**(5), 2088–2105 (2020)

20. Gafni, O., Wolf, L., Taigman, Y.: Live face de-identification in video. In: Proceedings of the IEEE/CVF International Conference on Computer Vision, pp. 9378–9387 (2019)

21. Zhong, H., Liao, C., Squicciarini, A.C., Zhu, S., Miller, D.: Backdoor embedding in convolutional neural network models via invisible perturbation. In: Proceedings of the Tenth ACM Conference on Data and Application Security and Privacy, pp. 97–108 (2020)

# Seat Belt Wearing Detection Based on EfficientDet_Ad

Min Li[1], Menghan Ai[1(✉)], Peng Luo[2], and Chun Wang[1]

[1] Wuhan Textile University, Wuhan, China
2008031@wtu.edu.cn, yn20182@163.com
[2] Wuhan University, Wuhan, China
thornluo@whu.edu.cn

**Abstract.** For the existing safety belt target detection algorithm in the realm of electrical power scenarios, which faces challenges such as low precision in recognizing small targets, easy confusion of target features with the background, and limited computational resources on the intelligent monitoring platform. In this paper, we propose an EfficientDet-based safety belt detection algorithm, EfficientDet_Ad. Firstly, an enhanced feature extraction module is designed for multi-scale feature fusion, improving the capability to detect small targets. Secondly, a feature fusion attention module, FFAM, is constructed to enhance the focus on less prominent targets. Finally, the algorithm achieves a reduction in network parameters by introducing Ghost Conv and Channel Shuffle operations to reconstruct the MBConv module in the EfficientNet backbone. Analyzing the results of the comparative experiment and ablation study reveals that the proposed EfficientDet_Ad algorithm achieves an average precision of 90.12%, surpassing the EfficientDet algorithm by 6.64%, and outperforming other advanced object detection algorithms. Simultaneously, the detection speed reaches 55.7 frames per second. The comprehensive experimental results demonstrate the remarkable effectiveness of the algorithm in terms of accuracy and real-time performance.

**Keywords:** Safety Belt · Object Detection · EfficientDet

## 1 Introduction

In the power industry, aerial operations are indispensable, but accompanying safety issues are gradually becoming more pronounced. To ensure the safety of personnel, the industry has implemented a series of measures, including raising employee safety awareness, strengthening regulatory and enforcement efforts, and introducing advanced safety technologies and equipment. However, in recent years, aerial operations continue to represent the most severe category of accidents in the power industry, with an accident rate as high as 30.26% [1]. Moreover, Due to the unique environmental conditions of power operation sites, the difficulty and risks associated with aerial operations are significantly higher than those in other conventional construction sites. Therefore, the urgent need to effectively and in real-time monitor workers wearing safety harnesses in operational zones is a critical issue that requires resolution [2]. However, current monitoring primarily relies on manual methods, resulting in insufficient coverage and limited real-time monitoring capabilities.

In recent years, deep learning technology, leveraging its powerful algorithmic advantages, has successfully been applied in the industrial and safety control domains. This includes the detection of safety helmets, work attire, and other safety protective equipment. It has not only achieved intelligent supervision and management of operations in these relevant fields but has also effectively addressed persistent issues in safety supervision and management, such as low coverage, poor timeliness, and high costs associated with human resources in supervision.However, despite some progress made by existing deep learning methods in the task of safety harness detection, there are still certain challenges that need further resolution.

Traditional safety harness detection algorithms commonly face challenges in handling multi-scale features, primarily manifesting as ease in detecting large objects and neglect of small objects. This may lead to the omission or misidentification of certain safety harnesses in practical situations, triggering potential safety risks, and even causing serious accidents. Additionally, safety harnesses have a low effective pixel ratio, meaning the actual area is relatively small compared to the annotated bounding box area. Safety harness targets are dispersed in the image, with features not well-focused, making them prone to confusion with the background [3], rendering detection networks challenging in feature extraction. Furthermore, previous research has predominantly focused on specific resource requirements, while in actual power scenarios, systems typically have diverse resource constraints. For instance, monitoring devices may be limited by power consumption and computational capabilities, necessitating the completion of safety harness detection tasks within finite resources.

In addressing the aforementioned challenges, this study focuses on designing a lightweight network-based object detection algorithm named EfficientDet_Ad. By integrating lightweight network structures, specialized scenario optimizations, and effective training strategies, the development of the EfficientDet_Ad algorithm aims to provide an innovative and efficient solution for safety belt detection in power scenarios. This solution is tailored to meet practical requirements and contribute to new technological advancements for the safety and reliability of power systems.

The structure of this paper is as follows: Sect. 2 reviews related work, Sect. 3 provides an in-depth exploration of the key concepts behind the EfficientDet_Ad algorithm, Sect. 4 extensively describes the source and size of the dataset, Sect. 5 presents the experimental design and discusses the results. Finally, Sect. 6 concludes the entire paper.

## 2 Related Work

Currently, both domestically and internationally, there has been extensive research in the field of safety supervision at work sites, with early emphasis on hardware devices and process management. These methods include, but are not limited to, sensors, surveillance cameras, and process monitoring. For example, J. Yi et al. [4] proposed an intelligent online monitoring device for safety harnesses during elevated work. However, this device requires the use of multiple sensors and hardware modules to achieve the monitoring of safety harness status, increasing the complexity and cost of supervision. Additionally, sensors are susceptible to external interference, leading to false alarms.A. Ma et al. [5] introduced an intelligent belt for real-time posture monitoring of personnel working on elevated power grids. While traditional methods like these can to some extent maintain the safety of work sites, they suffer from issues such as high costs, low efficiency, and poor adaptability to specific scenarios.

Recently, computer vision-based methods have gained prominence in the field of safety control at work sites. Researchers are increasingly leveraging visual technologies to detect situations such as the wearing of safety helmets, safety harnesses, and the use of tools by workers. For instance, J. Lv et al. [6] employed the YOLOv3 algorithm to train a safety helmet detection model. Through the collaborative efforts of cloud and edge computing, they addressed issues like the inability to detect the absence of safety helmets in real-time and resource inefficiency in traditional construction site monitoring systems. Methods that combine vision with technologies such as deep learning utilize image and video data for intelligent monitoring of safety conditions. In comparison to traditional approaches, vision-based methods offer advantages such as strong real-time capabilities, high adaptability, and relatively lower costs.

Concerning deep learning detection algorithms for safety harnesses at work sites, J. Li et al. [7] proposed a target detection model for safety violations in substations. They utilized the Mask R-CNN algorithm based on region-based relationship features to establish and train the model for safety harness detection. However, their approach of generating region proposals through sliding windows not only requires substantial computational resources and time for training and inference but also results in poorer detection performance when dealing with targets of varying scales. Fang Weili et al. [8] introduced a two-stage deep convolutional network to detect whether workers are wearing safety harnesses during work. The approach first detects the presence of workers and then determines whether they are wearing safety harnesses. However, this complex two-stage process is less suitable for real-time scenarios with high demands, such as power operations. Single-stage object detection algorithms like YOLO and SSD proposed by Redmon et al. [9,10] are suggested for their speed, which generally meets the real-time requirements for safety harness detection in power scenarios. However, their detection accuracy tends to be lower than two-stage detectors. Zheng Yi et al. [11] presented a multi-step safety harness detection method based on the SSD object detection algorithm.

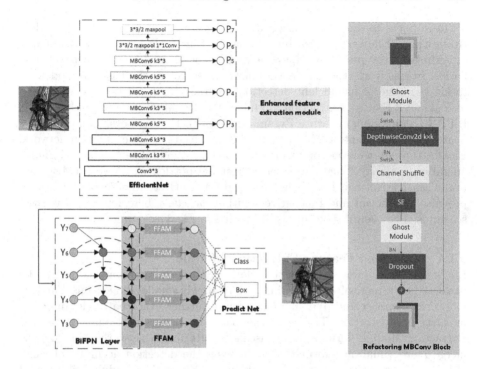

**Fig. 1.** EfficientDet_Ad Structure

# 3   Method Design

## 3.1   EfficientDet_Ad

EfficientDet is collectively referred to as a series of scalable and efficient object detectors known for their characteristics of structural simplicity, high model expansion efficiency, and superior performance. [12] The model leverages a pre-trained network, EfficientNet, from the ImageNet dataset as its backbone. It introduces BiFPN as the feature network, extracting features (P3, P4, P5, P6, P7) from the 3rd to 7th layers of the backbone and iteratively employs bidirectional feature fusion from top to bottom and bottom to top. The fused features are then fed into the classification and bounding box regression networks to generate target categories and predicted bounding boxes. The weights of the classification and bounding box regression networks are shared across all layers of features.

However, due to the complexity of the operational field environment, the detection effectiveness of small targets faces challenges. Additionally, the discernibility between target features and background features is not distinct. Coupled with practical constraints such as limited computational resources and memory on the power intelligent monitoring platform, these factors collectively impose limitations on the practical application of EfficientDet in real-world scenarios.

In response to the aforementioned challenges, this paper introduces an algorithm named EfficientDet_Ad, built upon the EfficientDet model, with the aim of addressing the practical requirements of safety belt detection in power scenarios. In this work, the EfficientDet network serves as the baseline model. To tackle the issue of insufficient detection accuracy for small targets, we design an Enhanced Feature Extraction Module for multiscale feature fusion before the BiFPN (Bidirectional Feature Pyramid Network). Furthermore, we introduce a Feature Fusion Attention Module into the enhanced feature extraction network. Finally, through a clever combination of the Ghost module and Channel Shuffle operation, we reconstruct the inverted residual bottleneck network (MBConv) in the EfficientNet backbone. The proposed EfficientDet_Ad detection algorithm provides an efficient and innovative solution for safety belt detection in power scenarios. The overall structure is illustrated in Fig. 1.

### 3.1.1 Enhanced Feature Extraction Module

In the electrical power scenario, the relatively stable camera perspective results in safety belt targets often appearing with relatively smaller dimensions. Furthermore, the complex and dynamic background further exacerbates the difficulty in safety belt detection. Therefore, this paper introduces an Enhanced Feature Extraction Module, forming a multiscale feature fusion network. This aims to merge more semantic information, enhancing the detection accuracy of small objects. The structure of the Enhanced Feature Extraction Module is illustrated in Fig. 2.

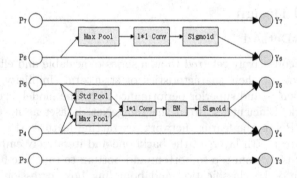

**Fig. 2.** Enhanced Feature Extraction Module Structure

Firstly, features are extracted from the intermediate layers (P4, P5, P6, corresponding to lower, middle, and higher-level feature maps) of the backbone feature network. Global feature information is captured through AvgPool and StdPool operations on P4 and P5 layers, as well as MaxPool operation on the P6 layer, enhancing contextual awareness. Subsequently, $1 \times 1$ convolutional layers are utilized to promote inter-channel dependencies, boosting feature representation capabilities. Feature distributions are normalized through BN normalization (except for the P6 layer), and Sigmoid activation functions are employed to generate channel weights ranging from 0 to 1. This assigns appropriate weights to each channel, optimizing the contribution of features. Finally, the computed weights are applied to layers P4, P5, and P6, creating new feature layers. These layers serve as input to the BiFPN, where the feature fusion process takes place. The BiFPN iteratively performs top-down and bottom-up operations during feature fusion to enhance the fusion of semantic information. The aim of this process is to improve the overall performance of object detection. The specific formulas are given in Formula 1–3:

$$\mu_c = \frac{1}{HW} \sum_{i=1}^{H} \sum_{j=1}^{W} X_{i,j} \tag{1}$$

$$\xi_c = \sqrt{\frac{1}{HW} \sum_{i=1}^{H} \sum_{j=1}^{W} (X_{i,j} - \mu_c)^2} \tag{2}$$

$$g(x) = [\mu_c, \xi_c] \tag{3}$$

In this context, Where H and W respectively represent the height and width of the feature map. $X_{i,j}$ denotes the elements in the input feature map, with $i$ and $j$ representing row and column indices. $\mu_c$ represents the feature vector obtained after AvgPool operation, and $\xi_c$ represents the feature vector obtained after StdPool operation. $g(x)$ represents the concatenation result of AvgPool and StdPool.

After obtaining the pooling information, we introduce one-dimensional convolution to capture inter-channel correlations. This convolution operation assists in extracting complex associations between features, enabling a more comprehensive representation of the structural information in the input data. Subsequently, through normalization and Sigmoid operations, we obtain the channel feature map weights $S_{4,5}$. Ultimately, utilizing these computed weights, we recalibrate the original input, facilitating effective information extraction and weight adjustment for the input feature map. Consequently, the output of layers P4 and P5 can be expressed using Formula 4.

$$Y_{4,5} = S_{4,5}X \tag{4}$$

In layer P6, we initially obtain the feature vector through MaxPool operation. Subsequently, by employing convolution and Sigmoid operation, we derive the feature map weights $S_6$. The final output of layer P6 can be represented by the following formulas, Formula 5 and 6, In this equation, $M_c$ represents the output of the MaxPool operation, $p$ denotes the size of the pooling window, and $b$ stands for the bias term.

$$M_c = \max_{i=1,j=1}^{p} (X_{ij}) + b \tag{5}$$

$$Y_6 = S_6X \tag{6}$$

### 3.1.2    Introducing Feature Fusion Attention Module

In the safety belt detection task, due to the similarity in color between safety belts and the background electrical poles in power scenarios, and the influence of multiple factors such as lighting changes and varied poses of workers, occurrences of missed detection and false alarms are common. To overcome this issue, this paper introduces an innovative and efficient Feature Fusion Attention Module (FFAM). The architecture of FFAM is illustrated in Fig. 3.

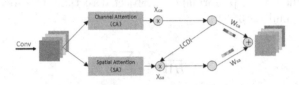

**Fig. 3.** The FFAM structure diagram of the feature fusion attention module

Specifically, the FFAM takes the intermediate feature map $X \in \mathbb{R}^{C \times H \times W}$ generated by the BiFPN as input and outputs an enhanced feature map $X_{\text{afam}} \in \mathbb{R}^{C \times H \times W}$ with the same scale. Within this process, channel attention maps $X_{\text{ca}}$ and spatial attention maps $X_{\text{sa}}$ are generated on the same input feature map using channel attention functions $f_{\text{ca}}$ and spatial attention functions $f_{\text{sa}}$, respectively. It is noteworthy that the channel attention feature map is the result of applying the channel attention map to the input feature map, while the spatial attention feature map is generated from spatial directional attention maps and channel attention maps. Due to the different generation processes of channel attention feature maps and spatial attention feature maps, we enhance the flow of attention information between them through Local Cross-Dimensional Interaction (LCDI). This interaction mechanism contributes to better integrating feature information in both channel and spatial directions, thereby improving the model's abstract representation and understanding of input data. Finally, the enhanced feature map is obtained by combining the channel-wise trainable vector $W_{\text{ca}} \in \mathbb{R}^{1 \times 256}$ from the channel attention map and the channel-wise trainable vector $W_{\text{sa}} \in \mathbb{R}^{1 \times 256}$ from the spatial attention map.

In the FFAM, our focus is on optimizing the feature maps to better capture the seatbelt targets. To achieve this, we delve into the intrinsic correlations among channel features and the spatial feature responses of the feature maps. Simultaneously, we introduce a mechanism of LCDI to strengthen the flow of information between channel attention feature maps and spatial attention feature maps. This mechanism, based on local regions, encourages the model to interact more intensively with both channel and spatial information, improving the capture of features relevant to less prominent targets.

### 3.1.3    Reconstruct the Inverted Residual Bottleneck MBConv Block

For the detection of safety belts in power operation scenes, research on neural networks often tends to focus on applications on mobile devices. We understand that, compared to traditional convolutions, Ghost Conv can generate the same number of feature maps with fewer parameters and lower computational complexity. Therefore, in the reconstructed MBConv Block, as shown in Fig. 1, this study replaces the traditional $1 \times 1$ convolution operation, which serves for dimensionality changes, with the Ghost module.

During the operation of a traditional convolutional layer, the convolution kernel (filter) slides over the input data, performing element-wise multiplication with each position of the input data. The results are then summed up, and the bias term is added. This process typically requires a large number of FLOPs, often in the hundreds of thousands. Additionally, the output feature maps of the convolutional layer often contain a considerable amount of redundancy, with some feature maps being similar to each other. Generating these redundant feature maps one by one demands a significant number of FLOPs and parameters, which we consider unnecessary.

The implementation of the Ghost module utilized in this paper consists of two steps. In the first step, regular convolutional operations are employed to obtain some internal feature maps (Ghosts). These internal feature maps typically originate from smaller-sized conventional convolution filters. Subsequently, a cost-effective linear transformation is applied to each internal feature map to generate the output of the Ghost module, as illustrated in Formula 7.

$$Y' = X * f' + b \tag{7}$$

In this context, $*$ represents convolutional operations, $b$ stands for bias terms, $X \in \mathbb{R}^{c \times h \times w}$ represents the input data in the original convolutional layer, $c$ is the number of input channels, and $h$ and $w$ are the height and width of the input data, respectively. $Y' \in \mathbb{R}^{m \times h' \times w'}$ denotes the output of the original convolution. Here, $m$ represents the number of generated internal feature maps, and finally, $f' \in \mathbb{R}^{c \times k \times k \times m}$ represents the convolutional kernel used, where $k \times k$ denotes the kernel size of the filter.

The second step involves generating Ghost feature maps. To obtain the desired number of feature maps, a series of cost-effective linear operations are applied to the internal features of each internal feature map obtained in the first step, generating additional Ghost feature maps. These linear operations can be accomplished through a linear transformation function $\Phi_{ij}$, as shown in Formula 8.

$$y_{ij} = \Phi_{ij}(y'_i), \forall i = 1, 2, \ldots, m, \quad j = 1, 2, \ldots, s \tag{8}$$

In the above formula, $\Phi_{ij}$ represents the linear transformation function for generating $y'_i$, the $j$-th Ghost feature map. $y'_i$ represents the $i$-th feature map of the internal feature maps, where $i$ denotes the sequence number of $m$ internal feature maps, and $j$ represents the $j$-th linear transformation applied to each internal feature map. As shown in Figure 4, for each feature map in the internal feature maps, $(s - 1)$ linear transformations (plus one Identity operation) can be performed, resulting in the generation of $(s - 1) \times m + m = s \times m = n$ Ghost feature maps by the Ghost module.

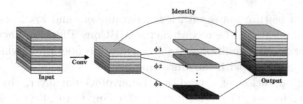

**Fig. 4.** Ghost module

Furthermore, since the DWConv in the MBConv module changes the operation from simultaneously affecting all channels of the input image to being responsible for only one channel, although this reduces the number of parameters and computational costs in the safety belt detection task, it fails to fully exploit the feature information from different channels at the same spatial position. Especially in safety belt images, there may be various complex visual features, such as texture, color, and shape, distributed across different channels.

To more effectively address the safety belt detection task, we introduce the channel shuffle operation to promote better integration of different channel features without adding excessive computational burden. This helps the model to comprehend multi-channel information at the same position more comprehensively, enhancing its ability to capture details and complex structures in safety belt images.

## 4    Data Set Source and Size

Currently, most image datasets can be obtained by searching with keywords on search engines. However, images from specific scenarios like high-altitude electrical work often suffer from low resolution and are predominantly used for commercial purposes, posing challenges for dataset construction. Additionally, some publicly available datasets are mostly binary classification data (*Not wearing* and *Wearing*), lacking the complexity needed to represent the intricacies of power scenarios.

Considering the factors mentioned above, this paper will use a self-built safety belt wearing dataset for model evaluation. The dataset was obtained by capturing photos and videos in actual power operation scenarios, including different lighting conditions, viewing angles, and scene types. In the end, we selected a total of 3334 images containing 4433 targets. For the safety belt detection task outlined in this study, the dataset underwent categorization employing the annotation tool LabelImg, resulting in three distinct classes: "Not wearing" (913 instances), "Wearing" (1661 instances), and "Improperly wearing" (1859 instances). as the Fig. 5 shows.

In addition, we conducted an analysis of the actual dataset of safety belt targets to understand the distribution of targets of different sizes in the dataset. However, due to the varied definitions of target sizes in different scenarios, there is currently no unified standard. Existing methods for defining target sizes can be broadly categorized into two types: those based on relative scale and those based on absolute scale.

Not Wearing          Wearing          Improperly wearing

**Fig. 5.** Classification of data sets

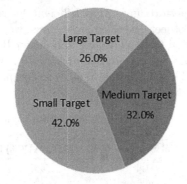

**Fig. 6.** Distribution of Target Sizes

However, the definition based on relative scale poses certain difficulties in effectively evaluating the detection performance of models on targets of different scales. It is also susceptible to the influence of data preprocessing and model structure. Therefore, we are considering adopting an absolute scale definition method [13–15] to precisely define small targets.

Considering the particularities of safety harness as a target in power scenarios, generic standards may not be entirely suitable. Therefore, I have chosen to draw inspiration from the CityPersons dataset [16], which defines small targets as objects with a height less than 75 pixels.

Additionally, I considered the definitions of target sizes in other datasets such as the aerial image dataset DOTA and the face detection dataset WIDER FACE. In the end, we defined targets with pixel values below $45 \times 75$ as small targets, those between $[45 \times 75, 150 \times 250]$ as medium targets, and those above $150 \times 250$ as large targets. The distribution of target sizes is shown in Fig. 6. It's worth noting that small targets constitute the majority of all targets in the dataset. This reflects the fact that in actual power operation scenes, most workers are at a distance from the camera. This emphasizes the need for breakthroughs in small target detection for better identification of whether workers are wearing safety belts in subsequent algorithmic research.

## 5    Experiments

### 5.1    Lab Environment

In this section, we will evaluate the effectiveness of the proposed method through a series of experiments. All experiments were conducted on an NVIDIA Tesla A30 24GB GPU. The primary dependencies for the deep learning framework include Python 3.8.17, CUDA 11.6, CUDNN 8302, and PyTorch 1.13.0. The batch size during training was set to 4, and the Adam optimizer was utilized with a learning rate of 0.001 and a weight decay coefficient of 0.0005.

### 5.2    Experimental Results and Analysis

To validate the superior performance of the EfficientDet_Ad algorithm compared to other commonly used object detection algorithms, we conducted comparative experiments with SSD, YOLOv3, YOLOv8, and Faster R-CNN. To ensure a fair comparison, all algorithms were trained and tested on the same experimental platform with the same dataset. The results of the comparative experiments are presented in Table 1.

**Table 1.** Object Detection Algorithm Comparison

| Network model | Storage Size (/MB) | mAP(%) | FPS(f/s) |
|---|---|---|---|
| SSD | 91.4 | 74.65 | 56.6 |
| YOLOv3 | 234.2 | 81.57 | 49.3 |
| YOLOv8 | 145.6 | 83.34 | 52.3 |
| Faster R-CNN | 107 | 84.60 | 13.6 |
| EfficientDet | 15.7 | 83.48 | 52.7 |
| EfficientDet_Ad | 10.1 | 90.12 | 55.7 |

From Table 1, it can be observed that the EfficientDet_Ad algorithm used in this study outperforms other object detection algorithms in terms of mAP values. The model size of EfficientDet_Ad is approximately 1/23 of YOLOv8, and its detection speed is four times that of Faster R-CNN. While SSD, as a representative of single-stage object detection algorithms, exhibits good speed performance, its detection accuracy is the lowest. Faster R-CNN, as a typical two-stage detection algorithm, achieves better detection accuracy performance compared to the EfficientDet algorithm. However, its detection speed is only 13.6 frames/s, which may not meet real-time requirements for monitoring platforms. The YOLO series algorithms impress with their speed and accuracy in object detection tasks. However, considering the specificity of power scenarios, where applications may need to run on embedded or edge devices, there could be stricter requirements on model size. YOLO series models have relatively large sizes, which might pose challenges in deploying them on monitoring platforms in power scenarios. Furthermore, the EfficientDet_Ad algorithm proposed in this paper improves the mAP by 6.64% compared to the EfficientDet algorithm, achieving a detection speed of 55.7 frames/s, a 5% improvement, making it fully capable of real-time monitoring in power scenarios.

Next, we further substantiate the impact of the designed Enhanced Feature Extraction Module, Feature Fusion Attention Module (FFAM), and the reconstructed MBConv module on various detection performance metrics of the EfficientDet algorithm through ablation experiments. Using EfficientDet as the baseline model, we conduct six sets of experiments to analyze the performance of each module in this paper. The experimental results are presented in Table 2:

**Table 2.** Object Detection Algorithm Comparison

| Enhanced Feature Extraction Module | FFAM | Refactoring MBConv Block | Storage Size (/MB) | mAP (%) | FPS (f/s) | AP | | |
|---|---|---|---|---|---|---|---|---|
| | | | | | | $AP_s$ | $AP_m$ | $AP_l$ |
| | | | 15.7 | 83.48 | 52.7 | 67.24 | 89.88 | 89.84 |
| ✓ | | | 15.8 | 86.64 | 53.1 | 80.16 | 89.91 | 90.24 |
| | ✓ | | 16.0 | 87.15 | 52.4 | 73.33 | 92.26 | 94.38 |
| | | ✓ | 9.8 | 83.21 | 56.3 | 68.46 | 88.59 | 90.54 |
| ✓ | ✓ | | 16.1 | 90.25 | 52.9 | 82.31 | 91.85 | 93.69 |
| ✓ | ✓ | ✓ | 10.1 | 90.12 | 55.7 | 82.09 | 91.45 | 93.47 |

From the table, it can be observed that the mAP value of the Efficient-Det algorithm is 83.48%, while the proposed EfficientDet combined with the Enhanced Feature Extraction Module achieves an mAP value of 86.64%, improving detection accuracy by 3.16%. Moreover, through a comparative analysis of the changes in Average Precision (AP) for different target scales before and after incorporating the Enhanced Feature Extraction Module into the Efficient-Det algorithm, we observe that the introduced module significantly improves the average precision detection results for small target objects in the dataset by 12.92%. For large and medium-sized target objects, the detection accuracy is also slightly improved. We can reasonably conclude that the module significantly improves the detection accuracy of small targets without sacrificing the detection accuracy of large and medium-sized targets. Furthermore, we observe that the addition of the Feature Fusion Attention Module (FFAM) increases the mAP by 3.67% compared to the baseline model and significantly improves AP for targets of different scales. Finally, with the integration of the reconstructed MBConv module, as shown in the experimental data in the table, the proposed Efficient-Det_Ad algorithm achieves a model size of only 9.8MB, a reduction of 37% compared to the original network, significantly reducing device resource consumption and improving the cost-effectiveness of the model. The FPS is 56.3 frames/s, representing a 6.8% improvement over the original network. In summary, EfficientDet_Ad retains the advantages of high model efficiency and support for compound scaling in real-world applications, while achieving improvements in platform deployment, small target detection, and overall detection accuracy.

EfficientDet Algorithm          EfficientDet_Ad Algorithm
detection results                detection results

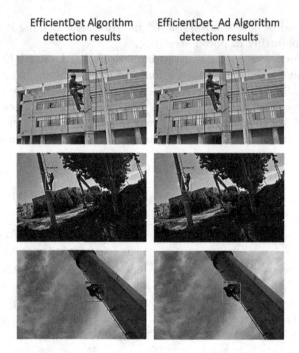

**Fig. 7.** Visual detection results of EfficientDet and EfficientDet_Ad.

## 5.3   Visualization of Experimental Results

Next, we will present the visual detection results of our dataset under different scenarios using the EfficientDet and EfficientDet_Ad algorithms. By observing the detection results on the left and right sides of Figure 7, we observe a clear trend. As the target size decreases, the detection performance faces greater challenges. Specifically, the proposed EfficientDet_Ad algorithm demonstrates better adaptability, especially in handling detection of targets at different scales.

Figure 8 illustrates the achievements of our algorithm in addressing misjudgments caused by background interference. This set of results reveals the effectiveness of the proposed FFAM in alleviating misjudgments resulting from background interference. These visualizations not only demonstrate the changing trend in algorithm performance but also emphasize the adaptability of the proposed EfficientDet_Ad algorithm to target detection tasks in different scenarios and scales, providing robust support for solving real-world problems.

Furthermore, in conjunction with the results of the ablation experiments in Sect. 5.2, it remains challenging to visually compare the impact of EfficientDet models before and after the addition of FFAM on images where detecting the status of seatbelt wearing is difficult due to background interference. To address this issue, we introduce the observation method of heatmaps to delve into the specific regions the model focuses on in the images. This allows us to validate the effectiveness of incorporating the FFAM module.

EfficientDet Algorithm          EfficientDet_Ad Algorithm
detection results                detection results

**Fig. 8.** Addressing the misjudgment issues arising from background interference.

**Fig. 9.** Comparison of thermal maps before and after the addition of FFAM

According to the detection results in Figure 9, we observe that in certain scenarios, such as those with complex background interference or overlap between the seatbelt target and utility poles, the features extracted by the baseline network are relatively coarse, leading to misjudgments in seatbelt detection. However, the model with FFAM performs more effectively in these situations, concentrating its detection focus more precisely on the waist area of the human body and the region where the seatbelt is located. This successfully achieves accurate predictions of seatbelt wearing status in elevated scenarios. Therefore, it is evident that the algorithm incorporating the FFAM module, as employed in this study, demonstrates higher accuracy in feature extraction, effectively enhancing the model's performance in complex scenes.

## 6   In Conclusion

This paper proposes a safety belt detection algorithm named EfficientDet_Ad. Firstly, by designing an enhanced feature extraction module that achieves multi-scale feature fusion, the algorithm improves the detection capability for small targets, adapting to scenarios in the power industry where safety belts appear at different scales. Secondly, a Feature Fusion Attention Module (FFAM) is constructed within the enhanced feature extraction network to enhance the visual saliency of safety belt targets. This allows the network to focus more on learning features in the target region, thereby improving detection accuracy. Finally, the MBConv module is restructured to reduce network parameters, optimizing the network structure for the task of object detection and improving computational efficiency. In summary, the proposed EfficientDet_Ad algorithm has achieved significant success in safety belt target detection, surpassing the original algorithm and other advanced algorithms in various performance metrics. This demonstrates the effectiveness of the proposed method in detecting safety belt targets and provides valuable insights for the intelligent inspection of power grid construction in the future.

**Acknowledgements.** We thank reviewers for their valuable comments and help. This project is supported by the Education Commission of Hubei Province (No. D2021701).

# References

1. Yan, Y., Zhang, S., Liang, Z., Sheng, W.: Analysis on statistics and patterns of fatal accidents in my country's electric power enterprises from 2016 to 2021. Safety **44**, 46–51 (2023)
2. 2008 engineering construction standard specification guidance and revision plan (first batch) (continued to be completed). Engineering construction standardization, pp. 36–38 (2008)
3. Li, W.: Analysis of falling accidents from heights in power construction projects and research on preventive measures. Comput. enthusiast (popular version) **11**, 65–66 (2021)
4. Yi, J., et al.: An intelligent on-line monitoring device for safety belt under high-altitude operation. Eng. constr. stand. 1–6 (2022)
5. Ma, A., et al.: Smart belt for real-time posture monitoring of grid workers at heights. In:2023 IEEE Sustainable Power and Energy Conference (iSPEC), pp. 1–5 (2023)
6. Lv, J., Hao, X., Feng, M., Jia, Z.: Research on worksite's video image safety helmet detection method based on cloud-edge cooperation. In: 2022 3rd International Conference on Big Data, Artificial Intelligence and Internet of Things Engineering (ICBAIE), pp. 405–409 (2022)
7. Li, J., Ren, Q., Wu, J.: Intelligent video recognition of violation behavior in substation site based on mask R-CNN. In: Engineering Construction Standardization, pp. 183–186 (2022)
8. Fang, W., Ding, L., Luo, H., Love, P.E.D.: Falls from heights: a computer vision-based approach for safety harness detection. Autom. Constr. **91**, 53–61 (2018)
9. Redmon, J., Divvala, S., Girshick, R., Farhadi, A.: You only look once: unified, real-time object detection. In: Proceedings of the IEEE Conference on Computer Vision and Pattern Recognition (CVPR), pp. 779–788 (2016)
10. Redmon, J., Farhadi, A.: Yolo9000: better, faster, stronger. In: Proceedings of the IEEE Conference on Computer Vision and Pattern Recognition (CVPR), pp.7263–7271 (2017)

11. Ltd. Beijing Haoyunda Intelligent Innovation Technology Co. Determine other helmet and seat belt detection methods based on deep neural network:. (CN201910237877.5), 07 2019
12. Tan, M., Pang, R., Le, Q.V.: EfficientDet: scalable and efficient object detection (2020)
13. Chen, C., Liu, M., Tuzel, O., Xiao, J.: R-CNN for small object detection. In: Computer Vision–ACCV 2016: 13th Asian Conference on Computer Vision, Taipei, Taiwan, November 20-24, 2016, Revised Selected Papers, Part V 13, pp. 214–230 (2017)
14. Torralba, A., Fergus, R., Freeman, W.T.: 80 million tiny images: a large data set for nonparametric object and scene recognition. IEEE Trans. Pattern Anal. Mach. Intell. **30**, 1958–1970 (2008)
15. Simonyan, K., Zisserman, A.: Very deep convolutional networks for large-scale image recognition. arXiv preprint arXiv:1409.1556 (2014)
16. Zhang, S., Benenson, R., Schiele, B.: CityPersons: a diverse dataset for pedestrian detection. In: Proceedings of the IEEE Conference on Computer Vision and Pattern Recognition, pp. 3213–3221 (2017)
17. Guo, M., et al.: Attention mechanisms in computer vision: a survey. Comput. Visual Media **8**(3), 331–368 (2022)
18. Hou, Q., Zhou, D., Feng, J.: Coordinate attention for efficient mobile network design. In: Proceedings of the IEEE/CVF Conference on Computer Vision and Pattern Recognition, pp. 13713–13722 (2021)
19. Wang, Q., Wu, B., Zhu, P., Li, P., Zuo, W., Hu, Q.: ECA-Net: efficient channel attention for deep convolutional neural networks. In: Proceedings of the IEEE/CVF Conference on Computer Vision and Pattern Recognition, pp. 11534–11542 (2020)
20. Shanti, M.Z.: A novel implementation of an AI-based smart construction safety inspection protocol in the UAE. IEEE Access **9**, 166603–166616 (2021)
21. Yao, Z., Song, X., Zhao, L., Yin, Y.: Real-time method for traffic sign detection and recognition based on YOLOv3-tiny with multiscale feature extraction. Proc. Inst. Mech. Eng. Part D: J. Autom. Eng. **235**(7), 1978–1991 (2021)
22. Zeng, L., Sun, B., Zhu, D.: Underwater target detection based on faster R-CNN and adversarial occlusion network. Eng. Appl. Artif. Intell. **100**, 104190 (2021)

# DHNet: A Depthwise Separable Convolution-Based High-Resolution Full Projector Compensation Network

Yuqiang Zhang, Huamin Yang$^{(\boxtimes)}$, Cheng Han, and Chao Zhang

Changchun University of Science and Technology, Changchun, Jilin, China
yanghuamin@cust.edu.cn

**Abstract.** The increasing application scenarios of projectors across various fields have made them indispensable tools. However, achieving optimal display effects in diverse scenarios presents challenges for projectors. In this study, we propose a novel high-resolution projector compensation method, named *DHNet*, which integrates a channel and spatial attention module into a depthwise separable convolution-based network. Our method effectively captures spatial information and exploits inter-channel associations, thereby enhancing the network's capability to handle projection distortions. Experimental results demonstrate that our method achieves comparable compensation performance to state-of-the-art methods while effectively reducing the network's parameters, making it more lightweight.

**Keywords:** High resolution · Full projector compensation · Depthwise separable convolution · Attention mechanism

## 1 Introduction

The projector is now a common tool for education, meetings, and entertainment. However, it faces challenges in achieving optimal geometric and photometric effects with increasing application scenarios. Traditional methods for addressing these distortions [1–4] typically require a carefully crafted sampling strategy by experienced individuals. Additionally, geometric calibration and photometric compensation are usually done independently, potentially causing mutual interference. Thus, efficient, robust, and widely applicable methods are crucial for effective distortion calibration. Recently, there has been a surge in deep learning methods for projector compensation [5–9], using convolutional neural networks for end-to-end projector compensation learning. However, their effectiveness is limited by low-resolution datasets, restricting their application. To overcome this, a novel high-resolution projector compensation method [10] has been proposed, combining the network architecture of CompenNeSt++ [9] with pixel shuffle [11]. This method handles high-resolution images effectively, especially with limited graphic processing units (GPU) memory. Although these methods mitigate projection distortions, convolution-based networks struggle with spatial perception and exploiting feature correlations. To address this, we integrate a channel and spatial attention module into our depthwise separable convolution-based compensation network, *DHNet*. In our experimental evaluations, *DHNet* achieves comparable results to state-of-the-art methods while significantly reducing network parameters by 71.2%.

(a) Surface     (b) Uncompensated     (c) DHNet     (d) Ground Truth

**Fig. 1. Projector full compensation.** (a) shows the warped textured projection surface, (b) is the uncompensated pro jection image, (c) displays the full compensation result of (b) and (d) presents the desired projected image.

## 2 Methods

### 2.1 Full Compensation Formulation

The end-to-end formulation for full projector compensation is derived through an image pair learning approach [7]. Following this methodology, let $I_h$ denote the high-resolution desired projected image, $S$ represent the projection surface, and $G$ denote the global lighting. After projecting $I_h$ onto $S$, the resulting uncompensated image $\tilde{I}_h$ is captured by the camera:

$$\tilde{I}_h = \mathcal{T}(\mathcal{F}(I_h; G, S)) \tag{1}$$

where the function $\mathcal{F} : \mathbb{R}^{H_1 \times W_1 \times 3} \rightarrow \mathbb{R}^{H_1 \times W_1 \times 3}$ represents the process within the procam system responsible for photometrically transforming a projector input image into an uncompensated camera-captured image, while $\mathcal{T} : \mathbb{R}^{H_1 \times W_1 \times 3} \rightarrow \mathbb{R}^{H_2 \times W_2 \times 3}$ denotes the process of geometrically warping a projector input image to the camera-captured image.

Full projector compensation aims to find a compensated projector input image $I_h^*$ such that, when projected onto the surface S, the ideal viewer-perceived image $I_h'$, which is an optimal affine transformation of $I_h$, can be obtained as follows:

$$I_h' = \mathcal{T}\big(\mathcal{F}(I_h^*; G, S)\big) \tag{2}$$

Given the challenge of directly obtaining the properties of $G$ and $S$, a camera-captured projection surface $\tilde{S}$ is introduced to implicitly capture these two factors. Moreover, only the area illuminated by the projector is necessary, which allows us to approximate $\tilde{S}$ by the effective subregion of the camera-captured $\mathcal{T}^{-1}(\tilde{S})$. Subsequently, the compensated projector input image can be derived as follows:

$$I_h^* = \mathcal{F}^\dagger\Big(\mathcal{T}^{-1}(I_h'); \mathcal{T}^{-1}(\tilde{S})\Big) \tag{3}$$

Here, $\mathcal{T}^{-1}$ denotes the inverse function of $\mathcal{T}$, while $\mathcal{F}^\dagger$ represents the pseudo-inverse function of $\mathcal{F}$. However, it is evident that this formulation lacks a closed-form solution. Consequently, a learning-based method is introduced to approximate the solution. Similar to the transition from Eq. (2) to Eq. (3), starting with Eq. (1), we can derive:

$$I_h = \mathcal{F}^\dagger \left( \mathcal{T}^{-1}(\tilde{I}_h); \mathcal{T}^{-1}(\tilde{S}) \right) \tag{4}$$

This formulation allows for compensation to be performed by learning data pairs such as $(\tilde{I}_h, I_h)$, along with a captured surface image $\tilde{S}$. The key to solving this problem lies in employing a neural network $\pi^\dagger$ to learn the parameters $\theta$ of the composite function described in Eq. (3) and Eq. (4). The primary objective of this learning process is to minimize the discrepancy between the network-inferred image $\hat{I}_h$ and $I_h$:

$$\theta = \arg\min_{\theta'} \sum_i \mathcal{L}\left( \hat{I}_{h,i} = \pi^\dagger_{\theta'}(\tilde{I}_{h,i}; \tilde{S}_h), I_{h,i} \right) \tag{5}$$

where $i$ denotes the index of training image pairs within the designated training set, while $\mathcal{L}$ signifies the employed loss function. In pursuit of optimizing the network parameters and bolstering its learning efficacy for the compensation task, we employ a composite of loss functions encompassing $L_1$, $L_2$, and $L_{SSIM}$. Specifically, $L_1$ denotes the Mean Absolute Error, $L_2$ signifies the Mean Square Error, and $L_{SSIM}$ represents the Structural Similarity Index Measure error.

$$\mathcal{L} = L_1 + L_2 + L_{SSIM} \tag{6}$$

## 2.2 Network Design

While traditional convolution-based methods offer comprehensive compensation, the pursuit of improved optimization in geometric and photometric projector compensation persists. Previous research [9, 10] has validated that a dual-branch Siamese network structure, utilizing both captured projection images and projected surface images as inputs, possesses superior prior information compared to single-branch network structures. This configuration demonstrates enhanced capability in projector compensation. Therefore, we incorporate such architectures into the design of our networks, as illustrated in Fig. 2.

Based on the geometric compensation framework introduced in CompenNeSt++ [9], we refine the sampling grid to a resolution of $1024 \times 1024$. This adjustment enhances compensation for the high-resolution geometric features present in both the surface and uncompensated images. Additionally, the High-Resolution Warping Network (HR WarpingNet) facilitates the generation of an orthogonal view image from the geometrically distorted input. To further enhance the understanding of photometric information within surface image and uncompensated images, while also ensuring the efficiency of the photometric compensation network, we incorporate depthwise separable convolutions into the network architecture which termed as DSCNet. In the DSCNet encoder, after two convolutional downsampling steps, we encode photometric information through depthwise separable convolutions, each followed by ReLU activation. At the network bottleneck, we incorporate Convolutional Block Attention Module (CBAM) [12] to extract both channel and spatial information from feature maps. This information is then seamlessly integrated with the encoder's output through element-wise addition. Similarly, in the decoder, we utilize multiple depthwise separable convolutional operations to decode the information. This process is followed by two upsampling steps, each comprising a transpose convolution and an activation function. Finally, the compensated image is generated through a convolution operation with ReLU activation. Furthermore, by employing skip connections, we integrate information from shallower network layers as residuals into deeper layers, effectively enhancing network stability.

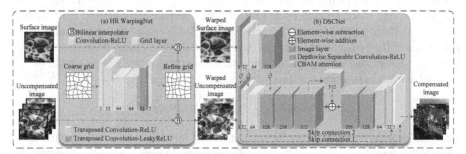

**Fig. 2. Architecture of the proposed *DHNet*.** (a) Illustrates the high-resolution warping network, which refines the initially generated coarse grid. Following bilinear interpolation, the warped surface image and the uncompensated image are fed into (b) the depthwise separable convolution-based network for further compensation. Ultimately, the compensated image is generated.

When using convolutional kernels of the same size, employing depth separable convolutions can lead to a reduction in the overall number of parameters in the network compared to traditional convolution operations. Consequently, by increasing the number of channels without a corresponding increase in parameters, the network's capacity for fitting data can be enhanced. However, in depthwise convolution, each channel's information is only related to its respective input, disregarding inter-channel correlations. This limitation may hinder the network's effectiveness in learning compensation information. To mitigate this, we employ the CBAM attention mechanism at the network's bottleneck. This enhances the network's ability to extract features from channel information, while also strengthening its capacity to capture spatial information from feature maps.

## 2.3 CBAM Attention

The significance of attention has been studied extensively in the previous literature. Attention not only tells where to focus, it also improves the representation of interests [12]. In particular, the CBAM module effectively captures both channel and spatial features through its two key components: the channel attention module and the spatial attention module, as illustrated in Fig. 3.

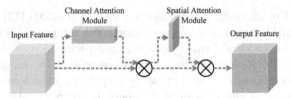

**Fig. 3.** The structure of CBAM attention.

The channel attention module primarily focuses on the channel dimension of the feature map. When given a feature map $F \in \mathbb{R}^{H \times W \times C}$, the spatial information within the feature map is aggregated by employing both average pooling and max pooling operations. These pooled features are subsequently fed into a weight-shared multi-layer perceptron (MLP) to generate channel features. Finally, the channel features are combined through element-wise summation, and the resulting output is processed by the sigmoid activation function $\sigma$ to produce a channel attention map $M_c \in \mathbb{R}^{1 \times 1 \times C}$.

$$M_c(F) = \sigma(MLP(AP(F)) + MLP(MP(F))) \tag{7}$$

Here, AP denotes the average pooling operation and MP denotes the max pooling operation. Subsequently, the channel attention features are element-wise multiplied with the input feature map, resulting in feature maps enhanced with channel attention information.

$$F' = M_c(F) \otimes F \tag{8}$$

where $\otimes$ denotes element-wise multiplication.

The spatial attention module primarily focuses on the spatial dimension of the feature map. To compute the spatial attention, average pooling and max pooling operations are applied along the channel axis of $F'$. The pooled highlighting features are then concatenated along the channel axis and convolved by a standard convolutional layer to generate a spatial attention map $M_s \in \mathbb{R}^{H \times W \times 1}$.

$$M_s(F') = \sigma\left(f^{7 \times 7}([AP(F'); MP(F')])\right) \tag{9}$$

where $f^{7 \times 7}$ represents a convolution operation with the kernel size of $7 \times 7$. Subsequently, we obtain the refined feature map $F'' \in \mathbb{R}^{H \times W \times C}$, incorporating both channel and spatial attention. This is achieved through the operation:

$$F'' = M_s(F') \otimes F' \tag{10}$$

After integrating the CBAM module at the network bottleneck, we validated its efficacy in feature extraction through ablative experiments in Subsect. 3.2. The CBAM module harnesses a robust spatial and channel feature replenishment capability, bolstering the network's ability to adeptly manage spatial structures and geometric relationships within the data, thus amplifying the efficacy of full compensation.

# 3 Experimental Evaluations

To validate the effectiveness of the proposed method, we conducted comparative experiments and module ablation experiments using the dataset provided by CompenHR [10]. This high-resolution benchmark dataset comprises 21 subsets captured at various poses, with each subset containing 500 training image pairs and 200 testing image pairs. The experimental setup includes an Intel i7-12700K CPU, Nvidia RTX 3090 GPU, 64GB DDR5 memory, and Ubuntu 22.04 operating system. PyTorch was utilized for constructing networks, while parameter optimization during training employed the Adam optimizer. Additionally, StepLR scheduler was utilized to dynamically adjust the learning rate within the optimizer throughout the training process. In the comparative experiments, we contrasted our proposed DHNet with CompenNet++, CompenNeSt++, and CompenHR. In the ablation experiments, we compared the proposed modules with the baseline network.

## 3.1 Comparative Experiments

We utilized the Peak Signal-to-Noise Ratio (PSNR), Root Mean Square Error (RMSE), Structural Similarity Index (SSIM), and $\Delta E$ [13] to evaluate each method. We trained and validated 21 individual subsets separately, and calculated the average values of the results obtained from these subsets. The quantified results obtained are presented in Table 1, while the visualized results are depicted in Fig. 4.

**Table 1.** Average quantified comparison results of different methods on 21 subsets

| Model | PSNR↑ | RMSE↓ | SSIM↑ | $\Delta E$↓ |
|---|---|---|---|---|
| CompenNet++ | 20.3898 | 0.1659 | 0.5945 | 8.0296 |
| CompenNeSt++ | 20.5425 | 0.1629 | 0.6002 | 7.6060 |
| CompenHR | 20.7232 | 0.1596 | 0.5936 | 7.7291 |
| DHNet | **20.9530** | **0.1555** | **0.6185** | **7.4611** |

In the table, the symbol ↑ indicates that a larger value corresponds to better compensation results, while the symbol ↓ indicates that a smaller value corresponds to better compensation results. For each trained subset, the model parameters of CompenNet++, CompenNeSt++ CompenHR, and *DHNet* are respectively: 1.1521M, 0.8331M, 0.8876M, and 0.5184M. Utilizing depthwise separable convolution, our network model reduces parameter count by 71.2% compared to CompenHR. Meanwhile, our method's compensation performance is comparable to various state-of-the-art methods.

## 3.2 Module Ablation Experiments

In the module ablation experiments, we compared *DHNet* with the baseline network CompenNeSt++. Chosen for its substantial impact in projection full compensation,

CompenNeSt++ exhibits exceptional performance. We then evaluated *DHNet* 's compensation results with and without the CBAM attention module. Quantified results are summarized in Table 2, while visual comparisons are depicted in Fig. 5.

In the baseline network, the bottleneck layer features 256 channels, while our approach employs 512 channels. This augmentation in channel count at the bottleneck layer bolsters the network's nonlinear modeling capacity, enabling it to effectively accommodate complex information within the existing architecture. Furthermore, the integration of the CBAM module allows the network to adaptively learn correlations among different channels, thereby amplifying its responsiveness to pivotal channels. Following the incorporation of the CBAM module, the *DHNet* network showcased improvements of 0.7% in PSNR, a decrease of 1.7% in RMSE, a 0.9% enhancement in SSIM, and a 0.5% reduction in $\triangle E$. Moreover, the CBAM module facilitates the allocation of varying weights to different spatial regions of the feature map, thereby augmenting its ability to capture crucial image structures and content. Consequently, this enhancement significantly improves projector compensation efficacy.

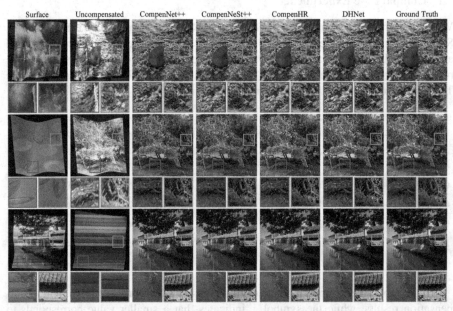

**Fig. 4. The compensation results of different methods.** The red and blue bounding boxes contain details of the compensated images. Through these details, we can observe that *DHNet* exhibits more intricate details compared to other methods, along with color restoration capabilities that are comparable or superior to other state-of-the-art methods.

**Table 2.** Module ablation experiment results

| Module | PSNR↑ | RMSE↓ | SSIM↑ | $\Delta E$↓ |
|---|---|---|---|---|
| Baseline | 20.5425 | 0.1629 | 0.6002 | 7.6060 |
| DHNet w/o CBAM | 20.8162 | 0.1582 | 0.6129 | 7.4970 |
| DHNet | **20.9530** | **0.1555** | **0.6185** | **7.4611** |

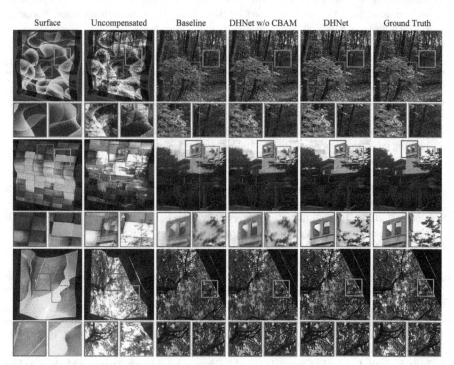

**Fig. 5. The ablation experiment results.** Compared with the baseline network, our *DHNet* benefits from a higher number of channels, enabling it to learn diverse feature representations that encompass texture and color information.

## 4   Conclusion

In this paper, we introduce a novel method, *DHNet*, designed to tackle high-resolution geometric and photometric full compensation. Through the integration of lightweight modules, we effectively diminish the network parameters, facilitating its deployment on hardware with limited resources without compromising the precision of projector full compensation. However, the higher resolution of input image pairs compared to the compensated image resolution poses a challenge in achieving real-time performance for high-resolution projector full compensation. Addressing this issue is pivotal for integrating the compensation method across a wide range of practical scenarios, an aspect worth exploring in future research endeavors.

**Acknowledgements.** This work is partially supported by the Natural Science Foundation of Jilin Province (Grant No. 20220101134JC), the Natural Science Foundation Project of Chongqing, Chongqing Science and Technology Commission (Grant No. CSTB2022NSCQ-MSX1240).

# References

1. Ashdown, M., Okabe, T., Sato, I., Sato, Y.: Robust content-dependent photometric projector compensation. In: 2006 Conference on Computer Vision and Pattern Recognition Workshop (CVPRW'06), pp. 6–6 (2006)
2. Dehos, J., Zeghers, E., Renaud, C., Rousselle, F., Sarry, L.: Radiometric compensation for a low-cost immersive projection system. In: Virtual Reality Software and Technology (2008)
3. Wenhai, Z., Haisong, X., Weige, L.: Radiometric compensation algorithm for color reproduction of projection display on patterned surface. Chin. Opt. Lett. **8**(4), 388–391 (2010)
4. Madi, A., Ziou, D.: Color constancy for visual compensation of projector displayed image. Displays **35**, 6–17 (2014)
5. Kageyama, Y., Iwai, D., Sato, K.: Efficient distortion-free neural projector deblurring in dynamic projection mapping. IEEE trans. Vis. Comput. Graph. (2024)
6. Kageyama, Y., Iwai, D., Sato, K.: Online projector deblurring using a convolutional neural network. IEEE Trans. Visual Comput. Graphics **28**, 2223–2233 (2022)
7. Huang, B., Ling, H.: CompenNet++: end-to-end full projector compensation. In: 2019 IEEE/CVF International Conference on Computer Vision (ICCV), 7164−7173 (2019)
8. Huang, B., Ling, H.: End-to-end projector photometric compensation. In: 2019 IEEE/CVF Conference on Computer Vision and Pattern Recognition (CVPR), 6803−6812 (2019)
9. Huang, B., Sun, T., Ling, H.: End-to-end full projector compensation. IEEE Trans. Pattern Anal. Mach. Intell. **44**, 2953–2967 (2020)
10. Wang, Y., Ling, H., Huang, B.: CompenHR: efficient full compensation for high-resolution projector. In: 2023 IEEE Conference Virtual Reality and 3D User Interfaces (VR), pp. 135–145 (2023)
11. Shi, W., et al.: Real-time single image and video super-resolution using an efficient sub-pixel convolutional neural network. IEEE Conf. Comput. Vis. Pattern Recogn. (CVPR) **2016**, 1874–1883 (2016)
12. Woo, S., Park, J., Lee, J., Kweon, I.: CBAM: Convolutional Block Attention Module. ArXiv, abs/1807.06521 (2018)
13. Sharma, G., Wu, W., Dalal, E.N.: The CIEDE2000 color-difference formula: Implementation notes, supplementary test data, and mathematical observations. Color. Res. Appl. **30**, 21–30 (2005)

# Denoising Implicit Feedback
# for Extractive Question Answering

Xinrong Hu[1], Jingxue Chen[1], Zijian Huang[1], Xun Yao[1(✉)], and Jie Yang[2(✉)]

[1] Wuhan Textile University, Wuhan, China
{hxr,yaoxun}@wtu.edu.cn, {2215363054,2115363096}@mail.wtu.edu.cn
[2] University of Wollongong, Wollongong, Australia
jiey@uow.edu.au
https://csai.wtu.edu.cn/info/1242/2636.htm

**Abstract.** The Extractive Question Answering (EQA) is a fundamental task in Natural Language Processing domain, focusing on the identification of a correct answer span (a sequence of continuous words) over the given question and passage. Recent years have witnessed a dramatically increasing interest in harnessing the Large Language Models (LLMs) for EQA. Yet, the existence of missing labeled training data in many EQA datasets has a negative impact on model training. These missing labeled instances can be attributed to inaccuracies in label annotations, format inconsistencies, and *etc.* Consequently, this paper introduces a novel training algorithm, termed *Adaptive Denoising Training (ADT)* to adaptively manipulate missing labeled instances during the training process. Specifically, the proposed ADT is characterized by an adaptive loss function, to dynamically adjust the contribution (or weights) of missing labeled data in each iteration, thereby minimizing their impact on model training. Extensive experiments over three benchmarks demonstrate that the proposed ADT algorithm achieves notable improvement compared to conventional training methods. Additionally, ADT also achieves strong performance in low-resource settings.

**Keywords:** Extractive Question Answering · Adaptive Training · Missing Labeled Training Data

## 1 Introduction

Machine Reading Comprehension (MRC) is a dynamic and active research area within the field of Natural Language Processing. One of the core tasks in MRC is Extractive Question Answering (EQA). EQA involves providing a model with a passage and a corresponding question, with the goal of comprehending both the passage and the question, and accurately identifying the answer within the passage. This task serves as a fundamental benchmark for a range of downstream applications, including chatbot development, online recommendation systems, and information retrieval [1–3].

In recent years, there has been a growing fascination with harnessing Large Language Models (LLMs) for Extractive Question Answering (EQA), where these models typically serve as context encoders to extract semantic embeddings

N. Magnenat Thalmann et al. (Eds.): CASA 2024, CCIS 2374, pp. 375–387, 2025.
https://doi.org/10.1007/978-981-96-2681-6_27

for input question-passage pairs. A substantial body of literature has evolved in this domain. Notably, attention mechanisms, as introduced in [4], synergize passage and question features, enhancing the model's ability to comprehend relevant information within the passage concerning the given question [5,6]. The imposition of constraints on the model's output features has been explored as a means to refine the accuracy of answer localization [7]. Additionally, ensemble models, which amalgamate distinctive strengths from various models [8], provide diverse perspectives on data information, thereby amplifying predictive accuracy.

Although aforementioned methods have achieved notable answering accuracy, they continue to have difficulty with one problem of the **missing labeled training data**. These missing labeled instances can be, for instance, attributed to missing label annotations, as depicted in Table 1. In this example, Lobund attained independent status as a dedicated research organization in the 1940 s, and by 1950, it was elevated to the status of an Institute. However, the annotation only includes 'the 1940 s,' which qualifies as a missing labeled annotation. Additionally, other factors, such as format inconsistencies, when annotating date-type labels, the encountered formats might be "1928 s," or even "1928." Such noise adversely affects model training. Previous approaches aimed to address this by excluding some dirty data from the dataset to enable the model to accurately interpret the data. However, most methods have focused on offsetting the impact of dirty data on the model by increasing the quantity of samples [9].

To address this, we introduce an Adaptive Denoising Training (ADT) strategy for the extractive question answering task, designed to dynamically remove missing labeled data encountered during the training process. The ADT strategy consists of two components: 1) Adaptive Data Filtering (ADF), dynamically

**Table 1.** A missing labeled training data example in SQuAD(1.1) [10] The highlighted portion is the complete answer in the passage.

---

**Passage**: ...But the objective was not merely to answer Pasteur's question but also to produce the germ free animal as a new tool for biological and medical research. This objective was reached and for years Lobund was a unique center for the study and production of germ free animals and for their use in biological and medical investigations. Today the work has spread to other universities. In the beginning it was under the Department of Biology and a program leading to the master's degree accompanied the research program. In the 1940 s Lobund achieved independent status as a purely research organization and in 1950 was raised to the status of an Institute. In 1958 it was brought back into the Department of Biology as integral part of that department, but with its own program leading to the degree of PhD in Gnotobiotics.

---

**Question**: Around what time did Lobund of Notre Dame become independent?
**Answers**: the 1940 s.

---

allocating weights to each training data point to mitigate the impact of missing labeled data on model optimization, and 2) Weighted Loss Fusion (WLF),
employing a weighted approach to merge the losses generated from the training
data. We evaluated our proposed methods on SQuAD (1.1) [10], NewsQA [11],
and NaturalQ [12] datasets. The results demonstrate a significant performance
improvement compared to standard training.

Our main contributions are summarized as follows:

- To the best of our knowledge, this represents one of the earliest attempts to
  dynamically remove missing labeled samples during the training process in
  the context of EQA tasks.
- We propose Adaptive Denoising Training, which dynamically prunes the missing labeled data interactions. More precisely, we utilize the loss of individual
  samples to estimate a selection probability, subsequently fusing these losses
  through a weighted approach.
- The method we proposed was applied to three EQA datasets, and extensive experiments validated the effectiveness of ADT in improving the model's
  accuracy in answering questions. Simultaneously, a series of ablation studies
  were conducted.

## 2    Related Work

In recent years, significant advancements have been made in the field of extractive question-answering, thanks to the widespread adoption of large-scale pre-
trained language models (PLMs) such as BERT [1] and RoBERTa [3]. These
PLMs serve as powerful content encoders, capable of extracting nuanced knowledge representations from input paragraphs and questions. In the context of
extractive question-answering models, a multi-classifier is typically trained to
identify the start and end positions of answers within the text. The text segment between these positions is considered the selected candidate answer. In
cases where the answer consists of a single word, the start and end positions
overlap. Compared to traditional encoding models, large-scale pretrained language models demonstrate superior proficiency in content encoding, leading to
enhanced performance in extractive question-answering tasks.

Driven by the remarkable success of PLMs, a variety of enhancement techniques have been introduced, often incorporating human reading strategies to
improve answer prediction. For example, approaches like those in [7] employ
hierarchical attention mechanisms to estimate matching relationships between
questions, paragraphs, and answers. [13] introduce hierarchical attention mechanisms that simulate a bi-directional reading process, emphasizing key aspects
such as highlighting and self-assessment. Strategies for multi-turn reasoning, as
explored in [14],involve techniques such as rapid scanning, focused exclusion,
and meticulous reading. Work like that in [6] introduces a chunk-based attention mechanism that adeptly predicts context closely related to the answer, with
similar methodologies echoed in [15]. In [8], an attention adapter, combining

gate control mechanisms with PLMs, aims at answer identification. Further, [16], propose amalgamating contextual representations from intermediate PLM layers with entity and relational data from external Knowledge Graphs.

Alternatively, another line of research focuses on an embedding-centric strategy. One such method revolves around modifying input tokens to create customized examples [17], effectively altering the input embeddings. Moreover, approaches like those presented in [18] fortify model resilience by introducing Gaussian noise into the features. Furthermore, [19] explores the analysis of variations in token embeddings, culminating in the development of a robust encoder capable of adapting to these fluctuations.

## 3   Proposed Method

In this section, the proposed Adaptive Denoising Training (ADT) algorithm is detailed, which comprises two key components: Adaptive Data Filtering (ADF) and Weighted Loss Fusion (WLF). As depicted in Fig. 1, ADT begins with the utilization of the ADF component to estimate weights of each training sample based on its loss value. These weights subsequently determine the selection probability (of those samples) at the next iteration. Subsequently, the WLF component is employed to calculate the final loss by performing a weighted sum across selected training samples.

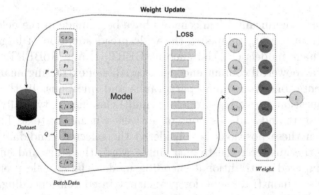

**Fig. 1.** ADT Method Dynamics: Weight Calculation, Sample Selection, and Model Update.

### 3.1   Problem Formulation

Extractive Question Answering (EQA) tasks revolve around analyzing a given input pair comprising a question ($q$) and an associated passage ($p$). The core objective is to meticulously discern and pinpoint the precise start and end positions within passage ($p$) that demarcate the correct answer span ($\alpha_{s/e}$).

Specifically, the input of EQA is a tokenized sequence, $X = [\text{CLS}]q_1q_2 \ldots q_{|q|}[\text{SEP}]p_1p_2 \ldots p_{|p|}[\text{SEP}]$, where $q_i$ represents the $i$-th token from the question $q$, and $p_j$ represents the $j$-th token from the passage $p$. Subsequently, the encoder $\mathbf{F}$, often a Pre-trained Language Model (PLM) like RoBERTa [3], is utilized to generate the subsequent probability distribution:

$$p\left(p_i = a_{s/e}\right) \triangleq \frac{\exp\left(\mathrm{MLP}^{s/e}\left(\mathbf{F}\left(p_i\right)\right)\right)}{\sum_j^{|p|} \exp\left(\mathrm{MLP}^{s/e}\left(\mathbf{F}\left(p_j\right)\right)\right)} \tag{1}$$

where $\mathbf{F}(p_i)$ denotes the extracted feature of $p_i$, while $\mathrm{MLP}^{s/e}$ symbolizes a multilayer perception network (often with one hidden layer) designed for the prediction of the answer span's start and end. Subsequently, the loss function for EQA is defined as follow:

$$\mathcal{L}_{EQA} \triangleq -\sum_i^{|p|} \mathbb{1}\left(p_i = a_{s/e}\right) \log p\left(p_i = a_{s/e}\right) \tag{2}$$

where $\mathbb{1}(\cdot)$ represents the indicator function that yields a value of 1 if the condition is true, and 0 otherwise. In essence, the primary objective of this module is to minimize the $\mathcal{L}_{EQA}$ loss by utilizing labeled original samples.

## 3.2 Adaptive Denoising Training

In the traditional EQA training process, random batches of data are selected from the dataset to train the model. This may involve training the model with missing labeled training data that are difficult for the model to fit. Moreover, each training sample is assigned an equal weight, implying that missing labeled training data and clean samples carry the same weight. This is detrimental to the model training process.

In the ADF component, to avoid this, we employ Eq. (3) to dynamically adjust the weight of each training sample based on its loss.

$$\omega = \begin{cases} \left(\frac{e^l - e^{-l}}{e^l + e^{-l}}\right)^\beta & \text{if } 0 < r \le x\% \\ \left(e^{-l}\right)^\beta & \text{if } x\% < r < 1 \end{cases} \tag{3}$$

where $r$ represents the percentage during the entire program's training process, and the loss $l$ is equivalent to loss $\mathcal{L}_{EQA}$. Additionally, $\beta$ is a numeric factor utilized to control the relationship between weight and loss curves.

ADF component comprises two stages, as illustrate in Fig. 2. Stage A covers the initial $x\%$ of training where larger loss values aid learning as the model is not effectively trained yet. Smaller-weighted data might be considered missing labeled data during this phase. Stage B represents the latter 1-$x\%$ of training, where the model has stabilized. Larger loss values might indicate missing labeled data, and minimizing learning from this subset becomes crucial. Additionally, the EQA model calculates the corresponding weight $\omega$ or each training data $k$, which influences the probability($\mathrm{Pro}_k = \omega_k$) of the sample being chosen by the model in the next iteration.

In the ADF component, we assume that data with smaller weights $\omega$, are more likely to be missing labeled data. However, currently, we lack theoretical proof to substantiate this assumption. To avoid this subjectivity, we split the dataset into two parts: $m$, containing a larger proportion of data with higher $\omega$ values (considered clean samples), and $n$, containing a smaller proportion of data with lower $\omega$ values (considered missing labeled data). We then sample from both $m$ and $n$ sets in specific proportions, ensuring each batch includes data points with smaller $\omega$ values, avoiding the complete exclusion of potentially normal data.

---

**Algorithm 1:** Adaptive Denoising Training

---

**Input**: the set of all trainable parameters $\Theta$, the maximum number of iterations $T_{max}$, training dataset $D$, learning rate $\eta$, mini-batch size $N$, $\beta$
**Output**: the optimized parameters $\Theta^*$ for EQA model.
1 Initialize the weights $\omega$ of each training sample $i \in D$;
2 Divide the dataset $D$ into sets $m$ and $n$;
3 **for** $T = 1 \rightarrow T_{max}$ **do**
4 　 **Sample** mini-batch data $\tilde{D}$ from $m$ and $n$ with the certain proportions;
5 　 **Obtain** $\mathcal{L}_{EQA}$ and $\omega$ using the Eq. (2) and Eq. (3);
6 　 **Update** the data in sets $m$ and $n$ based on the $\omega$;
7 　 **Obtain** $\omega_p$ using the Eq. (4);
8 　 **Update** $\Theta_T = \Theta_{T-1} - \eta \triangledown \frac{1}{|\tilde{D}|} \sum \omega_k \mathcal{L}_{EQA}(N, \beta|\Theta_{T-1})$;
9 **end**

---

Due to the traditional model training approach, typically employing an average loss fusion method to update the model, implying equal importance for each training sample at that step, we believe this method fails to distinguish the

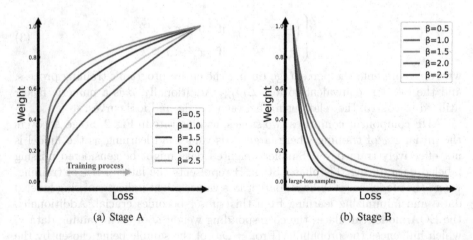

(a) Stage A                    (b) Stage B

**Fig. 2.** Relationship Between Weights $\omega$ and Losses $l$ Across Stages A and B.

significance of each individual sample. Therefore, in the WLF component, we employ a weighted fusion approach, as shown in Eq. (4).

$$\omega_k = \frac{\omega_i}{\sum_{j=0}^{|N|} \omega_j} \tag{4}$$

where $|N|$ represents the batch size, $i$ and $j$ respectively denote the $i$-th and $j$-th samples within that batch. Furthermore, $\omega_k$ represents the weighted fusion of sample $k$.

In summary, the final loss $\mathcal{L}_{SCE}$ is as follows:

$$\mathcal{L}_{SCE} = \omega_k \mathcal{L}_{EQA} \tag{5}$$

Our proposed ADT algorithm's detailed workflow is depicted in the algorithm 1.

## 4  Experiments

In our experiments, we utilized three datasets: SQuAD (1.1) [10], NewsQA [11], and NaturalQ [12]. The information for these datasets is presented in Table 2, where 'Dataset' represents the dataset name, 'Domain' signifies the domain covered by the dataset, and '#Train' and '#Test' indicate the quantity of training and testing instances, respectively.

**Table 2.** Dataset Overview for SQuAD(1.1), NewsQA, and NaturalQ

| Dataset | Domain | #Train | #Test |
|---------|--------|--------|-------|
| SQuAD(1.1) | Wikipedia | 86588 | 10507 |
| NewsQA | News articles | 74160 | 4212 |
| NaturalQ | Wikipedia | 104071 | 12836 |

The baseline model used in the experiments is RoBERTa-Base [3], which is a pre-trained model based on the Transformer encoder architecture. It utilizes a 12-layer attention mechanism [9] and has a maximum token length capacity of 512. RoBERTa-Base is pre-trained through masked language modeling on text data and has demonstrated good performance on extractive question-answering tasks.

The experiments were conducted on a machine with four Tesla K80 GPUs. The learning rate was set to $2e^{-5}$, and the batch size for each GPU was 16. Additionally, $\beta$ was set to 1.5, and a dropout rate of 0.1 was applied. We set $x$ to 80, with $m{:}n$ ratio at 1:4. Each batch is obtained by sampling data according to the ratio of 3 parts from $m$ to 1 part from $n$. The model was trained for 10 epochs. Each experiment was repeated ten times, and the average results were used as the final outcome.

## 4.1   Main Result

Table 3 provides the results of comparative experiments between our method and other mainstream algorithms and the other models have additional modules built on top of the Base. BLANC [7] utilizes block attention to focus more on the answer and reduce the offset in predicting answer start and end positions. SSMBA [17] randomly replaces some tokens with "[MASK]" and adds a reconstruction loss to predict these replaced tokens. SWEP [18] introduces Gaussian noise into the features to perturb the model and enhance its robustness. KALA [16] augments the initial contextual representation by incorporating information from the external Knowledge Graph related to entities and their relationships. PFA [19] is introduced to examine fluctuations in token embeddings, and a robust encoder is subsequently developed to withstand variations in embeddings with tolerance.

**Table 3.** ADT vs. Other Methods Performance Comparison

| Dataset | SQuAD | NewsQA | NaturalQ |
|---|---|---|---|
| Base | $90.3 \pm 0.2$ | $69.8 \pm 0.4$ | $79.6 \pm 0.2$ |
| BLANC [7] | $91.1 \pm 0.2$ | $70.7 \pm 0.5$ | $80.3 \pm 0.1$ |
| SSMBA [17] | $90.1 \pm 0.3$ | $69.2 \pm 0.2$ | $79.8 \pm 0.2$ |
| SWEP [18] | $91.0 \pm 0.1$ | $71.7 \pm 0.1$ | $80.2 \pm 0.3$ |
| KALA [16] | $90.9 \pm 0.4$ | $72.7 \pm 0.3$ | $80.1 \pm 0.4$ |
| PFA [19] | $92.4 \pm 0.1$ | $73.3 \pm 0.4$ | $82.2 \pm 0.3$ |
| ADT | $\mathbf{92.9} \pm 0.1$ | $\mathbf{73.8} \pm 0.2$ | $\mathbf{82.9} \pm 0.4$ |

We can observe that the ADT model outperforms other models in terms of F1 scores (2PR / (P + R), where P is precision and R is recall) across the SQuAD, NewsQA, and NaturalQ datasets. Compared to the baseline (Base model), it achieves a 2.6%, 4.0%, and 3.3% improvement in performance, respectively. When compared to the second-highest models in each dataset, ADT improves SQuAD by 0.5% compared to PFA, enhances NewsQA by 0.5% over PFA, and boosts NaturalQ by 0.7% over PFA. In terms of model speed, since the ADT model does not introduce additional computational overhead, its testing speed is the same as the Base model. Furthermore, ADT effectively utilizes each data sample, enabling it to train the model more rapidly, resulting in faster model training speeds.

## 4.2   Analysis

The adaptive denoising training (ADT) method introduced in this study, through its two core components - adaptive data filtering (ADF) and weighted loss fusion (WLF) - significantly improves the ability of extractive question answering models to deal with noise. Robustness and accuracy when using data. The application of the ADT method on data sets such as SQuAD (1.1), NewsQA and NaturalQ shows better performance than traditional training methods. These improvements are mainly attributed to ADT's ability to effectively reduce the negative impact of mislabeled data on model training.

**Adaptive Data Filtering (ADF):** ADF dynamically adjusts its weight by evaluating the loss value of each data point. This mechanism allows the model to gradually reduce the number of high-loss data points (often noisy or mislabeled data) during the iterative process. dependence. This not only improves the quality of training data, but also increases the sensitivity and learning efficiency of the model to clean data.

**Weighted Loss Fusion (WLF):** By weighted fusion of losses, WLF enables the model to pay more attention to those data points with higher weights (i.e., better quality) during the training process. This weighting mechanism ensures the effective utilization of information during the model optimization process, thereby enhancing the model's ability to solve complex problems.

### 4.3  Ablation Study

The ablation experiments below employed RoBERTa-Base as the baseline model and SQuAD as the test dataset. Each experiment was iterated ten times, and the resultant averages were calculated using the F1 [6] scoring formula.

**On the Model Breakdown.** We can observe that adding the ADF component to the base model results in an improvement of 2.1% over the original baseline model, and adding the WLF component improves it by 1.9% from Table 4. When both components are used simultaneously, there is an overall improvement of 2.6%. This indicates that the ADF and WLF components have a synergistic effect when used together.

**Table 4.** F1 Score Impact by ADT Components

|  | Base | Base ADF | Base WLF | ADT |
|---|---|---|---|---|
| SQuAD | 90.3 | 92.4 | 92.2 | 92.9 |

**On the Low-Resource Fine-Tuning.** Figure 3 presents a comparative analysis of data volume ablation. The figure illustrates the performance of the Base, PFA, and ADT models when using training data at 20%, 40%, 60%, 80%, and 100% of its full capacity. The graph indicates that the ADT model consistently performs well across these different data volumes, without a significant drop in model performance as data volume decreases. ADT shows stable and effective performance in low-data-volume extractive question-answering tasks, achieving an F1 score of 91.4% at a 40% data volume.

**On the Impact of $\beta$.** Since the value of $\beta$ impacts the weight of each sample, affecting the probability of selecting missing labeled data during the training

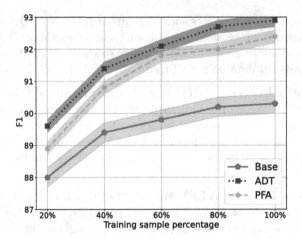

**Fig. 3.** F1-Accuracy by Training Sample Size

process, we conducted experiments with different $\beta$ values in the ADT model, where $\beta=\{0.5, 1.0, 1.5, 2.0, 2.5\}$, as shown in Fig. 4. The experimental outcomes indicate that the algorithm performs optimally when $\beta$ is set to 1.5. The performance is 0.8% lower when selecting $\beta$ as 0.5 compared to 1.5, possibly due to the model training process including more missing labeled data at this value, thereby compromising its performance.

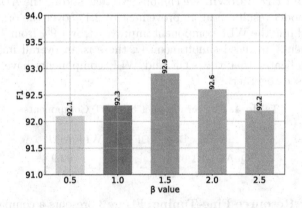

**Fig. 4.** The impact of different $\beta$ values on F1.

**On the Training Process.** The training of ADT is divided into two phases. The value of $x$ represents the percentage of data used for the first phase, and 1-$x$% is used for the second phase. The comparative experimental results for different values of $x$ are shown in Table 5. When $x$ is set to 0, it means that the first phase is skipped, and the model directly enters the second phase. The primary task of the second phase is to stabilize the model. If the model starts directly in the second phase, it can suppress the model's learning. The results show that compared to the Base model, the performance is 0.2% lower. This indicates that suppressing the model at the beginning has a negative impact on it.

**Table 5.** Results by Training $x$ Ratios.

| $x$ | 0 | 20 | 40 | 60 | 80 | 100 |
|---|---|---|---|---|---|---|
| F1 | 90.1 | 91.2 | 91.9 | 92.4 | 92.9 | 92.7 |

When $x$ is set to 100, it means that the second phase is skipped entirely. Skipping the second phase makes it easier for the model to overfit in the later stages. This is because the larger loss values for missing labeled data in the later stages will enhance its learning. Therefore, the chances of overfitting the model increase. The experimental results also show that when $x$ is set to 100, the performance decreases by 0.2% compared to when $x$ is set to 80. For other values of $x$, from 20 to 80, the performance steadily improves.

**On the Data Partitioning.** In specific experiments, the data is divided into two parts, $m$ and $n$, based on the weight of each data point. Here, $m$ represents the portion with higher weights, and n represents the portion with lower weights. Data is sampled from $m$ and $n$ at a certain ratio for model training. In our experiments, we used a ratio of 3:1.

**Table 6.** ADT Model Performance by $m{:}n$ Ratios

| $m:n$ | 1:9 | 1:4 | 2:3 | 3:2 | 4:1 | 9:1 |
|---|---|---|---|---|---|---|
| F1 | 91.7 | 92.9 | 92.6 | 92.4 | 92.4 | 92.3 |

Table 6 provides comparative experimental results for different $m:n$ ratios. From the table, it can be observed that the ADT model performs best when the $m:n$ ratio is 1:4. This ratio achieves a balance between data with higher and lower weights in each sampling. When the ratio is 9:1, it's clear that oversampling of data with lower weights hinders the accurate extraction of data that has a positive impact on the model. In summary, the model tends to perform better when the $m$ ratio is relatively small.

**On the Sampling Ratios.** In the experiments, a batch size of 16 was used, and these 16 data points were sampled from both $m$ and $n$. The different quantities of data sampled from $m$ and $n$ can also affect the prediction performance. Here, we kept the $m:n$ ratio fixed at 1:4, and Table 7 provides comparative experimental results for different quantities of data sampled from $m$ and $n$ in this scenario.

**Table 7.** Effects of Sampling Ratios on Results.

| | $1:0$ | $3:1$ | $1:1$ | $1:3$ | $0:1$ |
|---|---|---|---|---|---|
| F1 | 92.5 | 92.9 | 92.6 | 92.4 | 92.0 |

From Table 7, it can be observed that when the sampling ratio is 1:0, each batch of data contains no samples with lower weights. This heavy reliance on the screening provided by Eq.(5);introduces subjectivity and can be seen in the results where the model doesn't perform at its best under this ratio. When the sampling ratio is 0:1, it completely abandons the sampling of data with higher weights, causing the model to miss out on more challenging data. As a result, the model's performance is 0.2% lower than when using WLF component alone.

## 5 Conclusion

In conclusion, while ADT represents a substantial advancement in EQA training methodologies, ongoing efforts in addressing its limitations and exploring new applications will be crucial for its evolution and wider adoption.This paper introduced Adaptive Denoising Training (ADT), a novel approach designed to improve model robustness in Extractive Question Answering by dynamically managing missing labeled data. While ADT shows promise in enhancing model accuracy and handling noisy data, it faces limitations such as its performance dependency on specific datasets and parameter settings, and increased computational overhead.

Future research should focus on diversifying test datasets, automating parameter optimization for ADT, and improving algorithmic efficiency. These efforts are crucial for broadening ADT's real-world applicability in diverse and dynamic environments. Additionally, leveraging future technological advancements and interdisciplinary collaboration could further enhance ADT's scalability and efficiency, moving towards more robust and versatile EQA systems.

## References

1. Devlin, J., Chang, M.W., Lee, K., Toutanova, K.: BERT: pre-training of deep bidirectional transformers for language understanding. arXiv preprint arXiv:1810.04805 (2018)
2. Joshi, M., Chen, D., Liu, Y., Weld, D.S., Zettlemoyer, L., Levy, O.: SpanBERT: improving pre-training by representing and predicting spans. Trans. Assoc. Comput. Linguist. **8**, 64–77 (2020)
3. Liu, Z., Lin, W., Shi, Y., Zhao, J.: A robustly optimized BERT pre-training approach with post-training. In: China National Conference on Chinese Computational Linguistics, pp. 471–484. Springer (2021)
4. Vaswani, A., et al.: Attention is all you need. Adv. Neural Inf. Proc. Syst. **30** (2017)
5. Zhang, S., Zhao, H., Yuwei, W., Zhang, Z., Zhou, X., Zhou, X.: Dcmn+: dual co-matching network for multi-choice reading comprehension. In: Proceedings of the AAAI Conference on Artificial Intelligence, vol. 34, pp. 9563–9570 (2020)
6. Wang, S., Yu, M., Chang, S., Jiang, J.: A co-matching model for multi-choice reading comprehension. arXiv preprint arXiv:1806.04068 (2018)
7. Seonwoo, Y., Kim, J.H., Ha, J.W., Oh, A.: Context-aware answer extraction in question answering. arXiv preprint arXiv:2011.02687 (2020)
8. Wang, R., et al.: K-adapter: Infusing knowledge into pre-trained models with adapters. arXiv preprint arXiv:2002.01808 (2020)

9. Zhu, H., Dong, L., Wei, F., Wang, W., Qin, B., Liu, T.: Learning to ask unanswerable questions for machine reading comprehension. arXiv preprint arXiv:1906.06045 (2019)

10. Rajpurkar, P., Zhang, J., Lopyrev, K., Liang, P.: Squad: 100,000+ questions for machine comprehension of text. arXiv preprint arXiv:1606.05250 (2016)

11. Trischler, A., et al.: NewsQA: a machine comprehension dataset. arXiv preprint arXiv:1611.09830 (2016)

12. Kwiatkowski, T., et al.: Natural questions: a benchmark for question answering research. Trans. Assoc. Comput. Linguist. **7**, 453–466 (2019)

13. Sun, K., Yu, D., Yu, D., Cardie, C.: Improving machine reading comprehension with general reading strategies. arXiv preprint arXiv:1810.13441 (2018)

14. Zhang, C., et al.: Read, attend, and exclude: multi-choice reading comprehension by mimicking human reasoning process. In: Proceedings of the 43rd International ACM SIGIR Conference on Research and Development in Information Retrieval, pp. 1945–1948 (2020)

15. Luo, D., et al.: Evidence augment for multiple-choice machine reading comprehension by weak supervision. In: Farkaš, I., Masulli, P., Otte, S., Wermter, S. (eds.) ICANN 2021. LNCS, vol. 12895, pp. 357–368. Springer, Cham (2021). https://doi.org/10.1007/978-3-030-86383-8_29

16. Kang, M., Baek, J., Hwang, S.J.: Kala: knowledge-augmented language model adaptation. arXiv preprint arXiv:2204.10555 (2022)

17. Ng, N., Cho, K., Ghassemi, M.: SSMBA: self-supervised manifold based data augmentation for improving out-of-domain robustness. arXiv preprint arXiv:2009.10195 (2020)

18. Lee, S., Kang, M., Lee, J., Hwang, S.J.: Learning to perturb word embeddings for out-of-distribution QA. arXiv preprint arXiv:2105.02692 (2021)

19. Yao, X., Ma, J., Hu, X., Yang, J., Guo, Y., Liu, J.: Towards robust token embeddings for extractive question answering. In: International Conference on Web Information Systems Engineering, pp. 82–96. Springer (2023)

# Iterative Consistent Attentional Diffusion Model for Multi-Contrast MRI Super-Resolution

Jia Chen[1], Tong Zhang[1], Fei Fang[1]([⊠]), Huanrong Jiang[2]([⊠]), Yajie Meng[1], and Jinlong Qin[1]

[1] Wuhan Textile University, Wuhan, China
fangfei369@163.com, myj@hnu.edu.cn
[2] New H3C Technologies Co., Ltd., Hangzhou, China
18907172836@189.cn

**Abstract.** The multi-contrast Magnetic Resonance Imaging (MRI) super-resolution (SR) seeks to improve MR image resolution by leveraging multiple contrasts. Traditional diffusion-based methods, however, introduce complex conditional constraints, such as LR and multi-contrast MR images, often yielding inconsistent results. Moreover, existing techniques struggle to accurately capture both global and local relationships between the various multi-contrast MR images and their corresponding low-resolution (LR) counterparts. To overcome these limitations, we propose a novel approach: an iterative consistent attentional diffusion model for multi-contrast MRI SR. Our model comprises an iterative diffusion model, which mitigates complex conditional constraints by iteratively separating SR and diffusion process, and a consistent attentional fusion network. The latter effectively marries global and local correlations across multi-contrast and LR MR images through innovative pyramid cross-attention and deformable channel attention mechanisms. We have also developed a dual balance loss function that finely balances denoising with super-resolution enhancement. Experimental results demonstrate the effectiveness of our method in advancing MRI SR.

**Keywords:** magnetic resonance imaging · diffusion model · multi-contrast super-resolution

## 1 Introduction

Magnetic Resonance Imaging (MRI) is a commonly used medical imaging technique for diagnosing different types of tissues in the human body, including soft tissues such as organs, muscles, and nerves. However, obtaining high-resolution (HR) Magnetic Resonance (MR) images in clinical practice can be challenging due to factors such as equipment and scanning parameters [1]. Image super-resolution (SR) technology can enhance the quality of MR images by reconstructing low-resolution (LR) images into HR images without requiring any hardware changes [2].

© The Author(s), under exclusive license to Springer Nature Singapore Pte Ltd. 2025
N. Magnenat Thalmann et al. (Eds.): CASA 2024, CCIS 2374, pp. 388–401, 2025.
https://doi.org/10.1007/978-981-96-2681-6_28

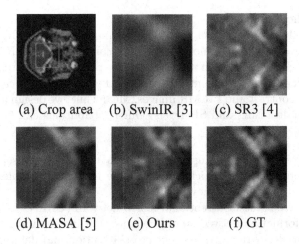

(a) Crop area    (b) SwinIR [3]    (c) SR3 [4]

(d) MASA [5]    (e) Ours    (f) GT

**Fig. 1.** The comparison of four MRI SR methods.

Deep learning-based methods have made significant achievements in single-contrast MRI SR in recent years. Shi *et al.* [6] extended SRCNN [7] using local residual blocks and global residual networks to perform SR reconstruction on 2D MR images. Feng *et al.* [8] proposed T2Net with combined SR and image reconstruction, which has better artifact removal effects than using single-contrast SR alone. Although the implementation process of single-contrast MRI SR is relatively simple, it ignores that the MR images of different contrasts can provide complementary information to each other, which is beneficial to the improvement of the SR image quality.

Multi-contrast MRI SR [5, 9–12] can utilize the multi-parameters characteristic of MRI to solve the above problems. Li *et al.* [9] used the cascaded Swin-Transformer [13] to capture the long-range features of multi-scale images and learned context features, which is an extension of the MASA-SR [5] on MR images. In recent years, diffusion models have been preliminarily used in natural image SR [4, 11, 14–16]. Saharia *et al.* [4] first introduced conditional diffusion models into image SR, iteratively improving the quality of image super-resolution. In the field of MRI SR, Mao *et al.* [11] first introduced diffusion models into multi-contrast MRI SR, where multi-contrast MR images serve as conditions for the diffusion model.

Nevertheless, these methods still have some limitations. Firstly, the diffusion-based methods introduce complex conditional constraints, such as LR and multi-contrast MR images, which can lead to inconsistent SR results (**Figure 1(c)**). Secondly, the global and local correlations between multi-contrast and LR MR images have not been fully captured, which leads to the lack of tissue detail information in the results, as shown in **Figure 1(b)** and **Figure 1(d)**. Furthermore, in processing MR images, the denoising process of the diffusion model may not completely remove the noise in SR images, as shown in **Figure 1(c)**.

To solve these shortcomings, in this paper, we propose an iterative consistent attentional diffusion model (ICADM) for multi-contrast MRI SR. We first propose an iterative diffusion model to achieve consistent MRI SR by iteratively separating the SR and diffusion model. Next, we present a consistent attentional fusion network (CAFN) to transfer and fuse the global and local correlations between multi-contrast and LR MR images. Meanwhile, we design a loss function to balance the denoising and SR levels. Our contributions can be summarized as follows:

1) We propose an iterative diffusion model (IDM) to iteratively separate the SR and diffusion processes, which alleviates the impact of complex conditional constraints on the consistency of SR results.
2) We present a consistent attentional fusion network (CAFN) to learn complementary information between multi-contrast MR images and LR MR images through parallel pyramid consistent cross-attention and deformable channel attention.
3) We design a dual balance loss function that balances the prediction noise and SR capability of the diffusion model, which can effectively remove the Gaussian noise introduced by the diffusion model.

## 2    Related Work

### 2.1    Multi-contrast MRI SR

Most of the existing multi-contrast MRI SR methods [5,9–12,17–19] achieve high-quality image super-resolution by learning the complementary information between different contrast MR images. Feng et al. [12] learned features of multi-contrast images at different stages of convolution. However, CNN-based methods cannot establish long-distance dependencies, making learning the global correlation between images difficult. In order to solve this problem, many researchers [9,10,17,19] used Transformer to expand the receptive field information of image feature extraction. For instance, Cao et al. [20] proposed a deformable attention transformer to match the correspondence and transfer the relevant texture between LR and Ref images. Zou et al. [17] showed the advantages of combining deformable convolutions with Transformers to extend the receptive field of CNNs. Although the above methods have achieved remarkable results, they are difficult to capture the complex distribution characteristics of MR images, thus generating more realistic and natural high-resolution images.

### 2.2    MRI Diffusion Model

The diffusion model is a probabilistic generative model, with its generation process divided into forward diffusion and inverse denoising processes. The forward diffusion process involves continuously adding noise to high-resolution MR images. In contrast, the inverse denoising process removes noise from the images, iteratively generating new images with high fidelity and quality. As diffusion

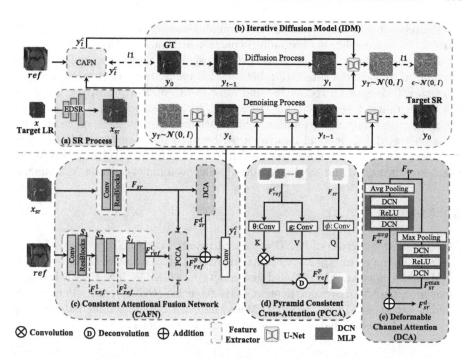

**Fig. 2.** The overall architecture of ICADM. The target LR image $x$ and the reference image $ref$ are first processed through the SR process and consistent attentional fusion network (CAFN) in sequence to perform SR and feature fusion, respectively. Finally, the target SR image $y_0$ is obtained by the iterative diffusion model (IDM).

models advance, researchers are beginning to explore the role of diffusion models in the field of MRI [4,11,14–16,21,22]. Khader *et al.* [21] used a conditional diffusion model to generate synthetic images from 3D medical images, expanding the medical image data. Saharia *et al.* [4] first introduced conditional diffusion models into image SR, iteratively improving the quality of image super-resolution. Mao *et al.* [11] demonstrated that diffusion models can enhance SR quality by leveraging multi-contrast MR images. However, these methods introduce bicubic upsampling LR or high-resolution ref as conditions into the diffusion model, which increases the complexity of the diffusion model conditions and leads to inconsistent SR results. Therefore, we consider decoupling the SR and diffusion processes and iterating the SR results in the denoising process of the diffusion model.

## 2.3 Attention Mechanism

The attention mechanism is a method to help the model focus on the information of interest in the task by calculating the weights of different parts of the input data. In recent years, it has been widely used in the field of MRI super-resolution [8,11,18,23–25]. Feng *et al.* [8] used hard and soft attention to establish the relationship between reconstruction and super-resolution. Mao *et al.* [11] learned the relationship between multi-contrast MR images through the channel attention mechanism. Georgescu *et al.* [18] designed a multi-head self-attention mechanism to learn the correlation between LR reference and LR target images. Li *et al.* [24] designed a rectangle-window cross-attention transformer to establish longer-range dependencies in MR images without increasing computational complexity and fully using reference information. However, these methods only focus on the global or local dependencies between multi-contrast MR images. Therefore, we propose a novel cross-attention and deformable channel attention to explore the global and local dependencies between multi-contrast MR images.

## 3   Method

The overall architecture of ICADM for multi-contrast MRI SR proposed in this paper is illustrated in Fig. 2. Our ICADM consists of an iterative diffusion model (IDM) and a consistent attentional fusion network (CAFN). The CAFN includes a feature extractor, a pyramid context cross-attention (PCCA), and a deformable channel attention (DCA) module. Meanwhile, we design a dual balance loss function (DB-loss) to balance the levels of SR and denoising.

### 3.1   Iterative Diffusion Model (IDM)

For diffusion-based methods, multi-contrast MRI SR methods introduce LR images and reference images as constraint conditions, which leads to inconsistent SR results compared to the ground-truth (GT) images. Therefore, our iterative diffusion model separates the SR and diffusion model and uses the SR result as a condition for the denoising process of the diffusion model, as shown in Fig. 2. Specifically, given a GT image $y_0$ and a LR image $x$, to mitigate the influence of the $x$ on the SR process of diffusion model, we first utilize a basic SR model such as EDSR to obtain the SR images $x_{sr}$, which further alleviates the resolution gap between $y_0$ and $x$. Then, during the diffusion process of the diffusion model, noise is progressively added to $y_0$ to generate the noisy image $y_t$ at time $t$, and in the progress $x_{sr}$ is conditionally concatenated into $y_t$ to complete noise prediction. Finally, in the denoising process of the diffusion model, we obtain the target SR image $y_0$ after using the predicted noise values under the constraint of $x_{sr}$.

### 3.2   Consistent Attentional Fusion Network (CAFN)

Given the multi-contrast HR reference MR image $ref$ and $x_{sr}$ of size $H \times W$, we first extract features from each of them separately. In Fig. 2(c), the shallow features of $x_{sr}$ are extracted using stacked layers including Convolution, ReLU, BatchNorm and LayerNorm. These shallow features are then input into ResNet Blocks to extract deep features $F_{sr}$ of size $H \times W$. For the reference image $ref$, we utilize a set of pyramid scale factors $S = \{s_1, s_2, \ldots, s_i\}(i =$

$1, 2, \ldots, n$), and apply down-scaling operations and convolution layers to obtain the shallow pyramid features of size $\frac{H}{s_i} \times \frac{W}{s_i}$. Subsequently, the extracted features are fed into ResNet Blocks to obtain deep pyramid features $F_{ref}^i = \{F_{ref}^1, F_{ref}^2, F_{ref}^3, \ldots, F_{ref}^i\}$ where $i$ is the pyramid scale factors, that is used to capture long-range dependencies.

After completing the extraction of deep features, the pyramid features $F_{ref}^i$ are inputted into PCCA for cross-transfer and fusion to obtain cross-transfer features $F_{ref}^p$ with global and local correlations. However, PCCA is not sufficient to eliminate the contrast difference between $ref$ and $x_{sr}$. Therefore, we input the deep feature $F_{sr}$ into the DCA to obtain an enhanced feature representation $F_{sr}^d$. Then, $F_{ref}^p$ and $F_{sr}^d$ are fused by element-wise addition, and the fusion result is sampled using convolution layers to obtain the integrated features $y_t^c$ of $ref$ and $x_{sr}$. Finally, $y_t^c$ is concatenated with the noise image as the input for the next time step of the diffusion model. Next, we obtain $F_{ref}^p$ and $F_{sr}^d$ separately through PCCA and DCA, respectively.

### 3.2.1 Pyramid Contextual Cross-Attention (PCCA)

Our pyramid contextual cross-attention (PCCA) module is used to transfer the features from $i$-th levels pyramid features $F_{ref}^i$ to $F_{sr}$, as shown in Fig. 2(d). Formally, we use feature map $a$ to represent the input feature $F_{sr}$, and feature map $b$ to represent the input pyramid features $F_{ref}^i$. The pyramid contextual cross-attention can be expressed as:

$$C_k = \frac{1}{\sigma(a, F_{ref}^i)} \sum_{b \in F_{ref}^i} \sum_{j \in b} f(a_k, b_j) g(b_j), \tag{1}$$

where $k, j$ are index on the input $a$ and $b$ and output $C$ respectively, the function $f$ computes pair-wise affinity between two input features, $g$ is a feature transformation function that generates a new representation of $b_j$, and the output response $C_k$ obtains information from the multi-scale pyramid feature $b$ by summing over all positions $j$ and is normalized by a scalar function $\sigma(a, F_{ref}^i)$. To enhance the long-range correlation between features, we set a correlation neighborhood of size $r \times r$ feature blocks when calculating the correlation between two input features. Only when the neighborhoods of both features are correlated will they be considered highly correlated.

For the correlation function $f$, we use a Gaussian function to compute the pair-wise correlation between two input features: $f(a_k, b_j) = e^{\phi(a_k)^T \theta(b_j)}$, where $\phi(a_k) = W_\phi a_k$ and $\theta(b_j) = W_\theta b_j$. For feature transformation function $g$, we use simple linear embedding: $g(b_j) = W_g b_j$. Specifically, we first use $F_{sr}$ as the query $(Q)$ and multiple levels of feature pyramids $F_{ref}^i$ as both the key $(K)$ and value $(V)$. Then, the $Q$, $K$, and $V$ are fed into three separate 1x1 convolution layers, namely $W_\phi$, $W_\theta$ and $W_g$, to extract features, denoted as $\phi$, $\theta$ and $g$ respectively, as shown in Fig. 2(d).

Finally, we utilize a convolution operation to compute the correlation between $Q$ and $K$. The cross-attention correlation scores, which are normalized using the softmax function, are then combined with V and fed into a deconvolution layer to obtain the final PCCA feature transformation result $F_{ref}^p$.

### 3.2.2  Deformable Channel Attention (DCA)

However, relying solely on the PCCA may result in structural and brightness discrepancies, which may lead to inaccurate SR results. To eliminate both differences between $F_{ref}^p$ and $F_{sr}$, we adopt deformable channel attention (DCA) to enhance the multi-channel correlation in the input feature $F_{sr}$.

As shown in Fig. 2(e), the DCA module consists of two pooling layers and two Deformable convolution network (DCN) MLP networks. Each DCN MLP network consists of two $1 \times 1$ DCNs and one ReLU layer. We calculate the global and local correlations between multiple channels of $F_{sr}$ separately. On the one hand, our DCA applies an average pooling layer to compute the average value for each channel in the feature map $F_{sr}$ of size $H \times W \times C$. Then, the computed channel average values are inputted into the DCN MLP network to adaptively obtain the global channel feature $F_{sr}^{avg}$ for $F_{sr}$. On the other hand, we use a max pooling layer to select the maximum value for each channel in the feature map $F_{sr}$. Similarly, we utilize a DCN MLP network to learn the enhanced local multi-channel correlations and obtain the local channel feature $F_{sr}^{max}$ for $F_{sr}$. Finally, we use addition to fuse the global channel features $F_{sr}^{avg}$ and the local channel features $F_{sr}^{max}$ and obtain the final deformable channel attention feature $F_{sr}^d$. Deformable channel attention (DCA) is computed by:

$$
\begin{aligned}
F_{sr}^d = \sigma(DCNMLP(AvgPooling(F_{sr}))+ \\
\sigma(DCNMLP(AvgPooling(F_{sr})))),
\end{aligned}
\tag{2}
$$

where $\sigma$ represents the sigmoid activation function.

### 3.3  Dual Balance Loss Function (DB-Loss)

Existing methods [4,11] do not establish a mapping relationship between GT images and SR models. We argue that the multi-contrast MRI SR results should be faithful to the original images, while the noise introduced by the diffusion model should also be eliminated. Therefore, we design a dual balance loss function to train our model.

As shown in Fig. 2, in forward mapping, our network acts as a regularizer to guide the LR images to learn the reference information and learns the noise level using U-Net. In the backward mapping, we minimize the L1 norm to ensure the consistency between the predicted noise $y_T$ and the random noise $\epsilon$, as well as the consistency between CAFN and GT image. The DB-loss $\mathcal{L}$ is defined as follows:

$$
\begin{aligned}
\mathcal{L} = \lambda_{SR}\mathcal{L}_{SR} + \lambda_\epsilon\mathcal{L}_\epsilon \\
= \lambda_{SR}\|f_c(x_{sr}, I_{ref}) - I_{GT}\|_1 \\
+\lambda_\epsilon\|y_T - \epsilon\|_1,
\end{aligned}
\tag{3}
$$

where $x_{sr}$ denotes the SR image after the SR process, $I_{ref}$ is the reference MR image, $\mathcal{L}_{SR}$ represents the L1 norm between the image generated by the

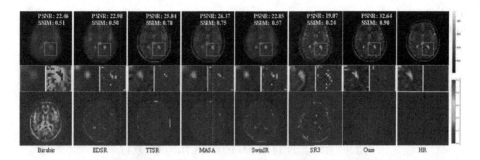

**Fig. 3.** Qualitative comparison of different SR methods on IXI dataset with 4× enlargement scale. The SR MR images and the corresponding error maps are provided. Ours recovers more accurate anatomical structures than others, as shown in the inset image.

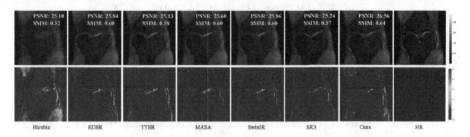

**Fig. 4.** Qualitative results of different SR methods on fastMRI dataset with 4× enlargement scale. The SR MR images and the corresponding error maps are provided.

consistent attentional fusion network $f_c$ and $I_{GT}$, and $\mathcal{L}_\epsilon$ is defined to minimize the L1 norm to ensure the consistency between $y_T$ and $\epsilon$.

Moreover, $\lambda_{SR}$ and $\lambda_\epsilon$ are two variables used to indicate the weights of two losses. Both variables range between 0 and 1.

## 4   Experiments

### 4.1   Datasets

We evaluate our model on the public fastMRI dataset [27] and IXI dataset [28].

**fastMRI.** Data from more than 1,500 fully sampled knee MRIs obtained on 3 and 1.5 T magnets and DICOM images from 10,000 clinical knee MRIs also obtained at 3 or 1.5 T. The raw dataset includes coronal proton density-weighted images with and without fat suppression.

**IXI.** IXI Dataset is a collection of 600 MR brain images from normal, healthy subjects. The data has been collected at three different hospitals in London: Hammersmith Hospital using a Philips 3T system (details of scanner parameters), Guy's Hospital using a Philips 1.5T system (details of scanner parameters), and the Institute of Psychiatry using a GE 1.5T system (details of the scan parameters not available at the moment).

**Table 1.** Quantitative comparison on two different datasets with 2× enlargement scale, in terms of PSNR, SSIM and MSE.

| Dataset | fastMRI | | | IXI | | |
|---|---|---|---|---|---|---|
| Scale | 2× | | | 2× | | |
| Metrics | PSNR | SSIM | MSE | PSNR | SSIM | MSE |
| Bicubic | 27.25 | 0.68 | 6.91 | 24.63 | 0.71 | 14.24 |
| EDSR [26] | 28.70 | 0.75 | 0.06 | 27.94 | 0.87 | 0.12 |
| TTSR [10] | 29.14 | 0.82 | 0.05 | 28.75 | 0.88 | 0.11 |
| SwinIR [3] | 28.67 | 0.86 | 0.06 | 28.65 | 0.75 | 0.17 |
| SR3 [4] | 27.70 | 0.79 | 5.67 | 26.17 | 0.73 | 13.23 |
| McMRSR [9] | 30.28 | 0.88 | 1.82 | 33.88 | 0.87 | 0.98 |
| DisC-Dif [11] | 29.89 | 0.86 | 2.31 | 34.64 | 0.91 | 1.29 |
| ours | **30.93** | **0.89** | **0.04** | **35.38** | **0.93** | **0.09** |

**Table 2.** Quantitative comparison on two different datasets with 4× enlargement scale, in terms of PSNR, SSIM and MSE.

| Dataset | fastMRI | | | IXI | | |
|---|---|---|---|---|---|---|
| Scale | 4× | | | 4× | | |
| Metrics | PSNR | SSIM | MSE | PSNR | SSIM | MSE |
| Bicubic | 25.10 | 0.52 | 69.06 | 22.46 | 0.51 | 95.35 |
| EDSR [26] | 25.84 | 0.60 | 36.23 | 22.98 | 0.58 | 75.11 |
| TTSR [10] | 25.13 | 0.58 | 42.23 | 25.04 | 0.78 | 47.87 |
| MASA-SR [5] | 25.60 | 0.60 | 37.03 | 26.37 | 0.75 | 35.93 |
| SwinIR [3] | 25.86 | 0.60 | 35.89 | 22.85 | 0.57 | 81.75 |
| SR3 [4] | 25.24 | 0.57 | 55.70 | 19.07 | 0.24 | 352.91 |
| McMRSR [9] | 26.23 | 0.62 | 33.78 | 30.96 | 0.88 | 1.32 |
| DisC-Dif [11] | 25.87 | 0.60 | 34.54 | 31.43 | 0.88 | 1.55 |
| ours | **26.56** | **0.64** | **32.45** | **32.64** | **0.90** | **0.69** |

As shown in Table 3, for the fastMRI dataset [27], we use the PD-weighted images as reference images and the FS-PD images as target images. Similarly, for the IXI dataset [28], we use the PD-weighted images as reference images and the T2-weighted images as target images.

To build the training and testing datasets, we downsample the GT images (256×256) using 2× and 4× bicubic interpolation to generate the LR images. To obtain the validation datasets, we transform the images to the k-space using the Fourier transform, crop them, and then use the inverse Fourier transform to obtain the LR validation set.

## 4.2   Implementation Details

The ICADM for MRI SR proposed in this paper is implemented in PyTorch on an NVIDIA Tesla V100 GPU (16GB). In our implementation, we set $\lambda_{SR} = 0.099$ and $\lambda_\epsilon = 0.9$ to control the level of SR and denoising. Due to computational limitations, we scale down the size of the testing and training data proportionally. Inspired by DDPM [14], we use the Adam optimizer for model training with the learning rate of $10^{-4}$ and the step of 200. In the SR process, we use the official EDSR code as the training network. In the EDSR training network, we set channel $= 64$. In CAFN, we set the PCCA pyramid levels to 5, the number of channels in DCA to 64, and the ratio of 1x1 convolution hyperparameters to 16.

## 4.3   Evaluation Metrics

We use peak signal-to-noise ratio (PSNR) and structural similarity (SSIM) to evaluate the SR performance. PSNR measures the ratio between the maximum possible power of a signal and the power of noise that affects the fidelity of the signal. SSIM provides a more comprehensive measure of similarity between images by taking into account how humans perceive images, making it a valuable tool in image quality assessment and image processing tasks. Moreover, we use Mean Squared Error (MSE) to measure the consistency between LR and down-sampled SR.

**Table 3.** Two datasets used to evaluate the proposed.

| Datasets | fastMRI [27] | IXI [28] |
|---|---|---|
| Reference | PD | PD |
| Target | FS-PD | T2 |
| Train/Valid/Test | 226/45/45 | 377/100/100 |

## 4.4   Qualitative Evaluation

We compare our ICADM with single-contrast and multi-contrast SR methods, namely EDSR [26], TTSR [10], MASA-SR [5], SwinIR [3] and SR3 [4]. Figure 3 shows our SR results with 4× enlargement scale on the IXI dataset. The green box indicates the enlarged local region and its corresponding error map, where the texture becomes more pronounced as the SR quality deteriorates. It can be observed that our method successfully reconstructs the complex anatomical structures in the MR images. Additionally, compared to SR3 [4], our results exhibit less noise.

To validate the superiority of our model in global structure SR and the robustness of the model, we conduct 4× upscaling tests on the fastMRI dataset, as shown in Fig. 5. The experimental results show that our model can reconstruct MR images with a single background structure and enhance significant features in LR images compared to other methods.

## 4.5  Quantitative Evaluation

We quantitatively compare our ICADM with single-contrast and multi-contrast SR methods, namely EDSR [26], TTSR [10], MASA-SR [5], SwinIR [3] and SR3 [4], McMRSR [9] and DisC-Dif [11]. As shown in Table 1 and Table 2, we calculate the scores of all the evaluation metrics scores on different datasets under the condition of 4× and 2× upscaling, and our method consistently outperformed the existing methods with the highest evaluation scores. The quantitative results demonstrate that our model has achieved high-quality SR on MR images.

**Table 4.** Ablation study on different variant models under IXI dataset with 4× enlargement scale.

| Variant | PSNR↑ | SSIM↑ | MSE↓ |
|---|---|---|---|
| *w/o* CAFN | 30.77 | 0.85 | 3.34 |
| *w/o* DCA | 30.89 | 0.89 | 1.23 |
| *w/o* SR-loss | 30.95 | 0.88 | 1.57 |
| SR | **32.64** | **0.90** | **0.69** |

## 4.6  Ablation Study

In this section, we perform three ablation experiments to show the effectiveness of the iterative diffusion model (IDM), consistent attentional fusion network (CAFN) and the DB-loss in our model. We conduct ablation studies on the 4× down-sampled IXI dataset. As shown in Table 4, we test three variations of our model, namely *w/o* CAFN, *w/o* DCA, and *w/o* SR-loss.

As shown in Table 4, the results of the *w/o* CAFN ablation study still outperform other methods, which indicates that even after removing CAFN, our IDM can improve the super-resolution quality of MR images. Moreover, removing DCA and using only PCCA and IDM can still improve the consistency and structural similarity of SR images, which indicates that our CAFN can establish global and local dependencies between LR and reference images. Experimental details on the pyramid levels of PCCA are presented in Sect. 2 of the supplementary materials. Finally, when the removal of the SR-loss and the retention of only the noise prediction loss, the MSE value of the model increases, which indicates that our proposed DB-loss helps to balance the SR and denoising levels.

Also, we conduct further experiments to test the effectiveness of the pyramid levels in the PCCA component of CAFN. Figure 5 provides qualitative ablation results using different levels of the pyramid with 4× enlargement scale on IXI dataset [28]. The green box indicates the selected local region, and the image below the green box represents the enlarged region corresponding to the local area.

The experimental results indicate that the pyramid structure with 4 levels has a stronger ability to capture local and global correlations compared to the pyramid structure with 3 levels. It can transfer more detailed information and sharper edges.

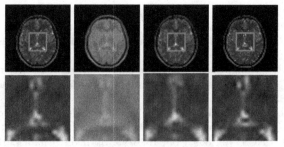

(a) HR    (b) Reference(c) 3 levels  (d) 4 levels

**Fig. 5.** Qualitative results of pyramid levels on IXI dataset with 4× enlargement scale.

## 5    Conclusion

In this work, we propose a novel iterative consistent attentional diffusion model for multi-contrast MRI super-resolution method. First, although multiple conditional constraints can help the diffusion model regulate the quality of image generation, complex conditional constraints will increase the inconsistency of the results. Therefore, our method iteratively separates the SR and diffusion processes, which alleviates the influence of complex conditional constraints on the consistency of SR results. Secondly, in exploring multi-contrast MR image correlation, our method cross-learns the global and local spatial features of MR images and expands the receptive field between channels through deformable convolution, further narrowing the structure and brightness gap between multi-contrast MR images. Finally, we design a dual balance loss function to balance the noise prediction and SR ability of the diffusion model. Extensive experiments have demonstrated the potential of our method in clinical practice. In the future, we will further explore the potential of the diffusion model in the field of unsupervised MRI super-resolution and reduce the sampling time and complexity of the diffusion model.

## References

1. Plenge, E., et al.: Super-resolution methods in MRI: can they improve the trade-off between resolution, signal-to-noise ratio, and acquisition time? Magn. Reson. Med. **68**(6), 1983–1993 (2012)
2. Van Reeth, E., Tham, I.W.K., Tan, C.H., Poh, C.L.: Super-resolution in magnetic resonance imaging: a review. Concepts Magn. Reson. Part A **40**(6), 306–325 (2012)
3. Liang, J., Cao, J., Sun, G., Zhang, K., Van Gool, L., Timofte, R.: SwinIR: image restoration using swin transformer. In: Proceedings of the IEEE/CVF International Conference on Computer Vision, pp. 1833–1844 (2021)
4. Saharia, C., Ho, J., Chan, W., Salimans, T., Fleet, D.J., Norouzi, M.: Image super-resolution via iterative refinement. IEEE Trans. Pattern Anal. Mach. Intell. **45**(4), 4713–4726 (2022)

5. Lu, L., Li, W., Tao, X., Lu, J., Jia, J.: MASA-SR: matching acceleration and spatial adaptation for reference-based image super-resolution. In: Proceedings of the IEEE/CVF Conference on Computer Vision and Pattern Recognition, pp. 6368–6377 (2021)

6. Shi, J., Liu, Q., Wang, C., Zhang, Q., Ying, S., Haoyu, X.: Super-resolution reconstruction of MR image with a novel residual learning network algorithm. Phys. Med. Biol. **63**(8), 085011 (2018)

7. Dong, C., Loy, C.C., He, K., Tang, X.: Learning a deep convolutional network for image super-resolution. In: Fleet, D., Pajdla, T., Schiele, B., Tuytelaars, T. (eds.) ECCV 2014. LNCS, vol. 8692, pp. 184–199. Springer, Cham (2014). https://doi.org/10.1007/978-3-319-10593-2_13

8. Feng, C.-M., Yan, Y., Fu, H., Chen, L., Xu, Y.: Task transformer network for joint MRI reconstruction and super-resolution. In: de Bruijne, M., et al. (eds.) MICCAI 2021. LNCS, vol. 12906, pp. 307–317. Springer, Cham (2021). https://doi.org/10.1007/978-3-030-87231-1_30

9. Li, G.: Transformer-empowered multi-scale contextual matching and aggregation for multi-contrast mri super-resolution. In: Proceedings of the IEEE/CVF Conference on Computer Vision and Pattern Recognition, pp. 20636–20645 (2022)

10. Yang, F., Yang, H., Fu, J., Lu, H., Guo, B.: Learning texture transformer network for image super-resolution. In: Proceedings of the IEEE/CVF Conference on Computer Vision and Pattern Recognition, pp. 5791–5800 (2020)

11. Mao, Y., Jiang, L., Chen, X., Li, C.: Disc-diff: disentangled conditional diffusion model for multi-contrast MRI super-resolution. In: International Conference on Medical Image Computing and Computer-Assisted Intervention (2023)

12. Feng, C.M., Fu, H., Yuan, S., Xu, Y.: Multi-contrast MRI super-resolution via a multi-stage integration network. In: International Conference on Medical Image Computing and Computer-Assisted Intervention (2021)

13. Liu, Z., et al.: Swin transformer: hierarchical vision transformer using shifted windows. In: Proceedings of the IEEE/CVF International Conference on Computer Vision, pp. 10012–10022 (2021)

14. Ho, J., Jain, A., Abbeel, P.: Denoising diffusion probabilistic models. Adv. Neural. Inf. Process. Syst. **33**, 6840–6851 (2020)

15. Song, Y., Ermon, S.: Generative modeling by estimating gradients of the data distribution. Adv. Neural Inf. Process. Syst. **32** (2019)

16. Gao, S., et al.: Implicit diffusion models for continuous super-resolution. In: Proceedings of the IEEE/CVF Conference on Computer Vision and Pattern Recognition, pp. 10021–10030 (2023)

17. Zou, B., Ji, Z., Zhu, C., Dai, Y., Zhang, W., Kui, X.: Multi-scale deformable transformer for multi-contrast knee MRI super-resolution. Biomed. Signal Process. Control **79**, 104154 (2023)

18. Georgescu, M.I., et al.: Multimodal multi-head convolutional attention with various kernel sizes for medical image super-resolution. In: Proceedings of the IEEE/CVF Winter Conference on Applications of Computer Vision, pp. 2195–2205 (2023)

19. Yang, G., et al.: Model-guided multi-contrast deep unfolding network for MRI super-resolution reconstruction. In: Proceedings of the 30th ACM International Conference on Multimedia, pp. 3974–3982 (2022)

20. Cao, J., et al.: Reference-based image super-resolution with deformable attention transformer. In: European Conference on Computer Vision, pp. 325–342. Springer (2022)

21. Khader, F., et al.: Denoising diffusion probabilistic models for 3D medical image generation. Sci. Rep. **13**(1), 7303 (2023)

22. Wang, J., Levman, J., Pinaya, W.H.L., Tudosiu, P.D., Cardoso, M.J., Marinescu, R.: InverseSR: 3D brain MRI super-resolution using a latent diffusion model. In: International Conference on Medical Image Computing and Computer-Assisted Intervention, pp. 438–447. Springer (2023)

23. Lyu, J., Wang, S., Tian, Y., Zou, J., Dong, S., Wang, C., Aviles-Rivero, A.I., Qin, J.: STADNet: spatial-temporal attention-guided dual-path network for cardiac cine MRI super-resolution. Med. Image Anal. **94**, 103142 (2024)

24. Li, G., et al.: Rethinking multi-contrast MRI super-resolution: rectangle-window cross-attention transformer and arbitrary-scale upsampling. In: Proceedings of the IEEE/CVF International Conference on Computer Vision, pp. 21230–21240 (2023)

25. Li, G., Lyu, J., Wang, C., Dou, Q., Qin, J.: WavTrans: synergizing wavelet and cross-attention transformer for multi-contrast MRI super-resolution. In: International Conference on Medical Image Computing and Computer-Assisted Intervention, pp. 463–473. Springer (2022)

26. Lim, B., Son, S., Kim, H., Nah, S., Lee, K.M.: Enhanced deep residual networks for single image super-resolution. In: Proceedings of the IEEE Conference on Computer Vision and Pattern Recognition Workshops, pp. 136–144 (2017)

27. Zbontar, J., et al.: fastMRI: an open dataset and benchmarks for accelerated MRI. arXiv preprint arXiv:1811.08839 (2018)

28. IXI Dataset (2015). https://brain-development.org/ixi-dataset.

# Author Index